ID0208089

THE CORRESPONDENCE OF
EDMUND BURKE

THE CORRESPONDENCE OF
EDMUND BURKE

VOLUME X

INDEX VOLUME
COMPILED BY
BARBARA LOWE
P. J. MARSHALL
JOHN A. WOODS

CAMBRIDGE UNIVERSITY PRESS

THE UNIVERSITY OF CHICAGO PRESS
CHICAGO, ILLINOIS
1978

Published by the Syndics of the Cambridge University Press
The Pitt Building, Trumpington Street, Cambridge CB2 1RP
Bentley House, 200 Euston Road, London NW1 2DB
296 Beaconsfield Parade, Middle Park, Melbourne 3206, Australia
and
The University of Chicago Press
Chicago 60637

First published 1978

Library of Congress Catalog Card Number: 58–5615

International Standard Book Numbers:

0 521 21024 0 Cambridge edition

0–226–11562–3 Chicago edition

PRINTED IN GREAT BRITAIN
AT THE UNIVERSITY PRESS, CAMBRIDGE

CONTENTS

PREFACE

Three scholars have taken the main responsibility for this index volume. Dr John Woods originally intended to complete the whole of it single-handed. Although that proved to be impossible because of his other duties, he did a very large amount of the essential labour. Specific sections, such as Additional Letters and the Errata and Addenda, are entirely his, and every part of the volume owes much to his skill and exactitude. When he was forced to resign his main task we were fortunate to find a worthy successor for him. Mrs Barbara Lowe is not a professional Burke scholar, or even a professional historian, but being highly trained, imaginative, and an experienced indexer, she knew how to deal with an exacting assignment. She could profit in some degree from beginnings already made, but the crucial challenge which faced her—that of mastering the detail of 4500 pages of difficult texts and notes—was inescapably hers. The volume as it stands is her achievement. She was guided in its preparation by Dr Peter Marshall, who, having a sabbatical leave for the academic year 1974-75, put his scholarly judgement and his exceptional knowledge of Burke at her disposal for a period of more than twelve months. Dr Marshall is characteristically modest about his immense contribution, but the General Index could never have been finished without his devoted assistance.

Those sections of the volume which contain Additional Letters, Errata and Addenda and the General Index are not likely to puzzle the reader, who expects to find them here. One section—that which is entitled *A Full Listing of Burke Correspondence*—may need a word of explanation. This edition has not been confined to printing letters by Burke himself. Some letters written to him and some 'surrounding letters' have also been added when they cast important light on his affairs. The number of these could not be large. There was never any question of printing all that survive. None the less this wider background of correspondence, though we could not include it entire, deserves attention. Scholars dealing with an active politician want to know the full range of his contacts and the extent of his involvement in countless affairs. And almost any readers of a major author may want to explore his social world, discover the sources of his ideas, and judge the effects he had on his contemporaries. The *Full Listing* tries to give an inquiring student access to all Burke letters for which manuscripts or printed texts survive.

ACKNOWLEDGEMENTS

The *Full Listing*, even more than other parts of this volume, is a co-operative enterprise. The work of hunting out and recording Burke letters has been going on for decades. The General Editor and Dr Milton S. Smith brought out a *Checklist* volume in 1955:[1] that is, three years before Volume One of the *Correspondence* appeared. In compiling it they had had years of assistance from Dr Robert A. Smith. Two extremely generous patrons had also given them aid. Dr Wilmarth S. Lewis subsidized an ambitious survey of autograph dealers' catalogues in the British Museum, as a means of tracking down surviving manuscripts. Dr James M. Osborn besides purchasing Burke letters and making them available—as he has done through the whole life of this edition—arranged to have the Index Society publish the *Checklist* volume. Since its publication virtually every person connected with the Burke editorial team has taken part in the long process of correcting and expanding our lists.

As Volume Ten completes the *Correspondence*, we would like in it to thank all those who have helped our long endeavour. Those who helped by granting permission to publish their Burke letters are named in the Source Lists of the volumes, with expressions of our gratitude. Some who have helped in other ways—by finding new letters, by supplying transcriptions, by giving hints where to look for new materials—have not been acknowledged publicly, largely because they were so numerous. But they have our sincerest thanks. Those who have been our major sponsors from the beginning to the end of the project have been acknowledged repeatedly, but it is a pleasure to name them again. The Earl Fitzwilliam, owner of Burke's private papers, is certainly the first of these. By depositing his Burke manuscripts and permitting their publication he made the *Correspondence* possible. Dr James M. Osborn—next to the Earl the chief owner of Burke materials—has also helped us by permissions, by purchases, by advice, and in other ways. The Librarians and staff of the Sheffield Central Library and the North-amptonshire Record Society have given us willing efficient service for many years. Two American universities—the University of Chicago and the University of Massachusetts—have been our academic sponsors. The University of Sheffield, and especially Professor George R. Potter of its History Department, anticipated and satisfied innumerable local needs. The Carnegie Corporation of New York, whose generous grant

[1] *A Checklist of the Correspondence of Edmund Burke. Arranged in Chronological Order and Indexed under the Names of 1200 Correspondents.* By Thomas W. Copeland and Milton Shumway Smith. Printed for the Index Society at the University Press, Cambridge, 1955.

of funds enabled us to start editorial operations in 1953, made us two supplementary grants to continue and conclude them. Mrs Albert Woods assisted us at the end with a magnificent private gift.

Amherst, Massachusetts   THOMAS W. COPELAND

September 1977

ADDITIONAL LETTERS

In Volume Nine of the *Correspondence* (pp. 381–472) we printed a few dozen letters which had come to our notice too late to be put in their proper chronological places in our first eight volumes. Since the publication of Volume Nine, a few more such letters have appeared: 23 of them wholly new to us, 11 merely better texts of letters we had published incompletely or from inferior sources.

These are annotated, completely or by a few necessary additions to earlier notes, on the principles already explained in Volume Nine. The short titles given to their manuscript and printed sources are explained in the *Key Lists* below (pp. 195–203). In texts—as is normal in our volumes—words, names, figures or parts thereof which are either wholly or partly illegible are put within angular brackets: ⟨ ⟩.

To PATRICK NAGLE—21 *October* 1767

Source: MS Osborn Collection.

Printed in vol. I, 328–30, from the *New Monthly Magazine*.

My dear Sir,

I am almost apprehensive that my long Silence[1] has put even your goodnature and forgiveness to a Trial, and that you begin to suspect me of some Neglect of you. I assure you that there are but very few things which could make me more uneasy than your entertaining such a Notion. However to avoid all risque of it, though I have very little to say, I will trouble you with a Line or two; if it were only to tell you, that we always keep a very strong, and very affectionate memory of our friends in Roches Country. Katty and our friend Courtney, I believe, can tell you that we never passed a day without a Bumper to your health, which, if it did you no good, was a real pleasure to ourselves. I take it for granted that the party was not much worse for their ramble, not Totally grown foppish by their Travels—I mean to except Garret; who certainly will be undone by his jaunt—he will be like those ingenious Farmers in Gulliver who carry on their husbandry in the most knowing manner in the world, but never have any Crop. To complete his ruin, you will tell him, I have not forgot the young Bull which I mentioned to him; but I find I antedated my promise a little; for he was not calved when Garret was here. However my Lord Rockingham has had one of the finest Bull Calves that can be; he is of an immense size; though when I left Yorkshire he was not more than 7 weeks old. His Sire is one of the Largest I have ever seen; and before he was bought by his present owner was let to Co⟨ver⟩ at half a Guinea a time. He is of the short horned Holderness breed; and undoubtedly his kind would not do for your pastures; but he will serve to cross the strain and mend your Breed. I take the Calf to be too young to travel; but by the time he is a year old, I fancy the best method of sending him, will be to get some careful fellow who comes from your County to harvest in England to take charge of him on his return. Let this man, if such can be found, call upon me and he shall have further directions. You see I encourage Garrett in his *idle Schemes*; My Use of this phrase puts me in mind of my Uncle James; (indeed I wanted nothing to put me in mind of him). I heard lately from Ned Barret of his illness,

[1] MS: Silences

3

which gives me a most sincere concern; I hope to hear shortly that he is better. I am told too that poor James Hennessy of Cork is [in] a bad way. He was as sensible and gentlemanlike a man as any in our part of the County—and I feel heartily for him and for his Wife.

Be so good to remember us all most affectionately to John, to Mr Courtney and Mrs Courtney—thank them for the pleasure we had in their Company last Summer—give Garrett the enclosed memorandum; If you should find it inconvenient to give us a line yourself, he will be so good as to let us hear from him soon; not but that we are much obliged to him for the Letters he has written to us, and to our friend English—assure him that when we have any good news, he will be the first to hear it. Farewell my dear Sir—all here are very truly yours; and believe me your ever affectionate Nephew

EDM BURKE

Octr 21. 1767.

Pat. Nagle behaves very well, is exceedingly attentive to his Business; and upon my word, from what I see of him, I think him a decent and intelligent young fellow. He has repaid me the 20 Guineas he had from me.

To JAMES DODSLEY—[*ante* 2 *June* 1774]

Source: MS Osborn Collection

Rockingham presumably wanted the copies of Pope's Homer for the debate on 2 June 1774 in the House of Lords on the 'Act for Relief of Booksellers . . . by vesting the Copies of printed Books in the Purchasers'.

James Dodsley (1724–97), acting at first with his brother Robert (1703–64), was Burke's publisher for most of his life.

Mr Burkes compliments to Mr Dodsley and not knowing where Mr Johnston[1] lives begs that Mr Dodsley would request him to be at Lord Rockinghams at Grosvenor Square this day at eleven or soon after and to bring with him the genuine and spurious Popes Homer[2] a Volume of each.

[1] William Johnston, a recently retired bookseller, had been actively involved in the attempts made by the London booksellers, supported by Burke, to obtain a Bill strengthening copyright (*Journals of the House of Commons*, XXXIV, 588–90).

[2] Alexander Donaldson (d. 1794), a Scottish bookseller, was a leading opponent of the Bill. His edition of Pope's Homer was specifically criticised by James Mansfield (1734–1821), counsel for the London booksellers, for suppressing many of Pope's notes (*Parliamentary History*, XVII, 1097).

4

To JOHN NOBLE—25 [*June*] 1778

Source: MS Osborn Collection.

Endorsed (by John Noble): Westminster 25 July 1778 | Edd Burke | an[sr]d 18 Sepr. The naval action described shows that the letter was written in June.

John Noble (1743–1828) was one of Burke's leading Bristol supporters. For the naval action described, see vol. III, 461, 464, 465.

My dear Sir,

A Stroke has been struck on the Coast of France. The Licorne and Pallas Frigates, hovering about the Fleet, and refusing to come to, are taken. The former fired her Broadside, and then struck. The Arethusa engaged the La Belle Poule a French Frigate for two hours. She was much damaged and lost in killed and wounded about 40. The Frenchman escaped. Some say the Arethusa was engaged with more than one; but of this I have no positive account. A French armed Schooner is taken also after a sharp engagement by one of our Sloops of War. Adieu. My Dear Sir, it is late. I have only to wish my Gossip[1] and you all happiness.

Most sincerely Yours
EDM BURKE

Westmr July 25. 1778

To WILLIAM EDEN—29 *September* 1779

Source: MS Osborn Collection.

This is Burke's letter to William Eden (1744–1814), later (1789) 1st Baron Auckland, about David Brown Dignan (*c.* 1755–80); see vol. IV, 133–5.

Dear Sir,

The Letter I take the Liberty of enclosing to you, is you will allow, of a very extraordinary kind, as it comes from a very extraordinary personage. I really think it is written with very great ability. All the general Topics seem to me handled in a very masterly manner; and there is little or nothing feeble in it except what is owing to the radical weakness of the Cause. Is it not shocking that a man capable of such things should Spend his Youth wheeling a barrow of Gravel at Woolwich amidst the outcasts of Society? Although I suppose he deserves his punishment as well as others that suffer along with him, yet that

[1] Presumably Mrs Noble had acted as godmother on an occasion when Burke himself was godfather—perhaps for Edmund Burke Smith (1775–1851); see vol. III, 131.

rigorous Justice, which considers nothing but the Crime, and totally forgets all persons and Circumstances, is perhaps too nearly allied to cruelty. Motives of humanity led you to bring into Parliament the Bill under which this unhappy man suffers,[1] and the same Motives will lead you in this Particular to interpose so far, as that the hard Labour, and other the most severe parts of his punishment may be remitted; and that a very young person, Liberally educated, and of a Slight make and constitution, may be employd in some way more suitable to him; and have even a few hours for such reading as may tend to correct his Vices. Mere punishment can hardly have that operation. It is not necessary that I should apologize to you for the trouble I give you: For a mind like yours will have a sympathy with Talents, however they may be abused, disgraced, or degraded. I have the honour to be with great regard and esteem

Dear Sir
Your most obedient
and humble Servant
EDM BURKE

Beconsfield Septr 29. 1779.

To LORD KENMARE—22 *January* 1780

Source: MS copy National Library of Ireland.

Thomas Browne, 4th Viscount Kenmare (1726–95), was a leading member of the Irish Catholic community.

Rt Honble Lord Viscount Kenmare

My Dear Lord

I have to ask pardon for a seeming neglect in Not answering instantly the Letter with which your Lordship honoured me by Mr Brown.[2] I was at that time ill, and much occupied, and every paper of the kind which your Lordship wished to see, was left in the Country, when I got there, I was not immediatly able to put my hands upon any of them, it is fourteen years ago Since I desisted from a pretty laborious work which I had undertaken upon the Subject of the penal System of Ireland.[3]

---

[1] See vol. III, 251–2, 252–3.
[2] Valentine Browne (1754–1812), Kenmare's only son. The letter he delivered is missing.
[3] The Tracts on the Popery Laws.

Except a prelimenary part, upon more general grounds, and a sort of popular abstr⟨act⟩ of that Body of Statutes, I found nothing at all in such order, as could make it of the least use; and a Business of some importance and difficulty, in which I have (perhaps imprudently) engaged,[1] and the necessity of some Relaxation on account of my health, rendered it utterly impracticable to digest my loose papers into any intelligible order. Very fortunately a Set of men have started up in Ireland since that period, of such Liberal Spirits, as well as of such powerfull Talents that they want no sort of assistance from me. The Gentlemen whom your Lordship has named in your letter are far more conversant, than I could ever have been in the Subject of their own Laws, and if it Suited me to engage again in the design, which I had formerly projected, I should probably apply to the very Gentlemen; not to give them any new lights, but to receive lights from them, and to receive with great docility the means of correcting my Errors. Another[2] circumstance that takes away from the Loss that your Lordsh⟨ip's⟩ partiality might imagine in this incurable disorder of my papers; It is that much the greater part were employed on the Subject of these Restraints on property: and all Reflections on that matter are rendered nearly unnecessary[3] by the wise Act of our last Session,[4] whatever defects it might have I take it for granted, will be very easily removed.

Merely to gratify your Lordship's Curiosity, for it can be of little use in Other Respects, I send by Mr Broughell,[5] *The View of the penal Laws*[6]. I got that part copied out, when Lord Richard Cavindishe's Bill, for the Relief of the Roman Catholicks from the English Act,[7] was in agitation, as a prelimenary to what was intended in Ireland; and I communicated it with good effect, to Lord North, to My Lord Chancellor,[8] The Attorney General,[9] The Lord advocate of Scotland,[10] and to some other Gentlemen besides my own particular Friends. Though of no use to the Gentlemen of the Bar in Ireland, it was of some here, where the Subject was less known, and where a long reading of acts of Irish Parliaments was a thing not to be expected[11]

---

[1] His plan of economic reform.
[2] MS: And other
[3] MS: necessary
[4] The Catholic Relief Act of 1778.
[5] Thomas Braughall (*c.* 1730–1803), of the Catholic Committee.
[6] MS copies in the National Library of Ireland and at Sheffield (R 103).
[7] Introduced by Lord Richard Cavendish (1751–81), second son of the Duke of Devonshire, in May 1778, to enable Ireland to pass its own Catholic Relief Act; see vol. III, 449.
[8] Edward Thurlow, 1st Baron Thurlow (1731–1806).
[9] Alexander Wedderburn (1733–1805), M.P. for Bishop's Castle.
[10] Henry Dundas (1742–1811), later (1802) 1st Viscount Melville, M.P. for Edinburghshire.
[11] MS: exspected

from either of Business or pleasure. I do most Sincerely wish your Lordship success in your endeavours for the future Relief of so large a part of your distressed Countrymen, your labours are now the more generous, because men of your quality and Fortune are already[1] relievd from a great part of your particular grivances, but indeed there are still much very much to be done, whether the time be favourable or not, I am not at all a Judge; and I fear that any interference of mine upon Irish affairs, would[2] be not so well taken at your Side of the Water, where I am supposed by Several, as I hear, not much to understand or to regard your Interests.[3]

I cannot conclude without giving your Lordship my best thanks for your kind protection of my kinsman Mr Neagle.[4] I have the honour to be with the greatest Regard and Esteem, My Lord Your Lordships most Obedient and Humble Servant.

EDMOND BOURKE

Charless Street January 22d. 1780

To SIR WILLIAM HAMILTON—29 *August* 1780

Source: MS Osborn Collection.

An extract of this letter was printed in vol. IV, 266 from *Sotheby Catalogue*, 22 April 1912, no. 150. Sir William Hamilton (1730–1803) was British Envoy at Naples.

Dear Sir,

I have so little Interest at home that I am willing to try whether I have any abroad; and if I should so far succeed in this adventure as to receive any token of Sir William Hamiltons regard I shall be indemnified in honour for what I may not have been so fortunate as to obtain in influence here.

The young Gentleman who will have the honour of delivering this to you is Mr Noble a very near relation to a Merchant of the very first Credit and Estimation in the City of Bristol, and one to whom I have been indebted for a long train of the most important and the kindest obligations. It is impossible for me to make any adequate requital to him; but the way in which I may approach the most nearly to it is by availing myself of my little power with my friends. Mr Noble is going to settle

---

[1] MS: alread
[2] MS: woul
[3] For Kenmare's reply see vol. IV, 203–4.
[4] Garrett Nagle (d. *c.* 1791), of Ballyduff; see vol. IV, 20.

in Business in the City of Naples; and I take the Liberty of most earnestly intreating your Countenance and protection to him. You will find him in all respects worthy of it; as he is a young man of strict honour, an excellent understanding, and a liberal and manly address.

I beg pardon for the Liberty I take but your known kindness to your deserving Countrymen, and your partiality to your friends induce me to flatter myself, that I shall find excuse for my application, and I hope effect from it. It is impossible for me to receive any favour more grateful to me, or that I shall more chearfully acknowlege than your protection to this young Gentleman.

I have the honour to be with Sentiments of the most respectful attachment

Dear Sir

Your most faithful

and obedient humble Servant

EDM BURKE

Bristol Aug. 29. 1780.

You will be so good as to present my most respectful Compliments to Lady Hamilton.

To the EARL OF HARDWICKE—5 *April* 1781

Source: MS Public Record Office of Northern Ireland (Caledon Papers, D. 2433/69/18).

Endorsed: Mr B—ke.

Philip Yorke, 2nd Earl of Hardwicke (1720–90), published *Walpoliana* in 1781.

Mr Burke presents his compliments and most grateful Acknowlege-ments to Lord Hardwicke for the honour his Lordship has done Mr Burke in the communication of his interesting and well selected Anecdotes concerning Sir Robert Walpole,[1] and will certainly restrain the participation of his pleasure in them to the Limits Lord Hardwicke has prescribed. Whatever the faults of the Minister, whose Life Lord Hardwicke has sketched, might have been, he was a *safe* Minister for this Country. His moderation of Temper did great things in difficult times, with no expence of blood, and not a great deal of expence of the publick Treasure. His Temperance with regard to peace Establishments (though they were greater perhaps than necessary) proved a foundation

[1] Sir Robert Walpole (1676–1745).

for the great things that followed and would have been sufficient to have supported any Fabrick of Grandeur if the same spirit had continued to govern the publick Councils.

Charles Street April 5. 1781.

To LORD MACARTNEY—15 *October* 1781

Source: Bodleian Library (Clark MSS).

Endorsed: Mr E. Burke M.P.| Beaconsfield 18 Oct. 1781| Rec June 1782
Per Dunkin.

George Macartney, 1st Baron Macartney (1737–1806), later (1794) 1st Earl Macartney, was an old friend of Burke's. In 1780 Burke had opposed his appointment as Governor of Madras, but once Macartney arrived in India, more cordial relations were restored by letter. A brief extract from this letter was printed in vol. IV, 377.

My dear Lord,

Your appointment has been but too well justified in the call which the distresses of your Province have made for great Abilities. I confess I suspected from the Tenour of the System which had long prevailed on the Coromandal Coast that an heavy Calamity of some kind or other must speedily have fallen upon it; and when your predecessors[1] short Letter was read in the general Court as a preservative against the spreading of my apprehensions I was silenced without being at all satisfied.[2] You enter indeed into a province harrassed and endangerd; which will, in the first instance, require all your exertions to defend it; and after it has been defended, all your wisdom to restore it. Your Task is difficult. But I have no doubt that you will acquit yourself with honour. Circumstances did not permit me to have a share in your appointment;[3] but I can say with Truth that no man wishes you success more cordially than I do.

To talk to you of publick affairs in my situation is little more than to repeat the Newspaper. As to my share of them it has been in the manner it has continued in for many years and in which it is likely to continue longer. India Business had a good share in the last Session. But it

---

[1] MS: precessors
[2] Haidar Ali of Mysore (*c.* 1722–82) had invaded the Carnatic and defeated a British army. Burke is presumably referring to letters from the former Governor, Sir Thomas Rumbold, 1st Baronet (1736–91), M.P. for Shaftesbury, read at the Company's General Court on 17 November 1780 (India Office Records, B/260, p. 19).
[3] For Burke's opposition to Macartney's appointment see vol. IV, 323–5.

employd without much agitating us. The confusions in Bengal, and the dangers in the Carnatick forced that Business upon [us] whether we would or not. The opposition concurred with the Ministry in almost all particulars relative to it. In my opinion the Salvation of that Country, and of this too, as far as it depends upon India (and that is a great deal) must depend upon our making an impartial review of our Conduct there. As far as it has chosen[1] to extend its Views the Secret Committee seems to have made an unexceptionable report.[2] We shall see, whether in the next Session, they will perfect their plan, and proceed upon it. Hitherto the Committee—multa et praeclara minatus,[3] has raised an expectation. A leading man in that Committee, and indeed in all Parliamentary affairs on the side of Ministry[4] hinted to me that an impeachment or a Bill of pains and penalties will be the consequence.[5] But you must not think me splenetick: I apprehend that no such remedy will be applied, but the grand favourite Nostrums of new offices, new Salaries, and new powers will be all the publick Issue of this Enquiry. The way to these Objects will indeed be full of menace and Bustle; but I fear in this it will end, or it will end in nothing. The last Act has given Government a more full and avowed share in Indian affairs than the act of 1774.[6] In that indeed the interference was implied, and the means of power in Effect amply given. I cheerfully agreed to it in the meeting, I had at Lord Norths, I think before your departure, on Condition that the propositions agreed upon in Behalf of the Tanjorines, and the other Natives, should be carried into execution.[7] On that head I have had since both from Robinson[8] and the Lord advocate[9] the fullest assurances of the determination of Government. But whether their promptitude has been correspondent to their intentions I know not. None of us opposed that Measure of power to Ministry as we had done on the former occasion. By the first act they obtaind the power substantially; and it may be of some use and some Check that they should obtain it formally and visibly. If our Bengal Committee could have passed the Bill through the Lords, on the Ideas on which it

[1] MS: it chosen
[2] The largely ministerial Secret Committee set up to enquire into the war in the Carnatic had made its first report on 27 June and 5 July 1781.
[3] Multa et praeclara minatus; having threatened great and glorious things (Horace, *Satires*, II, 3, 9).
[4] Presumably Henry Dundas, the Lord Advocate.
[5] A Bill of Pains and Penalties against Rumbold was in fact sponsored by the Secret Committee.
[6] Burke is comparing the Regulating Act of 1781 (21 Geo. III, c. 65) with the original Act of 1773 (13 Geo. III, c. 63).
[7] See vol. IV, 327–8.
[8] John Robinson (1727–1802), Secretary to the Treasury, M.P. for Harwich.
[9] Dundas

went so successfully through the House of Commons, I really think it would have done a great deal towards the Settlement of that Country.[1] The Chancellour[2] cut it short in many parts of it, and destroyd the regularity and system of the whole. I regret this without venturing to censure a man of his great parts, and having too all the reason in the world to thank him for his partiality to myself, in his publick declaration, that he went so far as he did, from his confidence in me; and on that Ground he would receive the rejected parts in another Session. That he did not Object to the matter, which seemd not improper; but that it would be much more to his mind, when the provisions should appear not so much to owe their origin to personal disputes and political Interests.[3] He gave more to me than I merited; as full as much, at least, was due to Genl Smith,[4] and Mr Rouse,[5] and other Gentlemen of the Committee, aided with extraordinary good information from without.

Things here are pretty much as you left them. Our Statesmen promised themselves rather too much from the advantage of a new Enemy. The Dutch War has answerd some purposes of resentment, and some of avarice. That Nation has sufferd; and individuals here have been enriched. But a moderate and a ballancing power has been lowerd; and others over great and not better disposed have been aggrandized. The first has felt the injury to the quick, and the latter are not over grateful for Benefits that were never intended for them. I fancy some applications more humiliating than effectual have been made to your old friends of Russia for their healing interposition to obtain a separate peace.[6] We are certainly rather sick of the Dutch War, notwithstanding all the plunder had and expected. As to the French and spaniards they are formidable in Force and sufferd to grow into a great and formidable superiority. But their want of Skill, or want of concert, has hitherto proved a sort of antidote to their power.

The American War seems to be in a *fair way* of dying a natural Death notwithstanding the attempts of France and England to make it

---

[1] The Bengal Judicature Act of 1781 (21 Geo. III, c. 70) was the work of the Select Committee, in which Burke had played a very prominent part.

[2] Thurlow

[3] Amendments to the Judicature Bill were inserted by the House of Lords on 12 and 13 July 1781.

[4] General Richard Smith (d. 1803), M.P. for Wendover.

[5] Charles William Boughton Rouse (1747–1821), later (1794), 9th Baronet, M.P. for Evesham.

[6] Negotiations in the autumn of 1781 for an end to hostilities with the Dutch through Russian mediation are described in I. de Madariaga, *Britain, Russia and the Armed Neutrality of 1780*, London, 1962, pp. 317 ff. Macartney had been Envoy to Russia 1764–7.

die by Violence. When it departs, sit illi terra levis[1]—we may well apply Vanbruggs epitaph to it—Oh Earth lie light on him, though he—laid many an heavy load on thee.[2]

Our friend Fox desires to be rememberd to you. He gains daily ground in Esteem and popularity with the Nation and with his Constituents. His situation in Westminster is such as I hope will secure him in future not only from defeat but from attack. You will have pleasure in hearing that all his Debts are either paid or settled—and that he is perfectly at his Ease.[3]

Adieu, my Dear Lord! Let this Letter have some value, if not from its Writer, at least from its bearer, our most worthy friend Dunkin.[4] By this you know through what dangers poor Will Burke has arrived to your Protection.[5] Pray Let him find consolation and amends in your friendship and power. I need not tell you that there is nothing so near my heart as his Success—I trust it is not far from your own. Let us see, I entreat, that in some one part of the World, there is one man, with whom old friends out of play are not out of regard. I have the honour to be with very sincere affection and high Esteem ever

My dear Lord
Your Lordships
most faithful
and Obedient humble Servant
EDM BURKE

Beconsfield Octr 15. 1781.

To WILLIAM EDEN—[circa 5 April 1782]

Source: MS Osborn Collection.

This letter almost certainly belongs to Eden's brief visit to England between 4 and 9 April 1782 (see vol. IV, 432–4).

Dear Sir,

I anticipated your obliging request, and the moment I heard of your arrival went to Sir John Edens[6] to look for you and left my Name. I wrote by the last post to Ireland[7] to thank you for the very kind polite,

---

[1] Let the earth lie lightly on it.
[2] The epitaph to Sir John Vanbrugh (1664–1726) by Abel Evans (1679–1737).
[3] See vol. IV, 377.
[4] William Dunkin (d. 1807) was going to India to practise as a barrister at Calcutta.
[5] For William's hazardous journey to India, see vol. IV, 379.
[6] Sir John Eden, 4th Baronet (1740–1812), William Eden's brother.
[7] Perhaps the letter of 5 April (see vol. IV, 432–3).

and every way handsome manner in which you conferred a real Obligation on me, by the Service you did my friend.[1] I am with great regard Dear Sir

ever sincerely Yours

EDM BURKE

I shall be at home and very happy to see you tomorrow at eleven or before as you please.

To LORD MACARTNEY—23 *September* [1783]

Source: Bodleian Library (Clark MSS).

Endorsed: Answer'd | Mr Ed Burke | Sept. 23. 1783.

Burke is answering Lord Macartney's letter from India of 17 October 1782 (see vol. V, 41–4).

Bath Septr 23.

My dear Lord,

I have just received intelligence in this place that a Vessel is to be instantly dispatched with an account of the Definitive Treaty. Remote as I am from London, and by no means in a condition of informing you of any thing at all clear or satisfactory with regard to publick affairs, I could not omit the Chance of the Vessel going to India, without a word to thank you heartily for your most friendly remembrance of me, and for the kind expressions you are so good to use with regard to your own and my old friend.[2]

I never for a moment doubted of two things; I mean of your incorruptible integrity, and of the incurable corruption of the person with whom you were unhappily connected. It was a thing absolutely impossible that two persons so perfectly dissimilar[3] should ever agree. Your being ill at the very fountain of pollution is to me worth a thousand proofs of the purity and rectitude of your Conduct.[4] Your affair has not yet had a parliamentary discussion, though all the papers were before the select Committee.[5] I have been out of Town so long on a Tour for my very necessary relaxation[6] that I cannot say whether the Ministers have

---

[1] Stephen Thurston Adey; see vol. IV, 287, 432, and below, pp. 22–3.
[2] William Burke.
[3] MS: dissimelar
[4] Burke is commenting on Macartney's quarrel with Paul Benfield (*c.* 1740–1810), M.P. for Cricklade; see vol. V, 43.
[5] See above, p. 12.
[6] Burke is reported to have arrived in Bath on 1 September (*Morning Herald*, 5 September 1783).

decided any thing on them or not. It indeed matters little for the present. The Nabob of Arcots scurrility[1] (for it is no more) or the scurrility put into his, and his sons mouth,[2] has had no Effect; and it is of no importance to look into this part of Mr Hastings's Conduct,[3] until he can be made sensible, that there is an authority somewhere in this Country that can call him to an account for his having so openly and avowedly cast off all pretence of obedience to the orders of the Court of directors, and the provisions of an Act of Parliament.[4] I am thoroughly convinced that the Court of directors itself must have some capital reform before it is fit for the exercise of the authority committed to it. Your Letter has made an impression upon me in many particulars, and no part of it either with regard to yourself or the publick has escaped me. This is all I can say for the present. I wish my power were more.[5] Adieu my Dear Lord—God preserve you in the honourable and virtuous struggle you are engaged in, and give you an honourable and successful issue. Remember me affectionately to my worthy friends Staunton[6] and Boyd;[7] and believe me ever My dear Lord

> Your Lordships
> most faithful
> and affectionate humble Servant
> EDM BURKE

Oh remember, that Will Burke is the man living most dear to me; and the quarter in which I am capable of receiving the most sensible obligation.

To LORD MACARTNEY—⟨13⟩ *January* 1785

Source: MS Osborn Collection.

Endorsed: Mr Ed Burke | London 25 Jany 1785.

My dear Lord,

I have begun several letters to your Lordship; I think no fewer than four or five. On all of these (to use a phrase of the House of Commons)

[1] Walajah Muhammad Ali, Nawab of the Carnatic (d. 1795), had complained bitterly about Macartney's treatment of him (for copies of his protests, see India Office Records, Home Miscellaneous, 324).

[2] The Amir ul-umara (d. 1788), second son of the Nawab, supported his father in these disputes.

[3] Hastings was threatening to intervene on the side of the Nawab; see vol. v, 43.

[4] Presumably the 1773 Regulating Act (13 Geo. III, c. 63).

[5] Burke was working on the provisions of Fox's India Bills at this time.

[6] George Leonard Staunton (1737–1801), later (1785) 1st Baronet; Macartney's secretary.

[7] Hugh Macauley Boyd (1746–94), Macartney's assistant secretary.

I have been ready to report a progress, and to move for leave to sit again. But I assure you, that the evanescent State of our Politicks has been such, that whilst I was writing you the State of them at any time, they alterd essentially; and I should have been obliged to contradict at the end of my Letter the representation I made in the beginning. I fairly own, that I never was able to catch 'the Cynthia of the minute'.[1]

There is one thing fixed however, which gives me great satisfaction, and upon which I may congratulate the publick, that is your Lordships confirmation in the Government of Madrass.[2] I shall certainly very soon trouble your Lordship with my thoughts upon some of the extraordinary instructions which you have receivd. Your State has hitherto been critical for want of Instructions. It will become more critical by your receiving them. You proposed a Scheme for redeeming all affairs and satisfying *all* Interests in the Carnatick. As much as sailed with *private* Interests has been receivd. The East is left to chance at best; and the *foundation* of the whole System is taken away. I confess I had my Doubts on the Scheme, as it stood entire and complete in all its parts. Neither you nor I can approve of it mangled as it is.[3]

I am now to recommend to your Lordships particular attention and civilities[4] Mr Tilghman[5] who does me the favour to present this to you. I shall take your protection to him as a very great kindness to myself. But he well merits friendship and regard on his own account, as he is a person of great merit experience and understanding, (and if I may add, what to all good minds must strongly recommend him) of no small suffering for his Virtues. He is a relation of Mr Francis and is on his way to Bengal to practice the profession of a Lawyer.

> I am, my Dear Lord,
> Your Lordships
> most affectionate and faithful
> humble Servant
> EDM BURKE

Charles Street Jany ⟨13⟩ 1785.

[1] Pope, *Moral Essays*, II, 20.
[2] Macartney had been reappointed Governor on 2 September.
[3] In the autumn of 1784 the Directors of the East India Company drafted a despatch intended to resolve urgent problems facing the Company at Madras: relations between the Nawab of Arcot and the Raja of Tanjore and the debts owed by both to the Company and to private creditors. This despatch was drastically amended by the Board of Control in ways that Burke was later to denounce in his *Speech on the Nabob of Arcot's Debts*. The scheme of Macartney's to which Burke refers was probably one for eventually paying off the debts; it is dated 30 October 1781 (India Office Records, Home Miscellaneous, 246, pp. 421–35).
[4] MS: civilities to
[5] Richard Tilghman (d. 1787), a cousin of Philip Francis (1740–1818); see vol. v, 95.

To LADY MACARTNEY—17 *February* 1785

Source: Bodleian Library (Clark MSS). Printed in vol. v, 207, from Clark, *Gleanings from an Old Portfolio*, I, 279.

Madam,

I take it for granted you are informed that Lord Macartney is chosen Governour General of Bengal. Permit me to wish your Ladyship Joy of this appointment so pleasant to all your friends and so beneficial to the publick. I have the honour to be, with Mrs Burkes most respectful Compliments and with the highest respect

Madam

Your Ladyships

most obedient

and most humble

Servant

EDM BURKE

Charles Street

Feb. 17. 1785.

To HUGH ELLIOT—29 *July* 1786

Source: MS National Library of Scotland.

Hugh Elliot (1752–1830) was a brother of Sir Gilbert Elliot, 4th Baronet (1751–1814), later (1813) 1st Earl of Minto. Sir Gilbert was contesting Berwick at a by-election; see vol. v, 276–7, 279–80.

Dear Sir,

I can I am afraid do no great Service to your Brother and my excellent friend in this Contest. Some friends of mine are doing what they can. But I am full of anxiety and wish to know whether in any way such a thing as I am can be turned to use. Pray let me know what aspect things bear. Believe me there are very few Events about which I can be more sollicitous than I am concerning the fate of the Berwick Election. I have the honour to be with very real respect and regard

Dear Sir

Your most faithful

and obedient humble Servant

EDM BURKE

Beconsfield July 29. 1786

Are there any freemen of Berwick at Bristol?

To JOHN S. BARROW—1 *October* 1786

Source: *Annals of the Fine Arts*, V (1820), no. 16, pp. 110–11.

An extract from this letter was printed in vol. V, 283–4. The recipient was then thought to be William Sharp (1749–1824), a line engraver. The letter had in fact appeared in print in *Annals of the Fine Arts* in 1820 and has been reprinted from that magazine in *Philological Quarterly*, L (1971), 675–7. Thus the recipient is now known to be John S. Barrow, who described himself in 1820 as 'Jeweller &c. No. 1, Little Compton Street, Soho, Citizen of the World in a Sky Parlour— the fate of most geniuses'. Barrow explained the circumstances of the composition of the letter:

The following anecdote relative to the late Honourable Edmund Burke is communicated in gratitude to his memory, principally to introduce a letter which he sent to Alderman Carr, [John Carr (1723–1807)] of York, to be delivered to the person by whom this anecdote is communicated. My occupation was that of a diamond jeweller. In the summer of 1786 I was going to York on foot: when I had got six miles on the Uxbridge road, I heard a voice behind me saying to a servant on horseback, 'Ask that gentleman how far he is going before he stops.' The carriage having reached me, the person within it asked me if I would step in? I declined, as I was going to stop at a village called South Hall, about a mile distant. 'Do, Sir, come in, it will rest you a little.' His manner was so very persuasive that I got in: he was reading Buffon's Natural History in French.

We had some interesting conversation, and, among other things, I had shown him the first or second attempt I had made at engraving, with which he seemed surprised and pleased. From circumstances, I thought he was a gentleman farmer. But we arrived at last at a very handsome mansion, and he introduced me to a lady and two gentlemen as an ingenious young man that he had met with on the road, whose name was Barrow. After dinner he took me to see his paintings; and then I asked him to whom I was so much obliged for such uncommon civility? 'When you return to London, go to Sir Joshua Reynolds', and ask for Burke of Beaconsfield', and at the same time put 10s. 6d. in my hand, observing, as I was a foot-traveller I should find it convenient on the road: it was wrapped in a piece of paper. I omitted to observe, that I had long had a desire to see, or, if possible, be acquainted with the Mr Burke who made a farewell speech to the people of Bristol, that made a very lasting impression on me; consequently the first house I came to after leaving Beaconsfield, I inquired whether it was Burke the member of parliament that lived where I had dined; and on being informed it was, I was much gratified to think I had my desire accomplished in so extraordinary a manner.

On my arrival at York I wrote a very warm imagined letter to my patron at Beaconsfield; and on my return to London, I went immediately to Sir Joshua's, and finding Mr Burke was still at Beaconsfield, I went there, and there he entertained me some days; and on going with him into his study the day of my arrival, he put the following letter into my hand, saying, 'I give you this, Sir, to let you see I did not neglect answering yours.' It was enclosed to Mr Carr, who was to give it to me; but I having left York, he returned it to Mr Burke; and is as follows:—

Beaconsfield, October 1, 1786

Sir,

I am much obliged to you for your letter from York, and for your receiving so kindly the trifling accommodation that it fell in my way by accident to afford you: I should, however, be exceedingly concerned if it should become the means of raising in your mind expectations which it may not be in my power to answer, and of inducing you to engage in pursuits which all your abilities and industry may not enable you to succeed in. My circumstances are such as oblige me to keep within narrow bounds, and will not suffer me to show that countenance to talents I wish to show whenever I meet them. Your case, I assure you, is one of those which makes the reserves which prudence and justice indispensably require, somewhat painful to me.

Not being able to undertake to support you in your studies as a painter, I cannot, in conscience and honour, encourage you to abandon wholly the business to which you are bred, and which is a very respectable trade.

I do not, however, mean at all to discourage you from the study of design, so far as is compatible with that employment which must be the foundation of your support and your retreat, in case your progress in the arts, or the encouragement you meet with, should not equal our mutual wishes.

Whether you can arrive at sufficient eminence as a painter to answer any good purpose, must be, in a great measure, uncertain; but, at any rate, whatever progress you make in design, though not sufficient to accomplish you as a painter, cannot fail of being of very great advantage in all those trades that are conversant in decoration, which are many, and some of them lucrative. I shall certainly, therefore, when we meet in town next winter, recommend you to the Academy—to Sir Joshua Reynolds, provided your progress in drawing be such as will entitle you to learn there; and we shall talk further on the further steps you are to take.

Your communicating your ideas to me in so open and friendly a manner, will, I hope, justify the liberty I take in recommending to you to put a little restraint on your imagination, relative to your views in life.

The spirit of enterprise and adventure I certainly do not mean wholly to damp, as it is the source of every thing which improves and adorns society; but, at the same time, it is more frequently the cause of the greatest disappointments, miseries and misfortunes, and sometimes of dangerous immoralities.

You seem to feel too much disgust at humble but honest situations in life, and to form too slight an opinion of those whom the order of Providence has destined to those situations. This is a serious mistake, whether it regards the happiness or the virtue of men, which are neither of them much less in one condition than in another.

Your own happiness is deeply concerned in not giving yourself over too much to the guidance of your imagination.

You will excuse the liberty I take, as proceeding from my very good wishes for you; and you will do me the favour to believe me, Sir,

Your most obedient and humble servant,
EDMUND BURKE

P.S. I enclose this to Mr Carr, of York, upon whom you will wait as soon as you can.

To UNKNOWN—5 [*December*] 1787

Source: MS Osborn Collection.

Endorsed: Edmund Burke Esqr | Decr 5. 1787.

This letter seems clearly to be connected with the appointment of a committee of the House of Commons to consider Hastings's Answer to the Article of Impeachment against him. Since the Committee was appointed on 5 December, the date endorsed on the letter, it is likely that Burke's 5 November is an error.

An extract of this letter was printed in vol. v, 358. Its recipient was probably Welbore Ellis (1713–1802), later (1794) 1st Baron Mendip, M.P. for Weymouth and Melcombe Regis. According to Burke, Ellis felt himself 'unequal at his time of life to the labour' of serving on the Committee (vol. v, 362). Ellis was certainly a man of 'long parliamentary and official Experience'.

My dear Sir,

The Duke of Portland has informed me that we are not to have the honour and advantage of your support in an undertaking which I had flatterd myself had the good fortune to obtain your Countenance. This is a loss to us which we shall not be able to repair; and I am very sorry for it. The advanced time of Life which you urge was one of my reasons in addition to your knowlege and ability, in wishing your assistance; as men of long parliamentary and official Experience would add much to the authority of our proceeding. If other infirmities prevent our having the honour which we proposed, I sincerely lament the Cause of the loss, as well as the loss itself, as I am with great Esteem and respect

Dear Sir

Your most faithful

and obedient humble Servant

EDM BURKE

Gerard Street Nov. 5. 1787

To SIR WILLIAM HAMILTON—29 *December* 1787

Source: MS The Chequers Trust.

This letter, published here by permission of the Trustees of the Chequers Trust, was kindly transcribed for us by Mr Anthony Hobson.

Dear Sir,

It has been my fortune to be always much in your Debt for your extraordinary goodness to the friends I have taken the liberty of recommending to you, without any power of return except in entertaining for you those sentiments of sincere respect which I have in common with too many others to leave me a great deal of merit in that particular. I am once again to make trial of your partiality. Mr Hutchinson[1] a young Gentleman who is a friend of my Son, and one to whom he wishes every advantage and every satisfaction in his travels, is ambitious of being presented to you; and an ambition so well directed, we think, ought not to be discouraged. He will have the honour of waiting on you at Naples. I shall be extremely happy, if this young Gentleman should have the good fortune, as I have no doubt he will, of meriting your protection whilst he stays in your Sphere of wonders.

I remain here, as you see, tied down as usual; but with an hope of drawing in some tolerable time to the end of my long struggle with the disorders of our Oriental Government. You are in a Country,[2] which was in its day, the scene of similar agitations. It is less glorious now; but less guilty too; and perhaps not less happy. You, I am sure spend your time there in a way in which every wise man ought to wish to pass the period of his mature age; in a soft Climate, in an honourable and useful, but not too laborious an employment; with all the busy transactions of the world near enough to you to keep up an Interest, but not so near as to trouble your repose; with all the monuments of the Bustle of the antient world very near you, and indeed all about you,

[1] Probably Richard Hely Hutchinson (1756–1825); see vol. v, 289.
[2] MS: County

but so as to be Objects only of elegant curiosity, and Philosophical Speculation; with the ruins of art, and the ruins of Nature too in your Neighbourhood, only to teach you how to regenerate the[1] former, and to shew you how the world is regenerated from the latter. (Excuse this ugly blot, but your Vulcanos deface everything.) Enjoy my dear Sir this situation, which nothing but the self Love of your friend could wish to call you from, and do me the favour to believe me with the most perfect respect and most cordial regard

Dear Sir
Your most faithful and
obedient humble servant
EDM BURKE

Beaconsfield Dec. 29. 1787.

The Duke of Portland has been led by his publick spirit to let your fine Vase out of his Hands; and it is to be hoped that Wedgwood will make a good Copy of it in his Ware.[2] It is returned, but the Copy I have not yet seen. Pray can you favour me with the printed account of the Births, Burials, and Lists of population which I understand are printed sometimes in Naples.

To STEPHEN THURSTON ADEY—[29] *June* 1788

Source: MS Osborn Collection.

Endorsed: Burkes Letter.

29 June 1788 was a Sunday. An extract from this letter was printed in vol. IX, 434.

My dear friend,

It was with the most real and heartfelt concern, that Mrs Burke and I received your Letter yesterday morning. I was in hopes, that these violent Commercial Storms would not have reached the family of a friend in whose welfare we took a deeper Interest than in that of any commercial house in the world. You must be deeply affected for your father,[3] even independently of what you suffer yourself. I hope that the

---

[1] There is a blot in the MS at this point.
[2] William Henry Cavendish Bentinck, 3rd Duke of Portland (1738–1809), had purchased the Portland Vase, previously owned by Hamilton, at the sale of his mother's museum. Josiah Wedgwood (1730–95) had originally intended to buy it in order to copy it. Portland allowed him to produce his copy, which he duly did.
[3] George Adey (d. 1801).

competency which you suppose will be left, will be found to turn out on the most ample side of competence. I shall be in Town the day you receive this—that is tomorrow and will see you if I can. Be assured, that it is highly flattering to us, that you find any consolation in our Sympathy and regard: If you do, you have them in the fullest measure. You deserve them if ever man did, for your kind, zealous, and steady friendship to this family; and for the amiable and honourable qualities, which ought to ensure you a friend and well wisher in every one that knows you. Our Sympathy is all which in our very powerless State we have to give. God give you better fortune; and more effective friends; more sincere you cannot have. Believe me with the most cordial affection ever

My dear Adey
Your most faithful
and obliged friend and humble Servant
EDM BURKE

Beconsfield Sunday 28. June 1788.

I have received a Letter from Little Carter[1] by the Thetis from India,[2] enclosing Bills for near eleven hundred pound more. I shall deposit them at your house. He has made a tolerable adventure of it for the time.

To JAMES NORTHCOTE—*January* 1790

Source: MS Osborn Collection.

Addressed: Northcote Esqr | Clifford Street | Bond Street.

Only the signature is in Burke's hand.

A similar letter to that written by Burke to Richard Cosway; see vol. VI, 78. James Northcote (1746–1831) was a portrait painter, once assistant to Reynolds and later his biographer.

Sir

I am much interested from the Value I have for an Old and Approved friend[3] in favor of a Young Gentleman, Mr Sanders,[4] whom he protects.—You know his Merit, because the Academy has acknowledged it—He wishes, and I wish that He may have the means of encreasing it,

---

[1] Not identified.
[2] The arrival of the *Thetis* was reported from Deal on 25 June (*Public Advertiser*, 27 June).
[3] Not identified.
[4] John Sanders (1768–1826); see vol. VI, 78.

and making himself worthy of being one Day of your Body by his being sent to Rome under your Protection.—I shall be much obliged to you for your Vote and have the Honor of being

Sir

Your most obedient Servant
EDM BURKE

Gerrard Street
 January 1790
— Northcote Esqr

To JOHN HATSELL—[*November* 1790]

Source: Northamptonshire Record Office (Young of Orlingbury MSS)

Endorsed: Letter from Mr Burke [?] To J. Hatsell Esqr.

John Hatsell (1743–1820), Clerk of the House of Commons, explains the circumstances in which this letter was written in a memorandum added to its second sheet:

This Letter from Mr Burke, arose, from my having express'd to him, whilst Mr *Fox* was standing by us in the H. of Cs my thanks for his publication relating to the French Revolution—Mr B. wish'd at the time to stop me, but as I persever'd to express in the strongest terms, my admiration at the Performance, and my opinion of its' utility, Mr B. hastily turn'd away, under pretence of speaking to another person—As soon as he was gone, Mr Fox said, Do you sincerely think what you said? I replied—Very sincerely—For, I confess, that in point of writing, wit, eloquence; politicks, philosophy, elegance, and every other *word*, that you Yourself or Mr Pitt could add of approbation, I think I know no Book that goes beyond it—But, said Mr Fox, sure it is inferior to Burke's other publications, Don't you think, He could have written better on this subject? To which I answer'd, Perhaps he might—but, Mr Fox, do You know any person that could have wrote so well? To which He gave me no answer.

My dear Sir,

   When you did me the honour to speak to me yesterday, I broke from you, in what might appear a rude and abrupt manner, and put a sudden stop to the conversation. I beg you not to think, that I felt indifferent to your approbation. I have ever courted it, and ever shall; and in the last critical measure, my having receivd it, is a most sincere Satisfaction to me. But I had reasons, just at that instant, for wishing, that a conversation so kind and flattering to me, should be discontinued; I feard it might draw out something which I did not wish to hear. Great Pains are taken to make ill blood where no ill blood ought to exist.

This is the Truth—and it is my apology for what was the furthest thing in the world from my heart, any thing like a Slight of your[1] opinions. Burn this. I am with the most perfect respect and regard

My dear Sir

Your most faithful

and obliged humble Servant

EDM BURKE

Duke Street St James's
Friday morn.

To JOHN KING—*4 December* 1791

Source: MS Osborn Collection.

This is Burke's letter of congratulation to John King (1760–1830) on his promotion to be Under-Secretary of State for the Home Department; see vol. VI, 454.

My dear John

My Brothers Letter brought us good news late last Night to compensate for a bitter Night and a leaky roof. We never sat up to better purpose. I congratulate you, your family, your friends, your protectors, and the publick service, on your promotion. It does indeed Great Credit at present, and it will do more in future, to those who brought you forward. Lord Grenville[2] has shewn sense, friendship, and a generous disposition. May you and they derive much advantage and honour from it. Mrs Burke desires me to tell you of the General Joy—adieu My Dear King

and believe me in all fortunes

most affectionately yours

EDM BURKE

Beconsfield 4. Decr 1791.

---

[1] MS: yours
[2] William Wyndham Grenville, 1st Baron Grenville (1759–1834), the Foreign Secretary.

To JOHN WILMOT—9 *October* 1792

Source: MS Osborn Collection.

This is Burke's acknowledgement of a letter from John Wilmot (*c.* 1749–1815), M.P. for Coventry, of 6 October 1792 (see vol. VII, 234–5).

Dear Sir,

I am extremely obliged to you for the favour of your Letter, and as much so for the arrangement it announces. I shall be always happy when you follow the dictates of your own good heart and your excellent understanding, and defye and renounce the Morning Chronicle and all his works. My observations on the conduct of our worthy Guests is exactly the same as yours.

I have the honour to be with the most sincere respect and Esteem

Dear Sir

Your most faithful
and obedient Servant

Bath Octr. 9. 1792.

To UNKNOWN—7 *March* 1793

Source: MS Osborn Collection.

The third page of the manuscript is torn.

An extract from this letter was printed in vol. VII, 358. The recipient and his 'valuable work' have not been identified.

My dear Sir,

I really thought I had very long since answerd the Letter which accompanied your valuable work. Nobody could be more sensible, than I was, and am of the Honour I receiv'd, or of the Service which such things, so executed, must prove to the world at this time. But procrastination first, and then some as little excusable degree of oblivion, may perhaps be more easily accounted for than justified—by domestick cares, and anxieties for the health of those we Love; some painful sollicitudes for the publick, and that croud of smaller Duties which you speak of, and of which, not the most important, but the most urgent are those that are most numerous and nearest. If I had husbanded my time with the greatest exactness and regulated my mind and conduct with the greatest Care, so as not to suffer any thing in my Business to fall into Confusion, or to see persons that I am not bound to see, or to eat drink or sleep more than Nature requires, or to go into Company that I am not necessitated to frequent, or to continue longer in it than prudence prescribes, perhaps this and innumerable Errours of the same kind might be avoided. They who know my way of Life will not be surprised that I am not very punctual, particularly in answering Letters. I cannot be very exact, but the fact nearly is, that being known to take a considerable Interest in the fate of seventy thousand Gentlemen, driven by the doctrines which you combat from their Country, I have had Letters innumerable Sent to me from abroad; I cannot as I said, be very exact, but I think the Postage alone of Books and Letters has not cost me within this year not much less than forty pound. My House too has never been shut to any human Creature for 27 years past.

Considering this mass of human infirmity, domestick attention, and various greater and smaller avocations so ⟨ ⟩ you, a⟨ ⟩ reasons for my ⟨ ⟩ some ones he *has* ⟨ ⟩ to your goodness than to his ⟨ ⟩ most exceedingly honourd by your ⟨ ⟩ and shall find myself happy in receiving ⟨ ⟩

I have the honour to be with great Esteem and respect
Sir

Your most obedient
and humble Servant
EDM BURKE

Duke Street March 7. 1793.

To EVAN NEPEAN—14 [*July*] 1793

Source: MS Osborn Collection.

Addressed: Evan Nepean Esqr| &c &c &c

Endorsed: Beaconsfield 14 July 1793 | Rt H: Edmd Burke | (Pte) | Ry 15.
Burke was trying to help the Duchesse de La Trémoille in July 1793.

An extract from this letter was printed in vol. VII, 378.

Dear Sir,

Tho' I attribute your readiness to oblige the Dutchess de la Tremouille,[1] to your politeness and humanity to an exiled foreign

---

[1] Louise-Emmanuelle, *née* de Châtillon (1763–1814), wife of Charles-Bretagne-Marie-Joseph, Prince de Tarente and Duc de La Trémoille (1764–1839).

Lady of great distinction, yet I take part of it to myself; and am much obliged to you for your ready kindness and attention. Mr Dundas observed to me that the affair was not in his Department: this I knew very well; and hope he will excuse my irregularity; because I have the honour of something more of intimacy with him than with the other Ministers. I had therefore taken the Liberty of making my application to him, rather as an acquaintance, with whom I have many years sat in Parliament, than as to a Minister of Department—Be so good to tell him this as my apology for the trouble I had given him in my two Notes.[1] Your kindness on that occasion encourages me to trouble you to send by the first Government express the little pacquet I enclose to a young man a relation of mine, who serves, I beleive, at present as a volunteer in the Austrian Army.[2] But as I have given him a Letter of recommendation to Col. St Leger,[3] He may be heard of, I take it, at the Duke of Yorks head quarters.

I beg pardon for this Trouble and have the honour to be with great respect and regard

Dear Sir
Your most obedient
and humble Servant
EDM BURKE

Beconsfield June 14. 1793.

To JOHN WILMOT—24 *November* 1793

Source: MS Osborn Collection.

Endorsed: J. Wilmot Esqr.

Burke's signature—on the verso of the single sheet—has been cut away, removing several words and parts of words on the recto.

This is part of Burke's correspondence relating to the proposed removal of the French *émigré* clergy from Winchester (see vol. VII, 491–2, 497–9).

Dear Sir,

I have strong reason to fear, that some persons perform ill Offices to the French Clergy; as the Ministers shew ⟨a general⟩ good disposition towards them. I will, without de⟨lay take the Liberty⟩ of laying my thoughts and wishes on this Subject ⟨before⟩ Mr Pitt. I must at the

---

[1] One is that of 10 July (see vol. VII, 377–8), the other is missing, unless it is that of 27 June (vol. VII, 377).
[2] James Nagle (d. 1801); see vol. VII, 376.
[3] Colonel John Hayes St Leger (1756–1800), M.P. for Okehampton, Deputy Adjutant General to Frederick, Duke of York (1963–1827). The letter is missing.

same time beg leave to suggest to you, that a strong Letter on this subject to him from the Committee itself,[1] will have a much greater weight with him than any sollicitation of mine. This is a fatal measure, especially at this time, and cannot fail of having the very worst effects, not only on the unhappy sufferers but on Government itself. I should think, that if the Marquis of Buckingham[2] took up the matter a little strongly he could not fail of success. He has done great things for that place, and this last effort would crown all. The Marchioness[3] appeard there like a protecting Angel.

I have the honour to be with great respect and regard

Dear Sir

Your most faithful

and obedient humble Servant

Beconsfield Nov. 24. 1793.

To [George Croker Fox]—*2 May* 1794

Source: MS Osborn Collection.

Endorsed: Ed: Burke | 1794 | [in pencil] To G Croker Fox | Grove Hill.

It is not known what connexion George Croker Fox (1752–1807) had with Pierre-Gaëton Dupont (1762–1817), translator of the *Reflections* into French.

Sir,

I am infinitely obliged to you for your kind attention in forwarding to me the Letter of my worthy and unfortunate friend Mr Dupont.[4] Your Humanity on all such occasions makes this nothing new either to you or to me. I really think the national Character itself obliged to you on these and many other accounts. I have the honour to be with great Respect and regard

Sir

Your most obedient and humble

Servant

EDM BURKE

Duke Street

St James's May 2. 1794.

Will you be so good as to shew my friend the Civilities you are so well disposed to.

[1] The Wilmot Committee.
[2] George Nugent Temple Grenville, 1st Marquess of Buckingham (1753–1813).
[3] Mary Elizabeth, *née* Nugent (d. 1812).
[4] Dupont was back in England by August, when he witnessed Burke's will (see vol. IX, 378). The letter is missing.

To SIR HERCULES LANGRISHE—13 *March* 1795

Source: MS copy Public Record Office, Dublin (Kilkenny 38).

Sir Hercules Langrishe, 1st Baronet (1731–1811) wrote to Burke on 5 March 1795 to explain and defend the Bill which Henry Grattan (1746–1820) was sponsoring, which would complete the emancipation of the Catholics (MS copy Public Record Office, Dublin, Kilkenny 38). It was for supporting this Bill that Burke's patron William Fitzwilliam, 4th Earl Fitzwilliam (1748–1833), was forced to give up the office of Lord Lieutenant of Ireland (see vol. VIII, xiv–xvii).

My Dear Sir

I give you a thousand thanks for the instance of your good nature, which came to my hands Yesterday. It is of a piece with all your kindness, to recollect a miserable broken spirited Old Man, wholly out of the World, except when reluctantly drawn into it by some very vexatious Business to myself, or to my friends. I can do very little as to the explanation of the Catholic Bill. I have never dined out of my own House in Company since my Disaster, and probably never may. But on this occasion, as far as I can find, there is no great mischief to arise from my want of means of Circulating in Society the lights you are so good to furnish. The Bill is perfectly understood in its Spirit; That is, that it is a measure to quiet the minds of Three Millions of people, at a far less expence to Government, than what serves, as an inadequate Compensation, to disquiet the mind of one Clerk of the Castle. The opposition to it, is also perfectly well understood in its Spirit. That it is a measure to get rid of an Excellent Man, and Lord Lieutenant; and when that End is answered, it is to be passed to reconcile the minds of the people to a new one. Passed it will be, no doubt of it;—This is the course always adopted for the honor of Parliament. A measure is to be at first rejected, or postponed as improper; and then received as necessary.

My Dear Sir Hercules! I am but a very poor Polititian. It is fit therefore that I should quit the Field. May you long continue in it with Honour and success.

Believe me with much Affection Ever truly Yours

EDMUND BURKE

Nerot's Hotel March 13th 1795

I am in Town expecting every Day to see on his return my Old friend Earl Fitzwilliam, in his new Character of a deposed Tyrant.

To SIR HERCULES LANGRISHE—26 *May* 1795

Source: MS copy Public Record Office, Dublin (Kilkenny 38).

Printed in vol. VIII, 253–7, from *Works* (Bohn), VI, 56–61; (Little, Brown), VI, 375–84.

My Dear Sir

If I am not as early as I ought to be in my acknowledgments for your very kind Letter, pray do me the Justice to attribute my failure to its real cause, a want of the most ordinary power of exertion; owing to the impressions made upon an Old, and infirm Constitution by private misfortune and by public calamity. It is true I make occasional efforts to rouse myself to some thing better, but I soon relapse into that state of langour, which must be the habit of my body and understanding, to the end of my short, and cheerless existence in the World.

I am sincerely grateful for your kindness in connecting the interest you take in the sentiments of an Old Friend, with the able part you take in the Service of your Country. It is an instance, among many, of that happy temper which has always given a Character of amity to your Virtues and a good natured direction to your Talents—Your Speech on the late Catholic Question, I read with much satisfaction—It is solid, It is convincing; It is eloquent, and it ought on the spot to have produced that Effect, which it's Reason, and that contained in the other excellent Speeches on the same side the Question, cannot possibly fail, (tho with less pleasant consequences) to produce hereafter. What a sad thing it is, that the grand Instructor *Time*, has not yet been able to teach the grand Lesson, of his own value; and that in every Question of Moral and political prudence it is the Cause of the Moment, which renders the Measure serviceable, or useless, anxious, or salutary. In the Catholic Question I considered only one point. Was it at the time, and in the circumstances, a measure which tended to promote the concord of the Citizens? I have no difficulty in saying it was; and as little in saying that the present concord of the Citizens was worth buying at a critical Season, by granting a few *Capacities*, which probably no one Man now living is likely to be served or hurt by. When any Man tells *you or me*, that, if those places were left in the Discretion of a Protestant Crown, and these Memberships in the Discretion of Protestant Electors, or Patrons, that We should have a Popish Official System, and a Popish Representation, capable of overturning the Establishment, He only insults our Understandings. When any man tells this to Catholics, he insults their Understandings, and he galls their feelings. It is not the Question of the Places and Seats, it is the *real* hostile Disposition, and the pretended Fears that leave stings in the minds of the people. I really thought that in the total of the late circumstances, with regard to persons, to things, to principles, and to measures, was to be found a Conjuncture favourable to the introduction, and to the perpetuation of a general Harmony; producing a general Strength, which to that hour Ireland was never so happy as to enjoy—My sanguine hopes are blasted, and I must consign my feelings on that terrible disappointment to the same patience in which I have been obliged to bury the vexation I suffered on the defeat of the other great, just, and honourable causes in which I had some share; and which have given more of Dignity, than of Peace and advantage, to a long laborious Life. Tho perhaps a want of success might be urged as a reason for making me doubt of the Justice of the part I have taken, yet untill I have other Lights than one Side of the debate has furnished me, I must see things, and feel them too, as I see, and feel them. I think I can hardly overrate the malignity of the principles of the Protestant Ascendency, as they affect Ireland; or of Indianism, as they affect these Countries, and as they effect Asia, or of Jacobinism, as they affect all Europe, and the state of human Society itself. The last is the greatest Evil; but it readily combines with the others, and flows from them.

Whatever breeds discontent at this time, will produce that great master mischief most infallibly. Whatever tends to persuade the people, that the *few*, called by whatever name you please, religious or political, are of opinion, that their interest is not compatible with that of the *many*, is a great point gained to Jacobinism. Whatever tends to irritate the Talents of a Country, which at all times, and at these particularly, have a mighty Influence on the public mind, is of infinite service to this formidable Cause. Unless where Heaven has mingled uncommon ingredients of Virtue in the Composition.

Talents naturally gravitate to Jacobinism. Whatever ill Humours are afloat in the State, they will be sure to discharge themselves in a mingled Torrent in the *Cloaca maxima* of Jacobinism; therefore people ought well to look about them. The Physicians are to take care that they do nothing to irritate this Epidemic distemper. It is a foolish thing to have the better of a Patient in a dispute—The Complaint, or its cause, ought to be removed, and wise and lenient Arts ought to precede the necessity of vigour. They ought to be the *Ultima*, not the *Prima*, not the sola ratio, of a wise Government. God forbid, that on a worthy occasion Authority should want the means of force; or the disposition to use it. But where a prudent and enlarged Policy does not precede it, and attend it too; where the Hearts of the better sort of the people do not go with the hands of the Soldiery, you may call your Constitution what you will; In Effect it will consist of three parts (orders if you please) Cavalry Infantry, and Artillery, and of nothing else, or better. I agree with you in your dislike of the Discourses in *Francis Street*—But I like as little some of those in *College Green*. I am even less pleased with the Temper that predominated in the latter, as better things might have been expected in the regular Family Mansion of public Discretion, than in a new and hasty assemblage of unexperienced Men; congregated under Circumstances of no small invitation. After people have taken your Tests, prescribed by yourselves, as proofs of their Allegiance; to be marked as Enemies, Traitors, or at best as suspected and dangerous persons; and that they are not to be believed on their Oaths, we are not to be surprised if they fall into a passion, and talk as Men in a passion do, intemperately and Idly. The worst of the matter is this, you are partly leading, partly driving into Jacobinism, that description of your people, whose religious principles, Church Polity, and habitual discipline,[1] might make them an Invincible Dyke against that Inundation. This you have a thousand mattocks and Pick Axes lifted up to demolish. You make a sad Story of the Pope 'O sere Studiorum'—It will not be difficult to get many called Catholics, to laugh at this fundamental part of their Religion. Never doubt it—You have succeeded in part, and you may succeed completely. But in the present State of Men's minds, and affairs, do not flatter yourselves, that they will piously look to the Head of our Church, in the place of that Pope, whom you make them forswear, and out of all Reverence to whom, you bully, and rail, and buffoon them. Perhaps you may succeed in the same manner with all the other Tenets of Doctrine and Usages of Discipline[2] amongst the Catholics.—But what security have you, that, in the Temper, and on the Principles on which they have made this change, they will stop at the exact sticking place? You have marked in *your* Articles! you have no Security for any thing but that [they] will become what are called French Jacobins, and reject the whole together. No Converts will now be made in a considerable number from one of our Sects to the others, upon really Religious Principles—Controversy moves in another direction. Next to Religion *Property*, is the great point of Jacobin attack. Here many of the Debaters in your Majority, and their Writers, have given these Jacobins all the assistance their hearts can wish. When the Catholics desire places and Seats, you tell them, that this is the only Pretext, (tho' Protestants might suppose it just *possible*, that men should like your places and snug Burroughs for their own Merits,) but that their real view is to strip Protestants of their

---

[1] MS: dicipline
[2] MS Dicipline

Property. To my certain knowledge, untill those Jacobin Lectures were opened in the House of Commons, they never dreamt of any such thing. But now the great Professors may stimulate them to enquire (on the new Principles) into the nature of Property. If you treat Men as Robbers; why Robbers sooner or later, they will become. A third point of Jacobin attack, is an old traditionary *constitution*. You are apprehensive for yours, which leans from its perpendicular, and does not stand firm on it's Theory. I like Parliamentary Reforms as little as any man, who has Boroughs to sell for money or Peerages in Ireland, but it passes my Comprehension in what manner it is, that men can be reconciled to the practice, or merits of a Constitution, the Theory of which is in Litigation, by being practically excluded from any of its advantages. Let us put ourselves in the place of these people, and try an experiment of the effects of such procedure on our own Minds!

Unquestionably we should be perfectly satisfied, when We were told, that Houses of Parliament, instead of being places of Refuge for popular Liberty, were Citadels for keeping us in order as a conquered People. Indeed my Dear Sir, there is not a single particular in the Francis St Declamations, which has not to your and to my certain knowledge been taught by the Zealous ascendants; sometimes by doctrine, sometimes by example, always by provocation. Remember the whole of 1781 and 1782 in Parliament, and out of Parliament; at this very day, and in the worst Acts and Designs, observe the Tenor of the objections with which the College Green Orators of the Ascendency reproach the Catholics. You have observed, no doubt, how much they rely on the Affair of Jackson. Is it not pleasant to hear Catholics reproached for a supposed Connection, with whom? With Protestant Clergy men, with Protestant Gentlemen! With Mr Jackson, with Mr Rowan &c &c—But Egomet mi Ignosco. Conspiracies and Treasons are priviledged pleasures, not to be profaned by the impure and unhallowed Touch of Papists. Indeed all this will do well enough with detachments of dismounted cavalry, and fencibles from Ireland, but let us not say to Catholics, by way of *argument*, that they are to be kept in a degraded State, because some of them are no better than many of us Protestants. The thing I disliked most in some of their Speeches (those I mean of the Catholics) was what is called the Spirit of Liberality, so much and so diligently taught by the Ascendants, by which they are ready to abandon their own Interests, and to merge them in the general discontents of the Country. As to the Dissolution of the Committee, there were in it a Majority to my knowledge of very sober, and well intentioned Men; and there were none in it, but such, who if not continually goaded, and irritated, might be made useful to the tranquility of the Country. It is right always to have a few of every description, thro' whom you may quietly operate on the many; both for the Interest of the Description, and for the general Interest. Excuse my Dear Friend, if I have a little tired your patience. You have brought this trouble on yourself, by your thinking of a Man forgotten, and who has no objection to be forgot by the World. These things we discussed together four or five and thirty years ago. We were then, and at bottom ever since, of the same Opinion on the Justice and policy of the whole, and of every part of the penal System. You and I and every body must now and then ply and bend to the occasion, and take what can be got; but very sure I am, that whilst there remains in the Law any Principle whatever, which can furnish to certain polititians an excuse for raising an Opinion of their own Importance as necessary to keep their fellow Subjects in order, the obnoxious people will be fretted, harrassed, irritated; provoked to discontent and disorder, and practically excluded from the partial advantage from which the Letter of the Law does not exclude them

Adieu my Dear Sir. Believe me ever truly Yours
EDMUND BURKE

Beaconsfield May 26 1795

To UNKNOWN LORD—3 *August* 1795

Source: MS Osborn Collection.
Only the signature is in Burke's hand.

This letter is almost identical with that to Dr Brocklesby of the same date (see vol. VIII, 293–4). The subject matter is explained in the annotation of that letter.

Beaconsfield Aug 3rd 1795

My dear Lord,

I beg leave to inform your Lordship that the Living of Albrighton in the gift of the Governors of Christs Hospital is vacant. Mr Richards of Oriel College Oxford is a Candidate for it. I am confident that I shall be excus'd in the Liberty I take in expressing my most ardent wishes in his favour, because I am certain it is doing the best service in my power to the Cause of Literature and of the Church. Mr Richards has been bred in Christs Hospital school. What honor he has done the place of his Education appears by his having obtain'd not only the two University prizes, but also an occasional prize, offered for the best poem on 'the Aboriginal Britons'.

These with his known reputation for Literature and morals will I hope be more prevalent with the Governors of the trust than any personal Consideration whatever.

> I have the honour to be
> my dear Lord
> Your Lordship's most faithful
> and obedient humble Servant
> EDM BURKE

Your Lordship will much oblige me by interesting any of your friends who are Governors for Mr Richards.

To SIR HERCULES LANGRISHE—3 *February* 1796

Source: MS copy Public Record Office, Dublin (Kilkenny 38).

My Dear Sir

Several years ago I visited Ireland in company with one who wished cordially well to that Country, and who might have made me more interesting than I could hope to be on my own account.[1] At that time I endeavoured to engage your favour and protection for a Gentleman who has the honour of serving in a little Office under you. I thought that Mr Mason[2] and yourself might have helped him to some promotion, or at least contrived to make the Office in which he served, capable of answering the purposes for which it was given to him, or in some way unload it from the burthen that so reduced it in its value. With the Commissioners for these six years I have had no success. This Mr Kiernan[3] is a person, whom by every motive which can affect a Man, I am bound to serve, and my Duty is strongly enforced by good Opinion, by affection and by relation. I have known, I think, every Lord Lieutenant, or Secretary, and sometimes both, who have been in Ireland for these thirty six years. I do not think there was one Viceroyal Reign, during that time, in which the Principal, or some Minister under him, and sometimes both the one and the other, have not professed a regard for me, and a disposition to do me a kindness. From not one of them have I obtained a benefit that I recollect, great, or

---

[1] Burke had visited Ireland in 1786 with Richard Burke, Jr.

[2] John Monck Mason (1726–1809).

[3] Francis Kiernan (d. *c.* 1809). He managed Burke's Irish affairs, had been clerk to his brother Garrett (*c.* 1725–65) and had married a daughter of Garrett Nagle (d. *c.* 1791). He held the office of Examinator and Comptroller of the Collector's account of Incidents.

small, for a single friend. It was not that they thought me a Man who had no friend, or who had cared nothing about those I had. With the knowledge, which my worthy friend Kiernan has of these kind expressions of regard with which I have been honoured, not only by the Castle Ministers, but by Men like yourself, of rank and consequence in your Country, and in high Official Situation, that he is jealous, and uneasy, and full of doubts of my Disposition to serve him. But I have been more unfortunate, than Culpable, towards him, and towards others. Despairing of all power of being otherwise useful to my friend, I have not cast off all hope, that I may at least be able to screen him from what is real oppression, and to keep to his little Office what in Justice and reason, ought to be inseparable from it. I therefore recommended his Memorial to your consideration. I think his Claim to be of Strict Justice, but I have learned to consider justice as a favour; and from you, I am sure, justice will always be mingled with kindness, to those you are inclined to think worth your notice. You know I have long been an humble Admirer of your Talents and lover of your Amiable Qualities and a respecter of your Virtues. I have the honour to be with the most entire regard, the remains of your poor friend and humble Servant

EDMUND BURKE

Beaconsfield Feby 3d 1796

Langrishe replied that he had presented Kiernan's memorial to John Jeffreys Pratt, 2nd Earl Camden (1759–1840), later (1817) 1st Marquess Camden, the Lord Lieutenant, who raised Kiernan's salary from £200 to £300 per annum (MS copy Public Record Office, Dublin, Kilkenny 38).

To SIR HERCULES LANGRISHE—8 *April* 1796

Source: MS copy Public Record Office, Dublin (Kilkenny 38).

This is Burke's acknowledgement of the help given to Kiernan (see the previous letter).

My Dear Friend

I am infinitely obliged to you for the kind concern you are pleased to take in me, and in what concerns me most, The interests of the few friends who are yet lingering with me on this unpleasant side of the Grave. You may be sure that I feel it as no small consolation that I enjoy the friendship of one of the most benevolent and social Minds, that ever existed in the World; and that anything that I can do can be tolerated by one of the best Judgments in it. This I have to say on my private account; as to the public, I shall say little; because I have little that is pleasant to say. No man respects and values the Lord Lieutenant[1] more than I do. He is an excellent, able, and well tempered man; and on this occasion he has acted to me with great kindness and generosity. What is going on in our unhappy Country, I consider as no fault that is his, but the consequence of the System in which he is engaged, and the representations he receives. Most men in his Situation would suffer things to go on, as he suffers, or must suffer them to proceed. But I am sure you will excuse me for my Weakness, (if weakness it is) in differing from you and him; and in regarding all the late proceedings with a degree of Scorn, abhorrence, and indignation, which I should in vain attempt to express; and which I should be very little disposed to express to you, if I were not quite sure that actively you were never the adviser, Executor, or the proximate, or remote, cause of any of them.

You have in Ireland a young Man, whom I valued as an old friend of mine; a person of great honour, Talents, and a most clear, accurate and sound understanding. I wonder they have suffered Ireland to rob us[2] at this rate. I speak of Mr Elliot.[3] Pray remember me to him; and tell him that his friend Mrs Burke, who has lately been ill indeed, tho' still rather lame, begins to mend apace, and never forgot his goodness to her.

Adieu my Dear Sir Hercules, and believe me with very unfeigned respect and Affection Most truly and Gratefully Yours

EDMUND BURKE

April 8th 1796

To ABBÉ AUGUSTIN BARRUEL
Source: Les Fontaines, Chantilly.
Only the signature is in Burke's hand.

Printed in vol. IX, 319–20, from Clifford, *Application of Barruel's Memoirs of Jacobinism.*

1 May 97

Sir,

I cannot easily express to you how much I am instructed and delighted by the first Volume of your History of Jacobinism. The whole of the

[1] Lord Camden.
[2] MS: as
[3] William Elliot (d. 1818), Under-Secretary for the Military Department in Ireland.

wonderful Narrative is supported by documents and Proofs with the most juridical regularity and exactness. Your Reflexions and reasonings are interspersed with infinite Judgment and in their most proper places, for leading the sentiments of the Reader and preventing the force of plausible objections. The tendency of the whole is admirable in every point of View, political, Religious, and let me make use of the abused word, philosophical. So far as I can presume to judge of a French Style, the language is of the first water. I long impatiently for the second Volume. But the great object of my Wishes is, that the Work should have a great circulation in France, if by any means it can be compassed: and for that end, I should be glad upon the scale of a poor Individual to become a liberal Subscriber.

I am yet in a miserable state of Health; and if I advance at all it is very slowly and with many fallings back. I forgot to say, that I have known myself personally five of your principal Conspirators; and I can undertake to say from my own certain knowledge, that so far back as the year 1773 they were busy in the Plot you have so well described and in the manner and on the Principle which you have so truly presented. To this I can speak as a Witness.

I have the honour to be, Sir, with great Respect and Gratitude Your most obedient and humble servant

E DM B URKE

Bath 1st May 1797

To D R M OORE—n.d.

Source: Trinity College, Dublin.
Addressed: To | Dr. Moore | Clarges Street | London
Endorsed: Edmund Burke | Esqr
Franked: Free | Edm Burke
Postmarked: OC FREE

Burke's correspondent may well be Dr William Moore (*c.* 1766–1832), physician to Frederick, Duke of York (1763–1827), in the Netherlands. The letter is therefore probably to be dated October 1793.

Mr Burke presents his Compliments to Dr Moore, and will be extremely happy in seeing him here any day this Week before Thursday; The sooner the better, as he is quite disengaged Until then. He will be so good as to thank Col. Craufurd[1] for his very obliging intentions, and to assure him how much Mr B. will be honourd by seeing him here with Dr Moore.

Beconsfield Sunday Evening.

[1] Possibly Charles Cregan Craufurd (1761–1821), Aide de Camp to the Duke of York.

To UNKNOWN—n.d.

Source: British Museum.

MS fragment of a letter bound into *The Poetical Works of Lord Byron*, London, 1839, vol. 1, part 1, between pp. 6 and 7, in the British Museum (C. 44. e).

time admits you to come over instantly, or whether ⟨   ⟩ will not do—though on the whole—if you found it not very inconvenient—I wish to see you some time in the day.

Very sincerly Yours
EDM BURKE

To UNKNOWN—n.d.

Source: Incomplete draft in Fitzwilliam MSS (Northampton), (A.xxxi.9).
Endorsed: On Tests and | Instructions to | Representatives.

I always receive with pleasure, and when my time admits am ready to acknowlege with gratitude the favour of any communication which may assist me in forming just Ideas of my publick Duty, or in performing it with propriety and effect. As you have done me the honour to address[1] me with more civility than I had any right to expect [I] answer your Letter merely for your own Satisfaction and mean to go no further; having neither leisure nor inclination to enter in to anything like controversy on a Business on which my sentiments and reasons are already so fully explained in more publication than one.[2]

I do not know nor have ever heard of any Law whatsoever, either by positive Statute or parliamentary usage, which requires a Member of the House of Commons to obey the orders of a Majority of his constituents; If I knew of such I should certainly ⟨submit⟩ to it in all Matters to which human Laws are competent. But the most direct and positive Statute should never make me submit to be the instrument of any set of men in forming such regulations as I am sorry to see that you recommend, because they are contrary as I conceive to the immutable Laws of Nature, and the principles of Essential Justice as well as to all reason and good policy. Many of the things you wish to be enacted, are unfortunately enacted to your hands and I assure you Sir that nothing but my inability to overturn that whole Structure, I mean the

---

[1] Burke first wrote 'addressed' and in rephrasing his sentence neglected to alter it.
[2] Most obviously in *The Speech to the Electors of Bristol*.

penal Laws about religion, could make a single Letter of them stand for half an hour. So that if you think they are good for any thing you have reason to rejoice that I have but little power in this Kingdom. I do not say this Sir, as if I had ever receivd Orders from the constituents whom I had the honour to serve, at any time to support measures of that Nature and tendency. But if I had receivd such orders, neither Law nor reason could bind me to the smallest attention to them.

I am sorry you are not pleased

ERRATA AND ADDENDA

Abbreviations used: dn, dating note; hn, head-note; tn, tail-note.

VOLUME ONE

p. 146. 'Mr Jack Burke' is probably John Bourke (*c.* 1742–95).

p. 164, n. 1, line 7. The note is in Edmond Malone's hand.

p. 182. The first Hamilton letter is printed from the original at Sheffield.

p. 189, n. 3. Alexander Wedderburn seems more probable than Joseph Warton.

p. 204. The 'bas-relief of Eurus' is one face of the Tower of the Winds at Athens.

p. 216, n. 1. The marriage of Michael Courtenay and Catherine Nagle took place at St Mary Le Bone, London, on 17 July 1767 (*The Registers of Marriages of St Mary Le Bone, Middlesex, 1754–1775*, ed. W. B. and R. R. B. Bannerman, *Harleian Society*, XLVIII, 1918, 73).

p. 217, n. 1. Clogher was sold to Edmund Nagle of Clogher; see vol. III, 417.

p. 228, n. 3. Section 3 should read: Garrett Nagle of Ballynahalisk, the son of Uncle James of Ballywalter.

p. 253, line 13. unwholsom.

p. 265, n. 1. The notes are on the *Speech on American Taxation*.

p. 266, lines 7 and 8. Probably from 'A great city is a great solitude': Erasmus borrowing from Strabo.

p. 276, n. 2. It was John Fitzgibbon (*c.* 1718–80), father of the future Lord Clare, who defended the Whiteboys.

p. 280, n. 1. The notes are on *Speech on American Taxation*.

p. 287, n. 4. *West Ham Gleanings* is a MS in possession of Newham Borough, Stratford Reference Library.

p. 288, n. 4. The Trinity textbook was Jean Le Clerc's *Logica sive Ars Ratiocendi*.

p. 318dn. The beginning is in fact not imperfect; see vol. IX, 390–1.

p. 323, line 26. For 'Patience' the MS has 'Patence'.

p. 331. John Ellis (d.1776) was the Agent of the Linen Board.

p. 345, n. 9. The Attorney General was William De Grey (1719–1800), later (1781) 1st Baron Walsingham.

p. 359, n. 2. The anecdote appears in *Ménagiana ou les Bons Mots et remarques critiques, historiques, morales et d'érudition de Monsieur Ménage Recueillis par ses Amis. Troisième edition* ... *plus correcte que les précédentes,* Paris, Chez Florentine Delaulne ... 1715 (4 vols), I, 306–7.

VOLUME TWO

p. 10, n. 3. Bulstrode was about three miles from Beaconsfield.

p. 106, n. 5. The spelling should be Fergusson.

p. 142, n. 1. For 'see below, p. 189' read 'see above, p. 89'.

pp. 180, n. 5; 239, n. 3. The spelling should be Baker.

p. 181. The original MS shows that 'Lare' is a misreading (see vol. IX, 395–6).

p. 213dn. The spelling of the names of Burke's secretary should be here and elsewhere Clement Nevill Zouch.

p. 359, n. 8. Burke did not write directly to Warren Hastings but through intermediaries.

pp. 550, 551. Caroline Williams, later the wife of General Bigoe Armstrong, was not married at this time.

VOLUME THREE

p. 112, line 26. For 'national' read 'rational'.

p. 118. Mrs John Noble seems to have been wrongly identified. She appears to be Elizabeth (d. 1792), daughter of Richard Hatt.

p. 213. *Endorsed* (by Boswell): Edmund Burke/to/Bennet Langton.

p. 240, n. 6. One of these letters is now printed in vol. IX, 406–8.

p. 268, n. 5. The quotation is from Swift, 'A description of a City shower', line 41.

p. 285, n. 2. Hewitt's instructions are in his papers now in the University of London (MS 522).

p. 304, n. 1. Bulstrode is about three miles from Beaconsfield.

p. 335. This letter is *Addressed*: 'David Garrick Esqr.'.

p. 446, hn. Span's letter of 30 April 1778 is entered in Masters' Letter-books (MS Society of Merchant Venturers).

VOLUME FOUR

pp. xiii, xv. The Yorkshire County Meeting was held on 30 December 1779.

p. 22, hn. Noble was not in fact a member of the Society of Merchant Venturers.

p. 45, n. 3. The Roman Catholic Address was of 1 May 1778.

p. 97, n. 4. The reference to Walker King's sister may be not to his sister-in-law but to his sister Anne.

p. 106, hn. The records of Gosling's Bank have the history of this bond. General Armstrong had married Caroline Williams, who held the chief mortgage on Beaconsfield.

p. 108, hn. It would be more accurate if 'The normal procedure' were changed to 'One common procedure'.

p. 133, hn. Dignan had stood at Hindon in 1777.

p. 146, line 9. For 'FitWilliams' read 'Fitzwilliams'.

p. 180, n. 2. The note assumes a rather literal interpretation of the word 'miscarriage' in the text. It would be better without the first sentence.

p. 203, n. 2. Burke's letter to Kenmare of 22 January 1780 is printed above, pp. 6–8.

p. 266, dn. Noble's son was John Hatt Noble.

p. 301, text line 15. 'in Covent Garden'.

p. 323, hn. For evidence showing the connexion between Paul Benfield and Macartney see Dame Lucy Sutherland, 'Lord Macartney's appointment as Governor of Madras, 1780', *English Historical Review*, XC (1975), 523–35.

pp. 358–60. Burke is answering a letter of Eden of 18 April 1781 (Richard Bourke MSS, National Library of Ireland). The favour done by Eden for Burke was helping John Bourke (*c.* 1742–95).

p. 461. The 'Mr John Bourke', the subject of this letter, was John Bourke (*c.* 1742–95) and not John Bourke (*c.* 1722–1806).

VOLUME FIVE

p. 142. The letter to Boswell [15 April 1784] is *Addressed*: James Boswell Esqr.

p. 167, n. 5. The Elliots' new habitation was at Swanage.

p. 211, n. 5. Burke is quoting Swift's 'Elegy on Mr Partrige', lines 89–90: '*Triumphant* Star! Some Pity show On *Coblers Militant* below'. Swift of course had Cowley in mind.

p. 293, dn. In fact Samuel Parr was married and had two daughters.

p. 307, n. 4. Ewart was born at Troqueer.

p. 326, dn. There is another copy in the New York Public Library.

p. 366, n. 2. This is the wrong Charles Goring. The correct one is identified in vol. VII, 181 n. 4.

p. 375. The postmark should read: FREE S.

p. 379. The letter to Sir Peter Burrell is in fact in Richard Burke, Sr's hand. He was out of the country until April.

p. 401. *Addressed*: Arthur Young Esq. *Endorsed*: 7/8/8/2 Mrs Burke.

p. 405, n. 4. Adey's father's affairs were clearly financial as well as domestic; see above, pp. 22–3.

p. 445, hn. The cross-reference at the end should be to p. 431.

VOLUME SIX

pp. 6–7. The recipient of this letter was in fact the Rev. Thomas Maurice (1754–1824), poet and orientalist. See T. Maurice, *Memoirs of the Author of Indian Antiquities*, London, 1819–20, II, 188.

p. 11, n. 6. Bulstrode is about three miles from Beaconsfield.

p. 14. The copy of the Fox letter is at Northampton.

p. 14, n. 3. Alexander Blair is listed in *Boyle's New Fashionable Court and Country Guide*, 1796, as living at 5 Portland Place and Beaconsfield, Bucks.

p. 55. There is a copy of this letter in the India Office Library.

p. 63, n. 4. The note should read: See above, pp. 54–5.

p. 93, hn. There is a copy of Mercer's letter of 19 February 1790 in the Macartney Collection, in Deccan College, Poona.

p. 95, n. 2. The note should read: Burke is referring to his Establishment Act of 1782 and to his reform of the Pay Office.

p. 98, tn. There is a copy of Mercer's letter of 8 November in the Macartney Collection in Deccan College, Poona.

p. 192, hn. The letter of John Hely Hutchinson of 13 December 1790 is now in the Hyde Collection.

p. 230. The Boswell letter is a draft rather than a copy.

p. 288, n. 4. This should read: Elisabeth-Philippine-Marie-Hélène (1764–94), 'Madame Elisabeth', sister of Louis XVI.

pp. 302–4. William Smith did not add Cusack to his name until 1800.

p. 339, n. 4. The Russian Ambassador (strictly speaking Minister) was Count Semen Romanovich Vorontsov (1744–1832); see vol. VII, 337.

p. 362, n. 1. The cross-reference should be to p. 341.

p. 365, n. 1. Most of the parish of Mohill is in County Leitrim.

p. 426. Bukaty's first name should be spelt 'Franciszek'.

p. 441, dn. Another copy of this letter is owned by Professor Frederick W. Hilles.

p. 478, line 14. For 'honour' read 'horrour'.

VOLUME SEVEN

p. 4, n. 4. The letter from Langrishe was sold in 1959; see vol. IX, 467.

p. 23, n. 3. Delete the 'R' from GOVERNMENT.

p. 161, nn. 3 and 4. Delete 'r' from Governments.

p. 213, n. 5. The letter is missing.

p. 273, line 21. For 'Hoary' read 'Strong'.

p. 323, n. 1. The paragraph in fact was published in the sale catalogue of Reynolds's collection of paintings of Old Masters in 1795 (A. Graves and W. V. Cronin, *A History of the Works of Sir Joshua Reynolds*, London, 1899–1901, IV, 1614).

p. 336, n. 3. Probably Reynolds's executors were offering Catherine his collection of Old Masters.

p. 349. This letter is certainly to Sir Hercules Langrishe. It is a reply to Langrishe's letter of 20 February (MS copy Public Record Office, Dublin, Kilkenny 38).

p. 451. The original of the letter to Henry Dundas, advertised by John Fleming of New York, has the date 16 October 1793.

VOLUME EIGHT

p. 40, line 13. For 'on' read 'or'.

p. 59, n. 4. For 'Whethan' read 'Whetham'.

p. 116, line 1. For 'September' read 'October'.

p. 124, n. 2. For Carrick-on-Shannon read Carrick-on-Suir.

p. 142. This letter was addressed to John King and not to Walker King; see IX, 442–3.

p. 148, n. 5. Delete the 'r' from Government.

p. 150, n. 1. The cross-reference should be: (see above, p. 137, and below, pp. 173, 186–7).

p. 396, line 13 of text. 'so' should read 'No'.

pp. 413, n. 4; 416, n. 3; 419, n. 8; 422 n. 2. The letter from Loughborough is now in the Osborn Collection. It is quoted in vol. IX, 62 n. 2.

VOLUME NINE

p. 8, n. 1. The letter is missing.

p. 99, line 2 of dn. For 'wichh' read 'which'.

p. 132, tn. The last phrase should be: de ma traduction.

p. 168, n. 1. Loughlinstown is south of Dublin.

pp. 202, 209. 'Mr Baxter' is Richard Baxter (1615–91), the Nonconformist divine. For the anecdote to which Burke is referring see the *Morning Chronicle*, 6 December 1777.

p. 236, line 1. 'confidentially' is correctly spelt in the MS.

p. 344, n. 4. Walker King; see next letter.

p. 349, n. 1. For '141' read '181'.

A FULL LISTING OF BURKE CORRESPONDENCE

To deal with the entire range of Edmund Burke's correspondence one must attend not only to the 1900-odd letters written by him, which occupy most of the pages of the present edition. There is a much larger body of letters written to him, preserved in his private papers at Sheffield and Northampton and in various other manuscript and printed collections. There are also, as those familiar with his habits know, quite a few letters written for him, by the members of his immediate family. When under the pressure of business Burke often allowed his wife, his brother, his son, his father-in-law, or his close friend and distant relation William Burke to help him out with his correspondence. And, since he was a politician, there are also a few 'public letters': compositions like the *Letter to a Member of the National Assembly* or the *Letter to a Noble Lord*, which though given epistolary form were obviously designed for wide circulation in print. These last have been excluded from our volumes, as they are essentially pamphlets not letters, but they cannot be wholly ignored by students of Burke's correspondence. They were often addressed to the recipients of his other letters, and when carelessly cited (e.g. as his 'letter to M. de Menonville') are able to cause confusion.

The following lists are intended for scholars who want to make use of the full range of the Burke correspondence. They include all surviving letters by or to Edmund himself, not merely those we have printed or cited in this edition. They do not include quite all letters by and to the members of his family, but do attempt to name all those likely to tell us about Edmund's affairs. Both William Burke and Richard Burke, Sr— Edmund's brother—had some political correspondence of their own. William was an Under-Secretary in the Home Office from July 1765 to February 1767, and many of his letters are preserved in the Public Record Office;[1] he was also while in India between 1782 and 1792 a Deputy Paymaster of His Majesty's Forces in the East, and many of his letters survive in the India Office and elsewhere.[2] Richard, Sr, was

---

[1] Many are printed in the *Calendar of Home Office Papers in the Reign of George III*, ed. Joseph Redington, 4 vols., London 1878.
[2] A few items from William's India correspondence are in the Fitzwilliam Museum, Cambridge, a few more in the Library of the University of Pennsylvania in Philadelphia, and a few in the Royal Library, The Hague. A few are to be found in the records of the Paymaster General's Office (P.R.O., P.M.G. 1/104).

Secretary to the Treasury in the second Rockingham Ministry and again under the Fox–North Coalition.[1] Official letters of both men are here omitted on principle—with however a few exceptions, when they happen to be written to persons with whom Edmund also corresponded. Richard Burke, Jr—Edmund's son—although he too lived on the fringe of politics, presents a simpler case. None of his letters were strictly official and they were almost always concerned with his father's causes. We have included all of Richard's letters which are known to us.[2] Finally, these lists take some account of the public letters. Those written to Burke's ordinary correspondents will be found under their proper dates in the first list. In the second, more detailed list, footnotes will give their printed titles and (at least for the more important of them) the pages on which they are described in Todd's *Bibliography*.[3]

It is too much to hope that any lists, however comprehensive, can anticipate and satisfy all the demands of scholars. A specialist pursuing, say, the full story of Burke's relations with Charles James Fox may not be content to be told of every single surviving letter that passed between the two men. He may want to know of further letters which did not survive, but which chance references tell us were written. The present lists have had to stop at real, still-accessible letters. But scholars desiring more than that have at least one further resource. In the recording of lost letters the *Checklist* published in 1955 is more exhaustive than our present *Full Listing*, and may still be consulted. It has been corrected by our later researches, so that when it differs from the *Listing* on, say, conjectural dates, the latter should be trusted. But it still has occasional uses. It has guided our volume-editors in many of their tasks, and all acknowledge the large debt which they owe to its compilers.

[1] Half a dozen letters dated from 'Treasury Chambers' have been omitted from our list. No considerable body of Richard's correspondence has been found.

[2] There is one embarrassing deficiency in our record of them. A few are preserved in the Public Record Office, and at an early stage of our researches they were listed with proper dates but without proper P.R.O. references. We certainly might omit these altogether—rather than track every one of them down again—but some scholars may be helped by being told of their existence, even if we can now tell them nothing more.

[3] *A Bibliography of Edmund Burke*. By William B. Todd. London, 1964.

A CHRONOLOGICAL SURVEY

This list is intended to give a panoramic view of the entire Burke correspondence. As it can accomplish this end more readily by keeping to a highly simplified form, it ignores many of the complications and discriminations of the Alphabetical List which follows. No distinction is here made between complete and incomplete letters, certain and merely probable dates. Letters by Edmund himself are listed in roman type, those by other members of the Burke family in italic type, but no initials are provided here to identify which member of the family wrote or received a particular letter. Nothing shows whether a letter has been printed in this edition or not—though any written by Edmund himself certainly will have been. In a word, the appearance of a letter in this list proves only that a full or partial text survives. For further information the reader should proceed to the more detailed entry under the correspondent's name in the Alphabetical List.

1744

APRIL
p 14   to Shackleton

MAY
10   to Shackleton
a 24   to Shackleton
24   to Shackleton
29   to Shackleton

JUNE
9   to Shackleton
11   to Shackleton
c 14   to Shackleton
21   to Shackleton
26   to Shackleton
29   to Shackleton

JULY
5   to Shackleton
7   to Shackleton
10   to Shackleton
14   to Shackleton

OCTOBER
15   to Shackleton

NOVEMBER
1   to Shackleton
24   to Shackleton

1745

JANUARY
25   to Shackleton
31   to Shackleton

FEBRUARY
5   to Shackleton
16   to Shackleton
23   to Shackleton

MARCH
c 5   to Shackleton
12   to Shackleton
15   to Shackleton
19   to Shackleton

JULY
4   to Shackleton
16   to Shackleton

AUGUST
16   to Shackleton

OCTOBER
15   to Shackleton

NOVEMBER
2   to Shackleton
12   to Shackleton

DECEMBER
7   to Shackleton
28   to Shackleton

1746

JANUARY
16   to Shackleton

FEBRUARY
15   to Shackleton

APRIL
26   to Shackleton

MAY
c 15   to Shackleton
c 24   to Shackleton

JUNE
1   to Shackleton

JULY
12   to Shackleton
25, 31   to RBsr and Shackleton

AUGUST
19   to Shackleton

NOVEMBER
29   to RBsr and Shackleton

DECEMBER
5   to Shackleton
19   to Shackleton
27   to Shackleton

1747
JANUARY
24 to Shackleton
FEBRUARY
*c*3 to Shackleton
*p*3 to Shackleton
21 to Shackleton
MARCH
*c*5 to Shackleton
*c*12 to Shackleton
21 to Shackleton
MAY
28, 29 to Shackleton
AUGUST
22 to Shackleton
OCTOBER
17 to Shackleton
NOVEMBER
21 to Shackleton
DECEMBER
24 to Shackleton

1748
FEBRUARY
2 to Shackleton
MAY
— to Shackleton

1749
JANUARY
5 to Shackleton

1750
NOVEMBER
— to WB
— fr WB
c— to M. Smith
c— fr M. Smith

1751
FEBRUARY
26 to Shackleton
APRIL
5 to Shackleton
AUGUST
31 to Shackleton

1752
SEPTEMBER
28 to Shackleton
— to Dr. Nugent

1753
JUNE
— *to Dr. Nugent*

1755
MARCH
11 to R. Burke, EB's
father

1757
AUGUST
*c*7 to Emin
10 to Shackleton

1759
APRIL
17 to P. Nagle
SEPTEMBER
*c*6 to R. Dodsley
10 to Adam Smith
24 to Mrs. Montagu
OCTOBER
6 to Mrs. Montagu
11 to P. Nagle
NOVEMBER
20 fr O'Hara

1760
APRIL
10 fr O'Hara
SEPTEMBER
10 to Vesey

1761
JANUARY
16 fr Mrs. Kempe
JULY
3 to O'Hara
10 to O'Hara
AUGUST
25 to Shackleton

SEPTEMBER
8 to Shackleton
MONTH NOT KNOWN
— to Dennis

1762
MAY
1 fr Wilcocks
AUGUST
10 fr O'Hara
*a*23 to O'Hara
OCTOBER
9 *to O'Hara*
30 to O'Hara
NOVEMBER
20 *to O'Hara*
23 to O'Hara
25 to O'Hara
DECEMBER
9 to O'Hara
12 to O'Hara
30 to O'Hara

1763
MARCH
4 to Mrs. Montagu
— to W. G. Hamilton
APRIL
*p*19 to Shackleton
20, 21 *fr Corsar*
23 to Ridge
25 to Mrs. Montagu
JULY
4 fr O'Hara
26 fr O'Hara
29 to Mrs. Montagu
29 to Wedderburn
MONTH NOT KNOWN
— fr Dr. Sleigh

1764
FEBRUARY
9 to J. Dodsley
MARCH
29 to Shackleton
APRIL
12 *to Shackleton*
— *to G. Grenville*

JUNE
21 fr Garrick

JULY
17 to Shackleton
24 fr O'Hara

AUGUST
16 fr Eliza Bourke and
     D. Murphy

SEPTEMBER
20 fr O'Hara
27 fr O'Hara

OCTOBER
14 fr Hutchinson

NOVEMBER
20 fr O'Hara

DECEMBER
15 fr Dr. Curry
31 to W. Young

1765

JANUARY
14 fr O'Hara

FEBRUARY
a12 fr W. G. Hamilton
a12 to W. G. Hamilton
a12 fr W. G. Hamilton
a12 to W. G. Hamilton
24 fr Dr. Curry
26 to Jephson
28 fr Dr. Leland

MARCH
6 fr Abbé Desfrançois

APRIL
8 fr W. G. Hamilton
10 to W. G. Hamilton
25 fr O'Conor

MAY
9 fr Flood
18 to Flood
p29 to J. M. Mason
30 fr Flood
— to Hutchinson

JUNE
8 fr Dr. Curry
10 fr W. Fitzherbert
17 fr Dr. Sleigh
23 fr C. Townshend
25 to C. Townshend

28 fr J. M. Mason

JULY
4 to O'Hara
9 to O'Hara
p10 *to Gen. Conway*
11 to O'Hara
16 to Garrick
17 fr Garrick
19 fr O'Hara
25 to Garrick
27 fr Flood
27 fr Dr. Leland
27 fr Vesey
30 fr O'Hara

AUGUST
6 fr J. M. Mason

SEPTEMBER
26 fr Macartney
27 fr Bn. Tyrawley

OCTOBER
a1 fr C. Lloyd
1 to C. Lloyd
4 *to Devisme*
11 *to E. of Bessborough
     and Bn. Grantham*
14 to P. Nagle
15 fr O'Hara

NOVEMBER
4 *fr Unknown*
4 *fr Unknown*
6 fr Barry
7 *fr S. Garbett*
8 *to Barry*
8 *fr G. Cooper*
22 fr O'Hara
28 fr O'Hara
a30 *to Dempster*

DECEMBER
4 *to Weston*
5 fr Barry
10 to G. Cooper
11 fr Sir W. Meredith
17 fr O'Hara
c20 fr Barry
23 *fr J. Pownall*
p23 to Macartney
24 to O'Hara
24 fr O'Hara

24 to Ridge
29 *fr Dr. Markham*
p30 to P. Nagle
31 to O'Hara
— fr Garrick

1766

JANUARY
1 fr Sir W. Meredith
9 fr Dr. Leland
10 fr O'Hara
a14 to RBsr
18 fr Garrick
18 to O'Hara
25 fr O'Hara
— to M. of
     Rockingham

FEBRUARY
6 to Mrs. French
7 to Wm. Pitt
8 fr J. Marriott
9 fr A. Henderson
11 *to Barry*
11 fr O'Hara
19 *fr Stephens*
20 fr O'Hara
21 *fr Macartney*
26 fr J. Marriott
— fr Barry

MARCH
1 fr E. Murphy
1, 4 to O'Hara
4 *fr Dr. Leland*
4 fr O'Hara
7 *fr G. Cooper*
a8 fr Ridge
8 fr Ridge
10 fr O'Hara
11 to O'Hara
12 *to G. Cooper*
13 fr O'Hara
14 fr Gen. Graeme
18 fr O'Hara
20 fr R. Fitzgerald
20 fr O'Hara
22 fr O'Hara
23 *to Barry*
23 *fr Sir W. Meredith*

25 *fr O'Hara*
27 to O'Hara
29 to O'Hara
31 *to Fraser*
APRIL
 8 to O'Hara
 8 fr O'Hara
 9 *fr G. Cooper*
 9 fr M. of Rockingham
10 fr O'Hara
15 fr O'Hara
21 to O'Hara
23, 24 to O'Hara
30 fr O'Hara
p 30 fr O'Hara
MAY
 3 fr T. Lee
 7 *to Vct. Beauchamp*
11 fr Rawlinson
c 13 to Barry
15 fr O'Hara
23 fr Rawlinson
24 to O'Hara
29 fr E. of Hertford
31 fr O'Hara
JUNE
12 fr Merchants at
      Lancaster
12 fr Wilkes
13 *to Macartney*
16 to Sir G. Savile
27 *to Barry*
30 *fr G. Cooper*
30 *fr G. Cooper*
JULY
 4 to Wilkes
 8 fr Ridge
17 to D. of Portland
18 to E. of Dartmouth
19 fr Reilly
22 *to J. Marriott*
29 *to Macartney*
29 to O'Hara
AUGUST
 4 fr Teisseirez
 5 *to Barry*
 5 *to Macartney*
14 *fr O'Hara*

16 fr Barry
19 to O'Hara
21 to M. of Rockingham
25 fr O'Hara
30 *to Shackleton*
— to Shackleton
SEPTEMBER
 4 *fr Macartney*
18 fr O'Hara
24 fr Barry
29 *to Macartney*
30 fr Garrick
30 *to J. Marriott*
OCTOBER
 4 *to O'Hara*
 7 *to Barry*
10 *to Barry*
19 to Shackleton
21 to O'Hara
21 fr Shackleton
24 *to Macartney*
25 *to Mrs. Hennessy*
25 *to Shackleton*
28 to Shackleton
30 *to Macartney*
31 fr O'Hara
— *fr F. Garbett*
— *fr F. Garbett*
NOVEMBER
 1 fr M. of Rockingham
 2 fr Barry
 4 fr F. A. Daly
 6 to P. Nagle
11 fr O'Hara
p 11 to O'Hara
18 *to Shackleton*
19 *fr Stanley*
p 25 *to O'Hara*
27 to O'Hara
28 *fr G. Cooper*
29 fr Dr. Leland
29 to O'Hara
DECEMBER
 2 to O'Hara
 3 *to Barry*
 6 fr O'Hara
 7 fr O'Hara
12 *to Macartney*

12 *fr O'Hara*
23 to O'Hara
25 fr Shackleton
27 *to O'Hara*
MONTH NOT KNOWN
— fr Sir G. Baker
— *to Macartney*
— to G. Nagle

1767
JANUARY
 1 *to E. of Shelburne*
 2 fr O'Hara
 4 fr W. Dowdeswell
c 8 to W. Dowdeswell
13 fr O'Hara
15 to O'Hara
17 fr Ridge
20 fr Faulkner
21 *fr Wolfall*
26 fr Dr. Cleaver
26 fr W. Dowdeswell
FEBRUARY
 7 fr O'Hara
13 fr Barry
15 *to Shackleton*
16 fr M. Howard
a 19 to Barry
20 fr O'Hara
25 to Mayor of Dublin
28 to O'Hara
— *fr Ridge*
MARCH
 7 to O'Hara
12 fr O'Hara
14 to O'Hara
17 to O'Hara
18 *to M. of Rockingham*
20 fr O'Hara
23 fr Rawlinson
27 fr O'Hara
28 to O'Hara
30, 31 to O'Hara
— fr M. of Rockingham
APRIL
 4 fr Dr. Leland
16 to Ms. of Rockingham
18 to O'Hara

26	to Barry	**NOVEMBER**		**JUNE**	
28	to Ms. of Rockingham	4	fr M. of Rockingham	9	to O'Hara
MAY		8	fr Lord G. Cavendish	13	to Garrick
5	to O'Hara	9	fr Sir W. Meredith	17	fr Garrick
10	fr Rawlinson	11	to E. of Bessborough	17	to Garrick
15	fr O'Hara	11	fr E. of Bessborough	19, 20	fr Moffatt
23	fr Barry	11	fr Dempster	25	fr Earl Verney
26	fr W. Dowdeswell	12	to O'Hara	**JULY**	
JUNE		14	fr O'Hara	9	fr O'Hara
4	to O'Hara	22	*fr Shackleton*	12	fr Garrick
16	fr O'Hara	26	*to O'Hara*	16	fr Garrick
26	fr Sir W. Meredith	27	to O'Hara	18	to M. of Rockingham
—	fr Barry	**DECEMBER**		19	to Barry
—	to G. Nagle	2	fr O'Hara	22	fr Mrs. Gataker
—	*fr Wedderburn*	5	fr O'Hara	25	to D. of Portland
JULY		11	to O'Hara	26	fr O'Hara
5	fr D. of Richmond	19	fr O'Hara	30	fr D. of Portland
16	to M. of Rockingham	22	*to O'Hara*	30	to D. of Portland
21	fr F. Montagu			**AUGUST**	
28	fr Hutchinson	**1768**		16	fr M. of Rockingham
AUGUST		**JANUARY**		**SEPTEMBER**	
1	to M. of Rockingham	12	fr Dr. J. Lee	1	to O'Hara
3	to Hutchinson	13	to D. of Portland	25	fr WB
16	fr O'Hara	14	fr M. of Rockingham	*a*26	to Dempster
18	to M. of Rockingham	16	fr D. of Portland	26	fr Dempster
24	to Barry	**FEBRUARY**		27	fr E. Murray
*a*27	*to O'Hara*	*c*1	to O'Hara	27	fr M. of Rockingham
30	fr D. of Newcastle	9	fr O'Hara	30	fr Barry
30	to D. of Newcastle	11	fr O'Hara	—	fr Reynolds
31	fr M. of Rockingham	16	fr O'Hara	**OCTOBER**	
SEPTEMBER		20	to O'Hara	10	*to Barry*
*p*4	fr WB	**MARCH**		29	fr Tomkyns
8	*fr O'Hara*	3	fr O'Hara	**NOVEMBER**	
20	fr Hutchinson	6	to G. Nagle	18	fr Royds
24	*fr C. Hargrave*	9	to M. of Rockingham	26	fr S. Garbett
OCTOBER		10	fr O'Hara	—	fr Barry
6	fr M. of Rockingham	*a*17	*fr Bn. Bruce*	**DECEMBER**	
12	fr Lord J. Cavendish	29	fr J. M. Mason	1	to D. of Portland
20	fr Rawlinson	**APRIL**		2	to Mrs. Montagu
21	to P. Nagle	11	to O'Hara	27	to G. Nagle
*a*22	fr O'Hara	15	to Barry	**MONTH NOT KNOWN**	
22	fr O'Hara	19	fr O'Hara	—	*to JB*
22	to Ms. of Rockingham	21	fr O'Hara		
27	to O'Hara	**MAY**		**1769**	
28	fr Sir W. Meredith	1	to Shackleton	**JANUARY**	
*p*30	to E. of Hardwicke	10	*fr O'Hara*	4	fr W. Dowdeswell
31	fr Lord G. Cavendish	22	fr Barry	5	fr Dr. J. King
31	fr M. of Rockingham	—	fr Ms. of Rockingham	*c*20	to Unknown

25   fr Moffatt
FEBRUARY
17   fr O'Hara
MARCH
7   fr Sjt. Glynn
16   fr Shackleton
25   fr Harward
APRIL
8   fr Barry
MAY
2   *fr O'Hara*
9   to E. of Charlemont
15   fr M. of Rockingham
16   *to Mrs. French*
16   fr O'Hara
18   fr Dr. G. Campbell
19   fr E. of Charlemont
31   to O'Hara
31   fr M. of Rockingham
JUNE
1   to O'Hara
13   to M. of Rockingham
14   fr T. Lloyd
15   to Garrick
24   fr RBsr
29   fr M. of Rockingham
JULY
2   to M. of Rockingham
7   *to M. of Rockingham*
8   fr Barry
8   fr C. Townshend
9   to M. of Rockingham
17   fr Sir W. Meredith
17   fr M. of Rockingham
20   fr W. Dowdeswell
22   fr Cornwall
26   fr Harward
30   to M. of Rockingham
—   fr O'Hara
AUGUST
10   fr W. Dowdeswell
13   to M. of Rockingham
20   fr O'Hara
21   to Whately
23   fr Whately
24   fr W. Fitzgerald
28   fr Sir W. Meredith
28   to O'Hara

30   fr Whately
SEPTEMBER
1   fr M. of Rockingham
1, 3   fr M. of Rockingham
2   fr D. of Richmond
5   fr W. Dowdeswell
6   to M. of Rockingham
7   fr Sir A. Abdy
7   fr Whately
8   to M. of Rockingham
9   to M. of Rockingham
12   fr E. of Albemarle
13   to M. of Rockingham
16   to Barry
18   to Garrick
24   fr J. Stewart
26   fr O'Hara
27   to O'Hara
OCTOBER
1   *to O'Hara*
7   *fr O'Hara*
7   fr. J. Stewart
8   to Barry
9   to M. of Rockingham
15   fr E. of Albemarle
15   fr M. of Rockingham
20   to E. of Hardwicke
24   to O'Hara
29   to M. of Rockingham
NOVEMBER
4   fr Sir A. Abdy
4   fr O'Hara
4   fr M. of Rockingham
6   to M. of Rockingham
p6   to M. of Rockingham
8   fr Barry
12   to O'Hara
22   fr O'Hara
24   to M. of Rockingham
30   fr O'Hara
DECEMBER
5   to M. of Rockingham
8   fr Shackleton
9   fr M. of Rockingham
18   to M. of Rockingham
MONTH NOT KNOWN
—   fr Barry

—   *fr Unknown*
1770
FEBRUARY
3   fr W. Bourke
8   to G. Nagle
21   *fr G. Fitzgerald*
MARCH
p8   fr Lord J. Cavendish
c12   to Earl Verney
22   fr Dr. Leland
APRIL
3, 6   *to Dennis*
17   fr E. of Clanricarde
19   to Shackleton
22   to D. of Portland
24   *to Barry*
26   fr G. Scott
28   fr Shackleton
MAY
6   to Shackleton
10   fr O'Hara
17   fr N. Bourke
19   fr Dr. Leland
21   to O'Hara
31   fr O'Hara
—   fr Barry
JUNE
5   to E. of Shelburne
10   fr D. of Richmond
11   fr Dr. Leland
a20   *to O'Hara*
20   to O'Hara
21   fr Franks
21   fr Dr. Johnson
29   fr A. Nagle
30   fr G. E. Howard
JULY
8   fr W. Dowdeswell
AUGUST
6   to Sir W. Young
9   to O'Hara
a15   to Shackleton
20   fr S. Garbett
SEPTEMBER
4   fr D. of Manchester
5   fr M. of Rockingham
7, 8   to M. of Rockingham

8 fr Barry
11 to G. Nagle
23 to M. of Rockingham
26 fr M. of Rockingham

OCTOBER

3 *to Garrick*
6 fr G. E. Howard
14 fr D. of Richmond
21 to A. Young
29 fr Pridie

NOVEMBER

*a*17 fr Barry
17 fr Barry
18 fr Gov. Wentworth
20 fr Barry
23 fr O'Hara

DECEMBER

4 to Wolfall
7 *to Barry*
8 *to O'Hara*
15 fr M. of Rockingham
18 to M. of Rockingham
29 to M. of Rockingham
31 to O'Hara

1771

JANUARY

1 *fr O'Hara*
*a*2 *fr Capt. Stott*
2 to G. Nagle
3 fr M. of
    Rockingham
9 to A. Young
13 fr Barry
15 fr M. of Rockingham
*p*20 to Editor, *London*
    Chronicle
30 fr M. of Rockingham

FEBRUARY

*c*2 to W. Dowdeswell
2 fr W. Dowdeswell
3 fr M. of Rockingham
3 fr M. of Rockingham
9 fr M. of Rockingham
14 fr M. of Rockingham
16 to M. of Rockingham

MARCH

2 to D. of Portland

9 fr Franks
11 fr O'Hara
*p*12 to Unknown
27 to M. of Rockingham
27 to M. of Rockingham
27 fr W. Dowdeswell
    and M. of Rocking-
    ham
28 to O'Hara

APRIL

2 to O'Hara
14 fr O'Hara

MAY

3 fr Garrick
6 to G. Nagle
— *to O'Hara*

JUNE

5 to Unknown
9 to J. Cruger
9 to De Lancey
9 to R. R. Livingston
*a*15 *to Sir F. Norton*
*a*15 *fr Sir F. Norton*
21 fr M. of Rockingham

JULY

11 fr O'Hara
12 *to M. of Rockingham*
*p*14 to O'Hara
16 *fr Garrick*
20 to Mrs. Montagu
24 to Mrs. Montagu
26 *to Garrick*
*a*31 to Shackleton

AUGUST

6 to N.Y. Assembly
23 to G. Nagle
30 fr O'Hara
30 fr M. of Rockingham

SEPTEMBER

10 to O'Hara
10 to A. Young
26 to W. Baker

OCTOBER

1 to W. Baker
2 to Capt. Therry
8 fr M. of Rockingham
8 fr Trecothick
14 fr O'Hara

*p*14 to A. Young
15 fr C. Townshend
17 to C. Townshend

NOVEMBER

9 to Bp. of Chester
*p*9 to Bp. of Chester
17 fr O'Hara
18 to O'Hara
20 to C. Price
20 fr C. Townshend
24 to C. Townshend

DECEMBER

2 fr Franks
4 to De Lancey
4 to N.Y. Assembly
8 fr Skynner
8 to Skynner
18 to O'Hara
27 fr M. of Rockingham
27 fr Capt. Stott
28 fr O'Hara
— *to O'Hara*

MONTH NOT KNOWN

— fr Barry

1772

JANUARY

2 fr H. Archdeacon
28 fr Ridge

FEBRUARY

2 *to O'Hara*
*a*6 to Cts. of Huntingdon
7 to Shackleton
19 to Macartney
22 *fr O'Hara*
27 fr Dr. Hallifax

MARCH

5 *fr O'Hara*
13 *to O'Hara*
14 to Sjt. Glynn
24 *to Ridge*

APRIL

1 *fr O'Hara*

MAY

5 fr W. Dowdeswell
6 to N.Y. Assembly
16 fr Pickard
17 fr Gregory

56

20 to Unknown

JUNE

1 to O'Hara
c3 fr J. Banks
12 fr Unknown
12 fr M. of Rockingham
13 fr M. of Rockingham
17 *to Shackleton*
30 to J. Cruger
30 to De Lancey
30 to N.Y. Assembly

JULY

6 fr D. of Portland
12 to G. Nagle
14 fr O'Hara
24 to Barry
30 to O'Hara
31 fr Macleane

AUGUST

2 fr Macleane
4 to D. of Richmond
4 fr Dempster
a10 to E. of Suffolk
15 fr Thurlow
19 to Wickham
20 to De Lancey
20 to N.Y. Assembly
23 fr O'Hara
29 fr S. Garbett
— fr N.Y. Assembly
— *to O'Hara*

SEPTEMBER

a2 *to O'Hara*
a4 to E. of Charlemont
4 to E. of Charlemont
5 to Garrick
8 fr E. of Charlemont
11 fr O'Hara
21 fr Garrick
30 to O'Hara
— to Dempster

OCTOBER

a7 to Duane
18 fr W. Dowdeswell
22 *to O'Hara*
24, 27, 28 fr M. of Rockingham
27 to W. Dowdeswell

27 fr M. of Rockingham
29 to M. of Rockingham
30 to J. Stewart
31 fr O'Hara

NOVEMBER

3 fr W. Dowdeswell
6 fr Adm. Keppel
6, 7 to W. Dowdeswell
8 fr W. Dowdeswell
8 *fr O'Hara*
11 to M. of Rockingham
12 fr G. E. Howard
15 fr D. of Richmond
p15 to D. of Richmond
a17 to Unknown
19 to M. of Rockingham
20 fr M. of Rockingham
23 to M. of Rockingham
25 fr D. of Richmond
26 to M. of Rockingham

DECEMBER

2 fr D. of Richmond
4 fr G. E. Howard
5 fr W. Dowdeswell
5 to D. of Portland
9 fr G. E. Howard
9 *fr G. E. Howard*
18 to D. of Portland
a22 fr Bp. of Chester
22 fr T. King
31 to De Lancey
31 to N.Y. Assembly

1773

JANUARY

3 to Shackleton
5 fr M. of Rockingham
7, 10 to M. of Rockingham
11 to JB
12 to JB
14 fr J. Cruger
17 *to JB*
20 *to JB*
20 to WB
24 to Comte de Lauraguais

FEBRUARY

2 fr J. Cruger
3 fr T. King
4 to JB
4 to RBjr and T. King
9 fr RBjr and T. King
9 fr M. of Rockingham
14 to WB
p14 fr RBjr and T. King

MARCH

1 fr J. Cruger
3 fr N.Y. Minority
4 *fr O'Hara*
14 fr D. of Richmond
26 to O'Hara
p27 fr G. E. Howard

APRIL

3 fr O'Hara
4 fr Gen. Burgoyne
6 fr J. Cruger
7 fr De Lancey
7 fr Duane
8 fr N.Y. Assembly
12 fr Comte de Lusigny
16 to J. Cruger
16 to N.Y. Assembly
21 fr Unknown
26 fr RBjr and T. King
29 fr O'Hara

MAY

1 fr T. King
6 *fr Carr*
18 fr Wedderburn
18 to Wedderburn
22 to O'Hara
22 *fr Carr*
24 fr O'Hara
27 fr D. of Richmond
31 fr Bp. of Auxerre

JUNE

1 *fr T. King*
3 fr Kelly
3 fr O'Hara
5 fr Drumgold
15 to J. Pownall
23 fr W. Gordon
24 fr J. Cruger
29 to Garrick

3-2

JULY
2 to N.Y. Assembly
3 fr N.Y. Assembly
4 to Garrick
7 fr De Lancey
9 *to Capt. King*
18 to D. of Portland
23 fr G. E. Howard
26 fr M. of Rockingham

AUGUST
2 to De Lancey
2 to N.Y. Assembly
3 fr J. Cruger
19 to M. of Rockingham
20 to O'Hara

SEPTEMBER
4 to Mrs. Montagu
11 fr Mrs. Montagu
20 fr M. of Rockingham
20 fr Ms. of Rockingham
21 to M. of Rockingham
29 to M. of Rockingham

OCTOBER
4 *fr T. King*
6 fr J. Cruger
12 to J. Bourke
16 fr Sir C. Bingham
20 to M. of Rockingham
23 fr Gen. C. Lee
27 to J. Bourke
27 to Francis
27 fr Francis
30 to Sir C. Bingham
31 to Sjt. Glynn

NOVEMBER
2 to Sjt. Glynn
2 fr N.Y. Assembly
7 fr Sir C. Bingham
7, 11 to M. of Rocking-
ham
7 fr Wickham
*a*11 fr Dodwell
12 fr M. of Rockingham
16 to M. of Rockingham
16 to M. of Rockingham
17 fr E. of Clanricarde
17 fr Joyce
18 fr M. of Rockingham

19 to O'Hara
27 fr W. Baker
27 fr Chev. de Ganay
*a*29 fr Sir C. Bingham
29 fr Sir C. Bingham

DECEMBER
7 to N.Y. Assembly
11 to O'Hara
*p*13 fr M. of Rockingham
18 fr O'Hara
22 to O'Hara
24 fr O'Hara
26 fr Drumgold

MONTH NOT KNOWN
— fr Unknown

1774

JANUARY
5 to De Lancey
5 to N.Y. Assembly
5 to Wickham
6 to O'Hara
8 fr M. of Rockingham
17 fr Borcke
*p*17 to Borcke
30 fr M. of Rockingham

FEBRUARY
1 to Gen. C. Lee
2 to N.Y. Assembly
2 to M. of Rockingham
12 fr Adm. Keppel
21 fr R. Devereux

MARCH
13 fr C. Scott
*a*31 to RBsr

APRIL
*a*4 *to JB*
4 to W. King
5 fr Marquise Du
Deffand
6 to N.Y. Assembly
9 fr W. King
29 fr Bayley

MAY
4 fr J. Cruger
4 to N.Y. Assembly
5 to Mrs. Thrale
*c*5 fr Whitefoord

6 *to O'Hara*
10 to E. of Bessborough
14 fr M. of Rockingham
20 fr Camplin
28 to Cleaver
30 to N.Y. Assembly
31 fr N.Y. Assembly

JUNE
1 fr Cleaver
1 fr M. of Rockingham
*a*2 to J. Dodsley
*a*10 fr Wedderburn
15 fr Dr. Leland
20 to Bp. of Chester
20 to Mrs. Thrale
21 fr Bp. of Chester
21 to W. King
26 fr Dr. Leland
27 fr Dr. Leland
28 to Davies
28 fr Dr. Wilson

JULY
1 to Dr. Wilson
9 to Barry
11 fr Barry
11 fr Dr. Wilson
13 to Barry
13 fr H. Cruger
*a*16 to Unknown
21 fr Ds. of Richmond
23 fr W. Burgh
24 to John Lee

AUGUST
2 to N.Y. Assembly
20 fr John Lee
26 fr Plumer

SEPTEMBER
2 *to O'Hara*
7 to Mrs. Dowdeswell
9 fr Tomlinson
13 fr M. of Rockingham
15 to W. King
18 fr W. Dowdeswell
18, 25 to M. of Rocking-
ham
25 *fr Earl Verney*
26 fr D. of Richmond
26 fr Earl Verney

*p*26 to D. of Richmond
27 fr M. Morris
28 fr S. Hayes
28 fr Earl Verney
29 fr Bollan
29, 30 to D. of Portland
29 fr D. of Portland
30 fr W. Baker
— to Bn. Holland

OCTOBER

1 fr Champion
1 fr Champion
1 fr D. of Portland
*a*2 *to D. of Portland*
2 fr E. of Abingdon
2 to D. of Portland
2 fr D. of Portland
2 *fr D. of Portland*
2 fr M. of Rockingham
3 fr Champion
3 fr Adm. Keppel
3 fr Adm. Keppel
*c*4 to D. of Portland
4 fr E. of Abingdon
*p*4 fr E. of Abingdon
5 *to Bullock*
5 to Champion
5 fr M. of Rockingham
7 to E. of Bessborough
7 to Champion
7 fr Champion
7 to D. of Portland
8 fr E. of Bessborough
8 fr Champion
9 fr Champion
9 to M. of Rockingham
9 fr M. of Rockingham
11 fr M. of Rockingham
11 *to Shackleton*
12 *fr O'Hara*
16 fr Dunning
17 fr Mrs. Dowdeswell
17 fr M. of Rockingham
18 fr Vct. Clare
19 *fr D. of Portland*
21 fr Greaves
21 *to D. of Portland*
22 *to O'Hara*

25 *to D. of Portland*
25 to M. of Rockingham
26 *to D. of Portland*
26 *fr M. of Rockingham*
27 *to D. of Portland*
28 *to D. of Portland*
29 to H. Lloyd
31 fr Carter
— to Unknown

NOVEMBER

1 *to WB*
1 *to M. of Rockingham*
2 to Mrs. French
2 to O'Hara
3 fr Prattinton
4 fr C. Barrow
4 *to Col. Bentinck*
5 *to D. of Portland*
8 to JB
8 *fr D. of Portland*
12 fr M. of Rockingham
12 *fr M. of Rockingham*
15 *fr Mrs. Dowdeswell*
15 fr Kerr
*c*15 to Sir A. Elton
16 fr Rawlinson
18 fr W. Baker
19 to Champion
19 to Joseph Smith
20 fr Champion
24 *to Champion*
24 fr W. Chapman
24 *to D. of Portland*
29 *to Champion*
29 fr M. of Rockingham
29 fr Joseph Smith

DECEMBER

5 *to WB*
*a*8 fr Merchants at
    Bristol
12 fr T. King
15 fr Clerke
16 fr Gen. C. Lee
17 fr Symons
18 fr W. Baker
19 fr Franklin
20 fr Danet
*a*22 fr Champion

22 *to Champion*
23 *to Champion*
24 fr Durbin
26 fr W. Baker
*a*28 fr Unknown
28 fr Merchants at Bristol
*a*30 *to O'Hara*

1775

JANUARY

2 fr Champion
2 fr G. E. Howard
2 *fr G. E. Howard*
3 fr Champion
3 to N.Y. Assembly
4 *to Champion*
5 to Champion
5 fr Champion
5 to D. of Portland
5 to M. of Rockingham
5 to Champion
7, 8 fr M. of
    Rockingham
8 fr D. of Portland
9 *to Champion*
10 to Champion
10 fr Jackson
12 to M. of Rockingham
12 fr Woodward
14 fr Champion
14 fr Shackleton
14 fr J. and T. Williams
15 to Barry
15 fr O'Keefe
16 fr Jacob
18 fr R. Smith
18 fr Citizens of Bristol
18 fr Greaves
19 fr Champion
19 fr Fry, Fripp & Co.
20 to Champion
20 to Citizens of Bristol
21 to Hutchinson
21 fr Champion
22 fr M. of Rockingham
23 fr O'Hara
23 fr Turton
24 fr M. of Rockingham

59

24	*to Champion*	2	fr James Harford	14	to Mullett
24	fr Champion	4	*fr Champion*	*p*14	*to O'Hara*
24	to M. of Rockingham	4	fr P. Farr	15	fr O'Hara
25	fr O'Hara	4	fr Joseph Smith	15	fr Mullett
27	fr Davison	6	*to Champion*	18	fr J. Phillips
30	fr J. and T. Williams	6	to Robert Smith	24	fr Robert Smith
31	fr Ms. of Rockingham	9	fr Robert Smith	26	to O'Hara
—	fr Independent	9	to Champion	26	fr Woodward
	Society, Bristol	9	to Huish	30	fr Symons
—	fr Gov. Johnstone	11	fr Huish		MAY
—	fr Unknown	12	*fr Champion*	1	fr P. Farr
	FEBRUARY	13	fr Robert Smith	1	fr R. Harford
1	fr H. Cavendish	13	fr Champion	1	to Adam Smith
2	fr W. Mason	14	to De Lancey	3	fr O'Hara
6	fr M. of Rockingham	14	to N.Y. Assembly	4	fr J. Cruger
6	fr Ridge	16	fr J. Anderson	4	fr Job Watts
7	fr R. Udny	17	fr Fry	4	fr Unknown
8	fr Merchants at	20	to Champion	8	fr Hatsell
	Birmingham	22	fr Champion	9	fr Glasgow
8	fr D. of Richmond	22	fr Champion	9	to D. of Portland
9	to W. Burgh	22	*to Champion*	*a*10	*to D. of Portland*
9	fr M. of Rockingham	22	fr Frank	10	fr E. of Dartmouth
11	fr Rickards	22	fr M. of Rockingham	10	fr Sir F. Norton
13	fr M. of Rockingham	23	fr Lane	11	to E. of Dartmouth
18	fr W. Burgh	24	to Champion	12	fr Eden
18	fr Peckard	24	to Robert Smith	12	to Eden
19	fr Lord North	*p*24	fr Champion	15	fr Franklin
19	fr Ms. of Rockingham	25	fr Hutchinson	17	fr M. of Rockingham
*c*21	to Champion	26	*fr Champion*	19	fr E. of Carlisle
*c*21	fr Farr	29	fr Ms. of Rockingham	21	to Eden
21	to Noble	29	to Champion	21	fr Sir W. Bagot
22	fr M. of Rockingham	30	fr Robert Smith	21	fr Eden
22	to Joseph Smith		APRIL	22	*fr O'Hara*
22	to Huish	1	fr Greaves	22	fr M. of Rockingham
23	fr Champion	4	fr Robert Smith	24	*to Champion*
23	*to Champion*	4	fr Champion	25	fr Gov. Johnstone
23	*to Champion*	5	fr Champion	27	fr P. Farr
25	fr Champion	5	fr N.Y. Assembly	*c*28	to O'Hara
25	*to Champion*	6	fr Dr. Haliday		JUNE
25	fr James Harford	6	to Robert Smith	1	fr Unknown
25	fr Huish	8	fr Champion	3	to Champion
—	fr Champion	10	fr James	*a*4	fr Gov. Johnstone
—	*to Champion*	10	fr Quarme	4	fr Unknown
—	fr Greaves	12	*to D. of Portland*	5, 18	fr O'Hara
—	fr Withers	12	*to Champion*	7	fr Mrs. Dowdeswell
	MARCH	13	fr Evans	7	to N.Y. Assembly
1	*to Champion*	13	to Mullett	7	fr Unknown
2	fr Champion	14	fr Mullett	9	*to Champion*

10	*to Champion*	18	to Langton	26	*to Champion*
13	to Mrs. Dowdeswell	18	*to J. Robinson*	27	*to Champion*
16	fr D. of Richmond	20	fr E. of Rochford	28	*to Champion*
16	fr M. of Rockingham	24	fr Noble	29	*to Champion*
20	fr Champion	24	fr M. of Rockingham	p29	*fr Champion*
20	fr P. Farr	25	fr Ridge	30	*fr O'Hara*
21	fr Mrs. Dowdeswell	26	to D. of Richmond	30	fr Unknown
23	fr M. of Rockingham	27	fr Champion	—	*to Champion*
a25	to Noble	29	*to Champion*	—	*to Champion*
28	to Champion	30	fr P. Farr		
28	*to Shackleton*	—	*to Champion*		

JULY

OCTOBER

NOVEMBER

8	fr American Congress	1	to Champion	2	fr M. of Rockingham
11	fr M. of Rockingham	c1	to Champion	3	fr Lord J. Cavendish
18	to Pieter Camper	1	to Sir G. Savile	7	fr M. of Rockingham
19	to Champion	1	to M. of Rockingham	7	*fr W. Salkeld*
24	fr Noble	2	*to Champion*	8	fr G. Rice
24	*to D. and Ds. of*	2	fr Langton	9	fr Dr. Haliday
	Portland	2	to D. of Portland	10	*to Champion*
25	*to D. of Portland*	3	*to Champion*	10	*to O'Hara*
26	to O'Hara	3	to La Grange and	p12	*fr Dr. Johnson*
27	fr Unknown		Livingston	16	*to Champion*
28	fr Bright	4	fr W. Baker	16	fr John Watts
28	*to D. of Portland*	5	fr W. Baker	18	*fr O'Hara*
		5	to Count Darcy	21	fr Committee at
AUGUST		5	fr D. of Portland		Westbury, Wilts.
4	fr O'Hara	7	fr P. Farr	25	fr D. of Richmond
4	to M. of Rockingham	8	*to Champion*	—	fr Bn. Craven
6	to Almon	10	fr Unknown	—	fr Dr. Barnard
9	*to J. Dodsley*	11	to T. Hayes		
9	fr O'Hara	11	fr Ridge	**DECEMBER**	
13	fr Champion	12	fr Dr. J. Sharp	4	fr Beresford
14	fr Champion	13	fr Comte de Sarsfield	11	fr P. Farr
17	to O'Hara	14	*fr Champion*	12	fr Merchants at
20	fr Champion	14	fr P. Farr		Bristol
21	fr A. Lee	16	fr Loscombe	14	fr P. Farr
22	fr W. Baker	17	*to Champion*	15	to Champion
22	to A. Lee	17	to Champion	15	fr Sir G. Cooper
22, 23	to M. of	18	fr P. Farr	a18	*to O'Hara*
	Rockingham	19	fr P. Farr	18	fr Robinson
23	to W. Baker	20	to Champion	23	fr Mrs. Dowdeswell
28	fr O'Hara	20	to Thistlethwaite	24	fr P. Farr
—	to W. King	23	to Champion	26	fr E. of Stair
		23	fr Champion	27	fr Capt. Nugent
SEPTEMBER		23	fr J. Ellis	28	to Champion
3	fr C. Dowdeswell	23	fr Ms. of Rockingham	29	fr O'Hara
6	to J. Robinson	a25	*to D. of Portland*	30	to Mrs. Dowdeswell
11	fr M. of Rockingham	25	fr Lord J. Cavendish	—	*to Champion*
14	to M. of Rockingham			—	*to Champion*
16	to E. of Suffolk				

MONTH NOT KNOWN

—   fr Chambers

— fr C. O'Hara, Jr.
— fr 'Amor Patriae'
— to Searle

1776

JANUARY

1 fr Drumgold
1 fr E. of Stair
1 fr Capt. Nugent
4 to Ms. of Rockingham
5 *to WB*
*p*6 to M. of Rockingham
7 *fr Champion*
7 to O'Hara
10 fr Webb
14 *to Champion*
16 fr T. Townshend
17 fr Rouquet
19 *to Hannah More*
26 fr Mrs. Dowdeswell
27 fr G. E. Howard
28 *to D. of Portland*
— fr Champion
— *fr Champion*

FEBRUARY

5 fr Ridge
6 fr P. Farr
6 fr Garrick
7 fr P. Farr
8 to Champion
9 to P. Farr
10 fr Dr. Barnard
10 fr Mrs. Montagu
10 to Mrs. Montagu
12 fr P. Farr
13 fr Adm. Keppel
13 fr Lane
16 fr P. Farr
20 *to Champion*
21 to Ms. of Rockingham
21 fr Adm. Keppel
22 to Champion
23 fr Adm. Palliser
24 fr Lord J. Cavendish
27 fr Rumbold
— fr E. of Stair
— fr E. of Stair

MARCH

1 *to Champion*
4 *to D. of Portland*
8 *to D. of Portland*
14 fr Citizens of Bristol
14 fr P. Farr
16 fr Adm. Palliser
17 fr Eden
17 to Eden
18 fr Eden
19 to Champion
19 fr Sir G. Cooper
20 fr Pennington & Biggs
22 fr O'Neill
25 *to M. of Rockingham*
28 fr Sir G. Savile
— *to Champion*

APRIL

*c*1 to Sir G. Savile
3 to Champion
12 fr Ms. of Rockingham
13 fr Ms. of Rockingham
20 fr Sir J. Colthurst
22 to Champion
23 to Col. St. Paul
27 fr Hutchinson

MAY

2 fr Giddy
3 to Mrs. Montagu
3 to M. of Rockingham
3 to Ms. of Rockingham
*a*15 *to D. of Portland*
22 to Thistlethwaite
*p*23 to Champion
30 to Champion

JUNE

2 fr M. of Rockingham
*a*4 to A. Young
4 to E. of Charlemont
4 to D. of Portland
4 fr D. of Portland
8 fr Dempster
13 to Strachey
21 fr Unknown
*p*22 to Dr. Johnson
25 to Bowden
*c*25 to Dr. R. Robinson

28 fr Blaquiere
28 *to D. of Portland*
— *to Champion*
— to Unknown
— *fr Champion*

JULY

*c*1 to Capt. Thompson
2 *fr Capt. King*
3 fr M. of Rockingham
4 to M. of Rockingham
6 to Sir J. Blaquiere
11 to J. Bourke
*a*12 *to M. of Rockingham*
12 fr M. of Rockingham
15 to Unknown
23 *to Champion*
23 fr P. Farr
25 *to D. of Portland*
27 fr Mullett

AUGUST

1 fr P. Farr
2 to G. Nagle
8 to Dr. Barnard
10 fr Noble
10 *to D. of Portland*
11 to Shackleton
12 to Eden
14 to Eden
*a*15 to Champion
15 *to Champion*
16 to D. of Portland
17 fr Fox
21 *to D. of Portland*
21 fr Mrs. Dowdeswell
22 *to D. of Portland*
26 fr D. of Richmond

SEPTEMBER

25 *to D. of Portland*

OCTOBER

2 *to Champion*
9 to Champion
9 fr J. Hickey
10 to Champion
10 fr D. of Richmond
13 fr Fox
13 fr M. of Rockingham
22 fr M. of Rockingham
25 fr Sir T. Bunbury

28 fr R. Watson
29 *to Champion*
29 fr G. E. Howard
31 fr D. of Richmond
— *to Champion*

NOVEMBER

*a*2 fr Sir G. Cooper
2 to Champion
*p*2 fr Sir G. Cooper
*a*4 to Noble
4 fr Capt. King
6 *to Champion*
6 fr P. Farr
7 fr Stephens
8 fr Stephens
*c*8 to Champion
9 *to Champion*
12 fr Unknown
14 to G. Nagle
14 fr Stanley
15 fr Stephens
16 to Garnett
27 fr D. of Richmond
29 fr Mauvillon

DECEMBER

9 to Champion
13 fr W. Baker
13 to D. of Portland
15 to Dr. Brocklesby
18 *to Champion*
19 fr G. Gordon
*a*22 fr Champion
22 to Champion
30 fr John Lee
31 fr Sir G. Cooper

MONTH NOT KNOWN

— *fr Champion*
— fr S. Hayes
— fr Sadler
— fr Sadler
— to Masères

1777

JANUARY

3 fr Sir G. Cooper
6 to M. of Rockingham
6, 7 fr M. of Rockingham
7 fr M. of Rockingham

12 *to Champion*
13 to Champion
13 fr Noble
15 to Champion
16 fr C. Morris
21 to Champion
22 fr Sir A. Elton
*c*22 *to Champion*
24 fr John King, of
    Bristol
27 to Champion
29 fr G. E. Howard
30 to Sir A. Elton
— fr Champion
— *fr Champion*

FEBRUARY

10 *to D. of Portland*
11 to D. of Portland
13 *to D. of Portland*
15 *to Champion*
15 fr Cumberland
17 fr Champion
17 *to Champion*
18 fr Maj. Cartwright
*p*18 to Maj. Cartwright
19 fr Fry, Fripp & Co.
21 to Champion
21 *to Champion*
21 to Huish
22 *to D. of Portland*
23 fr Champion
25 fr Huish
26 fr Turton

MARCH

4 *to Sir J. Reynolds*
*a*7 *to D. of Portland*
10 *to Shackleton*
17 *to Champion*
17 fr Worrall
18 *to Champion*
24 fr Farell & Jones
24 fr Garnett
26 *to Champion*
26 fr G. E. Howard
28 *fr Garrick*
28 to Ms. of Rockingham

APRIL

1 fr Ms. of Rockingham

2 *to Champion*
2 to Ms. of Rockingham
3 to Champion
4 fr Unknown
5 fr Farell & Jones
6 fr Fear
10 fr Garnett
12 fr Reynolds, Getly
    & Co.
16 fr Hawkswell
*p*18 to Champion
26 *to Champion*
26 fr Unknown
29 *to Champion*
29 to Garrick
29 fr Garrick
— fr Sir G. Cooper

MAY

2 to Barry
2 to Champion
5 *to Champion*
9 to Champion
14 to Garnett
14 *fr T. King*
21 to J. Bourke
27 fr Cappe
27 *to Champion*
28 fr Hutchinson
30 fr Gen. Oglethorpe
*c*30 to M. of Rockingham
31 fr Ross & Mill
31 fr Shoolbred
— fr Shackleton

JUNE

2 fr Kearney
2 to Gen. Oglethorpe
3 fr W. Harris
5 to Lord North
5 fr Robertson
5 *fr Champion*
8 to M. of Rockingham
9 to Francis
9 to Robertson
9 fr M. of Rockingham
10 to Robertson
13 to Champion
18 to Richardson
25 *to Champion*

26	to Champion	5	to M. of Rockingham	MARCH		
26	fr Worrall	6	fr Pulteney	3	fr Boswell	
28	fr Unknown	7	fr D. of Manchester	4	fr Span	
—	fr Dempster	9	to W. Baker	a14	fr Unknown	
JULY		11	fr Pery	14	fr Unknown	
3	to Champion	13	fr Col. Gordon	14	fr Span	
3	fr Dempster	13	fr J. Pownall	15	fr D. of Richmond	
3	to Garnett	21	fr Francis	15	fr Unknown	
9	to Champion	29	fr Wilcox	17	to Sir J. Durbin	
21	to Dr. Brocklesby	—	to J. Bourke	20	to Ds. of Devonshire	
21	to Izard	—	fr T. Townshend		and Cts. Spencer	
AUGUST		DECEMBER		20	fr Abbé Raynal	
c11	to Noble	1	to Champion	26	to Daubeny	
11	to Champion	3	fr Walpole	26	to P. Stephens	
26	to E. of Abingdon	3	to Wedderburn	27	to Daubeny	
28	fr E. of Abingdon	3	to Wedderburn	31	to Span	
30	fr Dr. Haliday	3	fr Wedderburn	APRIL		
—	to Birt	3	fr M. of	2	fr Span	
SEPTEMBER			Rockingham	2	to Champion	
1	to Francis	4	to Wedderburn	3	to Noble	
3	to G. Nagle	6	fr D. of Manchester	3	fr P. Stephens	
a5	to Hargrave	7	to Champion	4	to Champion	
6	fr Mrs. Montagu	7	fr M. of Rockingham	7	fr W. King	
8	fr Fox	9	to G. Nagle	9	to Mrs. Champion	
8	fr Garnett	16	to M. of Rockingham	9	to Span	
12	to Garnett	18	fr Francis	9	fr Vesey	
16	to Shackleton	c19	to Unknown	11	to Champion	
18	to Champion	20	fr A. Montgomery	11	fr Comerford	
21	to Garnett	24	fr Wilcox	11	to Strachey	
25	to Champion	25	fr W. Baker	13	fr Nesbitt	
—	to M. of Rockingham	MONTH NOT KNOWN		13	fr Span	
OCTOBER		—	to Garrick	14	to Champion	
1	fr Francis	—	fr Drumgold	14	fr Warren	
2	fr M. of Rockingham			23	to Span	
6	to D. of Portland	**1778**		24	to Noble	
7	to Chetwynd	JANUARY		27	fr Harford, Cowles &	
8	to Fox	4	fr Petrie		Co.	
9	fr W. Baker	4	to D. of Portland	29	fr Dr. Curry	
11	fr Vesey	4	to M. of Rockingham	30	fr Span	
12	to W. Baker	14	to D. of Portland	—	to Champion	
16	to Raja of Tanjore	31	fr P. Farr	MAY		
22	fr W. Baker	—	fr Jones	2	fr W. Baker	
26	to G. Nagle	FEBRUARY		2	to Harford, Cowles &	
26	fr M. of Rockingham	7	fr Dr. Dickens		Co.	
NOVEMBER		12	fr Unknown	2	fr Unknown	
1	to Stewards of Bell	14	fr Lord J. Cavendish	3	fr Hawkswell	
	Club, Bristol	16	to Vct. Weymouth	5	fr Harford, Cowles &	
1	to Champion	26	fr Span		Co.	

10	to E. of Surrey	*a*18	to Sir G. Cooper	3	fr J. Pownall
12	to Harford, Cowles &	*a*18	fr Bn. Thurlow	4	*to Champion*
	Co.	*a*18	to Bn. Thurlow	5	fr Stevens
12	to Span	18	to Pery	6	fr Boswell
14	fr G. E. Howard	19	to Champion	8	*to Champion*
16	fr G. E. Howard	20	fr Sir G. Cooper	11	to Span
16	*fr G. E. Howard*	23	*to Champion*	14	to Mrs. Dowdeswell
19	to Pery	28	fr Pery	20	to RBjr
25	fr Pery	29	*to G. Cook*	26	fr T. Erskine
27	fr J. Ponsonby	31	fr Sir G. Cooper	29	fr D. of Portland
31	to Champion		AUGUST		DECEMBER

JUNE

		1	fr Fox	3	fr M. Miller Jr.
2	to Pery	1	fr O'Halloran	9	fr M. of Rockingham
3	to Unknown	1	fr M. of Rockingham	11	fr M. of Rockingham
*c*3	to Unknown	1	fr Wilcox	14	*to Francis*
7	fr Dr. Curry	*p*1	to Adm. Keppel	17	fr Sir L. O'Brien
8	fr Pery	3	*fr Unknown*	23	fr Ms. of Rockingham
11	*to D. of Portland*	4, 5	fr Pery	24	to Francis
13	*fr Russel*	5	fr Pery	29	fr M. of Rockingham
14	fr J. Murray	11	fr Gardiner	—	*fr Ms. of Rockingham*
14	*to D. of Portland*	11	fr Vct. Kenmare		MONTH NOT KNOWN
16	to Pery	11	fr Pery	—	*to Champion*
17	fr Pery	12	fr Dr. Curry	—	fr Dr. Johnson
18	fr Hawkswell	12	fr Adm. Keppel		
20, 23	fr Dr. Curry	12	to Pery		**1779**
20	fr Sir L. O'Brien	12	fr Pery		JANUARY
21	fr Pery	16	*to D. of Portland*	1	to W. Ellis
22	fr St. John	17	fr W. O'Hara	2	fr M. of
23	fr M. of Rockingham	18	fr Dr. Curry		Rockingham
24	to Pery	23	to Champion	4	*fr W. King*
25	to Noble	24	to Gardiner	5	*fr Unknown*
25	fr Earl Nugent	25	to G. Nagle	6	*to Champion*
25	to Pery	26	fr Pery	12	to Miss Pelham
26	to Pery		SEPTEMBER	13	fr Rogers
26	to Pery	4	fr Yorke	14	fr Miss Pelham
*p*28	*to Champion*	21	to Mrs. Waller	16	*to Champion*
—	fr Fox		OCTOBER	19	*to Trimbuck Sambagee*
—	fr Bn. Thurlow	1	fr D. of Richmond	24	fr Fox
—	*to Vct. Weymouth*	3	to Noble	26	fr Wallis
	JULY	4	to Champion	29	*to Francis*
1	fr Pery	9	to Champion		FEBRUARY
2	fr Wedderburn	21	*to Champion*	3	to J. Almon
3	to Pery	23	*fr Trimbuck Sambagee*	4	*fr Gov. Johnstone*
10	fr Pery	26	fr Span	11	to Miss Pelham
15	fr Sir T. Bunbury	28	*fr Raja of Tanjore*	17	fr Carr
15	fr Sir L. O'Brien	—	fr Fox	20	fr Dr. Haliday
17	*to Mr. and Mrs.*		NOVEMBER	22	fr Boswell
	Champion	1, 2	*fr Unknown*	25	fr Brooks

28	fr Jones	12	to M. Miller	9	fr W. Baker
—	fr Vct. Lumley	20	fr Garth	9	*to Champion*
MARCH		21	to Ms. of Rockingham	9	fr Dermott
1	to Boswell	21	to Noble	12	*to D. of Portland*
1	*to Champion*	22	to Garth	13	to Champion
1	to M. Miller	22	fr M. Miller	14	to Dr. Curry
12	to Jones	22	fr M. Miller	17	to Dermott
16	fr Sir H. Hill	25	to M. Miller	18	*to D. of Portland*
18	*fr Raja of Tanjore*	25	to Shackleton	19	*to D. of Portland*
19	fr Hilton	26	to M. Miller	20	*to D. of Portland*
22	fr M. Miller	28	to M. Miller	21	fr Dr. Dickens
*a*24	to Noble	—	fr Dr. Hay	22	to Champion
24	to M. Miller	—	fr Dr. Hay	22	to Champion
24	fr Stephens	JUNE		23	fr Dermott
25	fr Bowie	3	*to Champion*	26	*to Champion*
26	fr Unknown	4	fr Sir L. O'Brien	27	*to D. of Portland*
29	fr Unknown	5	fr Camplin	29	to Champion
29	*fr Hawkswell*	8	fr Bowie	31	fr Gen. Burgoyne
30	fr E. of Charlemont	12	fr Dr. G. Campbell	SEPTEMBER	
*a*31	to Noble	12	to Dr. Erskine	1	to Gen. Burgoyne
31	to Bowie	13	fr M. of Rockingham	3	*to D. of Portland*
APRIL		15, 16	to Champion	4	fr Dr. Curry
10	fr Shackleton	19	fr Durbin	4	*to D. of Portland*
10	fr Unknown	21	to M. of Rockingham	5	*to D. of Portland*
10	fr Worrall	22	*to Champion*	5	*to D. of Portland*
13	fr M. Miller	24	to Coxe	5	*to D. of Portland*
14	fr M. Miller	24	fr Durbin	8	*to Champion*
16	to M. Miller	*p*24	to G. Nagle	12	*to Champion*
16	fr Stephens	25	*to D. of Portland*	*a*13	*to D. of Portland*
17	fr African Committee	JULY		16	fr Dignan
17	to M. Miller	3	fr Camplin	*a*22	*to D. of Portland*
19	fr Forster	4	to Camplin	22	*to D. of Portland*
22	fr M. Miller	4	to W. King	*a*23	*to D. of Portland*
24	fr Bowie	12	fr Dr. Hay	23	*to D. of Portland*
24	fr Dr. Erskine	16	fr Dr. Erskine	23	fr Ms. of Rockingham
27	fr Dr. Johnson	16	fr P. Farr	24	to D. of Portland
30	to M. of Rockingham	18	*to Champion*	25	to Dignan
MAY		18	fr D. of Portland	25	to E. of Upper Ossory
1	*to D. of Portland*	21	to Champion	26	fr Lord G. Cavendish
1	*to D. of Portland*	26	to John Lee	27	fr Earl Fitzwilliam
5	to Noble	26	*to D. of Portland*	29	to Eden
5	fr M. of Rockingham	AUGUST		*a*28	*to D. of Portland*
6	to Noble	4	fr W. Baker	29	fr D. of Portland
6	fr Worrall	4	*to D. of Portland*	29	*fr D. of Portland*
8	fr M. of Rockingham	6	fr Dr. Curry	30	to E. of Upper Ossory
9	to M. of Rockingham	7	fr Dr. Dickens	OCTOBER	
11	to Worrall	7	fr M. of Rockingham	3	to Ms. of Rockingham
12	*to Champion*	8	to M. of Rockingham	6	*to D. of Portland*

8	fr Eden	26	to Almon	12	fr Unknown
9	*to D. of Portland*	29	*to Champion*	14	fr Unknown
10	fr Dignan	—	*to Mr. and Mrs.*	15	fr J. Morton
12	*fr Unknown*		*Champion*	15, 16	*to D. of Portland*
14	to Champion	MONTH NOT KNOWN		18	fr Vct. Kenmare
14	*to Champion*	—	fr Unknown	20	fr Cheveley
14	to E. of Upper Ossory			20	fr J. Morton
14	*fr Unknown*	**1780**		23	fr Capt. Blankett
14	fr Popham	JANUARY		25	fr Ms. of Rockingham
15	to Champion	1	to T. Burgh	26	to Ms. of Rockingham
16	to D. of Portland	1	fr Ms. of Rockingham	28	to Awdry
17	to M. of Rockingham	2	to Ms. of Rockingham	28	to Jepson
18	*to Champion*	2	to D. of Bolton	MARCH	
19	*to Champion*	4	fr Ms. of Rockingham	2	fr Boswell
19	*to Sir T. Kent*	5	to Flood	2	fr Townsend
19	fr Hawkswell	6	fr M. of Rockingham	3	fr Vaughan
20	*to Sir T. Kent*	6	fr Ms. of Rockingham	4	fr A. Murphy
20	*to D. of Portland*	7	to M. of Rockingham	4	fr T. Williams
20	*to D. of Portland*	8	*to Mrs. Champion*	4	fr Unknown
27	fr Hawkswell	9	fr Ms. of Rockingham	6	to Kenyon
*a*30	*to D. of Portland*	9	to Ms. of Rockingham	6	to Rix
—	*fr Raja of Tanjore*	13	fr M. of Rockingham	6	to Townsend
—	fr Gen. Burgoyne	14	fr D. of Portland	7	fr C. Barrow
NOVEMBER		15	fr D. of Portland	7	to Ds. of Devonshire
3	fr M. of Rockingham	*a*16	to Ms. of Rockingham	7	fr John J. Smith
5	to Champion	16	to D. of Portland	*p*8	fr Mainwaring
5	fr W. King	16	to Ms. of Rockingham	11	fr Symons
5	*to D. of Portland*	16	fr Ms. of Rockingham	*p*11	fr Symons
6	to Adm. Keppel	17	fr Dignan	14	fr Unknown
15	*to Champion*	17	fr D. of Portland	15	fr Earl Talbot
15	fr Ms. of Rockingham	*p*17	fr Ms. of Rockingham	17	fr Braughall
19	fr Dr. W. Chapman	18	fr Dempster	17	fr J. Morton
23	fr Eden	18	*to Ms. of Rockingham*	*p*20	to Unknown
23	to Eden	20	fr Sir H. Harbord	31	fr M. of Rockingham
25	to Unknown	22	fr Dignan	31	fr M. of Rockingham
27	fr M. of Rockingham	22	to Vct. Kenmare	APRIL	
DECEMBER		24	to Champion	4	to J. Harford
6	fr J. Powell of Bristol	25	fr Smyth	4	to Merlott
8	fr Dr. W. Chapman	27	fr T. Burgh	6	to Vct. Mahon
9	to M. Miller	27	fr Unknown	8	fr Committee of
9	to J. Powell of Bristol	31	fr Brice and J. Harford		Merchants at Bristol
*p*9	fr Unknown	31	fr Smyth	12	to Chairman of
11	fr Unknown	FEBRUARY			Buckinghamshire
14	to E. of Shelburne	3	fr Hutchinson		Meeting
21	fr Dr. W. Chapman	7	*fr Trimbuck Sambagee*	12	to Noble
22	fr Archibald Dalzel	7	fr Unknown	15	fr Committee of
22	fr Dr. Hay	*a*8	fr Constituents at		Merchants at Bristol
24	fr T. Burgh		Bristol	16	to Wedderburn

a19	to Unknown	21	fr Necker	—	fr Ms. of Rockingham
20	*to D. of Portland*	a22	fr Unknown	OCTOBER	
25	to J. Hill	24	to Vct. Courtenay	1	to D. of Portland
29	fr Donston	28	*to D. of Portland*	2	fr Jenkinson
MAY		—	*to Champion*	2	to Jenkinson
5	fr Necker	AUGUST		3	to E. of Hillsborough
6	to Shackleton	4	*to Champion*		and Vct. Stormont
p8	to D. of Richmond	4	fr Wyvill	3	to Vct. Stormont
9	*to Mr. J. Cartwright*	6	fr Barrington	3	fr Jenkinson
16	to Champion	10	to Job Watts	3	fr Vct. Stormont
20	fr Miles	11	*to Champion*	4	fr Vct. Stormont
20	fr Shackleton	11	to Noble	4	to Vct. Stormont
22	to Wynn	14	to Wyvill	5	to Noble
24	to Champion	18	fr C. Barrow	5	to D. of Portland
JUNE		18	*to Earl Waldegrave*	a6	*to Champion*
1	*to Jenkinson*	19	*to Staunton*	10	fr Bn. Loughborough
2	*to Champion*	a20	*to D. of Portland*	a12	fr Dr. Haliday
6	to Sir E. Swinburne	22	*to Jenkinson*	15	to Champion
7	*to Champion*	29	to Sir W. Hamilton	18	fr E. of Hillsborough
7	to Unknown	31	*fr D. of Portland*		and Vct. Stormont
c7	to Unknown	SEPTEMBER		19	to E. of Hillsborough
7	fr Unknown	3	to D. of Portland		and Vct. Stormont
8	fr Noble	4	*to Champion*	p20	fr R. Burke, distant
12	fr Sir A. Elton	7, 8	to M. of Rocking-		relative
13	to Shackleton		ham	25	to C. Barrow
15	fr Earl Bathurst	a8	*to D. of Portland*	25	to Jenkinson
15	to Bn. Loughborough	8	*to D. of Portland*	28	fr Sir A. Elton
18	fr Noble	8	*to M. of Rockingham*	NOVEMBER	
18	fr Lord North	9	*to D. of Portland*	1	to Sir A. Elton
19	fr Lord North	9	*to M. of Rockingham*	2	to Champion
20	*to Champion*	10	to C. Barrow	2	fr J. Scott
22	fr Madan	15	fr Fox	3	*to Champion*
24	fr Bn. Petre	17	fr Gen. Burgoyne	7	fr Capt. Waldegrave
26	fr Unknown	17	fr Ms. of Rockingham	8	fr Capt. Waldegrave
29	*to Champion*	18	fr C. Barrow	9	fr Dr. Browne
JULY		18	fr Earl Nugent	15	to Hutchinson
1	fr C. Barrow	19	fr Prince Dashkov	16	to Jenkinson
7	fr Bn. Petre	22	fr Bns. Craven	17	*to Champion*
10	fr Vct. Courtenay	23, 26, 28	*to D. of*	28	*to Champion*
10	to Bn. Thurlow		*Portland*	DECEMBER	
15	fr C. Butler	25	fr T. Burgh	1	fr Irving and Touchet
17	fr E. of Mansfield	26	to Champion	2	to Unknown
17	to Bn. Loughborough	27	to J. Harford	6	to Weddell
18	to Earl Bathurst	27, 28	to Ms. of	12	fr Sir W. Hamilton
18	*to Champion*		Rockingham	14	fr E. of Effingham
18	to Sir G. Cooper	29	to Adm. Keppel	18	fr Capt. Blankett
19	fr Earl Bathurst	30	to Jenkinson	20	fr Bn. Loughborough
21	*to Mrs Champion*	—	fr Ms. of Rockingham	21	fr Adm. Keppel

23	*fr J. Robinson*	26	fr Fisher	14, 24, 30	fr Sir J.
27	*to Champion*	27	fr Crabbe		Reynolds
27	fr Gregory	APRIL		15	to Franklin
27	fr Vct. Kenmare	2	to Noble	15	to Molini
MONTH NOT KNOWN		5	to E. of Hardwicke	*a*17	to D. of Portland
—	fr Henderson	7	*to Champion*	19	fr D. Long
—	fr Lord R. Spencer	10	to Tighe	24	fr Crabbe
—	fr Warburton	11	fr Tighe	24	fr Unknown
—	fr M. of Rockingham	18	fr Eden	24	*fr Crabbe*
—	fr Sir G. Savile	*a*20	fr J. Henderson	—	to Ragunath Rao
—	fr Princess Dashkova	25	*to Mr. and Mrs.*	SEPTEMBER	
			Champion	2	to Champion

1781

		26	to Noble	5	to Mrs. Hennessy
JANUARY		MAY		11	to Molini
2	to Noble	3	fr Adm. Keppel	15	fr G. Goold
*c*4	fr Bn. Loughborough	9	to Bourn	17	fr E. of Bessborough
6	*fr T. King*	10	fr John Trumbull	18	fr Bn. Petre
7	to Champion	19	fr John Trumbull	*p*18	to Bn. Petre
7	to Champion	26	fr Dempster	28	*to Bn. Macartney*
9	*fr Septchêner*	29	*to Bn. Macartney*	OCTOBER	
14	*to Champion*	JUNE		3	fr Crabbe
20	*to Champion*	5	fr Sir F. Basset	3	fr Cursetji Manuar
25	to Unknown	9	fr S. Garbett		and Manuar
30	to O'Beirne	*p*13	to Jones		Ratanji
—	*fr Eliot*	22	fr Wren	4	to Sir T. Bunbury
FEBRUARY		25	to Mrs. Thrale	4	*to Champion*
14	fr MacMahon	25	fr Staunton	*a*11	to D. of Portland
15	fr Capt. Blankett	25	fr John Trumbull	*a*13	fr Molini
15	fr Sir G. Savile	26	fr Crabbe	13	fr Humund Rao
16	to Dr. Warton	30	to Mrs. Gwatkin	13	fr D. of Portland
18	fr J. Harford	JULY		14	fr Cursetji Manuar
18	fr M. of Rockingham	6	to Rev. J. Logan		and Manuar
24	fr Sir L. O'Brien	7	fr Earl Bathurst		Ratanji
—	fr Crabbe	10	fr M. of Rockingham	15	fr Franklin
MARCH		12	to E. of Hillsborough	15	fr J. Kent
2	fr Capt. Blankett	12	to Vct. Stormont	15	to Bn. Macartney
2	to Capt. Blankett	16	*fr Capt. King*	23	fr Hodgson
2	fr Unknown	21	fr Gen. Burgoyne	*a*24	to D. of Portland
7	to Dagge	28	to Eden	24	fr Cursetji Manuar
8	fr M. of Rockingham	28	to Dr. Haliday	NOVEMBER	
9	to Noble	28	fr Adm. Keppel	5	fr D. of Portland
10	fr Bp. of Killaloe	—	fr Unknown	6	to Noble
10	*fr Mme. Parisot*	AUGUST		6	fr J. Harford, Noble,
13	fr Lushington	2	fr Gen. Burgoyne		and Span
13	to Mrs. Champion	2	fr Sir J. Reynolds	12	to D. of Portland
16	*to Champion*	3	to J. Udny	14	*to Champion*
21	fr Sir T. Rumbold	8	*fr Huick*	18	*to Bn. Macartney*
23	to Sir T. Rumbold	10	fr Sir J. Reynolds	19	fr Gen. Burgoyne

28 fr Curson	17 *to Bn. Macartney*	30 fr Allen
— *to Champion*	18 to M. of Rockingham	30 fr Joseph Smith
DECEMBER	21 to Vct. Kenmare	31 fr Capt. Backhouse
2 to Bourdieu	27 fr Unknown	31 fr Nodin
3 fr Curson	28 *to Champion*	— fr O'Bryen
3 to Staunton	28 to Franklin	— fr H. Howison
5 to Lord North	MARCH	APRIL
5 to Bourdieu	1 fr Wren	1 fr Jones
6 to Bourdieu	3, 4 *to Champion*	1 fr Pearson
6 fr Bridgen	5 fr D. of Portland	1 fr Unknown
6 *to Francis*	7 to Sir G. Elliot	2 fr Dillon Lee
14 to Lord North	7 to John Lee	2 fr Peckell
15 fr Franklin	7 fr Poole	3 fr O'Donel
16 to Bourdieu	8 fr Storer	3 fr Symons
17 *to Champion*	9 fr J. Geddes	3 fr Sir J. Thorold
18 to Bourdieu	9 fr Thomas	3 fr Unknown
*p*20 to Franklin	11 fr Bacon	4 fr Bp. of Killaloe
22 fr Warburton	11 fr Sir T. Rumbold	4 fr Poole
24 to O'Beirne	12 *to Champion*	4 to Elwin
26 to Kenyon	12 to Francis	5 to Eden
— fr Gen. Burgoyne	13 fr Bn. Petre	*c*5 to Eden
— fr Laurens	14 fr Vct. Kenmare	*c*5 to M. of Rockingham
MONTH NOT KNOWN	16 *to Champion*	5 fr Bn. Loughborough
— fr Crabbe	17 fr Jones	6 fr T. Burgh
— *fr Mrs. Vesey*	17 fr Vct. Kenmare	6 *to Mrs. French*
— fr Unknown	18 fr Boswell	6 *to Mrs. French*
	20 *to Champion*	6 fr Dr. Gray
1782	21 *to Bn. Macartney*	6 fr Heaton
JANUARY	22 fr Eden	6 fr Hutchinson
4 to Kenyon	22 to M. of Rockingham	6 fr Bn. Loughborough
5, 6 *to Champion*	*p*23 to Jones	6 fr Unknown
7 fr Gen. Smith	24 *to Champion*	7 *to Mrs. French*
11 fr Francis	25 fr Chrysel	7 fr Sheridan
12 to Ds. of Portland	25 to O'Bryen	8 fr Bembridge
15 *to Mr. and Mrs.*	25 fr Petrie	8 fr Blaquiere
Champion	25 to John Lee	8 fr R. Daly
17 fr D. of Portland	26 fr Dundas	8 fr Peckard
22 fr Noble	27 to H. Laurens	9 fr Bn. Loughborough
28 fr Staunton	27 to Preston	9 fr Fox
29 *to Bn. Macartney*	*p*27 fr Preston	*p*9 to Hutchinson
30 fr Noble	*p*27 to WB	10 fr Dr. Gray
FEBRUARY	28 fr Sir G. Cooper	10 fr Dr. J. G. King
4 fr Hodgson	28 fr John Craufurd	10 to Dr. J. G. King
4 fr Vct. Kenmare	29 fr Boone	11 fr Kearney
*p*4 to Gen. Vaughan	29 *to Mr. and Mrs.*	12 fr Jones
9 fr Braughall	*Champion*	13 fr G. Smith
9 fr Lindo	29 fr Dr. Monsey	13 *fr Mrs. Vesey*
9 fr Pryce	29 fr Capt. Orme	13 to R. Fitzpatrick

14	fr Sir G. Cooper	3	for Sir T. Rumbold	5	fr Jones		
14	*to M. of Rockingham*	4	fr C. Barrow	5	fr Vct. Kenmare		
p 14	to Unknown	4	fr Unknown	7	*to Bn. Macartney*		
15	fr Hoheb	5	fr Sir W. Chambers	7	to O'Beirne		
15	fr Unknown	5	fr Du Buisson	7	*fr Stephens*		
a 16	to Crabbe	5	fr Sir T. Rumbold	9	fr Dr. Berkenhout		
16	fr Crabbe	6	fr J. Geddes	11	fr C. Butler		
16	fr Glover	6	fr Pine	12	to E. of Charlemont		
16	fr Grosvenor	7	fr Jones	13	fr Bembridge		
16	*fr C. Mason*	*a* 8	to E. of Lisburne	13	fr St. Valier		
18	fr Boswell	*a* 8	to E. of Lisburne	14	*to Nepean*		
19	*to Gen. Carleton*	8	fr E. of Lisburne	16	fr Committee of		
19	fr Hutchinson	8	to E. of Lisburne		Master Coopers		
20	fr Braughall	8	*to Gen. Carleton*	17	fr Channon		
21	fr T. Burgh	8	*to Knox*	17	fr Unknown		
21	to Dagge	8	fr Pollock	18	fr Sir W. Chambers		
23	to Boswell	9	fr Bowen	19	fr P. G. Craufurd		
23	to Gen. Conway	9	fr Hutchinson	19	fr Sir G. Howard		
23	fr Gen. Conway	9	fr Jeans	21	*fr S. Wright*		
23	fr Curzon	10	fr Dunant	23	to A. Stuart		
23	to Bn. Digby	12	fr Jeans	23	fr A. Stuart		
23	fr Secker	13	fr Lean	24	fr T. Browne		
23	fr Speed	14	fr Mason	25	fr T. Browne		
23	fr Stanhope	14	fr Henry	25	fr Secker		
24	*to Gen. Haldimand*	*p* 14	fr Declonard	25	*to Bn. Macartney*		
24	*fr W. King*	15	fr Crabbe	26	fr Blenman		
24	to M. of Rockingham	16	*fr T. Bourke*	26	*to T. Townshend*		
24	fr Stanhope	16	fr Judith Edwards	29	fr J. Harford		
25	to WB	17	fr Sir J. Dalrymple	JULY			
26	fr L. Gordon	18	fr Scudamore	1	fr E. of Buchan		
26	*to Gen. Haldimand*	18	*to Shackleton*	1	fr Adam Smith		
26	fr Dr. Haliday	18	fr Channon	2	*to Fox*		
26	fr Capt. Jervis	21	fr Sir T. Bunbury	3	to Fox		
26	fr Dundas	*a* 22	*to Gen. Haldimand*	3	to Earl Fitzwilliam		
27	to M. of Rockingham	22	fr Jennings	3	fr Earl Fitzwilliam		
27	to R. Fitzpatrick	24	fr H. Goldsmith	4	fr A. Anderson		
27	*to Bn. Macartney*	24	fr Tonge	4	*to Dundas*		
30	fr Boswell	25	to D. of Portland	4	fr T. Townshend		
31 [sic]	fr Sloper	26	fr C. Butler	6	fr Adam Smith		
—	fr Percy	27	fr T. Burgh	7	fr Bn. Loughborough		
—	fr D. of Portland	27	fr Peckard	7	to Walpole		
MAY		29	fr Bembridge	7	*to Walpole*		
1	fr Dr. Carlyle	29	fr M. Goldsmith	7	*to Bn. Macartney*		
1	fr Bp. of London	31	fr Gen. Haviland	8	*fr T. Townshend*		
1	fr Joseph Palmer	—	fr Chev. O'Gorman	9	fr O'Neale		
2	fr Shackleton	JUNE		10	fr Lieut. Broughton		
3	fr Dr. Browne	2	fr Bp. of Killaloe	10	to T. Townshend		
3	fr Coggan	4	*to Gen. Carleton*	11	to Brooke		

71

11	*to Dundas*	21	*fr Williamson*	**1783**	
11	fr Mrs. Reeves	22	fr RBjr	JANUARY	
13	fr Buck	23	fr Bn. Lucan	8	fr Earl Fitzwilliam
13	to Lord J. Cavendish	25	fr Tonson	10	to Gen. Burgoyne
*p*13	fr Lord J. Cavendish	27, 29	*to Bn. Macartney*	11	fr D. of Portland
14	fr W. Baker	30	fr Thoroton	12	to Strettell
16	to Barré	OCTOBER		16	fr Godwin
17	to Bn. Loughborough	1	*to Bn. Macartney*	22	fr Popkin
18	to Lords Commis-	3	*to Bn. Macartney*	28	fr M'Carthy
	sioners of the	8	fr Jones	29	to Unknown
	Treasury	12	to Weddell	FEBRUARY	
*p*18	fr Rose	15	*to Bn. Macartney*	3	fr Gregory
19	fr Boswell	17	fr Bn. Macartney	5	fr Noble
20	fr D. of Portland	20	fr Hutchinson	8	to Francis
22	fr W. Baker	21	*to Bn. Macartney*	12	*to Bn. Macartney*
22	fr Sir L. O'Brien	25	fr Dunant	20	fr E. of Charlemont
29	to Miss Burney	29	to Unknown	24	*to Hippisley*
AUGUST		NOVEMBER		25	fr Jones
1	fr D. Rice	5	fr Bn. Macartney	MARCH	
2	*to Dundas*	7	*to Bn. Macartney*	1	to Dundas
4	*to Champion*	7	*fr Pitt*	3	to Bullock
4	fr R. Fitzpatrick	8	*to Pitt*	3	to Shackleton
5	*to Champion*	9	*to Bn. Thurlow*	4	fr Adm. Pigot
10	to Franklin	20	to Ms. of Rockingham	4	fr D. of Portland
10	fr Vane	21	fr J. M. Mason	5	fr Prost Deroyer
12	fr Gen. Burgoyne	21	fr D. of Portland	6	fr Boone
12	*to Champion*	*p*21	to J. M. Mason	8	fr Deputy Patent
15	fr Boswell	22	fr Gen. Burgoyne		Searchers
15	*fr Gen. Carleton*	22	fr P. Conway	12	fr R. Hill
16	*fr Ds. of Portland*	*p*25	to RBjr	13	fr Bembridge
17	*fr B. Watson*	—	fr Laurens	14	fr Barré
20	fr O'Beirne	DECEMBER		15	fr D. of Portland
*a*22	to J. Dodsley	4	fr Mme. Parisot	16	fr Bridges
24	fr Hansard	11	fr Priestley	19	fr A. L. Pigott
26	fr Gen. Burgoyne	17	*fr Gen. Burgoyne*	19	to D. of Portland
26	fr Crabbe	18	*to Bn. Macartney*	19	fr Rouse
27	fr Gen. Conway	23	fr Boswell	20	*to A. L. Pigott*
27	to O'Beirne	24	to Gen. Burgoyne	20	fr D. of Portland
28	to O'Beirne	26	fr Jepson	20	fr D. of Portland
29	to O'Beirne	28	to Crabbe	21	to John Lee
30	fr Bn. Macartney	29	to Francis	24, 25	fr RBsr
SEPTEMBER		31	*fr Lady C. Wentworth*	24	fr Bn. Petre
1	to Boswell	MONTH NOT KNOWN		28	fr Lord North
2	*fr T. Burgh*	—	fr Bns. Craven	—	*fr Barré*
2	fr D. of Portland	—	*fr Mme. de Wardener*	APRIL	
11	fr Dr. Warren	—	fr Unknown	2	fr D. of Portland
12	to RBjr	—	fr W. M. Pitt	4	fr Unknown
19	*to Bn. Macartney*	—	fr Ms. of Rockingham	*p*4	fr A. L. Pigott

5	*to Mrs. French*	
7	fr Elwin	
10	fr Eliza Newton	
11	fr Capt. Desborow	
11	fr Keene	
11	*fr T. King*	
13	fr Dr. Hay	
14	fr Keene	
15	fr Adam Smith	
15	fr Barwell	
17	to Bembridge	
17	fr Sir T. Kent	
17	to John Powell	
20	fr Jonathan Trumbull	
22	fr Robert Molesworth	
22	fr Barwell	
27	fr Adam	
30	fr Trafford	
—	fr W. M. Pitt	

MAY

1	fr Little and M'Gru- gar	
3	fr Boothby	
4	fr Sir T. Dundas	
5	to Windham	
p 5	fr Dean Marlay	
15	fr Stennett	
16	to A. L. Pigott	
18	fr Bembridge	
20	*to Mrs. French*	
a 21	to O'Beirne	
23	fr Bembridge	
a 24	fr John Powell	
24	fr Blair	
28	to Francis	
28	fr Roberts	
30	fr Keene	
30	fr Mrs. Montagu	

JUNE

1	fr Bembridge
2	to W. M. Pitt
4	to Champion
8	*to Elliot*
9	*to Shackleton*
10	to Windham
16	fr E. of Charlemont
20	to Adam Smith
22	fr Earl Fitzwilliam

23	to Brunton
25	fr Col. Vallancey
25	fr Laurens

JULY

8	fr W. Thomson
12	*to Bn. Macartney*
15	fr A. Thomson
19	to Selwyn
—	*to JB*
—	*fr RBjr*

AUGUST

4	*to JB*
5	to E. of Charlemont
5	to T. Walpole
6	fr Lt. Col. Camac
	fr Bn. Macartney
8	fr Boswell
12	fr RBsr
13	to Boswell
13	fr RBsr
14	fr Sir G. Elliot
15	fr Todd
15	to Col. Vallancey
16	to O'Beirne
17	*to JB*
22	*to JB*
23	fr D. Rice
23	*to Bn. Macartney*
26	*to Champion*
28	*to Gen. Haldimand*
29	*to Carteret and Bn. Foley*
29	*to Carteret and Bn. Foley*
29	*to Fraser*
29	*to Fraser*
a 30	fr J. Henderson
30	to J. Henderson

SEPTEMBER

6	*to O'Beirne*
8	fr Unknown
13	*to Champion*
15	fr O'Halloran
17	*to Champion*
23	to Bn. Macartney
23	*to Bn. Macartney*
24	fr Fox
29	fr E. of Cholmondeley

OCTOBER

1	*fr Richard Molesworth*
1	fr Jonathan Trumbull
2, Nov 6	fr Dunkin
11	fr Gen. Carleton
14	fr Bn. Macartney
18	fr Sir W. Chambers
20	to Unknown
22	*to Bn. Macartney*
23	to Francis
23	fr Eliza Newton
28	fr Crabbe
31	*fr Hudleston*
—	fr A. L. Pigott

NOVEMBER

5	fr WB
6	*to Mrs. French*
10	fr Gen. Carleton
11	*fr Bn. Macartney*
12	to Cawthorne
14	*fr Kearney*
16	*to Bn. Macartney*
17	*fr Bn. Macartney*
18	*to Bn. Macartney*
20	fr Boswell
20	*to Bn. Macartney*
23	*to D. of Portland*

DECEMBER

3	fr J. Call
6	fr Dr. Leechman
15	*to Gen. Haldimand*
16	*to Bn. Macartney*
19	to Dr. Burney
19	fr Earl Temple
23	fr W. Miller

MONTH NOT KNOWN

—	fr Crabbe
—	fr Sheridan
—	fr Clerks at Pay Office
—	fr J. Henderson
—	fr Windham
—	fr R. Lee
—	fr Unknown

1784

JANUARY

1	to Noble

3	fr Boswell	17	to Eden	18	fr Earl Fitzwilliam
8	*to Boyd*	**JUNE**		22	fr Shackleton
22	to Richardson	3	fr Cawthorne	23	fr R. C. Lee
31	fr Boswell	3	fr Herbert	*a*28	fr Richardson
31	fr Dunkin	13	fr Laurens	30	*fr Capt. King*
31	fr Bn. Macartney	15	fr Sir J. Dalrymple	**OCTOBER**	
—	fr G. A. North	16	fr Dr. Leechman	1	fr Bembridge

FEBRUARY

13	fr Hoheb	20	fr W. Baker	2	to RBjr
27	fr Sir W. Jones	20	to C. O'Hara, Jr.	2	to Bembridge

MARCH

		22	to W. Baker	2	to Champion
1	*fr Rose*	24	fr Orde	*p*2	*to RBsr*
8	fr Sir S. Hannay	—	fr Bn. Loughborough	4	fr Powney
8	to Sir S. Hannay	**JULY**		7	*fr Capt. King*
8	*fr Bn. Macartney*	3	to Bn. Sydney	13	to Sir J. Blaquiere
10	*fr Topping*	6	fr Sir J. Dalrymple	14	to Windham
10	*fr Topping*	8	fr Sir J. Dalrymple	15	to Windham
10	*to Topping*	11	to C. O'Hara, Jr.	15	to Sir G. Elliot
13	fr RBjr	15	fr J. Bourke	18	*fr Capt. King*
16	to Dr. Smith	15	fr Francis	22	fr Adey
21	fr Mitchell	15	fr Bn. Loughborough	27	*fr W. King*
22	*to Bn. Macartney*	17	fr Bn. Sydney	28	fr Todd
22	*to Bn. Macartney*	20	fr Andrew Dalzel	**NOVEMBER**	
26	to Sir G. Elliot	20	fr Francis	3	to Sir G. Elliot
27	to Sir W. Lee	24	fr Colquhoun	3	*to W. King*
—	*fr RBjr*	27	fr Francis	6	fr Sir J. Blaquiere
—	*to Bn. Macartney*	28	fr Bn. Macartney	*p*6	to Sir J. Blaquiere

APRIL

		29, 30	fr Sir G. Elliot	8	fr Unknown
7	fr Dundas	30	fr D. of Portland	9	*fr Capt. Young*
8	fr Sir J. Dalrymple	**AUGUST**		13	fr J. Hamilton
10	fr Boswell	1	fr Sir G. Elliot	15	*to Hippisley*
12	fr Boswell	2	fr Desmoulins	15	fr Dr. Leechman
13	fr Sir J. Dalrymple	3	to Sir G. Elliot	15	fr Lushington
13	fr Sir W. Jones	*p*5	to Sir G. Elliot	15	fr Millar
13	fr Sir W. Forbes	9	fr Joyce	19	to W. King
15	to Boswell	10	fr Gen. Bruce	20	*fr Capt. Young*
15	fr Robertson	14	fr Richardson	22	fr Sir G. Elliot
25	fr Earl Fitzwilliam	16	fr Millar	22	to C. O'Hara, Jr.
29	fr Francis	22	fr Bns. Macartney	*p*22	to M. Ridge

MAY

		23	fr Bns. Macartney	28	to O'Beirne
5	fr R. C. Lee	24	fr Sir J. Reynolds	*p*28	*to O'Beirne*
6	to Sir W. Lee	25	fr Bn. Foley	**DECEMBER**	
7	*to Champion*	25	*to Bn. Macartney*	4	fr Bn. Loughborough
10	to E. of Carlisle	25	fr Bns. Macartney	4	to Bn. Thurlow
11	fr Grant	31	*fr Bn. Macartney*	6	fr Bn. Thurlow
11	fr Sir W. Lee	31	*fr Bn. Macartney*	8	*fr T. King*
13	fr Eden	—	to Sir G. Elliot	13	to Mary Shackleton
13	fr Earl Fitzwilliam	**SEPTEMBER**		13	fr Bn. Thurlow
		5	*to Mrs. Champion*	14	fr Bn. Thurlow

14	to Bn. Thurlow
18	fr Sir J. Reynolds
19	fr Earl Fitzwilliam
20	fr Bn. Thurlow
23	fr Capt. Waldegrave
30	fr A. Geddés
30	*to Bn. Macartney*

MONTH NOT KNOWN

—	*to Champion*
—	fr Davers
—	fr D. Long
—	fr Windham

1785

JANUARY

7	*to RBjr*
13	to Bn. Macartney
19	fr Millar
21	to Staunton
21	*to Staunton*
26	fr D. of Portland

FEBRUARY

15	fr Boswell
16	fr Dr. Leechman
17	to Bns. Macartney
17	*to Staunton*
a21	*to Hippisley*
27	to Staunton

MARCH

9	fr Crabbe
12	fr RBjr
18	fr C. Peat
21	*to Bn. Macartney*
22	fr Sir J. Dalrymple
23	fr Sir J. Dalrymple
24	fr H. Keeling
30	fr Sir J. Dalrymple

APRIL

2	fr E. Keeling
3	fr Sir J. Dalrymple
4	fr John Lee
5	fr Dr. Clarke
7	to Staunton
p7	fr J. Bourke
8	fr Sir J. Blaquiere
10	to Unknown
10	to Staunton
17	fr Millar

MAY

1	fr Dr. Leechman
c7	to Windham
14	fr Dr. Leechman

JUNE

4	*to Bn. Macartney*
11	fr Staunton
15	to Staunton

JULY

4	fr Ms. of Rockingham
4	to Staunton
6	to Staunton
11	to Staunton
15	*to Bn. Macartney*
18	fr D. of Portland
22	*fr Comtesse de Genlis*
p27	to Staunton
—	to W. King

AUGUST

1	to Fullarton
6	fr Windham
7	to E. of Charlemont
7	to Hutchinson
12	fr Bn. Sydney
26	fr Robertson
p28	*fr Ms. of Rockingham*
29	fr Fullarton

SEPTEMBER

4	*to JB*
6	to Ds. of Argyll
25	*fr Earl Fitzwilliam*
25	fr Windham
c30	to Francis
—	to WB

OCTOBER

2	fr Earl Fitzwilliam
12	fr Comtesse de Genlis
12	to O'Beirne
18	fr Shackleton
18	fr Yonge
20	fr Windham
22	fr Wodsworth
26	to Shackleton
28	to Sir G. Elliot

NOVEMBER

9	*to JB*
10	fr RBsr
13	fr Millar

14	to Francis
21	to Windham
22	*to Bruere*
23	to Francis

DECEMBER

5	fr Shackleton
10	to Francis
14	to Francis
20	fr Boswell
21	fr Shackleton
23	to Francis
24	*to RBjr*
25	fr RBjr
25	*fr Emin*
27	to T. Burgh
30	*to RBjr*

MONTH NOT KNOWN

—	to Dr. Beaufort

1786

JANUARY

1	*to RBjr*
4	to Boswell
8	to Sir G. Elliot
9	fr Porcher
9	to Sir G. Staunton
14	*fr Hawkswell*
a15	*to RBsr*
15	fr Depont
17	*to Gen. Sloper*
19	to Mary Palmer

FEBRUARY

7	fr Boswell
8	to Boswell
8	to D. of Manchester
9	to Boswell
10	fr Boswell
10	fr Boswell
10	*fr Kiernan*
13	fr Middleton
c20	to Sir G. Elliot
c24	to Sir G. Staunton

MARCH

3	fr Gregory
10	fr J. Miller
13	fr Porcher
20	*fr Boswell*
20	fr Gen. Cowper

a22   to Mary Shackleton
24   fr Dr. Dodge
26   fr Sir J. Dalrymple
27   fr T. Burgh
APRIL
19   *fr Buller*
22   fr H. Geddes
28   fr Crabbe
MAY
5   to Bolts
c5   *to Zouch*
14   fr J. Burke
15   fr Dr. Dodge
18   fr Crespigny
18   fr Mrs. Davison
19   fr Jenison
29   fr E. of Buchan
JUNE
a1   to Francis
2   *to Shackleton*
4   fr J. Champion
p19   to Miss Burney
27   fr Adair
28   fr Barrety
JULY
6   fr Mrs. Cropley
7   to E. of Buchan
8   fr Sheils
24   *to Sir G. Staunton*
29   to H. Elliot
AUGUST
6   to Francis
7   *to Mrs. Francis*
8   fr D. of Portland
a11   to E. Waller
a12   *to JB*
14   *to RBsr*
16   to Adey
17   to E. Waller
c17   to E. Waller
p17   to E. Waller
c20   to Mrs. Francis
22   fr RBsr
—   fr Ds. of Portland
SEPTEMBER
6   fr Sir G. Elliot
12   to D. of Portland
26   to Sir G. Elliot

26   *to Sir G. Elliot*
29   to O'Beirne
OCTOBER
1   to J. Barrow
12   to Mrs. French
12   to Shackleton
15   *to Francis*
22   to E. of Charlemont
p25   *to Mrs. French*
a—   *fr Homer*
NOVEMBER
3   to Francis
c8   to Francis
11   to Hutchinson
17   fr Podesta
29   to Col. Vallancey
—   to Homer
DECEMBER
7   to Adam Smith
14   to Sir G. Elliot
a15   fr John King
15   to Francis
15   *to the Misses Francis*
20   to Adam Smith
22   *to Porcher*
23   *fr Porcher*
25   fr E. of Buchan
MONTH NOT KNOWN
—   fr Beckford

1787

JANUARY
1   to Sir G. Elliot
c2   to Francis
3   *to Shackleton*
12   fr Brandes
13   fr Unknown
a14   *to Porcher*
14   *fr Porcher*
17   fr Bn. Earlsfort
FEBRUARY
3   to Francis
21   *fr Mrs. Morritt*
27   to Francis
27   fr Pitt
MARCH
14   to Michie
16   fr Michie

21   fr T. Morton
25   to Dundas
26   fr Dundas
29   to Dundas
30   fr Michie
31   fr T. Morton
APRIL
1   to Dundas
4   to Dundas
5   to Dundas
7   to Dundas
13   to Dundas
14   to Dundas
20   to Dundas
20   to Mrs. Francis
MAY
4   to P. of Wales
9   fr S. Johnson
10   to Sir G. Elliot
13   fr Unknown
25   fr Thicknesse
28   to Shackleton
JUNE
1   to E. of Charlemont
1   to Dundas
5   to Shackleton
9   to Dr. Parr
12   *fr Mrs. Morritt*
12   fr Adm. Rodney
15   fr Lambert
17   to Earl Fitzwilliam
19   to RBjr
JULY
1   to T. Burgh
10   to E. of Charlemont
12   fr D. of Portland
23   to RBsr
SEPTEMBER
9   to W. Sharp
10   *to Sir C. Barrow*
10   fr Earl Fitzwilliam
23   fr D. of Portland
OCTOBER
3   *to W. W. Grenville
   and Bn. Mulgrave*
5   fr RBjr
5   to RBjr
5   *to Champion*

9 fr *Mme. Parisot*
c10 fr RBjr
11 to RBjr
11 to Dundas
17 to Sir G. Elliot
20 fr Troward
29 to Dundas

NOVEMBER

1 to Dundas
7 to Gen. Burgoyne
18 fr *Mme. Parisot*
19 *to RBsr*
20 fr E. of Buchan
21 to RBsr
30 *fr John and W. King*
— *fr Vcts. Torrington*
— *fr Vcts. Torrington*
— *fr Unknown*

DECEMBER

5 to Unknown
7 to Dundas
8 fr Dundas
9 to Dundas
10 to Francis
a12 to Sir G. Elliot
13 to Lady Elliot
18 to Francis
20 fr Wilks
24 fr Dundas
28 fr M. of Titchfield
29 to Sir W. Hamilton

MONTH NOT KNOWN

— fr John Stuart

1788

JANUARY

2 fr R. Hudson
c3 to Francis
6, 9 *fr John and W. King*
8 to Sir P. Burrell
p8 fr Sir P. Burrell
9 *fr D. and Ds. of Portland*
13 fr Bn. Loughborough
24 fr Dr. W. Hamilton
30 to Fawkener
30 fr Citizens of Malton

FEBRUARY

3 fr Sheridan
11 fr Windham
12 to Malone
p17 fr Goring
a29 *fr Francis*
— to Sir P. Burrell

MARCH

28 to Adey

APRIL

2 fr Unknown
2 fr T. Sparkes
6 fr Boswell
7 to Paterson
8 to Boswell
10 fr Steele
13 to Francis
15 to Lords of the Treasury
16 fr Boswell
18 to Sheridan
22 fr Boswell
— to Sir P. Burrell

MAY

1 to Cornwall
4 to Gen. Burgoyne
5 *fr Bp. of Auxerre*
9 to Shackleton
17 fr Lymburner
20 fr Merchants Trading to Quebec
26 to Counsel for the Managers
28 fr D. Young
— to Hippisley

JUNE

a3 to Sir P. Burrell
a19 to A. Young
20 to T. Steele
23 to Sir G. Elliot
a25 fr D. Long
25 to RBjr and RBsr
25 *to Earl Cornwallis*
p25 fr RBjr
26 fr Carr
26 *to Earl Cornwallis*
29 to Adey

JULY

1 to RBjr
2 fr Dr. Brocklesby
9 *fr Sec'y Hay*
9 *fr Sec'y Hay*
9 fr D. of Portland
10 fr Sir W. Pepperrell
15 *to Earl Cornwallis*
p15 *fr Sec'y Hay*
17 to Dr. Brocklesby
24 fr Laurence
24 fr D. of Portland
26 fr Dempsy
26 fr Laurence
27 fr Philips
30 fr Ms. of Rockingham

AUGUST

1 to Dr. Burney
5 to Francis
7 fr Paine
8 fr Dr. Burney
8 fr Ms. of Rockingham
10 to Unknown
11 *to G. Robinson*
11 *fr G. Robinson*
16 fr Laurence
18 to Laurence
22 fr Thomisdeen
26 fr Stockdale
29 fr MacIntyre
p29 to Christie

SEPTEMBER

3 to Sir G. Elliot
6 *to G. Robinson*
11 to Unknown
14 to Francis
14 *to G. Robinson*
15 *fr Col. Murray*
17 to RBjr
19 to RBjr
21 to RBjr
23 *to Col. Murray*
23 *fr Col. Murray*
25 *to W. W. Grenville and Bn. Mulgrave*
28 fr Sir G. Elliot

OCTOBER

10 *fr Col. Murray*

12 *to W. W. Grenville
and Bn. Mulgrave*
20 *fr T. Osborne*
23 *to Col. Murray*
25 fr Laurence

NOVEMBER

7 fr Ds. of Portland
9, 12 *fr Mme. Parisot*
11 *to Champion*
13 *fr Col. Murray*
14 *to Col. Murray*
15 fr Pitt
24 *to Earl Cornwallis*
24 to RBsr and RBjr
*p*24 to Fox

DECEMBER

1 to C. O'Hara, Jr.
5 *fr Col. Murray*
5 fr D. of Portland
8 fr O'Beirne
11 to Sheridan
12 *to Col. Murray*
14 fr Colles
16 *to Earl Cornwallis*
16 *fr Hawkswell*
17 *to Earl Cornwallis*
25 to Windham
26 *to Earl Cornwallis*
26 *to Col. Murray*
27 *fr Col. Murray*
28 fr Ms. of Rockingham
29 fr Adam

MONTH NOT KNOWN

— *to the Misses Francis*
— *to Hickey*
— *fr Hickey*
— *fr Hickey*
— *to Hickey*
— *fr Hickey*
— *to Hickey*
— *fr Mme. Parisot*

1789

JANUARY

1 *fr Sec'y Hay*
6 to Capt. Payne
*c*24 to Windham
29 *fr Col. Murray*

29 to D. of Portland

FEBRUARY

8 fr P. of Wales
11 to Francis
24 to T. Burgh
*p*25 to Sheridan

MARCH

3 *to Crabbe*
12 to Malone
15 *to Holland*
17 *fr Mme. Parisot*
19 to E. of Charlemont
19 to Grattan
24 fr E. of Charlemont
26 to Mrs. Sheridan
29 to T. Burgh
29 to Emin
30 *fr O'Beirne*
30 fr Sheridan
30 to Sheridan
— fr Grey

APRIL

4 to E. of Charlemont
6 fr Nawab of the
Carnatic
7 fr Windham
8 *to Earl Cornwallis*
8 *to Col. Murray*
11 fr Sir Wm. Scott
22 to Unknown
22 fr Bn. Thurlow
25 to Sir J. Reynolds
30 to W. W. Grenville

MAY

1 to F. Montagu
5 fr Bright
8, 9 to Bright
11 fr Bright
11 to Fox
26, 27 to E. of Charle-
mont
26 to Mrs. Fitzherbert
29 fr E. of Charlemont

JUNE

8 to W. W. Grenville
22 *fr Decrétot*
29 *fr Decrétot*

30 *to Unknown*

JULY

4 fr E. of Charlemont
10 to E. of Charlemont
12 fr Earl Fitzwilliam
25 fr Sir J. Reynolds
28 to W. King

AUGUST

4 to Maurice
4 to W. W. Grenville
6 fr Earl Fitzwilliam
9 to E. of Charlemont
25 fr Shee

SEPTEMBER

1 to Thompson
2 to Capt. Cuppage
9 to Fox
14 *fr Mme. Parisot*
15 fr Windham
23 fr Mary Shackleton
24 to Capt. Payne
27 to Windham
28 fr Capt. Payne

OCTOBER

1 to Capt. Payne
8 fr Col. Vallancey
*p*8 to Col. Vallancey
*c*10 to RBjr
18 fr Sir G. Staunton

NOVEMBER

3 fr Laurence
4 fr Depont
7 fr J. Browne
11 to RBjr
12 to Earl Fitzwilliam
15 to Francis
— to Depont
— fr Depont

DECEMBER

11 to Francis
15 *fr Hawkswell*
17 to Francis
26 fr B. Edwards
29 fr Depont
29 fr Sir G. Elliot

MONTH NOT KNOWN

— fr Unknown

1790

JANUARY

2	fr Francis
3	to Sir G. Elliot
6	fr Bn. Loughborough
p6	to Sir G. Elliot
12	to Dolphin
15	fr J. Browne
17	fr Paine
23	to Jerningham
—	to Bp. of Carlisle
—	to Northcote
—	to Cosway
—	to Unknown

FEBRUARY

4	fr Bright
8	fr Bp. of Killaloe
13	fr Bright
18	to Bright
19	fr Francis
19	fr Capt. Mercer
19	fr Meyer
20	to Francis
20	*to Francis*
22	fr W. Wright
26	to Capt. Mercer
p27	fr Plumb
p27	to Royal Irish Academy

MARCH

5	*fr T. King*
10	to Francis
14	to Noble
27	fr Laurence
p29	to Duport

MAY

6	fr Paine
12	fr Cloots
19	*fr Sir G. Staunton*
22	*to Shackleton*
23	to Earl Spencer
25	to E. of Charlemont
27	*fr Lady C. Wentworth*
28	to Shackleton
31	fr Bp. of Killaloe

JUNE

6	*fr Sir G. Elliot*
10	*fr Mme. Parisot*

a11	*fr Earl Fitzwilliam*
11	*fr Earl Fitzwilliam*
11	*to Sir G. Elliot*
22	to W. Baker
25	to W. Baker
c25	to RBjr
26	fr E. of Charlemont
27	*fr Earl Fitzwilliam*
p27	*fr Earl Fitzwilliam*

JULY

2	to E. of Charlemont
14	*to Earl Fitzwilliam*
15	*fr Earl Fitzwilliam*
29	*to Earl Fitzwilliam*
30	to Lady Eleanor Butler and Sarah Ponsonby

AUGUST

8	*fr Earl Fitzwilliam*
13	fr Dr. Hussey
16	*to Earl Fitzwilliam*
21	*fr Earl Fitzwilliam*
27	*to Earl Fitzwilliam*
28	*fr Dr. Hussey*
31	*to Earl Fitzwilliam*
—	to Cloots
—	*to Earl Verney*

SEPTEMBER

8	*to Earl Fitzwilliam*
9	fr Gen. Burgoyne
15	*fr Earl Fitzwilliam*
27	*to Earl Fitzwilliam*
28	to Capt. Cuppage
28	to Unknown
30	*fr Decrétot*

OCTOBER

10	*to Earl Fitzwilliam*
14	*fr Earl Fitzwilliam*
14	fr Laurence
15	fr Taubman
18	*to Earl Fitzwilliam*
20	*fr Earl Fitzwilliam*
20	fr Laurence
23	fr Mme. de Calonne
24	*to Earl Verney*
25	*fr John Allen*
25	to Calonne
c25	to Swift

27	fr Dupont
27	to Francis
27	to Windham
28	to Dupont
28	to Sir G. Elliot

NOVEMBER

a1	*to Earl Fitzwilliam*
1	fr Dr. Brocklesby
2	fr W. W. Grenville
3	fr Gen. Burgoyne
3, 4	fr Francis
4	fr Comtesse de Boufflers
4	*fr Kearney*
4	fr Walpole
5	fr Sir W. Lee
6	fr Sir G. Elliot
6	fr Bn. Loughborough
6	fr Unknown
7	fr Bp. of Carlisle
8	fr Capt. Mercer
8	*to Shackleton*
9	to Bp. of Carlisle
10	fr Dr. S. Cooper
10	*fr J. French*
11	*to Earl Cornwallis*
11	fr Cumberland
13	to Cumberland
14	to Dr. Falconer
14	fr Lord J. Cavendish
a17	fr Dr. Falconer
17	fr Dr. Falconer
17	fr Menonville
18	to Jerningham
19	fr Sir G. Elliot
19	to Francis
a22	fr Unknown
23	*to Earl Fitzwilliam*
23	to Sir Wm. Scott
25	to Addington
27	fr M. of Buckingham
29	to Sir G. Elliot
c29	to Malone
30	fr Dr. Browne
30	fr Dupont
—	fr Sir P. Burrell
—	to Hatsell
—	to Chev. de La

Bintinaye
— to Chev. de La
 Bintinaye
— to Lady Anne
 Lindsay

DECEMBER
1 fr Landon
2 to Addington
2 fr John Trumbull
4 to Francis
4 fr Trevor
4 fr Travis
6 fr Depont
10 fr Jephson
11 fr Comtesse de
 Boufflers
12 fr Comtesse
 d'Osmond
13 fr Dupont
13 fr J. Eyre
13 fr Dr. Falconer
13 fr Hutchinson
13 *fr Hawkswell*
18 fr Abbé Damartin
18 to Hutchinson
*a*21, 22 fr Oxford
 Graduates
21 *fr Shackleton*
22 to Windham
22 fr Lawson
28 fr Unknown
29 fr Perregaux
30 fr Comtesse de
 Montrond

MONTH NOT KNOWN
— to Addington
— fr Unknown

1791
JANUARY
2 to Unknown
2 fr Adam
4 to Adam
4 fr J. Geddes
5 fr Capt. Woodford
8 to Comtesse
 d'Osmond
9 to Unknown

12 fr R. Smith
13 *to Unknown*
*a*18 fr Jerningham
18 to Jerningham
18 fr Unknown
19 fr Marquise de
 Lanascal
19 to Menonville
20 fr Morizot
21 fr Demoiselle de Vic
24 to Vicomte de Cicé
24 fr Col. Ironside
25 to Comtesse de
 Montrond
25 fr Sir J. Reynolds
26 to Unknown
28 fr Lord R. Fitzgerald
31 fr Bp. of St. Davids
— to Trevor

FEBRUARY
*a*1 fr WB
5 fr T. Goold
*c*8 to Sir J. Banks
8 to D. of Clarence
9 fr Bishop
9 fr Calonne
9 fr Unknown
11 to Capt. Woodford
11 fr Capt. Woodford
14 fr Ogilvie
14 fr Pitt
16 fr Fernyhough
17 to Unknown
18 fr Pitt
21 fr Dupont
21 fr Kearney
21 fr Millett
22 fr Gen. de Blangy
24 fr Rector of Stowford
25 fr Bn. Grenville
26 fr Coats
28 fr Comtesse de
 Hautoÿ
28 fr Percy

MARCH
1 fr Mlle. de Livry
3 fr C. Stewart
4 fr S. Devereux

5 fr Boswell
7 to Boswell
9 fr Abbé Foullon
9 fr Marquise de Tilly
11 fr Morizot
11, Apr 27 fr Menonville
12 fr Percy
13 fr Bp. of Amiens
15 *to Sir G. Elliot*
16 fr Steell
17 fr Millett
19 fr White
20 to Duchesse de Biron
20 *fr Hippisley*
21 *to WB*
23 fr Duchesse de Biron
23 fr Bn. Grenville
24 fr Duchesse de Biron
24 fr Unknown
25 fr Duchesse de Biron
26 fr Dr. Dodge
— to Chev. de La
 Bintinaye
— *to Hickey*

APRIL
1 fr Comtesse de Faÿ
2 fr Mounier
3 to E. of Carhampton
*c*3 *fr Hippisley*
4 fr E. of Carhampton
7 fr Duchesse de
 Choiseul
7 fr Sir S. Lushington
8 fr Rouse
11 *fr O'Beirne*
12 fr Rouse
16 fr Wisemore
20 fr Bn. Grenville
21 fr Comte de Bressÿ
22 to Dundas
23 fr Bp. of Amiens
*p*23 fr Marquis de Duras
*a*25 fr Unknown
29 fr Capt. Woodford
— fr Duchesse de Biron

MAY
1 to J. King
1 *to Unknown*

5	*to Nepean*		Tollendal	29	*to Earl Fitzwilliam*
6	fr Burges	21	fr Comte de Murat-	30	*fr T. King*
6	*to O'Beirne*		Montferrand	30	fr Leonetti
8	fr Meyer	23	fr Rougemont	31	to Bp. of Salisbury
*p*8	to Meyer	26	to Burges	31	to Bn. Southampton
9	fr Francklyn	26	fr Marquis de Bouillé	—	fr Laurence
10	fr Comte de La	26	fr Burges	**AUGUST**	
	Galissonnière	27	to Bp. of Carlisle	1	fr Laurence
10	fr Lenoir	28	fr Burges	2	to Laurence
12	fr Unknown	29	fr Burges	3	fr Rougemont
15	*fr Bp. of Auxerre*	29	fr Terray	3	fr Bp. of Salisbury
15	fr Dr. Hay	29	to Burges	4	to Earl Fitzwilliam
15	fr Vicomtesse de	30	fr W. Smith	4	fr John King
	Pellagrüe	—	fr Unknown	5	to RBjr
16	fr Mme. Gaulard	**JULY**		5	fr Earl Camden
16	fr Unknown	1	to Dundas	5	to Swift
19	fr Bowles	1	fr Faydel	6	*to Louis XVI*
23	fr Comtesse de	4	fr Nicolaïdes	6	fr Sir Wm. Scott
	Boufflers	4	fr Unknown	7	fr Archbp. of Aix
24	fr Chev. de La	5	to Bn. Auckland	7	*fr Committee of French*
	Bintinaye	5	Lord R. Fitzgerald		*Nobility*
24	fr Lawson	6	to Bp. of Carlisle	7	fr Comte de Lally-
27	fr Bp. of Amiens	7	fr Dupont		Tollendal
27	fr Réverseau	11	fr RBsr	7	fr Bp. of Salisbury
28	to Calonne	12	fr Pinson de Méner-	*p*7	*to Committee of French*
29	fr Dupont		ville		*Nobility*
29	fr Earl Fitzwilliam	13	to Marquis de Bouillé	8	fr RBjr
30	fr C. Morris	13	*to JB*	8	to E. of Charlemont
31	to Francis	13	to Swift	8	fr Laurence
—	*fr Earl Fitzwilliam*	14	fr Dupont	8	fr Comte de Mont-
JUNE		15	to Archbp. of Aix		losier
1	to Abbé Foullon	15	fr RBjr	8	*fr Poissonnier-*
1	to Chev. de Rivarol	16	fr Abbé de Bonneval		*Desperrières*
3	fr Unknown	16	fr Boswell	9	to RBjr
5	to Earl Fitzwilliam	17	to Swift	9	fr Gen. Conway
6	fr Vct. de La-	19	fr RBsr	9	*to Dundas*
	moignon	20	to Boswell	9	fr Bp. of London
6	fr Unknown	*c*20	fr Calonne	9	fr E. of Mansfield
7	to J. Fowke	*c*20	to Calonne	10	to RBjr
8	fr Beauchamp	*c*20	fr Calonne	11	fr Dupont
8	fr Dupont	21	fr RBsr	12	fr Bn. Auckland
*a*16	fr B. Waller	21	fr Dupont	12	fr Comtesse de
16	fr Comtesse de Faÿ	22	to W. Smith		Boufflers
16	*fr Holliday*	23	to Bp. of Salisbury	12	fr Dundas
16	to B. Waller	24	to RBsr	12	fr Bn. Hawkesbury
17	fr Pinson de Méner-	25	*fr O'Beirne*	13	fr E. of Charlemont
	ville	27	fr Bp. of Raphoe	13	*fr Comte de Vaudreuil*
20	fr Comte de Lally-	27	to Swift	*p*15	fr Archbp. of Aix

16	to RBjr	12	fr Sir F. Basset	*a*7	fr RBjr		
16	fr RBjr	12	fr Col. St. Leger	*a*8	fr King of Poland		
16	*to Calonne*	13	fr Deluc	8	fr RBjr		
17	fr Archbp. of Aix	14	to D. of Dorset	8	*fr Pitt*		
17	to RBjr	14	*to Calonne*	8	fr Count Vorontsov		
17	fr RBsr	14	fr Drake	9	to Chev. de La		
17	to D. of Dorset	14	fr Sir A. Hume		Bintinaye		
*c*17	to Marie Antoinette	15	*fr Byrne*	11	*to Calonne*		
18	to RBjr	15	*to Calonne*	12	*fr Marquis de La*		
18	to RBjr	17	fr Bn. Grenville		*Queuille*		
18	*fr Shackleton*	17	to Comte de	13	to Chev. de La		
19	*fr Poissonnier-*		Provence		Bintinaye		
	Desperrières	18	to Dundas	13	*fr Pitt*		
20	fr D. of Dorset	18	fr Earl Fitzwilliam	14	*to Chev. de La*		
21	to D. of Dorset	18	to Chev. de La		*Bintinaye*		
22	fr Mme. de Rivarol		Bintinaye	18	to RBjr		
23	fr Hutchinson	20	fr RBjr	*p*21	*to Dundas*		
24	*fr Bp. of Arras*	20	fr Dr. Dodge	24	*fr C. Nugent*		
25	to RBjr	20	to Dundas	27	fr Unknown		
25	fr Marquise de	20	*fr Dundas*	28	to RBjr		
	Closelle	20	fr Marquis de La	NOVEMBER			
25	fr Chev. de Freire		Queuille	*c*1	to RBjr		
25	fr RBjr	21	fr Lord J. Cavendish	1	to Catherine II		
26	fr Comte de	21	to Bn. Grenville	2	to J. King		
	Provence	22	fr Dundas	2	to Chev. de La		
27	fr Weddell	23	to Dundas		Bintinaye		
28	fr Sir R. Chambers	23	fr Bn. Grenville	4	fr W. Smith		
28	*to Chev. de La*	24	fr Laurence	8	fr Wolfe		
	Bintinaye	26	to RBjr	9	*fr Calonne*		
29	to Bembridge	26	fr Dundas	11	fr John King		
30	*to Dundas*	27	fr Count Vorontsov	12	fr John King		
SEPTEMBER		28	*to Calonne*	*c*12	to John King		
1	to RBjr	28	to Earl Fitzwilliam	14	fr Unknown		
2	fr RBjr	28	to Chev. de La	18	fr John King		
4	fr A. Peat		Bintinaye	20	fr Villers		
5	fr Sir F. Basset	30	to Dundas	21	to Earl Fitzwilliam		
6	*to Calonne*	30	fr Pitt	21	fr Archbp. of Nisibis		
6	*fr Calonne*	OCTOBER		26	fr Earl Fitzwilliam		
6	to Hutchinson	2	to Chev. de La	DECEMBER			
6	to D. of Dorset		Bintinaye	2	fr Abbesse de		
7	fr Calonne	2	fr Count Vorontsov		Moucler		
10	*to Dundas*	4	*to Calonne*	4	to John King		
10	fr RBjr	4	*fr Comte de Vaudreuil*	5	to RBsr		
10	to Chev. de La	5	*fr Calonne*	5	fr Glasse		
	Bintinaye	5	fr Fawkener	6	*to Calonne*		
11	to D. of Dorset	6	to Bukaty	8	*fr Calonne*		
11	to Chev. de La	6	fr Dundas	9	to Bp. of Norwich		
	Bintinaye	6	*fr Dundas*	10	fr Sir H. Langrishe		

13	to RBjr	9	fr Calonne	29	*fr J. Lewis*	
14	to Archbp. of Nisibis	9	*fr Hobart*	MARCH		
15	to RBjr	11	fr Bp. of Antwerp	*c*1	*fr RBjr*	
15	fr RBjr	11	*to Hobart*	1	*fr W. King*	
16	fr W. Baker	11	fr Archbp. of Nisibis	2	to Bn. Hawkesbury	
16	to RBjr	12	to RBjr	2	fr Bn. Hawkesbury	
16	to Lord Hailes	12	*to Dundas*	3	*fr John King*	
16	*fr W. King*	12	fr I. Geoghegan	3	fr Windham	
*p*16	*to Dundas*	12	fr Lord Hailes	5	fr Abbé de La	
*p*16	*to Dundas*	13	to RBjr		Bintinaye	
17	*fr Hawkswell*	13	*fr Hobart*	*c*8	to RBjr	
19	*to RBsr*	14	*to Hobart*	8	to Abbé and Chev.	
21	fr Earl Camden	16	fr Macdonald		de La Bintinaye	
23	*fr C. Nugent*	18	fr Troward	10	fr Dempster	
24	fr A. Murphy	20	*fr Dundas*	*c*11	to Abbé de La	
*a*25	*to Dundas*	*p*20	*to Dundas*		Bintinaye	
*a*25	*to Dundas*	21	fr Francis	*c*11	to RBjr	
*a*25	*to Dundas*	23	to Francis	13	to Bp. of Salisbury	
25	*fr Dundas*	*a*25	fr RBjr	14	*to Dundas*	
25	*to Dundas*	26	to RBjr	17	fr Malone	
25	*to Dundas*	27	to Abbé and Chev.	18	to Malone	
26	fr Bischoff		de La Bintinaye	20	to RBjr	
26	*to Calonne*	*c*29	fr RBjr	20	*fr W. King*	
27	*to Dundas*	29	to RBjr	21	*fr Dundas*	
28	*fr Hawkswell*	31	to Weddell	22	to Dundas	
29	to E. of Charlemont	FEBRUARY		23	to RBjr	
30	fr Maj. Swiney	1	to Mrs H. W.	25	fr Dundas	
—	to Calonne		Bunbury	25	to W. King	
—	*to Dundas*	1	*fr Chev. de La*	30	fr Bukaty	
			Bintinaye	*p*30	fr Bukaty	
MONTH NOT KNOWN		2	fr Lawson	—	*to Hickey*	
Mon	fr Dundas	3	fr Earl Camden	APRIL		
—	*to Catholic Committee*	7	fr Bn. Grenville	3	to Sir G. Elliot	
	in Ireland	9	*to John King*	5	*to Shackleton*	
—	*to Hickey*	9	fr Bn. Grenville	9	to Dundas	
—	to Rougane	11	fr John King	10	to Chev. de La	
—	to Unknown	15	fr Brand		Bintinaye	
—	fr Unknown	19	to RBjr	17	fr Laurence	
—	fr Unknown	*p*19	to RBjr	18	fr RBjr	
		20	fr D. Smith	18	*to Dundas*	
1792		22	to Dempster	18	to Chev. de La	
JANUARY		23	fr RBjr		Bintinaye	
1	to RBjr	23	*to Metcalfe*	19	*to Chev. de La*	
1	fr RBjr	*a*28	fr King of Poland		*Bintinaye*	
2	to John King	28	to King of Poland	19	fr Chev. de La	
*p*3	to RBjr	28	to Metcalfe		Bintinaye	
7	*to Hobart*	29	to RBjr	19	*fr Shackleton*	
8	to RBjr	29	to Dr. Dodge	19	to Joseph Hill	

MAY

6 *to Dundas*
7 fr Mary Brady
8 to Deluc
12 fr Cazalès
13 *to Capt. Cuppage*
14 *to Dundas*
16 *to WB*
16 to Capt. Cuppage
16 *fr Dundas*
17 *fr Keogh*
24 fr O'Leary
27 to Bn. Loughborough
28 *fr Byrne*
29 to Lord Hailes
30 to W. Markham, Jr.

JUNE

1 fr Mrs. Crotty
2 *to Bn. Hawkesbury*
5 *to Dundas*
*p*7 to Capt. Grey
8 *to D. of Portland*
13 fr Earl Camden
13 fr Bn. Loughborough
13 to Bn. Loughborough
*a*17 *to Dundas*
17 *to Catholic Committee
   in Ireland*
17 *to Dundas*
18 to Abbé and Chev.
   de La Bintinaye
20 to Hill
22 *fr Dundas*
23 to Metcalfe
24 to Hill
27 to Hill

JULY

10 to Malone
10 to Metcalfe
20 *to Dundas*
23 *to Dundas*
26 *fr Keogh*
29 to RBjr
29 to RBjr
29 *to Dundas*
30 *fr Catholic Committee
   in Ireland*
30 fr Gattoni

31 *to Dundas*
31 fr Laurence

AUGUST

1 *to J. King*
1 *fr Dundas*
1 fr Shippen
3 *to Dundas*
3 *to Bn. Hawkesbury*
3 to Abbé de La
   Bintinaye
4 *fr Earl Fitzwilliam*
5 *fr Bn. Hawkesbury*
7 *to Bn. Hawkesbury*
7 to Unknown
15 *to Earl Fitzwilliam*
15 fr Unknown
15 fr Unknown
16 fr Unknown
*a*17 fr Earl Fitzwilliam
17 to Burges
17 *to WB*
17 to Earl Fitzwilliam
18 to Bn. Grenville
19 fr Bn. Hawkesbury
19 fr Knight
22 to RBjr
24 to RBjr
24 to RBjr
24 to Mrs. Crewe
24 to Chev. de Grave
28 fr Laurence
29 fr Laurence
30 to Dr. Lind
30 fr Savy
31 fr Unknown
— fr E. Dowdeswell
— fr Laurence

SEPTEMBER

1 fr RBjr
3 fr RBjr
3 to WB
*c*4 to RBjr
6 fr Bn. Grenville
7 to W. King
8 to Mrs. Leadbeater
*c*8 fr RBjr
9, 10 to RBjr
9 fr Bn. Sheffield

12 fr D. of Portland
13 fr Bp. of St.-Pol-de-
   Léon
*p*13 to Bp. of St.-Pol-de-
   Léon
14 to Unknown
15 fr Bn. Loughborough
16 to W. King
18 to W. King
*c*19 to Dundas
19 fr Bowles
19 to Bn. Grenville
*a*20 to W. King
20 to W. King
21 fr Dundas
*c*21 fr J. King
21 fr Bp. of St.-Pol-de-
   Léon
23 fr Hume
25 fr Harrison
25 *fr Sandouville*
27 fr Bruandet
27 fr Earl Fitzwilliam
28 fr Vicomtesse de
   Cambis
28 fr Abbé Somers
— *to Dundas*

OCTOBER

1 to RBjr
2 to Wilmot
5 to Earl Fizwilliam
6 *to Earl Fitzwilliam*
6 fr Wilmot
8 to Dundas
8 to Dundas
8 fr Mme. Nugent
8 fr D. of Portland
9 to Wilmot
10 fr RBjr
12 fr Molesworth
13 fr C. G. and J.
   Greenwood
*p*13 to Sandouville
14 to Baring
14 to Molesworth
14 fr E. Dowdeswell
*a*16 *to Catholic Committee
   in Ireland*

84

16	fr RBjr
16	to Dr Hughes
17	fr Baring
17	to RBjr
17	to Bn. Sheffield
19	fr Dundas
21	fr Bn. Sheffield
23	to Earl Fitzwilliam
25	fr Huet
26	to Adam
26	to Sir G. Elliot
27	fr RBjr
28	to Dundas
29	fr Anstruther
29	fr Lasmartres
29	fr Laurence
30	fr Mme. Phoenix

NOVEMBER
2	to RBjr
4	*to Bn. Grenville*
5	*to Bn. Hawkesbury*
6, 7, 10	to RBjr
8	fr Laurence
14	fr Windham
14	*fr Mme d'Assigny*
15	fr Windham
18	to RBjr
18	to Bp. Moylan
19	fr Bp. Moylan
*a*21	fr RBjr
*p*21	to RBjr
23	to Abbé de La Bintinaye
25	*to W. Smith*
26	*fr W. Smith*
27	fr Bn. Loughborough
27	*to W. Smith*
28	to Bn. Loughborough
29	to Earl Fitzwilliam
29	fr Capt. Woodford
30	fr Bn. Loughborough

DECEMBER
1	fr Bn. Grenville
3	fr Dr. Hussey
6	to Bn. Grenville
8	fr Laurence
10	fr Laurence
11	fr Laurence

*a*13	to Cts. of Inchiquin
16	fr Malone
18	*fr Hawkswell*
19	fr E. of Upper Ossory
22	fr Pitt
27	*to Dundas*
27	to Dundas
28	fr Castley
29	fr Unknown
30	fr Nott
31	fr Overton
31	fr Abbé Somers

MONTH NOT KNOWN
—	fr Bn. Loughborough
—	*fr Dr. Browne*
—	to RBjr
—	*to Unknown*
—	fr Unknown

1793

JANUARY
2	*fr Dundas*
9	*fr Marquis de Las Cases*
9	fr Repton
11	fr Capt. Harness
12	fr Bn. Loughborough
13	to Repton
16	fr Woolley
17	to Catherine II
*c*17	to Malone
19	fr Andrezel
19	fr Bn. Loughborough
20	to Capt. Harness
20	fr J. Butler
22	to E. of Upper Ossory
23	*to Dundas*
24	to Nepean
27	to Bn. Loughborough
28	fr Baron de Cormatin-Desotteux
28	fr Lafon
31	fr Count Vorontsov
—	to Burges

FEBRUARY
3	fr Bertier de Sauvigny
8	fr Gentz

*p*8	to Gentz
10	fr Pitt
15	fr Vicomte de Cicé
15	fr Count Vorontsov
*p*18	to Sir H. Langrishe
20	fr Fullarton
20	fr Sir H. Langrishe
24	fr Heatly
28	*to Grattan*
28	to Whig Club

MARCH
*p*2	to W. Smith
5	to A. Young
6	to Sir H. Hoghton
6	fr Dr. Maxwell
7	to Sir L. Parsons
7	to Unknown
7	fr Unknown
8	to Grattan
12	fr Woolley
20	*fr Grattan*
*c*20	*fr Dr. Browne*
23	*to Earl Fitzwilliam*
23	fr Bn. Loughborough
*p*23	*fr Earl Fitzwilliam*
25, 26	fr Grattan

APRIL
8	fr Batley
10	fr Batley
12	fr Abbé Somers
19	fr Abbé Somers
20	fr Sambourne

MAY
2	fr Unknown
5	*fr Cazalès*
6	*to Malone*
6	fr A. Murphy
*p*6	fr John King
15	fr Marquis de St. Ange
18	fr Vicomte de Retz
26	to A. Murphy
28	fr Duc d'Havré et de Croy
29	*to RBjr*

JUNE
2	to Unknown
5	fr Magenis

7	fr C. Grey	31	*to Earl Fitzwilliam*	18	*fr Noble*
7	to Dundas	SEPTEMBER		23	fr Comte d'Artois
12	fr King of Poland	1	fr Bn. Loughborough	23	to Col. St. Leger
15	*fr Noble*	7	fr Hippisley	*c*24	fr Bp. of St.-Pol-de-
22	fr Vct. Beauchamp	7	fr Pius VI		Léon
24	*to Bn. Hawkesbury*	8	fr Prince of Saxe-	24	to Windham
26	fr Vct. Beauchamp		Coburg	25, 26	to RBjr
27	to Comte de Mercy-	9	fr Unknown	25	to Dundas
	Argenteau	14, 15	to Dr. Burney	26	fr Bn. Grenville
27	to Dundas	14	fr Deyzac	26	*to John King*
JULY		15	to WB	27	*fr Drennan*
*a*3	to Wills	*c*15	to Mrs. Crewe	27	to Dundas
6	fr Bukaty	16	to Sir G. Elliot	27	to Gen. O'Hara
10	to Dundas	18	to Sir G. Elliot	28	*to Dundas*
12	fr Dundas	18	fr Hippisley	28	*to Bn. Hobart*
14	to Nepean	22	to Sir G. Elliot	29	fr Dundas
18	*fr Unknown*	22	*to W. Elliot*	29	fr Bn. Grenville
19	fr Comte de Mercy-	24	fr Hippisley	29	to J. King
	Argenteau	29	*fr Noble*	NOVEMBER	
23	fr Unknown	29	to D. of Portland	1	*fr Hennessy*
24	*to Unknown*	29	to Earl Fitzwilliam	1	fr Windham
27	fr Gen. Dalton		and D. of Portland	2	*fr Dundas*
29	to Joseph Hickey	OCTOBER		4	*to Dundas*
*p*29	fr Bn. Loughborough	1	fr Comte de Mercy-	4	to Windham
30	*to Dundas*		Argenteau	5	*to Dundas*
31	fr D. of Portland	1	*fr J. and J. H. Noble*	6	to Comte d'Artois
31	fr Wilde	2	to Windham	*c*6	to Windham
—	*to W. King*	3	to Hippisley	7	to RBjr
AUGUST		4	*fr Comte de Vaugiraud*	7	fr Windham
1	to D. of Portland		*de Rosnay*	8	fr S. Douglas
4	*to J. King*	5	fr E. of Charlemont	9	*fr Hobart*
6	to Gen. Dalton	6	fr Col. St. Leger	10	*fr Cazalès*
*c*6	to Comte de Mercy-	7	*fr Noble*	*c*10	to Windham
	Argenteau	8	to Dundas	11	to RBjr
8	fr Prince de Carency	10	*to Bn. Grenville*	13	fr Comte de Serent
8	*fr Earl Fitzwilliam*	10	fr Dr. Hall and	13	fr Voisins
*a*11	*fr Earl Fitzwilliam*		Dr. Young	14	to S. Douglas
11	*to Earl Fitzwilliam*	10	fr D. of Portland	14	fr Windham
14	fr Chev. de Grave	13	fr Dundas	17	*fr Earl Fitzwilliam*
15	fr Dr. Hussey	14	to Dundas	19	fr E. of Malmesbury
16	*to Earl Fitzwilliam*	*c*14	*to Cazalès*	19	*fr Noble*
17	fr Windham	16	to Comte de Mercy-	19	to Sir G. Elliot
18	to Windham		Argenteau	20	fr Hippisley
20	to Windham	16, 17	*fr Cazalès*	23	fr Comte de Coigny
*a*22	fr Windham	17	fr Abbé Mann	24	to Wilmot
22	fr James Craufurd	17	*fr Noble*	25	fr Comte de Coigny
23	to Windham	17	fr Dr. Young	25	to Dr Hughes
27	*fr Earl Fitzwilliam*	17	*to Sir G. Elliot*	25	to Windham

26   *fr A. M. Campbell*
27   fr M. of Buckingham
27   fr Hippisley
28   fr Comte de Coigny
28   to Dolphin
29   to Earl Fitzwilliam

DECEMBER

1   to M. of Buckingham
5   *fr Noble*
6   to Bp. Moylan
7   *to Nepean*
8   to A. Murphy
12   *fr Noble*
15   to Nepean
16   *fr Cazalès*
16   *to Bn. Hawkesbury*
17   to Capt. Cuppage
18   *fr Cazalès*
18   fr Chev. O'Gorman
19   *fr Hawkswell*
20   fr Ferris
20   fr Bp. Moylan
21   fr D. of Portland
23   *fr M. of Hertford*
23   *to Bn. Hawkesbury*
28   *fr Worrall*
30   fr S. Douglas
30   *fr J. Lewis*
*p*30   to S. Douglas

MONTH NOT KNOWN

—   *fr R. Bruce*
—   *to Dundas*
—   fr G. Johnson
—   to Bn. Loughborough

1794

JANUARY

1   fr Ferris
3   fr Bp. of St.-Pol-de-
    Léon
4   *to Dundas*
    to Dr. Brocklesby
    to Hippisley
8   to Windham
8   *to Windham*
10   to RBjr
10   fr W. Smith
11   fr Bn. Loughborough

12   *to Earl Fitzwilliam*
12   to Bn. Loughborough
13   to Capt. Woodford
14   fr Abbé Mann
15   fr Bn. Loughborough
15   to Unknown
18   fr Windham
19   fr Echalon
19   fr D. of Portland
20   fr Pitt
20   to D. of Portland
21   to Pitt
23   *fr J. Lewis*
24   *fr Drennan*
27   *to Earl Fitzwilliam*
29   *fr Earl Fitzwilliam*
30   to Dolphin

FEBRUARY

1   to Windham
8   *to Charles Townshend*
9   *fr Charles Townshend*
11   *fr Windham*
14   fr Wigglesworth
15   fr Monsignor Leardi
16   to Francis
17   *to Sir P. Burrell*
21   *to Bp. of Auxerre*
*p*21   *fr Bp. of Auxerre*

MARCH

14   to Addington
17   *fr Cazalès*
17   fr Wigglesworth
17   fr Capt. Woodford
18   *to Earl Fitzwilliam*
28   fr Wigglesworth

APRIL

5   to Wigglesworth
5   to Addington
10   to Astle
11   fr Pitt
13   fr Windham
16   to Ley
18   to Ley
19   to Ley
21   fr Ley
22   to Ley
22   *to Pitt*
23   fr Ley

23   fr Watkins
24   fr Ley
24   *to West*

MAY

2   to G. C. Fox
7   to Addington
13   fr James Craufurd
22   *fr Col. Boismarnier*
22   fr Marquis de La
    Queuille
23   *to Grattan*
26   fr J. Edwards

JUNE

1   to U. Price
7   fr Hippisley
10   *fr Cazalès*
10   fr Ley
10   to Windham
11   fr D. of Portland
19   *to Windham*
21   to Earl Fitzwilliam
*p*21   *to W. King*
24   to Bn. Hawkesbury
25   fr Pitt
25   to Pitt
26   fr Earl Fitzwilliam
27   *to Earl Fitzwilliam*
*c*27   *to Windham*
28   to Earl Fitzwilliam
30   to Pitt
—   fr Unknown

JULY

5   fr James Craufurd
7   fr Cérat
9   fr E. of Traquaire
*c*18   *to Mrs. T. Haviland*
28   *to G. Hennessy*
29   to Wallis
31   to Laurence

AUGUST

*p*2   fr Laurence
3   fr Pinson de
    Ménerville
4   fr Earl Fitzwilliam
4   fr Bp. of St.-Pol-de-
    Léon
*p*4   to Earl Fitzwilliam
7   *fr Vct. Sydney*

9	*to Francis*	8	to Windham	12	to Bn. Loughborough
15	to Windham	12	fr A. Browne	14	to Sir G. Colebrooke
16	fr Kennedy	15	to Windham	15	fr Vct. Milton
17	to Windham	15	fr Windham	16	fr S. Douglas
20	fr Bp. Moylan	16	to Windham	20	to E. of Chatham
22	fr Comte d'Artois	16	to Windham	20	to Ivernois
26	fr Grattan	18	fr Windham	21	fr E. of Chatham
28	fr Comte d'Hading	19	to Bn. Loughborough	22	to Windham
28	to W. King	20	to Windham	29	to Comtesse
30	fr Pitt	21	to Earl Fitzwilliam		d'Osmond
31	to Earl Fitzwilliam	21	fr Earl Fitzwilliam	*c*30	to Abbé de La
31	to W. King	21	fr Windham		Bintinaye
31	to Pitt	*p*21	to Windham	30	to Windham
31	to Pitt	23	fr Bn. Loughborough	MONTH NOT KNOWN
—	to W. King	28	to Windham	—	*to West*
SEPTEMBER		*p*28	to WB	—	fr Wilks
1	fr Comte de Séerent	NOVEMBER		—	fr Windham
3	to Grattan	1	to Dr. Hughes	—	fr Clemenceau
5	to Abbé de La	2	to Laurence	—	to T. Goold
	Bintinaye	2	to Bn. Loughborough	—	*to Col. Ross*
9	to Earl Fitzwilliam	4	to Dundas	—	to Unknown
12	fr Lady Anne Barnard	5	to Dundas		
14	to John King	6	to Bn. Loughborough	**1795**	
*c*14	to W. King	7	to Earl Fitzwilliam	JANUARY	
*c*14	to W. King	11	fr Monsignor Erskine	7	to Windham
14	to D. of Portland	12	fr Wigglesworth	8	to Addington
16	fr James Craufurd	14	to WB	8	to Windham
17	to W. King	*c*16	to Bp. of Auxerre	10	fr Francis
18	fr Pitt	18	fr Earl Fitzwilliam	10	fr Francis
19	to Pitt	*c*22	to Mrs. Crewe	10	fr Wigglesworth
23	fr Grattan	*c* 22	to Earl Fitzwilliam	10	to Bn. Loughborough
*c*26	to Earl Fitzwilliam	24	to Wilmot	15	to Wallis
*c*28	to Lady Anne Barnard	25	to D. of Portland	16	to Inspector General
	and A. Barnard	30	to Abbé d'Héral		of Accounts
28	to Abbé de La	30	to W. King	18	to Unknown
	Bintinaye	DECEMBER		18	to Wallis and
28	to Windham	1	fr Comtesse		Troward
—	fr J. Adair		d'Osmond	20	fr Addington
—	fr Cathcart	8	to Comtesse	20	fr W. Smith
OCTOBER			d'Osmond	21	to Addington
1	to Cts. Spencer	8	to Abbé de La	21	fr Addington
1	fr Bp. of Clonfert		Bintinaye	21	to Laurence
1	fr Grattan	10	fr Comtesse	29	fr Dr. Hussey
2	to WB		d'Osmond	29	to W. Smith
3	*to Laurence*	12	fr Bp. of Auxerre	FEBRUARY	
5	fr Mrs. Leadbeater	12	to WB	*c*2	to Windham
	and Mrs. Shackleton	12	to Grattan	4	to Dr. Hussey
7	to Windham	12	to Grattan	6	to Wilmot

8	to J. King
9	fr Wilmot
a10	to Dr. Hussey
10	to Earl Fitzwilliam
12	to Wilmot
13	fr Kearney
19	fr Grattan
19	fr Dr. Hussey
20	fr Bp. of Clonfert
23	to Windham
24	to W. Elliot
24	to Wallis and Troward
c26	to Earl Fitzwilliam
27	fr Dr. Hussey
28	fr Dr. Hussey

MARCH

2, 3	to Grattan
p2	to Addington
3	fr Dr. Hussey
4	fr Earl Fitzwilliam
5	to Addington
c5	to Dundas
5	to Grattan
5	to Dr. Hussey
5	fr Sir H. Langrishe
5	fr Windham
6	to Windham
9	fr Earl Fitzwilliam
11	to D. of Devonshire
11	fr Grattan
11	to Bn. Grenville
11	*to Lady Anne Barnard*
c13	to Mrs. Crewe
13	to Earl Fitzwilliam
13	to Sir H. Langrishe
14	fr Grattan
c14	fr Dr. Hussey
17	to Dr. Hussey
19	fr Byrne and Keogh
19	to Earl Spencer
20	to Grattan
20	fr Earl Fitzwilliam
21	fr Earl Fitzwilliam
21	to Dr. Hussey
c23	to Mrs. Crewe
25, 26	to Earl Fitzwilliam

—	to Addington
—	to Addington
—	to Dundas
—	fr Bp. of Ossory

APRIL

1	to Windham
3	fr Cathcart
3	fr Earl Fitzwilliam
6	fr Earl Fitzwilliam
11	to Earl Fitzwilliam
c12	to Earl Fitzwilliam
14	to Earl Fitzwilliam
15	fr Grattan
18	to Mrs. Crewe
20	to Noble
c30	to Laurence

MAY

6	fr Abbé Lubersac
8	to Abbé Lubersac
9	fr Earl Fitzwilliam
10	to Earl Fitzwilliam
13	to Dundas
14	fr Dundas
15	to Earl Fitzwilliam
c15	to W. Smith
18	to Dr. Hussey
21	to E. of Inchiquin
22	to Laurence
22	to Malone
26	to Sir H. Langrishe
28	to Commissioners for Public Accounts

JUNE

5	to Dundas
6	fr Earl Fitzwilliam
9	to Dr. Hussey
9	to Windham
21	to W. Elliot
21	fr E. Hay
26	to E. Hay
27	to Windham
28	fr Lord J. Cavendish
28	to Earl Fitzwilliam
28	fr D. of Portland
30	fr Earl Fitzwilliam
30	to W. King

JULY

1	to Lord J. Cavendish

1	to Laurence
1	to D. of Portland
5	to Earl Fitzwilliam
p5	fr Earl Fitzwilliam
13	fr Archbp. Troy
14	fr Goring
19	fr E. Hay
20	fr Decotte
26	fr Grattan
30	to Windham
—	to Mrs. Crewe

AUGUST

2	to Pitt
3	to Dr. Brocklesby
3	to Unknown
a5	to Mrs. W. Haviland
5	to Dolphin
6	to Mrs. W. Haviland
8	to Earl Fitzwilliam
9	fr Earl Fitzwilliam
p11	to Mrs. Crewe
12	to Earl Fitzwilliam
16	to Earl Fitzwilliam
24	to Dr. Hussey
25	fr Comte d'Artois
27	fr Archbp. of Bordeaux
30	to Dundas
31	fr Dundas

SEPTEMBER

2	to Dundas
3	to Abbé de La Bintinaye
4	to Mrs. T. Haviland
4	to Windham
8	fr E. of Moira
13	to W. Smith
14	to Dundas
15	fr E. Hay
15	to D. of Portland
15	to Windham
16	fr B. Anderson
17	to John King
26	to Dr. Hussey
29	fr Bp. of St.-Pol-de-Léon

OCTOBER

2	fr D. of Portland

2	fr Semple Lisle	14	fr Semple Lisle	8	fr Earl Fitzwilliam
3	to D. of Portland	15	fr Semple Lisle	8	fr P. Howard
5	to Dr. Burney	17	to Earl Fitzwilliam	8	fr Bn. Loughborough
10	to Windham	17	fr Semple Lisle	11	fr Bowles
10	to Capt. King	17	fr Windham	11	to W. King
12	to Abbé de La	18	to Dr. Hussey	11	to Abbé de La
	Bintinaye	19	fr Abbé Du Boys		Bintinaye
19	to J. E. Devereux	19	to Windham	11	to Laurence
25	fr Cursetji Manuar	21	fr Dr. Hussey	c12	to Bowles
26	to John King	21	fr Semple Lisle	13	fr C. O'Conor
28	fr Bn. Auckland	22	to Hippisley	13	fr C. Stewart
28	to Pitt	24	to Harwood	14	fr Peltier
28	to Pitt	24	to Unknown	15	fr Laurence
30	to Bn. Auckland	26	fr Ludgate	17	to Mrs. Crewe
31	fr Earl Fitzwilliam	27	fr Semple Lisle	c17	to Dundas

NOVEMBER

c4	to Dundas		**FEBRUARY**	c17	to Dundas
7	to Pitt	3	to Sir H. Langrishe	c17	to Dundas
a17	to Windham	p3	to Dundas	c17	to Laurence
17	to Windham	p3	fr Sir H. Langrishe	17	fr Laurence
18	fr L. Campbell	8	fr Fénelon	c17	to Bn. Loughborough
25	to Windham	12	fr Comte de Coigny	c17	to Bn. Loughborough
c26	to Capt. Woodford	12	fr Laurence	c17	to Bn. Loughborough
27	to Dr. Hussey	18	fr Earl Fitzwilliam	a21	fr Earl of Lucan
p30	to W. King	22	fr Marquis de	21	fr Moser
			Jumilhac	21	fr Dr. Pargeter

DECEMBER

2	*to Laurence*	22	to W. King	23	to W. King
6	to Dundas	24	to Noble	24	fr M. of Buckingham
8	fr Reeves	25	to Unknown	p24	to W. King
9	to Earl Fitzwilliam	25	fr Gifford	25	fr Bp. of St.-Pol-de-
16	to Earl Fitzwilliam	25	fr Laurence		Léon
16	to Major Cuppage	26	to Mrs. Crewe	26	fr Laurence
p16	to Major Cuppage	c27	to Laurence	26	fr Bp. of St.-Pol-de-
17	fr Earl Fitzwilliam	29	fr Mitford		Léon

MONTH NOT KNOWN

—	*fr Mrs. Crewe*	29	fr A. Murphy	28	fr Bp. of St.-Pol-de-
—	to Unknown	c—	to Nash		Léon
—	to Unknown		**MARCH**	28	to Windham
		2	fr Trench	29	to T. Townshend

1796

		3	to Mrs. Crewe	30	fr Wilde
	JANUARY	6	to Dundas	—	to W. King
5	to Unknown	6	to Earl Fitzwilliam		**APRIL**
5	to J. Nugent	c6	to D. of Portland	1	fr Malone
7	to Earl Fitzwilliam	6	to Windham	3	fr Hamille
10	fr Earl Fitzwilliam	7	to Addington	5	to Malone
10	fr Abbé de Levizac	7	to Gifford	5	to Moser
10	fr Sir R. Woodford	7	to Abbé de La	6	fr Comte de Coigny
11	to Sir J. Scott		Bintinaye	6	fr Bp. of St.-Pol-de-
		7	to Bn. Loughborough		Léon
		7	to Windham	8	to Sir H. Langrishe

12	fr Abbé de Lageard de Cherval	26, 29	fr M. of Buckingham	11	fr Swift
13	fr T. Townshend	26	fr Bp. of St.-Pol-de-Léon	13	fr Mrs. Pickar
14	fr G. Fitzgerald			14	fr Dr. Hussey
c15	fr Major Cuppage	28	to W. King	18	fr Comte d'Artois
16	fr T. Goold	28	fr Bp. of St.-Pol-de-Léon	20	fr E. Elliott
16	fr Bp. of St.-Pol-de-Léon			20	fr Keogh
		30	to Bp. of St.-Pol-de-Léon	26	to Dr. Hussey
18	fr Earl Camden			28	fr J. Forbes
25	fr Sinclair	JUNE		28	to Laurence
27	to A. Young	1	to M. of Buckingham	AUGUST	
—	to W. King	2	to M. of Buckingham	1	fr Vicomte de Frondeville
MAY		2	to Windham		
1	to Adey	4	to W. King	1	to Windham
1	fr Abbé Maraine	5	to Dr. Douglass	11	fr Bp. of St.-Pol-de-Léon
2	fr W. King and Bp. of St.-Pol-de-Léon	5	fr Comtesse de La Bourdonnaÿe		
				12	fr Abbé Maraine
2	to Abbé Maraine	5	fr Windham	12	to Earl Spencer
3	fr Bp. of St.-Pol-de-Léon	7	to Windham	16	fr Earl Spencer
		9	fr Dancel	22	fr D. of Portland
4	fr Bn. Arundell	10	fr Baron Du Pac Bellegarde	23	to Earl Fitzwilliam
5	to Earl Spencer			23	to Edward Nagle
11	fr Bp. of St.-Pol-de-Léon	10	fr Savignac	25	fr Vicomte de Frondeville
		11	to Laurence		
p14	to W. King	12	fr M. of Buckingham	25	to Louis XVIII
p14	to W. King	13	fr French Committee	26	to Laurence
17	fr Marquis d'Autichamp	13	fr Marquis de Lanascal	26	fr Comtesse de Montrond
19	to Unknown	17	fr Barentin	26	fr Windham
21	fr Bp. of St.-Pol-de-Léon	18	fr Dr. Hussey	27	to Windham
		20	to Geoghegan	30	fr Earl Fitzwilliam
21	to Unknown	21	fr Dr. Douglass	SEPTEMBER	
22	to Bp. of St.-Pol-de-Léon	22	to Geoghegan	2	to Earl Fitzwilliam
		22	fr Marquis de Lanascal	2	fr Comtesse de Jupeaux
22	fr Vicomtesse de Mauny	23	fr E. Elliott	2	to Laurence
23	fr Bp. of St.-Pol-de-Léon	26	to W. King	3	to John King
		27	fr Barentin	6	to Laurence
24	to M. of Buckingham	29	fr Semple Lisle	11	to Windham
24	fr Bp. of St.-Pol-de-Léon	—	to Bp. of St.-Pol-de Léon	c14	to Unknown
				15	to Laurence
25	to Dr. Hussey	—	fr Edward Nagle	15	fr Waller
c25	to Bp. of St.-Pol-de-Léon	JULY		17	fr Earl Fitzwilliam
		3	fr Comte de Berville	19	to Dr. Brocklesby
25	to Bp. of St.-Pol-de-Léon	5	to Dr. Hussey	20	to Venables
		8	fr C. Long	23	to Earl Fitzwilliam
p25	to Bp. of St.-Pol-de-Léon	9	fr Earl Fitzwilliam	23	*to Venables*
		11	to Earl Fitzwilliam	25	fr Abbé Edgeworth
				25	fr Unknown

91

26	to Earl Fitzwilliam
28	fr Earl Fitzwilliam
29	to Venables

OCTOBER

6	to Laurence
10	to Laurence
13, 14	fr Laurence
24	to W. King
24	to Mrs. Venables
*p*24	to W. King
26	to Lushington
29	fr Brandes
30	to Earl Fitzwilliam

NOVEMBER

1	to Windham
3	fr J. Therry
4	to W. King
4	fr J. W. Ridge
6	fr T. Townshend
7	to Edward Nagle
7, 8	to Mrs. Crewe
10	fr Earl Fitzwilliam
11	to Windham
16	fr Keogh
16	to J. Therry
17	to Keogh
18	to Laurence
20	to Earl Fitzwilliam
22	fr French *emigrés* at Jersey
22	fr Laurence
23	to Ms. of Buckingham
23	to Mrs. Crewe
23	to W. King
23	to Laurence
24	fr Keogh
24	fr Laurence
25	to Laurence
25	to Windham
27	fr Earl Fitzwilliam
29	fr Douce & Rivington
30	to Earl Fitzwilliam
30	fr Dr. Hussey

DECEMBER

1	to Jenkins
2	fr Laurence

3	fr Boisdarcy
5	fr Earl Fitzwilliam
6	to Earl Fitzwilliam
6	to Venables
7	fr Earl Fitzwilliam
7	to Earl Fitzwilliam
8	to Laurence
9	fr Earl Fitzwilliam
9	to Laurence
9	to Capt. Woodford
*p*9	to Earl Fitzwilliam
*p*9	to Dr. Hussey
10	fr Laurence
13	to Laurence
14	fr Earl Fitzwilliam
14	to Laurence
15	to Earl Fitzwilliam
15	fr Laurence
16	to Laurence
18	to Earl Fitzwilliam
18	to Jerningham
18	to Laurence
18	to Windham
19	fr Laurence
20	to Earl Fitzwilliam
20	to Laurence
20	fr Windham
21	to W. King
22	fr Mackintosh
23	to Laurence
23	to Mackintosh
23	to Windham
24	fr Laurence
24	fr Windham
25	to Laurence
25	to Windham
27	to Mrs. Crewe
27	to Lord F. Cavendish
28	to Earl Fitzwilliam
28	to Laurence
28	to D. North
28	fr Sherlock
29	to Lord F. Cavendish
29	to Earl Fitzwilliam
29	fr P. O'Conor
30	to W. King

MONTH NOT KNOWN

—	fr Abbé Maraine

—	to M. Lewis

1797

JANUARY

1	fr Earl Fitzwilliam
4	to Earl Fitzwilliam
5	to Windham
6	fr Windham
9	fr Earl Fitzwilliam
9	to Windham
17	*to Venables*
17	fr Windham
18	fr Madgett
25	to W. King
26	fr Comte de Châtillon
26	to Mrs. W. King
29	to Dr. Parry
30	fr Duhigg
31	fr Sir L. Parsons

FEBRUARY

2	to Mrs. H. W. Bunbury
2	fr Laurence
3	fr M. de Roquefeuil
8	fr Lord F. Cavendish
8	fr Laurence
9	fr Laurence
10	*fr Major Cuppage*
10	fr Windham
10	fr Unknown
10, 12	to Laurence
11	fr Windham
12	to Windham
14	fr Dr. Brocklesby
14	fr Laurence
15	fr Fowler
15	to Laurence
17	fr Windham
20	fr Laurence
*p*20	to Laurence
24	fr Laurence
24	fr Marquis de St. Aulaire
*a*27	fr Unknown
28	fr Laurence
—	to Unknown

MARCH
1   to Canning
1   to Laurence
3   fr Laurence
5   to Laurence
c5 to Laurence
5   fr Unknown
7   fr John King
7   fr Laurence
8   to Sir L. Parsons
11 fr Kennedy
13 *fr Adey*
14 fr Laurence
14 fr Vicomte de
    Segonzac
15 to Earl Fitzwilliam
16 to Laurence
17 fr Laurence
c18 fr Laurence
18 fr Abbé Maraine
21 to Lord F. Cavendish
21 to W. King
a22 to Laurence
22 fr Laurence
28 fr Laurence
28 fr Monbrun
29 to Laurence
29 fr Laurence
29 to Bp. of Waterford
30 to Laurence
30 to Windham

APRIL
1   fr Laurence
2   fr Bp. of Waterford
3   to Laurence

3   fr Laurence
10 fr Laurence
11 to Laurence
12 fr Laurence
12 fr Laurence
14 fr Malone
16 to Malone
c16 to Heirs of Prince
    Potemkin
17 fr Earl Fitzwilliam
23 *to Venables*
25 fr Laurence
25 fr Windham
26 to Earl Fitzwilliam
26 to Windham
27 fr Troward
28 fr Laurence
28 to Prince of Würt-
    temberg
29 fr Laurence
30 fr Windham

MAY
a1 fr Abbé Barruel
1   to Abbé Barruel
1   to Gifford
1   to Bn. Loughborough
1   to Troward
2   fr Malone
3   fr Bn. Loughborough
4   to Malone
6   fr Prince of Würt-
    temberg
7   to Earl Fitzwilliam
8   fr Sir J. Hippisley
8   fr Laurence
8   *to Capt. Woodford*

9   fr Bp. of Waterford
11 fr Laurence
12 to Bp. of Waterford
12 to Laurence
15 fr Earl Fitzwilliam
16 fr Abbé Barruel
16 to Bp. of Waterford
16 to W. King
16 to Windham
18 to Laurence
18 fr Laurence
21 to Mrs. Crewe
21 to Earl Fitzwilliam
22 to Bp. of Waterford
23 to Mrs. Leadbeater
23 to Troward
23 to A. Young
28 fr Mrs. Leadbeater
    and A. Shackleton
30 fr Laurence
31 to Capt. Woodford

JUNE
1   to Laurence
4   to Earl Fitzwilliam
5   to Laurence
6   to Unknown
9   fr Troward
18 to Earl Fitzwilliam
25 to Abbé de La
    Bintinaye

JULY
3   to Unknown
a9 *to Fox*
9   *fr Windham*

93

AN ALPHABETICAL LIST OF THE CORRESPONDENCES

In this list each of Burke's correspondences is presented, chronologically arranged, under the name of the correspondent. Identifications are as simple as possible, being generally confined to full names. Peers are placed under their peerage rather than their family names. Ecclesiastical and a few official posts are mentioned, but only those which were held in the period of the correspondence. Cross-references are kept to a minimum. The reader may always seek fuller information in the General Index.

If the manuscript of a letter has survived, the entry in our date-column embodies a report on the authenticity of its date. If the whole date is as certain as it can be—that is, if the year, month, and day are on the manuscript in the writer's hand—the date-entry for that letter will be printed without brackets. If however any one of the three parts has been supplied editorially—however conclusive the reasons—that part will be enclosed in square brackets. Where no manuscript survives and the date has been taken from a printed work, it will appear as it does in that work unless there is obvious reason to call it into question. The abbreviations which appear in dates—*a* for *ante*, *p* for *post*, *c* for *circa*—are perhaps self-explanatory.

The second column of each letter-entry reports on the direction. 'EB to' means that Edmund Burke wrote the letter to, 'EB fr' that he received it from, the correspondent named. In this list there are distinguishing initials for each member of the Burke family: 'JB' for Jane, Edmund's wife; 'RBSr' for Richard, his brother; 'RBJr' for Richard his son; 'WB' for William Burke. Dr Christopher Nugent, Edmund's father-in-law, appears occasionally, with his full surname.

The third column reports on where the letter is to be found. If it has been printed in this edition, there will be a simple volume-and-page reference in roman type. The reader can find the letter at its proper place in our volumes, with a full report on its manuscript or printed location, the existence of copies or drafts, the condition of the original and similar details. If we have *not* printed a letter but know where to send the reader to a manuscript or printed text, that information will appear in the third column. Bold-face capital letters stand for manuscript collections, bold-face figures for printed works.* Where both are

* For *Key Lists* of MS and printed sources, see below, pp. 195–203.

known, we give them on successive lines, the capital normally standing alone, the figure being followed by volume-and-page references. When a letter has not survived entirely, it may be described as an extract, abstract, or a mere reference ('ext', 'abs', or 'ref').

ABDY, Sir Anthony Thomas, 5th
   Baronet
1769 Sept 7   EB fr   A
1769 Nov 4   EB fr   A

ABINGDON, Willoughby Bertie,
   4th Earl of
[1774 Oct 2]   EB fr   A
[1774 Oct 4]   EB fr   A
[1774 Oct p 4]   EB fr   A
1777 Aug 26   EB to   III, 368–70
1777 Aug 28   EB fr   A
    1 II, 177–8

ACCOUNTS, Inspector General of
1795 Jan 16   EB to   VIII, 115–17

ADAIR, James
1794 Sept   EB fr   D
    4 50829–30
ADAIR, William
1794 Sept   EB fr   A

ADAM, William
1783 Apr 27   EB fr   V, 89–91
[1788] Dec 29   EB fr   V, 434–6
1791 Jan 2   EB fr   B
1791 Jan 4   EB to   VI, 197–9
1792 [Oct] 26   EB to   VII, 278–9

ADDINGTON, Henry; Speaker of
   the House of Commons 1789–1801
[1790 Nov 25]   EB to   VI, 175–6
[1790 Dec 2]   EB to   VI, 187
[1790]   EB to   VI, 196
[1794 Mar 14]   EB to   VII, 533–4
[1794 Apr 5]   EB to   VII, 536
[1794 May 7]   EB to   VII, 540–1
1795 Jan 8   EB to   VIII, 110–12

1795 Jan 20   EB fr   A
1795 Jan 21   EB to   VIII, 122–3
1795 Jan 21   EB fr   A
1795 Mar 5   EB to   VIII, 177–8
[1795 Mar]   EB to   VIII, 219–21
[1795 Mar]   EB to   VIII, 221–2
1796 Mar 7   EB to   VIII, 404–5

ADEY, Stephen Thurston
1784 Oct 22   EB fr   B
1786 Aug 16   EB to   V, 268–9
1788 Mar 28   EB to   V, 380
1788 June [29]   EB to   IX, 434; X, 22–3
1796 May 1   EB to   IX, 468
1797 Mar 13   JB fr   A

AFRICAN COMMITTEE (Committee of the Company of Merchants trading to Africa)
See also CAMPLIN
1779 Apr 17   EB fr   A

AIX, Jean de Dieu-Raymond de Cucé de Boisgelin, Archbishop of
[1791] July 15   EB to   VI, 293–5*
1791 Aug 7   EB fr   B
[1791 Aug p 15]   EB fr   B
1791 Aug 17   EB fr   B

ALBEMARLE, George Keppel,
   3rd Earl of
1769 Sept 12   EB fr   A
[1769 Oct 15]   EB fr   BA
n.d.   EB fr   BA

ALLEN, John
1790 Oct 25   RBjr fr   B

    * Published in *Lettre de M. Burke à M. l'Archevêque d'Aix; et réponse de M. l'Archevêque d'Aix à M. Burke* (Todd, 175).

ALLEN, Robert
1782 Mar 30 EB fr **A**

ALMON, John
1775 Aug 6 EB to III, 184
1779 Feb 3 EB to IV, 42
[1779 Dec 26] EB to IV, 175
[1779] EB to IX, 429–30

AMERICAN CONGRESS
1775 July 8 EB and **X**
     others fr

AMIENS, Louis-Charles
 Machault, Bishop of
1791 Mar 13 EB fr **B**
1791 Apr 23 EB fr **B**
1791 May 27 EB fr **B**

ANDERSON, Alexander
1782 July 4 EB fr **A**

ANDERSON, Benjamin
1795 Sept 16 EB fr **H**

ANDERSON, John
1775 Mar 16 EB fr **A**

ANDREZEL, Barthélemy-Philbert
1793 Jan 19 EB fr **B**

ANSTRUTHER, John
1792 Oct 29 EB fr **A**
n.d. EB fr **A**

ANTWERP, Corneille-François
 Nelis, Bishop of
1792 Jan 11 EB fr **A**

ARCHDEACON, Henry
1772 Jan 2 EB fr **A**

ARGYLL, Elizabeth (*née* Gunning),
 Duchess of
[1785 Sept 6] EB to V, 222

ARMAGH, Archbishop of
See ROBINSON

ARRAS, Louis-François-Marc-
 Hilaire de Conzié, Bishop of
1791 Aug 24 RBjr fr **B**

ARTOIS, Charles-Philippe de
 Bourbon, Comte d'; later
 'Monsieur'; later Charles X, King of
 France
1793 Oct 23 EB fr VII, 454–6
1793 Nov 6 EB to VII, 472–5
1794 Aug 22 EB fr VII, 573
1795 Aug 25 EB fr **A**
1796 July 18 EB fr **A**

ARUNDELL, Henry Arundell, 8th
 Baron
1796 May 4 EB fr **A**

ASSIGNY, Madame d'; wife of
 Claude-Antoine d'Assigny
1792 Nov 14 RBjr fr **B**

ASTLE, Thomas
[1794 Apr 10] EB to VII, 536–7

ASTON, Abigail
n.d. EB to IX, 470

AUCKLAND, 1st Baron
See EDEN

AUTICHAMP, Jean-Thérèse-
 Louis de Beaumont, Marquis d'
1796 May 17 EB fr **B**

AUXERRE, Jean-Baptiste-Marie
 Champion de Cicé, Bishop of
1773 May 31 EB fr **B**
1788 May 5 RBjr fr **B**
1791 May 15 RBjr fr **B**
1794 Feb 21 RBjr to **B**
[1794 Feb *p* 21] RBjr fr **B**
[1794 Nov *c* 16] EB to VIII, 77–8
1794 Dec 12 EB fr **B**

AWDRY, John
1780 Feb. 28	EB to	IV, 206–7

BACKHOUSE, Captain Thomas
1782 Mar 31	EB fr	A

BACON, John
1782 Mar 11	EB fr	A

BAGOT, Sir William, 6th
  Baronet
[1775 May 21]	EB fr	A

BAKER, Sir George
[1766]	EB fr	A

BAKER, William
1771 Sept 26	EB to	II, 240–2
1771 Oct 1	EB to	II, 242–3
1773 Nov 27	EB fr	II, 492–3
1774 Sept 30	EB fr	A
1774 Nov 18	EB fr	A
1774 Dec 18	EB fr	A
1774 Dec 26	EB fr	A
[1775 Aug 22]	EB fr	A
		1 II, 44–6
[1775 Aug 23]	EB to	III, 196–8
1775 Oct 4	EB fr	A
1775 Oct 5	EB fr	A
1776 Dec 13	EB fr	A
1777 Oct 9	EB fr	A
		1 II, 186–7
[1777 Oct 12]	EB to	III, 388–90
1777 Oct 22	EB fr	A
		1 II, 187–90
1777 Nov 9	EB to	III, 401–2
1777 Dec 25	EB fr	A
		II, 205–7
1778 May 2	EB fr	III, 439–40
1779 Aug 4	EB fr	IV, 108–10
1779 Aug 9	EB fr	A
1782 July 14	EB fr	A
1782 July 22	EB fr	A
1784 June 20	EB fr	V, 153–4
1784 June 22	EB to	V, 154–6
[1790 June 22]	EB to	VI, 120
1790 June 25	EB to	VI, 121–2
1791 Dec 16	EB fr	A

BALDWYN, Charles
1782 May 18	EB fr	A

BANKS, Joseph; later (1781) 1st
  Baronet
[1772 June c 3]	EB fr	II, 307–8
[1791 Feb c 8]	EB, RBjr	VI, 220
	and others to	

BARENTIN, Charles-Louis-
  François de Paule de
1796 June 17	EB fr	B
1796 June 27	EB fr	B

BARING, Francis
1792 Oct 14	EB to	VII, 265–7
1792 Oct 17	EB fr	A
		59 I, 229

BARNARD, Andrew
[1794 Sept c 28]	EB to,	VIII, 26
	and Lady Anne	
	Barnard	

BARNARD, Lady Anne
[1790 Nov]	EB to	VI, 186–7
1794 Sept 12	EB fr	AX
[1794 Sept c 28]	EB to,	VIII, 26
	and Andrew Barnard	
1795 Mar 11	JB to	AX

BARNARD, Thomas; later (1780)
  Bishop of Killaloe
[1775 Nov]	EB fr	A
[1776 Feb] 10	EB fr	A
1776 Aug 8	EB to	III, 285–6
1781 Mar 10	EB fr	A
1782 Apr 4	EB fr	A
		1 II, 463–6
1782 June 2	EB fr	A
1790 Feb 8	EB fr	A
1790 May 31	EB fr	A
n.d.	EB to	IX, 444

BARRÉ, Isaac
1782 July 16	EB to	V, 18–19
[1783 Mar 14]	EB fr	V, 73–4
[1783 Mar]	WB fr	

BARRETY, Joseph
1786 June 28 EB fr   **A**

BARRINGTON, Daines
1780 Aug 6   EB fr   **A**

BARROW, Charles, later (1784) 1st
  Baronet
1774 Nov 4   EB fr   **A**
1780 Mar 7   EB fr   **A**
1780 July 1   EB fr   **A**
1780 Aug 18   EB fr   **A**
1780 Sept 10   EB to   IV, 281
1780 Sept 11   EB to   IX, 464
1780 Sept 14   EB to   IX, 464
1780 Sept 18   EB fr   **A**
1780 Oct 25   EB to   IV, 316–17
1782 May 4   EB fr   **A**
1787 Sept 10   RB[sr] to   IX, 466

BARROW, John S.
1786 Oct 1   EB to   X, 18–20

BARRUEL, Abbé Augustin
[1797 May a 1]   EB fr   **B**
1797 May 1   EB to   IX, 319–20
1797 May 16   EB fr   **B**

BARRY, James
1765 Oct 26   WB to   **5** I, 27–8
1765 Nov 6   EB fr   **5** I, 24–6
1765 Nov 8   WB to   **5** I, 28–9
1765 Dec 5   EB and   **A**
          WB fr   **1** I, 86–92
[1765 Dec c 20]   EB and   I, 220–2
          WB fr
1766 Feb 11   RBsr to   I, 237–8
[1766 Feb]   EB fr   **5** I, 46–8
1766 Mar 23   WB to   I, 245–6
[1766 May c 13]   EB and   I, 253–4
          Dr Nugent to
1766 June 27   WB to   **5** I, 43–4
1766 Aug 5   RBsr to   **5** I, 48–9
1766 Aug 16   EB fr   **5** I, 49–52
1766 Sept 24   EB fr   **5** I, 56–60
1766 Oct 7   WB to   **5** I, 60–2
1766 Oct 10   WB to   **5** I, 55–6
1766 Nov 2   EB fr   **5** I, 65–6

1766 Dec 3   WB to   **5** I, 76–7
1767 Feb 13   EB and   **5** I, 77–82
          WB fr
[1767 Feb a 19]   EB and   I, 292–5
          WB to
1767 Apr 26   EB to   I, 307–9
1767 May 23   EB and   **A**
          WB fr   **1** I, 116–29
[1767 June]   EB fr   **5** I, 97–101
[1767] Aug 24   EB and   I, 322–4
          WB to
1768 Apr 15   EB to   I, 349–50;
                    IX, 393
1768 May 22   [EB] fr   **5** I, 123–34
1768 July 19   EB to   II, 7–9
1768 Sept 30   EB fr   **5** I, 118–23
1768 Oct 10   WB to   **5** I, 101–3
[1768 Nov]   EB fr   **5** I, 108–17
1769 Apr 8   EB fr   **5** I, 158–64
1769 July 8   EB fr   **5** I, 170–4
1769 Sept 16   EB to   II, 81–3
[1769] Oct 8   EB to   II, 86–7
1769 Nov 8   EB fr   **5** I, 166–8
[1769]   EB fr   **5** I, 174–8
1770 Apr 24   WB to   **5** I, 187–9
[1770 May]   EB fr   **5** I, 179–86
1770 Sept 8   EB fr   **5** I, 207–16
[1770 Nov a 17]   EB and   **5** I, 189–91
          WB fr
1770 Nov 17   EB fr   **5** I, 194–5
[1770] Nov 20   EB fr   **5** I, 197–9
1770 Dec 7   WB to   **5** I, 195–6
1771 Jan 13   EB fr   **5** I, 199–
                    206
[1771]   EB fr   **5** I, 217–23
1772 July 24   EB to   II, 315
1774 July 9   EB to   III, 4–5
1774 July 11   EB fr   III, 6
1774 July 13   EB to   III, 7–9
1775 Jan 15   EB to   III, 99–100
1777 May 2   EB to   III, 336–7
n.d.   Dr. Nu-   **5** I, 145–6
          gent to

BARWELL, Richard
1783 Apr 15   EB fr   **3** VIII, 107
1783 Apr 22   EB fr   **3** VIII, 108–
                    9

BASSET, Sir Francis, 1st Baronet

1781 June 5	EB fr	A
1791 Sept 5	EB fr	A
1791 Sept 12	EB fr	A

BATHURST, Henry Bathurst, 2nd Earl

[1780 June 15]	EB fr	A
1780 July 18	EB to	IV, 256
[1780 July 19]	EB fr	A
[1781 July 7]	EB fr	A

BATLEY, Jeremiah

1793 Apr 8	EB fr	B
1793 Apr 10	EB fr	A

BAYLEY, Thomas Butterworth

1774 Apr 29	EB fr	A
		1 I, 455

BEAUCHAMP, Francis Seymour Conway, styled Viscount; later (1793) 1st Marquiess of Hertford

1766 May 7	WB to	I
		34 II, 42 abs 9 lines
[1793 June 22]	EB fr	A
[1793 June 26]	EB fr	A
1793 Dec 23	[RBjr] fr	A

BEAUCHAMP, R.

1791 June 8	EB fr	A

BEAUFORT, Dr. Daniel Augustus

1785	EB to	V, 375, n. 1

BECKFORD, Richard

[1786] Monday	EB fr	A

BEMBRIDGE, Charles

1782 Apr 8	EB fr	A
1782 May 29	EB fr	A
1782 June 13	EB fr	A
1783 Mar 13	EB fr	A
1783 Apr 17	EB to	V, 88–9
1783 May 18	EB fr	A
1783 May 23	EB fr	B
1783 June 1	EB fr	B

1784 Oct 1	EB fr	V, 169
[1784 Oct 2]	EB to	V, 171
1791 Aug 29	EB to	VI, 374–5

BENTINCK, Colonel

[1774 Nov 4]	WB to	H

BERESFORD John

1775 Dec 4	EB fr	A

BERKENHOUT [Dr. John]

1782 June 9	EB fr	A

BERTIER DE SAUVIGNY, Bénigne-Louis de

1793 Feb 3	EB fr	B

BERVILLE, Paul-Antoine-Joseph Vollant, Comte de

1796 July 3	EB fr	B

BESSBOROUGH, William Ponsonby, 2nd Earl of

1765 Oct 11	WB to, and Baron Grantham	I **34** I, 607, abs 4 lines
1767 Nov 11	EB to	I, 332–3
1767 Nov 11	EB fr	A
1774 May 10	EB to	IX, 464
1774 Oct 7	EB to	III, 60
1774 Oct 8	EB fr	A
1781 Sept 17	EB fr	A

BINGHAM, Sir Charles; later (1776) 1st Baron Lucan, (1795) 1st Earl of Lucan

1773 Oct 16	EB fr	A
1773 Oct 30	EB to	II, 474–81
1773 Nov 7	EB fr	A
[1773 Nov a 29]	EB fr	A
1773 Nov 29	EB fr	A
1782 Sept 23	EB fr	A
[1796 Mar a 21]	EB fr	B

BIRMINGHAM, Merchants at

1775 Feb 8	EB fr	**9** I, 286–7

BIRON, Amélie (*née* de Boufflers),
Duchesse de
1791 Mar 20	EB to	VI, 234–7
1791 Mar 23	EB fr	**B**
[1791 Mar 24]	EB fr	**A**
[1791 Mar 25]	EB fr	**B**

BIRT, Rev. James
[1777 Aug]	EB to	IX, 415–16

BISCHOFF, John
1791 Dec 26	EB fr	**A**

BISHOP, William Evans
1791 Feb 9	EB fr	**A**

BLAIR, Rev. Hugh
1783 May 24	EB fr	**A**

BLANGY, Lieutenant-General
Ducarne de
1791 Feb 22	EB fr	**B**

BLANKETT, Captain John
1780 Feb 23	EB fr	**A**
1780 Dec 18	EB fr	**A**
1781 Feb 15	EB fr	**B**
[1781 Mar 2]	EB fr	**A**
1781 Mar 2	EB to	IV, 339–40

BLAQUIERE, John; later (1784)
1st Baronet
1776 June 28	EB fr	**B**
1776 July 6	EB to	III, 279
1782 Apr 8	EB fr	**A**
[1784 Oct 13]	EB to	V, 174–7
1784 Nov 6	EB fr	V, 180–2
[1784 Nov *p* 6]	EB to	V, 182–7
1785 Apr 8	EB fr	**B**

BLENMAN, William
1782 June 26	EB fr	**A**

BOISDARCY, Lemoine de
1796 Dec 3	EB fr	**B**

BOISMARNIER, Colonel
1794 May 22	RBjr fr	**B**

BOLLAN, William
1774 Sept 29	EB fr	**A**

BOLTON, Harry Powlett, 6th Duke of
[1780 Jan] 2	EB to	IV, 178–9

BOLTON, Serjeant James Clayton
n.d. Monday	EB fr	**A**

BOLTS, William
1786 May 5	EB to	V, 262–4

BONNEVAL, Abbé Sixte-Louis-
Constant Ruffo, de
1791 July 16	EB fr	**B**

BOONE, Thomas
1782 Mar 29	EB fr	**A**
1783 Mar 6	EB fr	**A**

BOOTHBY, Francis
1783 May 3	EB fr	**A**

BORCKE [Adrian Heinrich von]
1774 Jan 17	EB fr	**A**
[1774 Jan *p* 17]	EB to	II, 511–14

BORDEAUX, Jérôme-Marie
Champion de Cicé, Archbishop of
[1795] Aug 27	EB fr	**A**

BOSWELL, James
1778 Mar 3	EB fr	**A**
		1 II, 207–9
1778 Nov 6	EB fr	**BE**
1779 Feb 22	EB fr	IV, 43–4
1779 Mar 1	EB to	IV, 44–7
1780 Mar 2	EB fr	**A**
1782 Mar 18	EB fr	**A**
1782 Apr 18	EB fr	**A**
1782 Apr 23	EB to	IV, 445
1782 Apr 30	EB fr	**A**
1782 July 19	EB fr	**A**
1782 Aug 15	EB to	**BE**
1782 Sept 1	EB to	V, 34–5
1782 Dec [26]	EB fr	**BE**
1783 Aug 8	EB fr	**BE**
1783 Aug 13	EB to	V, 105–6

Boswell, James (*cont.*)

1783 Nov 20	EB fr	**BE**
1784 Jan 3	EB fr	**BE**
1784 Jan 31	EB fr	**BE**
1784 Apr 10	EB fr	v, 138–9
1784 Apr 12	EB fr	v, 139–40
[1784 Apr 15]	EB to	v, 142
1785 Feb 15	EB fr	**A**
1785 Dec 20	EB fr	**BE**
1786 Jan 4	EB to	v, 248–50
[1786 Feb 7]	EB fr	**BE**
[1786 Feb 8]	EB to	v, 257–8
1786 Feb 9	EB to	v, 258–9
1786 Feb 10	EB fr	**BE**
[1786 Feb 10]	EB fr	**BE**
1786 Mar 20	RBjr fr	**BE**
1788 Apr 6	EB fr	**BE**
1788 Apr 8	EB to	v, 386–7
[1788] Apr 16	EB fr	**BE**
[1788] Apr 22	EB fr	**BE**
[1791 Mar 5]	EB fr	vi, 230–1
1791 [Mar] 7	EB to	vi, 231
1791 July 16	EB fr	vi, 297–8
1791 July 20	EB to	vi, 299–300

BOUFFLERS, Marie-Charlotte-Hippolyte (*née* Campet de Saujon), Comtesse de

1790 Nov 4	EB fr	**B**
1790 Dec 11	EB fr	**B**
1791 May 23	EB fr	**B**
1791 Aug 12	EB fr	**B**

BOUILLÉ, François-Claude-Amour, Marquis de

1791 June 26	EB fr	**S**
1791 July 13	EB to	vi, 289–92

BOURDIEU, James

1781 Dec 2	EB to	iv, 383–5
1781 [Dec] 5	EB to	iv, 387
1781 Dec 6	EB to	iv, 388–9
[1781 Dec 16]	EB to	iv, 390–3
[1781 Dec 18]	EB to	iv, 394–5

BOURKE, Mrs. Eliza

1764 Aug 16	EB fr,	**B**
	and D. Murphy	

BOURKE, John

[1773 Oct 12]	EB to	ii, 471
1773 Oct 27	EB to	ix, 463
1776 July 11	EB to	iii, 280–1
1777 May 21	EB to	iii, 340–2
[1777 Nov]	EB to	iii, 402–4
[1784 July 15]	EB fr	v, 159–60
[1785 Apr *p* 7]	EB fr	**A**
n.d.	EB to	ix, 470
	[John] Bourke	

BOURKE, Michael

1785	EB to	ix, 465

BOURKE, N[icholas]

1770 May 17	EB fr	**A**

BOURKE, Theobald

n.d.	EB to	ix, 470

BOURKE, Thomas

1782 May 16	RBsr fr	**A**

BOURKE, Walter

1770 Feb 3	EB fr	**B**

BOURN, Samuel

1781 May 9	EB to	iv, 350–1

BOWDEN, Rev. John

1776 June 25	EB to	iii, 274–5
n.d.	EB to	ix, 444–5

BOWEN, Thomas

1782 May 9	EB fr	**A**

BOWIE, Patrick

1779 Mar 25	EB fr	**A**
		1 ii, 253–5
1779 Mar [31]	EB to	iv, 53–7
1779 Apr 24	EB fr	**A**
1779 June 8	EB fr	**A**

BOWLES, John

1791 May 19	EB fr	**A**
1792 Sept 19	EB fr	**A**
1796 Mar 11	EB fr	**A**
		1 iv, 341–2

Bowles, John (*cont.*)
[1796 Mar *c* 12] EB to   VIII, 414–
                                  15

BOYD, Hugh
1784 Jan 8   WB to   A

BRADY, Mary
1792 May 7   EB fr   C

BRAND, Rev. John
1792 Feb 15   EB fr   A

BRANDES, Ernst
1787 Jan 12   EB fr   V, 305–8
1796 Oct 29   EB fr   A

BRAUGHALL, Thomas
1780 Mar 17   EB fr   A
1782 Feb 9   EB fr   B
1782 Apr 20   EB fr   A

BRESSŸ [Jean Lemulier de Bressÿ],
  Comte de
1791 Apr 21   EB fr   B

BRICE, Edward
1780 Jan 31   EB and   IV, 202–3
               H. Cruger fr, and
               Joseph Harford

BRIDGEN, Edward
1781 Dec 6   EB fr   **55** I, 77

BRIDGES, Brook Allen
1783 Mar 16   EB fr   A

BRIGHT, Richard
1775 July 28   EB fr   A
1789 May 5   EB fr   V, 469
1789 May 8, 9   EB to   V, 470–2
1789 May 11   EB fr   A
1790 Feb 4   EB fr   A
1790 Feb 13   EB fr   A
1790 Feb 18   EB to   VI, 82–5

BRISTOL, Bell Club, Stewards of
  the

1777 Nov 1   EB to   III, 394–8

BRISTOL, Citizens of
1775 Jan 18   EB and   A
               H. Cruger fr
1775 Jan 20   EB to   III, 101–3
1776 Mar 14   EB and   A
               H. Cruger fr

BRISTOL, Committee of Merchants
  at, interested in Insolvent Debtors
  Bill
See also HILL, James
1780 Apr 8   EB fr   A
1780 Apr 15   EB fr   A

BRISTOL, Constituents at
1760 Feb *a* 8   EB fr   **50** XX, 1383,
                               abs 2 lines

BRISTOL, Independent Society,
  Committee of
See also BRISTOL, Bell Club
[1775 Jan]   EB fr   A

BRISTOL, Merchants at, protesting
  against duty on Indian corn
See also ⎰FRANK, Thomas
         ⎱HARFORD, James
[1774 Dec *a* 8]   EB fr   A
1774 Dec 24   EB and   **16** VIII, No.
               H. Cruger   398 (Jan
                    to   12, 1775)
1774 Dec 28   EB fr   B

BRISTOL, Merchants at, protesting
  against the Prohibitory Act
1775 Dec 12   EB fr   A

BROCKLESBY, Dr. Richard
1776 Dec 15   EB to   III, 304–5
1777 July 21   EB to   III, 365
1788 July 2   EB fr   V, 406
1788 July 17   EB to   V, 407
1790 Nov 1   EB fr   A
1794 Jan 5   EB to   VII, 511–12
1795 Aug 3   EB to   VIII, 293–4

Brocklesby, Dr Richard (*contd.*)
1796 Sept 19	EB to	IX, 86
1797 Feb 14	EB fr	A
n.d.	EB to	IX, 445–7
	[Brocklesby]	

BROOKE, William
1782 July 11	EB to	V, 16–17

BROOKS, 'Ephm'
1779 Feb 25	EB fr	A

BROUGHTON, Alexander D.
1782 July 10	EB fr	A

BROWNE, Arthur
1780 Nov 9	EB fr	A
1782 May 3	EB fr	A
1790 Nov 30	EB fr	A
[1792]	RBjr fr	B
[1793 Mar *c* 20]	RBjr fr	B
[1794]	EB fr	B

BROWNE, Colonel James
1789 Nov 7	EB fr	A
1790 Jan 15	EB fr	A

BROWNE, Thomas
[1782] June 24	EB fr	A
[1782] June 25	EB fr	A

BRUANDET, S. J.
1792 Sept 27	EB fr	B

BRUCE, Robert
[1793]	RBsr fr	A

BRUCE, Thomas Bruce, 2nd
Baron
[1768 Mar *a* 17]	[WB] fr	A

BRUCE, General Thomas
[1784] Aug 10	EB fr	A

BRUERE, William
1785 Nov 22	WB to	F
	[Bruere]	

BRUNTON
1783 June 23	EB to	V, 99–100

BUCHAN, David Steuart Erskine,
11th Earl of
[1782 July 1]	EB fr	A
1786 May 29	EB fr	A
1786 July 7	EB to	V, 265
1786 Dec 25	EB fr	A
1787 Nov 20	EB fr	A

BUCK, Rev. Dr. Andrew
1782 July 13	EB fr	A

BUCKINGHAM, George Nugent
Temple Grenville, 3rd Earl Temple,
later (1784) 1st Marquess of
1783 Dec 19	EB fr	V, 119
[1790] Nov 27	EB fr	A
1793 Nov 27	EB fr	VII, 491–2
1793 Dec 1	EB to	VII, 497–9
1796 Mar 24	EB fr	VIII, 444
[1796 May 24]	EB to	IX, 16–20
1796 May 26, 29	EB fr	IX, 29–33
1796 June 1	EB to	IX, 39–42
1796 June 2	EB to	IX, 42–3
1796 June 12	EB fr	A

BUCKINGHAM, Mary Elizabeth
(*née* Nugent), Marchioness of
1796 Nov 23	EB to	IX, 127–9

BUCKINGHAMSHIRE Meeting,
Chairman of
1780 Apr 12	EB to	IV, 226–9

BUKATY, Franciszek
1791 Oct 6	EB to	VI, 426–8
1792 Mar 30	EB fr	A
[1792 Mar *p* 30]	EB fr	A
1793 July 6	EB fr	A

BULLER, Sir Francis, 1st Baronet
1786 Apr 19	RB[sr] fr	B

BULLOCK, Joseph
1774 Oct 5	RBsr to	III, 55–6

Bullock, Joseph (*cont.*)

| 1783 Mar 3 | EB to | V, 69–71 |

BUNBURY, Mrs. Henry William

| 1792 Feb 1 | EB to | VII, 63–4 |
| 1797 Feb 2 | EB to | IX, 469 |

BUNBURY, Sir Thomas Charles, 6th Baronet

[1776 Oct 25]	EB fr	A
1778 July 15	EB fr	A
1781 Oct 4	EB to	IV, 373–4
1782 May 21	EB fr	A
n.d.	EB to	IX, 447 (ref)
n.d.	EB to	IX, 447 (ref)
n.d.	EB to	IX, 447 (ref)

BURGES, James Bland

1791 May 6	EB fr	VI, 252–3
1791 June 26	EB fr	A
1791 June 26	EB to	VI, 278
1791 June 28	EB fr	A
1791 June 29	EB fr	A
[1791 June 29]	EB to	VI, 279
1792 Aug 17	EB to	VII, 168–70
[1793 Jan]	EB to	VII, 345

BURGH, Thomas

[1779 Dec 24]	EB fr	B
1780 Jan 1	EB to	A
		3 VI, 209–34*
1780 Jan 27	EB fr	IV, 201–2
1780 Sept 25	EB fr	B
1782 Apr 6	EB fr	A
1782 Apr 21	EB fr	A
[1782 May] 27	EB fr	A
1782 Sept 2	RBjr fr	A
1785 Dec 27	EB to	V, 247–8
1786 Mar 27	EB fr	A
1787 July 1	EB to	V, 340–2
1789 Feb 24	EB to	V, 448–50

* Published as *A Letter in Vindication of His Conduct* (Todd, 104–6).

| 1789 Mar 29 | EB to | V, 454–5 |

BURGH, William

1774 July 23	EB fr	A
1775 Feb 9	EB to	III, 110–13
1775 Feb 18	EB fr	A

BURGOYNE, General John

[1773] Apr 4	EB fr	A
1779 Aug 31	EB fr	A
1779 Sept 1	EB to	IV, 127–8
[1779 Oct]	EB fr	A
1780 Sept 17	EB fr	A
[1781] July 21	EB fr	A
1781 Aug 2	EB fr	A
		1 II, 417–19
[1781] Nov 19	EB fr	A
[1781 Dec]	EB fr	A
1782 Aug 12	EB fr	A
1782 Aug 26	EB fr	A
1782 Nov 22	EB fr	A
1782 Dec 17	RBjr fr	A
1782 Dec 24	EB to	V, 55–8
1783 Jan 10	EB to	V, 60–2
1787 Nov 7	EB to	V, 358–9
1788 May 4	EB to	V, 395–7
1790 Sept 9	EB fr	A
1790 Nov 3	EB fr	A

BURKE, Mrs Edmund ('JB'); Edmund's wife

1773 Jan 11	EB and RBjr to	II, 411–12
[1773] Jan 12	EB to	II, 413
[1773] Feb 4	EB to	II, 421–2
[1774] Nov 8	EB to	III, 74–5

BURKE, John

| 1786 May 14 | EB fr | A |

BURKE, Juliana
See FRENCH, Mrs.

BURKE, Richard; Edmund's father

| 1755 Mar 11 | EB to | I, 119–20 |

BURKE, Richard ('RBsr'); Edmund's brother

Burke, Richard (*cont.*)

1746 July 25, 31	EB to, and Shackleton	I, 68–70
1746 Nov. 29	EB to, and Shackleton	I, 72–3
[1766 Jan *a* 14]	EB and JB to	I, 230–1
[1769 June 24]	EB fr	II, 31–5
[1774 Mar *a* 31]	EB to	II, 524–5
[1783 Mar 24, 25]	EB fr	v, 79–82
1783 Aug 12	EB fr	A
1783 Aug 13	EB fr	B
[1785] Nov 10	EB fr	v, 235–8
[1786 Aug 22]	EB fr	A
		1 III, 46–8
[1787 July 23]	EB to	v, 344–5
1787 Nov 21	EB, JB and RBjr to	v, 359–60
1788 June 25	EB to, and RBjr	v, 403–5
[1788 Nov 24]	EB to, and RBjr	v, 426–7
[1791 July 11]	EB and JB fr	B
[1791 July 19]	EB fr	B
1791 July 21	EB fr	B
		62 74
[1791 July 24]	EB to	VI, 306–7
1791 Aug 17	EB fr	B
[1791 Dec 5]	EB to	VI, 454–5

BURKE, Richard ('RBjr');
Edmund's son

[1773 Feb 4]	EB to, and T. King	II, 419–21
1773 Feb 9	EB fr, and T. King	B
[1773 Feb *p* 14]	EB fr, and T. King	B
[1773 Apr 26]	EB fr, and T. King	B
1778 Nov 20	EB to	IV, 28–30
1782 Sept 12	EB to	v, 35–6
[1782 Sept 22]	EB fr	A
[1782 Nov *p* 25]	EB to	v, 51–3
[1783 July]	EB fr	B
[1784 Mar 13]	EB fr	v, 130–3

[1784 Oct 2]	EB to	v, 170–1
[1785 Mar 12]	EB fr	B
1785 Dec 25	EB fr	v, 246–7
1787 June 19	EB to	v, 339–40
[1787 Oct 5]	EB and JB fr	v, 346–7
1787 Oct 5	EB and JB to	v, 347–9
[1787 Oct *c* 10]	EB and RBsr fr	v, 349–50
[1787 Oct 11]	EB to	v, 350–2
1788 June 25	EB to, and RBsr	v, 403–5
[1788 June *p* 25]	EB fr	B
1788 July 1	EB to	v, 405–6
1788 Sept [17]	EB, JB and RBsr to	v, 418–19
1788 Sept [19]	EB to	v, 419–20
[1788] Sept 21	EB and RBsr to	v, 420–1
[1788 Nov 24]	EB and RBsr to	v, 426–7
[1789 Oct *c* 10]	EB to	VI, 29–30
1789 Nov 11	EB to	VI, 32–4
[1790 June *c* 25]	EB to	VI, 122–3
[1791 July 15]	EB and JB fr	VI, 295–7
1791 Aug 5	EB to	VI, 315–18
[1791 Aug 8]	EB fr	VI, 323–30
1791 Aug 9	EB to	VI, 332–4
[1791] Aug 10	EB and JB to	VI, 334–7
1791 Aug 16	EB to	VI, 339–41
[1791] Aug 16	EB and JB fr	VI, 342–7
[1791] Aug 17	EB to	VI, 347–8
1791 Aug 18	EB to	VI, 353
[1791] Aug 18	EB to	VI, 354–65
[1791] Aug 25	EB to	VI, 366–9
[1791] Aug 25	EB fr	VI, 369–73
1791 [Sept] 1	EB to	VI, 376–8
1791 Sept 2	EB fr	VI, 378–84
[1791] Sept 10	EB fr	VI, 386–91
[1791] Sept 20	EB fr	B
1791 Sept 26	EB to	VI, 409–15
[1791 Oct *a* 7]	EB fr	B
[1791 Oct 8]	EB fr	VI, 430–2
1791 Oct 18	EB to	VI, 438

Burke, Richard (*cont.*)

1791 Oct 28	EB to	VI, 439–40
[1791 Nov *c* 1]	EB to	VI, 440–1
1791 Dec 13	EB to	VI, 456–7
1791 Dec 15	EB to	VI, 461–3
[1791 Dec 15]	EB fr	VI, 463–4
1791 Dec 16	EB to	VI, 464–5
1792 Jan 1	EB to	VII, 3–5
1792 Jan 1	EB and JB fr	VII, 5–7
[1792 Jan *p* 3]	EB to	VII, 8–12
1792 [Jan] 8	EB to	VII, 15–17
[1792] Jan 12	EB to	VII, 20–2
1792 Jan 13	EB to	VII, 29–31
1792 Jan *a* 25	EB fr	VII, 39–40
1792 Jan 26	EB to	VII, 40–1
[1792 Jan *c* 29]	EB fr	VII, 43–7
1792 Jan 29	EB to	VII, 48–50
[1792] Feb 19	EB to	VII, 64–7
[1792 Feb *p* 19]	EB to	**3** VI, 61–80*
[1792 Feb 23]	EB fr	VII, 68–74
1792 Feb 29	EB to	VII, 80–4
1792 Mar [*c* 8]	EB to	VII, 92–5
[1792 Mar *c* 11]	EB to	VII, 97–8
1792 Mar 20	EB to	VII, 100–7
1792 Mar 23	EB to	VII, 118–20
[1792 Apr 18]	EB fr	**B**
[1792 July 29	EB to	VII, 157–62
[1792 July 29]	EB to	VII, 162–4
1792 Aug 22	EB to	VII, 178–9
[1792 Aug 24]	EB to	VII, 180–1
[1792 Aug 24]	EB to	VII, 181–2
[1792 Sept 1]	EB and JB fr	VII, 185–8
1792 Sept 3	EB and JB fr	VII, 188–9
[1792 Sept *c* 4]	EB to	VII, 196–7
[1792 Sept *c* 8]	EB fr	VII, 200–3
1792 Sept 9, 10	EB to	VII, 203–6
1792 Oct 1	EB to	VII, 223–5
[1792] Oct 10	EB fr	VII, 255–8
1792 [Oct 16]	EB and JB fr	VII, 267–9
1792 Oct 17	EB to	VII, 271–4

1792 Oct 27	EB and JB fr	**A**
1792 Nov 2	EB to	VII, 280–4
1792 Nov 6, 7, 10	EB to	VII, 284–8
[1792 Nov 18]	EB to	VII, 289–93
[1792 Nov *a* 21]	EB fr	VII, 294–7
[1792 Nov *p* 21]	EB to	VII, 298–301
[1792]	EB to	**B**
[1793] Oct [25,] 26	EB and Capt. Woodford to	VII, 462–3
1793 Nov 7	EB to	VII, 477–8
[1793 Nov 11]	EB to	VII, 483
[1793]	EB to	**B**
[1794 Jan 10]	EB to	VII, 515–16

BURKE, Richard; son of Walter Burke of Middleton

[1780 Oct *p* 20]	EB fr	**A**
		62 26n

BURKE, William; Edmund's 'cousin'

1750 Nov	EB to	I, 103–7
1750 Nov	EB fr	**A**
1753 July	EB to	**A**
		I, 325–8
[1767 Sept *p* 4]	EB fr	I, 325–8
1768 Sept 25	EB fr	**B**
[1773] Jan 20	EB to	II, 414–17
[1773 Feb 14]	EB to	II, 424–5
[1782 Mar *p* 27]	EB to	IV, 430–1
[1782] Apr [25]	EB to	IV, 447–8
1783 Nov 5	EB fr	**AX**
[1785 Sept]	EB to	V, 224–5
1791 Feb *a* 1	EB fr	**B**
1792 Sept 3	EB and JB to	VII, 189–96
[1793 Sept] 15	EB to	VII, 427–8
1794 Oct 2	EB to	VIII, 29–30
[1794 Oct *p* 28]	EB to	VIII, 65–7
1794 Nov 14	EB to	VIII, 76–7
[1794 Dec] 12	EB to	VIII, 95
n.d.	[EB] fr	**B**

* Published in *Works* as 'A Letter to Richard Burke, Esq., on Protestant Ascendency in Ireland' (Todd, 256).

BURKE Family, Letters between members of

Burke, family (*cont.*)

[1768]	RBjr to JB	A
[1773 Jan] 17	RBjr to JB	B
[1773 Jan 20]	RBjr to JB	II, 417–18
[1774 Apr *a* 4]	RBjr to JB	B
[1774 Nov 1]	RBsr to WB	B
[1774 Dec 5]	RBsr to WB	A
[1776 Jan 5]	RBsr to WB	A 1 I, 403–7
[1783 July]	RBjr to JB	B
1783 Aug 4	RBsr to JB	V, 101–2
[1783 Aug 17]	RBjr to JB	V, 111–12
[1783 Aug 22]	RBsr to JB	B
[1784 Mar]	RBjr to JB	B
[1784 Oct *p* 2]	RBjr to RBsr	B
1785 Jan 7	WB to RBjr	I
1785 Sept 4	RBjr to JB	B
1785 Nov 9	RBjr to JB	V, 231–5
[1785 Dec 24]	WB to RBjr	I
1785 Dec 30	WB to RBjr	I 62 31–2, 87–9 abs and ext
1786 Jan 1	WB to RBjr	N
1786 [Jan *a* 15]	RBjr to RBsr	B
[1786 Aug *a* 12]	RBjr to JB	B
[1786] Aug 14	RBjr to RBsr	B

1787 Nov 19	JB to RBsr	B
1791 Mar 21	JB to WB	VI, 237–9
[1791 July 13]	RBsr to JB	B
[1791 Dec 19]	RBjr to RBsr	B
[1792 Mar *c* 1]	RBjr to RBsr	VII, 86–9
1792 May 16	RBjr to WB	VII, 139–42
1792 Aug 17	RBjr to WB	A 1 III, 486– 502 part omitted
1793 May 29	RBsr to RBjr	VII, 368–70

BURNEY, Dr. Charles

1783 Dec [19]	EB to	V, 120
1788 Aug 1	EB to	V, 408–9
1788 Aug 8	EB fr	A
1793 Sept 14, 15	EB to	VII, 421–4
1795 Oct 5	EB to	VIII, 325

BURNEY, Frances

1782 July 29	EB to	V, 25–7
[1786 June *p* 19]	EB to	V, 265

BURRELL, Sir Peter, 2nd Baronet

1788 Jan 8	EB to	IX, 433–4
[1788 Jan *p* 8)	EB fr	AR
[1788 Feb]	EB to	V, 380
[1788 Apr]	RBsr to	V, 379; X, 45
[1788 June *a* 3]	EB to	V, 401
[1790 Nov]	EB fr	A
1794 Feb 17	JB to	AJ

BUTLER, Charles

1780 July 15	EB fr	A
[1782] May 26	EB fr	A
1782 June 11	EB fr	IV, 459

BUTLER, Eleanor Charlotte

1790 July 30	EB to, and Sarah Ponsonby	VI, 130–2

BUTLER, John
1793 Jan 20   EB fr   **A**

BYRNE, Edward
1791 Sept 15   RBjr fr   VI, 396–8
1792 May 28   RBjr fr   **A**
1795 Mar 19   EB fr,   **A**
                 and   **1** IV, 306–8
                 Keogh

CALL, John
[1783] Dec 3   EB fr   **E**

CALONNE, Charles-Alexandre de
1790 Oct 25   EB to   VI, 140–1
1791 Feb 9   EB fr   VI, 221–3
1791 May 28   EB to   VI, 257–8
[1791 July c 20] EB fr   VI, 300–1
[1791 July c 20] EB to   VI, 302
[1791 July c 20] EB fr   **A**
1791 Aug 16   RBjr to   **I**
1791 Sept 6   RBjr to   **I**
[1791 Sept 6]   RBjr fr   **I**
1791 Sept 7   EB fr   **I** F.O. 95/
                            632, No.
                            74
[1791 Sept 14]   RBjr to   **I**
[1791 Sept 15]   RBjr to   **I**
1791 Sept 28   RBjr to   **I**
1791 Oct 4   RBjr to   **I**
1791 Oct 5   RBjr fr   VI, 424–5
1791 Oct 11   RBjr to   **I**
1791 Nov 9   RBjr fr   **B**
1791 Dec 6   RBjr to   **I**
1791 Dec 8   RBjr fr   **B**
1791 Dec 26   RBjr to   **I**
[1791 Dec]   EB to   VI, 473–7
1792 Jan 9   EB fr   **B**

CALONNE, Madame de; wife of
  Charles-Alexandre de Calonne
[1790 Oct] 23   EB fr   **B**

CAMAC, Lt. Col. J.
1783 Aug 6   [EB] fr   **A**

CAMBIS, Gabrielle-Françoise-
  Charlotte (*née* d'Alsace-Hénin-

Liétard), Vicomtesse de
1792 Sept 28   EB fr   **B**

CAMDEN, Charles Pratt, 1st Earl
1791 Aug 5   EB fr   **A**
                            1 III, 228–9
1791 Dec 21   EB fr   **A**
1792 Feb 3   EB fr   **A**
1792 June 13   EB fr   **A**

CAMDEN, John Jeffreys Pratt, 2nd
  Earl
[1796] Apr 18   EB fr   **A**

CAMELFORD, Lady Anne (*née*
  Wilkinson)
n.d. Tuesday   RBjr fr,   **A**
                 and Baron
                 Camelford

CAMELFORD, Thomas Pitt, 1st
  Baron
n.d. Tuesday   RBjr fr,   **A**
                 and Lady
                 Camelford

CAMPBELL, Rev. Dr. George
1769 May 18   EB fr   **A**
1779 June 12   EB fr   **A**

CAMPBELL, L. D.
1795 Nov 18   EB fr   **A**

CAMPER, Pieter
1775 July 18   EB to   III, 178–9

CAMPLIN, Richard
1774 May 20   EB fr   **A**
                            1 I, 456
1779 June 5   EB fr   **A**
1779 July 3   EB fr   **A**
1779 July 4   EB to   IV, 95–6

CANNING, George
1797 Mar 1   EB to   IX, 267–70

CAPPE, Newcome
1777 May 27   EB fr   **A**

CARENCY, Paul, Prince de
1793 Aug 8   EB fr   A

CARHAMPTON, Henry Lawes
  Luttrell, 2nd Earl of
1791 Apr 3   EB to   VI, 243–6
                [E. of Carhampton]
[1791] Apr 4   EB fr   A

CARLETON, General Guy
1783 Oct 11   EB fr   I
1783 Nov 10   EB fr   I

CARLISLE, Bishop of
See DOUGLAS

CARLISLE, Frederick Howard,
  5th Earl of
[1775] May 19   EB fr   A
1784 May 10   EB to   V, 144–5

CARLYLE, Dr.
1782 May 1   EB fr   A

CARNATIC, Nawab of the
1789 Apr 6   EB fr   AG

CARR, Richard Cooban
1773 May 6   WB fr   A
1773 May 22   WB fr   A
1779 Feb 17   EB fr   A
1788 June 26   EB fr   A

CARTER, John
1774 Oct 31   EB fr   A

CARTERET, Henry Frederick
  Carteret, 1st Baron
1783 Aug 29   RBsr to,   A
                and Bn. Foley
1783 Aug 29   RBsr to,   A
                and Bn. Foley

CARTWRIGHT, Major John
1777 Feb 18   EB fr   A
                           18 I, 103–5
[1777 Feb p 18] EB to   III, 328–9

1780 May 9   RBjr to   12 III, 114–
                           16

CASTLEY, Thomas
1792 Dec 28   EB fr   A

CATHCART, David
1794 Sept   EB fr   B
1795 Apr 3   EB fr   A

CATHERINE II, Empress of
  Russia
1791 Nov 1   EB to   VI, 441–5
1793 Jan 17   EB,   VII, 335–7
                Malone and
                Philip Metcalfe to

CATHOLIC COMMITTEE
See IRELAND, Catholic
  Committee in

CAVENDISH, Lord Frederick
1796 Dec 27   EB to   IX, 209–11
1796 Dec 29   EB to   IX, 215
1797 Feb 8   EB fr   A
1797 Mar 21   EB to   IX, 288–9

CAVENDISH, Lord George
1767 Oct 31   EB fr   A
1767 Nov 8   EB fr   A
1779 Sept 26   EB fr   A

CAVENDISH, Henry; later (1776)
  2nd Baronet
1775 Feb 1   EB fr   A

CAVENDISH, Lord John
[1767] Oct 12   EB fr   A
[1770 Mar p 8] EB fr   II, 124–5
[1775 Oct 25]   EB fr   A
[1775 Nov 3]   EB fr   A
                           1 II, 86
[1776 Feb 24]   EB fr   A
[1778 Feb 14]   EB fr   B
[1782] July 13 EB to   V, 17–18
[1782 July p 13] EB fr   A
[1790] Nov 14   EB fr   VI, 160–1
[1791] Sept 21 EB fr   A

Cavendish, Lord John (*cont.*)

[1795 June 28]	EB fr	VIII, 277–8
1795 July 1	EB to	VIII, 281
n.d.	EB to	IX, 447–9

CAWTHORNE, Joseph

1783 Nov 12	EB to	V, 117
1784 June 3	EB fr	A

CAZALÈS, Jacques-Antoine-
  Marie de

[1792] May 12	EB fr	A
1793 May 5	RBjr fr	A
[1793 Oct *c* 14]	RB jr to	B
1793 Oct 17	RBjr fr	A
[1793] Nov 10	RBjr fr	A
1793 Dec 16	RBjr fr	A
[1793] Dec 18	RBjr fr	A
1794 Mar 17	RBjr fr	A
1794 June 10	RBjr fr	A

CÉRAT, Bernard-Jean-Joseph de

1794 July 7	EB fr	A

CHAMBERS, Sir Robert

1791 Aug 28	EB fr	A

CHAMBERS, Sir William

[1775]	EB fr	A
1782 May 5	EB fr	A
1782 June 18	EB fr	A
1783 Oct 18	EB fr	A

CHAMPION, John

1786 June 4	EB fr	A

CHAMPION, Richard

1774 Oct 1	EB fr	III, 42–8
1774 Oct 1	EB fr	A
1774 Oct 3	EB fr	J
1774 Oct 5	EB to	III, 54
1774 Oct 7	EB to	III, 60–1
1774 Oct [7]	EB fr	J
1774 Oct 8	EB fr	J
1774 Oct 9	EB fr	J
1774 Nov 19	EB to	III, 78–9
1774 Nov [20]	EB fr	J
1774 Nov 24	RBsr to	B

[1774 Nov 29]	RBsr to	B
1774 [Dec *a* 22]	EB and	J
	RBsr fr	
1774 Dec 22	RBsr to	B
1774 Dec 23	RBsr to	J
1775 Jan 2	EB fr	J
1775 Jan 3	EB fr	J
[1775] Jan 4	RBsr to	B
1775 Jan 5	EB to	III, 84–6
1775 Jan 5	EB fr	J
1775 Jan [5]	EB to	III, 87
1775 Jan 9	RBsr to	III, 93–4
1775 Jan [10]	EB to	III, 94–7
1775 Jan 14	EB fr	J
1775 Jan 19	EB fr	J
[1775 Jan 20]	EB to	III, 101
1775 Jan 21	EB fr	J
1775 Jan 24	EB fr	J
[1775] Jan 24	RBsr	B
	and WB to	
1775 [Feb *c* 21]	EB to	III, 116–17
1775 Feb 23	EB fr	J
1775 Feb 23	RBsr to	B
1775 Feb 23	WB to	B
1775 Feb 25	EB fr	J
[1775 Feb 25]	WB to	B
[1775 Feb]	WB to	J
[1775 Feb]	EB and	J
	JB fr	
1775 Mar 1	RBsr to	J
1775 Mar 2	EB and	III, 123–6
	JB fr	
1775 Mar 4	RBsr fr	J
1775 Mar 6	JB to	J
1775 Mar 9	EB to	III, 131–3
1775 Mar 12	JB fr	J
1775 Mar 13	EB fr	J
1775 Mar 20	EB to	III, 138
1775 Mar 22	EB fr	J
1775 Mar 22	EB fr	J
[1775] Mar 22	RBsr to	III, 139–40
1775 Mar 24	EB to	III, 142–3
1775 [Mar *p* 24]	EB fr	J
1775 Mar 26	RBsr fr	J
1775 Mar 29	EB and	III, 143–5
	RBsr to	
[1775] Apr 4	EB fr	J
[1775 Apr 5]	EB fr	J

1775 Apr 8	EB fr	**A**
[1775 Apr 12]	[WB] to	**J**
[1775 May 24]	JB and	**B**
	WB to	
1775 June 3	EB and	III, 162–3
	RBsr to	
[1775 June 9]	RBsr to	**B**
[1775 June 10]	RBsr to	**B**
1775 June 20	EB fr	**A**
[1775] June 28	EB to	III, 175–6
1775 July 19	EB to	III, 179–80
1775 Aug 13	EB fr	**A**
[1775 Aug 14]	EB fr	**A**
1775 Aug 20	EB fr	**A**
[1775 Sept 27]	EB fr	**A**
1775 Sept 29	[WB] to	**J**
1775 [Sept]	[RBsr] to	**J**
[1775 Oct 1]	EB to	III, 220–1
[1775 Oct c 1]	EB to	III, 221
1775 Oct 2	[RBsr] to	**J**
1775 Oct 3	WB to	**J**
[1775 Oct 8]	RBsr to	**B**
1775 Oct 14	WB fr	**J**
[1775 Oct 17]	EB to	III, 230–1
1775 Oct 17	RBsr to	**B**
[1775 Oct 20]	EB to	III, 232–3
[1775 Oct 23]	EB and	III, 233–4
	RBsr to	
1775 Oct 23	EB fr	**J**
1775 Oct 26	JB to	**B**
[1775 Oct 27]	RBsr to	**B**
[1775 Oct 28]	RBsr to	**B**
[1775 Oct 29]	WB to	**B**
1775 [Oct p 29]	JB fr	**J**
[1775 Oct]	RBjr to	**J**
[1775 Oct]	WB to	**J**
[1775 Nov 10]	WB to	**B**
[1775] Nov 16	WB to	**B**
		8 160–1
		ext ½p.
1775 Dec 15	EB to	III, 238–9
1775 Dec 28	EB to	III, 239–41
[1775 Dec]	WB to	**B**
[1775 Dec]	WB to	**B**
[1776] Jan 7	RBsr fr	**8** 163 ext
		1p.
1776 Jan 14	WB to	**B**
1776 [Jan]	EB fr	**8** 207 extp ½.

1776 [Jan]	RBsr fr	**8** 207 ext
		6 lines
[1776 Feb 8]	EB to	III, 247–8
[1776 Feb 20]	RBsr to	**B**
[1776 Feb 22]	EB to	III, 250–1
[1776 Mar 1]	WB to	**B**
[1776 Mar 19]	EB and	III, 253–5
	RBsr to	
[1776 Mar]	RBsr to	**B**
[1776] Apr 3	EB to	III, 259–60
1776 Apr 22	EB to	III, 260–1
[1776 May p 23]	EB to	III, 268
1776 May 30	EB to	III, 268–9
1776 June	WB fr	**8** 190–2
[1776 June]	JB and	**B**
	RBsr to	**8** 165–6
		ext ½p.
1776 July 23	JB to	**B**
		8 167 ext
		½ p.
[1776 Aug a 15]	EB to	III, 288–9
1776 Aug 15	WB to	**B**
		8 168–9
		ext ½ p.
1776 Oct 2	JB to	III, 291–2
1776 Oct 9	EB to	III, 292
1776 Oct 10	EB to	III, 292–3
1776 Oct 29	WB to	**B**
		8 172 ext
		½p.
1776 [Oct]	WB to	**8** 172
		5 lines
1776 Nov 2	EB and	III, 298–
	RBsr to	300
1776 Nov 6	WB to	**B**
[1776 Nov c 8]	EB to	III, 300–1
[1776 Nov 9]	RBsr to	**B**
1776 Dec 9	EB to	III, 302–3
[1776 Dec 18]	WB to	**B**
		8 180 ext
		½p.
[1776 Dec a 22]	EB fr	**8** 179
[1776 Dec 22]	EB to	III, 305–6
[1776]	RBsr fr	**8** 192
[1777] Jan 12	WB to	III, 317–18
[1777 Jan 13]	EB to	III, 318–19
1777 Jan 15	EB to	III, 319–20
[1777 Jan 21]	EB to	III, 320–1

1780 Jan 24	EB to	IV, 199–200
[1780 May 16]	EB to	IV, 238–9
1780 May 24	EB to	IV, 240–1
[1780 June 2]	WB to	B
1780 June 7	RBsr to	A
		1 II, 350–2
[1780 June 20]	WB to	B
1780 June 29	JB to	B
1780 July 18	JB and	B
	WB to	62 83 ext
		7 lines
[1780 July]	RBsr and	B
	WB to	
1780 Aug 4	RBjr to	B
1780 Aug 11	JB to	B
1780 Sept 4	WB to	B
1780 Sept 26	EB to	IV, 293–4
[1780 Oct a 6]	WB to	B
1780 Oct 15	EB and	IV, 315
	JB to	
1780 Nov [2]	EB to	IV, 318–19
[1780 Nov 3]	RBsr to	B
1780 Nov 17	WB to	B
1780 Nov 28	WB to	B
1780 Dec 27	RBsr to	B
[1781 Jan 7]	EB to	IV, 328–30
1781 Jan 7	EB to	IV, 330–3
1781 Jan 14	RBsr to	B
[1781 Jan 20]	RBsr to	B
1781 Mar 16	RBsr to	A
		1 II, 403–6
1781 Apr 7	JB to	B
1781 Sept 2	EB to	IV, 369–70
1781 Oct 4	RBsr to	B
1781 Nov 14	JB to	B
[1781 Nov]	JB and	B
	RBsr to	
1781 Dec 17	JB to	B
1782 Jan 5, 6	RBsr to	B
1782 Jan 15	JB to,	B
	and Mrs. Champion	
1782 Feb 28	JB to	B
1782 Mar 3, 4	JB and	B
	RBjr to	
1782 Mar 12	JB to	B
1782 Mar 16	JB to	B
1782 Mar 20	JB to	B
	[Champion]	

[1782 Mar 24]	JB to	B
1782 Mar 29	JB to	B
1782 Aug 4	RBsr to	B
1782 Aug 5	WB to	B
1782 Aug 12	RBjr to	A
1783 June 4	EB to	v, 96–7
[1783 Aug] 26	JB to	B
1783 Sept 13	RBsr to	v, 113–14
1783 Sept 17	RBsr to	B
1784 May 7	JB to	B
1784 Oct 2	EB to	v, 172–4
[1784]	WB to	B
1787 Oct 5	WB to	B
1788 Nov 11	WB to	B
n.d. Sunday	EB and	IX, 449
	WB to	

CHAMPION, Mrs. Richard

1778 Apr 9	JB to	B
[1779 Dec]	JB to,	B
	and Champion	
[1780 Jan 8]	JB to	B
1780 July 21	JB to	B
[1781 Mar] 13	EB and	IV, 343
	JB to	
1781 Apr 25	JB to	B
1782 Jan 15	JB to,	B
	and Champion	
1784 Sept 5	JB to	B
		62 101n
		ext 2 lines

CHANNON, L.

1782 May 18	EB fr	A
1782 June 17	EB fr	A

CHAPMAN, William

1774 Nov 24	EB fr	A

CHAPMAN, Rev. Dr. W.

1779 Nov 19	EB fr	A
1779 Dec 8	EB fr	A
1779 Dec 21	EB fr	A

CHARLEMONT, James Caulfeild, 1st Earl of

1769 May [9]	EB to	II, 22–5

Charlemont, 1st Earl of (*cont.*)

1769 May 19	EB fr	**A**	
			1 I, 163–7
[1772 Sept *a* 4]	EB to		II, 546–7
1772 Sept 4	EB to		II, 332–3
1772 Sept 8	EB fr	**A**	
1776 June 4	EB to		III, 270–1
1779 Mar 30	EB fr	**A**	
1782 June 12	EB to		IV, 459–60
1783 Feb 20	EB fr	**A**	
1783 June 16	EB fr	**A**	
1783 Aug 5	EB to		V, 102–3
1785 Aug 7	EB to		V, 219–20
1786 Oct [22]	EB to		V, 286–7
1787 June 1	EB to		V, 333
1787 July 10	EB to		V, 343
1789 Mar 19	EB to		V, 451–2
1789 Mar 24	EB fr	**B**	
			29 89, 367–8 ext 1 p
1789 Apr 4	EB to		V, 458–62
1789 May 26, 27	EB to		V, 474–8
1789 May 29	EB fr	**A**	
			29 368
1789 July 4	EB fr	**A**	
			29 368–9
1789 July 10	EB to		VI, 1–4
1789 Aug 9	EB to		VI, 9–12
1790 May 25	EB to		VI, 117–19
1790 June 26	EB fr		VI, 123–4
1790 July 2	EB to		VI, 124–5
1791 Aug 8	EB to		VI, 330–2
1791 Aug 13	EB fr	**A**	
			1 III, 250–2 part omitted
1791 Dec 29	EB to		VI, 472
1793 Oct 5	EB fr	**A**	

CHATHAM, John Pitt, 2nd Earl of

1794 Dec 20	EB to		VIII, 100–1
1794 Dec 21	EB fr	**I**	

CHÂTILLON, Comte de

1797 Jan 26	EB fr	**B**	

CHESTER, Bishop of
See MARKHAM

CHETWYND, George

1777 Oct ⟨7⟩	EB to		III, 380

CHEVELEY, Jameneau

1780 Feb 20	EB fr	**A**	

CHOISEUL, Louise-Honorine (*née* Crozat du Châtel), Duchesse de

1791 Apr 7	EB fr	**B**	

CHOLMONDELEY, George James Cholmondeley, 4th Earl of

1783 Sept 29	EB fr	**A**	

CHRISTIE, Thomas

[1788 Aug *p* 29]	EB to		V, 412

CHRYSEL, Christopher

1782 Mar 25	EB fr	**A**	

CICÉ, Augustin-Marie Champion de Cicé, Vicomte de

1791 Jan 24	EB to		VI, 206–8
1793 Feb 15	EB fr	**B**	

CLANRICARDE, John Smith de Burgh, 11th Earl of

1770 Apr 17	EB fr	**A**	
1773 Nov 17	EB fr	**A**	

CLARE, 1st Viscount
See NUGENT, 1st Earl

CLARENCE, William, Duke of; later William IV, King of England

1791 Feb 8	EB to		VI, 219–20

CLARKE, Rev. Dr. Thomas Brooke

1785 Apr 5	EB fr	**A**	

CLEAVER, John

1767 Jan 26	EB fr	**A**	
1774 May 28	EB to		II, 537–8

Cleaver, John (*cont.*)
1774 June 1   EB fr   **B**

CLEMENCEAU
French judge
[1794]   EB fr   **B**

CLERKE, Robert
1774 Dec 15   EB fr   **A**

CLONFERT, Bishop of
See MARLAY

CLOOTS, Jean-Baptiste du Val-de-
Grace ('Anacharsis'), Baron de
1790 May 12   EB fr   VI, 109–15*
[1790 Aug]   EB to   VI, 135–6

CLOSELLE, Marquise de
1791 Aug 25   EB fr   **B**

COATS, William
[1791 Feb 26]   EB fr   **A**

COGGAN, Charles Thomas
1782 May 3   EB fr   **A**

COIGNY, Ange-Augustin-Gabriel
Franquetot, Comte de
1793 Nov 23   EB fr   **B**
1793 Nov 25   EB fr   **B**
[1793 Nov 28]   EB fr   **B**
1796 Feb 12   EB fr   **B**
[1796] Apr 6   EB fr   **B**

COLEBROOKE, Sir George, 2nd
Baronet
1794 Dec 14   EB to   VIII, 99–
100

COLLES, Richard
1788 Dec 14   EB fr   **A**

COLQUHOUN, Patrick
1784 July 24   EB fr   **B**

* Published as *Addresse d'un Prussien
à un Anglais*, Paris, 1790.

COLTHURST, Sir John Conway,
2nd Baronet
1776 Apr 20   EB fr   **A**

COMERFORD, Garrett
1778 Apr 11   EB fr   **B**

CONWAY, General Henry Seymour
[1765 July *p* 10]   WB to   **I**
[1782] Apr 23   EB to   IV, 444
1782 Apr 23   EB fr   **BE**
1782 Aug 27   EB fr   **A**
1791 Aug 9   EB fr   **A**

CONWAY, P.
1782 Nov 22   EB fr   **A**

COOK, George
1778 July 29   WB to   **B**

COOPER, Sir Grey, 3rd Baronet
1765 Nov 8   WB fr   **I** 34 I,
619–20,
ext 4 lines
1765 Dec 10   EB to   I, 219
[Cooper]
1766 Mar 7   WB fr   **I** 34 II,
23, abs 4
lines
1766 Mar 12   WB to   **I** 34 II,
23–4, abs
6 lines
1766 Apr 9   WB fr   **I** 34 II,
34, abs 4
lines
1766 June 30   WB fr   **I** 34 II,
55, abs 8
lines
1766 June 30   WB fr   **I** 34 II,
55, abs 4
lines
1766 Nov 28   WB fr   **I** 34 II,
95, abs 3
lines
[1775 Dec 15]   EB fr   **A**
1776 Mar 19   EB fr   **A**
[1776 Nov *a* 2]   EB fr   **8** 175
7 lines

[1776 Nov p 2]	EB fr	**8** 176 abs 7 lines	
1776 Dec 31	EB fr	A	
1777 Jan 3	EB fr	A	
[1777 Apr]	EB fr	A	
1778 July a 18	EB to	3 VI, 205 abs 3 lines	
1778 July 20	EB fr	**B** 3 VI, 205 ext 5 lines	
1778 July 31	EB fr	**B**	
1780 July 18	EB to	IV, 257–8	
1781 [Dec 1]	EB to	**50** XXII, 766, abs 2 lines	
1781 Dec 3	EB fr	**50** XXII, 766, abs 3 lines	
1782 Mar 28	EB fr	A	
1782 Apr 14	EB fr	A	

COOPER, Rev. Dr. Samuel

1790 Nov 10	EB fr	A	

CORK, Bishop of
See **MOYLAN**

CORMATIN-DESOTTEUX,
Pierre-Marie-Félicité, Baron de

1793 Jan 28	EB fr	**B**	

CORNWALL, Charles Wolfran

[1769] July 22	EB fr	A	
1788 May 1	EB to	V, 393–5	

CORNWALLIS, Charles Cornwallis 2nd Earl

1788 June 25	WB to	**I**	
1788 June 26	WB to	**I**	
1788 July 15	WB to	**I**	
1788 Nov 24	WB to	**I**	
1788 Dec 16	WB to	**I**	
1788 Dec 17	WB to	**I**	
1788 Dec 26	WB to	**I**	
1789 Apr 8	WB to	**I**	
1790 Nov 11	WB to	**I**	

CORSAR, Frederick

1763 Apr 20, 21	WB fr	**B** **62** 53n abs and ext 1p	

COSWAY, Richard

1790 Jan	EB to	VI, 78	

COUNSEL FOR THE MANAGERS

1788 May 26	EB to	V, 398–9	

COURTENAY, William Courtenay, 2nd Viscount

1780 July 10	EB fr	A	
1780 July 24	EB to	IV, 258–60	

COWPER, General Spencer

1786 Mar 20	EB fr	A	

COXE, Richard Hippisley

1779 June 24	EB to	IV, 92	

CRABBE, George

[1781 Feb]	EB fr	IV, 337–9	
[1781] Mar 27	EB fr	A **1** II, 413–15	
[1781] June 26	EB fr	**BE**	
1781 Aug 24	EB fr	A **1** II, 429–31	
[1781] Aug 24	JB fr	A	
1781 Oct 3	EB fr	**B**	
[1781]	EB fr	A	
1782 Apr a 16	EB to	**20** 107, abs 6 lines	
1782 Apr 16	EB fr	A **1** II, 475–6	
1782 May 15	EB fr	IV, 453–4	
[1782] Aug 26	EB fr	A	
1782 Dec 28	EB to	V, 59	
1783 Oct 28	EB fr	A	
[1783] Wednesday	EB fr	A	
1785 Mar 9	EB fr	V, 208	
1786 Apr 28	EB fr	A	
1789 Mar 3	RBjr to	**35** 201n, ext 7 lines	

CRAUFURD, James; later (1797) 2nd Baronet

1793 Aug 22	EB fr	A
1794 May 13	EB fr	A
1794 July 5	EB fr	A
1794 Sept 16	EB fr	A

CRAUFURD, John

[1782] Mar 28	EB fr	A

CRAUFURD, P. George

1782 June 19	EB fr	A

CRAVEN, Lady Elizabeth (née Berkeley), Baroness

[1780 Sept 22]	EB fr	A
[1782] Saturday	EB fr	A

CRAVEN, William Craven, 6th Baron

[1775 Nov]	EB fr	A

CRESPIGNY, Philip

1786 May 18	EB fr	A

CREWE, Mrs. John

1792 Aug 24	EB to	IX, 467
[1793 Sept c 15]	EB to	VII, 424–6
1794 Nov [c 22]	EB to	VIII, 80–4
[1795 Mar c 13]	EB to	VIII, 188
[1795 Mar c 23]	EB to	VIII, 215–16
[1795 Apr 18]	EB to	VIII, 233–4
[1795 July]	EB to	VIII, 462
[1795 Aug p 11]	EB to	VIII, 299–305
[1795] Wednesday	JB fr	B
1796 Feb 26	EB to	VIII, 394–5
1796 Mar 3	EB to	VIII, 399–401
1796 Mar 17	EB to	VIII, 442–3
1796 Nov 7, 8	EB to	IX, 106–8
1796 Nov 23	EB to	IX, 129–31
1796 Dec 27	EB to	IX, 206–9
1797 May 21	EB to	IX, 356–7

CROPLEY, Mrs William

1786 July 6	EB fr	A

CROTTY, Mrs David

1792 June 1	EB fr	C

CRUGER, Henry, Jr.

1774 July 13	EB fr	III, 10–11

CRUGER, John

1771 June 9	EB to	II, 213
1772 June 30	EB to	II, 308–10
1773 Jan 14	EB fr	A
1773 Feb 2	EB fr	A
1773 Mar 1	EB fr	A
1773 Apr 6	EB fr	A
1773 Apr 16	EB to	II, 428–30
1773 June 24	EB fr	A
1773 Aug 3	EB fr	A
1773 Oct 6	EB fr	A
1774 May 4	EB fr	A
1775 May 4	EB fr	R
		30 298–9, abs and ext 6 lines

CULLEN, C.

1792 Jan 2	EB fr	A

CUMBERLAND, Richard

[1777] Feb 15	EB fr	A
1790 Nov 11	EB fr	A
		9 II, 111 ext ½p
1790 Nov 13	EB to	VI, 157–8

CUPPAGE, Captain William; later (1794) Major

1789 Sept 2	EB to	VI, 13–14
1790 Sept 28	EB to	VI, 137–8
1792 May 13	WB to	A
		62 74n, 91 ext 8 lines
1792 May 16	EB to	VII, 142
1793 Dec 17	EB to	VII, 506
1795 Dec 16	EB to	VIII, 359
[1795 Dec p 16]	EB to	VIII, 360–1
[1796 Apr c 15]	EB fr	VIII, 458–9

[1797] Feb 10	JB fr	A
n.d. Wednesday EB to		IX, 450

CURRY, Dr. John

1764 Dec 15	EB fr	A
1765 Feb 24	EB fr	A
1765 June 8	EB fr	I, 201–3
1778 Apr 29	EB fr	A
1778 June 7	EB fr	A
1778 June 20, 23	EB fr	A
1778 Aug 12	EB fr	A
1778 Aug 18	EB fr	A
		1 II, 237–8
1779 Aug 6	EB fr	A
		1 II, 281–2
[1779 Aug 14]	EB to	IV, 117–20
1779 Sept 4	EB fr	A
		1 II, 305–8

CURSETJI Manuar

1781 Oct 3	EB fr, and Manuar Ratanji	A
1781 Oct 14	EB fr, and Manuar Ratanji	A
1781 Oct 24	EB fr	B
1795 Oct 25	EB fr	A

CURSON, Samuel

1781 Nov 28	EB fr	A
1781 Dec 3	EB fr	A

CURZON, A[ssheton]

1782 Apr 23	EB fr	A

DAGGE, Henry

1781 Mar 7	EB to	IV, 340–1
1782 Apr 21	EB to	IV, 443

DALRYMPLE, Sir David
See **HAILES**

DALRYMPLE, Sir John, 4th Baronet

1782 May 17	EB fr	A
1784 Apr 8	EB fr	B
[1784] Apr 13	EB fr	B
1784 June 15	EB fr	A
[1784] July 6	EB fr	A
[1784] July 8	EB fr	A
[1785] Mar 22	EB fr	B
[1785] Mar 23	EB fr	A
1785 Mar 30	EB fr	A
[1785] Apr 3	EB fr	B
[1786] Mar 26	EB fr	A

DALTON, Lieutenant General Edward, Count

1793 July 27	EB fr	VII, 379–80
1793 Aug 6	EB to	VII, 381–5

DALY, F. A.

1766 Nov 4	EB fr	B

DALY, Richard

1782 Apr 8	EB fr	A

DALZEL, Andrew

1784 July 20	EB fr	B

DALZEL, Archibald

1779 Dec 22	EB fr	A

DAMARTIN, Abbé M. R.

1790 Dec 18	EB fr	B

DANCEL, [Jean-Charles-Richard]

1796 June 9	EB fr	B

DANET, M.

1774 Dec 20	EB fr	A

DARCY, Count Patrick

1775 Oct 5	EB to	III, 228–9

DARTMOUTH, William Legge, 2nd Earl of

[1766 July 18]	EB to	I, 260–1
[1775 May 10]	EB fr	A
[1775 May 11]	EB to	III, 155

DASHKOV, Prince Pavel Mikhailovich

1780 Sept 19	EB fr	A

DASHKOVA, Princess Ekaterina
Romanovna

[1780]	EB fr	A

DAUBENY, [John]

1778 Mar 26	EB to	IX, 418–19
1778 Mar 27	EB to	IX, 419

DAULIS, Bishop of
See HAY

DAVERS, Sir Charles, 6th Baronet

[1784] Sunday	EB fr	A

DAVIES, Thomas

1774 June 28	EB to	II, 545–6

DAVISON, [Alexander]

1775 Jan 27	EB fr	A

DAVISON, Mrs. Elizabeth

1786 May 18	EB fr	A

DECLONARD, Masterson

[1782 May p 14]	EB fr	A

DECOTTE, Peter

1795 July 20	EB fr	A

DECRÉTOT, Jean-Baptiste

1789 June 22	RBjr fr	B
1789 June 29	RBjr fr	B
1790 Sept 30	RBjr fr	B

DE LANCEY, James

1771 June 9	EB to	II, 215–18
1771 Dec 4	EB to	II, 289–92
1772 June 30	EB to	II, 311–12
1772 Aug 20	EB to	II, 326–30
1772 Dec 31	EB to	II, 398–9
1773 Apr 7	EB fr	A
1773 July 7	EB fr	A
1773 Aug 2	EB to	II, 445–7
1774 Jan 5	EB to	II, 504–7
1775 Mar 14	EB to	III, 137–8

DELUC, Jean André

1791 Sept 13	EB fr	B

1792 May 8	EB to	VII, 138

DEMPSTER, George

[1765 Nov a 30]	WB to	I
1767 Nov 11	EB fr	A
[1768 Sept a 26]	EB to	IX, 394
1768 Sept 26	EB fr	A
1772 Aug 4	EB fr	II, 321–3
[1772 Sept]	EB to	II, 339–40
1776 June 8	EB fr	A
[1777 June]	EB fr	A
1777 July 3	EB fr	A
1780 Jan 18	EB fr	A
1781 May 26	EB fr	A
1792 Feb 22	EB to	VII, 67–8
1792 Mar 10	EB fr	A

DEMPSY, Joannes

1788 July 26	EB fr	A

DENNIS, William

1757 May p 6	EB fr	**10** 210, abs 1 line
[1761]	EB to	I, 143–4 (abs)
[1770] Apr [3, 6]	WB to	II, 126–9

DEPONT, Charles-Jean-François

1786 Jan 15	EB fr	B **22** VIII (1951), 172–3
1789 Nov 4	EB fr	VI, 31–2
[1789 Nov]	EB to	VI, 39–50
1789 Dec 29	EB fr	VI, 59–61
1790 Nov 1	EB to	**3** III, 333–563*
1790 Dec 6	EB fr	B **22**†
[1790]	EB fr‡	A

* Burke's *Reflections* (Todd, 142–66).
† Published as *Answer to the Reflections*; see *English*, VIII (1951), 175–8.
‡ Written, according to Nichols, *Literary History* (VI, 123–5), not by Depont but by Thomas Pitt, 1st Baron Camelford.

DERMOTT, Anthony
1779 Aug 9   EB fr   **A**
                             1 II, 290
[1779] Aug 17   EB to   IV 120–1
1779 Aug 23   EB fr   **A**

DESBOROW, Captain Lieutenant
  John
1783 Apr 11   EB fr   **A**

DESFRANÇOIS, Abbé Louis-
  Antoine
1765 Mar 6   EB fr   I, 187–8

DESMOULINS, John
1784 Aug 2   EB fr   **A**

DEVEREUX, J. E.
1795 Oct 19   EB to   VIII, 327–9

DEVEREUX, Robert
1774 Feb 21   EB fr   **A**

DEVEREUX, Sidney
1791 Mar 4   EB fr   **42** LXIX
                             (Jan–June
                             1791), 604

DEVISME, Louis   **AD**
1765 Oct 4   WB to

DEVONSHIRE, William Cavendish
  5th Duke of
1795 Oct 11   EB to   VIII, 183–5

DEVONSHIRE, Georgiana (*née*
  Spencer), Duchess of
[1778 Mar 20] EB to,   III, 421–3
                 and Countess
                 Spencer
1780 Mar 7   EB to   IV, 212–13

DEYZAC
1793 Sept 14   EB fr   **B**

DICKENS, Rev. Dr. Samuel
1778 Feb 7   EB fr   **A**
1779 Aug 7   EB fr   **A**

1779 Aug 21   EB fr   **A**

DIGBY, Henry Digby, 7th Baron
1782 Apr 23   EB to   IV, 445–6

DIGNAN, David Brown
1779 Sept 16   EB fr   **B**
1779 Sept 25   EB to   IV, 133–5
[1779] Oct 10   EB fr   **B**
1780 Jan 17   EB fr   **B**
1780 Jan 22   EB fr   **B**

DILLON LEE, Charles; later
  (1787) 12th Viscount Dillon
1782 Apr 2   EB fr   **B**

DODGE, Rev. Dr. Robert
1786 Mar 24   EB fr   **A**
1786 May 15   EB fr   **A**
1791 Mar 26   EB fr   VI, 239–40
1791 Sept 20   EB fr   **A**
1792 Feb 29   EB to   VII, 84–6

DODSLEY, James
1764 Feb 9   EB to   I, 174–5
                 [J. Dodsley]
[1774 June *a* 2] EB to   X, 4
1775 Aug 9   RBsr to **AB**
1782 Aug [*a* 22] EB to   V, 30–1
n.y. Apr 7   RBjr to **E**
n.d.   EB to   IX, 450
                 [J. Dodsley]

DODSLEY, Robert
[1759 Sept *c* 6] EB to   I, 127–8
n.d.   EB to   IX, 470

DODWELL, Henry
1773 Nov *a* 11 EB fr   **A**

DOLPHIN, Oliver
1790 Jan 12   EB to   VI, 66–7
1793 Nov 28   EB to   VII, 493–4
1794 Jan 30   EB to   IX, 467
1795 Aug 5   EB to   VIII, 295

DONSTON, George
1780 Apr 29   EB fr   **A**

DORSET, John Frederick Sackville,
  3rd Duke of

1791 Aug 17	EB to	VI, 348–9
1791 Aug 20	EB fr	A
		1 III, 283–5
1791 Aug 21	EB to	VI, 365–6
1791 Sept 6	EB to	VI, 385–6
1791 Sept 11	EB to	VI, 393
1791 Sept 14	EB to	VI, 394–6

DOUCE & RIVINGTON

1796 Nov 29	EB fr	A

DOUGLAS, John, Bishop of
  Carlisle; later (1791) Bishop of
  Salisbury

[1790 Jan]	EB and others to	VI, 77
1790 Nov 7	EB fr	A
1790 Nov 9	EB to	VI, 157
1791 June 27	EB to	VI, 278–9
1791 July 6	EB to	VI, 282–3
1791 July 23	EB to	VI, 305
1791 July 31	EB to	VI, 308–10
1791 Aug 3	EB fr	A
1791 Aug 7	EB fr	A
1792 Mar 13	EB to	VII, 98

DOUGLAS, Sylvester; later (1800)
  1st Baron Glenbervie

1793 Nov 8	EB fr	A
1793 Nov 14	EB to	VII, 484–7
1793 Dec 30	EB fr	B
[1793 Dec p 30]	EB to	VII, 509–11
1794 Dec 16	EB fr	A

DOUGLASS, John, Catholic Vicar-
  apostolic of the London District,
  Bishop in partibus 1790–1812

1796 June 5	EB to	IX, 45–6
1796 June 21	EB fr	B

DOWDESWELL, Charles William

1775 Sept 3	EB fr	AL

DOWDESWELL, Edward
  Christopher

[1792 Aug]	EB fr	A

1792 Oct 14	EB fr	A

DOWDESWELL, William

[1767] Jan 4	[EB] fr	P
1767 Jan [c 8]	EB to	I, 289–90
1767 Jan 26	EB fr	B
1767 May 26	EB fr	B
1769 Jan 4	EB fr	P
1769 July 20	EB fr	A
1769 Aug 10	EB fr	II, 53–4
1769 Sept 5	EB fr	II, 69–71
1770 July 8	EB fr	P
[1771 Feb c 2]	EB to	II, 189
1771 Feb 2	EB fr	II, 190
1771 Mar [27]	EB fr, and M. of Rockingham	II, 204–5
1772 May 5	EB fr	P
1772 Oct 18	EB fr	P
1772 Oct 27	EB to	II, 349–53
1772 Nov 3	EB fr	II, 360–1
1772 Nov 6, 7	EB to	II, 361–6
1772 Nov 8	EB fr	II, 366–7
1772 Dec 5	EB fr	P
1774 Sept 18	EB fr	AL

DOWDESWELL, Mrs. William

1774 Sept [7]	EB to	III, 21–2
[1774] Oct 17	EB fr	AL
[1774] Nov 15	WB fr	A
1775 June 7	EB fr	AL
1775 June 13	EB to	III, 168–9
1775 June 21	EB fr	AL
[1775] Dec 23	EB fr	AL
1775 Dec 30	EB to	III, 241–2
[1776] Jan 26	EB fr	A
[1776] Aug 21	EB fr	AL
1778 Nov 14	EB to	IV, 27–8

DRAKE, William, Jr.

1791 Sept 14	EB fr	A

DRENNAN, William

1793 Oct 27	RBjr fr	A
1794 Jan 24	RBjr fr	A

DROMORE, Bishop of
See PERCY

DRUMGOLD, Colonel John			
1773 June 5	EB fr	**B**	
1773 Dec 26	EB fr	**A**	
1776 Jan 1	EB fr	**A**	
[1777]	EB fr	**B**	
DUANE, James			
1772 Oct [a 7]	EB to		II, 341–2
1773 Apr 7	EB fr	**A**	
DUBLIN, Archbishop of			
See TROY			
DUBLIN, Lord Mayor of			
See SANKEY			
DU BOYS, Abbé [Sebastien-			
Geneviéve]			
1796 Jan 19	EB fr	**B**	
DU BUISSON, Peter			
1782 May 5	EB fr	**A**	
DU DEFFAND, Marie (née de			
Vichy-Champrond), Marquise			
1774 Apr 5	EB fr	**A**	
		1 I, 454–5	
DUHIGG, Bartholomew			
1797 Jan 30	EB fr	**A**	
DUNANT, William			
1782 May 10	EB fr	**B**	
1782 Oct 25	EB fr	**A**	
DUNDAS, Henry			
[1782 Mar 26]	EB fr	**A**	
[1782 Apr 26]	EB fr	**A**	
1782 July 4	RBsr to	**P**	
1782 July 11	RBsr to	**P**	
1782 Aug 2	RBsr to	**P**	
1783 Mar 1	EB to		V, 67–9
1784 Apr 7	EB fr		V, 136–7
1787 Mar 25	EB to		V, 312–15
[1787] Mar 26	EB fr		V, 315–16
[1787 Mar 29]	EB to		V, 316–17
1787 Apr 1	EB to		V, 317–19
[1787] Apr 4	EB to		V,319–20

1787 Apr 5	EB to		V, 320–1
1787 Apr 7	EB to		V, 322–4
[1787 Apr 13]	EB to		V, 324–5
1787 Apr 14	EB to		V, 326
1787 Apr 20	EB to		V, 328–9
1787 June 1	EB to		V, 333–5
1787 Oct 11	EB to		V, 352–3
[1787 Oct 29]	EB to		V, 355–6
1787 Nov 1	EB to		V, 356–7
1787 Dec 7	EB to		V, 360–3
1787 Dec 8	EB fr		V, 363–4
1787 Dec 9	EB to		V, 364–6
1787 Dec 24	EB fr		V, 371
[1791 Apr 11]	EB fr	**A**	
1791 Apr 22	EB to		VI, 249–52
[1791 July 1]	EB to		VI, 279–80
1791 Aug 9	RBjr to	**C**	
[1791] Aug 12	EB fr	**A**	
1791 Aug 30	RBjr to	**AF**	
1791 Sept 10	RBjr to	**AF**	
1791 Sept 18	EB to		VI, 400–1
[1791 Sept 20]	EB to		VI, 403–4
1791 Sept 20	RBjr fr		VI, 404–5
1791 Sept 22	EB fr	**B**	
1791 [Sept] 23	EB to		VI, 409
			IX, 437–8
1791 Sept 26	EB fr		VI, 415
1791 Sept 30	EB to		VI, 418–22
1791 Oct 6	EB fr		VI, 428–9
1791 Oct 6	RBjr fr		VI, 429–30
[1791 Oct p 21]	RBjr	**AL**	
[1791 Dec p 16]	RBjr to		VI, 467–9
[1791 Dec p 16]	RBjr to	**I**	
[1791 Dec a 25]	RBjr to	**I**	
[1791 Dec a 25]	RBjr to	**I**	
[1791 Dec a 25]	RBjr to	**I**	
1791 Dec 25	RBjr fr		VI, 469–70
1791 Dec 25	RBjr to	**I**	
1791 Dec 25	RBjr to	**I**	
1791 Dec 27	RBjr to		VI, 471
[1791 Dec]	RBjr to	**I**	
[1792 Jan] 12	RBjr to		VII, 22–9
[1792] Jan 20	RBjr fr		VII, 33–4
[1792 Jan p 20]	RBjr to		VII, 34–7
1792 Mar 14	RBjr	**AL**	
1792 Mar 21	RBjr fr	**A**	
1792 Mar 22	EB to		VII, 107–17
[1792] Mar 25	EB fr	**A**	

Dundas, Henry (*cont.*)

1792 Apr 9	EB to	VII, 122–5
1792 Apr 18	RBjr to	VII, 126–8
1792 [May] 6	RBjr to	VII, 130–8
1792 May 14	RBjr to	AM
1792 May 16	RBjr fr	A
1792 June 5	RBjr to	AL
[1792 June *a* 17]	RBjr to	I
1792 June 17	RBjr to	I
1792 June 22	RBjr fr	A
1792 July 20	RBjr to	A
1792 July 29	RBjr to	I
1792 July 29	RBjr to	AL
1792 July 31	RBjr to	A
		1 IV, 61–4
1792 Aug 1	RBjr fr	A
		1 III, 482–3
1792 Aug 3	RBjr to	I
[1792 Sept *c* 19]	EB to	VII, 215–17
	[Dundas]	
1792 Sept 21	EB fr	VII, 223
[1792 Sept]	RBjr to	I
1792 Oct 8	EB to	VII, 246–8
1792 Oct 8	EB to	VII, 248–55
1792 Oct 19	EB fr	VII, 275–6
1792 Oct 28	EB to	VII, 279–80
1792 Dec 27	RBjr to	VII, 324–8
[1792 Dec 27]	EB to	VII, 328
1793 Jan 2	RBjr fr	A
1793 Jan 23	RBjr to	I
1793 June 7	EB to	VII, 371–4
1793 June 27	EB to	VII, 377
	[Dundas]	
1793 July 10	EB to	VII, 377–8
1793 July 12	EB fr	B
1793 July 30	RBjr to	I
1793 Oct 8	EB to	VII, 445–6
1793 Oct 13	EB fr	VII, 449–50
1793 Oct 16	EB to	VII, 451; X, 46
[1793 Oct 25]	EB to	VII, 464
1793 Oct 27	EB to	VII, 465–6
1793 Oct 28	RBjr to	I
1793 Oct 28	RBjr to	I
[1793] Oct 29	EB fr	VII, 468
1793 Nov 2	RBjr fr	I
1793 Nov 4	RBjr to	I
1793 Nov 5	RBjr to	I

1793	RBjr to	IX, 467
1794 Jan 4	RBjr and I	
	Dr. Hussey to	
1794 Nov 4	EB to	VIII, 71–2
1794 Nov 5	EB to	VIII, 72–3
[1795 Mar *c* 5]	EB to	VIII, 177
		IX, 443–4
[1795 Mar]	EB to	VIII, 218
1795 May 13	EB to	VIII, 239–41
1795 May 14	EB fr	VIII, 241
1795 June 5	EB to	VIII, 260–1
1795 Aug 30	EB to	VIII, 309–10
1795 Aug 31	EB fr	VIII, 310
1795 Sept 2	EB to	VIII, 310–11
1795 Sept 14	EB to	VIII, 316
[1795 Nov *c* 4]	EB to	VIII, 337
1795 Dec 6	EB to	VIII, 353–5
[1796 Feb *p* 3]	EB to	VIII, 384–6
1796 Mar 6	EB to	VIII, 401–2
[1796 Mar *c* 17]	EB to	VIII, 435–6
[1796 Mar *c* 17]	EB to	VIII, 436–7
[1796 Mar *c* 17]	EB to	VIII, 437–42
n.d. Sunday	RBsr to	P

DUNDAS, Sir Thomas, 2nd Baronet

[1783] May 4	EB fr	A

DUNKIN, William

1783 Oct 2, Nov 6	EB fr	A
1784 Jan 31	EB fr	B

DUNNING, John

1774 Oct 16	EB fr	A
n.d. Wednesday	E.B. fr	A

DU PAC BELLEGARDE, Baron

1796 June 10	EB fr	B

DUPONT, Pierre-Gaëton

[1789 Nov]	EB fr	B
	[Dupont]	
[1790 Oct 27]	EB fr	VI, 144–5
1790 Oct 28	EB to	VI, 145–9*
1790 Nov 30	EB fr	VI, 183–5
1790 Dec 13	EB fr	VI, 189–91
1791 Feb 21	EB fr	VI, 227–9

* Published in *Two Letters on the French Revolution* (Todd 171–2).

Dupont, Pierre-Gaëton (*cont*)

1791 May 29	EB fr	VI, 259–62
[1791 June 8]	EB fr	B
		38 XXV, No. 1 (Mar 1953), 49
1791 July 7	EB fr	VI, 283–9
1791 July 14	EB fr	B
		38 XXV, No. 1 (Mar 1953), 54–7
1791 July 21	EB fr	B
		38 XXV, No. 1 (Mar 1953), 58–9
1791 Aug 11	EB fr	VI, 337–9

DUPORT, Adrien-Jean-François

[1790 Mar *p* 29]	EB to	VI, 104–9

DURAS, Amédée-Bretagne-Malo de Durfort, styled Marquis de

[1791 Apr *p* 23]	EB fr	B
n.d.	EB fr	B

DURBIN, John; later (1778) knighted

1774 Dec 24	EB fr	A
1778 Mar 17	EB to	III, 420–1
	[Durbin]	
1779 June 19	EB fr	A
1779 June 24	EB fr	A

EARLSFORT, 1st Baron
See SCOTT

ECHALON, Degraindorge d'

1794 Jan 19	EB fr	B

EDEN, William; later (1789) 1st Baron Auckland

[1775 May 12]	EB fr	III, 156
[1775 May 12]	EB to	III, 157
[1775 May 21]	EB to	III, 157

[1775 May 21]	EB fr	III, 158
[1776] Mar 17	EB fr	III, 251–2
1776 [Mar] 17	EB to	III, 252–3
[1776] Mar 18	EB fr	A
		1 II, 94–5
1776 Aug 12	EB to	III, 287; IX, 413–14
[1776 Aug 14]	EB to	III, 287–8
	[Eden]	
1779 Sept 29	EB to	X, 5–6
[1779] Oct 8	EB fr	B
[1779] Nov 23	EB fr	A
1779 Nov 23	EB to	IV, 170
1781 Apr 18	EB fr	AL
1781 July 28	EB to	IV, 358–60
1782 Mar 22	EB fr	A
		1 II, 459–61
1782 Apr 5	EB to	IV, 432–3
[1782 Apr *c* 5]	EB to	X, 13–14
1784 May 13	EB fr	V, 145–9
1784 May 17	EB to	V, 150–1
1791 July 5	EB to	VI, 280–1
1791 Aug 12	EB fr	A
		1 III, 247–9
1795 Oct 28	EB fr	VIII, 333
1795 Oct 30	EB to	VIII, 334–5

EDGEWORTH DE FIRMONT, Abbé Henry Essex

1796 Sept 25	EB fr	A

EDWARDS, Bryan

1789 Dec 26	EB fr	A

EDWARDS, Judith

1782 May 16	EB fr	A

EDWARDS, J., Jr.

1794 May 26	EB fr	B

EFFINGHAM, Thomas Howard, 3rd Earl of

1780 Dec 14	EB fr	A

ELIOT, Edward Craggs Eliot, later (1784) 1st Baron

[1781 Jan]	JB fr	A

ELLIOT, Lady (Anna Maria
  Amyand); wife of Sir Gilbert
  Elliot, 4th Baronet

| 1787 Dec 13 | EB to | V, 368–9 |

ELLIOT, Sir Gilbert, 4th Baronet

[1782 Mar 7]	EB to	IX, 465
1783 Aug 14	EB fr	V, 106–7
1784 [Mar] 26	EB to	V, 134–5
1784 July 29, 30	EB fr	V, 162–4
1784 Aug 1	EB fr	B
[1784] Aug 3	EB to	V, 164–6
1784 Aug [p 5]	EB to	V, 166–7
[1784 Aug]	EB to	V, 168–9
1784 Oct 15	EB to	V, 178–9
1784 Nov 3	EB to	V, 179–80
1784 Nov 22	EB fr	V, 189–90
1785 Oct 28	EB to	V, 229–31
1786 Jan 8	EB to	V, 250–1
[1786 Feb c 20]	EB to	V, 259–60
[1786 Sept 6]	EB fr	V, 276–7
1786 Sept 26	EB to	V, 279–80
1786 Sept 26	RBjr to	C
1786 Dec 14	EB to	V, 298–300
1787 Jan 1	EB and JB to	V, 302–4
1787 May 10	EB to	V, 331–2
1787 Oct 17	EB to	V, 353–5
[1787 Dec a 12]	EB to	V, 367
1788 June 23	EB to	V, 402–3
1788 Sept 3	EB to	V, 413–15
1788 Sept 28	EB fr	V, 421–4
1789 Dec 29	EB fr	A
1790 Jan 3	EB to	VI, 61–4
[1790 Jan p 6]	EB to	VI, 64–5
1790 June 6	JB fr	A
1790 June 11	JB to	C
1790 Oct [28]	EB to	VI, 149–50
1790 Nov 6	EB fr	VI, 155–7
1790 Nov 19	EB fr	A
1790 Nov 29	EB to	VI, 176–80
[1791 Mar 15]	RBjr to	C
1792 Apr 3	EB to	VII, 121–2
1792 [Oct] 26	EB to	C
[1793 Sept 16]	EB to	VII, 428–9
[1793 Sept 18]	EB to	VII, 430–1
1793 Sept 22	EB to	VII, 431–6

| [1793] Oct 17 | RBjr to | C |
| 1793 Nov 19 | EB to | VII, 488–9 |

ELLIOT, Hugh

| 1786 July 29 | EB to | X, 17 |

ELLIOT, John
Correspondent at Bartholomew Close

| 1783 June 8 | RBsr to | C |

ELLIOT, William

1793 Sept 22	RBjr to	A
1795 Feb 24	EB to	VIII, 157–60
1795 May 26	EB to	B
		3 V, 109–29*
1795 June 21	EB to	VIII, 267–9

ELLIOTT, Ebenezer, Jr.

| [1796 June 23] | EB fr | A |
| 1796 July 20 | EB fr | A |

ELLIS, John

| [1775 Oct 23] | EB fr | A |

ELLIS, Rev. William

| 1779 Jan 1 | EB to | IV, 36 |

ELTON, Sir Abraham Isaac, 4th
  Baronet

[1774 Nov c 15]	EB to	III, 77–8
1777 Jan 22	EB fr	A
		1 II, 136–8
1777 Jan 30	EB to	III, 325–7
1780 June 12	EB fr	A
1780 Oct 28	EB fr	A
		1 II, 394–5
1780 Nov 1	EB to	IV, 317–18

ELWIN, Peter

| 1782 Apr 4 | EB to | IV, 431–2 |
| 1783 Apr 7 | EB fr | A |

* Published in *Two Letters on the Conduct of our Domestick Parties* (Todd, 255).

EMIN, Joseph
1757 Aug [*c* 7]   EB and   I, 120–2
               WB to
1785 Dec 25   RBjr fr   I
1789 Mar 29   EB to   V, 455–7

ERSKINE, Monsignor Charles
1794 Nov 11   EB fr   B
n.d. Saturday   EB fr   A

ERSKINE, Rev. Dr. John
1779 Apr 24   EB fr   IV, 62–4
1779 June 12   EB to   IV, 83–8
1779 July 16   EB fr   IV, 102–5

ERSKINE, Thomas
[1778] Nov 26   EB fr   A

EVANS
1775 Apr 13   EB fr,   A
             and others

EYRE, James
1790 Dec 13   EB fr   A

FALCONER, Dr. William
1790 Nov 14   EB to   VI, 158–60
1790 [Nov *a* 17] EB fr   A
1790 Nov 17   EB fr   A
1790 Dec 13   EB fr   A

FARR, Paul
[1775 Feb *c* 21] EB fr   J
1775 Mar 4   EB fr   III, 126–7
1775 May 1   EB fr   A
1775 May 27   EB fr   A
1775 June 20   EB fr   A
1775 Sept 30   EB fr   A
1775 Oct 7   EB fr   A
1775 Oct 14   EB fr   A
1775 Oct 18   EB fr   A
1775 Oct 19   EB fr   A
1775 Dec 11   EB fr   A
1775 Dec 14   EB and   AZ
            H. Cruger fr
1775 Dec 24   EB fr   A
1776 Feb 6   EB and   B
            H. Cruger fr

1776 Feb 7   EB fr   A
[1776 Feb 9]   EB and   III, 248–9
            H. Cruger to
1776 Feb 12   EB fr   A
1776 Feb 16   EB fr   A
1776 Mar 14   EB fr   A
1776 July 23   EB fr   A
1776 Aug 1   EB fr   A
1776 Nov 6   EB fr   A
1778 Jan 31   EB fr   A
1779 July 16   EB fr   A

FARRELL & JONES
Virginia Merchants
1777 Mar 24   EB fr   A
1777 Apr 5   EB fr   A

FAULKNER, George
1767 Jan 20   EB fr   B

FAWKENER, William
1788 Jan 30   EB to   V, 376–7
1791 Oct 5   EB fr   A

FAŸ, Elizabeth (*née* Hamilton),
   Comtesse de
[1791] Apr 1   EB fr   B
1791 June 16   EB fr   B

FAYDEL, Jean-Félix
1791 July 1   EB fr   B

FEAR, John
1777 Apr 6   EB fr   A

FÉNELON, Claude-Etienne
   Salignac de Fénelon, Chevalier de
1796 Feb 8   EB fr   B

FERNYHOUGH, Rev. William
1791 Feb 16   EB fr   A

FERRIS, Richard
1793 Dec 20   EB fr   B
1794 Jan 1   EB fr   B

FISHER, Richard
1781 Mar 26   EB fr   A

FITZGERALD, Gerald
1796 Apr 14   EB fr   A

FITZGERALD, Gibbon
1770 Feb 21   WB fr   A

FITZGERALD, Lord Robert
1791 Jan 28   EB fr   A
1791 July 5   EB to   VI, 281–2
                [Fitzgerald]

FITZGERALD, Robert
1766 Mar 20   EB fr   B
n.y. June 22   WB fr   B

FITZGERALD, William
1769 Aug 24   EB fr   A

FITZHERBERT, Mrs. Thomas
1789 May 26   EB to   V, 478–9

FITZHERBERT, William
1765 June 10   EB fr   A

FITZPATRICK, Richard
1782 [Apr] 13   EB to   IV, 442
1782 Apr 27   EB to   IV, 450–1
1782 Aug 4   EB fr   A

FITZWILLIAM, William
  Fitzwilliam, 4th Earl
1779 Sept 27   EB fr   A
1782 July [3]   EB to   V, 6–7
[1782 July 3]   EB fr   V, 7–8
1783 Jan 8   EB fr   A
[1783] June 22 EB fr   A
[1784] Apr 25   EB fr   A
[1784 May 13]   EB fr   V, 149–50
1784 Sept 18   EB fr   A
1784 Dec 19   EB fr   A
[1785 Sept 25] RBsr fr   V, 223
[1785 Oct 2]   EB fr   A
1787 June 17   EB to   V, 338–9
1787 Sept 10   EB fr   A
[1789] July 12 EB fr   A
[1789] Aug 6   EB fr   A
1789 Nov 12   EB to   VI, 34–7

[1790 June a 11] RBjr fr   A
[1790 June 11]   RBjr fr   A
[1790 June 27]   RBjr fr   A
[1790 June p 27] RBjr fr   A
1790 July 14   RBjr to   B
[1790 July 15]   RBjr fr   A
1790 July 29   RBjr to   VI, 125–30
[1790] Aug 8   RBjr fr   A
1790 Aug 16   RBjr to   B
[1790 Aug 21]   RBjr fr   A
1790 Aug 27   RBjr to   B
1790 Aug 31   RBjr to   B
[1790] Sept 8   RBjr to   B
[1790] Sept 15   BRjr fr   A
1790 Sept 27   RBjr to   B
1790 Oct 10   RBjr to   B
[1790] Oct 14   RBjr fr   A
1790 Oct 18   RBjr to   B
[1790 Oct 20]   RBjr fr   A
[1790 Nov a 1]   RBjr to   B
[1790] Nov 23   RBjr to   B
[1791] May 29   EB fr   A
[1791 May]   [RBjr] fr A
1791 June 5   EB to   VI, 271–6
1791 July 29   RBjr to   B
1791 Aug 4   EB to   VI, 312–14
1791 Sept 18   EB fr   VI, 401–2
1791 Sept 28   EB to   VI, 415–17
1791 Nov 21   EB to   VI, 449–53
[1791 Nov 26]   EB fr   A
[1792] Aug 4   RBjr fr   A
[1792] Aug 15   RBjr to   B
[1792 Aug a 17]   EB fr   A
1792 Aug 17   EB to   VII, 170–3
[1792] Sept 27   EB fr   A
1792 Oct 5   EB to   VII, 227–34
1792 Oct 6   RBjr to   VII, 235–46
1792 Oct 23   EB to   VII, 276–8
1792 Nov 29   EB to   VII, 306–18
[1793 Mar 23]   RBjr to   B
[1793 Mar p 23]   RBjr fr   A
1793 Aug 8   RBjr fr   VII, 394–5
[1793 Aug a 11]   RBjr fr   A
1793 Aug 11   RBjr to   B
1793 Aug 16   RBjr to   VII, 396–
                            410
1793 Aug 27   RBjr fr   VII, 416–19
1793 Aug 31   RBjr to   B

Fitzwilliam, 4th Earl (*cont.*)

[1793 Sept 29]	EB to,	**H**
	and D.	**3** v, 7–63*
	of Portland	
[1793] Nov 17	RBjr fr	**A**
1793 Nov 29	EB to	VII, 494–7
1794 Jan 12	RBjr to	**A**
1794 Jan 27	RBjr to	**A**
1794 Jan 29	RBjr fr	**A**
1794 Mar 18	RBjr to	**B**
1794 June 21	EB to	VII, 552–3
1794 June 26	EB fr	VII, 555
1794 June 27	RBjr to	VII, 555–6
1794 June 28	EB to	VII, 558–9
1794 Aug 4	EB fr	VII, 566–7
[1794 Aug *p* 4]	EB to	VII, 567–9
1794 Aug 31	EB to	VII, 578–9
1794 Sept 9	EB to	VIII, 8–9
[1794 Sept *c* 26]	EB to	VIII, 20–3
1794 Oct 21	EB to	VIII, 53–7
1794 Oct 21	EB fr	VIII, 57–9
1794 Nov 7	EB to	VIII, 74–6
[1794] Nov 18	EB fr	VIII, 78
[1794 Nov *c* 22]	EB to	VIII, 78–80
1795 Feb 10	EB to	VIII, 144–8
[1795 Feb *c* 26]	EB to	VIII, 161–2
1795 Mar 4	EB fr	VIII, 169–72
1795 Mar 9	EB fr	VIII, 180–2
1795 Mar [13]	EB to	VIII, 188–96
1795 Mar 20	EB fr	VIII, 209–10
1795 Mar 21	EB fr	VIII, 211–12
1795 Mar 25, 26	EB to	VIII, 216–18
1795 Apr 3	EB fr	VIII, 223
1795 Apr 6	EB fr	VIII, 224–5
[1795 Apr 11]	EB to	VIII, 225–6
[1795 Apr 12]	EB to	VIII, 226–30
[1795 Apr 14]	EB to	VIII, 230–1
[1795 May 9]	EB fr	VIII, 237–8
1795 May 10	EB to	VIII, 238–9
1795 May 15	EB to	VIII, 242–3

[1795 June 6]	EB fr	VIII, 262
[1795 June 28]	EB to	VIII, 276–7
[1795 June 30]	EB fr	VIII, 278–9
1795 July 5	EB to	VIII, 285–7
[1795 July *p* 5]	EB fr	VIII, 287–8
1795 Aug 8	EB to	VIII, 296–8
[1795] Aug 9	EB fr	VIII, 298–9
1795 Aug 12	EB to	VIII, 305–6
1795 Aug 16	EB to	VIII, 306–8
[1795 Oct 31]	EB fr	VIII, 336
1795 Dec 9	EB to	VIII, 357–8
1795 Dec 16	EB to	VIII, 358–9
1795 Dec 17	EB fr	VIII, 361–2
1795	EB to	**3** VI, 9–112*
1796 Jan 7	EB to	VIII, 367–8
[1796 Jan *p* 7]	EB fr	**A**
[1796] Jan 10	EB to	VIII, 368–9
1796 Jan [17]	EB to	VIII, 373–4
1796 Feb 18	EB fr	VIII, 386–8
1796 Mar 6	EB to	VIII, 402–3
1796 Mar 8	EB fr	VIII, 410–11
[1796] July 9	EB fr	IX, 55–6
1796 July 11	EB to	IX, 56–7
1796 Aug 23	EB to	IX, 67–8
1796 Aug 30	EB fr	IX, 74–6
1796 Sept 2	EB to	IX, 77–80
[1796] Sept 17	EB fr	**A**
1796 Sept 23	EB to	IX, 88–90
1796 Sept 26	EB to	IX, 90
[1796 Sept 28]	EB fr	**A**
1796 Oct 30	EB to	IX, 101–2
1796 Nov 10	EB fr	**A**
		1 IV, 355–9
1796 Nov 20	EB to	IX, 120–4
[1796] Nov 27	EB fr	IX, 136–8
1796 Nov 30	EB to	IX, 139
1796 Dec 5	EB fr	IX, 144–6
1796 Dec 6	EB to	IX, 146–7
[1796] Dec 7	EB fr	**A**
		1 IV, 378–9
1796 Dec 7	EB to	IX, 148–50
1796 Dec 9	EB fr	IX, 155–8
[1796 Dec *p* 9]	EB to	IX, 158–61
[1796 Dec 14]	EB fr	IX, 175–7

* Published in *Works* as 'Observations on the Conduct of the Minority' (Todd, 207–12).

* Published in *Works* as 'Fourth Letter on the Proposals for Peace' (Todd, 256).

Fitzwilliam, 4th Earl (*cont.*)

1796 Dec [15]	EB to	IX, 177–8
1796 Dec 18	EB to	IX, 180–2
1796 Dec 20	EB to	IX, 188–90
1796 Dec 28	EB to	IX, 211–12
1796 Dec 29	EB to	IX, 216
[1797 Jan 1]	EB fr	IX, 218–20
1797 [Jan] 4	EB to	IX, 220–1
[1797 Jan 9]	EB fr	IX, 227–9
1797 Mar 15	EB to	IX, 282–4
[1797] Apr 17	EB fr	A
[1797] Apr 26	EB to	IX, 317
1797 May 7	EB to	IX, 330–1
[1797] May 15	EB fr	IX, 340–1
1797 May 21	EB to	IX, 355–6
1797 June 4	EB to	IX, 367
1797 June 18	EB to	IX, 370–1
n.d.	EB fr	A
Wednesday		

FLOOD, Henry

1765 May 9	EB fr	I, 191
[1765] May 18	EB to	I, 192–5
1765 May 30	EB fr	A
[1765] July 27	EB fr	B
1780 Jan 5	EB to	IV, 181–2

FOLEY, Thomas Foley, 2nd
Baron

1783 Aug 29	RBsr to,	A
	and Carteret	
1783 Aug 29	RBsr to,	A
	and Carteret	
1784 Aug 25	EB fr	B

FORBES, J.

1796 July 28	EB fr	A

FORBES, Sir William

[1784 Apr 13]	EB fr	B

FORSTER, Johann Reinhold

1779 Apr 19	EB fr	A

FOULLON, Abbé Honoré-Charles-
Ignace

1791 Mar 9	EB fr	B
1791 June 1	EB to	VI, 263–4

FOURNÈS, Jules-Marie-Henri de
Faret, Marquis de

n.y. Nov 14	RBjr fr	B

FOWKE, Joseph

[1791 June 7]	EB to	VI, 276–7

FOWLER, Rev. Henry Bond

1797 Feb 15	EB fr	A

FOX, Charles James

1776 Aug 17	EB fr	III, 290–1
[1776] Oct 13	EB fr	III, 294
[1777] Sept 8	EB fr	A
		1 II, 181–2
1777 Oct 8	EB to	III, 380–8
[1778 June]	EB fr	A
		1, II, 225–6
[1778] Aug 1	EB fr	A
[1778 Oct]	EB fr	A
[1779] Jan 24	EB fr	IV, 38–41
1780 Sept 15	EB fr	IV, 282–4
[1782 Apr 9]	EB fr	A
[1782 July 2]	[RBjr] to	V, 3–5
[1782 July 3]	EB to	V, 5–6
1783 Sept 24	EB fr	D
[1788 Nov *p* 24]	EB to	V, 427–9
1789 May 11	EB to	V, 472–4
1789 Sept 9	EB to	VI, 14–15
[1797 July *a* 9]	JB to	IX, 372–3
n.d. Tuesday	EB fr	A

[FOX, George Croker]

1794 May 2	EB to	X, 29

FRANCE, King of
See LOUIS XVI

FRANCE, Queen of
See MARIE ANTOINETTE

FRANCIS, Philip

[1773 Oct 27]	EB to	II, 473
1773 Oct 27	EB fr	IX, 463
1777 June 9	EB to	III, 348–9
1777 Sept 1	WB to	A
		1 II, 179–
		81

Francis, Philip (*cont.*)

1777 Oct 1	WB fr	**A**
		1 II, 183–6
1777 Nov 21	EB fr	**F**
1777 Dec 18	WB fr	**F**
1778 Dec 14	WB to	**A**
		1 II, 244–7
1778 Dec 24	EB to	IV, 32–5
1779 Jan 29	WB to	**C**
1781 Dec 6	JB to	**F**
1782 Jan 11	EB fr	**F**
[1782 Mar 12]	EB to	IV, 420–1
[1782 Dec 29]	EB to	V, 59–60
[1783 Feb 8]	EB to	V, 65
[1783 May 28]	EB to	V, 95
[1783 Oct 23]	EB to	V, 116
1784 Apr 29	EB fr	V, 142–3
1784 July 15	EB fr	**A**
1784 July 20	EB fr	V, 160–1
1784 July 27	EB fr	V, 161–2
[1785 Sept *c* 30]	EB to	V, 224
1785 Nov 14	EB to	V, 239
1785 Nov 23	EB to	V, 240
1785 Dec 10	EB to	V, 241–4
1785 Dec 14	EB to	V, 244–5
1785 Dec 23	EB to	V, 245–6
[1786 June *a* 1]	EB to	V, 264–5
1786 Aug 6	EB to	V, 265–7
1786 Oct [15]	RBsr to	**F**
1786 Nov 3	EB to	V, 288
[1786 Nov *c* 8]	EB to	V, 288–9
1786 Dec 15	EB to	V, 300
[1787 Jan *c* 2]	EB to	V, 304–5
[1787 Feb 3]	EB to	V, 308
1787 Feb 27	EB to	V, 308–9
[1787 Dec 10]	EB to	V, 366–7
1787 Dec 18	EB and other Managers of Hastings Impeachment to	V, 370–1*
[1788 Jan *c* 3]	EB to	V, 372
[1788 Feb *a* 29]	WB fr	**63** 373–5, ext 3 pp.
[1788 Apr 13]	EB to	V, 387

* Published as *A Letter to Philip Francis* (Todd, 138–9).

[1788 Aug 5]	EB to	V, 409
1788 Sept 14	EB to	V, 416–18
[1789 Feb 11]	EB to	V, 447
[1789] Nov 15	EB to	VI, 38–9
1789 Dec 11	EB to	VI, 50–5
1789 Dec 17	EB to	VI, 55–8
[1790] Jan 2	EB fr	**A**
		1 III, 85–8
1790 Feb 19	EB fr	VI, 85–7
[1790] Feb 20	EB to	VI, 88–92
1790 Feb 20	RBjr to	**A**
		1 III, 132–4
[1790 Mar 10]	EB to	VI, 99–100
1790 Oct 27	EB to	VI, 142
1790 Nov 3, 4	EB fr	VI, 150–5
1790 Nov 19	EB to	VI, 170–3
[1790 Dec 4]	EB to	VI, 188–9
[1791] May 31	EB to	VI, 262
1792 Jan 21	EB fr	**A**
		1 III, 376–8
1792 Jan 23	EB to	VII, 38–9
[1794 Feb 16]	EB to	VII, 533
1794 Aug 9	WB to	**F**
1795 Jan 10	[EB] fr	**A**
n.d.	EB to	IX, 451

FRANCIS, Mrs. Philip

1786 Aug 7	JB to	**AJ**
[1786 Aug *c* 20]	EB to	V, 276
1787 Apr 20	EB to	V, 326–7
n.d.	JB to	**AJ** [Mrs. Francis]
n.d.	JB to	**AJ** [Mrs. Francis]

FRANCIS, Miss

n.d.	RBjr to	**54** (27 Feb 1892)

FRANCIS, The Misses

[1786] Dec 15	RBjr to	**AJ**
n.y. Apr 18	RBsr to	**AJ**
n.d.	RBjr to	**54** (27 Nov 1897), abs 3 lines

FRANCKLYN, Gilbert **AJ**

1791 May 9	EB fr	**A**

FRANK, Thomas

[1775] Mar 22	EB fr	A	

FRANKLIN, Benjamin

1774 Dec 19	EB fr	III, 80–1	
1775 May 15	EB fr	A	
		1 II, 27–8	
1781 Aug 15	EB to	IV, 362–5	
1781 Oct 15	EB fr	IV, 378	
1781 Dec 15	EB fr	A	
[1781 Dec *p* 20]	EB to	IV, 395–7	
1782 Feb 28	EB to	IV, 418–19	
1782 Aug 10	EB to	V, 27–8	

FRANKS, Moses

1770 June 21	EB fr	A	
1771 Mar 9	EB fr	A	
1771 Dec 2	EB fr	A	

FRASER, William

[1766 Mar 31]	WB to	I	
1783 Aug 29	RBsr to	I	
1783 Aug 29	RBsr to	I	

FREIRE, Chevalier de

1791 Aug 25	EB fr	A	

FRENCH, Mrs. Patrick William (Juliana, *née* Burke); Edmund's sister

1766 Feb 6	EB and JB to	I, 235–6 IX, 389–90	
1769 May 16	Mrs. B, Edmund's mother to	Q	
1774 Nov 2	EB to	III, 73–4	
[1782] Apr 6	RBsr to	IV, 437	
1782 Apr 6	JB to	IV, 438	
1782 Apr 7	RBjr to	IV, 438–9	
1783 Apr 5	JB to	V, 86	
1783 May 20	JB to	**9** II, 66–8	
1783 Nov 6	RBsr to	W	
1786 Oct 12	EB to	V, 284–5	
[1786 Oct *p* 25]	RBjr to	V, 287	

FRENCH COMMITTEE

1796 June 13	EB fr	B	

FRENCH NOBILITY, Committee of

1791 Aug 7	RBjr fr	A	
		1 IV, 531	
1791 Aug *p* 7	RBjr to	A	
		1 IV, 532–3	

FRONDEVILLE, Thomas-Louis-César-Lambert, Vicomte de

1796 Aug 1	EB fr	B	
1796 Aug 25	EB fr	B	

FRY, Joseph

1775 Jan 19	EB fr	A	
1775 Mar 17	EB fr	A	

FRY, FRIPP & CO.

1777 Feb 19	EB fr	A	

FULLARTON, William

1785 Aug 1	EB to	V, 216–18	
	[Fullarton]		
1785 Aug 29	EB fr	B	
		62 87 ext 5 lines	
1793 Feb 20	EB fr	B	

GANAY, Paul-Louis, Chevalier de

1773 Nov 27	EB fr	A	

GARBETT, Samuel

1768 Nov 26	EB fr	A	
1770 Aug 20	EB fr	A	
1772 Aug 29	EB fr	A	
1781 June 9	EB fr	A	

GARDINER, Luke

1778 Aug 11	EB fr	A	
		1 II, 233–7	
1778 Aug [24]	EB to	IV, 16–18	

GARNETT, Henry

1776 Nov 16	EB to	III, 301–2	
1777 Mar 24	EB and H. Cruger fr	AZ	
1777 Apr 10	EB and H. Cruger fr	AZ	
1777 May 14	EB to	III, 340	

Garnett, Henry (*cont.*)

1777 July 3	EB to	III, 357–61
1777 Sept 8	EB fr	AZ
1777 Sept 12	EB to	III, 374
1777 Sept 21	EB to	III, 376

GARRICK, David

1764 June 21	[EB] fr	U
		25 I, 417–18
1765 July 16	EB to	I, 211–13
[1765 July 17]	EB fr	BD
		25 II, 468–9
[1765] July ⟨25⟩	EB and WB to	I, 213
[1765 Dec]	EB fr	A
		25 II, 476
[1766] Jan 18	EB fr	I, 233–4
[1766] Sept 30	EB fr	A
		25 II, 545–6
[1768] June 13	EB and RBsr to	I, 353–4
1768 June 17	EB fr	I, 354–6
[1768 June 17]	EB to	I, 356
1768 July 12	EB fr	II, 1–2
[1768] July 16	EB fr	II, 2–3
1769 June 15	EB to	II, 31
1769 Sept 18	EB to	II, 83–4
1770 Oct 3	RBsr to	BD
		25 I, 401–2
1771 May 3	EB fr	A
		1 I, 253
[1771] July 16	WB fr	A
		25 II, 748–50
1771 July 26	RBsr to	BD
1772 Sept 5	EB to	II, 333–4
[1772] Sept 21	EB fr	BD
1773 June 29	EB to	II, 438
[1773 July 4]	EB to	II, 443
1776 Feb 6	EB fr	A
		25 III, 1069
[1777 Mar 28]	JB fr	A
		25 III, 1157–8
[1777 Apr 29]	EB to	BD
		25 III, 335–6

[1777 Apr 29]	EB fr	A
		25 III, 1163
[1777]	WB to	BD
n.d.	EB to	IX, 451–2
n.d.	EB to	IX, 470
n.d.	WB to	IX, 470

GARRICK, Mrs. David

n.d.	EB to	IX, 452

GARTH, James

1779 May 20	EB fr	I
1779 May 22	EB to	IV, 77–8

GATAKER, Mrs. Thomas

1768 July 22	EB fr	A

GATTONI, Jule Cesar

1792 July 30	EB fr	A

GAULARD, Madame

[1791] May 16	EB fr	B

GEDDÉS, A.

1784 Dec 30	EB fr	A

GEDDES, H.

1786 Apr 22	EB fr	A

GEDDES, John

1782 Mar 9	EB fr	B
1782 May 6	EB fr	B
1791 Jan 4	EB fr	A

GENLIS, Stéphanie-Félicité (*née* Ducrest de Saint-Aubin), Comtesse de

1785 July 22	JB fr	B
1785 Oct 12	EB fr	V, 226–7

GENTZ, Friedrich

1793 Feb 8	EB fr	VII, 346–7
[1793 Feb *p* 8]	EB to	VII, 347–8

GEOGHEGAN, Ignatius

1792 Jan 12	EB fr	A
1796 June 20	EB to	IX, 48–9
1796 June 22	EB to	IX, 49–50

GIDDY, Rev. Edward
1776 May 2   EB fr   A

GIFFORD, John
[1796] Feb 25   EB fr   VIII, 391
1796 Mar 7   EB to   VIII, 407–8
1797 May 1   EB to   IX, 320–1

GLASGOW, George
1775 May 9   EB fr   A

GLASSE, George Henry
1791 Dec 5   EB fr   A

GLOVER, Richard
1782 Apr 16   EB fr   A

GLYNN, Serjeant John
[1769 Mar 7]   EB fr   A
1772 Mar 14   EB to   IX, 398–
                           400
[1773 Oct 31]   EB to   IX, 401–2
1773 Nov 2   EB to   IX, 402
n.d.   EB to   IX, 452–3

GODEFROY, [Denys-Joseph]
n.d.   EB fr   A

GODWIN, William
1783 Jan 16   EB fr   V, 63–4

GOLDSMITH, Henry
1782 May 24   EB fr   B

GOLDSMITH, Maurice
1782 May 29   EB fr   B

GOOLD, George
1781 Sept 15   EB fr   A
                           1 II, 432–3

GOOLD, Thomas
1791 Feb 5   EB fr   A
[1794]   EB to   VIII, 107
1796 Apr 16   EB fr   A

GORDON, G.
1776 Dec 19   EB fr   A

GORDON, L.
1782 Apr 26   EB fr   A

GORDON, Colonel William
1777 Nov 13   EB fr   B

GORDON, William
1773 June 23   EB fr   A

GORING, Charles
[1788 Feb p 17] EB fr   A
1795 July 14   EB fr   A

GRAEME, General David
1766 Mar 14   EB fr   A

GRANT, James
1784 May 11   EB fr   A

GRATTAN, Henry
1789 Mar 19   EB to   V, 453
1793 Feb 28   RBjr to   VII, 351–3
1793 Mar 8   EB to   VII, 360–2
[1793] Mar 20   RBjr fr   VII, 362–3
[1793] Mar, 25, EB fr   VII, 363–6
  26
1794 May 23   RBjr to   VII, 541–7
[1794] Aug 26   EB fr   A
                           1 IV, 229–30
1794 Sept 3   EB to   VIII, 3–7
[1794 Sept] 23 EB fr   VIII, 19
[1794] Oct 1   EB fr   VIII, 27–9
1794 Dec 12   EB to   VIII, 95–6
1794 Dec 12   EB to   VIII, 96–7
1795 Feb 19   EB fr   VIII, 149–
                           51
1795 Mar 2, 3   EB to   VIII, 164–7
1795 Mar 5   EB to   VIII, 173–5
[1795] Mar 11   EB fr   VIII, 185–8
[1795] Mar 14   EB fr   VIII, 196–7
1795 Mar 20   EB to   VIII, 205–8
1795 Apr 15   EB fr   VIII, 232–3
[1795] July 26 EB fr   VIII, 289–90

GRAVE, Pierre-Marie, Chevalier de
1792 Aug 24   EB to   VII, 182–3
1793 Aug 14   EB fr   A
                           1 IV, 130–1

GRAY, Dr. John

1782 Apr 6	EB fr	A
1782 Apr 10	EB fr	A

GREAVES, William

1774 Oct 21	EB fr	A
1775 Jan 18	EB fr	A
[1775 Feb]	EB fr	A
1775 Apr 1	EB fr	A

GREENWOOD, C. G.

1792 Oct 13	EB fr,	A
	and J. Greenwood	

GREENWOOD, John

1792 Oct 13	EB fr,	A
	and C. G. Greenwood	

GREGORY, Robert

1772 May 17	EB fr	A
1780 Dec 27	EB fr	A
1783 Feb 3	EB fr	A
1786 Mar 3	EB fr	A

GRENVILLE, George

[1764 Apr]	WB to	AK

GRENVILLE, Thomas

[1795 Mar 11]	EB to	VIII, 183

GRENVILLE, William Wyndham Grenville, 1st Baron

1787 Oct 3	WB to,	I P.R.O.
	and Bn.	30/8/361
	Mulgrave	
1788 Sept 25	WB to,	I
	and Bn. Mulgrave	
1788 Oct 12	WB to,	I P.M.G.
	and Bn.	1/104
	Mulgrave	
[1789 Apr 30]	EB to	IX, 434–6
1789 June 8	EB to	IX, 436
1789 Aug 4	EB to	VI, 8–9
1790 Nov 2	EB fr	A
1791 Feb 25	EB fr	I
1791 Mar 23	EB fr	A
1791 Apr 20	EB fr	VI, 248–9
1791 Sept 17	EB fr	VI, 398

1791 Sept 21	EB to	VI, 405–8
1791 Sept 23	EB fr	B
1792 Feb 7	EB fr	A
[1792] Feb 9	EB fr	A
1792 Aug 18	EB to	VII, 173–8
1792 Sept 6	EB fr	A
		1 III, 532–3
1792 Sept 19	EB to	VII, 217–19
1792 Nov 4	RBjr to	I
[1792 Dec 1]	EB fr	A
1792 Dec 6	EB to	VII, 319
1793 Oct 10	RBjr to	B
1793 Oct 26	EB fr	VII, 464–5
[1793 Oct 29]	EB fr	B
[1796 Feb]	EB to	3 V, 173–
[Bn.		229*
Grenville]		

GREY, Charles

[1789 Mar]	EB fr	A
[1793 June 7]	EB fr	VII, 370–1

GREY, Captain John

[1792 June *p* 7]	EB to	VII, 147–9

GROSVENOR, W. L.

1782 Apr 16	EB fr	A

GWATKIN, Mrs. Robert Lovell

1781 June 30	EB and	IV, 353–4
	Sir J. Reynolds to	

HADING, Comte d'

1794 Aug 28	EB fr	B

HAILES, Sir David Dalrymple, styled Lord

1791 Dec 16	EB to	VI, 466–7
1792 Jan 12	EB fr	A
1792 May 29	EB to	VII, 144–6

HALIDAY, Dr. Alexander Henry

1775 Apr 6	EB fr	A
1775 Nov 9	EB fr	A
1777 Aug 30	EB fr	B

* Published as *A Letter to a Noble Lord* (Todd, 186–93).

Haliday, Dr. Alexander Henry (*cont.*)

1779 Feb 20	EB fr	**A**
[1780 Oct *a* 12]	EB fr	**B**
1781 July 28	EB to	IV, 360–1
1782 Apr 26	EB fr	**A**

HALL, Dr. George

[1793] Oct 10	EB fr,	**A**
	and Dr. Young	

HALLIFAX, Dr. Samuel

1772 Feb 27	EB fr	**A**

HAMILLE, Henry

1796 Apr 3	EB fr	**A**

HAMILTON, Joseph

1784 Nov 13	EB fr	**B**

HAMILTON, William Gerard

[1763 Mar]	EB to	I, 163–6
[1765 Feb *a* 12]	EB fr	I, 178–9
[1765 Feb *a* 12]	EB to	I, 179–81
[1765 Feb *a* 12]	EB fr	I, 182
[1765 Feb *a* 12]	EB to	I, 182
1765 Apr 8	EB fr	**A**
		1 I, 63
1765 Apr 10	EB to	I, 188–9

HAMILTON, Sir William

1780 Aug 29	EB to	IV, 266; x, 8–9
1780 Dec 12	EB fr	**A**
1787 Dec 29	EB to	IX, 466; x, 21–2
n.d. 'Wensday'	EB fr	**A**

HAMILTON, Dr. William

1788 Jan 24	EB fr	V, 375–6

HANNAY, Sir Samuel, 3rd Baronet

1784 Mar 8	EB fr	V, 129
1784 Mar 8	EB to	V, 129–30

HANSARD, Hugh Joseph

1782 Aug 24	EB fr	**A**

HARBORD, Sir Harbord, 2nd Baronet

1780 Jan 20	EB fr	**A**

HARDWICKE, Philip Yorke, 2nd Earl of

[1767 Oct *p* 30]	EB to	I, 332
1769 Oct 20	EB to	II, 95–6
1781 Apr 5	EB to	X, 9–10

HARFORD, James

1775 Feb 25	EB fr	**A**
[1775 Mar 2]	EB fr	**A**

HARFORD, Joseph

1780 Jan 31	EB and H. Cruger fr, and Brice	IV, 202–3
1780 Apr 4	EB to	IV, 218–22
1780 Sept 27	EB to	IV, 294–9
1781 Feb 18	EB fr	**A**
1781 Nov 6	EB fr, Noble and Span	**A**
1782 June 29	EB fr	**A**

HARFORD, Richard

1775 May 1	EB fr	**A**

HARFORD, COWLES & CO.

1778 Apr 27	EB fr	**A**
1778 May 2	EB to	III, 440–4*
1778 May 5	EB fr	III, 444–5
1778 May 12	EB to	III, 445–6

HARGRAVE, Christopher

1767 Sept 24	WB fr	**BC**
[1777 Sept *a* 5]	EB to	III, 372–4

HARNESS, Captain William

[1793 Jan 11]	EB fr	**B**
1793 Jan 20	EB to	VII, 340–1

HARRIS, W.

1777 June 3	EB fr	**L**

HARRISON, Edward

1792 Sept 25	EB fr	**A**

HARWARD, William

[1769] Mar 25	EB fr	**A**

* Published in *Two Letters on the Trade of Ireland* (Todd, 91–2).

Harward, William (*cont.*)
1769 July 26   EB fr   **A**

HARWOOD, William
1796 Jan 24   EB to   VIII, 383–4

HASTINGS IMPEACHMENT,
  Counsel for the Managers of the
1788 May 26   EB to   V, 398–9

HATSELL, John
[1775 May 8]   EB fr   **A**
[1790 Nov]   EB to   X, 24–5

HAUTOŸ, Comtesse de
1791 Feb 28   EB fr   **A**

HAVILAND, Mrs. Thomas;
  Burke's niece
[1794 July *c* 18]   RBjr to   VII, 560
1795 Sept 4   EB to   VIII, 313–14

HAVILAND, General William
1782 May 31   EB fr   **A**

HAVILAND, Mrs. William
[1795 Aug *a* 5]   EB to   VIII, 294
[1795 Aug 6]   EB to   VIII, 296
n.d.   EB to   IX, 453
n.d.   EB and JB to   IX, 453–4
n.d.   EB to   IX, 454

HAVRÉ, Joseph-Anne-Auguste-
  Maximilien, Duc d', et de Croy
1793 May 28   EB fr   **B**

HAWKESBURY, Charles
  Jenkinson; later (1786) 1st Baron
[1780] June 1   WB to   **D**
                   4 38404 f. 166
1780 Aug 22   WB to   **D**
                   4 38404 f. 172
1780 [Sept] 30   EB to   IV, 303–5

1780 Oct 2   EB fr   **D**
                   4 38308 f. 12
1780 Oct 2   EB to   IV, 306–7
1780 Oct 3   EB fr   **B**
1780 Oct 25   EB to   IX, 465
[1780 Nov 16]   EB to   IV, 320
1791 Aug 12   EB fr   **A**
1792 Mar 2   EB to   VII, 89–90
[1792 Mar 2]   EB fr   **A**
1792 June 2   RBjr to   **A**
                   4 38227 ff. 345–8
1792 Aug 3   RBjr to   **D**
                   4 38472 f. 145
1792 Aug 5   RBjr fr   **D**
                   4 38472 f. 147
1792 Aug 7   RBjr to   **D**
                   4 38472 f. 148
1792 Aug 19   EB fr   **A**
                   4 38310 f. 79
1792 Nov 5   RBjr to   **D**
                   4 38228 ff. 107–9
1793 June 24   RBjr to   **D**
                   4 38229 f. 42
1793 Dec 16   RBjr to   VII, 504–5
[1793 Dec 23]   RBjr to   **D**
                   4 38472 f. 177
1794 June 24   EB to   VII, 553–4

HAWKINS, Rev. Dr. James,
  Bishop of Raphoe 1780–1807
1791 July 27   EB fr   **A**

HAWKSWELL, Richard
1777 Apr 16   EB fr   **L**
1778 May 3   EB fr   **L**
1778 June 18   EB fr   **L**
1779 Mar 29   EB fr   **L**
1779 Oct 19   EB fr   **L**
1779 Oct 27   EB fr   **L**

Hawkswell, Richard (*cont.*)

1786 Jan 14	RBsr fr	L
1788 Dec 16	RBsr fr	L
1789 Dec 15	RBsr fr	L
1790 Dec 13	RBsr fr	L
1791 Dec 17	RBsr fr	L
1791 Dec 28	RBsr fr	L
1792 Dec 18	RBsr fr	L
1793 Dec 19	RBsr fr	L

HAY, Edward

1795 June 21	EB fr	VIII, 270–1
1795 June 26	EB to	VIII, 272–3
1795 July 19	EB fr	A
1795 Sept 15	EB fr	A

HAY, George, Catholic Bishop of
Daulis and Vicar-apostolic of the
Lowland District of Scotland

[1779 May]	EB fr	A
[1779 May]	EB fr	A
1779 July 12	EB fr	IV, 99–102
1779 Dec 22	EB fr	A
1783 Apr 13	EB fr	A
1791 May 15	EB fr	A

HAYES, Samuel

[1774 Sept 28]	EB fr	A
[1776]	EB fr	A

HAYES, Thomas

1775 Oct 11	EB to	III, 229–30

HEATLY, C.

1793 Feb 24	EB fr	A

HEATON, John

1782 Apr 6	EB fr	B

HENDERSON, Archibald

1766 Feb 9	EB fr	A

HENDERSON, John

[1780]	EB fr	A
[1781 Apr 20]	EB fr	A
[1783 Aug *a* 30]	EB fr	A
1783 Aug 30	EB to	V, 112–13
[1783]	EB fr	A

HENNESSY, Mrs. Ellen; Burke's
cousin

1766 Oct 25	Mrs. Bsr	**1** I, 111–14
	to	
1781 Sept 5	EB to	IV, 370–1

HENNESSY, George

1793 Nov 1	RBjr fr	A
1794 July 28	RBjr to	AN

HENRY, J. B.

1782 May 14	EB fr	A

HÉRAL, Abbé Emmanuel-
Alexandre-Joseph d'

1794 Nov 30	EB to	VIII, 86–9

HERBERT, J.

1784 June 3	EB fr	A

HERTFORD, Francis Seymour
Conway, 1st Earl of

1766 May 29	[EB] fr	A

HICKEY, John

1776 Oct 9	EB fr	B

HICKEY, Joseph

1793 July 29	EB to	IX, 440–1

HICKEY, William

[1788]	WB to	**26** III, 339 abs and ext 6 lines
[1788]	WB fr	**26** III, 339–40 abs ½ p
[1788]	WB fr	**26** III, 340 4 lines
[1788]	WB to	**26** III, 340–1 abs 5 lines
[1788]	WB fr	**26** III, 341 abs 3 lines
[1788]	WB to	**26** III, 341 abs and ext ½ p
[1791 Mar]	WB to	**26** IV, 24–5 abs ½ p

Hickey, William (*cont.*)

[1791]	WB to	**26** IV, 59
		abs 9 lines
[1792 Mar]	WB to	**26** IV, 70
		abs 5 lines

HILL, Sir Hugh, 1st Baronet

1779 Mar 16	EB fr	**A**

HILL, James

1780 Apr 25	EB to	IV, 231–2

HILL, Joseph

1792 Apr	EB to	IX, 467
	[Joseph] Hill	
[1792] June 20	EB to	IX, 439–40
1792 June 24	EB to	VII, 154
	[Joseph Hill]	
[1792 June 27]	EB to	VII, 155
	[Joseph Hill]	

HILL, [Sir] Richard [2nd Baronet]

1783 Mar 12	EB fr	**A**

HILLSBOROUGH, Wills Hill,
  1st Earl of

1780 Oct 3	EB to,	IV, 307–10
	and Vct. Stormont	
1780 Oct 18	EB fr,	**B**
	and Vct. Stormont	
1780 Oct 19	EB to,	IV, 316
	and Vct. Stormont	
1781 July 12	EB to	IV, 356–8
		IX, 430–1

HILTON, William

1779 Mar 19	EB fr	**A**

HIPPISLEY, John Coxe; later
  (1796) 1st Baronet

1783 Feb 24	WB to	**AS**
	[Hippisley]	
1784 Nov 15	WB to	**AB**
[1785 Feb *a* 21]	WB to	**AS**
[1788 May]	EB to	V, 400
[1791 Mar] 20	RBjr fr	**B**
[1791 Apr *c* 3]	RBjr fr	**B**
[1793] Sept 7	EB fr	**A**

[1793] Sept 18	EB fr	**B**
1793 Sept 24	EB fr	**B**
1793 Oct 3	EB to	VII, 439–45
1793 Nov 20,	EB fr	**B**
27		**4** 37848
		ff. 303–10
1793 Nov 27	EB fr	**B**
		4 37848
		ff. 325–8
1794 Jan 8	EB to	VII, 512–13
1794 June 7	EB fr	**B**
1796 Jan 22	EB to	VIII, 380
[1797] May 8	EB fr	**A**

HOBART, Major Robert

1792 Jan 7	RBjr to	VII, 13–14
1792 Jan 9	RBjr fr	VII, 18–19
1792 Jan 11	RBjr to	VII, 19–20
1792 Jan 13	RBjr fr	**A**
1792 Jan 14	RBjr to	VII, 32
1793 Oct 28	RBjr to	**I**
		24 III, 114–
		15n
1793 Nov 9	RBjr fr	**A**

HODGSON, William

1781 Oct 23	EB fr	**B**
1782 Feb 4	EB fr	**B**

HOGHTON, Sir Henry, 6th Baronet

[1793 Mar 6]	EB to	VII, 357–8

HOHEB, Samuel

1782 Apr 15	EB fr	**A**
1784 Feb 13	EB fr	**A**

HOLLAND, Stephen Fox, 2nd
  Baron

1774 Sept	EB to	IX, 403

HOLLIDAY, J.

1791 June 16	RBjr fr	**A**

[HOMER, Henry]

[1786 *a* Oct]	RBsr fr	**A**
	[Homer]	
[1786 Nov]	EB to	V, 293–6
	[Homer]	

HOPE, John
n.d.   EB fr   A

HOPKINSON
[1782 Apr *a* 26]   RBsr fr   A

HORNE, George, Bishop of Norwich
1791 Dec 9   EB to   VI, 455–6

HORSLEY, Rev. Dr. Samuel,
   Bishop of St. Davids 1788–93
1791 Jan 31   EB fr   A

HOWARD, [Sir] George
1782 June 19   EB fr   A

HOWARD, Gorges Edmund
1770 June 30   EB fr   A
1770 Oct 6   EB fr   A
1772 Nov 12   EB fr   A
1772 Dec 4   EB fr   A
1772 Dec 9   EB fr   A
1772 Dec 9   WB fr   A
[1773 Mar *p* 27] EB fr   A
1773 July 23   EB fr   A
1775 Jan 2   EB fr   A
1775 Jan 2   WB fr   A
1776 Jan 27   EB fr   A
1776 Oct 29   EB fr   A
1777 Jan 29   EB fr   A
1777 Mar 26   EB fr   A
1778 May 14   EB fr   A
1778 May 16   EB fr   A
1778 May 16   WB fr   A

HOWARD, Martin, Jr.
Chief Justice of Province of North
   Carolina
1767 Feb 16   EB fr   A

HOWARD, Philip
1796 Mar 8   EB fr   A

HOWISON, Henry
[1782 Mar]   EB fr   A

HUDLESTON, John
1783 Oct 31   WB fr   **AI**

HUDSON, [Robert]
1788 Jan 2   EB fr   **B**

HUET, Julien-Michel
1792 Oct 25   EB fr   **B**

HUGHES, Rev. David
1792 Oct 16   EB to   VII, 269–71
[1793] Nov 25   EB to   IX, 441–2
1794 Nov 1   EB to   VIII, 67–8

HUICK, J.
1781 Aug 8   [RBjr] fr   **B**

HUISH, Mark
1775 Feb [22]   EB to   III, 121–3
1775 Feb 25   EB fr   A
1775 Mar 9   EB to   III, 129–30
1775 Mar 11   EB fr   A
1777 Feb 21   EB to   III, 331
1777 Feb 25   EB fr   A

HUME, Sir Abraham, 2nd Baronet
1791 Sept 14   EB fr   A
1792 Sept 23   EB fr   A

HUMUND RAO, Bramin, Maratha
   agent
1781 Oct 13   EB fr   A

HUNTINGDON, Selina (*née*
   Shirley), Countess of
[1772 Feb *a* 6]   EB to   II, 298–9

HUSSEY, Rev. Thomas; later (1797)
   Catholic Bishop of Waterford
1790 Aug 13   EB fr   VI, 132–3
[1790] Aug [28]   RBjr fr   VI, 134
[1792] Dec 3   EB fr   A
[1793] Aug 15   EB fr   VII, 395–6
[1795] Jan 29   EB fr   VIII, 124–6
1795 Feb 4   EB to   VIII, 136–
                                       40
[1795 Feb *a* 10]   EB to   VIII, 142–4
1795 Feb 19   EB fr   VIII, 151–4
[1795 Feb 27]   EB fr   VIII, 162–3
[1795] Feb 28   EB fr   VIII, 163–4
1795 Mar 3   EB fr   VIII, 168–9

Hussey, Rev. Thomas (*cont.*)

1795 Mar 5	EB to	VIII, 175–6
[1795 Mar *c* 14]	EB fr	VIII, 198
1795 Mar 17	EB to	VIII, 199–205
1795 Mar 21	EB to	VIII, 212–15
1795 May 18	EB to	VIII, 245–50
[1795 June 9]	EB to	VIII, 262–5
1795 Aug 24	EB to	VIII, 308–9
1795 Sept 26	EB to	VIII, 322
[1795 Nov 27]	EB to	VIII, 351–2
1796 Jan 18	EB to	VIII, 378
[1796] Jan 21	EB fr	VIII, 379–80
1796 May 25	EB to	IX, 20–1
[1796] June 18	EB fr	A **1** IV, 346–7
[1796 July 5]	EB to	IX, 53–4
1796 July 14	EB fr	A
1796 July 26	EB to	IX, 60–1
1796 Nov 30	EB fr	IX, 140–3
[1796 Dec *p* 9]	EB to	IX, 161–72
[1797 Mar 29]	EB to	IX, 298
1797 Apr 2	EB fr	IX, 302–4
1797 May 9	EB fr	A **1** IV, 444–6
1797 May 12	EB to	IX, 331–2
1797 May 16	EB to	IX, 341–5
1797 May 22	EB to	IX, 357–8

HUTCHINSON, John Hely

1764 Oct 14	EB fr	A
[1765 May]	EB to	I, 198–201
1767 July 28	EB fr	B
1767 Aug 3	EB to	I, 318–20 IX, 390–1
1767 Sept 20	EB fr	A
1775 Jan [21]	EB to	III, 103–5 IX, 404–6
1775 Mar 25	EB fr	A
1776 Apr 27	EB fr	A
1777 May 28	EB fr	B
1780 Feb 3	EB fr	B
1780 Nov 15	EB to	IV, 461
1782 Apr 6	EB fr	IV, 434–6
[1782 Apr *p* 9]	EB to	IV, 440–1
1782 Apr 19	EB fr	A
1782 May 9	EB fr	A
1782 Oct 20	EB fr	A

1785 Aug 7	EB to	V, 220–1
1786 Nov 11	EB to	V, 289–90
1790 Dec 13	EB fr	IX, 466
1790 Dec 18	EB to	VI, 192–3
1791 Aug 23	EB fr	A **1** III, 289
1791 Sept 6	EB to	VI, 384–5

INCHIQUIN, Murrough O'Brien,
5th Earl of

1795 May 21	EB to	VIII, 250

INCHIQUIN, Countess of
See PALMER

INSPECTOR GENERAL
See ACCOUNTS, Inspector
General of

IRELAND, Catholic Committee in
See also

BRAUGHALL DERMOTT
BYRNE   KEOGH
CURRY

[1791]	[RBjr] to	**B** [Catholic Committee]
1792 June 17	RBjr to	**65** I, 209–10 ext
[1792 July 30]	RBjr fr	VII, 164–6
1792 Oct *a* 16	RBjr to	**64** I, 144 abs and ext 6 lines

IRELAND, Primate of
See ROBINSON

IRONSIDE, Colonel Gilbert

1791 Jan 24	EB fr	A

IRVING, John

1780 Dec 1	EB fr, and Touchet	A

IVERNOIS, Francis d'

1794 Dec 20	EB to	VIII, 101

IZARD, Ralph

1777 July [21]	EB to	III, 364–5

JACKSON, Thomas			
1775 Jan 10	EB fr	A	

JACOB, John W.			
1775 Jan 16	EB fr	A	

JAMES, William			
1775 Apr 10	EB fr	A	

JEANS, Thomas			
1782 May 9	EB fr	A	
1782 May 12	EB fr	A	

JENISON, F[rancis, Count Jenison
  Walworth
Chamberlain to the Elector Palatine of
  Bavaria]
1786 May 19   EB fr   A

JENKINS, Edward
1796 Dec 1   EB to   IX, 143–4

JENKINSON, Charles
See HAWKESBURY

JENNINGS, Richard
  Downing
1782 May 22   EB fr   A

JEPHSON, Robert
[1765] Feb 26   EB to   I, 186–7
1790 Dec 10   EB fr   A

JEPSON, John Wilkins
1780 Feb 28   EB to   IV, 207–9
1782 Dec 26   EB fr   A

JERNINGHAM, Edward
1790 Jan 23   EB to   VI, 76
1790 Nov 18   EB to   VI, 170
[1791 Jan a 18]   EB fr   VI, 203–4
1791 Jan 18   EB to   VI, 204–5
1796 Dec 18   EB to   IX, 183–4

JERSEY, French émigrés at
See also LA BINTINAYE
1796 Nov 22   EB fr   B

JERVIS, Captain John
1782 Apr 26   EB fr   A

JOHNSON, Godschall
[1793]   EB fr   A

JOHNSON, Dr. Samuel
1770 June 21   EB fr   II, 145–6
[1775 Nov p 12]   JB fr   III, 236–7
[1776 June p 22]   EB and   III, 273–4
                        others to
[1778]   EB fr   **57** II, 129
                        abs and
                        ext 4 lines
1779 Apr 27   EB fr   IV, 64

JOHNSON, Samuel; Examiner of
  East Indian Correspondence
1787 May 9   EB fr   A

JOHNSTONE, George
[1775 Jan]   EB fr   A
[1775 May 25]   EB fr   A
[1775 June a 4]   EB fr   A
1779 Feb 4   WB fr   B

JONES, William; later (1783)
  knighted
[1778 Jan]   EB fr   A
                        37 I, 257–8
1779 Feb 28   EB fr   A
                        37 I, 286–7
1779 Mar 12   EB to   IV, 48–9
[1781 June p 13]   EB to   IV, 352
1782 Mar 17   EB fr   A
                        37 II, 520–3
[1782 Mar p 23]   EB to   IV, 424–5
[1782] Apr 1   EB fr   A
                        37 II, 523–4
1782 Apr 12   EB fr   A
                        37 II, 531–2
1782 May 7   EB fr   A
                        37 II, 536–8
1782 June 5   EB fr   A
                        37 II, 550–1
1782 Oct 8   EB fr   V, 37–8
1783 Feb 25   EB fr   V, 65–7
1784 Feb 27   EB fr   V, 127–8

Jones, William (*cont.*)
1784 Apr 13   EB fr   v, 140–2

JOYCE, Peter Hyacinth
1784 Aug 9   EB fr   A

JOYCE
1773 Nov 17   EB fr   A

JUMILHAC, Pierre-Marie
  Chapelle, Marquis de
1796 Feb 22   EB fr   B

JUPEAUX, Comtesse de
1796 Sept 2   EB fr   A

KEARNEY, John
1795 Feb 13   EB fr   C

KEARNEY, Michael
Fellow of Trinity College, Dublin
1777 June 2   EB fr   B
1782 Apr 11   EB fr   A
1783 Nov 14   RBsr fr   A
1790 Nov 4   RBsr fr   A

KEARNEY, Michael
1791 Feb 21   EB fr   A

KEELING, Eugene
1785 Apr 2   EB fr   A

KEELING, Herbert
1785 Mar 24   EB fr   B

KEENE, Whitshed
1783 Apr 11   EB fr   A
[1783] Apr 14   EB fr   A
1783 May 30   EB fr   A

KELLY, John
1773 June 3   EB fr   A

KEMPE, Mrs.
1761 Jan 16   EB fr   A

KENMARE, Thomas Browne,
  4th Viscount

1778 Aug 11   EB fr   A
1780 Jan 22   EB to   x, 6–8
1780 Feb 18   EB fr   IV, 203–4
1780 Dec 27   EB fr   A
1782 Feb 4   EB fr   IV, 400–2★
1782 Feb 21   EB to   IV, 405–18
1782 Mar 14   EB fr   IV, 421–2
1782 Mar 17   EB fr   B
1782 June 5   EB fr   A

KENNEDY, Patrick
1794 Aug 16   EB fr   B
1797 Mar 11   EB fr   A

KENT, John
1781 Oct 15   EB fr   A
1791 Sept 16   EB fr   †

KENT, Sir Thomas
1779 Oct 19   [RBsr] fr   58
1779 Oct 20   RB[sr] to   58
                [T. Kent]
1783 Apr 17   [EB] fr   58

KENYON, Lloyd
1780 Mar 6   EB to   IV, 211–12
1781 Dec 26   EB to   IV, 398–9
1782 Jan 4   EB to   IV, 399

KEOGH, John
1792 May 17   RBjr fr   A
1792 July 26   RBjr fr   A
1795 Mar 19   EB fr,   A
                and   1 IV, 306–8
                Byrne
1796 July 20   EB fr   IX, 59–60
1796 Nov 16   EB fr   A
[1796] Nov 17   EB to   IX, 112–16
1796 Nov 24   EB fr   B

KEPPEL, Admiral Augustus Keppel,
  1st Viscount
1772 Nov 6   EB fr   A

★ Published as *A Letter to a Peer of Ireland* (Todd, 121–2).
† Published as *Lettre de John Kent à M. Burke* [1791].

Keppel, Admiral Augustus (*cont.*)

1774 Feb 12	EB fr	A	
[1774] Oct 3	EB fr	A	
[1774] Oct 3	EB fr	A	
1776 Feb 13	EB fr	A	
1776 Feb 21	EB fr	A	
[1778 Aug *p* 1]	EB to	IV, 13–14	
1778 Aug 12	EB fr	H	
1779 Nov 6	EB to	IV, 168–9	
1780 Sept 29	EB to	IV, 303	
1780 Dec 21	EB fr	A	
1781 May 3	EB fr	A	
1781 July 28	EB fr	A	
n.d. Monday	EB fr	A	

KERR, Rev. Joseph

1774 Nov 15	EB fr	A	

KIERNAN, Francis

1786 Feb 10	RBjr fr	B	

KILLALOE, Bishop of
See BARNARD

KING, Lieutenant Henry

1795 Oct 10	EB to	VIII, 326	

KING, Rev. Dr. James; father of
Walker King

1769 Jan 5	EB fr	A	

KING, Captain James; brother of
Walker King

1773 July 9	JB to	B	
1776 July 2	JB fr	B	
1776 Nov 4	EB fr	B	
1781 July 16	JB fr	A	
1784 Sept 30	JB fr	B	
1784 Oct 7	JB fr	A	
1784 Oct 18	JB fr	A	

KING, Rev. Dr. John Glen

[1782 Apr 10]	EB fr	A	
1782 Apr 10	EB to	IV, 441	

KING, John, brother of Walker King

1786 Dec *a* 15	EB fr	49 II, 253 abs 2 lines	

[1787 Nov 30]	RBsr fr,	A and W. King	
1788 Jan 6, 9	RBsr fr,	A and W. King	
1791 May 1	EB to	IX, 436–7	
[1791] Aug 4	EB fr	A	
1791 Nov 2	EB to	IX, 439	
[1791] Nov 11	EB fr	B	
[1791 Nov *c* 12]	EB to	VI, 446–8	
[1791] Nov 12	EB fr	B	
[1791] Nov 18	EB fr	B	
1791 Dec 4	EB to	C	
[1792 Jan 2]	EB to	VII, 7–8	
[1792] Feb 9	RBjr to	C	
[1792] Feb 11	EB fr	B	
1792 Mar 3	RBjr fr	A	
1792 Aug 1	RBjr to	IX, 467	
[1792 Sept *c* 21]	EB fr	A [J. King]	
[1793 May *p* 6]	EB fr	A	
1793 Aug 4	RBjr to	A	
1793 Oct 26	RBjr to	A	
1793 Oct 29	EB to	IX, 441	
1794 Sept 14	EB to	VIII, 12–14	
1795 Feb 8	EB to	VIII, 142; IX, 442–3	
1795 Sept 17	EB to	VIII, 320–2	
1795 Oct 26	EB to	VIII, 329–30	
1796 Sept 3	EB to	IX, 82–3	
1797 Mar 7	EB fr	A	

KING, John

1777 Jan 24	EB fr	A	

KING, Rev. Thomas; brother of
Walker King

1772 Dec 22	EB fr	II, 394–5	
1773 Feb 3	EB fr	A	
[1773 Feb 4]	EB to,	II, 419–21 and RBjr	
1773 Feb 9	EB fr,	B and RBjr	
[1773 Feb *p* 14]	EB fr,	B and RBjr	
[1773 Apr 26]	EB fr,	B and RBjr	

King, Rev. Thomas (*cont.*)

1773 May 1	EB fr	A
1773 June 1	JB fr	A
1773 Oct 4	JB fr	A
1774 Dec 12	EB fr	A
1777 May 14	JB fr	A
1781 Jan 6	JB fr	A
1783 Apr 11	JB fr	A
1784 Dec 8	JB fr	A
1790 Mar 5	JB fr	A
1791 July 30	JB fr	A

KING, Rev. Dr. Walker

1774 Apr 4	EB to	II, 525–6
[1774 Apr 9]	EB fr	AJ
1774 June 21	EB to	II, 544–5
1774 Sept 15	EB to	III, 26–8
[1775 Aug]	EB to	III, 198–200
[1778 Apr 7]	RBjr fr	A
[1779 Jan 4]	JB fr	A
1779 July 4	JB, WB and EB to	IV, 97–8
1779 Nov 5	EB fr	IV, 165–8
[1782 Apr 24]	WB fr	A
		1 II, 476–82
1784 Oct 27	JB fr	A
1784 Nov 3	JB to	A
1784 Nov 19	EB to	V, 189
[1785] July	EB to	V, 215–16
[1787 Nov 30]	RBsr fr, and John King	A
1788 Jan 6, 9	RBsr fr, and John King	V, 373–4
[1789 July 28]	EB to	VI, 5–6
[1791] Dec 16	RBsr fr	A
1792 Mar 1	RBjr fr	A
[1792] Mar 20	RBjr fr	A
[1792 Mar] 25	EB to	VII, 120
[1792 Sept] 7	EB to	VII, 197–8
[1792 Sept 16]	EB to	VII, 213
[1792 Sept 18]	EB to	VII, 214–15
[1792 Sept *a* 20]	EB to	VII, 219–21
1792 Sept 20	EB to	VII, 222
[1793 July]	RBjr to	C
[1794 June *p* 21]	RBjr to	C
1794 Aug 28	EB to	VII, 573–4

[1794 Aug 31]	EB to	VII, 579
1794 Aug	EB to	IX, 468
[1794 Sept *c* 14]	EB to	VIII, 14
[1794] Sept [*c*. 14]	EB to	VIII, 15–16
1794 Sept 17	EB to	VIII, 16
[1794] Nov 30	EB to	VIII, 89–90
1795 June 30	EB to	VIII, 279–80
[1795 Nov *p* 30]	EB to	VIII, 353
[1796 Feb 22]	EB to	VIII, 388–9
[1796 Mar 11]	EB to	VIII, 412
1796 Mar 23	EB to	VIII, 443
[1796 Mar *p* 24]	EB to	VIII, 445
[1796 Mar]	EB to	VIII, 453
[1796 Apr]	EB to	VIII, 460–1
1796 May 2	EB fr, and Bp of St.-Pol-de-Léon	B
[1796 May *p* 14]	EB to	IX, 9–11
[1796 May *p* 14]	EB to	IX, 11
[1796 May 28]	EB to	IX, 33–4
1796 June 4	EB to	IX, 44
1796 June 26	JB and EB to	IX, 51–2
1796 Oct 24	EB to	IX, 97
[1796 Oct *p* 24]	EB to	IX, 97–9
1796 Nov 4	EB to	IX, 103–4
[1796] Nov 23	EB to	IX, 131–2
[1796] Dec 21	EB to	IX, 191–2
1796 Dec 30	EB to	IX, 217–18
1797 Jan 25	EB to	IX, 231–3
[1797] Mar 21	EB to	IX, 290–1
1797 May 16	EB to	IX, 345–6
n.d.	EB to	IX, 454–5
n.d.	EB to	IX, 455
n.d.	EB to	IX, 470
n.d.	EB to	IX, 470
n.d.	EB to	IX, 471
n.d.	JB to	C
n.d.	JB to	C

KING, Mrs. Walker

[1797 Jan 26]	EB to	IX, 233–4

KNIGHT, Richard Payne

1792 Aug 19	EB fr	A

   * Published as *Lettre écrit au très honorable Edmund Burke*, Florence, 1791.

   † Published as *Seconde lettre de M. de Lally-Tollendal à M. Burke*, Londres et Paris, 1792.

LAMBERT, R.
1787 June 15   EB fr   **A**

LAMOIGNON, Anne-Pierre-
Chrétien, Vicomte de
1791 June 6   EB fr   **B**

LANASCAL, Jacques-Yves-
Joseph-Marie de Quemper Marquis de
1796 June 13   EB fr   **B**

LANASCAL, Marie-Marguerite-
Françoise-Julie (*née* de La Boessière),
Marquise de
1791 Jan 19   EB fr   **B**
1796 June 22   EB fr   **B**

LANCASTER, Merchants at
See also RAWLINSON
1766 June 12   EB fr   **A**
                        1 I, 104

LANDON, James
1790 Dec 1   EB fr   **A**

LANE, John
1775 Mar 23   EB fr   **A**
1776 Feb 13   EB fr   **A**

LANGRISHE, Sir Hercules, 1st
Baronet
1791 Dec 10   EB fr   IX, 467
1792 Jan 3   EB to   **3** IV, 243–
                        306*
[1793 Feb *p* 18] EB to   VII, 349–51
1793 Feb 20   EB fr   **AT** Kil-
                        kenny 38
1795 Mar 5   Eb fr   **AT** Kil-
                        kenny 38
1795 Mar 13   EB to   X, 30
1795 May 26   EB to   VIII, 253–7;
                        X, 31–5
1796 Feb 3   EB to   X, 36–7
[1796 Feb *p* 3] EB fr   **AT** Kil-
                        kenny 38
1796 Apr 8   EB to   X, 37–8

* Published as *A Letter to Sir
Hercules Langrishe* (Todd, 176–9).

LANGTON, Bennet
1775 Sept 18   EB to   III, 213–14
1775 Oct 2   EB fr   **A**

LA QUEUILLE, Jean-Claude-
Victor, Marquis de
1791 Sept 20   EB fr   **B**
1791 Oct 12   RBjr fr   **B**
1794 May 22   [EB] fr   **B**

LAS CASES, Marie-Joseph-
Emmanuel-Auguste-Dieudonné,
Marquis de
1793 Jan 9   RBjr fr   **B**

LASMARTRES, [Gabriel]
1792 Oct 29   EB fr   **B**

LAURAGUAIS, Louis-Léon-
Félicité de Brancas, Comte de
1773 Jan 24   EB to   II, 418–19

LAURENCE, Dr. French
1788 July 24   EB fr   **2** 1–3
[1788 July 26]   EB fr   **2** 6–7
1788 Aug 16   EB fr   V, 410–11
1788 Aug 18   EB to   V, 411–12
1788 Oct 25   EB fr   **E**
                        2 7–9
1789 Nov 3   EB fr   **C**
                        2 9–10
1790 Mar 27   EB fr   **E**
                        2 14–15
[1790 Oct 14]   EB fr   **E**
                        2 10–12
1790 Oct 20   EB fr   **E**
                        2 12–14
[1791 July]   EB fr   **E**
                        2 242
1791 Aug 1   EB fr   **E**
                        2 15–16
[1791 Aug 2]   EB to   VI, 311–12
1791 Aug 8   EB f   **A**
1791 Sept 24   EB fr   **A**
                        1 III, 337–
                        41
1792 Apr 17   EB fr   **C**
                        2 17

Laurence, Dr. French (*cont.*)

1792 July 31	EB fr	E
		2 17–19
1792 Aug 28	EB fr	E
		2 19–21
1792 Aug 29	EB fr	E
		2 21–3
[1792 Aug]	EB fr	E
		2 29–30
1792 Oct 29	EB, JB	2 23–6
	and RBsr fr	
1792 Nov 8	EB fr	C
		2 27–8
1792 Dec 8	EB fr	VII, 320
[1792 Dec 10]	EB fr	VII, 320–1
1792 Dec 11	EB fr	E
		2 28
[1794 July 31]	EB to	VII, 561–2
[1794 Aug *p* 2]	EB fr	C
		2 31–3
1794 Oct 3	WB to	C
[1794 Nov 2]	EB to	VIII, 68–70
[1795 Jan 21]	EB to	VIII, 123–4
[1795 Apr *c* 30]	EB to	VIII, 235–6
1795 May 22	EB to	VIII, 251
1795 July 1	EB to	VIII, 282
1795 Dec 2	WB to	C
1796 Feb 12	EB fr	E
		2 36–7
1796 Feb [25]	EB fr	VIII, 392–4
[1796 Feb *c* 27]	EB to	VIII, 397–9
[1796 Mar 11]	EB to	VIII, 413–14
1796 Mar 15	EB fr	VIII, 415–18
[1796 Mar *c* 17]	EB to	VIII, 419–20
1796 Mar 17	EB fr	VIII, 420–1
1796 Mar 26	EB fr	VIII, 447–8
[1796 June 11]	EB to	IX, 47–8
1796 July 28	EB to	IX, 62–4
1796 Aug 26	EB to	IX, 70–1
1796 Sept 2	EB to	IX, 80–2
1796 Sept 6	EB to	IX, 83
[1796 Sept 15]	EB to	IX, 85–6
[1796 Oct 6]	EB to	IX, 92–3
1796 Oct 10	EB to	IX, 93–4
1796 Oct 13, 14	EB fr	IX, 94–6

1796 Nov 18	EB to	IX, 116–20
1796 Nov 22	EB fr	C
		2 79–81
1796 Nov [23]	EB to	IX, 124–7
1796 Nov 24	EB fr	A
		1 IV, 364–9
1796 Nov 25	EB to	IX, 133–4
1796 Dec 2	EB fr	C
		2 89–91
[1796 Dec 8]	EB to	IX, 150–2
1796 Dec 9	EB to	IX, 152–3
1796 Dec 10	EB fr	E
		2 92–5
[1796 Dec 13]	EB to	IX, 173–4
[1796 Dec 14]	EB to	IX, 174–5
1796 Dec 15	EB fr	C
		2 95–7
1796 Dec 16	EB to	IX, 178–80
1796 Dec 18	EB to	IX, 184
1796 Dec 19	EB fr	C
		2 102
1796 Dec 20	EB to	IX, 190–1
1796 Dec 23	EB to	IX, 196–7
1796 Dec 24	EB fr	A
1796 Dec 25	EB to	IX, 203–5
1796 Dec 28	EB to	IX, 212–13
1797 Feb 2	EB fr	E
		2 109–11
1797 Feb 8	EB fr	E
		2 111–13
1797 Feb 9	EB fr	IX, 235–6
1797 Feb 10, 12	EB and E. Nagle to	IX, 236–40
1797 Feb 14	EB fr	IX, 242–4
1797 Feb 15	EB to	IX, 244–7
1797 Feb 20	EB fr	IX, 248–50
[1797 Feb *p* 20]	EB to	IX, 251
1797 Feb 24	EB fr	IX, 252–3
1797 Feb 28	EB fr	E
		2 136–9
1797 Mar 1	EB to	IX, 263–7
1797 Mar 3	EB fr	E
		2 140–1
1797 Mar 5	EB to	IX, 270–2
[1797 Mar *c* 5]	EB to	IX, 273–5
1797 Mar 7	EB fr	IX, 275–6
1797 Mar 14	EB fr	IX, 280–2
1797 Mar 16	EB to	IX, 284–8

Laurence, Dr. French (*cont.*)

1797 Mar 17	EB fr	**E**	
			2 166–9
[1797 Mar *c* 18]	EB fr	**2** 157–62	
[1797 Mar *a* 22]	EB to	IX, 291–2	
1797 Mar 22	EB fr	**C**	
			2 163–6
1797 Mar 28	EB fr	IX, 292–4	
1797 Mar 29	EB to	IX, 294–6	
1797 Mar 29	EB fr	IX, 296–8	
1797 Mar 30	EB to	IX, 298–9	
1797 Apr 1	EB fr	**E**	
			2 177–8
[1797] Apr 3	EB to	IX, 304–6	
1797 Apr 3	EB fr	**E**	
			2 181–2
1797 Apr 10	EB fr	**E**	
			2 182–5
1797 Apr 11	EB to	IX, 306–8	
[1797 Apr 12]	EB fr	**E**	
			2 193–5
1797 Apr 25	EB fr	**E**	
			2 188–9
1797 Apr 28	EB fr	**E**	
			2 189–92
1797 Apr 29	EB fr	**E**	
			2 196–7
1797 May 8	EB fr	**E**	
			2 197–201
1797 May 11	EB fr	**E**	
			2 201–4
1797 May 12	EB to	IX, 332–40	
1797 May 18	EB fr	IX, 349–53	
[1797] May 18	EB to	IX, 353–5	
1797 May 30	EB fr	**E**	
			2 227–30
1797 June 1	EB to	IX, 364–6	
1797 June 5	EB to	IX, 368–9	
n.d.	RBsr to	**C**	
	[Laurence]		

LAURENS, Henry

1781 Dec	EB fr	**61** 383 abs	
		3 lines	
1782 Mar 27	EB to	IV, 428	
[1782 Nov]	EB fr	**A**	
1783 June 25	EB fr	**55**	
1784 June 13	EB fr	**A**	

LAWSON, Rev. Archibald

1790 Dec 22	EB fr	**A**	
1791 May 24	EB fr	**A**	
1792 Feb 2	EB fr	**A**	

LEADBEATER, Mrs.
See **SHACKLETON**

LEAN, Alexander

1782 May 13	EB fr	**A**	

LEARDI, Monsignor Paolo

1794 Feb 15	EB fr	**B**	

LEE, Arthur

1775 Aug 21	EB fr	**A**	
			1 II, 42
1775 Aug 22	EB to	III, 188–9	

LEE, General Charles

1773 Oct 23	EB fr	**A**	
1774 Feb 1	EB to	II, 517–18	
1774 Dec 16	EB fr	**A**	
			1 I, 508–15

LEE, John; barrister

1774 July 24	EB to	III, 12–13	
1774 Aug 20	EB fr	**A**	
1776 Dec 30	EB fr	**A**	
[1779] July 26	EB to	IV, 106–8	
[1782 Mar 7]	EB to	IV, 419–20	
[1782 Mar 25]	EB and	IV, 427	
	M. of Rockingham		
	to Lee		
[1783 Mar 21]	EB to	V, 77–9	
n.d.	[EB] fr	**A**	
n.d.	EB fr	**A**	

LEE, John; attorney at law

[1785] Apr 4	EB fr	**A**	

LEE, Dr. J.

1768 Jan 12	EB fr	**A**	

LEE, Richard

[1783]	EB fr	**A**	

LEE, Robert Cooper

1784 May 5	EB fr	A
1784 Sept 23	EB fr	A

LEE, Thomas

1766 May 3	EB fr	A

LEE, Sir William, 4th Baronet

1784 Mar 27	EB to	v, 135–6
1784 May 6	EB to	v, 143–4
1784 May 11	EB fr	A
1790 Nov 5	EB fr	A

LEECHMAN, William

1783 Dec 6	EB fr	v, 117–19
1784 June 16	EB fr	A
1784 Nov 15	EB fr	v, 187–8
1785 Feb 16	EB fr	A
1785 May 1	EB fr	A
1785 May 14	EB fr	A

LEEDS, Francis Godolphin Osborne, 5th Duke of

[1796]	EB fr	**D**
		4 27916
		f. 68

LELAND, Rev. Dr. Thomas

1765 Feb 28	EB fr	**B**
1765 July 27	EB and WB fr	A
		1 I, 81–5
1766 Jan 9	EB fr	A
		1 I, 94–7
1766 Mar 4	WB fr	**B**
1766 Nov 29	EB, RBsr and WB fr	**B**
1767 Apr 4	EB fr	**B**
1770 Mar 22	EB fr	A
		1 I, 221–4
1770 May 19	EB fr	A
1770 June 11	EB fr	A
		1 I, 225–8
1774 June 15	EB fr	A
1774 June 26	EB fr	A
		1 I, 459–61
1774 June 27	EB fr	A
		1 I, 461–4

LENOIR, Jean-Charles-Pierre

1791 May 10	EB fr	**B**

LEONETTI, Antonio

1791 July 30	EB fr	A

LEVIZAC, Abbé Jean-Pons-Victor-Lecontz de

1796 Jan 10	EB fr	**B**

LEWIS, John

1792 Feb 29	RBsr fr	**M** p. 15
1793 Dec 30	RBsr fr	A
1794 Jan 23	RBsr fr	A

LEWIS, M.

1796	EB to	IX, 469

LEY, John

[1794 Apr 16]	EB to	VII, 538
[1794 Apr 18]	EB to	VII, 538
[1794 Apr 19]	EB to	VII, 539
1794 Apr 21	EB fr	A
[1794 Apr 22]	EB to	VII, 539–40
1794 Apr 23	EB fr	**B**
1794 Apr 24	EB fr	A
1794 June 10	EB fr	A

LIND, Dr. James

1792 [Aug] 30	EB to	VII, 183–5

LINDO, Benjamin

1782 Feb 9	EB fr	A

LISBURNE, Wilmot Vaughan, 1st Earl of

[1782 May *a* 8]	EB to	IV, 452
[1782 May *a* 8]	EB to	IV, 452
[1782] May 8	EB fr	A
[1782 May 8]	EB to	IV, 453

LITTLE, William Charles

1783 May 1	EB fr, and M'Grugar	A

LIVINGSTON, Philip

1775 Oct 3	EB to, and La Grange	III, 226–7

LIVINGSTON, Robert R.
[1771 June 9]   EB to   II, 214

LIVRY, Philippine de
1791 Mar 1   EB fr   B

LLOYD, Charles
1765 [Oct *a* 1]   EB fr   A
1765 Oct 1   EB to   I, 214–15
                        IX, 388

LLOYD, Harford
1774 Oct 29   EB to   III, 69–70

LLOYD, Thomas
1769 June 14   EB fr   A

LOGAN, Rev. John
1781 July 6   EB to   IV, 354–5

LONDON, Bishop of
See LOWTH
     PORTEUS

[LONDON CHRONICLE, editor
   of the]
[1771 Jan *p* 20]   EB to   II, 186–8

LONG, Charles
[1796] July 8   EB fr   B

LONG, Dudley, later (1789) Dudley
   Long North
1781 Aug 19   EB fr   A
[1784] Tuesday   EB fr   A
1788 June *a* 25   EB fr   1 III, 76–7
1796 Dec 28   EB to   IX, 213–14

LOSCOMBE, Benjamin
1775 Oct 16   EB fr   A

LOUGHBOROUGH, Alexander
   Wedderburn, later (1780) 1st Baron
1763 July 29   EB to   I, 173–4
[1767 June]   [WB] fr   A
[1773 May 18]   EB fr   A
1773 May 18   EB to   II, 433
[1774 June *a* 10] EB fr   A

1777 Dec 3   EB to   III, 406
1777 [Dec] 3   EB to   III, 407
[1777 Dec 3]   EB fr   III, 407
1777 Dec 4   EB to   III, 408
1778 July 2   EB fr   A
                        1 II, 226–7
[1780 Apr 16]   EB to   IV, 230–1
1780 June 15   EB to   IV, 247–50
1780 July 17   EB to   IV, 255–6
1780 Oct 10   EB fr   A
1780 Dec 20   EB fr   IV, 323–5
[1781 Jan *c* 4]   EB fr   IV, 327–8
1782 Apr 5   EB fr   A
1782 Apr 6   EB fr   A
1782 Apr 9   EB fr   A
1782 July 7   EB fr   V, 14–15
1782 July 17   EB to   V, 19–21
1784 [June]   EB fr   A
1784 July 15   EB fr   A
[1784 Dec 4]   EB fr   A
1788 Jan 13   EB fr   A
[1790] Jan 6   EB fr   C
1790 Nov 6   EB fr   A
1792 May 27   EB to   VII, 143–4
[1792 June 13]   EB fr   VII, 149–50
1792 June 13   EB to   VII, 150–1
1792 Sept 15   EB fr   VII, 211–12
1792 Nov 27   EB fr   VII, 303–4
1792 Nov 28   EB to   VII, 304–6
1792 Nov 30   EB fr   VII, 318–19
[1792] Thursday EB fr   A
1793 Jan 12   EB fr   A
1793 Jan 19   EB fr   VII, 338–40
1793 Jan 27   EB to   VII, 344–5
[1793 Mar 23]   EB fr   A
[1793 July *p* 29]   EB fr   C
1793 Sept 1   EB fr   A
[1793]   EB to   17 VI, 232,
                        abs ½ p.
[1794 Jan 11]   EB fr   A
1794 Jan 12   EB to   VII, 516–19
[1794 Jan 15]   EB fr   VII, 524–5
[1794 Oct 19]   EB to   VIII, 43–50
[1794 Oct 23]   EB fr   A
1794 Nov 2   EB to   VIII, 70–1
[1794] Nov [6]   EB to   VIII, 73
1794 Dec 12   EB to   VIII, 98–9
1795 Jan 10   EB to   VIII, 114–15

Loughborough, 1st Baron (*cont.*)			
1796 Mar 7	EB to	VIII, 406–7	
1796 Mar 8	EB fr	C	
[1796 Mar *c* 17]	EB to	VIII, 422–3	
[1796 Mar *c* 17]	EB to	VIII, 423–5	
[1796 Mar *c* 17]	EB to	VIII, 425–35	
1797 May 1	EB to	IX, 322–3	
1797 May 3	EB fr	A	
n.d.	EB fr	A	
	[Bn. Loughborough]		
n.d.	EB fr	C	

LOUIS XVI, King of France

1791 Aug 6	RBjr to	VI, 318–20

LOWE, J.

1782 Apr 30	RBjr fr	A
1782 May 1	RBjr fr	A

LOWTH, Robert, Bishop of London

1782 May 1	EB fr	A

LUBERSAC DE LIBRON,
Abbé Charles-François

1795 May 6	EB fr	A
1795 May [8]	EB to	VIII, 236–7

LUCAN, 1st Baron and 1st Earl
of
See BINGHAM

LUDGATE, Robert

1796 Jan 26	EB fr	B

LUMLEY, George Augusta Lumley
Saunderson, styled Viscount

[1779 Feb]	EB fr	A

LUSHINGTON, Sir Stephen,
1st Baronet

1781 Mar 13	EB fr	A
1784 Nov 15	EB fr	A
1791 Apr 7	EB fr	F

LUSHINGTON, William

1796 Oct 26	EB to	IX, 99–100

LUSIGNY, Lazare-Guillaume de
Ganay, Comte de

1773 Apr 12	EB fr	A

LYMBURNER, Adam

1788 May 17	EB fr	B

MACARTNEY, Sir George; later
(1776) 1st Baron Macartney

1765 Sept 26	EB fr	A
1765 Dec [*p* 23]	EB & WB to	I, 222–3
1766 Feb 21	WB fr	A
		1 I, 101–2
1766 June 13	WB to	C
1766 July 29	WB to	C
1766 Aug 5	WB to	C
1766 Sept 4	WB fr	A
		51 37–9
1766 Sept 29	WB to	C
1766 Oct 24	WB to	C
1766 Oct 30	WB to	C
1766 Dec 12	WB to	C
[1766]	WB to	C
1772 Feb 19	EB to	II, 301
1781 May 29	WB to	AW
1781 Sept 28	WB to	AS
1781 Oct 15	EB to	IV, 377; X, 10–13
1781 Nov 18	WB to	AS
1782 Jan 29	WB to	AW
1782 Feb 17	WB to	AW
1782 Mar 21	WB to	AW
1782 Apr 27	WB to	AW
1782 June 7	WB to	AW
1782 June 25	WB to	AW
1782 July 7	WB to	AW
1782 Aug 30	EB fr	E
		51 204–6
1782 Sept 19	WB to	AW
1782 Sept 27, 29	WB to	AW
1782 Oct 1	WB to	AW
1782 Oct 3	WB to	AW
1782 Oct 15	WB to	AW

1782 Oct 17	EB fr	v, 41–4
1782 Oct 21	WB to	AW
1782 Nov 5		D
		4 22458,
		f. 80
1782 Nov 7	WB to	AW
1782 Dec 18	WB to	AS
1783 Feb 12	WB to	AS
1783 July 12	WB to	D
		4 29160
		f. 74
1783 Aug 11	EB fr	D
		4 22459,
		f. 161
1783 Aug 23	WB to	D
		4 29160
		f. 246
[1783] Sept 23	EB to	x, 14–15
1783 Sept 23	WB to	D
		4 29160
		ff. 387–8
1783 Oct 14	EB fr	v, 114–15
1783 Oct 22	WB to	AW
1783 Nov 11	WB fr	AI
1783 Nov 16	WB to	AS
1783 Nov 18	WB to	AS
1783 Nov 20	WB to	AS
1783 Dec 16	WB to	AS
1784 Jan 31	EB fr	v, 124–7
1784 Mar 8	WB fr	E
		51 226
1784 Mar 22	WB to	AI
1784 Mar 22	WB to	AI
[1784] Mar	WB to	AS
1784 July 28	EB fr	D
		51 227
1784 Aug 25	WB to	AI
1784 Aug 31	WB fr	AI
1784 Dec 30	WB to	AS
1785 Jan ⟨13⟩	EB to	x, 15–16
1785 Mar 21	WB to	AS
1785 June 4	WB to	AS
1785 July 15	WB to	AS

MACARTNEY, Lady Jane (née Stuart)

1784 Aug 22	EB fr	A
1784 Aug 23	EB fr	A

1784 Aug 25	EB fr	A
1785 Feb 17	EB to	v, 207; x,

M'CARTHY, F.

1783 Jan 28	EB fr	A

MACDONALD, Thomas

1792 Jan 16	EB fr	A

M'GRUGAR, Thomas

1783 May 1	EB fr,	A
	and Little	

MACINTYRE, Rev. Dr. Joseph

1788 Aug 29	EB fr	A

MACKINTOSH, James

1796 Dec 22	EB fr	IX, 192–4
1796 Dec 23	EB to	IX, 194–6

MACLEANE, Lauchlin

1772 July 31	EB fr	A
[1772 Aug 2]	EB fr	A

MACMAHON, Parkyns

1781 Feb 14	EB fr	A

MADAN, Robert

1780 June 22	EB fr	A

MADGETT, N.

1797 Jan 18	EB fr	A

MAGENIS, Father George

1793 June 5	EB fr	B

MAHON, Charles Stanhope, styled Viscount

1780 Apr 6	EB to	IV, 225–6

MAINWARING

[1780 Mar p 8]	EB fr	A

MALMESBURY, James Harris, 1st Baron

1793 Nov 19	EB fr	A
		1 IV, 200–1

MALONE, Edmond

[1788 Feb 12]	EB to	v, 378–9
1789 Mar 12	EB to	v, 451
[1790 Nov c 29]	EB to	VI, 181–2

Malone, Edmond (*cont.*)

1792 Mar 17	EB fr	**A**	
1792 Mar 18	EB to	VII, 99–100	
1792 July 10	EB to	VII, 155–6	
1792 Dec 16	EB fr	VII, 323–4	
[1793 Jan *c* 17]	EB to	VII, 337	
1793 May 6	RBjr to	**19** II, 28	
1795 May 22	EB to	VIII, 251–2	
1796 Apr 1	EB fr	VIII, 454	
1796 Apr 5	EB to	VIII, 455–6	
1797 Apr 14	EB fr	IX, 308–10	
1797 Apr 16	EB to	IX, 310	
1797 May 2	EB fr	IX, 325	
1797 May 4	EB to	IX, 326–9	
n.d. Thursday	EB to	IX, 455–6	
n.d.	EB to	IX, 471	

MANCHESTER, George Montagu, 4th Duke of

[1770] Sept 4	EB fr	**A**
[1777] Nov 7	EB fr	**A**
[1777] Dec 6	EB fr	**A**
[1786] Feb 8	EB to	V, 257

MANN, Abbé Theodore Augustus

1793 Oct 17	EB fr	**A**
1794 Jan 14	EB fr	**A**

MANSFIELD, William Murray, 1st Earl of

1780 July 17	EB fr	IV, 255
1791 Aug 9	EB fr	**A**

MANUAR RATANJI

1781 Oct 3	EB fr,	**A** and Cursetji Manuar
1781 Oct 14	EB fr,	**A** and Cursetji Manuar

MARAINE, Abbé Jean-Marin

1796 May 1	EB fr	**B**
1796 May 2	EB to	IX, 3–6
1796 Aug 12	EB fr	**B**
[1796] Thursday	EB fr	**B**
1797 Mar 18	EB fr	**B**

MARIE ANTOINETTE, Queen of France

[1791 Aug *c* 17]	EB to	VI, 349–52

MARKHAM, William; later (1771) Bishop of Chester

1765 Dec 29	WB fr	I, 225–7
1771 Nov 9	EB to	II, 250–2
[1771 Nov *p* 9]	EB to	II, 252–86
[1772 Dec *a* 22]	EB fr	II, 393–4
1774 June 20	EB to	II, 541–3
1774 June 21	EB fr	**A**

MARKHAM, William

1792 May 30	EB to	VII, 146–7

MARLAY, Richard; later (1787) Bishop of Clonfert

[1783 May *p* 5]	EB fr	**A**
1794 Oct 1	EB fr	**A**
1795 Feb 20	EB fr	VIII, 154–6

MARRIOTT, James

1766 Feb 8	EB fr	**A** **1** I, 97–8
1766 Feb 26	EB fr	**A** **1** I, 102–3
1766 July 22	WB to	I
1766 Sept 30	WB to	I

MASÈRES, Francis

[1776]	EB to	III, 306–8

MASON, Charles

1782 Apr 16	RBsr fr	**A**

MASON, Edward

1782 May 14	EB fr	**A**

MASON, John Monck

[1765 May *p* 29]	EB to	I, 195–8
[1765] June 28	EB fr	**B**
[1765] Aug 6	EB fr	**B**
[1768] Mar 29	EB fr	**A**
[1782] Nov 21	EB fr	V, 48–9
[1782 Nov *p* 21]	EB to	V, 49–51

MASON, Rev. William

[1775 Feb 2]	EB fr	**B**

MASTER COOPERS, Committee of
1782 June 16   EB fr   A

MAUNY, [Marie-Victoire (*née* Arnauld), Vicomtesse de]
1796 May 22   EB fr   B

MAURICE, Thomas
1789 Aug 4   EB to   VI, 6–8

MAUVILLON, Jakob
1776 Nov 29   EB fr   A

MAXWELL, Dr. William
1793 Mar 6   EB fr   A

MENONVILLE, François-Louis-Thibault de
1790 Nov 17   EB fr   VI, 162–9
1791 Jan [19]   EB to   3 IV, 3–55*
1791 Mar 11,   EB fr   VI, 232–3
     Apr 27

MERCER, Captain Thomas
1790 Feb 19   EB fr   9 II, 81–4
1790 Feb 26   EB to   VI, 92–8
1790 Nov 8   EB fr   A
                    9 II, 92–4
                    abs and
                    ext 1p

MERCY-ARGENTEAU, Florimond-Claude, Comte de
1793 June 27   EB to   VII, 376
1793 July 19   EB fr   Y
[1793 Aug *c* 6]   EB to   VII, 386–93
1793 Oct 1   EB fr   B
1793 Oct 16   EB to   VII, 451–2

MEREDITH, Sir William, 3rd Baronet
1765 Dec 11   EB fr   A
1766 Jan 1   EB fr   A
1766 Mar 23   EB fr   A

* Published as *A Letter to a Member of the National Assembly* (Todd, 166–70).

1767 June 26   EB fr   A
                    1 I, 129–30
1767 Oct 28   EB fr   A
1767 Nov 9   EB fr   A
1769 July 17   EB fr   A
1769 Aug 28   EB fr   A

MERLOTT, John
1780 Apr 4   EB to   IV, 223–5

METCALFE, Philip
[1792 Feb 23]   RBsr to   VII, 74
[1792 Feb 28]   EB to   VII, 79–80
[1792 June 23]   EB to   VII, 153–4
1792 July 10   EB to   VII, 156–7

MEYER, Friedrich Ludwig Wilhelm
1790 Feb 19   EB fr   A
1791 May 8   EB fr   A
[1791 May *p* 8]   EB to   VI, 256–7

MICHIE, John
1787 Mar 14   EB to   V, 309–11
1787 Mar 16   EB fr   V, 311–12
1787 Mar 30   EB fr   A

MIDDLETON, Matthew
1786 Feb 13   EB fr   A

MILES, William
1780 May 20   EB fr   A

MILLAR, John
1784 Aug 16   EB fr   A
1784 Nov 15   EB fr   B
1785 Jan 19   EB fr   A
1785 Apr 17   EB fr   A
1785 Nov 13   EB fr   A

MILLER, James
1786 Mar 10   EB fr   A

MILLER, Michael
1778 Dec 3   EB and   AZ
                    H. Cruger fr
1779 Mar 1   EB to   IV, 47–8
1779 Mar 22   EB and   AZ
                    H. Cruger fr

Miller, Michael (*cont.*)

1779 Mar 24	EB and	IV, 51–2	
	H. Cruger to		
1779 Apr 13	EB and	A	
	H. Cruger fr		
1779 Apr 14	EB and	A	
	H. Cruger fr		
1779 Apr 16	EB to	IV, 59	
1779 Apr 17	EB to	IV, 60–2	
1779 Apr 22	EB and	A	
	H. Cruger fr		
1779 May 12	EB to	IV, 73–4	
1779 May 22	EB fr	**AZ**	
1779 May 22	EB and	**AZ**	
	H. Cruger fr		
1779 May 25	EB to	IV, 81	
1779 May 26	EB to	IV, 82	
1779 May 28	EB to	IV, 82–3	
1779 Dec 9	EB to	IV, 173	

MILLER, William

1783 Dec 23	EB fr	**B**

MILLETT, Jo[seph]

1791 Feb 21	EB fr	**A**
1791 Mar 17	EB fr	**A**

MILTON, George Damer, styled
  Viscount

1794 Dec 15	EB fr	**A**

MITCHELL, William

1784 Mar 21	EB fr	**A**

MITFORD, William H. T.

[1796 Feb 29]	EB fr	**A**

MOFFATT, Thomas

1768 June 19,	EB fr	**A**
20		
1769 Jan 25	EB fr	**A**

MOIRA, Francis Rawdon-Hastings,
  2nd Earl of

1795 Sept 8	EB fr	**A**

MOLESWORTH, Richard

1783 Oct 1	WB fr	**F**

1792 Oct 12	EB fr	**F**
1792 Oct 14	EB to	VII, 267

MOLESWORTH, Robert

1783 Apr 22	EB fr	**A**

MOLINI, Peter

1781 Aug 15	EB to	IV, 365
1781 Sept 11	EB to	IV, 371–2
[1781 Oct *a* 13]	EB fr	**A**

MONBRUN, Alexandre de

1797 Mar 28	EB fr	**B**

MONSEY, Dr. Messenger

1782 Mar 29	EB fr	**B**

MONSIEUR
See ARTOIS PROVENCE

MONTAGU, Mrs. Edward

1759 Sept 24	EB to	I, 131–3	
1759 Oct 6	EB to	I, 133–4	
[1763 Mar 4]	EB to	I, 163	
		IX, 384	
1763 Apr [25]	EB to	I, 169–70	
[1763] July 29	EB to	I, 170–3	
		IX, 385–7	
1768 Dec 2	EB to	II, 19	
[1771 July 20]	EB to	II, 224–5	
1771 July 24	EB to	II, 225–6	
1773 Sept 4	EB to	II, 454–6	
1773 Sept 11	EB fr	II, 456–8	
[1776 Feb 10]	EB fr	**A**	
		1 II, 91–2	
1776 Feb 10	EB to	III, 249–50	
1776 May [3]	EB to	III, 265–6	
[1777 Sept] 6	EB fr	**BE**	
		60 99–100	
[1783] May 30	EB fr	**A**	
[n.y. Feb 10]	EB to	IX, 456	

MONTAGU, Frederick

[1767] July 21	EB fr	**A**
1789 May 1	EB to	V, 465–9

MONTGOMERY, Alexander

1777 Dec 20	EB fr	**A**

MONTLOSIER, François-
Dominique de Reynaud, Comte de
1791 Aug 8   EB fr   **B**

MONTROND, Angélique-Marie
(*née* Darlus du Taillis), Comtesse
de
1790 Dec 30   EB fr   **B**
1791 Jan 25   EB to   VI, 210–13
1796 Aug 26   EB fr   **B**

MOORE, Dr
n.d.   EB to   X, 39

MORE, Hannah
1776 Jan 19   RBsr to   **52** I, 60–1

MORIZOT, [Édmé-Étienne]
1791 Jan 20   EB fr   **B**
1791 Mar 11   EB fr   **B**

MORRIS, Charles
[1791 May 30]   [EB] fr   **B**

MORRIS, Corbyn
Commissioner of Customs
1777 Jan 16   EB fr   **A**

MORRIS, M.
1774 Sept 27   EB fr   **A**

MORRITT, Mrs. John
 Sawrey
1787 Feb 21   RBjr fr   **A**
1787 June 12   RBjr fr   **A**

MORTON, John
1780 Feb 15   EB fr   **A**
1780 Feb 20   EB fr   **A**
1780 Mar 17   EB fr   **A**

MORTON, Thomas
1787 Mar 21   EB fr   **A**
1787 Mar 31   EB fr   **A**

MOSER, Joseph
1796 Mar 21   EB fr   **A**
1796 Apr 5   EB to   VIII, 456–8

MOUCLER, Abbesse de
1791 Dec 2   EB fr   **B**

MOUNIER, Jean-Joseph
1791 Apr 2   EB fr   **B**
                    [Mounier]

MOYLAN, Francis, Catholic Bishop
 of Cork
1792 Nov 18   EB to   VII, 293–4
1792 Nov 19   EB fr   **B**
1793 Dec 6   EB to   VII, 499–
                                  500
1793 Dec 20   EB fr   VII, 506–8
1794 Aug 20   EB fr   **B**

MULLETT, Thomas
1775 Apr 13   EB to   III, 147–8
1775 Apr 14   EB fr   III, 148–9
1775 Apr 14   EB to   III, 149–
                                  50
1775 Apr 15   EB fr   III, 150–1
1776 July 27   EB fr   **A**

MURAT-MONTFERRAND,
 Comte de
1791 June 21   EB fr   **B**

MURPHY, Arthur
1780 Mar 4   EB fr   **A**
1791 Dec 24   EB fr   **A**
1793 May 6   EB fr   **23** 316
1793 May 26   EB to   VII, 367–8
1793 Dec 8   EB to   VII, 500–3
1796 Feb 29   EB fr   **A**

MURPHY, David
1764 Aug 16   EB fr,   **B**
                    and Eliza Bourke

MURPHY, Rev. Edward
1766 Mar 1   EB fr   **A**

MURRAY, Evan
1768 Sept 27   EB fr   **A**

MURRAY, James
1778 June 14   EB fr   **B**

New York Assembly (*cont.*)

1775 Jan 3	EB to	III, 81–3
1775 Mar 14	EB to	III, 133–6
1775 Apr 5	EB fr	**R**
		30 287 abs
		and ext
		2 lines
1775 June 7	EB to	III, 164–7

NEW YORK, Minority Members of
a Committee at

1773 Mar 3	EB fr	**A**

NICOLAÏDES, Stephanos

1791 [July] 4	EB fr	**A**

NISIBIS, Cesare Brancadoro,
Archbishop of

1791 Nov 21	EB fr	**B**
1791 Dec 14	EB to	VI, 457–61
[1792 Jan] 11	EB fr	**B**

NOBLE, John

1775 Feb 21	EB to	III, 117–18
1775 June [*a* 25]	EB to	III, 173–4
1775 July 24	EB fr	**A**
1775 Sept 24	EB fr	**A**
1776 Aug 10	EB fr	**H**
[1776 Nov *a* 4]	EB to	III, 300
1777 Jan 13	EB fr	**A**
1777 Mar	EB to	IX, 464
1777 Aug [*c* 11]	EB to	III, 365–6
[1778 Apr 3]	EB to	III, 424
1778 Apr 24	EB to	III, 437–9
1778 [June] 25	EB to	X, 5
1778 Oct 3	EB to	IV, 22–3
1779 Mar [*a* 24]	EB to	IV, 49–51
[1779 Mar *a* 31]	EB to	IV, 52–3
1779 May 5	EB to	IV, 66
		IX, 425–6
[1779 May 6]	EB to	IV, 68
		IX, 426
1779 May 21	EB to	IV, 75–7
1780 Apr 12	EB to	IV, 230
1780 June 8	EB fr	IV, 243–5
1780 June 18	EB fr	IV, 251–3
1780 Aug 11	EB to	IV, 263–4
1780 Oct 5	EB to	IV, 312–13

1781 [Jan] 2	EB to	IV, 325–7
1781 Mar 9	EB to	IV, 342
1781 Apr 2	EB to	IV, 347–8
1781 Apr 26	EB to	IV, 350
1781 Nov 6	EB to	IV, 380–1
1781 Nov 6	EB fr,	**A**
		Harford and Span
1782 Jan 22	EB fr	**A**
1782 Jan 30	EB fr	**A**
1783 Feb 5	EB fr	**A**
[1784] Jan 1	EB to	V, 121–2
1790 Mar 14	EB to	VI, 100–4
1793 June 15	RBsr fr	**A**
1793 Sept 29	RBsr fr	**A**
1793 Oct 1	RBsr fr,	**A**
		and J. H. Noble
1793 Oct 7	RBsr fr	**A**
1793 Oct 17	RBsr fr	**A**
1793 Oct 18	RB[sr] fr	**A**
1793 Nov 19	RBsr fr	**A**
1793 Dec 5	RBsr fr	**A**
1793 Dec 12	RBsr fr	**A**
1795 Apr 20	EB to	VIII, 235
1796 Feb 24	EB to	VIII, 389–90

NOBLE, John Hatt
Son of John Noble

1793 Oct 1	RBsr fr,	**A**
		and J. Noble

NODIN, J.

1782 Mar 31	EB fr	**A**

NORTH, Dudley Long see LONG,
Dudley

NORTH, Frederick North, styled
Lord

[1775] Feb 19	EB fr	III, 115
1777 June 5	EB to	III, 345–6
[1780 June 18]	EB fr	IV, 250–1
[1780 June 19]	EB fr	**A**
1781 Dec 5	EB to	IV, 386–7
[1781] Dec 14	EB to	IV, 389–90
1783 Mar 28	EB fr	V, 83–4

NORTH, George Augustus

[1784 Jan]	EB fr	**B**

NORTHCOTE, James
1790 Jan   EB to   x, 23–4

NORTON, Sir Fletcher
[1771 June *a* 15] WB to   A
[1771 June *a* 15] WB fr   A
1775 May 10   EB fr   A

NORWICH, Bishop of
See HORNE

NOTT, John
[1792 Dec 30]   EB fr   VII, 328–9

NUGENT, Dr. Christopher,
Burke's father-in-law
[1752] Sept   EB to   I, 115–18
1753 June   WB to   A

NUGENT, C.
[1791] Oct 24   RBjr fr   A
[1791] Dec 23   JB fr   B

NUGENT, John
1796 Jan 5   EB to   VIII, 367

NUGENT, Captain Nicholas
[1775] Dec 27   EB fr   B
1776 Jan 1   EB fr   B

NUGENT, Robert Nugent, 1st
  Viscount Clare; later (1776) 1st
  Earl (Nugent)
1774 Oct 18   EB fr   A
1778 June 25   EB fr   A
1780 Sept 18   EB fr   A

NUGENT, Madame
1792 Oct 8   EB fr   B

O'BEIRNE, Thomas Lewis; later
  (1795) Bishop of Ossory
1781 Jan 30   EB to   IV, 334–5
1781 Dec 24   EB to   IV, 397–8
1782 June 7   EB to   IV, 457–8
1782 Aug 20   EB fr   V, 28–30
1782 Aug 27   EB to   V, 31–2
[1782 Aug 28]   EB to   V, 33

1782 Aug 29   EB to   V, 33–4
[1783 May *a* 21] EB to   V, 93–4
1783 Aug 16   EB to   V, 110
1783 Sept 6   RB[sr] to IX, 465
[1784 Nov 28]   EB to   V, 195–6
[1784 Nov *p* 28] RBjr to   A
1785 Oct 12   EB to   V, 225–6
1786 Sept 29   EB to   V, 280–3
1788 Dec 8   EB fr   A
1789 Mar 30   RBjr fr   A
1791 Apr 11   RBjr fr   A, B
1791 May 6   RBjr to   VI, 253–5
1791 July 25   RBjr fr   A
[1795 Mar]   EB fr   B

O'BRIEN, Sir Lucius Henry, 3rd
  Baronet
1778 July 15   EB fr   A
1778 Dec 17   EB fr   A
1779 June 4   EB fr   A
1781 Feb 24   EB fr   A
1782 July 22   EB fr   A

O'BRYEN, Dennis
1782 Mar 25   EB to   IV, 425–6
[1782 Mar]   EB fr   A

O'CONOR, Charles; Irish
  antiquary
1765 Apr 25   EB fr   A

O'CONOR, Charles
1796 Mar 13   EB fr   A

O'CONOR, Patrick
1796 Dec 29   EB fr   A

O'DONEL, Hugh
1782 Apr 3   EB fr   A

OGILVIE, Thomas
1791 Feb 14   EB fr   A

OGLETHORPE, General James
  Edward
1777 May 30   EB fr   III, 343–4
1777 June 2   EB to   III, 344

O'GORMAN, Chevalier Thomas

[1782 May]	EB fr	**B**
1793 Dec 18	EB fr	**AL**

O'HALLORAN, Sylvester

1778 Aug 1	EB fr	**A**
1783 Sept 15	EB fr	**A**

O'HARA, Charles, Sr.

[1759] Nov 20	EB fr	**A**
[1760] Apr 10	EB fr	**A**
1761 July 3	EB to	I, 137–40
1761 July 10	EB to	I, 140–2
1762 Aug 10	EB fr	I, 144–6
[1762 Aug *a* 23]	EB to	I, 147–9
1762 [Oct] 9	EB, WB and Dr Nugent to	I, 149–51
[1762] Oct 30	WB and Dr Nugent to	
[1762] Oct 30	EB to	I, 151–3
1762 Nov 20	WB to	I, 153–4
[1762] Nov 23	EB to	I, 155–6
1762 Nov 25	EB to	I, 156–8
[1762] Dec 9	EB to	I, 158–60
1762 Dec 12	EB to	I, 160–1
1762 Dec 30	EB to	I, 161–3
[1763] July 4	EB fr	**A** 7 308–11
[1763] July 26	EB fr	**A** 7 311–13
[1764] July 24	EB fr	**A**
[1764] Sept 20	EB fr	**A**
1764 Sept 27	EB fr	**A**
[1764] Nov 20	EB fr	**A**
[1765] Jan 14	EB fr	**A**
[1765 July] 4	EB and WB to	I, 206–8
1765 July 9	EB to	I, 208–10
1765 July 11	EB to	I, 211
1765 July 19	EB fr	**A** 7 320–2
[1765] July 30	EB and WB fr	I, 214
1765 Oct 15	EB fr	**A**
[1765] Nov 22	EB fr	I, 218–19
[1765] Nov 28	EB fr	**A**
1765 Dec 17	EB fr	**A**
[1765] Dec 24	EB to	I, 223–4

[1765 Dec] 24	EB fr	**A**
[1765] Dec 31	EB to	I, 228–30
[1766] Jan 10	EB fr	**A**
[1766 Jan] 18	EB to	I, 231–3
[1766] Jan 25	EB fr	**A**
[1766] Feb 11	EB fr	**A**
[1766] Feb 20	EB fr	**A**
1766 Mar 1, 4	EB to	I, 239–41
[1766] Mar 4	EB fr	**A**
[1766] Mar 10	EB fr	**A** 7 334–8
[1766] Mar 11	EB to	I, 244–5
[1766] Mar 13	EB fr	**A**
[1766] Mar 18	EB fr	**A** 7 339–41
[1766] Mar 20	EB fr	**A**
[1766] Mar 22	EB fr	**A**
[1766] Mar 25	RBsr fr	**A**
[1766 Mar 27]	EB to	I, 246
[1766] Mar 29	EB to	I, 246–7
[1766] Apr 8	EB to	I, 248–9
[1766] Apr 8	EB fr	**A**
[1766] Apr 10	EB fr	**A**
[1766] Apr 15	EB fr	**A** 7 344–6
[1766 Apr 21]	EB to	I, 250
[1766 Apr] 23, 24	EB to	I, 251–2
[1766] Apr 30	EB fr	**A**
[1766 Apr *p* 30]	EB fr	**A**
[1766] May 15	EB fr	**A**
[1766 May] 24	EB to	I, 254–6
[1766] May 31	EB fr	**A**
[1766] July 29	EB to	I, 261–4
[1766] Aug 14	WB fr	**A** 7 355–6
[1766] Aug 19	EB to	I, 264–5
[1766] Aug 25	EB fr	**A** 7 358–9
[1766] Sept 18	EB fr	**A** 7 359–60
1766 Oct 4	WB to	I, 268–70
1766 Oct [21]	EB to	I, 271–3
[1766] Oct 31	EB fr	**A**
[1766] Nov 11	EB fr	**A**
[1766 Nov *p* 11]	EB to	I, 277–80
[1766 Nov *p* 25]	RBsr to	**G** 7 370–3

O'Hara, Charles Sr. (*cont.*)

[1769] Nov 30	EB fr	A	
		7 460–1	
[1770] May 10	EB fr	A	
		7 462–4	
1770 May 21	EB to	II, 137–40	
[1770] May 31	EB fr	A	
		7 469–71	
1770 [June *a* 20]	WB to	G	
		7 471–2	
1770 June 20	EB and Dr Nugent to	II, 143–5	
1770 Aug 9	EB to	II, 147–9	
1770 Nov 23	EB fr	A	
[1770 Dec 8]	WB to	G	
		7 478–80	
1770 Dec 31	EB to	II, 177–9	
[1771] Jan 1	WB fr	A	
[1771] Feb 17	EB fr	A	
		7 483–5	
1771 Mar 11	EB fr	A	
		7 485–6	
1771 Mar 28	EB to	II, 206–7	
1771 Apr 2	EB to	II, 207–10	
[1771] Apr 14	EB fr	A	
[1771 May]	WB to	G	
1771 July 11	EB fr	A	
		7 492–4	
[1771 July *p* 14]	EB to	II, 220–3	
1771 Aug 30	EB fr	A	
		7 498–500	
1771 Sept 10	EB to	II, 235–8	
1771 Oct 14	EB fr	A	
1771 Nov 17	EB fr	A	
1771 Nov 18	EB to	II, 286–8	
1771 Dec 18	EB to	II, 295–6	
1771 Dec 28	EB fr	A	
[1771 Dec]	WB to	G	
1772 Feb 2	WB to	G	
		1 512–16	
1772 Feb 22	WB fr	A	
1772 Mar 5	WB fr	A	
1772 Mar 13	WB to	G	
		7 516–21	
1772 Apr 1	WB fr	A	
1772 June 1	EB to	II, 305–7	
1772 July 14	EB fr	A	
[1772] July 30	EB to	II, 316–19	

1772 Aug 23	EB fr	A	
[1772 Aug]	WB to	G	
		7 529–30	
[1772 Sept *a* 2]	WB to	G	
1772 Sept 11	EB fr	A	
1772 Sept 30	EB to	II, 334–9	
1772 Oct 22	WB to	G	
		7 531–4	
1772 Oct 31	EB fr	A	
1772 Nov 8	WB fr	A	
1773 Mar 4	WB fr	A	
1773 Mar 26	EB to	II, 425–7	
1773 Apr 3	EB fr	A	
		7 541–3	
1773 Apr 29	EB fr	A	
[1773 May 22]	EB to	II, 434–6	
1773 May 24	EB fr	A	
1773 June 3	EB fr	A	
		7 546–7	
1773 Aug 20	EB to	II, 451–4	
1773 Nov 19	EB and WB to	II, 489–92	
1773 Dec 11	EB to	II, 495–6	
1773 Dec 18	EB fr	A	
		7 555–7	
1773 Dec 22	EB and Dr Nugent to	II, 500–1	
1773 Dec 24	EB fr	A	
1774 Jan 6	EB to	II, 507–10	
1774 May 6	WB to	G	
		7 563–7	
1774 Sept 2	WB to	G	
		7 567–70	
1774 Oct 12	RBsr fr	A	
1774 Oct 22	WB and Dr Nugent to	G	
		7 570–1	
[1774] Nov 2	EB to	III, 72–3	
[1774 Dec *a* 30]	WB to	G	
		7 572–4	
1775 Jan 23	EB fr	A	
		7 574–5	
1775 Jan 25	EB fr	A	
		7 576	
[1775 Apr *p* 14]	WB to	G	
		7 576–7	
1775 Apr 26	EB to	III, 151–2	
1775 May 3	EB fr	A	
		7 579–80	

O'Hara, Charles Sr. (*cont*)

1775 May 22	WB fr	A	7 581–2
[1775 May *c* 28]	EB to	III, 160–2	
1775 June 5, 18	EB fr	A	7 584–8
1775 July 26	EB to	III, 181–2	
1775 Aug 4	EB fr	A	7 590–1
1775 Aug 9	EB fr	A	7 591–3
1775 Aug [17]	EB to	III, 185–8	
1775 Aug 28	EB fr	A	7 596–8
[1775 Nov 10]	WB to	G	7 606–9
1775 Nov 18	WB fr	A	7 609–10
[1775 Dec *a* 18]	WB to	G	7 610–11
1775 Dec 29	EB fr	A	7 611–12
[1776] Jan 7	EB to	III, 243–7	
n.y. Mar 6	EB fr	A	

O'HARA, Charles, Jr.

[1775] Oct 30	Dr. Nugent fr	A	
[1775]	EB fr	A [C. O'Hara, Jr]	
1784 June 20	EB to	V, 152–3	
1784 July 11	EB to	V, 157–8	
1784 Nov 22	EB to	V, 190–2	
1788 Dec 1	EB to	V, 430	
n.d.	EB fr	G	

O'HARA, General Charles

1793 Oct 27	EB to	VII, 467

O'HARA, William Henry King

1778 Aug 17	EB fr	A

O'KEEFE, T.

1775 Jan 15	EB fr	A

O'LEARY, Arthur

1792 May 24	EB fr	C

O'NEALE, Michael

1782 July 9	EB fr	A

O'NEILL, Charles

1776 Mar 22	EB fr	A

ORDE, [Thomas]

[1784] June 24	EB fr	A

ORME, Captain Robert

1782 Mar 29	EB fr	A

OSBORNE, T.

1788 Oct 20	RB[sr] fr	AZ

OSMOND, Eleanor (*née* Dillon), Comtesse d'

1790 Dec 12	EB fr	B
1791 Jan 8	EB to	VI, 199–202
1794 Dec 1	EB fr	A
1794 Dec 8	EB to	VIII, 91–5
1794 Dec 10	EB fr	A
1794 Dec 29	EB to	VIII, 102–3

OSSORY, Bishop of
See O'BEIRNE

OSSORY, Earl of
See UPPER OSSORY

OVERTON, J.

1792 Dec 31	EB fr	A

OXFORD, Resident Graduates of the University of

[1790 Dec *a* 21]	EB fr	V

OXFORD, Vice-Chancellor of
See WILLS

PAINE, Thomas

1788 Aug 7	EB fr	K
1790 Jan 17	EB fr	VI, 67–76
1790 [May 6]	EB fr	**48** II, 497 abs 10 lines

PALLISER, Admiral Sir Hugh,
  1st Baronet
1776 Feb 23   EB fr   **A**
1776 Mar 16   EB fr   **A**

PALMER, [Rev.] Joseph
1782 May 1   EB fr   **A**

PALMER, Mary; later (1792)
  Countess of Inchiquin
1786 Jan 19   EB to   v, 252–7
[1792 Dec *a* 13]   EB to   VII, 321–3

PARGETER, Dr. William
1796 Mar 21   EB fr   **A**

PARISOT, Madame; wife of Jean-
  Baptiste-François-Pierre Parisot
1781 Mar 10   RBjr fr   **B**
1782 Dec 4   EB fr   **B**
1787 Oct 9   RBjr fr   **B**
1787 Nov 18   RBjr fr   **B**
1788 Nov 9   RBjr fr   **B**
[1788]   RBjr fr   **B**
1789 Mar 17   RBjr fr   **B**
1789 Sept 14   RBjr fr   VI, 16–20
1790 June 10   RBjr fr   **B**

PARR, Dr. Samuel
1787 June 9   EB to   v, 336–8

PARRY, Dr. Caleb Hillier
1797 Jan 29   EB to   IX, 234–5
[1797]   EB to   IX, 469

PARSONS, Sir Lawrence, 5th
  Baronet
1793 Mar 7   EB to   VII, 358–60
1797 Jan 31   EB fr   **C**
1797 Mar 8   EB to   IX, 277–80

PATENT SEARCHERS,
  Deputy
See also BRIDGES
1783 Mar 8   EB fr   **A**

PATERSON, George
1788 Apr 7   EB to   v, 381–6

PAYNE, Captain John Willett
[1789 Jan 6]   EB to   v, 436
1789 Sept 24   EB to   VI, 22–4
[1789] Sept 28   EB fr   VI, 26–7
1789 Oct 1   EB to   VI, 27–8
n.d. Sunday   EB fr   **A**
n.d. Saturday   EB fr   **A**
n.d.   EB to   IX, 456–7
         [Captain Payne]

PEARSON, Adam
1782 Apr 1   EB fr   **A**

PEAT, Alexander
1791 Sept 4   EB fr   **A**

PEAT, C.
1785 Mar 18   EB fr   **A**

PECHELL, Samuel
1782 Apr 2   EB fr   **A**

PECKARD, Rev. Peter
1775 Feb 18   EB fr   **A**
1782 Apr 8   EB fr   **A**
1782 May 27   EB fr   **A**

PELHAM, Frances
1779 Jan 12   EB to   IV, 37–8
1779 Jan 14   EB fr   **B**
[1779 Feb 11]   EB to   IV, 42–3

PELLAGRÜE, Vicomtesse de
1791 May 15   EB fr   **B**

PELTIER, Jean-Gabriel
1796 Mar 14   EB fr   **B**

PENN SCHOOL, French com-
  mittee for
1796 June 13   EB fr   **B**

PENNINGTON & BIGGS
1776 Mar 20   EB fr   **A**

PEPPERELL, [Sir William,
  1st Baronet]
1788 July 10   EB fr   **A**

PERCY, Thomas; Bishop of Dromore
[1782 Apr]   EB fr   **B**

PERCY, Thomas
1791 Feb 28   EB fr   VI, 229–30
1791 Mar 12   EB fr   **A**

PERREGAUX, Jean-Frédéric
1790 Dec 29   EB fr   **B**

PERY, Edmund Sexton
1777 Nov 11   EB fr   **A**
1778 May 19   EB to   III, 448–9
[1778] May 25   EB fr   III, 449–50
1778 June 2   EB to   III, 452–3
[1778 June] 8   EB fr   **A**
1778 June 16   EB to   III, 456–9
1778 June 17   EB fr   **A**
[1778] June 21 EB fr   **A**
1778 June 24   EB to   III, 459–60
1778 June 25   EB to   III, 460–2
1778 June 26   EB to   III, 462–4
1778 June 26   EB to   III, 464–5
[1778] July 1   EB fr   **A**
                           1 II, 223–4
1778 July 3   EB to   IV, 3–5
[1778] July 10 EB fr   **A**
                           1 II, 227–30
1778 July 18,   EB to   IV, 5–10
   [p 20]
[1778] July 28 EB fr   **A**
                           1 II, 230–1
[1778] Aug 4, 5 EB fr   **A**
[1778 Aug] 5   EB fr   **A**
[1778] Aug 11   EB fr   **A**
                           1 II, 232
1778 Aug 12   EB to   IV, 14–15
[1778] Aug 12   EB fr   **A**
[1778] Aug 26   EB fr   **A**
                           1 II, 239–
                           40

PETRE, Robert Petre, 9th Baron
[1780 June 24] EB fr   **A**
1780 July 7   EB fr   **A**
1781 Sept 18   EB fr   **A**
                           1 II, 436–7
[1781 Sept p 18] EB to   IV, 372–3

1782 Mar 13   EB fr   **A**
1783 Mar 24   EB fr   **A**

PETRIE, Samuel
1778 Jan 4   EB fr   **E**
                           36 III
                           (1940),
                           326–8
1782 Mar 25   EB fr   **E**

PHILIPS, Fr. C.
1788 July 27   EB fr   **A**

PHILLIPS, John
1775 Apr 18   EB fr   **A**

PHOENIX, Madame
[1792] Oct 30   EB fr   **B**

PICKAR, Mary
1796 July 13   EB fr   **A**

PICKARD, Rev. Edward
1772 May 16   EB fr   **A**

PIGOT, Admiral Hugh
1783 Mar 4   EB fr   **A**

PIGOTT, Arthur Leary
1783 Mar 19   EB fr   **A**
1783 Mar 20   RBjr to   v, 76
[1783 Apr p 4] EB to   v, 85
[1783 May 16]   EB to   v, 93
[1783 Oct]   EB fr   **A**
                           1 III, 22

PINE, William
1782 [May] 6   EB fr   **A**

PINSON DE MÉNERVILLE,
   Charles
1791 June 17   EB fr   **B**
1791 July 12   EB fr   **B**
1794 Aug 3   EB fr   **B**

PITT, William; later (1766) 1st Earl
   of Chatham
[1766 Feb 7]   EB to   I, 237
                [Pitt]

PITT, William

1782 Nov 7	RBjr fr	A
[1782 Nov 8]	RBjr to	A
1787 Feb 27	EB fr	A
1788 Nov 15	EB fr	v, 425–6
1791 Feb 14	EB fr	VI, 226
1791 Feb 18	EB fr	B
1791 Sept 30	EB fr	I
[1791] Oct 8	RBjr fr	A
1791 Oct 13	RBjr fr	VI, 436
1792 Dec 22	EB fr	VII, 324
[1793 Feb 10]	EB fr	VII, 348–9
[1794] Jan 20	EB fr	VII, 527
[1794 Jan] 21	EB to [Pitt]	VII, 529
[1794] Apr 11	EB fr	VII, 537
1794 Apr 22	RBjr to	I
1794 June 25	EB fr	VII, 554
1794 June 25	EB to	VII, 554–5
1794 June 30	EB to	VII, 559
1794 Aug 30	EB fr	VII, 574–5
1794 Aug 31	EB to	VII, 575–6
1794 Aug 31	EB to	VII, 577–8
1794 Sept 18	EB fr	VIII, 17
1794 Sept 19	EB to	VIII, 17–18
1795 Aug 2	EB to	VIII, 290–1
1795 Oct 28	EB to	VIII, 330–1
1795 Oct 28	EB to	VIII, 331–2
1795 Nov [7]	EB to	VIII, 337–8

PITT, William Morton

[1783 April]	EB fr	A
1783 June 2	EB to	v, 95–6

PIUS VI, Pope

1793 Sept 7	EB fr	VII, 419–21

PLUMB, Thomas

[1790 Feb p 27]	EB fr	A

PLUMER, William

1774 Aug 26	EB fr	A

PODESTA, Gio[vanni] Bat[tis]ta

1786 Nov 17	EB fr	A

POISSONNIER-DESPER-RIÈRES, L.

[1791] Aug 8	RBjr fr	B
[1791] Aug 19	RBjr fr	A

POLAND, King of
See STANISLAUS AUGUSTUS

POLLOCK, John

1782 May 8	EB fr	A

PONSONBY, John

1778 May 27	EB fr	A

PONSONBY, Sarah

1790 July 30	EB to, and Eleanor Butler	VI, 130–2

POOLE, R.

1782 Mar 7	EB fr	A
1782 Apr 4	EB fr	A

POPE
See PIUS VI

POPHAM, Stephen

1779 Oct 14	EB fr	D

POPKIN, J[ohn] B.

1783 Jan 22	EB fr	A

PORCHER, Josias Dupré

1786 Jan 9	EB fr	A
1786 Mar 13	EB fr	A
1786 Dec 22	WB to	T
1786 Dec 23	WB fr	T
[1787 Jan a 14]	WB to	T
1787 Jan 14	WB fr	T
n.d.	EB fr	I C 12/204/18

PORTEUS, Beilby, Bishop of London

1791 Aug 9	EB fr	A

PORTLAND, William Henry Cavendish Bentinck, 3rd Duke of

[1766 July 17]	EB to	I, 260

Portland, 3rd Duke of (*cont.*)

1768 Jan 13	EB to		I, 341
1768 Jan 16	EB fr	A	
1768 July 25	EB to		II, 9
1768 July 30	EB fr		II, 10
1768 July 30	EB to		II, 10–11
[1768 Dec 1]	EB to		II, 18
[1770 Apr 22]	EB and		II, 131–2
	D. of Manchester to		
1771 Mar 2	EB to		II, 200–1
1772 July 6	EB fr	A	
[1772 Dec 5]	EB to		II, 391
[1772 Dec 18]	EB to		II, 391–2
[1773 July 18]	EB to		II, 443–4
1774 Sept 29, 30	EB to		III, 40–2
1774 Sept 29	EB fr	A	
1774 Oct 1	EB fr	A	
[1774 Oct *a* 2]	WB to	H	
[1774] Oct 2	EB to		III, 50–1
1774 Oct 2	EB fr		III, 51–3
1774 Oct 2	WB fr	A	
[1774 Oct *c* 4]	EB to		III, 53
1774 Oct 7	EB to		III, 58–9
1774 Oct 19	JB fr	A	
[1774 Oct] 21	JB to	H	
[1774] Oct 25	JB to	H	
[1774 Oct 26]	WB to	H	
[1774 Oct 27]	WB to	H	
[1774] Oct 28	JB to	H	
1774 Nov 5	WB to	H	
1774 Nov 8	JB fr	A	
[1774 Nov 24]	WB to	H	
1775 Jan 5	EB to		III, 83–4
1775 Jan 8	EB fr	A	
1775 Apr 12	WB to	H	
[1775] May [9]	EB to		III, 153–4
[1775 May *a* 10]	WB to	H	
1775 July 24	WB to,	H	
	and Ds. of Portland		
1775 July 25	WB to	H	
1775 July 28	WB to	H	
1775 Oct 2	EB to		III, 225–6
1775 Oct 5	EB fr	A	
		1	II, 76–7
[1775 Oct 25]	WB to	H	
[1776 Jan 28]	WB to	H	
[1776 Mar 4]	WB to	H	

[1776 Mar 8]	WB to	H	
[1776 May *a* 15]	WB to	H	
[1776 June 4]	EB to		III, 271–2
1776 June 4	EB fr	A	
[1776 June 28]	WB to	H	
1776 July 25	WB to	H	
1776 Aug 10	WB to	H	
1776 Aug 16	EB to		III, 289–90
1776 Aug 21	WB to	H	
1776 Aug 22	WB to	H	
1776 Sept 25	WB to	H	
1776 Dec 13	EB to		III, 303–4
1777 Feb 10	WB to	H	
1777 [Feb] 11	EB to		III, 327–8
1777 Feb 13	WB to	H	
1777 Feb 22	WB to	H	
[1777 Mar *a* 7]	WB to	H	
1777 Oct 6	WB to	H	
1778 Jan 4	WB to	H	
[1778 Jan 14]	EB to		III, 417–18
1778 June 11	WB to	H	
[1778 June 14]	WB to	H	
1778 Aug 16	WB to	H	
1778 Nov 29	EB fr	A	
1779 May 1	WB to	H	
[1779 May 1]	WB to	H	
1779 June 25	WB to	H	
1779 July 18	EB fr	B	
1779 July 26	WB to	H	
1779 Aug 4	WB to	H	
1779 Aug 12	WB to	H	
1779 Aug 18	WB to	H	
1779 Aug 19	WB to	H	
1779 Aug 20	WB to	H	
1779 Aug 27	WB to	H	
1779 Sept 3	WB to	H	
1779 Sept 4	WB to	H	
1779 Sept 5	WB to	H	
1779 Sept 5	WB to	H	
[1779 Sept 5]	WB to	H	
[1779 Sept *a* 13]	WB to	H	
[1779 Sept *a* 22]	WB to	H	
[1779 Sept 22]	WB to	H	
[1779 Sept *a* 23]	WB to	H	
1779 Sept 23	WB to	H	
1779 Sept 24	EB to		IV, 129–33
[1779 Sept *a* 28]	WB to	H	
1779 Sept 29	EB fr		IV, 136–8

* Published in *Works* as 'Observations on the Conduct of the Minority' (Todd, 207–12).

Portland, Duchess of (*cont.*)

1782 Jan 12	EB to	IV, 400
1782 Aug 16	JB fr	A
[1786 Aug.]	EB fr	A
[1788 Nov] 7	EB fr	V, 424–5

POTEMKIN, Prince Gregory
Aleksandrovich; Heirs of

[1797 Apr *c* 16]	EB,	IX, 311
	Malone and	
	Philip Metcalfe	
	to	

POWELL, John
Cashier in the Pay Office

1783 Apr 17	EB to	V, 87–8
1783 May *a* 24	EB fr	50 XXIII, 903

POWELL, John; Master of
Merchants Hall, Bristol

1779 Dec 6	EB and H. Cruger fr	A
1779 Dec 9	EB to	IV, 171–2

POWNALL, John

1765 Dec 23	WB fr	I 34 I, 642–3 abs ½ p.
1773 June 15	EB to	II, 437–8
1777 Nov 13	EB fr	A
1778 Nov 3	EB fr	A

POWNEY, Penyston

1784 Oct 4	EB fr	A

PRATTINTON, William

1774 Nov 3	EB fr	A

PRESTON, James

1782 Mar 27	EB to	IV, 428–9
[1782 Mar *p* 27]	EB fr	A

PRICE, Chase

1771 Nov 20	EB to	IX, 397–8

PRICE, T.

n.y. Nov 24	EB fr	A

PRICE, Uvedale

1794 June 1	EB to	VII, 547–8

PRIDY, Robert J.

1770 Oct 29	EB fr	A

PRIESTLEY, Joseph

1782 Dec 11	EB fr	V, 53–4
1791 Jan 1	EB fr★	

PROST DEROYER, Pierre-
Antoine

1783 Mar 5	EB fr	B

PROVENCE, Louis-Stanislas-
Xavier de Bourbon, Comte de; later
'Monsieur'; later Louis XVIII, King
of France

1791 Aug 26	EB fr	VI, 373
1791 Sept 17	EB to	VI, 399–400
1796 Aug 25	EB to	IX, 69–70

PRYCE, Thomas

1782 Feb 9	EB fr	A

PUBLIC ACCOUNTS,
Commissioners for

1795 May 28	EB to	VIII, 258–60

PULTENEY, William

1777 Nov 6	EB fr	A

QUARME, George

[1775] Apr 10	EB fr	A

QUEBEC, Merchants trading to
Province of

1788 May 20	EB fr	B

RAGUNATH RAO

[1781 Aug]	EB to	IV, 367–8

RAPHOE, Bishop of
See HAWKINS

★ Priestley's *Letters to Edmund Burke occasioned by his Reflections*, Birmingham, 1791, contains thirteen letters, of which only one, the last, is dated.

RICHMOND, Mary (*née* Bruce),
  Duchess of
1774 July 21   EB fr   **A**

RICKARDS, John
1775 Feb 11   EB fr   **A**

RIDGE, John
[1763] Apr 23   EB to   I, 168–9
[1765] Dec 24   EB and   I, 225
                  Dr. Nugent to
[1766 Mar *a* 8]   EB and   I, 242–3
                  WB fr
[1766] Mar 8   EB fr   **A**
[1766] July 8   EB fr   **B**
1767 Jan 17   EB fr   **B**
                  62 76n ext
                  8 lines
[1767 Feb]   WB fr   **B**
1772 Jan 28   EB fr   **A**
                  7 509–11
[1772 Mar 24]   WB to   **G**
                  7 521–3
1775 Feb 6   EB, JB,   **B**
                  RBsr and WB fr
1775 Sept 25   EB and   **A**
                  RB[sr] fr **7** 599–
                                    604
[1775] Oct 11   EB fr   **A**
1776 Feb 5   EB fr   **B**

RIDGE, J. W.
1796 Nov 4   EB fr   **A**

RIDGE, Michael
[1784 Nov *p* 22] EB to   v, 192–5

RIVAROL, Madame; wife of
  Antoine de Rivarol
1791 Aug 22   EB fr   **B**

RIVAROL, Claude-François de; styled
  Vicomte de Rivarol
1791 June 1   EB to   VI, 265–70*
1791 June 12   EB fr

* Published, with Rivarol's reply, in
Lettre à M. le Vicomte de Rivarol (Todd,
175–6).

RIVINGTON
See DOUCE & RIVINGTON

RIX, William
1780 Mar 6   EB to   IV, 209–10

ROBERTS, Captain Benjamin
1783 May 28   EB fr   **A**

ROBERTSON, William
1777 June 5   EB fr   **A**
1777 June 9   EB to   III, 350–2
1777 June 10   EB to   III, 352
[1784] Apr 15   EB fr   **B**
[1785] Aug 26   EB fr   v, 221–2

ROBINSON, John
1775 Sept 6   EB to   III, 201–3
1775 Sept 18   RBsr to   I T. 1/516,
                                    fols 221 ff.
1775 Dec 18   EB fr   **A**
1780 Dec 23   RBsr fr   I T. 11/32,
                                    p. 458

ROBINSON, Richard, Archbishop
  of Armagh and Primate of All
  Ireland
[1776 June *c* 25] EB to   III, 275–6

ROCHFORD, William Henry
  Nassau de Zuylestein, 4th Earl of
1775 Sept 20   EB fr   **15**

ROCKINGHAM, Charles
  Watson Wentworth, 2nd Marquess
  of
[1766 Jan]   EB to   I, 234–5
[1766 Apr 9]   EB fr   **A**
1766 Aug 21   EB to   I, 266–7
1766 Nov 1   EB fr   **A**
[1767 Mar 18]   WB to   **A**
[1767 Mar]   EB fr   **A**
[1767 July 16]   EB to   I, 315–16
1767 Aug 1   EB to   I, 316–18
1767 Aug 18   EB to   I, 320–2
1767 Aug 31   EB fr   **A**
                  1 I, 146–9
1767 Oct 6   EB fr   **A**

Rockingham, 2nd Marquess of (*cont.*)		
1767 Oct 31	EB fr	A
1767 Nov 4	EB fr	A
1768 Jan 14	EB fr	A
1768 Mar 9	EB to	I, 347–8
1768 July 18	EB to	II, 3–6
1768 Aug 16	EB fr	II, 11–13
1768 Sept 27	EB fr	II, 15–16
1769 May 15	EB fr	II, 25
1769 May 31	EB fr	II, 27–8
1769 June 13	EB to	II, 30–1
[1769 June 29]	EB fr	II, 35–40
[1769] July 2	EB to	II, 40–2
1769 July 7	WB to	A
1769 July 9	EB to	II, 43–6
1769 July 17	EB fr	II, 46–9
1769 July 30	EB to	II, 50–3
1769 Aug 13	EB to	II, 54–5
1769 Sept 1	EB fr	II, 60–1
1769 Sept 1, 3	EB fr	II, 61–5
[1769 Sept 6]	EB to	II, 71–4
[1769] Sept 8	EB to	II, 74–5
1769 Sept 9	EB to	II, 75–7
1769 Sept 13	EB to	II, 78–81
1769 Oct 9	EB to	II, 87–9
1769 Oct 15	EB fr	II, 89–95
1769 Oct 29	EB to	II, 100–3
1769 Nov 4	EB fr	II, 104
1769 Nov 6	EB to	II, 104–8
[1769 Nov *p* 6]	EB to	II, 108–10
1769 Nov [24]	EB to	II, 112–14
1769 Dec 5	EB to	II, 114–16
1769 Dec 9	EB fr	II, 116–17
1769 Dec 18	EB to	II, 121–3
1770 Sept 5	EB fr	II, 151–4
[1770] Sept 7, 8	EB to	II, 154–8
1770 Sept 23	EB to	II, 159–62
1770 Sept 26	EB fr	II, 162–5
1770 Dec 15	EB fr	II, 169–72
[1770 Dec 18]	EB to	II, 172–3
1770 Dec 29	EB to	II, 174–6
1771 Jan 3	EB fr	II, 181–2
1771 Jan 15	EB fr	II, 184–5
[1771 Jan 30]	EB fr	II, 188
[1771 Feb 3]	EB fr	II, 190–2
1771 Feb 3	EB fr	A
1771 Feb 9	EB fr	A
1771 Feb 14	EB fr	II, 192–6

[1771 Feb 16]	EB to	II, 196–200
[1771 Mar 27]	EB to	II, 203–4
[1771 Mar 27]	EB to	II, 204
1771 Mar [27]	EB fr,	II, 204–5
	and W. Dowdeswell	
1771 June 21	EB fr	II, 218–20
1771 July 12	WB to	A
1771 Aug 30	EB fr	A
1771 Oct 8	EB fr	A
1771 Dec 27	EB fr	II, 296–8
1772 June 12	EB fr	A
1772 June 13	EB fr	A
1772 Oct 24, 27, 28	EB fr	II, 342–7
1772 Oct 27	EB fr	II, 347–9
1772 Oct 29	EB to	II, 353–7
1772 Nov 11	EB to	II, 368–70
1772 Nov 19	EB to	II, 378–9
1772 Nov 20	EB fr	II, 379–82
1772 Nov 23	EB to	II, 382–6
1772 Nov 26	EB to	II, 387–8
1773 Jan 5	EB fr	II, 401–2
1773 [Jan] 7, 10	EB to	II, 403–11
1773 Feb 9	EB fr	II, 423–4
1773 July 26	EB fr	II, 444–5
1773 [Aug] 19	EB to	II, 449–51
1773 Sept 20	EB fr	II, 458–9
1773 Sept 21	EB to	II, 460–4
1773 Sept 29	EB to	II, 464–70
1773 Oct 20	EB to	II, 472–3
1773 Nov 7, 11	EB to	II, 481–4
1773 Nov 12	EB fr	II, 484–7
1773 Nov 16	EB to	II, 487–8
[1773 Nov 16]	EB to	II, 488–9
1773 Nov 18	EB fr	II, 489
[1773 Dec *p* 13]	EB fr	II, 497–500
1774 Jan 8	EB fr	II, 510–11
1774 Jan 30	EB fr	II, 515–16
1774 Feb 2	EB to	II, 523–4
1774 May 14	EB fr	A
1774 June 1	EB fr	II, 540–1
1774 Sept 13	EB fr	III, 22–6
1774 Sept 18, 25	EB to	III, 28–36
1774 Oct 2	EB fr	III, 48–50
1774 Oct 5	EB fr	III, 56–7
[1774 Oct 9]	EB to	III, 61–2
1774 Oct 9	EB fr	III, 62–3

Rockingham, 2nd Marquess of (*cont.*)			
1774 Oct 11	EB fr	III, 63–4
1774 Oct 17	EB fr	III, 66
1774 Oct 25	EB to	III, 67–8
1774 Oct 26	JB fr	III, 68–9
1774 Nov 1	JB to	III, 71–2
1774 Nov 12	EB fr	III, 75–6
1774 Nov 12	JB fr	III, 77
1774 Nov 29	EB fr	III, 80
[1775 Jan] 5	EB to	III, 87–90
1775 Jan 7, 8	EB fr	III, 90–3
1775 Jan 12	EB to	III, 97–9
1775 Jan [22]	EB fr	III, 105
1775 Jan [24]	EB fr	III, 105–6
[1775 Jan 24]	EB to	III, 106–8
1775 Feb [6]	EB fr	III, 109
1775 Feb 9	EB fr	III, 113–14
1775 Feb 13	EB fr	III, 114–15
1775 Feb 22	EB fr	III, 120
[1775 Mar 22]	EB fr	III, 139
1775 May 17	EB fr	A
1775 May 22	EB fr	III, 158–9
1775 June 16	EB fr	III, 171–2
[1775] June 23	EB fr	III, 172–3
1775 July 11	EB fr	III, 176–8
1775 Aug 4	EB to	III, 182–4
1775 Aug [22], 23	EB to	III, 189–96
1775 Sept 11	EB fr	III, 203–6
1775 Sept 14	EB to	III, 206–11
1775 Sept 24	EB fr	III, 214–17
1775 Oct 1	EB to	III, 222–5
1775 Nov 2	EB fr	III, 234–5
1775 Nov 7	EB fr	III, 235–6
[1776 Jan *p* 6]	EB to	III, 242–3
1776 Mar 25	WB to	III, 255–6
1776 May [3]	EB to	III, 264–5
1776 June 2	EB fr	III, 269–70
1776 July 3	EB fr	III, 276–8
[1776 July 4]	EB to	III, 278
[1776 July *a* 12]	WB to	A
1776 July 12	EB fr	III, 281–3
1776 Oct 13	EB fr	III, 295–7
1776 Oct 22	EB fr	III, 297
1777 Jan 6	EB to	III, 308–15
1777 Jan 6, 7	EB fr	III, 315–17
1777 Jan 7	EB fr	A
[1777 May *c* 30]	EB to	III, 342–3
[1777] June 8	EB to	III, 346–7
1777 June 9	EB fr	III, 347
1777 Sept	EB to	III, 378–9
1777 Oct 2	EB fr	A
1777 Oct 26	EB fr	III, 392–3
1777 Nov 5	EB to	III, 398–400
1777 Dec 3	EB fr	III, 408
1777 Dec 7	EB fr	III, 411
[1777 Dec 16]	EB to	IX, 416–18
1778 Jan 4	WB to	A
1778 June 23	EB fr	A
1778 Aug 1	EB fr	IV, 11–12
1778 Dec 9	EB fr	IV, 30–1
1778 Dec [11]	EB fr	IV, 31
1778 Dec [29]	EB fr	IV, 35–6
1779 Jan 2	EB fr	A
[1779 Apr 30]	EB to	IV, 65–6
1779 May [5]	EB fr	IV, 67
1779 May 8	EB fr	IV, 69
[1779 May 9]	EB to	IV, 70–2
1779 June 13	EB fr	IV, 88–9
[1779 June 21]	EB to	IV, 91–2
[1779 Aug 7]	EB fr	IV, 110–12
1779 Aug 8	EB to	IV, 112–14
1779 Oct 17	EB to	IV, 155–9
[1779 Nov 3]	EB fr	IV, 159–64
1779 Nov 27	EB fr	IV, 171
1780 Jan 9	EB fr	IV, 183–7
[1780] Jan 7	EB to	IV, 188–90
1780 Jan 13	EB fr	IV, 192–3
1780 Mar 31	EB fr	IV, 216
1780 Mar 31	EB fr	IV, 216–18
1780 Sept 7, 8	EB to	IV, 275–8
1780 Sept 8	RBsr to	IV, 279
1780 Sept 9	RBsr to	IV, 280–1
[1780] Wednesday	EB fr	A
1781 Feb 18	EB fr	IV, 336
1781 Mar 8	EB fr	A
1781 July 10	EB fr	IV, 355–6
[1782 Feb 18]	EB to	IV, 404–5
1782 Mar 22	EB to	IV, 422–3
[1782 Apr *c* 5]	EB to	IV, 433–4
1782 Apr 14	RBsr to	A
[1782 Apr 24]	EB to	IV, 446
1782 Apr 27	EB to	IV, 448–50
n.d.	EB to	A
n.d.	JB to	AE

ROCKINGHAM,
Marchioness of

[1767 Apr 16]	EB to	I, 304–5
[1767 Apr 28]	EB to	I, 309–11
1767 Oct 22	EB to	IX, 392–3
[1768 May]	EB fr	A
[1773 Sept 20]	EB fr	A
[1775 Jan 31]	EB fr	III, 108–9
[1775 Feb 19]	EB fr	III, 116
[1775 Mar 29]	EB fr	III, 146–7
[1775 Oct 23]	EB fr	A
[1776] Jan 4	EB to	IX, 408–9
[1776 Feb 21]	EB to	IX, 409–10
[1776] Apr 12	EB fr	A
[1776 Apr 13]	EB fr	A
1776 May [3]	EB to	III, 262–4
[1777 Mar 28]	EB to	IX, 414
1777 Apr 1	EB fr	A
1777 Apr 2	EB to	IX, 415
[1778] Dec 23	EB fr	IV, 32
[1778 Dec]	JB fr	A
1779 May 21	EB to	IV, 74–5
1779 Sept 23	EB fr	IV, 128–9
1779 Oct 3	EB to	IV, 139–45
1779 Nov 15	EB fr	A
[1779 Dec *p* 14]	EB to	A
1780 Jan 1	EB fr	IV, 176–7
1780 Jan 2	EB to	IV, 177–8
1780 Jan 4	EB fr	IV, 179–80
1780 [Jan] 6	EB fr	IV, 187–8
1780 Jan 9	EB fr	IV, 190
[1780] Jan 9	EB to	IV, 191
[1780 Jan *a* 16]	EB to	IV, 193–5
1780 Jan 16	EB fr	IV, 195–6
1780 Jan 16	EB to	IV, 198–9
[1780 Jan *p* 17]	EB fr	A
1780 Jan 18	RBjr to	A
1780 Feb 25	EB fr	IV, 204–5
[1780 Feb 26]	EB to	IV, 205–6
1780 Sept 17	EB fr	IV, 284–6
1780 Sept 27, 28	EB to	IV, 299–302
[1780 Sept]	EB fr	A
[1780 Sept]	EB fr	A
1782 Nov 20	EB to	V, 45–7
[1782]	EB fr	AV
1785 July [4]	EB fr	A
[1785 Aug *p* 28]	JB fr	A

[1788] July 30	EB fr	A
1788 Aug 8	EB fr	A
1788 Dec [28]	EB fr	A
n.d. Sunday	EB fr	A
n.d. Sunday	EB fr	A
n.d. Sunday	EB fr	A
n.d. Tuesday	EB fr	A
n.d. Tuesday	EB fr	A
n.d. Saturday	EB to	IX, 457
n.d.	EB fr	IX, 471

RODNEY, Admiral George Brydges,
1st Baron

1787 June 12	EB fr	A

ROGERS, Bayley

1779 Jan 13	EB fr	A

ROQUEFEUIL, Augustin-Joseph,
Marquis de

[1797] Feb 3	EB fr	B

ROSE, George

[1782 July *p* 18]	EB fr	P
1784 Mar 1	RBsr fr	AJ

ROSS, Colonel [Alexander]

1794	WB to	IX, 468
1795	WB to	IX, 468

ROSS & MILL

1777 May 31	EB fr	A

ROSSIGNAC, L.

n.y. July 4	EB fr	B

ROUGANE, Claude-Constant

[1791]	EB to	VI, 477–9

ROUGEMONT, G.

1791 June 23	EB fr	B
1791 Aug 3	EB fr	B

ROUQUET, James

1776 Jan 17	EB fr	B

ROUSE, Charles William Broughton

1783 Mar 19	EB fr	A

Rouse, Charles William (*cont.*)

1791 Apr 8	EB fr	A
1791 Apr 12	EB fr	A

ROWE, M.

1775 Feb 22	RBsr fr	I T 27/31, p. 97

ROYAL IRISH ACADEMY

[1790 Feb *p* 27]	EB to	VI, 98–9

ROYDS, John

1768 Nov 18	EB fr	A

RUMBOLD, Sir Thomas, 1st Baronet

[1776 Feb 27]	EB fr	A
1781 Mar 21	EB fr	A
1781 Mar 23	EB to	IV, 343–7
1782 Mar 11	EB fr	A
[1782 May 3]	EB fr	A
1782 May 5	EB fr	A

RUSSEL, C.

[1778 June 13]	WB fr	H

RUSSIA, Empress of
See CATHERINE II

SADLER, James

[1776]	EB fr	A
[1776]	EB fr	A

SAINT-ANGE, Antoine-Louis Le Fèvre de Caumartin, Marquis de

1793 May 15	EB fr	I

ST. AULAIRE, Jean-Baptiste de Beaupoil, Marquis de

1797 Feb 24	EB fr	B

ST. DAVIDS, Bishop of
See HORSLEY

ST. JOHN, J[ohn]

1778 June 22	EB fr	A

ST. LEGER, Colonel John Hayes

1791 Sept 12	EB fr	A
1793 Oct 6	EB fr	A
1793 Oct 23	EB to	VII, 457–60
n.d. Monday	EB fr	A

ST. PAUL, Colonel Horace

1776 Apr 23	EB to	III, 262

ST.-POL-DE-LÉON, Jean-François de La Marche, Bishop of

1792 Sept 13	EB fr	B
[1792 Sept *p* 13]	EB to	VII, 207–10
1792 Sept 21	EB fr	B
[1793 Oct *c* 24]	EB fr	B
1794 Jan 3	EB fr	A
1794 Aug 4	EB fr	A
1795 Sept 29	EB fr	A
1796 Mar 25	EB fr	VIII, 445–6
1796 Mar 26	EB fr	B
[1796 Mar 28]	EB to	VIII, 448–51
1796 Apr 6	EB fr	B
1796 Apr 16	EB fr	B
1796 May 2	EB and W. King fr	B
1796 May 3	EB fr	B
1796 May 11	EB fr	IX, 8–9
1796 May 21	EB fr	IX, 12–13
[1796 May 22]	EB to	IX, 14–16
1796 May 23	EB fr	B
1796 May 24	EB fr	B
[1796 May *c* 25]	EB to	IX, 22–3
1796 May 25	EB to	IX, 23–8
[1796 May *p* 25]	EB to	IX, 28–9
1796 May 26	EB fr	B
1796 May 28	EB fr	IX, 34–5
1796 [May] 30	EB to	IX, 35–7
[1796 June]	EB to	IX, 52–3
1796 Aug 11	EB fr	B
n.d.	EB fr	B

ST. VALIER, Joly de

1782 June 13	EB fr	B

SALISBURY, Bishop of
See DOUGLAS

SALKELD, William
1775 Nov 7   WB fr   **BC**

SAMBOURNE, Thomas
1793 Apr 20   EB fr   **A**

SANDOUVILLE, Monsieur
  de
1792 Sept 25   RBjr fr   **B**
[1792 Oct *p* 13]   EB to   VII, 258–65

SANKEY, Edward; Lord Mayor of
  Dublin 1766–7
1767 Feb 25   EB to   I, 295–6

SARLABUS, Jean-Antoine de Mun,
  Marquis de
n.d.   EB fr   **B**

SARSFIELD, Jacques-Hyacinthe
  de Sarsfield, Comte de
1775 Oct 13   EB fr   **A**

SAUNDERS, Sir Charles
n.d. Sunday   EB fr   **A**

SAVIGNAC
1796 June 10   EB fr   **B**

SAVILE, Sir George, 8th
  Baronet
[1766] June 16   EB to   I, 258
1775 Oct 1   EB to   III, 222
[1776] Mar 28   EB fr   III, 256–8
[1776 Apr *c* 1]   EB to   III, 258
[1780]   EB fr   **A**
                   1, IV, 524–6
[1781 Feb 15]   EB fr   **A**

SAVY, Durouve de
1792 Aug 30   EB fr   **B**

SAXE-COBURG-SAALFELD,
  Friedrich Josias, Prince of
1793 Sept 8   EB fr   **A**

SCOTT, Charles
1774 Mar 13   EB fr   **A**

SCOTT, George
1770 Apr 26   EB fr   **D**
SCOTT, John; later (1784) 1st
  Baron Earlsfort
1780 Nov 2   EB fr   **A**
1787 Jan 17   EB fr   **A**

SCOTT, Sir John
1796 Jan 11   EB to   VIII, 369–70

SCOTT, Sir William
1789 Apr 11   EB fr   **A**
[1790] Nov 23   EB to   VI, 174
                   [Scott]
1791 Aug 6   EB fr   **A**
                   1 III, 230–1

SCUDAMORE, John
1782 May 18   EB fr   **A**

SEARLE, James
[1775]   EB to   IX, 408

SECKER, John
[1782] Apr 23   EB fr   **A**
1782 June 25   EB fr   **A**

SEERY, J. G.
1772 June 12   EB fr   **AA**

SEGONZAC, Pierre-François de
  Bardon, Vicomte de
1797 Mar 14   EB fr   **B**

SELWYN, George
1783 July 19   EB to   V, 100

SEMPLE LISLE, James George
1795 Oct 2   EB fr   **A**
1796 Jan 14   EB fr   **A**
1796 Jan 15   EB fr   **A**
1796 Jan 17   EB fr   **A**
1796 Jan 21   EB fr   **A**
1796 Jan 27   EB fr   **A**
1796 June 29   EB fr   **A**

SEPTCHÊNER
1781 Jan 9   RBjr fr   **B**

SÉRENT, Armand-Sigismonde-
  Félicité-Marie, Comte de
1793 Nov 13   EB fr   A
1794 Sept 1   EB fr   A
                   1 IV, 233-4

SHACKLETON, Abraham
1797 May 28   EB fr,   A
        and Mrs **1** IV, 454–
        Leadbeater

SHACKLETON, Mary; later
  (1791) Mrs William Leadbeater
1784 Dec 13   EB to   V, 200–1
[1786 Mar *a* 22] EB to   V, 261–2
1789 Sept 23   EB fr   **B**
1792 Sept 8   EB to   VII, 198–
                 200
1794 Oct 5   EB fr,   **B**
        and Mrs [Richard]
        Shackleton
1797 May 23   EB to   IX, 359–60
1797 May 28   EB fr,   A
        and A. **1** IV, 454–6
        Shackleton

SHACKLETON, Richard
1744 Apr [*p* 14] EB to   I, 1–3
1744 May 10   EB to   I, 4
[1744 May *a* 24] EB to   I, 5–7
1744 May 24   EB to   I, 7–10
1744 May 29   EB to   I, 10–11
1744 June 9   EB to   I, 11–15
1744 June 11   EB to   I, 15–17
[1744 June *c* 14] EB to   I, 17–19
1744 June 21   EB to   I, 19–21
1744 June 26   EB to   I, 21–3
[1744] June 29   EB to   I, 23–4
1744 July 5   EB to   I, 24–6
1744 July 7   EB to   I, 27–8
1744 July 10   EB to   I, 28–30
1744 July 14   EB to   I, 30–1
1744 Oct 15   EB to   I, 32–4
1744 Nov 1   EB to   I, 34–6
1744 Nov 24   EB to   I, 36–8
1745 Jan 25   EB to   I, 38–9
1745 Jan 31   EB to   I, 40–1
1745 Feb 5   EB to   I, 41–2

1745 Feb 16   EB to   I, 42–3
1745 Feb 23   EB to   I, 43–4
1745 [Mar *c* 5] EB to   I, 44–6
1745 Mar 12   EB to   I, 46–7
1745 [Mar] 15 EB to   I, 47–8
1745 Mar 19   EB to   I, 49–50
1745 July 4   EB to   I, 50–2
1745 July 16   EB and I, 52–4
        Newcomen Herbert
        to
1745 Aug 16   EB to   I, 54
[1745] Oct 15   EB to   I, 55
1745 Nov 2   EB to   I, 56
1745 Nov 12   EB to   I, 56–7
1745 Dec 7   EB to   I, 58
1745 Dec 28   EB to   I, 59–60
1746 Jan 16   EB to   I, 60–1
1746 Feb 15   EB to   I, 61–2
[1746] Apr 26   EB to   I, 62–3
1746 May [*c* 15] EB to   I, 63–4
1746 May [*c* 24] EB to   I, 64–5
1746 June 1   EB to   I, 65–6
1746 July 12   EB to   I, 67–8
1746 July 25,   EB to,   I, 68–70
    31   and RBsr
1746 Aug 19   EB to   I, 71
1746 Nov 29   EB to,   I, 72–3
        and RBsr
1746 Dec 5   EB to   I, 74–5
1746 Dec 19   EB to   I, 75–6
1746 Dec 27   EB to   I, 76–7
1747 Jan 24   EB to   I, 77–8
[1747 Feb *c* 3] EB to   I, 78–80
[1747 Feb *p* 3] EB to   I, 80–1
1747 Feb 21   EB to   I, 82–4
[1747 Mar *c* 5] EB to   I, 85–6
[1747 Mar *c* 12] EB to   I, 87–8
1747 Mar 21   EB to   I, 88–90
1747 May 28, EB and I, 90–4
    29   Dennis to
1747 Aug 22   EB and I, 94–5
        Dennis to
[1747 Oct 17] EB to   I, 96–9
1747 Nov 21   EB to   I, 99–100
1747 Dec [24] EB to   I, 100–1
1747 Dec [24] EB to   I, 100–1
1748 Feb 2   EB to   I, 101–2
1748 May   EB to   I, 102

Shackleton, Richard (*cont.*)

1748 May	EB to	I, 102
[1749] Jan 5	EB to	I, 102–3
1751 Feb 26	EB to	I, 108–9
1751 Apr 5	EB to	I, 109–10
1751 Aug 31	EB to	I, 110–11
1752 Sept 28	EB to	I, 112–14
1757 Aug 10	EB to	I, 123–5
1761 Aug 25	EB to	I, 142–3
1761 Sept 8	EB to	I, 143
1763 Apr [*p* 19]	EB to	I, 166–7
[1764 Mar 29]	EB to	I, 175
1764 Apr 12	RBsr to	C
1764 July 17	EB to	I, 175–6
1766 Aug 30	RBsr to	C
[1766 Aug]	EB to	I, 267–8
[1766 Oct 19]	EB to	I, 270–1
1766 Oct 21	EB fr	B
1766 Oct 25	RBsr to	C
1766 Oct 28	EB and RBsr to	I, 273–5
1766 Nov 18	RB sr to	C
1766 Dec 25	EB fr	A
1767 Feb 15	RBsr to	C
1767 Nov 22	RBsr fr	A
1768 May 1	EB to	I, 350–2
1769 Mar 3	EB fr	39 49–51
1769 Mar 16	EB fr	A
		40 II, 104–9
1769 Dec 8	EB fr	A
		47 LIII (1938), 1105 ext 4 lines
1770 Apr 19	EB to	II, 129–31
1770 Apr 28	EB fr	II, 133–5
1770 May 6	EB to	II, 135–6
[1770 Aug *a* 15]	EB to	II, 149–50
[1771 July *a* 31]	EB to	II, 226–8
1772 Feb 7	EB and RBsr to	II, 299–301
1772 June 17	RBsr to	C
1773 Jan 3	EB and RBsr to	II, 400–1
1774 Oct 11	RBsr to	III, 64–6
1775 Jan 14	EB fr	A
1775 June 28	RBsr to	C
1776 Aug 11	EB to	III, 286–7

1777 Mar 10	RBsr to	C
[1777 May]	EB fr	A
1777 Sept 16	EB to	III, 374–5
1779 Apr 10	EB fr	IV, 57–9
1779 May 25	EB to	IV, 78–80
1780 May 6	EB to	IV, 233–4
1780 May 20	EB fr	B
[1780 June 13]	EB to	IV, 245–7
1782 May 2	EB fr	C
		40 II, 128–32
1782 May 18	RBsr to	C
1783 Mar 3	EB to	V, 71–2
1783 June 9	RBsr to	C
1784 Sept 22	EB fr	A
1785 Oct 18	EB fr	C
		40 II, 134–5
1785 Oct 26	EB to	V, 228–9
1785 Dec 5	EB fr	C
		40 II, 136–7
1786 June 2	RBsr to	C
1786 Oct 12	EB to	V, 285–6
1787 Jan 3	RBjr to	C
[1787 May 28]	EB to	V, 332
[1787 June 5]	EB to	V, 336
[1788 May 9]	EB to	V, 397–8
[1790 May 22]	RBsr to	C
[1790 May 28]	EB to	VI, 119
1790 Nov 8	RBsr to	C
		9 311 ext 2 lines
1790 Dec 21	RBsr fr	C
1791 Aug 18	RBsr fr	C
1792 Apr 5	RBjr to	C
1792 Apr 19	RBjr fr	C
n.d.	EB to	IX, 458

SHACKLETON, Mrs. Richard

1794 Oct 5	EB fr, and Mrs. Leadbeater	B

SHARP, Rev. Dr. John

1775 Oct 12	EB fr	A

[SHARP, William]

1787 Sept 9	EB to	V, 345–6

SHARPE, [Philip]
n.d.   WB to **I** p.c. 1/11,
        bundle 54

SHEE, George; later (1795) 1st
 Baronet
1789 Aug 25 EB fr **A**

SHEFFIELD, John Baker Holroyd,
 1st Baron
1792 Sept 9 EB fr **A**
[1792 Oct 17] EB to VII, 274
1792 Oct 21 EB fr **A**

SHEILS, Philip
1786 July 8 EB fr **A**

SHELBURNE, William Petty, 2nd
 Earl of
1767 Jan 1 WB to **P**
[1770 June 5] EB to II, 140–1
[1779 Dec 14] EB to IV, 174–5

SHERIDAN, Charles Francis
n.d.   EB fr **A**

SHERIDAN, Richard Brinsley
[1782] Apr 7 EB fr IV, 439–40
[1783] Friday EB fr V, 121
[1788] Feb 3 EB fr V, 377–8
[1788] Apr 18 EB to V, 391–3
[1788 Dec 11] EB to V, 432
[1789 Feb p 25] EB to V, 450–1
[1789 Mar 30] EB fr V, 457
[1789 Mar 30] EB to V, 458

SHERIDAN, Mrs. Richard
 Brinsley
[1789 Mar 26] EB to V, 453–4

SHERLOCK, Thomas
1796 Dec 28 EB fr **A**

SHIPPEN, Thomas Lee
1792 Aug 1 EB fr **A**

SHOOLBRED, John
1777 May 31 EB fr **A**

SINCLAIR, Sir John, 1st Baronet
1796 Apr 25 EB fr **A**

SKYNNER, John
[1771] Dec 8 EB fr II, 294
[1771 Dec 8] EB to II, 294

SLEIGH, Dr. Joseph Fenn
1763   EB fr **9** I, 125 abs
        4 lines
1765 June 17 EB fr I, 203–4

SLOPER, Lieutenant General Robert
1786 Jan 17 WB to **F**

SLOPER, W[illiam]
1782 Apr 31 EB fr **A**
 [sic]

SMITH, Adam
1759 Sept 10 EB to I, 129–30
1775 May 1 EB to III, 152–3
1782 July 1 EB fr V, 3
1782 July 6 EB fr V, 9–10
1783 Apr 15 EB fr V, 86–7
1783 June 20 EB to V, 98–9
1786 Dec 7 EB to V, 296–8
1786 Dec 20 EB to V, 301–2

SMITH, Donald
1792 Feb 20 EB fr **C**

SMITH, George
1782 Apr 13 EB fr **A**

SMITH, John S.
1780 Mar 7 EB fr **A**

SMITH, Joseph
1774 Nov 19 EB to IX, 403–4
1774 Nov 29 EB fr **A**
1775 Feb 22 EB to III, 119–20
1775 Mar 4 EB fr **A**
1775   EB to IX, 464
1782 Mar 30 EB fr **A**

SMITH, Michael
[c. 1750] EB to I, 357–63

Smith, Michael (*cont.*)

[*c.* 1750]	EB fr	**14** I, XI–XV

SMITH, General Richard

1782 Jan 7	EB fr	**A**

SMITH, Robert

1775 Jan 18	EB and H. Cruger fr	
1775 Mar 6	EB to	III, 128–9
1775 Mar 9	EB and H. Cruger fr	
1775 Mar 13	EB fr	
1775 Mar 24	EB to	III, 140–2
1775 Mar 30	EB and H. Cruger fr	
1775 Apr 4	EB and H. Cruger fr	
1775 Apr 6	EB to	IX, 406–8
1775 Apr 24	EB and H. Cruger fr	

SMITH, R.

1791 Jan 12	EB fr [R.] Smith	**A**

SMITH, William; later (1800) William Cusack Smith

1791 June 30	EB fr	**53** 1–3
1791 July 22	EB to	VI, 302–5
1792 Nov 25	RBjr to	**A** **1** IV, 37–42
1792 Nov 26	RBjr fr	**A** **1** IV, 42–6
[1792 Nov 27]	RBjr to	**9** II, 223–6
[1793 Mar *p* 2]	EB to	VII, 355–6
1794 Jan 10	EB fr	**A**
1795 Jan 20	EB fr	VIII, 118–21
1795 Jan 29	EB to	VIII, 127–34
[1795 Jan *p* 29]	EB fr	**9** II, 286– 91 part omitted
[1795 May *c* 15]	EB to	VIII, 243– 5
1795 Sept 13	EB to	VIII, 315–16

SMITH, Dr. [Samuel]

1784 Mar 16	EB to	V, 133–4

SMYTH, Robert

1780 Jan 25	EB fr	**A**
1780 Jan 31	EB fr	**A**

SOMERS, Abbé Michael

1792 Sept 28	EB fr	**B**
1792 Dec 31	EB fr	**A**
1793 Apr 12	EB fr	**A**
1793 Apr 19	EB fr	**A**

SOUTHAMPTON, Charles Fitzroy, 1st Baron

1791 July 31	EB to	VI, 310–11

SPAN, Samuel

1778 Feb 26	EB and H. Cruger fr	**AZ**
1778 Mar 4	EB and H. Cruger fr	**AZ**
1778 Mar 14	EB and H. Cruger fr	**AZ**
1778 Mar 31	EB to	IX, 419–20
1778 Apr 2	EB and H. Cruger fr	**AZ**
1778 Apr 9	EB to	III, 426 IX, 421
1778 Apr 13	EB and H. Cruger fr	III, 429
1778 Apr 23	EB to	III, 431–6★
1778 Apr 30	EB fr	**AZ**
1778 May 12	EB to	III, 446–7 IX, 423–4
1778 Oct 26	EB fr	**AZ**
1778 Nov 11	EB to	IV, 26–7
1781 Nov 6	EB fr, J. Harford and Noble	**A**

SPARKES, T.

1788 Apr 2	EB fr	**A**

SPEED, Hugh

1782 Apr 23	EB fr	**A**

SPENCER, George John Spencer, 2nd Earl

1790 May 23	EB to	VI, 116–17

★ Published in *Two Letters on the Trade of Ireland* (Todd, 91–2).

Spencer, George John (*cont.*)		
1795 Mar 19	EB to	VIII, 205
1796 May 5	EB to	IX, 6–7
1796 Aug 12	EB to	IX, 65–6
1796 Aug 16	EB fr	A

SPENCER, Lavinia (*née* Bingham), Countess		
1794 Oct 1	EB to	VIII, 26–7

SPENCER, Margaret Georgiana (*née* Poyntz), Countess		
[1778 Mar 20]	EB to, and Duchess of Devonshire	III, 421–3

SPENCER, Lord Robert		
[1780] Friday	EB fr	A

STAIR, John Dalrymple, 5th Earl of		
1775 Dec 26	EB fr	A
[1776] Jan 1	EB fr	A
[1776 Feb]	EB fr	A
[1776 Feb]	EB fr	A

STANHOPE, L[ovell]		
1782 Apr 23	EB fr	A
1782 Apr 24	EB fr	A

STANISLAUS AUGUSTUS, King of Poland		
[1792 Feb *a* 28]	EB fr	9 II, 105 abs 3 lines
1792 Feb 28	EB to	VII, 76–9
1793 June 12	EB fr	VII, 374–5

STANLEY, Edward		
1766 Nov 19	WB fr	I 34 II, 95 abs 3 lines
1776 Nov 14	EB fr	A

STAUNTON, George Leonard; later (1785) 1st Baronet		
1780 Aug 19	RBsr to	C 56 251–3

[1781] June [25]	EB fr	A
1781 Dec 3	EB to	IV, 385–6
1782 Jan 28	EB fr	A
[1785 Jan 21]	RBsr to	C
[1785 Jan 21]	EB to	V, 206
1785 Feb 17	RBsr to	IX, 465
[1785 Feb 27]	EB to	V, 207
1785 Apr 7	EB to	V, 208–9
[1785 Apr 10]	EB to	V, 210
1785 June 11	EB fr	A
1785 June 15	EB to	V, 211–12
1785 [July] 6	EB to	V, 212
1785 July 6	EB to	V, 213
1785 July 11	EB to	V, 213
1785 [July *p* 27]	EB to	V, 213–15
1786 Jan 9	EB to	V, 251–2
[1786 Feb *c* 24]	EB to	V, 260
1786 July 24	RBsr to	C
1789 Oct 18	EB fr	A
1790 May 19	RBsr fr	A
n.d.	EB to	IX, 471

STEELE, Thomas		
1788 Apr 10	EB fr	33 78–9
1788 June 20	EB to	V, 402
n.d. Sunday 25th	EB fr	A [Thomas Steele]

STEELL, M. G.		
1791 Mar 16	EB fr	A

STENNETT, Rev. Dr. Samuel		
1783 May 15	EB fr	A

STEPHENS, Philip; later (1795) 1st Baronet		
1766 Feb 19	WB fr	I 34 II, 17 abs 3 lines
1776 Nov 7	EB fr	A
1776 Nov 8	EB fr	I ADM 2/ 735
1776 Nov 15	EB fr	A
1778 Mar 26	EB fr	AZ
1778 Apr 3	EB fr	I
1779 Mar 24	EB fr	AZ
1779 Apr 16	EB fr	AZ
1782 June 7	RBsr fr	A

STEVENS, Joseph
1778 Nov 5   EB fr   **AZ**

STEVENSON
n.d. Monday   EB fr   **A**

STEWART, Charles Edward
1791 Mar 3   EB fr   **A**
1796 Mar 13   EB fr   **A**

STEWART, John
1769 Sept 24   EB fr   **A**
1769 Oct 7   EB fr   **A**
1772 Oct 30   EB to   II, 357–60

STOCKDALE, Percival
1788 Aug 26   EB fr   **A**

STONEHEWER, Richard
n.d.   EB to   IX, 458

STORER, Anthony Morris
1782 Mar 8   EB fr   **A**

STORMONT, David Murray, 7th Viscount
1780 Oct 3   EB to, and E. of Hillsborough   IV, 307–10
1780 Oct 3   EB fr   **B**
1780 Oct 3   EB to   IV, 311
1780 Oct 4   EB to   IV, 311–12
1780 Oct 4   EB fr   **B**
1780 Oct 18   EB fr, and E. of Hillsborough   **B**
1780 Oct 19   EB to, and E. of Hillsborough   IV, 316
1781 July 12   EB to   IV, 356, ref

STOTT, Captain John
1771 Jan *a* 2   JB fr   **46** XIV (1824), 456, ext 5 lines
1771 Dec 27   EB fr   **A**

STOWFORD, Rector of
1791 Feb 24   EB fr   **A**

STRACHEY, Henry
1776 June 13   EB to   III, 272–3
1778 Apr 11   EB to   III, 428

STRETTELL, Thomas
1783 [Jan] 12   EB to   V, 62–3

STUART, Andrew
1782 June 23   EB fr   **AM**
[1782 June 23]   EB to   IX, 432–3

STUART, John (Ottobah Cuguano); a negro servant
[1787]   EB fr   **A**

SUFFOLK, Henry Howard, 12th Earl of
[1772 Aug *a* 10]   EB to   II, 323–5
1775 Sept 16   EB to   III, 212–13

SURREY, Charles Howard, styled Earl of
1778 May 10   EB to   IX, 422–3

SWIFT, William Thomas
[1790 Oct *c* 25]   EB to [Swift]   VI, 141–2
1791 July 13   EB to   VI, 292
1791 July 17   EB to   VI, 298–9
1791 July 27   EB to   VI, 308
1791 Aug 5   EB to   VI, 314–15
1796 July 11   EB fr   IX, 57–8

SWINBURNE, Sir Edward, 5th Baronet
[1780 June 6]   EB to   IV, 241–2

SWINEY, Major Matthew
1791 Dec 30   EB fr   **A**

SYDNEY, Thomas Townshend, later (1783) 1st Baron; later (1789) 1st Viscount
1776 Jan 16   EB fr   **A**

Sydney, Thomas Townshend
  (*cont.*)

[1777 Nov]	EB fr	**A**
1782 June 26	RBsr to	**F**
		62 85 abs
		2 lines
1782 July 4	EB fr	v, 8–9
1782 July 8	RBsr fr	**F**
1782 July 10	EB to	v, 15–16
1784 July 3	EB to	v, 156–7
1784 July 17	EB fr	**A**
1785 Aug 12	EB fr	**I**
1794 Aug 7	WB fr	**B**

SYMONDS, Thomas

1774 Dec 17	EB fr	**A**
1775 Apr 30	EB fr	**A**
1780 Mar 11	EB fr	**A**
[1780] Mar *p* 11	EB fr	**A**
1782 Apr 3	EB fr	**A**

TALBOT, William Talbot, 1st
  Earl

1780 Mar 15	EB fr	**A**

TANJORE, Raja of
See also TRIMBUCK
  SAMBAGEE

1777 Oct 16	WB to	**AH**
		MS 3441
1778 Oct 28	WB and	**D**
	Capt.	4 39846
	Walde-	ff. 145–7
	grave fr	
[1779 Mar 18]	WB and	**D**
	Capt.	4 39856
	Walde-	f. 227 ext
	grave fr	1 line
1779 Oct	WB and	**D**
	Capt.	4 39856
	Walde-	ff. 187–8
	grave fr	

TAUBMAN, John

1790 Oct 15	EB fr	**A**

TEISSEIREZ

1766 Aug 4	EB fr	**B**

TEMPLE, 3rd Earl
See BUCKINGHAM

TERRAY, Antoine-Jean

1791 June 29	EB fr	**B**

THERRY, John Joseph

1796 Nov 3	EB fr	**B**
1796 Nov 16	EB to	IX, 109–11

THERRY, Captain John

1771 Oct 2	EB to	II, 244

THICKNESSE, Philip

[1787] May 25	[EB] fr	**A**

THISTLETHWAITE, James

1775 Oct 20	EB to	III, 231–2
[1776] May 22	EB to	III, 267

THOMAS, William

1782 Mar 9	EB fr	**A**

THOMISDEEN, G. I.

1788 Aug 22	EB fr	**A**

THOMPSON, Captain Edward

[1776 July *c* 1]	EB to	IX, 411

THOMPSON, George Nesbitt

1789 Sept 1	EB to	VI, 12
		[G. N. Thompson]

[THOMPSON]

n.d.	EB fr	**B**
		[Thompson]

THOMSON, Alexander

1783 July 15	EB fr	**28** IV, 226
		abs ½p

THOMSON, W.

1783 July 8	EB fr	**A**

THOROLD, Sir John, 9th Baronet

1782 Apr 3	EB fr	**A**

THOROTON, Robert

[1782] Sept 30	EB fr	**A**

THRALE, Mrs. Henry

1774 May 5	EB to	II, 534–5
1774 June 20	EB to	II, 543
1781 June 25	EB to	IV, 352–3

THURLOW, Edward; later (1778)
1st Baron

1772 Aug 15	EB fr	**B**
[1778 June]	EB fr	**A**
1778 July a 18	EB fr	3 VI, 200 abs 3 lines
1778 July a 18	EB to	3 VI, 200 abs 4 lines
1780 July 10	EB to	IV, 254
[1782 Nov 9]	RBjr to	**A**
[1784 Dec 4]	EB to	V, 196–9
1784 Dec 6	EB fr	V, 199
[1784 Dec 13]	EB fr	**A**
1784 Dec [14]	EB fr	V, 201–2
[1784 Dec 14]	EB to	V, 203–5
[1784 Dec 20]	EB fr	**A**
[1789 Apr 22]	EB fr	**A**

TIGHE, William

1781 Apr 10	EB to	IV, 348–9
1781 Apr 11	EB fr	**A**

TILLY, [Jeanne-Antoinette-
Jacquine *née* Ameslon de Saint
Cher], Marquise de

1791 Mar 9	EB fr	**B**
n.d. Wednesday	EB fr	**B**

TITCHFIELD, William Henry
Cavendish Bentinck, styled
Marquess of

1787 Dec 28	EB fr	**B**

TODD, Anthony

1783 Aug 15	EB fr	**A**
1784 Oct 28	EB fr	**B**

TOMKYNS

1768 Oct 29	EB fr	**A**

TOMLINSON, Robert

1774 Sept 9	EB fr	**A**

TONGE, Thomas R.

1782 May 24	EB fr	**A**

TONSON, William

1782 Sept 25	EB fr	**A**

TOPPING, James

[1784 Mar 10]	RBjr fr	**B**
[1784 Mar 10]	RBjr to	**B**
[1784 Mar 10]	RBjr fr	**B**

TORRINGTON, Lucy (*née* Boyle),
Viscountess

[1787 Nov]	RBsr fr	**A**
[1787 Nov]	RBsr fr	**A**

TOUCHET, John

1780 Dec 1	EB fr, and Irving	**A**

TOWNSEND, James

1780 Mar 2	EB fr	**A**
1780 Mar 6	EB to	IV, 210–11

TOWNSHEND, Charles
Chancellor of the Exchequer 1766–7

1765 J[une] 23	EB fr	**A**
1765 June 25	EB to	I, 204–6

TOWNSHEND, Charles

1769 July 8	EB fr	**A**
1771 Oct 15	EB fr	**A** 1 I, 265–7
1771 Oct 17	EB to	II, 249–50
1771 Nov 20	EB fr	**A** 1 I, 272–4
1771 Nov 24	EB to	II, 288–9

TOWNSHEND, Charles

1794 Feb 8	WB to	**AP**
[1794] Feb 9	WB fr	**B**

TOWNSHEND, Thomas

[1796] Mar 29	EB to	VIII, 452–3
[1796] Apr 13	EB fr	**A**
1796 Nov 6	EB fr	**A**

TRAFFORD, Henry
1783 Apr 30   EB fr   **A**

TRAQUAIR, Charles Stewart,
  7th Earl of
1794 July 9   EB fr   **A**

TRAVIS, Rev. George
1790 Dec 4   EB fr   **A**

TREASURY, Lords Commissioners
  of the
1782 July 18   EB to   v, 21–3
1788 Apr 15   EB to   v, 388–91

TRECOTHICK, Barlow
[1771 Oct 8]   EB fr   II, 245–6

TRENCH, Frederick
1796 Mar 2   EB fr   **B**

TREVOR, John
1790 Dec 4   EB fr   **A**
[1791 Jan]   EB to   VI, 216–19

TRIMBUCK SAMBAGEE
1778 Oct 23   WB and   **D**
           Capt.   **4** 39856
           Walde-   ff. 143–4
           grave fr
1779 Jan 19   WB to   **AH**
           [Trim-   MS 3441
           buck
           Sambagee]
1780 Feb 7   WB and   **D**
           Capt.   **4** 39856
           Walde-   ff. 227–8
           grave fr

TROWARD, Richard
1787 Oct 20   EB fr   **A**
1792 Jan 18   EB fr   **A**
1795 Jan 18   EB to,   VIII, 117–
           and   18
           Wallis
1795 Feb 24   EB to,   VIII, 160
           and Wallis
1797 Apr 27   EB fr   **A**

1797 May 1   EB to   IX, 323–4
1797 May 23   EB to   IX, 360–1
1797 June 9   EB fr   **B**

TROY, John Thomas, Catholic
  Archbishop of Dublin
1795 July 13   EB fr   VIII, 288–9

TRUMBULL, John
1781 May 10   EB fr   **B**
1781 May 19   EB fr   **A**
1781 June 25   EB fr   **B**
1790 Dec 2   EB fr   **A**

TRUMBULL, Jonathan
1783 Apr 20   EB fr   **A**
1783 Oct 1   EB fr   **A**

TURTON, John
1775 Jan 23   EB fr   **A**
1777 Feb 26   EB fr   **A**

TYRAWLEY, James O'Hara, 2nd
  Baron
1765 Sept 27   EB fr   **A**

UDNY, John
1781 Aug 3   EB to   IV, 361–2

UDNY, Robert [Fullarton]
1775 Feb 7   EB fr   **A**

UPPER OSSORY, John Fitz-
  patrick, 2nd Earl of
1779 Sept 25   EB to   IV, 135–6
1779 Sept 30   EB to   IV, 138–9
1779 Oct 14   EB to   IV, 148–9
                          [E. of Upper
                          Ossory]
1792 Dec 19   EB fr   **A**
                          1 IV, 58
[1793] Jan 22   EB to   VII, 341–3

VALLANCEY, Colonel Charles
1783 June 25   EB fr   **A**
1783 Aug 15   EB to   v, 108–10
1786 Nov 29   EB to   v, 290–3
1789 Oct 8   EB fr   **A**

Vallancey, Colonel Charles (*cont.*)
[1789 Oct *p* 8] EB to VI, 29

VANE, Frederick
1782 Aug 10 EB fr A

VAUDREUIL, Joseph-Hyacinthe-
François de Paule Rigaud, Comte
de
[1791 Aug 13] RBjr fr A
1791 Oct 4 RBjr fr B

VAUGHAN, General John
[1782 Feb *p* 4] EB to IV, 402–3

VAUGHAN, [Richard]
1780 Mar 3 EB fr A

VAUGIRAUD DE ROSNAY,
Pierre-René-Marie, Comte de
1793 Oct 4 RBjr fr B

VENABLES, Thomas
1796 Sept 20 EB to IX, 87–8
1796 Sept 23 JB to C
1796 Sept 29 EB to IX, 91–2
1796 Dec 6 EB to IX, 147–8
1797 Jan 17 JB to Z
[1797] Apr 23 JB to IX, 469
1797 June JB to IX, 469

VENABLES, Mrs. Thomas
1796 Oct 24 EB to IX, 96–7

VERNEY, Ralph Verney, 2nd Earl
1768 June 25 EB fr A
[1770 Mar *c* 12] EB to II, 125
1774 Sept 25 WB fr A
1774 Sept 26 EB fr A
1774 Sept 28 EB fr A
[1790 Aug] RBjr to BC
1790 Oct 24 RBsr to BC

VESEY, Agmondesham
1760 Sept 10 EB to I, 136–7
1765 July 27 EB fr B
1777 Oct 11 EB fr B
1778 Apr 9 EB fr A

VESEY, Mrs. Agmondesham
[1781]   JB fr A
[1782] Apr 13 JB fr A
n.y. July 10 JB fr A

VIC, Demoiselle de
1791 Jan 21 EB fr B

VILLERS, François-Alexandre-
Léonard le Jolis de
1791 Nov 20 EB fr B

VOISINS, Mark-Gilbert de
1793 Nov 13 EB fr B

VORONTSOV, Count Semen
Romanovich
1791 Sept 27 EB fr A
1791 Oct 2 EB fr A
1791 Oct 8 EB fr A
1793 Jan 31 EB fr A
1793 Feb 15 EB fr A

WALDEGRAVE, John
Waldegrave, 3rd Earl
[1780 Aug 18] WB to D
       4 38404
       f. 170

WALDEGRAVE, Captain William
[1780] Nov [7] EB fr A
[1780] Nov 8 EB fr A
[1784] Dec 23 EB fr A

WALES, George Augustus
Frederick, Prince of; later George
IV, King of England
1787 May 4 EB to V, 329–31
[1789 Feb 8] EB fr V, 446–7

WALLER, Rev. Bryan
[1791 June *a* 16] EB fr A
1791 June 16 EB to VI, 277–8

WALLER, Edmund
[1786 Aug *a* 11] EB to V, 267–8
1786 Aug 17 EB to V, 269–73
[1786 Aug *c* 17] EB to V, 274–5

Waller, Edmund (*cont.*)
[1786 Aug *p* 17]   EB to   V, 275–6

WALLER, Mrs. Edmund
1778 Sept 21   EB to   IV, 21–2

WALLER
1796 Sept 15   EB fr   **A**

WALLIS, Albany
1779 Jan 26   EB fr   **A**
1794 [July] 29   EB to   VII, 560–
                          1
1795 Jan 15   EB to   VIII, 115
1795 Jan 18   EB to,   VIII, 117–
        and   18
        Troward
1795 Feb 24   EB to,   VIII, 160
        and Troward
1795   EB to   IX, 468

WALPOLE, Horace
1777 Dec 3   EB fr   **A**
                    44 LIV
                    (1939),
                    124
[1782 July 7]   EB to   V, 10–11
1782 July 7   RBjr to   V, 11–13
1790 Nov 4   EB fr   **A**

WALPOLE, Thomas
1783 Aug 5   EB to   V, 104–5

WARBURTON, John
1781 Dec 22   EB fr   **A**

WARBURTON
[1780] Monday   EB fr   **A**

WARDENER, Madame de
[1782] 13   RBjr fr   **B**
n.y. Apr 19   RBjr fr   **B**

WARREN, Peter
1778 Apr 14   EB fr   **A**

WARREN, Dr. Richard
1782 Sept 11   EB fr   **A**

WARTON, Dr. Joseph
1781 Feb 16   EB to   IV, 335–6

WATERFORD, Catholic Bishop
    of
See HUSSEY

WATKINS, Charles
[1794 Apr 23]   EB fr   **A**

WATSON, Brook
1782 Aug 17   RBsr fr   **P**

WATSON, Robert
1776 Oct 28   EB fr   **A**

WATTS, Job
1775 May 4   EB fr   **A**
1780 Aug 10   EB to   IV, 260–2

WATTS, John
1775 Nov 16   EB fr   **A**

WEBB, H. Arthur
1776 Jan 10   EB fr   **A**

WEDDELL, William
1780 Dec 6   EB to   IV, 322
1782 Oct 12   EB to   V, 38–40
1791 Aug 27   EB fr   **A**
1792 Jan 31   EB to   VII, 50–
                          63

WEDDERBURN, Alexander
See LOUGHBOROUGH

WENTWORTH, Lady
    Charlotte Watson
1782 Dec 31   JB fr   **B**
1790 May 27   RBjr fr   **A**

WENTWORTH, Sir John
1770 Nov 18   EB fr   **A**

WEST, James
1794 Apr 24   RBjr to   **D**
                    4 34728
                    f. 213

West, James (*cont.*)
[1794] Monday   RBjr to   **D**
4 34728
f. 215

WESTBURY, Wiltshire, Committee
at
1775 Nov 21   EB fr   **A**

WESTON, Edward
1765 Dec 4   WB to   **32** 397–8
ext ½p

WEYMOUTH, Thomas Thynne,
3rd Viscount
1778 Feb 16   EB to   III, 418–19
1778 June   WB to   **F**
62 8on
ext 2 lines

WHATELY, Thomas
[1769] Aug 21   EB to   II, 55–6
IX, 394–5
1769 Aug 23   EB fr   II, 56–7
1769 Aug 30   EB fr   II, 59–60
1769 Sept 7   EB fr   **A**

WHIG CLUB
[1793 Feb 28]   EB and   VII, 353–5
others to

WHITE, Patrick
1791 Mar 19   EB fr   **A**

WHITEFOORD, Caleb
[1774 May *c* 5]   EB fr   II, 535–7
[Whitefoord]

WICKHAM, William
1772 Aug 19   EB to   II, 325–6
1773 Nov 7   EB fr   **A**
1774 Jan 5   EB to   II, 501–2

WIGGLESWORTH, John
1794 Feb 14   EB fr   **I**
1794 Mar 17   EB fr   **I**
1794 Mar 28   EB fr   **I**
1794 Apr 5   EB to   VII, 535–6

1794 Nov 12   EB fr   **I**
1795 Jan 10   EB fr   **I**

WILCOCKS, Joseph
1762 May 1   EB fr   **A**

WILCOX, John
1777 Nov 29   EB fr   **A**
1777 Dec 24   EB fr   **A**
1778 Aug 1   EB fr   **A**

WILDE, John
1793 July 31   EB fr   **A**
1796 Mar 30   EB fr   **B**
n.d. Friday   EB fr   **A**

WILKES, John
1766 June 12   EB fr   I, 256–7
1766 July 4   EB to   I, 259–60

WILKS, Samuel
1787 Dec 20   EB fr   **A**
1794 Monday   EB fr   **B**

WILLIAMS, John
1775 Jan 14   EB fr,   **A**
and Thos. Williams
1775 Jan 30   EB fr,   **A**
and Thos. Williams

WILLIAMS, Thomas
1775 Jan 14   EB fr,   **A**
and J. Williams
1775 Jan 30   EB fr,   **A**
and J. Williams

WILLIAMS, T.
1780 Mar 4   EB fr   **A**

WILLIAMSON, James
1782 Sept 21   RBjr fr   **A**

WILLS, John; Vice-Chancellor of
Oxford 1792–6
1793 July *a* 3   EB to   **43** II,
154
abs 2
lines

WILMOT, John Eardley		
1792 Oct 2	EB to	VII, 225–7
1792 Oct 6	EB fr	VII, 234–5
1792 Oct 9	EB to	X, 26
1793 Nov 24	EB to	X, 28–9
1795 Feb 6	EB to	VIII, 140–1
1795 Feb 9	EB fr	C
1795 Feb 12	EB to	VIII, 148–9
WILSON, Dr. Thomas		
1774 June 28	EB fr	A
		1 I, 465–7
1774 July 1	EB to	III, 3–4
1774 July 11	EB fr	A
		1 I, 468–9
WINDHAM, William		
1783 May 5	EB to	V, 91–3
1783 June 10	EB to	V, 97–8
[1783]	EB fr	A
1784 Oct 14	EB to	V, 177
1784 Oct 15	EB to	V, 177–8
[1784] 20	EB fr	B
[1785 May c 7]	EB to	V, 210–11
[1785] Aug 6	EB fr	V, 218–19
[1785] Sept 25	EB fr	B
1785 Oct 20	EB fr	A
[1785 Nov 21]	EB to	V, 239
[1788 Feb 11]	EB fr	A
1788 Dec 25	EB to	V, 433–4
[1789 Jan c 24]	EB to	V, 436–45
1789 Apr 7	EB fr	V, 463–4
1789 Sept 15	EB fr	VI, 20–2
1789 Sept 27	EB to	VI, 24–6
1790 Oct 27	EB to	VI, 142–4
1790 Dec 22	EB to	VI, 193–5
[1792 Mar 3]	EB fr	A
[1792] Nov 14	EB fr	VII, 288–9
[1792] Nov 15	EB fr	A
1793 Aug 17	EB fr	VII, 411–12
1793 Aug 18	EB to	VII, 413–14
1793 Aug 20	EB to	VII, 414
[1793 Aug a 22]	EB fr	A
1793 Aug 23	EB to	VII, 415–16
1793 Oct 2	EB and Sir Gilbert Eliot to	VII, 438–9
[1793 Oct 24]	EB to	VII, 460–2
1793 Nov 1	EB fr	VII, 469–71

1793 Nov 4	EB to	VII, 471–2
[1793 Nov c 6]	EB to	VII, 476–7
1793 Nov 7	EB fr	VII, 478–80
[1793 Nov c 10]	EB to	VII, 480–3
1793 Nov 14	EB fr	VII, 487–8
1793 Nov 25	EB to	VII, 489–91
1794 Jan 8	EB to	VII, 514
1794 Jan 8	RBjr to	D
		6 94
[1794 Jan 18]	EB fr	VII, 525–6
[1794 Feb 1]	EB to	VII, 530–1
[1794] Feb 11	RBjr fr	VII, 531–2
[1794] Apr 13	EB fr	A
[1794 June 10]	EB to	VII, 548–9
1794 June 19	RBjr to	VII, 550–2
[1794 June c 27]	RBjr to	VII, 557–8
[1794 Aug 15]	EB to	VII, 570–1
1794 Aug 17	EB to	VII, 571–2
1794 Sept 28	EB to	VIII, 23–4
[1794 Oct 7]	EB to	VIII, 30
1794 Oct 8	EB to	VIII, 31
[1794 Oct 15]	EB to	VIII, 31–2
[1794 Oct] 15	EB fr	VIII, 32–3
1794 Oct 16	EB to	VIII, 33–5
[1794 Oct 16]	EB to	VIII, 35–42
[1794] Oct 18	EB fr	VIII, 43
1794 Oct 20	EB to	VIII, 50–2
1794 Oct 21	EB fr	VIII, 60–2
[1794 Oct p 21]	EB to	VIII, 62–3
1794 Oct 28	EB to	VIII, 64–5
1794 Dec 22	EB to	VIII, 101–2
1794 Dec 30	EB to	VIII, 103–5
[1794]	EB fr	A
1795 Jan 7	EB to	VIII, 108–9
1795 Jan 8	EB to	VIII, 113
[1795 Feb c 2]	EB to	VIII, 134–6
[1795 Feb 23]	EB to	VIII, 156–7
[1795 Mar 5]	EB fr	VIII, 178–9
[1795] Mar 6	EB to	VIII, 179–80
[1795 Apr 1]	EB to	VIII, 222
[1795] June 9	EB to	VIII, 265–7
[1795 June 27]	EB to	VIII, 273–4
[1795] July 30	EB to	VIII, 290
1795 Sept 4	EB to	VIII, 314
1795 Sept 15	EB to	VIII, 319–20
1795 Oct 10	EB to	VIII, 325

Windham, William (*cont.*)

[1795 Nov *a* 17]	EB to	VIII, 338–41
1795 Nov 17	EB to	VIII, 341–4
1795 Nov [25]	EB to	VIII, 345–7
1796 Jan 17	EB fr	VIII, 375–7
1796 Jan 19	EB to	VIII, 378–9
1796 Mar 6	EB to	VIII, 403–4
1796 Mar 7	EB to	VIII, 409–10
[1796 Mar 28]	EB to	VIII, 451
1796 June 2	EB to	IX, 43–4
1796 [June] 5	EB fr	A
[1796 June 7]	EB to	IX, 46–7
1796 Aug 1	EB to	IX, 64–5
1796 Aug 26	EB fr	IX, 71–3
[1796 Aug 27]	EB to	IX, 73–4
1796 Sept 11	EB to	IX, 84
[1796 Nov 1]	EB to	IX, 102–3
1796 Nov 11	EB to	IX, 108–9
1796 Nov 25	EB to	IX, 134–6
1796 Dec 18	EB to	IX, 185–6
1796 Dec 20	EB fr	IX, 187–8
1796 Dec 23	EB to	IX, 198–202
1796 Dec 24	EB fr	IX, 202–3
1796 Dec 25	EB to	IX, 205–6
1797 Jan 5	EB to	IX, 221–3
1797 Jan 6	EB fr	IX, 224–5
1797 Jan 9	EB to	IX, 225–7
[1797 Jan] 17	EB fr	IX, 229–31
[1797 Feb 10]	EB fr	A
[1797] Feb 11	EB fr	A
		1 IV, 427–8 part omitted
[1797] Feb 12	EB to	IX, 240–1
[1797 Feb] 17	EB fr	IX, 247–8
1797 Mar 30	EB to	IX, 299–302
1797 Apr 25	EB fr	IX, 312–14
1797 Apr 26	EB to	IX, 314–16
1797 Apr 30	EB fr	A
1797 May 16	EB to	IX, 347–9
1797 July 9	JB fr	A
n.d.	RBjr fr	A

WISEMORE, Henry

1791 Apr 16	EB fr	VI, 246–7

WITHERS, Thomas

[1775 Feb]	EB fr	A

WODSWORTH, N.

1785 Oct 22	EB fr	A

WOLFALL, Richard

1767 Jan 21	WB fr	**I**
1770 Dec 4	EB to	II, 167–9

WOLFE, Arthur

1791 Nov 8	EB fr	A

WOODFORD, Captain Emperor John Alexander

1791 Jan 5	EB fr	A
1791 Feb 11	EB to	VI, 223–6*
[1791] Feb 11	EB fr	A
1791 Apr 29	EB fr	A
1792 Nov 29	EB fr	A
1794 Jan 13	EB to	VII, 519–22
[1794] Mar 17	EB fr	A
[1795 Nov *c* 26]	EB to	VIII, 348–51
1796 Dec 9	EB to	IX, 153–5
1797 May 8	JB to	
1797 May 31	EB to	IX, 362–3

WOODFORD, Sir Ralph, 1st Baronet

1796 Jan 10	EB fr	A

WOODWARD, John

[1775] Jan 12	EB fr	A
1775 Apr 26	EB and H. Cruger fr	A

WOOLLEY, James

1793 Jan 16	EB fr	VII, 331–5
1793 Mar 12	EB fr	A

WORRALL, Samuel

1777 Mar 17	EB, H. Cruger, Coombe and Dunning fr	**AZ**
1777 June 26	EB fr	A

* Published in *Two Letters on the French Revolution* (Todd, 171–2).

Worrall, Samuel (*cont.*)
1779 Apr 10	EB and	**AZ**	
	H. Cruger fr		
1779 May 6	EB, H.	**AZ**	
	Cruger, Coombe		
	and Sir Jos Laroche		
	fr		
1779 May 11	EB to	IV, 73	

WORRALL, Samuel, Jr.
1793 Dec 28	RBsr fr	**M** p. 49

WREN, Thomas
1781 June 22	EB fr	**A**
1782 Mar 1	EB fr	**B**

WRIGHT, Sampson
1782 June 21	RBsr fr	**I**

WRIGHT, William
1790 Feb 22	EB fr	**B**

WÜRTTEMBERG, Frederick
William Charles, Prince of
1797 Apr 28	EB to	IX, 318–19
1797 May 6	EB fr	**A**

WYNN, Sir Watkin Williams, 4th
Baronet
1780 May 22	EB to	IV, 239–40

WYVILL, Christopher
1780 Aug 4	EB fr	**B**
1780 Aug 14	EB to	IV, 265

YARMOUTH, 1st Earl of
See BEAUCHAMP

YONGE, Philip
1785 Oct 18	EB fr	**A**

YORKE, Joseph; later (1788) 1st
Baron Dover
1778 Sept 4	EB fr	**A**

YOUNG, Arthur
1770 Oct 21	EB to	II, 165–7

1771 Jan 9	EB to	II, 182–4
1771 Sept 10	EB to	II, 238–40
[1771 Oct *p* 14]	EB to	II, 247–8
[1776 June *a* 4]	EB to	III, 270
[1788 June *a* 19]	EB to	V, 401
1793 Mar 5	EB to	VII, 356
1796 Apr 27	EB to	VIII, 459
1797 May 23	EB to	IX, 361–2

YOUNG, David
1788 May 28	EB fr	**A**

YOUNG, Dr. Matthew
[1793] Oct 10	EB fr,	**A**
	and Dr. Hall	
[1793] Oct 17	EB fr	VII, 453–4

YOUNG, William; later (1769) 1st
Baronet
1764 Dec 31	EB to	I, 176–7
	[William] Young	
1770 Aug 6	EB to	II, 146

YOUNG, Captain William
1784 Nov 9	JB fr	**A**
1784 Nov 20	JB fr	**A**

ZOUCH, Clement Nevill
[1786 May *c* 5]	RBsr to	**B**

UNKNOWN
1764 Jan	EB to	IX, 463
1765 Nov 4	RBsr fr	**A**
		62 54
1765 Nov 4	RBsr fr	**A**
		62 54 abs
		2 lines
1766 [Jan]	EB to	**31** 139 abs
		3 lines
[1769 Jan *c* 20]	EB to	II, 21–2
[1769]	WB fr	**I,** 284 abs
		5 lines
[1771 Mar *p* 12]	EB to	II, 201–3
[1771] June 5	EB to	IX, 397
1772 May 2	EB to	IX, 463
1772 May 20	EB to	II, 304–5
[1772 Nov *a* 17]	EB to	IX, 400–1

Unknown (*cont.*)		
1773 Apr 21	EB fr	**B**
[1773]	EB fr	**A**
[1774 July *a* 16]	EB to	III, 11–12
1774 Oct	EB to	III, 70–1
[1774 Dec *a* 28]	EB fr	**A**
[1775 Jan]	EB and	**A**
	H. Cruger	
	fr	
1775 May 4	EB fr	**A**
1775 June 1	EB fr	**A**
1775 June 4	EB fr	**A**
1775 June 7	EB fr	**B**
1775 July 27	EB fr	**A**
1775 Oct 10	EB fr	**A**
1775 Oct 30	EB fr	**A**
[1775]	EB fr	**A**
1776 June 21	EB fr	**A**
1776 [June]	EB to	IX, 464
1776 July 15	EB to	IX, 464
1776 Nov 12	EB fr	**8** 177 abs
		4 lines
1777 Apr 4	EB fr	**A**
		1 II, 152–4
1777 Apr 26	EB fr	**B**
1777 June 28	EB fr	**45**
		June 28,
		1777
[1777 Dec *c* 19]	EB to	III, 417
[1778] Feb 12	EB fr	**A**
[1778 Mar *a* 14]	WB fr	**D**
		4 39856
		ff. 3–17
1778 Mar 14	WB fr	**D**
		4 39856
		ff. 54–61
1778 Mar 15	WB fr	**D**
		4 39856
		ff. 61–2
1778 May 2	EB fr	**A**
1778 June 3	EB to	III, 453–4
[1778 June *c* 3]	EB to	III, 454–6
[1778 Aug 3]	WB and	**D**
	Capt.	**4** 39856
	Walde-	ff. 65–71
	grave fr	
1778 Nov 1, 2	WB and	**D**
	Capt.	**4** 39856

	Walde-	ff. 136–41
	grave fr	
1779 Jan 5	WB and	**D**
	Capt.	**4** 39856
	Walde-	ff. 149–54
	grave fr	
1779 Mar 26	EB fr	**A**
1779 Mar 29	EB fr	**A**
1779 Apr 10	EB fr	**A**
1779 Oct 12	WB and	**D**
	Capt.	**4** 39856
	Walde-	ff. 162–8
	grave fr	
1779 Oct 14	WB fr	**D**
		4 39856
		f. 173
[1779 Dec *p* 9]	EB to	IX, 429
1779 Dec 11	EB fr	**A**
[1779]	EB fr	**B**
[1780] Jan 27	EB fr	**A**
1780 Feb 7	EB fr	**A**
[1780] Feb 12	EB fr	**A**
[1780 Feb 14]	EB fr	**A**
1780 Mar 4	EB fr	**A**
1780 Mar 14	EB fr	**A**
[1780 Mar *p* 20]	EB to	IV, 214–15
[1780 Apr *a* 19]	EB to	IV, 231
1780 June 7	EB fr	**A**
[1780 June 7]	EB to	IV, 242
[1780 June *c* 7]	EB to	IV, 242–3
1780 June 26	EB fr	**A**
1780 July *a* 22	EB fr	**42**
		XLVIII
		(1780), 71
1780 Dec 2	EB to	IV, 320–1
[1781 Jan 25]	EB to	IV, 333
1781 Mar 2	EB fr	**A**
[1781 July]	EB fr	**A**
1781 Aug 24	EB fr	**A**
[1781]	EB fr	**A**
1782 Feb 27	EB fr	**A**
1782 Mar 22	EB to	IX, 465
1782 Apr 1	EB fr	**A**
1782 Apr 3	EB fr	**A**
1782 Apr 6	EB fr	**A**
[1782 Apr *p* 14]	EB to	IX, 432
1782 Apr 15	EB fr	**A**
1782 May 4	EB fr	**A**

Unknown (*cont.*)

1782 June 17	EB fr	A
1782 Oct 29	EB to	V, 45
[1782]	EB fr	A
1783 Jan 29	EB to	V, 64
1783 Apr 4	EB fr	A
1783 Sept 8	EB fr	A
1783 Oct 20	EB to	V, 115–16
[1783]	EB fr	A
1784 Aug 12	EB fr	B
1784 Nov 8	EB fr	B
1785 Apr 10	EB to	V, 209–10
1785	EB to	IX, 466
1785	RB[jr] to	V, 466
1787 Jan 13	EB fr	B
1787 May 13	EB fr	A
[1787 Nov]	RBsr fr	A
1787 [Dec] 5	EB to	V, 358; X, 20–1
1788 Apr 2	EB fr	A
1788 May 7	EB to	IX, 466
1788 Aug 10	EB to	IX, 466
1788 Sept 11	EB to	V, 416
[1788]	[RBjr] to	AJ
[1789 Apr 22]	EB to	V, 464–5
1789 June 30	RBsr to	Q
[1789]	[EB] fr	B
[1790 Jan]	EB to	VI, 78–82
1790 Sept 28	EB to	VI, 138–9
1790 Nov 6	EB fr	A
1790 Nov *a* 22	EB fr	21 Nov 22, 1790
1790 Dec 28	EB fr	A
[1790]	EB fr	C
1791 Jan 2	EB to	VI, 196–7
1791 Jan 9	EB to	VI, 202–3
1791 Jan 13	RBjr to	IX, 466
1791 Jan 18	EB fr	AY
1791 Jan 26	EB to	VI, 214–16
[1791 Feb 9]	EB fr	A
1791 Feb 17	EB to	IX, 466
1791 Mar 24	EB fr	A
[1791 Apr *a* 25]	EB fr	A
[1791] May 1	RBjr to	BC
1791 May 12	EB fr	A
[1791] May 16	EB fr	A
[1791] June 3	EB fr	A

1791 June 6	EB fr	A
1791 June 7	EB fr	A
[1791 June]	EB fr	A
1791 July 4	EB fr	B
[1791 Oct 27]	EB fr	A
[1791 Nov 14]	EB fr	A
[1791]	EB to	VI, 479–80
[1791]	EB to	A
[1791]	EB fr	A
[1791]	EB fr	A
1792 Aug 7	EB to	VII, 167–8
[1792] Aug 15	EB fr	B
[1792] Aug 15	EB fr	B
1792 Aug 16	EB fr	B
1792 Aug 31	EB fr	A
1792 Sept 14	EB to	VII, 210–11
[1792] Dec 29	EB fr	A
[1792]	EB, Fox and Sheridan fr	B
1793 Mar 7	EB to	VII, 358; X, 26–7
1793 Mar 7	EB fr	A
[1793] May 2	EB fr	A
1793 June 2	EB to	IX, 467
1793 July 18	RBjr fr	I 24 III, 110–11
1793 July 23	EB fr	A
1793 July 24	RBjr to	AL
1793 Sept 9	EB fr	A
1794 Jan 15	EB to	VII, 523
1794 June 30	EB to	IX, 467
[1794 June]	EB fr	A
1794 Sept 8	EB to	IX, 468
[1794]	EB to	VIII, 107–8
[1794]	EB to	A
1795 Jan 18	EB to	IX, 468
1795 June 2	EB to	IX, 468
1795 Aug 3	EB to	X, 35–6
[1795]	EB to	VIII, 363
[1795]	EB to	VIII, 364–5
1796 Jan 5	EB to	VIII, 365–6
1796 Jan 24	EB to	VIII, 381–2
[1796] Feb 25	EB to	VIII, 390
1796 May 19	EB to	IX, 12
[1796 May 21]	EB to	IX, 13–14
[1796 Sept *c* 14]	EB to	IX, 84–5

Unknown (*cont.*)					
			n.d.	EB to	IX, 460–1
1796 Sept 25	EB fr	**A**	n.d.	EB to	IX, 461
1796 Nov 9	EB to	IX, 469	n.d.	EB to	IX, 461
1797 Feb 10	EB fr	**A**	n.d.	EB to	IX, 462
[1797 Feb *a* 27]	EB fr	**A**	n.d.	EB to	IX, 462
[1797 Feb]	EB to	IX, 253–63	n.d.	EB to	IX, 471
1797 Mar 5	EB fr	**B**	n.d.	EB to	IX, 471
[1797] June 6	EB to	IX, 369–70	n.d.	EB to	IX, 471
1797 July 3	EB to	IX, 372	n.d.	EB to	IX, 472
n.y. Apr	EB fr	**A**	n.d.	EB to	IX, 472
n.d.	EB fr	**C**	n.d.	EB to	IX, 472
n.d.	EB to	IX, 459	n.d.	RBsr to	IX, 472
n.d.	EB to	IX, 459–60	n.d.	EB to	X, 40
n.d.	EB to	IX, 460	n.d.	EB to	X, 40–1

KEY LIST OF MS SOURCES

The following manuscript collections containing Burke letters are cited in this volume by bold-face capitals (**A**, **B**, **AA**, **AB**, etc.), or occasionally by the short titles ('Fitzwilliam MSS [Sheffield]', 'Osborn Collection') which they have borne elsewhere in this edition. The ten collections most important for Burke studies have been arbitrarily placed first in the list; others follow in the alphabetical order of their short titles.

A Fitzwilliam MSS (Sheffield)
Manuscripts belonging to the Earl Fitzwilliam; now on deposit with the Sheffield City Libraries. These were formerly at the Fitzwilliam family seat of Wentworth Woodhouse in Yorkshire and hence are sometimes cited by scholars under the name 'Wentworth Woodhouse MSS'. They include the main body of Burke's private papers.

B Fitzwilliam MSS (Northampton)
Manuscripts belonging to the Earl Fitzwilliam; now on deposit with the Northamptonshire Record Office, Delapré Abbey, Northampton. These were formerly at the Fitzwilliam family seat at Milton, Near Peterborough, and hence are sometimes cited by scholars under the name 'Milton MSS'. They include a portion—roughly a fifth—of Burke's private papers.

C Osborn Collection
The James Marshall and Marie-Louise Osborn Collection, now deposited in the Beinecke Library, Yale University, New Haven, Connecticut.

D British Museum
Department of Manuscripts, The British Library, Great Russell Street, London W.C.1.

E Bodleian Library
The Bodleian Library, Oxford.

F India Office Library
India Office Library, Orbit House, Blackfriars Road, London S.E. 1.

G O'Hara MSS
Manuscripts formerly in the possession of Donald F. O'Hara, Esq., Annaghmore, Collooney, Sligo. They are now on deposit with the National Library of Ireland, Kildare Street, Dublin 2.

H   Portland MSS (Nottingham)
Manuscripts from the collection of the Duke of Portland; now on deposit with the Library of the University of Nottingham, University Park, Nottingham.

I   Public Record Office
Public Record Office, Chancery Lane, London W.C.2.

J   Champion Letter-books
A collection of notebooks of Richard Champion, containing transcriptions of his correspondence. A single notebook, formerly first of the collection, is now in the New York Public Library. The main body of the notebooks is in the possession of Miss Phyllis Rawlins, Abbey Cottage, Denbigh, Wales.

K   American Philosophical Society
American Philosophical Society, 105 South 5th Street, Philadelphia 6, Pennsylvania.

L   Bristol Archives (Chamberlain's Letter Book)
Bristol Archives, Bristol Record Offices, Council House, College Green, Bristol 1.

M   Bristol Archives (Town Clerk's Letter Book)
Bristol Archives, Bristol Record Office, Council House, College Green, Bristol 1.

N   Cambridge University Library
The University Library, West Road, Cambridge.

O   The Chequers Trust
Chequers, Buckinghamshire.

P   Clements Library
William L. Clements Library, Ann Arbor, Michigan.

Q   Professor Thomas W. Copeland
Professor Thomas W. Copeland, 12 Halcourt Gardens, Amherst, Massachusetts 01002.

R   Dartmouth MSS
Manuscripts belonging to the Earl of Dartmouth, 12 Chester Street, London, S.W. 1; now on deposit with the William Salt Library, Eastgate Street, Stafford.

S   Fitzwilliam MSS (Milton)
Manuscripts in the possession of the Earl Fitzwilliam, Milton, Peterborough.

T   Fitzwilliam Museum, Cambridge
Fitzwilliam Museum, Trumpington Street, Cambridge.

U   Folger Library
The Folger Shakespeare Library, Washington 3, D.C.

Glynn MSS
    Manuscripts of the Glynn family, belonging to Lt. D. H. J. Glynn, R.N., Cannon Cottage, Upton Road, Chichester, Sussex.

W   Professor George H. Guttridge
    Professor George H. Guttridge, Box 6345, Carmel, California.

X   Harvard Library
    Harvard College Library, Cambridge 38, Massachusetts.

Y   Haus-, Hof-, und Staatsarchiv, Vienna
    Haus-, Hof-, und Staatsarchiv, Minoritenplatz 1, Vienna.

Z   Professor Frederick W. Hilles
    Professor Frederick W. Hilles, P.O. Box 525, Old Lyme, Connecticut 06371.

AA   Hull Trinity House
    Trinity House, Trinity House Lane, Hull.

AB   Hyde Collection
    Manuscripts belonging to Mrs. Donald Hyde, Four Oaks Farm, Somerville, New Jersey.

AC   Les Fontaines, Chantilly
    Les Fontaines, 60500 Chantilly, France.

AD   Wilmarth S. Lewis.
    Wilmarth Sheldon Lewis, Farmington, Connecticut.

AE   Little MSS
    Manuscripts owned by the late Professor D. M. Little of Harvard University, Cambridge 38, Massachusetts.

AF   London School of Economics Library
    British Library of Political and Economic Science, London School of Economics, Houghton Street, Aldwych, London, W.C. 2.

AG   Macpherson MSS
    Macpherson manuscripts in the library of the School of Oriental and African Studies, University of London, Malet Street, London W.C. 1.

AH   Madras Record Office
    Madras Record Office, Egmore, Madras 8.

AI   Madras Select Committee Proceedings
    Manuscripts cited under this title in these lists are all in Range D, vol. 27 of Madras Select Committee Proceedings in the India Office Library, Orbit House, Blackfriars Road, London S.E. 1.

AJ   Morgan Library
    The Pierpont Morgan Library, 33 East 36th Street, New York 16, New York.

AK Sir John Murray
Sir John Murray, 50 Albemarle Street, London, W. 1.

AL National Library of Ireland
The National Library of Ireland, Kildare Street, Dublin 2.

AM National Library of Scotland
The Trustees of the National Library of Scotland, George IV Bridge, Edinburgh 1.

AN Lady Neville
Lady Neville, Sloley Old Hall, Norwich, Norfolk.

AO New York Historical Society
New York Historical Society, 170 Central Park West, New York 24, New York.

AP New York Public Library
New York Public Library, Fifth Avenue and 42nd Street, New York 18, New York.

AQ Northamptonshire Record Office
Northamptonshire Record Office, Delapré Abbey, Northampton.

AR Northumberland County Record Office
County Record Office, Melton Park, North Gosforth, Newcastle upon Tyne.

AS Pennsylvania University Library
Charles Patterson Van Pelt Library, The University of Pennsylvania, Philadelphia 4, Pennsylvania.

AT Public Record Office, Dublin
Public Record Office of Ireland, Four Courts, Dublin 7.

AU Public Record Office of Northern Ireland
Public Record Office, 66 Balmoral Avenue, Belfast 9. The letter of Burke in the Caledon Papers is printed by kind permission of the Earl of Caledon.

AV Ramsden MSS
Manuscripts owned by Sir William Pennington Ramsden; now on deposit with the Central Library, Leeds 1.

AW Royal Library, The Hague
Koninklijke Bibliotheke, Lange Voorhout 34, The Hague.

AX Rylands Library
The University Library of Manchester, Oxford Road, Manchester M13 9PD.

AY Miss E. S. Scroggs
Miss E. S. Scroggs, 12 Vicarage Gate, London, W. 8.

AZ Society of Merchant Venturers
Society of Merchant Venturers, Merchants Hall, The Promenade, Clifton, Bristol 8.

BA Suffolk Record Office, Ipswich
Suffolk Record Office, Ipswich Branch, County Hall, Ipswich.
BB Trinity College, Dublin
Trinity College Library, Dublin University, College Street, Dublin 2.
BC Verney MSS
Manuscripts belonging to R. B. Verney, Esq., Claydon House, Bletchley, Buckinghamshire.
BD Victoria and Albert Museum
The Victoria and Albert Museum, Cromwell Road, South Kensington, London, S.W. 7.
BE Yale Library
The Sterling Memorial Library, Yale University, New Haven, Connecticut.

KEY LIST OF PRINTED SOURCES

The following printed works containing Burke letters are cited by bold-face figures (**1**, **2**, **3**, etc.) in this volume, or by their usual short titles '*Corr.* (1844)', '*Burke–Laurence Correspondence*'. Again the ten which are most important for Burke studies are arbitrarily placed first.

1 *Corr.* (1844)
Edmund Burke, *Correspondence between 1744 and 1797*, ed. Charles William, Earl Fitzwilliam and Sir Richard Bourke, 4 vols, London 1844.
2 *Burke–Laurence Correspondence*
The Epistolary Correspondence of Edmund Burke and French Laurence, London, 1827.
3 *Works*
The Works of Edmund Burke, 8 vols [Bohn's British Classics], London, 1854–89.
4 *Add. MSS*
Catalogue of Additions to Manuscripts in the British Museum. London, 1836– .
5 Barry, *Works*
James Barry, *Works*, 2 vols, London, 1809.
6 *Burke–Windham Correspondence*
Correspondence of Edmund Burke and William Windham, ed. J. P. Gilson, London, 1910.
7 Hoffman
Ross J. S. Hoffman, *Edmund Burke, New York Agent. With his*

Letters to the New York Assembly and Intimate Correspondence with Charles O'Hara 1761–1776, Philadelphia, 1956.

8 Owen

Hugh Owen, *Two Centuries of Ceramic Art in Bristol*, London, 1873.

9 Prior (2nd ed.)

James Prior, *Memoir of the Life of Edmund Burke*, 2nd ed., 2 vols, London, 1826.

10 Samuels

A. P. I. Samuels, *Early Life, Correspondence and Writings of Edmund Burke*, Cambridge, 1923.

11 *Adam Catalogue*

The R. B. Adam Library relating to Dr. Samuel Johnson and his Era, 3 vols, London, 1929; 4th vol., Buffalo, New York, 1930. Citations are from vol. I, the portion separately paged and entitled 'Letters of Edmund Burke'.

12 Almon, *Anecdotes*

Anecdotes of the Life of William Pitt, Earl of Chatham [compiled by J. Almon], 3rd ed., 3 vols, London, 1793.

13 *Annals of the Fine Arts*

Annals of the Fine Arts, London, 1817–20.

14 *Beauties of Burke*

The Beauties of the Late Right Hon. Edmund Burke [ed. C. H. Wilson], 2 vols, London, 1798.

15 Bristol Elections

'Bristol Elections 1774–90. Addresses, Squibs, Songs, etc.', a bound folio volume in which are pasted various election handbills, as well as addresses in pamphlet form. The unique copy is in the Central Library, College Green, Bristol 1, Gloucestershire.

16 *Bristol Gazette*

The Bristol Gazette and Public Advertiser, Bristol, 1767–1872.

17 Campbell, *Lives of the Chancellors*

John Campbell, 1st Baron Campbell, *The Lives of the Lord Chancellors and Keepers of the Great Seal*, 8 vols, London, 1845–69.

18 Cartwright, *Life of Cartwright*

Frances Dorothy Cartwright, *Life and Correspondence of Major Cartwright*, 2 vols, London, 1826.

19 Coleridge, *Life of Coutts*

Ernest Hartley Coleridge, *Life of Thomas Coutts*, 2 vols, London and New York, 1920.

20 Crabbe, *Life of Crabbe*
    The poetical Works of the Rev. George Crabbe, with his Letters and Journals, and his life, by his son, 8 vols, London, 1834.
21 *Edinburgh Herald*
    Edinburgh, 1790–1806.
22 *English*
    English. The Magazine of the English Association. Oxford, 1936– .
23 Foot, *Life of Murphy*
    Jesse Foot, *The Life of Arthur Murphy*, London, 1811.
24 Froude, *English in Ireland*
    James Anthony Froude, *The English in Ireland in the Eighteenth Century*, 3 vols, London, 1872.
25 Garrick, *Letters*
    David Garrick, *Letters*, ed. David M. Little and George M. Kahrl, 3 vols, Cambridge, Mass., 1963.
26 Hickey, *Memoirs*
    William Hickey, *Memoirs*, ed. Alfred Spencer, 4 vols, London, 1913–25.
27 Hilles, *Literary Career of Reynolds*
    Frederick W. Hilles, *Literary Career of Sir Joshua Reynolds*, Cambridge, 1936.
28 Hist. MSS Comm. (*American MSS*)
    Historical Manuscripts Commission Report on American MSS in the Royal Institute of Great Britain, 4 vols. London, 1904–9.
29 Hist. MSS Comm. (*Charlemont MSS*)
    Historical Manuscripts Commission, Thirteenth Report, Appendix 8, London, 1894.
30 Hist. MSS Comm. (*Dartmouth MSS*)
    Historical Manuscripts Commission, Fourteenth Report, Appendix 10, London, 1887–95.
31 Hist. MSS Comm. (*Lansdown MSS*)
    Historical Manuscripts Commission, Third Report.
32 Hist. MSS Comm. (*Underwood MSS*)
    Historical Manuscripts Commission, Tenth Report Appendix 1 (Charles Fleetwood Weston Underwood MSS), London, 1885.
33 *History of the Trial of Warren Hastings*
    The History of the Trial of Warren Hastings, Esq....containing the whole of the proceedings and debates in both Houses of Parliament... (a single volume containing eight parts), London, 1796.
34 *Home Office Papers*
    Calendar of Home Office Papers of the reign of George III. 1760..., ed. J. Redington, London, 1878.

35 Huchon, *Life of Crabbe*
René Huchon, *George Crabbe and His Times*, tr. Frederick Clarke, London, 1907.

36 *Huntingdon Library Quarterly*
Huntingdon Library Quarterly, San Marino, California, 1937– .

37 Jones, *Letters*
The Letters of Sir William Jones, ed. Garland Cannon, 2 vols, Oxford, 1970.

38 *Journal of Modern History*
Journal of Modern History, Chicago, 1929– .

39 Leadbeater, *Memoirs of Richard Shackleton*
Memoirs and Letters of R. and E. Shackleton, compiled by M. Leadbeater, London, 1849.

40 *Leadbeater Papers*
Mary Leadbeater, *Leadbeater Papers*, 2 vols, London, 1862.

41 Leslie and Taylor, *Life of Reynolds*
C. R. Leslie and T. Taylor, *Life and Times of Sir Joshua Reynolds*, 2 vols, London, 1862.

42 *London Chronicle*
London Chronicle, London, 1757–1823.

43 Minto, *Life of Elliot*
The Countess of Minto, *Life and Letters of Sir Gilbert Elliot*, 3 vols, London, 1874.

44 *Modern Language Notes*
Baltimore, 1886– .

45 *Morning Post*
The Morning Post, London, 1772–1800.

46 *New Monthly Magazine*
The New Monthly Magazine and Literary Journal (2nd series), London, 1821–1871.

47 *PMLA*
Publications of the Modern Language Association of America, Menasha, Wisconsin, 1884– .

48 Paine, *Works*
The Complete Writings of Thomas Paine, ed. Philip S. Foner, 2 vols, New York, 1945.

49 Parkes and Merivale, *Memoirs of Francis*
Memoirs of Sir Philip Francis, ed. J. Parkes and H. Merivale, 2 vols, London, 1867.

50 *Parliamentary Debates*
T. C. Hansard, *Parliamentary History of England: continued as Parliamentary Debates*, London, 1803– .

51 Robbins, *Life of Macartney*
Helen H. Robbins, *Our First Ambassador to China: an Account of the Life of George, Earl Macartney*, London, 1908.

52 Roberts, *Memoirs of Hannah More*
William Roberts, *Memoirs of the Life and Correspondence of Mrs. Hannah More*, 4 vols, London, 1834.

53 Smith, *Rights of Citizens*
The Rights of Citizens. Being an Examination of Mr Paine's Principles Touching Government. By a Barrister. [Dublin, 1791.]

54 *Sotheby Catalogue*
Sotheby and Company, 34 and 35, New Bond Street, London W. 1

55 South Carolina Historical Society, *Collections*
Collections of the South-Carolina Historical Society, 2 vols, Charleston, S.C., 1857–8.

56 Staunton, *Memoir of Staunton*
Sir George Thomas Staunton, *Memoir of the Life and Family of Sir Leonard Staunton*, London, 1823.

57 Stockdale, *Memoirs*
Percival Stockdale, *Memoirs of the Life and Writings of Percival Stockdale. Written by himself*, 2 vols., London, 1809.

58 *Suffolk Records*
The Suffolk Records, ed. Henry W. Aldred, London [1888].

59 Teignmouth, *Memoir of Teignmouth*
Charles John Shore, 2nd Baron Teignmouth, *Memoir of the Life and Correspondence of John, Lord Teignmouth*, 2 vols, London, 1843.

60 *Tenbury Letters*
The Tenbury Letters, ed. E. H. Fellowes and E. Pine, London, 1942.

61 Wallace, *Life of Laurens*
D. D. Wallace, *Life of Henry Laurens*, London, 1915.

62 Wecter
Dixon Wecter, *Edmund Burke and His Kinsmen* (University of Colorado Studies, Series B, vol. I, no. 1), Boulder, 1939.

63 Weitzman, *Hastings and Francis*
Sophia Weitzman, *Warren Hastings and Philip Francis*, Manchester, 1929.

64 Wolfe Tone, *Autobiography*
Theobald Wolfe Tone, *The Autobiography of Theobald Wolfe Tone 1763–1798*.

65 Wolfe Tone, *Life*
Life of Theobald Wolfe Tone, Written by Himself, and Continued by his Son, 2 vols, Washington, 1826.

GENERAL INDEX

The first and far the most important aim of this index has been to record all references to persons mentioned in the texts or annotation of the letters printed in our volumes. We have allowed ourselves one slight departure from absolute completeness in listing these. For a few individuals—Mrs Burke, Richard, Jr, Lady Rockingham—we have omitted references to their names in such routine compliments as usually appear at the ends of letters: 'Jane sends her love', 'Be so good to present Mrs Burke's and my humble Duty to Lady Rockingham', and so on. But even these minor mentions are not wholly lost. Any reader disappointed by their absence here may find them in the name-indexes of our nine previous volumes. There we did undertake to record every single reference to any named person.

Besides indexing individuals we have dealt very fully with groups: formal bodies, committees, ministries, political parties and 'connexions'. We have tried to be equally thorough with books and pamphlets, which normally appear under their authors' names or, when anonymous, under their titles. Burke's own writings are listed in alphabetical order at the end of his own entry; all references to them, whether in the texts of letters or in notes, have been included. We are less exhaustive in dealing with places. Those which particularly concern Burke's activities—as Beaconsfield, Buckinghamshire, Bristol, Dublin, Clogher—are treated fully, but we have not attempted to preserve every mention whatever of a place.

Subject entries of a more general kind are included, but with no attempt at an ideal fullness. Like places, subject entries are listed when they have direct and obvious relation to Burke himself: his occupations, his opinions, his health, and the like. To emphasize their highly personal character they are almost all put into the entry for 'Burke, Edmund'. Cross-references, however, send the reader to other persons or topics if there is any considerable amount of additional material. Where specific individuals are mentioned, the reader is urged to consult the *Alphabetical List of the Correspondences* (see above, pp. 94–194) on the chance that the individual may have been a regular correspondent with whom there were other relations.

Only five members of the Burke family are referred to by abbreviations: 'EB' stands for Edmund Burke; 'JB' for his wife, Jane: 'RBSr' for his brother Richard; 'RBJr' for his son Richard; 'WB' for William Burke.

Ailesbury, Countess of (Caroline Campbell), widow of the preceding, wife of Henry Seymour Conway, I, 321n4

Aimée, Lewis, Ballitore schoolboy, I, 9, 31

Ainslie, Sir Robert Sharpe (c. 1730–1812), British Ambassador to Turkey, IV, 379n6

Aishe, William (d. 1752), Vicar of Timolin, I, 42

Aitken, James (1752–77), 'John the Painter': executed for arson, III, 327; also mentioned, 366n4, 382, IV, 50n3

Aix, Archishop of, see Cucé de Boisgelin, Jean de Dieu-Raymond de

Alam II, Shah, see Shah Alam

Albemarle, 1st Duke of, see Monck, George

Albemarle, 3rd Earl of, see Keppel, George

Albert, François-Hector d', Comte de Rions (1728–1802), French Admiral, EB recommends to Windham, VIII, 31

Aldridge, Mr, of Bristol, III, 366

Alembert, Jean le Rond d' (1717–83), philosopher: Rousseau's *Letter* to, reviewed in *Annual Register*, VI, 81n2; quoted by French artisans, 113–14

Alexander the Great, I, 76, VII, 68

Alfred, King of Wessex: Asser's life of, V, 292n2; his translation of Boethius, VI, 466

Ali, Nizam of Hyderabad (ruled 1762–1802), IV, 346n1, V, 43n2, 319

Ali Ibrahim Khan, of Benares, private agent of Hastings, V, 316–17

Alison, Rev. Archibald (1757–1839), writer on 'taste', III, 266

Allan, Thomas (1725–98), Irish M.P., describes quarrel between EB and Rigby, II, 124hn

Allen, John
correspondence with, listed above, p. 95

Allen, John Carter (d. 1800), Rear Admiral, EB visits, V, 348

Allen, Dr Joseph (c. 1714–96), Master of Dulwich College, supports Surrey petition, II, 37

Allen, Margaret, see De Lancey, Mrs James

Allen, Robert
correspondence with, listed above, p. 96

Allen, William (1704–80), Chief Justice of Pennsylvania, II, 311n3, III, 138n3

Allonville's Corps, disbanded in 1796, IX, 71n3

Almack's Club, I, 208, IX, 416. *See also* Brooks's Club

Almas Ali Khan (d. 1808), revenue farmer in Oudh, Hastings's treatment of, V, 253–5, VIII, 160

Almodóvar del Rio, Duque d', *see* Jiménez de Góngora, Pedro

Almon, John (1737–1805), printer
correspondence with, listed above, p. 96
'Letter' to, attributed to Camden, II, 161; Rex v. Almon, 278 n 2; prints *Letters to Valens*, III, 233n3; publishes *Proceedings* of Keppel's Court-martial, IV, 36n1; his shop in Piccadilly, 98; EB sends corrections for *Substance of the Speeches*, 175; reports Yorkshire Association in his paper, 216

Alsop, Robert (d. 1785), Alderman of London and Governor of the Irish Society: sees Irish Absentee Tax correspondence, II, 482

Althorp, Viscount, see Spencer, George John and Spencer, John Charles

Alvensleben, Johann Friedrich Karl von (1714–95), Hanoverian Minister in London: and Regency question, V, 431tn, 446tn

Amelia, Princess (1711–86), aunt of George III, I, 318, 334n1

Amelia, Princess (1783–1810), daughter of George III, one of the three 'lives' of EB's first annuity, VIII, 292n3

America: EB's plan to go to, I, 123; liberty of Ireland saved in, 229; would require an army to enforce Stamp Act in, 289; 'more wild and absurd than ever', II, 77; constitutional dependence ought to be preserved, 290–1, 529, III, 181; 'infinite Objects of Curiosity' in, II, 517; distracted condition of (1774), 518; popular current set against, 528; American affairs not likely to come to crisis, III, 30; discontents of, affect Administration as little as division of Poland, 31; prospects of conciliation, 101–2, 105, 137; North's plan a scheme of senseless Tyranny, 118; EB cannot sit down to a table from which he has kicked away his Brethren, 118; infamous Bill for famishing the Four Provinces, 131–2; EB 'much fallen away' with concern for, 137n5, America hangs upon his conscience, 140; little prospect of conciliation after Concord, 160

war with America: Congress's idea of a defensive war ridiculous, III, 175; a Civil war from which the Empire can never recover, 181, 286–7, an

America (*cont.*)

impious war, 193; England seduced into, 183; the Spirit of America, 187, 195; effects of non-importation agreements on trade with America, 186–7, 191, 209, 246, 319, 358–9; threat to use Russian troops, 218; Ministers confused over, 224–5, 232; war against the interests of England, 229–30, 286–7; magnanimity of America, 245–6; North's scheme for 'Free Assembly' in New York, 298–9; EB defies Fast Day for America, 302–5; if freedom comes it will be through separation from England, 307; no system of representation in England acceptable, 307; events drawing to a crisis (1777), 309, 323; EB's proposals for conciliation, 310, IV, 394; war never approved of by him, III, 349, caused by ignoring human nature and history, 351; the Separation Acts, 359; a System of endless hopes and disappointments, 377; Liverpool merchants ruined, but love the war, 382; all parties growing sick of it, 405; fate of Burgoyne's army deplorable, but wasting and ruining the Country would be worse, 408–9; Minister for America ready to get rid of it, 409; EB supports recognition of American Independence, 419–20, 427hn; Commons accused of starting new war, 427; proposed concessions, 433, 452, refusal to renew them, IV, 89–90; the War that brought Wars, III, 441; losses due to folly and incompetence of Government, IV, 33; EB's motion on conduct of the war, 65; more glorious to let America govern herself than to attempt conquest, 87; Temper of the Ministry, 89–90; total failure of 'our absurd designs', 155; lost by one idle quarrel, 261; the War in a swift decay, 380; America the younger and 'not the inferior Branch of our Nation', 396; Conway's motion to end the war, 419; England an example of want of moderation in use of power, 455

France and America: French assistance, III, 349, IV, 87, X, 5; the 'French Treaty', III, 452–3; follies of Government add French war to American, IV, 33; America does not yet belong to France (1777), IX, 418; declaration of friendship between Directory and

America (1795), VIII, 358; American revolution not on a par with French, IX, 241

see also British Empire; Burgoyne, General John; Franklin, Benjamin; Laurens, Henry; New York Assembly

American Congress

correspondence with, listed above, p. 96

American Taxation, Speech on, see Burke, Edmund: Works

Amherst, Sir Jeffrey (1717–97), later (1776) 1st Baron Amherst, army officer: replaced as Governor of Virginia, II, 14; declines Supervisorship in India, 320hn; Commander-in-Chief, IV, 76; Grafton wishes replaced by Conway, 144; thanks Rockingham for actions at Hull, 160; receives news about Cherburg, V, 374; replaced by Duke of York, VIII, 149n2; orders issued by, in 1780, IX, 305–6

Letters to, by Andrew Stuart, IX, 432n1

Ami du Roi, see Newspapers

Amiens, Bishop of, *see* Machault, Louis-Charles

Amir-ul-umara (d. 1788), 2nd son of the Nawab of Arcot, X, 15; and Guntur Circar and Jagir lands, IV, 346

Amyand, Anna Maria, *see* Elliot, Lady

Amyand, Harriet Maria, *see* Harris, Lady

Anacreon, I, 101

Anderson, Adam (*c.* 1692–1765), historian of commerce: Laurence's notes on, VIII, 413, 421; also mentioned, 447, 454n3

Anderson, Alexander, V, 25n1, 110n2

correspondence with, listed above, p. 96

Anderson, Benjamin (*c.* 1733–1812), Vicar of Little Missenden

correspondence with, listed above, p. 96

his views on house proposed for refugee clergy at Penn, VIII, 318, 319, 320, 321

Anderson, David (1751–1825), friend of Hastings: his letter to Court of Directors sent to Dundas, V, 312; will probably attest garbled correspondence, 317; examined by Impeachment Committee, 321; directed to produce correspondence, 322; admits Revenue Committee a tool of its *diwan*, 328; principal instrument of Hastings, VII, 249; and nomination of Devi Singh, 250; also mentioned, V, 384n2

Anderson, John (1726–96), Professor at Glasgow, disagreement with Leechman, V, 187–8

Anderson, John (d. 1797), Bristol merchant

correspondence with, listed above, p. 96

Anderson, John (*cont.*)
EB's worthy friend, III, 120; against ceremonial entry into Bristol, 123hn; part owner of the *Valiant*, IV, 117n1; also mentioned, III, 131n5, IV, 243

Andrews, Dr Francis (*c.* 1718–74), Provost of Trinity College, Dublin: praises EB's speech on America, I, 243; campaigns against petitioning in Northampton, II, 51; his death, 541hn; his appointment 'unstatutable', VIII, 54

Andrezel, Barthélemy-Philbert d' (1757–1825)
correspondence with, listed above, p. 96

Angerstein, John Julius (*c.* 1735–1823), underwriter at Lloyd's: thinks proper advertising is everything, VII, 213

Angoulême, Duc d', *see* Bourbon, Louis-Antoine de

Angoulême, Duchesse d', *see* Marie Thérèse-Charlotte, 'Madame Royale'

Anguish, Thomas (d. 1785), Commissioner of Public Accounts, ordered to attend the House of Commons, V, 76hn, 93hn

Ankerville, Lord, *see* Ross, David

Anne, Queen of England, VIII, 447, IX, 174

Annesley, Francis Charles, 1st Earl of Annesley (1720–1802), alleged to have distributed arms, VII, 236–7

Annual Register, see Burke, Edmund, Works

Anstruther, John (1753–1811), M.P.
correspondence with, listed above, p. 96
lawyer for Impeachment Committee, V, 320, 355, VI, 199; a Manager, V, 371; opens Presents Article, VI, 58; at Beaconsfield, 65; goes through Benares charge, VII, 113; dines with party leaders at Portland's, 313–14; present at debate on resumption of Impeachment, 532; solicited on behalf of Harwood, VIII, 384; can bear witness to Hastings's habit of concealment, 440; also mentioned, IX, 282

Antiquaries, Society of, VIII, 350

Antiquaries of Scotland, Society of, V, 265hn

Antiquities, *see* Burke, Edmund, Opinions

Antwerp, Corneille-François Nelis, Bishop of
correspondence with, listed above, p. 96

Appeal from the New to the Old Whigs, see Burke, Edmund, Works

Apsley, 1st Baron, *see* Bathurst, Henry

Aranda, Conde d', *see* Abarca y Boleo, Pedro Pablo

Arbuthnot, John, farmer, dines with Lord Rockingham, II, 541

Arbuthnot, Marriot (*c.* 1711–94), Rear Admiral: sails from Jersey to America, IV, 69; French fleet instructed to intercept, 90n7; sickness of recruits brought to America by, 158; despatches from, 252n5; removed from command, 313n3

Arcedeckne, Chaloner (*c.* 1743–1809), M.P., visits EB with Francis, V, 244

Archdeacon, Henry (d. 1773), Cork merchant
correspondence with, listed above, p. 96
asks EB to become guardian of John Joseph Therry, II, 180n3, 244, IX, 396

Architecture, *see* Burke, Edmund, Opinions

Arcot, Nawab of, *see* Walajah Muhammad Ali

Arden, Richard Pepper (1744–1804), Solicitor General, and Powell-Bembridge affair, V, 90

Ardesoif, Abraham, member of The Society in Dublin, subscribes to *Poems on Several Occasions*, I, 98n3

Ardfert, Bishop of, *see* Teahan, Gerard

Arenberg, Louis-Engelbert, Duc d' (1750–1820), accident to, III, 229

Argyll, 3rd Duke of, *see* Campbell, Archibald

Argyll, 4th Duke of, *see* Campbell, John

Argyll, 5th Duke of, *see* Campbell, John

Argyll, Duchess of (Elizabeth Gunning, 1773–90), wife of the preceding
correspondence with, listed above, p. 96
EB breakfasts with at Inverary, V, 222

Aristocracy, *see* Burke, Edmund, Opinions

Aristophanes, EB compared to, VII, 152

Aristotle: his errors and absurdities, I, 45; *Poetics*, 94hn, VIII, 67; Ellis's translation of *Politics*, IV, 36

Arkwright, Richard (1732–92), riots against his textile machines, IV, 146n1

Armagh, Archbishop of, *see* Newcombe, William; Robinson, Richard; Stone, George

Armistead, Mrs (Elizabeth Bridget Cane, d. 1842), later (1795) wife of C. J. Fox, V, 304n3

Armstrong, Bigoe (d. 1794), Lieutenant-General: EB's financial involvement with, IV, 106; mortgage interest paid to, VIII, 14; also mentioned, X, 43, 44

Armstrong, Mrs Bigoe, *see* Williams, Caroline

Army Estimates, Speech on, see Burke, Edmund, Works

Armytage, Sir George, 3rd Baronet (1734–8), his Letter as Chairman of the Yorkshire meeting, II, 162

Arniston, Lord, *see* Dundas, Robert

Arnold, Benedict (1741–1801), American General: invades Canada, III, 246; badly wounded, 250; gives Burgoyne 'a slap', 394; at Saratoga, 409

Arras, Bishop of, *see* Conzié, Louis-François-Marc-Hilaire de

Arthur's Club, I, 208

Artois, Charles-Philippe de Bourbon, Comte d' (1757–1836), later (1795) 'Monsieur', and (1824) Charles X, King of France

correspondence with, listed above, p. 96

relationship with Calonne, VI, 140hn; his 'sanguine Hopes' at Turin, 218n1; at Schönbornslust, Coblenz, 301hn; goes with Calonne to Pillnitz, 344, 347; Emperor agrees to his propositions, 379–80, 406; returns *via* Vienna, 372, 380n5, 396; meets Monsieur on Pont Volant, 406–7, VII, 474; advised to see Emperor again, VI, 431

visits Russia, VII, 368; Captain Edmund Nagle asked to escort him to England, 368–9; apanage abolished, 389; made 'Lieutenant General of the Kingdom', 391n3; invited to command in La Vendée, 433n2, 454–5; asks EB's help for passage to France, 455–6, British Government refuse, 473–5; thinks help can come only from England, 504–5; invited to organise *émigré* troops in England, 573n2; not allowed to head expedition, VIII, 269; reported to be in the Thames, 353; letter of condolence on RBJr's death, VII, 573

as Monsieur, becomes Patron of *émigré* school at Penn, VIII, 446, IX, 5; is sent *Two Letters on a Regicide Peace*, 98; sends portraits to EB, 128

also mentioned, V, 232, VI, 257, 345n5, 373, 386dn, 400, 403tn, 414n5, 424hn, VII, 48n3

see also French Princes

Arundell, Henry, 8th Baron Arundell (1740–1808)

correspondence with, listed above, p. 96

asks admission for French boys to *émigré* school at Penn, IX, 8, 15, 24

Asaf-ud-daula, Nawab-Wazir of Oudh (d. 1797): Hannay commands his troops, V, 129hn, 331–2; increase in his debts, 148; and Almas Ali Khan, 253n2; Hastings accused of forcing him to confiscate Begums' estates, 303n1; presents from, 321n1, 322,

325n3, VI, 58; gives his Agent a pension, V, 323–4; Captain Thomas Edwards his aide-de-camp, 392n1; allowances paid by, 396n3; money owed to Marsac by, 397n2; signs testimonial for Hastings, 416n4; armed bands likely to seek service with, VII, 148; Hastings accused of breaking treaty with, VIII, 160n4, tries to settle affairs of, V, 128n7

Asgill, Sir Charles (*c.* 1763–1823), prisoner-of-war in America: condemned to death, then reprieved, IX, 186

Ashburton, 1st Baron, *see* Dunning, John

Ashurst, Sir William Henry (1725–1807), Judge of the King's Bench: helps Eden with his Bill, III, 251; charges 'combinations' with producing scarcity, VIII, 344

Asser (d. *c.* 909), monk, V, 292

Assigny, Claude-Antoine d', Seigneur de Laine, marries daughter of Madame Parisot, II, 422n2, VI, 16n3

Assigny, Madame Claude-Antoine d' (Marie Gabrielle Parisot, *c.* 1750–1815), wife of the preceding

correspondence with, listed above, p. 96

RBJr at Auxerre with, II, 422; flees from and returns to Auxerre, VI, 16–17; loses seigneurial rights at Laine, 18

Association for Preserving Liberty and Property against Republicans and Levellers, VII, 356n4, VIII, 346n3, 354; *see also* VII, 340–1, IX, 281

Associations: Richmond's plan for, to work for parliamentary reform, IV, 166–8; York County prepares plan of, 177n4, 216; Middlesex follows Yorks, 188; County Committees plan for, pledged to enforce test on candidates, 205n1; Wiltshire stays out, 206hn; Duke of Devonshire speaks in favour of in Lords, 213; Counties plan for, to support economical and parliamentary reform, 216hn; Rockingham and Shelburne agree on support for economical only, 217tn; Bucks rejects Yorks plan, 226hn, ends with two associations, 229 n; Pitt proposes general association to support Government, IX, 368

Astle, Thomas (1735–1803), keeper of records in Tower of London

correspondence with, listed above, p. 96

consulted by EB on records of Lord High Steward's Court, VII, 536–7

Astley's Riding School, VIII, 346n1

Aston, Abigail (*c.* 1734–1814), sister of Mrs Haviland
correspondence with, listed above, p. 96
dines with EB, VII, 4; well settled at Beaconsfield, 85; upset by Lord Inchiquin's marriage, 190; also mentioned, VIII, 294, 296, IX, 454, 470

Aston, Mary, *see* Balfour, Mrs William Charles Townley

Aston, Sir Richard (d. 1778), Judge of the King's Bench, gives verdict in favour of EB in dispute with Waller, III, 12

Aston, Salusbury, *see* Haviland, Mrs William

Atheism, *see* Burke, Edmund, Opinions

Atkins, Mr, dealer in lace, attacks Verney's interest at Wendover, II, 148n3

Atkinson, Richard (1735–85), M.P., one of the 'Arcot Squad', V, 197hn

Atkinson, Theodore, III, 146n1

Atkinson, Mrs Theodore (Frances Wentworth), widow of the preceding, *see* Wentworth, Mrs John

Atterbury, Francis (1662–1732), Bishop of Rochester, III, 313

Atwood, Mr, of Turley House, Bradford, EB stays with, I, 112n1

Aubrey, John (1739–1826), later (1786) 6th Baronet, M.P.: takes Chair at Buckinghamshire meeting, II, 76–7, 78; alters toast about Yorkshire, 79; helps prepare Bicester–Aylesbury Road Bill, 125hn; meets EB at Wendover election, 157; abandons idea of standing for County, III, 30; supports EB on New York Remonstrance, 165; elected for County, V, 143hn; his return challenged, 144tn; withdraws, VI, 120n7

Auchinleck, Lord, *see* Boswell, Alexander

Auckland, 1st Baron, *see* Eden, William

Auckland, Lady, *see* Eden, Mrs William

Augier, Mrs (d. 1771), sister of Dr Nugent, her last illness, II, 286

Augusta, Princess Dowager of Wales (1719–72): omitted from Regency Bill, I, 194n2; myth of Bute's influence through, II, 206n2

Augustus Frederick (1773–1843), later (1801) Duke of Sussex, son of George III: sent to Göttingen, V, 308n1

Aulne, Baron de l', *see* Turgot, Anne-Robert-Jacques

Aurangzeb (1618–1707), Mughal Emperor, VI, 171

Auriol, James Peter, cross-examined, VII, 370

Ausonius, I, 361n2

Aust, George (d. 1829), Under-Secretary of State, declaration to La Bintinaye, VI, 410, 412

Austin, Gilbert (*c.* 1753–1837), clergyman and tutor to Lord Charlemont's sons: intervenes on behalf of Borland, sentenced to transportation, VI, 8–9, 12

Austrian Netherlands: revolt against new form of government a good Cause, VI, 37, but a failure, 217, a revolt against innovation, 268; Emperor's mishandling of situation, 266–7; 'the best cultivated and most flourishing country of Europe', 267–8; flourishing, though Catholic, IX, 164; its annexation and renaming as Belgium, 265; also mentioned, V, 348

Autichamp, Jean-Thérèse-Louis de Beaumont, Marquis d'
correspondence with, listed above, p. 96

Autun, Bishop of, *see* Talleyrand-Périgord, Charles-Maurice de

Auxerre: EB visits with RBJr (1773), II, 411hn, 424; RBJr and Thomas King stay at, 415, 419n2, 421–2, 426, V, 52n2, VII, 584–6, 588–9; Captain James King stays at, V, 178, 179, 405n5, VII, 588–9; RBJr revisits (1780), 587, (1785), V, 235, VI, 366; Francis advised to rest at, V, 266; events in (1789), VI, 16–20. *See also* Parisot

Auxerre, Bishop of, *see* Champion de Cicé, Jean-Baptiste-Marie

Auxerre, Mayor of, flees from the town, VI, 17

Avonmore, 1st Baron, *see* Yelverton, Barry

Awdry, John, of Wotton
correspondence with, listed above, p. 97
sends thanks of Wiltshire Committee to EB, IV, 206–7

Aylesford, 3rd Earl of, *see* Finch, Heneage

Aymar, Chevalier d' (*c.* 1716–*p.* 1792), thrown in pond at the Tuileries, VI, 169

Ayrton, Richard, of Malton, IV, 322

Backhouse, Captain Thomas
correspondence with, listed above, p. 97

Bacon, Anthony (*c.* 1717–86), M.P. for Aylesbury, munitions contractor: says American news is false, III, 163; Sir William Lee advised to support, V, 135hn

Bacon, Francis (1561–1626): 'Letter of consolation' to Coke, II, 255; 'Of Unity in Religion', VI, 113; 'Of Cunning', 420

Barry, Barry Maxwell (*cont.*)
M.P., supports Catholic relief, III, 450, IV, 421

Barry, James (1741–1806), painter
correspondence with, listed above, p. 98
encouraged by EB, I, 203–4, sent abroad to study, 220, 323–4, II, 7hn, IX, 393, advised on his studies, I, 253, 292–4, 309, II, 8–9, 83; his views on art dealers, I, 323; copies paintings for EB, 221, 246, 292, II, 418n1; his letters 'worth keeping', 7–8; elected to Royal Academy, 315hn; EB fails to get a sitting from, III, 4–9; his *Inquiry into . . . the Arts of England* criticised, 99–100; inscribes print of Job to EB, 336
paintings: 'Adam and Eve', I, 324; portrait of EB, III, 9n, IV, facing p. xi; paintings for the Adelphi, III, 337n1
also mentioned, II, 417n2, 418

Barry, John, father of James Barry, I, 324, II, 87

Barry, Sir Nathaniel, 2nd Baronet (*c.* 1725–85), physician, V, 33, 187

Barthélemy, François, Marquis de (1747–1830), French Minister in London, VI, 191n3, 436n2, IX, 89n4

Barthélemy, Abbé Jean-Jacques (1716–95), copy of *Reflections* sent to, VI, 337

Bartolozzi, Francesco (1727–1815), engraver, VII, 99hn

Barton, Major Newton, VI, 209n4

Barwell, Edward (d. 1799), clerk without doors, House of Commons, III, 159, 222, V, 45

Barwell, Nathaniel (*c.* 1718–93), clerk without doors, House of Commons, III, 159, 222

Barwell, Richard (1741–1804), M.P.
correspondence with, listed above, p. 98
'apostle' of Hastings, IV, 431, V, 107, VI, 180, IX, 451; examined on Benares charge, VII, 371

Basil, Edmund (d. 1779), neighbour of EB at Beaconsfield, II, 71, III, 11, 22

Baskerville, John (1706–75), RBJr's copy of his Horace, VII, 600, VIII, 288

Basset, Sir Francis, 1st Baronet (1757–1835)
correspondence with, listed above, p. 99

Bastard, John Pollexfen (1756–1816), M.P., leads attempt to form third party, IX, 271n1, 275, 285

Bateman, John, 2nd Viscount Bateman (1721–1802), M.P., I, 149n2

Bath
EB consults Dr Nugent at, I, 115;

meets Champion and Harford at (1774), III, 54, 57–8, 65n2; passes through (1783), V, 113, X, 14; stays at (1790), VI, 137–8, antiquities discovered at, 139; visit to, for Mrs Burke's health (1792), VII, 180–3, 188, 196, 198, 200, 203–4, 206, 211–12, 223–4, 227, 258, 267, 284–5, VIII, 242; 'Heads for Consideration' written at, VII, 288n5, 309; a good place for strangers, 318
visit to, for health (1796), IX, 55, 61, 71, 72, 73, 74, 112, 454, 'melancholy Scenes' witnessed by Mrs Crewe, 77; EB returns much better for, 84, 86, 88, 89, 226, 230, 234; (1797), 105n6, 138, 229, 230–1, 235, 242, 255, 270tn, 277, 318hn, 325; would rather die at home than at Bath, 129, 354; a terrible place in winter, 139; the crowd at, frightens him, 226; does not drink the waters, 246, 283; has gained no benefit from, 354, 355, 358, 360, 361; prepares to quit, 358, 360, 361

Bath, 1st Earl of, *see* Pulteney, William

Bath, Marquess of, *see* Thynne, Thomas

Bath and Wells, Bishop of, *see* Moss, Charles; Willes, Edward

Bathurst, Henry, 1st Baron Apsley, 2nd Earl Bathurst (1714–91)
correspondence with, listed above, p. 99
Lord Chancellor, II, 176n1, 403; appointed Commissioner on Duke of Gloucester's marriage, 435; and Champion's patent, III, 158–9; opposes annuity for Chatham, 453n7; becomes Lord President, IV, 161n5; EB appeals to, for mercy to rioters, 256; also mentioned, 254hn

Batley, Jeremiah
correspondence with, listed above, p. 99

Battersby, William (1732–1812), III, 260

Battier, John Ralph, EB takes up his petition against seizure of turpentine III, 451

Baugh, Isaac, Alderman (d. 1786), V, 114

Bawn, Harry, servant of the Shackletons, I, 3, 10, 29, 72, 73, 75, 81

Baxter, Richard (1615–91), his last words, IX, 202, 209, X, 47

Baxter's Club, VII, 211n6

Bayle, Pierre, *Dictionnaire historique et critique*, I, 72; quoted by French artisans, VI, 113

Bayley, Thomas Butterworth (1744–1802)
correspondence with, listed above, p. 99

Bayly, John, fellow-student of EB, I, 2, 41, 52, 67

Bentinck, Hans William, 1st Earl of Portland (1649–1709), III, 290n4

Bentinck, William, 2nd Duke of Portland (1709–62), III, 304n1

Bentinck, Captain William, Count Bentinck (1764–1813): on EB's relations with Paine, VI, 75tn

Bentinck, Lord William Charles Augustus Cavendish, see Cavendish Bentinck, Lord William Charles Augustus

Bentinck, William Henry, 1st Duke of Portland, III, 304n1

Bentinck, William Henry Cavendish, 3rd Duke of Portland, see Cavendish Bentinck, William Henry

Bentinck, William Henry Cavendish, Marquess of Titchfield, see Cavendish Bentinck, William Henry

Bentinck, Lord William Henry Cavendish, see Cavendish Bentinck, Lord William Henry

Benyon, Richard (1746–96), M.P. for Peterborough, Fitzwilliam's borough, IX, 67; his death gives French Laurence a seat, 74

Beresford, Lady Frances Maria, see Flood, Lady Frances Maria

Beresford, George de la Poer, 1st Marquess of Waterford (1735–1800), VII, 236

Beresford, John (1738–1805), Irish M.P.
correspondence with, listed above, p. 99
leads opposition to Catholic franchise, VII, 71, VIII, 170, 192n3; goes to England to negotiate settlement, VII, 365; influence in Junto, VIII, 34n3; removed from office by Fitzwilliam, 137n1, 150, 185; a convicted peculator, 169, 170, 286, a 'stinking jobber', 171, 186–7, 192, 197; goes to England, 173; reinstated, 182; Fitzwilliam's letter to Carlisle on, 183, 281; Catholic hostility to, 195; Portland always intended to remove, 197; his removal the alleged reason for Fitzwilliam's recall, 209, 211; remains at Revenue Board, 226; Westmorland repudiates allegations against, 238n5; challenges Fitzwilliam to duel, 275, 276, 277; 'behaved very properly', 278
also mentioned, VIII, 32hn
see also Beresford family

Beresford, John Claudius (1766–1846), son of the preceding, his places in the revenue, VIII, 186–7

Beresford, Marcus (1764–97), son of John Beresford, Counsel to the Revenue Commissioners, VIII, 186, 209n2

Beresford, William (1743–1819), brother of John Beresford, Bishop of Ossory, later (1794) Archbishop of Tuam: his marriage, VII, 71n4; gets Archbishopric, VIII, 186

Beresford, Mrs William (Elizabeth Fitzgibbon, d. 1807), wife of the preceding, VII, 71n4

Beresford family: political influence in Ireland, VII, 71, VIII, 150n1, 173, IX, 338; Fitzwilliam accused of exalting Ponsonby family above, VIII, 228; Pelham sent to reconcile the two families, 195

Bergasse, Nicolas (1750–1832), avocat, withdraws from Assembly, VI, 115

Berkeley, George (1685–1753), Bishop of Cloyne, on the virtues of tar-water, I, 26n3

Berkeley, George Cranfield (1753–1818), Whig M.P.: defeated for Gloucestershire, III, 268n4; brings news of Keppel's action, 461; EB proposes as Union Club candidate, IV, 329–30

Berkeley, Joshua (d. 1807), RBJr's tutor at Oxford, II, 394, 538

Berkeley, Norborne (c. 1717–70), later (1764) 4th Baron Botetourt: Lord Talbot's second in duel with Wilkes, I, 150; becomes Governor of Virginia, II, 14; speech against taxing colonies, III, 80

Berkeley, Dr Robert, Irish doctor, II, 394n3

Berkenhout [Dr John, c. 1730–91]
correspondence with, listed above, p. 99

Berkshire, see County meetings

Bernard, Sir Francis, Governor of Massachusetts, II, 77n7

Bernard, Sir Robert, 5th Baronet (c. 1740–89), M.P., supporter of Bill of Rights: stimulates anti-ducal revolt in Bedford, II, 77n8; returned for Westminster, 131–2, III, 29n2

Bernstorff, Johann Hartwig Ernst, Count von (1712–72), First Minister to King of Denmark, II, 15

Bertie, Lord Robert, II, 249hn

Bertie, Willoughby, 4th Earl of Abingdon (1740–99)
correspondence with, listed above, p. 95
his interest sought in Buckinghamshire election, III, 34, 37; wants EB's help in petition from Berks County Meeting, 234–5; Walpole on, 368hn, 370tn; proposed Bill on Irish commerce, V, 103n2
Thoughts on the Letter of Edmund Burke Esq. to the Sheriffs of Bristol,

218

Bertie, Willoughby (*cont.*)
EB on, III, 369–70, 378–9, 394;
Richmond on, 398hn
also mentioned, II, 395
'Abingdonians', IV, 271
Bertier de Sauvigny, Anne-Ferdinand-
Louis de (1782–1864), brought to
England after his father's murder,
VI, 263
Bertier de Sauvigny, Bénigne-Louis de
(1777–1814)
correspondence with, listed above, p. 99
brought to England after his father's
murder, VI, 263
Bertier de Sauvigny, Louis-Bénigne-
François de (1737–89), Intendant of
Paris, murdered by mob, VI, 10n1,
263, IX, 186
Bertrand, M., *see* Dubu de Longchamp,
Jean-François
Bertrand de Molleville, Antoine-François,
Marquis de (1744–1818), Minister of
the Marine: speech on absent Navy
officers, VI, 457n1
Berville, Paul-Antoine-Joseph Vollant,
Comte de
correspondence with, listed above, p. 99
Besenval, Pierre-Joseph-Victor, Baron de
(1721–94), his crime of *lèse-nation*, VI,
45n2
Bessborough, 2nd Earl of, *see* Ponsonby,
William
Bessborough, Countess of (Lady Caroline
Cavendish), wife of the preceding,
III, 59n3
Bessborough, 3rd Earl of, *see* Ponsonby,
Frederick
Bethel, Slingsby (1617–97), *The Interests
of Princes and States*, VIII, 447
Béthune, Maximilien de, Duc de Sully,
his *Mémoires* quoted, VI, 147; also
mentioned, VIII, 419n5
Betty (Mrs Burke's dairymaid), IV, 117,
240, V, 437, VIII, 390
Bible: Pharisee and publican, I, 36;
Judith and Holofernes, 41; St Paul
on the Athenians, 86; the Land of Uz,
88; bread and stones, 169; Solomon
in all his glory, 362; no room at the
inn, II, 84; the hands of Esau, 133;
St Paul to the Corinthians, 134; the
Good Shepherd, 435; trust in Princes,
III, 281; weep with those that weep,
319; scribes and Pharisees, 356; the
wicked heart, IV, 196; charity, 206;
the body of Death, IV, 278, IX, 308;
perfect Love, IV, 284; the Ten Talents,
V, 249; Judas Iscariot, VI, 73; light

before men, 179; Barabbas, 291; do
unto others, 478; sparrows, VIII, 80;
false accusers, 113; 'Sampson', 134;
old wine in new bottles, 135; things
meet for repentance, 147–8; pearls
before swine, 408; the gospel preached
to the poor, IX, 343
also mentioned, VII, 59, 368n1, VIII, 137,
288n2
Binfield, Rev. Henry (1735–95), Rector
of Albrighton, VIII, 293n2
Bingham, Sir Charles, 7th Baronet (1735–
99), later (1776) 1st Baron and (1795)
1st Earl of Lucan
correspondence with, listed above, p. 99
opposes Absentee Tax, II, 474, 480–1,
484, 487, 491; supports repeal of
anti-Catholic laws, IV, 19; is sent
Two Letters, IX, 98; also mentioned,
II, 470, VI, 220, VIII, 98tn
Bingham, Lady (Margaret Smith, d. 1814),
wife of the preceding, II, 481
Bingham, Sir Henry, 3rd Baronet (d. *c.*
1714), M.P., IV, 19n2
Bingham, Lavinia, *see* Spencer, Countess
Bintinnaye, *see* La Bintinaye
Bird, Christopher Clapham (*c.* 1771–1861):
his mission to save Choiseul, VIII,
376, IX, 89; *émigré* business confided
to by Windham, 54
Bird, James, Catholic businessman of
Drogheda, charged with being a
Defender, VIII, 194
Birmingham
EB's visit to, II, 149; riots in, VI, 307,
311–13, 316, 420n4, VII, 119; the
Birmingham Socrates, 152; daggers
episode, 328
Birmingham, Merchants at
correspondence with, listed above, p. 99
Biron, Baron de, *see* Gontaut, Armand de
Biron, Duc de, *see* Gontaut, Armand-
Louis de; Charles de; Louis-Antoine de
Biron, Duchesse de (Amélie de Boufflers,
1751–94), wife of Louis-Antoine de
Gontaut, Duc de Biron
correspondence with, listed above, p. 100
persuades EB to modify passage on
Choiseul in *Reflections*, VI, 234–7;
also mentioned, 203, 204, 205, 315
Birt, Rev. James (*c.* 1717–1801), Canon of
Hereford, long-standing friend of EB,
VIII, 283
correspondence with, listed above, p. 100
exchange of gifts with EB, IX, 415–16
Birt, William, I, 167n5
Bischoff, John
correspondence with, listed above, p. 100

Bolton, Serjeant James Clayton (*cont.*)
tries to prevent RBJr's duel with Topping, v, 132

Bolts, William (*c.* 1740–1808), adventurer, v, 262hn
correspondence with, listed above, p. 100
Considerations on India Affairs praised by EB, v, 263; plan for expansion of French trade, 263n3

Bonal, François de, Bishop of Clermont-Ferrand (1734–1800), VI, 211–12

Bonaparte, Napoleon (1769–1821): suppresses rising against 1795 constitution, VIII, 358n1; 'Champion of the Protestant World', IX, 162–4, 260; also mentioned, VIII, 149n4, IX, 123

Bonneval, Abbé Sixte-Louis-Constant Ruffo de (1742–1820)
correspondence with, listed above, p. 100

Bonomi, Joseph (1739–1808), architect: designs obelisk for Juliana Burke, VI, 209

Boone, Thomas
correspondence with, listed above, p. 100

Booth, Barton, I, 142n1

Booth, Charles (*c.* 1726–92), Fellow of Brasenose College, Oxford, VII, 98

Booth, John, lecturer on natural philosophy in Dublin, I, 8, 10, 42, 44

Boothby, Francis
correspondence with, listed above, p. 100

Borcke [Adrian Heinrich von], Prussian diplomat
correspondence with, listed above, p. 100
offers to keep EB informed on foreign affairs, II, 512, 513

Borcke, Friedrich Wilhelm von (1693–1769), father of the preceding, Frederick the Great's Chancellor, II, 511hn

Bordeaux, Archbishop of, *see* Champion de Cicé, Jerôme-Marie

Borgia, Cesare (1476–1507), II, 246n1

Borland, Archibald, his petition for mitigation of sentence supported by EB, VI, 8–9, 12

Bosanquet, Jacob (*c.* 1756–1828), elected director of East India Company, v, 31tn

Boscawen, Admiral Edward (1711–61), I, 132

Boscawen, Mrs Edward (Frances Glanville, 1719–1805), wife of the preceding: and EB's application for Madrid consulship, I, 132; to be a 'substitute bookseller' for Fanny Burney's novels, v, 26n1

Boswell, Alexander, Lord Auchinleck (1706–82), Judge, father of James Boswell, IV, 444

Boswell, James (1740–95)
correspondence with, listed above, p. 100–1
quotes EB on Ossianic forgeries, I, 146n3; on foundation of Literary Club, 220n2, member of Club, VI, 220; on the Round Robin, III, 273–4hn; thinks Scotland not ready for Catholic toleration, IV, 43–4; on Edinburgh riots, 45n4, 46n2; EB solicits on behalf of, 444–5; delighted with speech on Economical Reform, v, 35; hopes for political post, 35n4; solicits EB's interest, 105–6; fears EB is offended with him, 138–9, 257–9, 386–7, VI, 230hn; invites EB to supper, v, 139–40, 142, 386–7; EB at his table for the first time, 387tn; answers Johnson on EB's lack of wit, 248hn, EB's response, 248–50; his reproducing of casual talk spreads alarm, 257–9, and cp VI, 298n1, 299; member of Johnson Memorial Committee, 77; quotes EB on Malone edition of Shakespeare, 181n1; denies authorship of squib against EB, 230–1; on Radical meeting at Crown and Anchor, 297; gets Paoli's sketch of EB printed, 297; wants record of EB's conversation with the King on *Life of Johnson*, 298, EB declines, 300; quotes EB on affection between parents and children, VII, 592n2
Journal of a Tour to the Hebrides, ed. 1, v, 248hn, ed. 2, 248–50, 257, VI, 298n1; *Letter to the People of Scotland*, v, 138n1; *Life of Johnson*, I, 220n2, 221n3, v, 139n1, 206tn, 248hn, 249n2, 257hn, VI, 77, VII, 67, 592n2, praised by the King, VI, 297–8, 300
also mentioned, I, 164hn, II, 545hn, v, 206tn, 276n2, VII, 67dn, x, 43, 45

Boswell, Mrs James (Margaret Montgomerie), wife of the preceding, v, 34n2

Boswell, James, Jr (1778–1822): records anecdote of EB, I, 198hn; *Memoir of Edmond Malone*, VIII, 455hn

Boswell, John (*c.* 1722–50), of Trinity College, Dublin, I, 52

Botetourt, 4th Baron, *see* Berkeley, Norborne

Bouche, Charles-François (1737–95), *avocat* and political writer, VI, 336

Boufflers, Amélie de, *see* Biron, Duchesse de

Boufflers, Comtesse de (Marie-Charlotte-Hippolyte Campet de Saujon, 1725–1800), VI, 205n3

British Empire (*cont.*)
never be restored, 181, 432; wrecked and in danger of being pillaged, 222; 'half our Empire' lost by one idle quarrel, IV, 261; Boston lost, only Halifax remains, III, 263–4; an unnatural tranquillity among a people who have just lost an Empire, 269; EB's divided feelings over decisive victory for either side, 286, 296, still hopes for a reunited Empire without direct representation, 307; and the planting of Georgia, 344; 'our departed Empire' forgotten by most, 423
Empire in India, IV, 394, V, 400; magnitude of, VIII, 431; dominion of, given into English hands by Divine providence, IX, 62
plight of formerly French West Indies as members of, 204
other references, III, 184, 230, IV, 57, 317hn, V, 221n1, 456, VII, 510, VIII, 41, 430
see also America; British Constitution; England; India; Ireland; Parliament

Brocklesby, Dr Richard (1722–97), EB's physician, I, 270
correspondence with, listed above, p. 102–3
commissions Barry to paint EB, III, 4–5, 6, 7, 9; sends EB a cod, 304–5; arranges hospital for EB's man, 365; makes an 'instant present' of £1000 to EB, V, 406–7; visits EB, VI, 307, IX, 127, 234; acts for Committee for French Refugee Clergy, VII, 234–5; attends RBJr in his last illness, 562, 563, acts as pall bearer, 570n; solicits EB for a friend's son, 511; EB solicits for George Richards, VIII, 293, X, 35
EB's faith in, IX, 86, not shared by Edward James Nagle, 86n3; 'thinks nothing' of EB's symptoms, 108; on EB's 'Observations on the Conduct of the Minority', 245, 254n1
also mentioned, IX, 232, 233

Brodrick, Alan, 1st Viscount Midleton (*c.* 1656–1728), VIII, 69
Brodrick, George, 4th Viscount Midleton (1754–1836), IX, 123n3
Broglie, Charles-François, Comte de (1719–81), VII, 273
Broglie, Victor-François, Duc de (1718–1804), Maréchal de France: his troops fail to suppress National Assembly, VI, 70, 206; also mentioned, VII, 273n4
Bromfield, Captain Philip, V, 344n3

Brooke, Henry (*c.* 1703–83), author, EB wishes for anecdotes of, I, 363
Brooke, Henry, Madras councillor, IV, 321n2
Brooke, William
correspondence with, listed above, p. 103
offers his interest for a borough, V, 16–17
Brooks, 'Ephm'
correspondence with, listed above, p. 103
Brooks's Club, formerly Almack's: EB a member of, V, 75–6, 80, 437, opposed to doctrines of, VI, 273; other members: Fox, IV, 377n1, Fitzwilliam, V, 150, Francis, 100; other references, 322, VII, 412, IX, 416n8
Broome, Ralph (d. 1805), pamphleteer, VIII, 434
Brothers, Richard (1757–1824), religious fanatic, V, 324n1, VIII, 363
Brough, Richard (b. *c.* 1724), fellow student of EB, I, 3, 47; cautioned with a 'vix', 49
Broughton, Alexander D.
correspondence with, listed above, p. 103
Broughton, J. P. (d. 1784), V, 384n3
Brown, Jacob, Rockingham's secretary, IV, 191; his inaccuracies, 194, 195n1, 196; also mentioned, 241n1, VI, 6n
Brown, John (d. before 1784), guardian of John Ridge Jr, V, 158n1
Brown, Josiah, IV, 133hn
Brown, Lancelot ('Capability', 1715–83), EB agrees with Uvedale Price's strictures on, VII, 548
Browne, Arthur (*c.* 1756–1805), Irish M.P., friend of EB, VII, 65
correspondence with, listed above, p. 103
supports Catholic petition, VII, 65n4; Senior Fellow of Trinity College, Dublin, VIII, 6n6; also mentioned, VI, 192n2, VIII, 32, 37n1
Browne, Colonel James (*c.* 1743–92), of the East India Company, V, 312tn
correspondence with, listed above, p. 103
Browne, John (1730–94), later 1st Baron Kilmaine, I, 84
Browne, Thomas, 4th Viscount Kenmare (1726–95), Irish Catholic peer
correspondence with, listed above, p. 142
his taste for improvements, II, 143, VII, 268; advises on boarding arrangements in France for RBJr, II, 415; kindness to Garrett Nagle, IV, 20, 94, IX, 428; consults EB on Bill for relaxing penal laws, IV, 20n6, 203–4, X, 6–8; Chairman of Catholic Committee, IV, 117hn; leads landed gentry group in Committee, VI, 397n2, VII, 6,

Burgoyne, General John (*cont.*)

74; refuses to go back to America as prisoner of war, 127hn, 154n3; resigns all preferments, 154, 164, 364; negotiations with Washington for his exchange as prisoner, 362hn; EB presents case to Franklin, 362–3; plan to exchange with Laurens, 363n2, 378, 383–5, 386, 388–92, 394; hostility of Ministers, 392, 395–7; their claim to have exchanged him for soldiers, 396–7

joins in talks with leaders of Rockingham party, IV, 171; Jane Burke stays with during Gordon riots, 245; false rumour of defeat at Preston, 282; appointed Commander-in-Chief in Ireland, 451, V, 62; his account of Portland's riding accident, 28n4; wishes to join actively in politics, 55hn; told to stay in Ireland, 55, 60hn, 61; dissuaded from resigning, 61n2; convalesces at Bath, 358–9; takes part in Hastings Impeachment, 358–9, 395–7; his pompous style, IX, 417

A Letter from Lieut. Gen. Burgoyne to his Constituents, IV, 154n3; *A State of the Expedition from Canada*, 127–8

also mentioned, IV, 419, 458, V, 371, VI, 138hn

Burke, Christopher (b. 1758), younger son of EB, I, 135–6, 142, 190; died an infant, 136n1

BURKE, EDMUND (1729–97)

Biographical outline

12 Jan 1729 birth in Dublin, 1, 102–3hn, II, 413n, III, 99

c. 1735–*c.* 40 lives mainly with maternal relations in County Cork, I, 79n3

1741–4 attends school at Ballitore, 1, 3, 34, 124

1744 enters Trinity College, Dublin, 1hn

1747 registered at Middle Temple, London, 103hn

1748 graduates from Trinity College, launches *The Reformer*, a periodical on the model of *The Spectator*, 102

1750 begins studying for the Bar in London, 103hn; forms friendship with WB, 103hn

1755 considers applying for post in the West Indies, 119hn; deserts the Law, 136hn; quarrels with his father, 119–20

1756 publishes *Vindication of Natural Society*, 127hn

1757 contracts with the Dodsleys to produce *An Essay Towards an Abridgment of English History*, 164n1; marries Jane Nugent, 115hn, 124; publishes *The Sublime and Beautiful*, 127hn

1758 birth of first son, Richard (RBJr), 136n1; contract with Dodsleys to edit the *Annual Register*, 127hn; birth of second son, Christopher (dies in infancy), 136n1

1759 applies for consulship at Madrid, 131–3; becomes secretary to William Gerard Hamilton, 138n3

1761–2 Hamilton becomes Chief Secretary to the Lord Lieutenant of Ireland; EB goes with him to Ireland, 142

1763 receives pension on Irish Establishment, 163–4

1763–4 returns with Hamilton to Ireland for another 'Parliament Winter', 167n4; applies for post as Agent to Conquered Isles, 177

1764 a founding member of the Literary Club, 220n2

1764–5 quarrels with Hamilton over terms of employment, 178–86; resigns pension, 186

1765 becomes private secretary to Marquess of Rockingham at the beginning of his first Administration, 211; brought into Parliament for Wendover by Earl Verney, 222–3; owes his seat to WB's stepping down, 223tn

1766 maiden speech, 232–3; his immediate success as a speaker, 238, 340; Rockingham Ministry falls, 260; receives offers from Pitt Ministry, remains in Opposition, 279, 294; publishes *A Short Account of a Late Short Administration*

1767 receives Freedom of City of Dublin, 295–6

1768 re-elected for Wendover, 351, II, 7; purchases Gregories, his country seat at Beaconsfield, I, 351, 353–4

1769 publishes *Observations on a State of the Nation*, II, 265n3; WB and Verney lose heavily in speculation in East India stock, 27–9

1770 publishes *Thoughts on the Cause of the Present Discontents*, 123tn appointed Agent to the General Assembly of New York, 213

1772 refuses Supervisorship for India, 319–20

1773 visits France with RBJr, 411–12

Burke, Edmund (*cont.*)

1774 delivers speech on American Taxation, 531hn; loses Wendover seat, III, 32–3; elected for Rockingham's seat at Malton, 66hn; accepts invitation to contest Bristol, 64; elected, 72–3; WB loses his seat, 73

1775 publishes *Speech on American Taxation*, 93hn; delivers and publishes *Speech on Conciliation*, 171n1

1777 WB goes to India and becomes Agent for Raja of Tanjore, 346–7; EB publishes *Letter to the Sheriffs of Bristol*, 334n2

1779 takes active part in defence of Keppel, IV, 35

1780 delivers and publishes *Speech on Economical Reform*, 203hn; declines poll at Bristol, 272, 280–1; offered and accepts seat at Malton, 322

1781 appointed to Select Committee on Justice in India, becomes its leading member, 352hn

1782 becomes Paymaster General in second Rockingham Administration, 423tn; RBJr his father's deputy, 437; WB Deputy Paymaster of Forces in East Indies, 430n1; sworn to the Privy Council, 430n3, 437; resigns office on Rockingham's death, V, 9tn

1783 returns to Pay Office in Fox–North Coalition, 86n3; writes 9th Report of Select Committee, 107n4; dismissed from office along with Fox and North, 119; elected Rector of Glasgow University, 117; speaks on Fox's India Bill, V, 129hn

1784 goes to Glasgow for Installation, 123n5; publishes *Representation to His Majesty*, a protest against dismissal of Coalition, 156n1

1785 delivers and publishes *Speech on the Nabob of Arcot's Debts*, 211–12

1786 prepares Articles of Charge against Warren Hastings, 259, 264; visits Ireland with RBJr, 284

1787 formal Impeachment of Hastings voted in Commons, 319tn

1788 Chairman of Committee of Managers for trial of Hastings, 370hn; makes Opening Speech in Westminster Hall, 379tn

1788–9 Regency crisis, V, 425

1789 delivers Speech on Presents Charge, 464–5; reacts mildly to storming of Bastille, VI, 10

1790 delivers and publishes *Speech on Army Estimates*, takes public stand against the Revolution, 82hn; publishes *Reflections on the Revolution in France*, 141n1

1791 publishes *Letter to a Member of the National Assembly*, 253tn; breaks with Fox in the House of Commons, 255tn; publishes *Appeal*, 308n4; RBJr goes on mission to émigrés at Coblenz, 315hn

1792 RBJr goes to Ireland as Agent for Catholic Committee, VII, 3hn; EB active on behalf of French refugee clergy in England, 215, 225; publishes 'Case of the Suffering Clergy', 219n2

1793 consulted by Ministers over French declaration of war, 348n3; resigns from Whig Club, 353–5; writes 'Observations on the Conduct of the Minority', 436

1794 *Report on the Lords' Journals*, 540tn; delivers final speech of Hastings Trial, 552hn; resigns from Parliament, 553–5; RBJr elected for Malton, 560, dies shortly after, 566hn; encourages Fitzwilliam to accept Lord Lieutenancy of Ireland, 558

1795 Fitzwilliam goes to Ireland, VIII, 80n2, is recalled, 161hn; EB takes his part, 176; receives pension from the Crown, 292, 330; pension attacked in House of Commons, 339n3

1796 publishes *Letter to a Noble Lord*, 388hn; writes Letters on a Regicide Peace in reply to pamphlet of Auckland, 333tn; publishes *Two Letters*, IX, 97; starts Third Letter, 99; founds school for émigré boys at Penn, VIII, 396–7

1797 death, IX, 373n1; burial in Beaconsfield Church, 374

Character: his youthful impudence, I, 24; 'too giddy', 32; unpunctual in correspondence, 127, 142, 296, 350, 352, VII, 145, careless in writing, VI, 440, with blots, 460, VII, 503, X, 22, and blurs, VI, 467; his 'air of anger', I, 233tn; the Novus Homo, II, 128, VII, 53; fits of dejection, II, 374, VII, 476, 478, 480; over-earnest, II, 452; his Temper, 451, VII, 205; 'a dried spunge', III, 389; his idleness, V, 250, 280–1, 355, 413, VI, 62, 65; pro-

Burke, Edmund (*cont.*)

crastination his evil spirit, v, 280, vi, 256, vii, 145, x, 26; cannot help his nature, vi, 109; love of order 460; 'too eager pursuits', vii, 17; his affairs always in a state of embarrassment and confusion, 591, x, 27; his sense of guilt, vii, 583, 595; his gift for gratitude, viii, 86, 291, 341; no enthusiast, ix, 238

Opinions on EB: Sir John Blaquiere, v, 181; Matthew Boulton, iii, 121n3; RBJr, vi, 92tn, vii, 404, 419tn, 550–2; Fanny Burney, v, 25hn, 120tn; George Canning, ix, 267hn, 270tn; Richard Champion, iii, 46–7; Robert Dallas, v, 309n2; George Dempster, vii, 68tn; Benjamin Franklin, iv, 378; Friedrich Gentz, vii, 346–7; George III, v, 430n2, vii, 578tn; William Godwin, v, 63–4; Henry Grattan, viii, 187–8, 196; Edward Hay, 264n5; George Hay, iv, 100; French Laurence, viii, 420, ix, 374; Sir James Mackintosh, 193, 195–6tn; Richard Marlay, viii, 155; Dr Markham, i, 133tn; Mrs Montagu, 131hn; William Pitt the Younger, vii, 554, viii, 335tn; Pope Pius VI, vii, 421n2; the King of Poland, vi, 426tn; Duke of Richmond, iii, 171; Adam Smith, v, 9; Edward Thurlow, iv, 9n2; William Windham, vi, 144tn

Portraits of: by James Barry, iii, 9n, iv, facing p. xi, problems of a sitting for, iii, 4–9; by John Hoppner, viii, frontispiece; by John Opie, vi, frontispiece; medallion portrait by T. R. Poole, ix, frontispiece; by Sir Joshua Reynolds, iii, facing p. xi, 8; with Rockingham (unfinished), ii, frontispiece; by George Romney, commissioned by Duke of Richmond, iii, 237–8, engraving by John Jones, v, frontispiece, 293hn, 336hn; commissioned by Ernst Brandes, 306; miniature by Richard Sisson, iii, 8; miniature by Gervase Spencer, 8; by Thomas Worlidge, i, v, facing p. xv, iii, 8; bust in Rockingham Mausoleum, v, 46n5. EB has no desire to be painted, iii, 7, never thought his portrait a business of consequence, 8

coat of arms, on a letter, vi, 259, on his sister's monument, 209

Farming: EB's farm at Theobalds Park, ii, 548–9. His model farm at 'Gregor-ies', Beaconsfield: first plans, ii, 13; produce from, sent to London home, 212; directions to his 'doer', 224; farm described by Arthur Young, 238; a season's farming (1771), 238–40, (1772), 314–15; advice on farm management, 316–19, 338–9. Bacon hogs, ii, 180, ix, 396; barley, ii, 124, vi, 101; cabbages, ii, 143, 237, 239; carrots, 165–7, 183, 238–9; celery, iii, 228; cheeses, iv, 240–1; clover, ii, 6, 233, 318, viii, 282; corn, ii, 400, v, 167, 168, viii, 306; deep ploughing, ii, 247–8; a Farming dinner, ix, 471; grass harvest, ii, 443; Harvest Home, vi, 137; hay harvest, ii, 235, 239, v, 408; horses, ii, 312, vi, 34, viii, 345, experiments in breeding, ii, 316, 337–8, 427; horse-hoeing, 144, 318, 319, 338; Indian corn, 183; old labourers at work, viii, 364; oxen at work, 342, 345; peas and beans, ii, 318–19; pigs, 180, 183, 212, ix, 396; potatoes, ii, 234, 316–18, 338, v, 231, sells them all, viii, 344; the roothouse or tea-house, iii, 181; sheep, v, 268, 437, experiments in breeding with Colchian ram, vi, 313–14, 401–2, 416, vii, 170; turkeys, v, 404; turnips, ii, 212, 223, 231–5, 236–7, 317, 338; wheat, 21, 124, 471, vi, 101, viii, 306, ix, 396. Farming at Clogher, *see* Clogher. Farming in France, ii, 414hn

Finances: payments for writing, i, 164n1, 190, account with Rivington, ix, 290; seriously affected by collapse of East India stock, ii, 28–9, 141; borrows from Garrick, 31, 32, 438, viii, 284; attempts to raise money on Gifford security, ii, 58, 85, 100, 111–12, 140; receives draft from Clogher, 159; Loyd's mortgage, 206, 210; debts to Verney, 550–1, vi, 271n2; raises purchase money for Gregories from Miss Williams, ii, 550–1, viii, 284, and from Admiral Saunders, ii, 549–50, viii, 443; exhausts his resources to pay off WB's debts, iii, 373; financial involvements with Hargrave, 372–4, iv, 77–8, 106; Rockingham cancels debts in his will, v, 8; receives gift of money from Dr Brocklesby, 406; financial relations with Fitzwilliam, vi, 271, 449, 452–3, vii, 495, 551, 569–70, 578, viii, 9, 13, 15, debts cancelled, 306; bequest from Reynolds, and cancellation of

Burke, Edmund (*cont.*)

debts, VII, 87n2, 141n5, IX, 328; postage expenses on refugee clergy, VII, 358; debt to Captain Woodford, VIII, 13n3; cannot always command £50, 86–7, is not master of a single guinea, 106; 'critical exigence' of his affairs, 284; tradesmen's bills, 284; debts to Ridge's executors, 284, 365–6; total debts in 1795, 292; bequest from Lord John Cavendish and cancellation of debts, IX, 215, 216, 289, farm bills paid with legacy, 290; debts to John Bourke, 52, 290; leaves all his property to his wife, 375–9. Pension: 'something permanent' rumoured for EB and his family, VII, 451tn, 550hn, 557hn; pension and peerage talked of, 550–2, 557; pension granted, 573–9, 'watering old withered stumps', 575tn; arrangements for pension, VIII, 13–18, attacked in Parliament, 339, defended by Grenville, 342n4, by Windham, 339n3. For EB's Irish pension, *see* Hamilton, William Gerard

Health: pain in his hip, I, 94, IX, 46, 55; fish bone in his throat, I, 251; tumour in wrist tendon, IV, 200; wasted by fatigue and lack of sleep, 218; reported to be dangerously ill, V, 225, dead, 228hn; eye strain, 325; very weak after an illness, 359, not very well, 364, 368, reduced by illness, 379; absent from duty, 393, Portland's concern for, 407–8; feeble and feverish, 470–1, 474; a cold and hoarse, VI, 38; bowel complaint, VII, 214, 222; indigestion, 431; gout, VIII, 126; his old windy complaint, IX, 46, the 'Vice in my Stomach', 56, 61, 63, 80, 108, an 'Aeolian Cave', 155; urged to consult specialist, 55, 56; suffers from pyloric stenosis, 56n2; goes to Bath, 61, 64, 112, 'the last retreat of hunted infirmity', 62; 'the expiring snuff of a farthing candle', 64; chalybeate recommended, 72, rejected, 73; leaves Bath much better, 84, 86, 88, 89; again ill, 97, 106, 112, 124; hours of ease and of uneasiness, 132; fits in the night, 134; everything fluctuating and precarious, 144; his storms rage with tenfold fury, 153, 178; spends days on his couch, 161, 183, 226; sleepless night, 173; 'the worst day I ever spent', 180, 184; walks two miles, 191; his decaying

flesh, 206; pain in the bowels, 216; his friends' concern, 225–6, 230–1; Bath again, 234–5, 236; symptoms change, 236, 246, 252; given a purgative, 241; mostly in bed, 255; more at ease, 267, 272, but unable to exert body or mind, 277, 283, 469; opiates worse than useless, 289; only the shadow exists, 317; seemed at the point of death, 321, decays very fast, 331; returns to Beaconsfield, 354–8, 360, 362; like a man dug out of his grave, 366; no diet or medicine serviceable, 371, 372; death bed message to Fox, 372–3; dies, 9 July 1797, 373–4; his funeral, 374, 375; pall bearers, 374n3; his Will, 375–9; his executors, 376. Other references, I, 140, III, 182, 300, V, 111, VII, 342

EB's doctors, *see* Blane, Dr Gilbert; Brocklesby, Dr Richard; Parry, Dr Caleb Hillier; Smyth, Dr James Carmichael

Humanitarian Activities: on behalf of Archibald Borland, sentenced to Botany Bay, VI, 8–9; a poor Blunderer sentenced to die, IX, 413–14; two London chairmen condemned to death, II, 21–2; George Crabbe, in search of a patron, IV, 337–9, 373–4, 453–4; David Brown Dignan, swindler, condemned to the hulks, IV, 133–5; pension for old Fowke, VI, 249; limitation to executions of Gordon rioters, IV, 254–8; French emigrant friends, IX, 372; Samuel Hoheb, Jew from St Eustatius, IV, 402–3, 452; Mrs Douglas Johnston, widow, VIII, 24; Robert Jones, condemned to death, II, 323–5; La Robrie, robbed and imprisoned, VII, 530–2; James Lisle, trickster, VIII, 327–30; a poor woman refused an ale-house licence, IV, 21–2; Major Maxwell, court-martialled, III, 272–3; relief for L-C Machault and Archbishop of Paris, IX, 322–3; a poor Woman, V, 380; Read and Smith, sentenced to the pillory for sodomy, IV, 230–1, 350–1; Edward Sheehy and other Irish Catholics due for execution, I, 249, 337; James Thistlethwaite, imprisoned for debt, III, 231–2, 267; Professor Wilde, suffering from mental breakdown, VIII, 98–9. Opposes lighter penalties for shipwreckers and plunderers, III, 212–13; supports Eden's plan for

Burke, Edmund (*cont.*)
  employing criminals at home, 251–3, 287–8, IX, 413–14

OPINIONS

Abstract and concrete: France concerned with man in the concrete, VI, 46, 48; opposed to legislation on an abstract principle, 102; has no great opinion of abstract humanity, 109; accused of treating his subjects in too much of a *concrete* way, 304; condemns the abstract mode, 304; rejects idea of an abstract principle of public law, VII, 176; on abstract principles in practical affairs, 435, advises Hussey to know men 'in their Concrete' before trusting them 'in their abstract', VIII, 202
  Advertising, VII, 213
  Antiquities: traffic in, I, 323; EB a lover of all, VI, 394; of Languages, 466; objects of 'elegant curiosity and philosophical speculation' in Naples, X, 22; Irish antiquities, *see* Ireland; *see also* Ossian
  Architecture: on Westminster Abbey, I, 358, 361; prefers ancient to modern style, II, 7–8; Knole preferable to the 'foppish Structures of this enlightened age', VI, 395
  Aristocracy: a good Aristocrat defined, VI, 202, EB an 'aristocrate in principle', VIII, 185; the nature of an Aristocratick party, VI, 450, VII, 52, 53, French revolution aimed at EB's party as, VI, 451, VII, 60; independent aristocracy a safeguard to the Constitution, 56, 160; Pitt's administration weak through lack of basis in, 310; alarming tendency of Aristocrats to engage in cause of democracy, 437, to be deluded by Jacobin hypocrisy, VIII, 301; madness and folly of, 216; cannot survive if not true to one another, 184–5. In France: fatal division between 'external and internal', VI, 432; fighting a Civil War in same party as EB, VII, 432. Treatment of, in *Thoughts on the Present Discontents*, II, 121, in *Reflections* and *Appeal*, VI, 450; EB accused of hurting the cause of, 336; his name proverbial for supporting, 405. On men 'of high Birth and great property', II, 373–4, 377–8, 'younger Branches of illustrious families', IV, 152, 'men the best born and the best bred', VII, 62. Other references, VI, 464, VII, 276, VIII, 139, 206, 287n2
  Atheism: wishes to see it crushed by the Established Church, II, 299; the most horrid blow society can receive, 426n1;

Chesterfield an atheist playing the part of a bigot, IV, 416; encouraged by newspapers, VII, 229; Oxford a bulwark against, 270. In France, VI, 173, VII, 160, 232; philosophers pollute the young with, VI, 270; persecutions of Christians by atheists, VII, 219n2; satellites of, savages and cannibals, VI, 478–9. Danger of, in Ireland, VII, 293, VIII, 5, 245, IX, 261.
  Balance of power: and partition of Poland, II, 429; destroyed by France, VII, 161, 162, 315; war with France not about, 438; other references, I, 173, IX, 387. Balance of Europe, VI, 106
  Character drawing: 'got into the trade' of, I, 72; character sketch of RBSr, VII, 596–8, of RBJr, 580–91, of Samuel Dyer, II, 334–5, of Lord Lyttelton, 454–5, of Sir Joshua Reynolds, VII, 75–6, VIII, 252
  Charity: wishes RBJr to avoid everything 'sordid, illiberal and uncharitable', II, 420, advises him on 'the article of *giving*', 420; appeals to Garrick to perform new plays in aid of Swift's Hospital, 333; on Christian charity, VI, 94; all the possible Charities of life ought to be cultivated, VII, 101; opposes private subscriptions for National affairs, 162; charity of individuals nothing to do with Ministers, 214–17; prudent discrimination necessary in, 220; too closely connected with sturdy beggars, 425; justice and, essential parts of religion, VIII, 128; rules of, 266; *see also above*, Humanitarian Activities, *below*, French Refugee clergy, Penn School
  Commerce: EB's knowledge of, I, 133tn, 239hn, II, 128, III, 46, 140; works on revision of commercial laws, I, 239–40, 246–8, 251–2, 255; labouring to improve and extend, 245; dislikes restrictions on, II, 480; Rockingham Party the protectors of, II, 243; landed and commercial interests united on corn question, 306n; true balance of trade found without curtailing natural rights, III, 434; 'trade is not a limited thing', 442. Effects of American crisis on, III, 95, 98, 120, 130, 186–7, 191, 216, 246, 367, IV, 24, 49–50; 'natural decay' of, III, 108; Restraining Bills (1775), 117–18, 131–2, 135; concern for Bristol trade, 142, 240, IV, 59, 73, 381; war 'a sort of substitute' for, III, 191; commercial Acts passed in 1777, 357–61; Irish trade concessions (1778) and Bristol, 426–7, 430–7, 440–4, 445–7, (1779), IV, 172, 173, (1782), V, 103; equal privileges for Ireland in every branch of, VIII, 246–7;

Burke, Edmund (*cont.*)
trade flourishing (1786), V, 296. East India trade, II, 397, V, 42n2, VIII, 424. French trade, effect of Revolution on, VI, 43, 208, 294, VII, 54; trade and the French war, 464, 487, IX, 164, 274; hopes of augmenting British trade by cession of French colonies, VIII, 231. Scottish trade, increased since Act of Union, III, 434–5. *See also* Africa Company; Bristol; Merchant Venturers; New York Assembly

Compromise: preferred in all disputes between great parties, VII, 350; the very condition of our existence, VIII, 82

Conversation: EB dumb in mixed company, I, 24–5; writes as he talks, 108; his conversation little seasoned with wit, V, 249; Dr Johnson on his conversation, I, 24n1, V, 248hn; Bland Burges on, 393, Sir James Mackintosh on, IX, 195tn; a conversation with Jane Burke, VI, 7n1, with George III, 238–9, with John Barrow, X, 18; on Mrs Crewe's conversation, VIII, 84tn

Democracy: in the new French constitution, VI, 25, 45, 54; the lamp-irons of the democratic fury, 80; injustices of, 96, crimes of, VIII, 216; Démocratie royale, VI, 268, VII, 60. In England: democratick notions of Dissenters, VII, 55–6; Pitt said to be in the Interest of, 355; the Aristocratick Interest and, VII, 437; and the Prince of Wales's marriage, VIII, 216; a Luxurious Table loved by, 305; definition of a compleat, IX, 266; other references, VII, 482

Education: of boys, proposes to write thoughts on, I, 69–70; of RBSr, 73; of children, advice on, 288–9, II, 544–5; of a young man, 537; plan of, for Irish Catholics, IV, 119n1, VIII, 200–3; advantages of a classical, V, 337; advice on a young peer's, VII, 495; of James King, 588; importance of religion to, VIII, 5–6, 28n2, 130; advice on caning, 446n1; punishment and, X, 6; *see also* Maynooth College; Penn School; Trinity College, Dublin; and *below*, Painting

Epitaphs, IX, 324, 360–1; Goldsmith's on the Burkes, II, 536–7; EB's on William Dowdeswell, III, 241–2, 243, IV, 27, on David Garrick, VII, 561, IX, 323–4, 360, 468, on Sir Joshua Reynolds, VII, 99–100, 322, on the Marquess of Rockingham, VI, 5–6, on George Thicknesse, VII, 38

Equality: and trade, III, 358, 434, 443, difference of opinion on, with Bristol tradesmen, 445; rage for, in Sardinia and America, 403; for Irish Catholics, IV, 17, 406, VII, 360, IX, 369; of all men, doctrine

preached by Knavery, IV, 25; ideal of justice and, for every part of the Empire, 121; Paine's levelling idea of, VI, 304; equal taxation a phantom, III, 433–4; Liberty and the just and equal rights of one's fellows, VI, 42, 45; other references, II, 256, VIII, 371

Events: must be trusted to, I, 263, III, 401, VI, 378; conduct but not principles to be guided by, III, 399; systems arise from, rather than guiding, V, 342; due more to accidents than a chain of certain causes, 414–15; no longer move in a beaten circle, VII, 496

Family: and Commonwealth, III, 457, VII, 594; family society pleasanter in France than in England, VIII, 88; father and son, IV, 152, EB's relations with his father, I, 71, 119–20, 121hn, 136, 139, 274, with his son, *see* RBJr; great families and the State, II, 377; advice on marriage, IV, 354; parents and children, V, 194, VII, 592–5, earnings of a little girl at spinning, I, 114; family as 'strict and faithful monitors', II, 254

Freedom: without justice and humanity only a mask, V, 351n1; moderation a necessary qualification for, VI, 10; social freedom, the freedom EB loves, 42; EB well known by all who value good order and, 162; has struggled against the Tyranny of, VII, 368; freedom of speech, II, 281, VI, 43; constitutional freedom, III, 438; Free Countries, 397–8; freedom of trade, II, 480, IV, 71, in provisions, IX, 361–2. *See also* Liberty

Gambling, VII, 594–5

Gardens: at Stowe, II, 104–5; Lord Kenmare's improvements, 143; landscape gardening, VII, 330; art of the picturesque, 547–8

History: EB reading, I, 68; comes out of furor historicus, 89; starts 'Abridgment of English History', 124n5, 164, 202n3; takes part in Curry's *Historical Memoir of the Irish Rebellion*, 201–2, IV, 117hn; urges Leland to undertake a new History of Ireland, II, 285, VII, 104; studies Irish History with uncommon care, II, 285, III, 275hn; on Robertson as a historian, 350–1, VII, 502; correspondence with Vallancey on ancient Irish history, V, 108–10, 290–3, VI, 29; his discovery of Sebright's Irish MSS, V, 108, 292; urges publication and translation of ancient Irish Monuments, 109, 291–2; defends his treatment of Henri IV in *Reflections*, VI, 145–9; is more affected by contem-

Burke, Edmund (*cont.*)
porary cruelty than anything he reads in history, 171; asks for historical proofs before writing on Avignon, 461; on sources for study of Kilkenny Confederation, VII, 104–5. History 'arrests the wings of time', I, 360, is a preceptor of Prudence, not of principles, II, 282; events made historical as much by distance of place as by remoteness of Time, 513; no need to go to History, the Great Map of Mankind is unrolled at once, III, 351; is directed by divine Providence, VI, 308n1; role cast for Louis XVI a subject for, 149; extraordinary events in, VII, 281, 284, VIII, 357; Hastings Impeachment of importance to English, 439; flight from Mediterranean the most disgraceful event in our History, IX, 109; other references, I, 141, IV, 25, 413, VI, 181, VII, 75

Innovation: wishes all things could be kept *where they are*, IV, 295, VII, 518–19; Governments should let sleeping dogs lie, IV, 417; warns all parties against approaching Spirit of, VI, 255; Netherlands rebellion one against, French Revolution a revolt of, 268; worst abuses of old Order better than boasted reforms of, VII, 384, 389; to be avoided by Irish Catholics, VIII, 204; resisted by the sound part of the people, IX, 119

Intuitive certainty, IX, 268

Law: common and statute, II, 217; criminal, III, 212, 252; of Nations, IV, 402–3; public Law of Europe, VII, 176; Laws and policy of Ireland, 443; Laws and the executive government, VIII, 69, 80, 126, 258, 282, 347, 423, 431; fundamental laws of the country, 131; the God of Law and order, IX, 48; punishment and, 168–9; Justice and, 169–70; House of Commons the Guardian of, 169. *See also* Nature

Liberty: the birthright of our species, VI, 41, another name for Justice, 42; Authority and, the most sacred things of all, VII, 367; EB a zealous advocate for, III, 65tn, applies his ideas of Civil to religious liberty, IV, 84; first lit up the flame of, in Depont, VI, 31, 33, 40, 59; regarded by some as enemy of, 104hn; upholds principles of morality and, in *Reflections*, 162, 192, VII, 52; the Pope's tribute to his noble arguments for, 420, 421n2. In England: of the Press, II, 187; would be none if ancient Whigs were like the modern, III, 290; contrasted with other nations, 398; 'wild unprincipled' liberty opposed by Commons when led by Whigs,

v, 143; an un-English liberty appearing, VII, 307, its 'bloody barren pole' set up by Revolutionary Societies, VIII, 370, 372. In France: England uncertain whether to applaud or blame struggle for, VI, 10; the Land of, throws off Yoke of Laws and morals, 24–5; EB would rejoice to see *practical* liberty established there, 399, 400; Government of Louis XVI more favourable to than Mirabeau's, 225, immense sacrifices of Louis for, IX, 186; 'oppressed liberty', VI, 290, VII, 160, 172, VIII, 248; Fox's view of the French Spirit of, VII, 315. In Ireland: constitutional liberty for Catholics, VII, 83; the perilous blessing of, VIII, 4. In Poland, VII, 78. Other references, I, 223n3, V, 294, VII, 144, 360–1, VIII, 371, 382

Medical profession, I, 139, 140, IX, 186, 225–6, 234–5, 246, 283, 371–2; quack medicines, VII, 209

Moderation: Rockingham's plan of freedom and, for America, I, 278; lessons of prudence and, from war, III, 307; should be taught in Ireland, 387; more suitable than loftiness towards America, 432; 'natural moderation' a necessary qualification for freedom, VI, 10; a powerful Virtue in formation of New Constitutions, 49–50; millions of good men less capable of, than the headiest of princes, 97; Walpole's Temper one of, X, 9

Monarchy: exists for the principles of property and order, VI, 413, and of our Liberties, VIII, 174; functions of, in France, VII, 263; cannot be extinguished by removing a King, 392–3; monarchical succession, safeguards for, VI, 268; *see also* Court; King's Friends

Morality: moralizing a thing EB 'uncapable' of, I, 22; Adam Smith's moral theory, 129n2; previous systems of, 129–30; an analogy with Physics and farming, II, 248; religion and, III, 457, IX, 260; interests of a community in, III, 457; politics and, VI, 47, VIII, 82, EB hoped Old Whigs would be an Asylum for moral and political principles, IX, 78; low place of forms in scale of moral agency, VI, 108; passion and, 269–70; spirituous liquors and, VII, 294; moral State of Mankind fills EB with dismay, 496. *See also* Prudence

Nature: in her terrible scenes, I, 39; the strong hand of, III, 401; no bad Chancellor, 457; King's recovery the 'decision' of, VI, 1; and the French Revolution, VII, 183; ties of, 474; satisfactions grounded in,

Burke, Edmund (*cont.*)

586; March of, 594; political independence for Ireland a struggle against, VIII, 247; is subservient to a moral end, 364; justice and, VIII, 206; Laws of, III, 374, IV, 416, IX, 84, X, 40, first law of, VI, 266; legislation of, 266; order of, IX, 220; nature of things, III, 403, VI, 392. Natural consequences in a natural situation, V, 299; natural guardians, IX, 5, interests of property, 125, justice, II, 284, leaders, III, 218, operation of things, I, 321, order of things, VII, 500; natural passions for fields and houses of one's own, III, 456; natural rights, 434, V, 70, VI, 102; natural style, VI, 89, sympathies, 89, wickedness, III, 244

Opposition: never a desirable thing to EB, I, 285, 291, II, 138; ground of, too contracted by Rockingham, 155, 260; EB not 'forward in laying the grounds', 259; dangerous and unsuitable methods for, 404–5, 411, 523; needs outside support, III, 192; conditions for taking risks in, 193–4; without a tolerably uniform attendance, carries a disreputable air, 314; general routine of, as divisive to Nation as an impeachment, IV, 142; systematic Opposition a dangerous plaything, VII, 306, EB's practices in, 177; proposed suspension of, 314; folly of staying in when taking office in public interest, VIII, 82

Painting: EB acts as patron to James Barry, I, 203, sends him to Rome to study, 220, advises him to study anatomy with the knife in his hand, 253–4; thinks drawing beauty with Truth and precision more important than composition, 253, 293; has Barry's copy of 'Alexander' in his dining-room, 292; encourages him to experiment in the Natural History of colouring, II, 9; finds it difficult to get a sitting with him, III, 5–9; criticises his 'Arts of England', 100. Assists George Barrett, I, 221n5; visits exhibition of Society of Arts, 254; on the superiority of Reynolds, 323, his pre-eminence in Portrait, VII, 75; thinks credit of artists not damaged by dealers in Taste, I, 323–4; buys pictures and marbles with his house, 'Gregories', II, 7, a 'collection of Antique Statues and Italian Pictures', 7n1; his house 'hung from Top to bottom with Pictures', 8; advice to Champion on colouring of his china, III, 261, to John Barrow on choosing a career as a painter, V, 283–4, X, 19–20; asks for a Toast to an English Tradesman at Royal Academy Dinner, V, 465; writes obituary for Sir

Joshua Reynolds, VII, 75–6, and a note on Reynolds's collection of pictures, 322–3; knows nothing of the Arts, 322, never hazarded sixpence for a Picture on his own judgment, 322; other references, V, 343, 368, IX, 447–8

Paper Currency: on the French *assignats*, VI, 51–4; 'fraudulent and violent scheme' of the new Regime, 360, VII, 55, 384, 389; warns Canning against Pitt's proposed Guinea notes, IX, 269, mortified by scheme, 271; objects to paying soldiers in paper, 299; EB's words quoted by Canning in 1826, 270tn

Party: EB makes his party position clear, I, 279; systematic action in public Business better in large Bodies, II, 263; Spirit of, IV, 25; on the nature of political parties, 79–80; cause for decline of, VI, 2; 'absolutely necessary' in 1789, 9–10; suspension of, essential in 1792, VII, 307; ought to be made for Politics, not politics for Party, 318; Ministry is *one* Thing, not composed of separate parties, VIII, 39; extinguished by dominance of Pitt and Fox, IX, 78; Third Parties, 271; *see also* Rockingham Party; Tories; Whigs

Passive obedience, IX, 171

Patronage: sacred trust of, VIII, 79, IX, 94; EB has no command of, IV, 425–6, 445, V, 62–3, 70, 99, 106, 112–13, 209, X, 8, 36; in France, VIII, 49; in Ireland, 9, 11–12, 42, 48–9, 69

The People: EB not moved by vulgar opinion, III, 192; not meant by God and nature to think and act without Guidance, 218, IV, 295; certain to follow anyone who gives a lead, III, 223, 'act on the condition of our Nature', VIII, 331; impart their Character to their Rulers, III, 396–7; their faults not *popular* vices (1777), 381–2; angry with the Ministry, IV, 25; their unaccountable temper (1779), 128; Opposition does not stand well with, 141; well disposed to vigorous effort, 158; their wish for economical reform, 208, can get it through 'constitutional interference' by petitioning, 210; a 'very great and decided majority of', must prevail, 220, 228; EB will always follow the popular humour, 274; very corruptible by Paine's flatteries, VI, 304; EB has only twice given way to popularity, IX, 274–5; and Jacobinism, X, 32

Poetry: EB deep in the study of, I, 68; absorbed in the furor poeticus, 89; feels the fatal Itch, 104; prefers rhyme to blank verse, III, 354; on Genius and familiar images, IV, 234; the practical part of, the

Burke, Edmund (*cont.*)
most difficult, V, 262; its triumphs the art of interesting the passions, VI, 265; EB not a good critic of Latin poetry, VII, 145; moderns more 'fastidious' than our predecessors in mechanical perfection, IX, 183; moral poetry, 461. Poets and philosophers, I, 147, V, 21, VI, 269–70; on the Earl of Buchan as a poet, V, 265, Rev. John Eustace, IX, 102, Oliver Goldsmith, IV, 234, Edward Jerningham, VI, 204, William Richardson, III, 354, Edmund Waller, I, 74; on Latin verse, VII, 145; William Smith meant by Nature for something 'more respectable and useful' than a poet, 356. Poems addressed to EB, VI, 6hn, 230, 277, IX, 183hn; poems by EB, I, 5–7, 12–15, 18, 29, 35, 79–80, 80–1, 86, 103–7, 115–18. *See also below*, Works; Leadbeater, Mrs William; Shackleton, Richard

Politics: centripetal force of, I, 353; one of the worst of follies, II, 237, EB regrets he ever meddled with, 238; his thoughts do not run on, 337; principles of true politics those of morality enlarged, II, 282; his own principles (*c.* 1791), IX, 446–7; a dinner without, IV, 47; sick of the game of, (1780), 273, sick of the political atmosphere, (1796), IX, 178; his political influence worn out in the Service of, V, 106; prudence always a virtue in, VI, 48, X, 32; political prudence, VIII, 139, 253, IX, 193; EB no politician, X, 30

Poor, relief of, I, 278, II, 398, IX, 155

Port, EB's favourite wine, III, 303, 305, IV, 73

Power: the Talons of, I, 352; natural interests and, of Ireland, II, 336–7; of bad Men, VI, 47; Great Powers reside in those who can make great Changes, 49; Italy deprived of, VII, 85; a corrupting thing, 101; EB's struggle against licentiousness of, 368; Pitt's power, VIII, 34, 39, necessary for rescue of Europe, 36, 190, supported by EB, 180; where real and solid, must be yielded to, 38–9; William Smith's analysis of, 131–2; power of an M.P. uncertain and indirect, 133; power of being just, what Governments are made for, 138; uttering hazardous opinions the privilege of, 272

Prescription, rights, of, VI, 95; prescriptive Government, VII, 434, religions, VIII, 130, right, VI, 44, usage, III, 112

Property: men of great, rarely as enterprising as others, II, 373, III, 381; equality and, 403; stability of, necessary for safety of a Country, 404, VII, 384, 388, monarchy and Aristocracy depend on, VI, 334; the 'homely rustick' of, laid in Ireland, IV, 15; morals and, 460; sacred principles of, VI, 94; the foundation of social Union, 108, first origin of Civil Society, VII, 359; landed property should have the lead in well regulated states, 594; the contest in Ireland between those with and those without, VIII, 272, IX, 188. In France: no security for, VI, 108, 173; war with France a war to prevent subversion of, VII, 381, perhaps the last struggle against Religion, morality and, 527–8; System of, undermined by new species of democracy, 437; cannot stand alone against Jacobinism, VIII, 243, the great point of Jacobin attack, 256, IX, 283, 330

Providence: wonders of, IV, 125; mysterious disposition of, VI, 37; Gifts of, 242; divine tactics of, 308n1; not to be struggled with, 358; wisdom lies in conforming to, 439, VII, 487; satisfaction found in common order of, natural and innocent, VII, 586; her hand in human affairs, 586, VIII, 100. EB the creature of, II, 26; his trust in, V, 359, VII, 227, 274, 472; submits to, 302; wishes to retire into the retreat allotted by, VI, 275; was placed in his station by, IX, 67, 70, 282–3. Hangs her Trophies on a perfect fool, IV, 456; Rockingham's death in the course and order of, V, 20; paper currency and, VII, 384; RBJr's death difficult to accept as a mere act of, 568; George III the grand instrument of, 577; Grattan favoured by, VIII, 4; a glorious Empire given to England by, IX, 62; advice to those destined for humble situations by, X, 20; other references, I, 285, II, 147, VI, 407, IX, 268. *See also* Nature; Religion

Provisions: scarcity of (1772), II, 359, (1773), 400, (1795), VIII, 337–8, 344; possible supplies from Africa and South America, 354–5; in France (1789), VI, 21n1, 37n2, 39, 43; free trade in, IX, 361–2; *Thoughts and Details* on, VIII, 337–8, 344, 459hn; *see also above*, Farming; *below*, Parliament, Corn Bills

Prudence, V, 250, VI, 267, VII, 48–9; Authority and, IX, 256; charity and, VII, 220; and Mr Cruger's friends, IV, 331; filial piety and, VII, 593; James King's manly prudence, VII, 588; in India and Ireland a misnomer for servile patience, VIII, 147, or for improvident timidity, 104; rules of circumspect, IX, 342; other references, I, 119, VIII, 37, 80, IX, 79; *see also* History, Politics

Burke, Edmund (*cont.*)

Public opinion: importance of, for Rockingham Party, II, 51–2, 138, III, 381; Bloomsbury Gang's defiance of, II, 296; direction of, must originate with a few, III, 190; Fox advised to lay his foundations deep in, 385; can do little in Ireland, 386; EB's companion, never his Guide, V, 255; Dissenters likely to be high in, VI, 307; a cementing principle in the Fabrick of Government, 459; newspapers as avenues to, 476; increasing dominion of, VIII, 36; and Cabinet crisis over Fitzwilliam, 50–1

Punishment, IV, 134; caning advocated for schoolboys, VIII, 446n1; evidence and, II, 324; death penalty, III, 287, IV, 254, 255–8, VIII, 327, IX, 413; penal labour, III, 251–3, 288, IX, 413, X, 5–6; the pillory, IV, 230–1; transportation, III, 252–3, VI, 8–9, VIII, 327–8

Religion: uneasiness over RBJr not justified by principles of, V, 225; nothing worth saving if religion destroyed, VII, 298; slavery and, 124; persecution of, in France, 220–1, VIII, 248; natural pre-eminence of, in education, VIII, 6; learning not to be separated from, 28n2; negative and positive religion, IX, 125, 261; danger to State of indifference to, 142; politics and, 261–2; other references, I, 42, 274, II, 309, VIII, 80, 89–90, 200–1. Christianity: early views on doctrine of Christ, I, 32–3, 35–6; EB respects whole Christian religion with all its divisions, IV, 84–5, is attached to it at large, VI, 215; sacramental test dishonourable to, 17; property and, 94; supports toleration as a Christian, IV, 261; danger to, from Jacobinism, VII, 513, VIII, 93, 130–2, 146, 245–6, 255–6, IX, 115, 349, from French sympathies of Dissenters, VII, 119; where justice and charity are, particular tenets no danger, VIII, 128, 246; wishes to see a primitive Christian Church in Ireland, 143; denying toleration to Catholics injurious to, IX, 211; meant for the common people, 343. God: the Author of our Nature, III, 442; distributor of his own blessings, VI, 95; and RBJr's death, VII, 569, VIII, 66, 81, 122, 147–8, IX, 375; the Great Disposer, VIII, 70–1, 103, 140; the heavy hand of, 71, EB's face marked by, 70; his mysterious councils, 80, his lessons, 87; our only Refuge, 216; the Creator's Eye of Reason and Design, 364; God of Law and Order, IX, 48; the Grand Remembrancer, the God *within*, 170; Master of the Drama, 340; other references, VII,

523, VIII, 6, 35, 267, IX, 260–1. *See also* Catholicism; Church of England; Dissenters; and *below*, Toleration

Rights: natural rights and commerce, III, 434; EB's natural right to take care of his own Interests, V, 70; prescriptive right of possession, VI, 44; rights of war, 47–8; rights of the people, Parliament's duty to protect, IX, 169; 'Right' as an abstract principle, impossible for Parliament to accept, VI, 102. Rights of man, VI, 48; theories of, in France, 46; a digest of anarchy, 167n5; French constitution founded on vices not rights of men, 210; civil society destroyed in name of, VII, 54; daggers stamped with, 334n3; Catastrophe inevitable once rights of man declared, 344; Dissenters and, 421; 'conspiracy' to realize in England, 544; Rights of Man sect, VIII, 302

Servility, II, 452

Slavery: EB acts against tax on Negroes imported into Jamaica, III, 131n5, 141; favours abolition of slave trade, VII, 122–5; his plan for reducing evils of the trade, 123–5, VIII, 451; proposal to provide 'a few Slaves' for Catholick Colony in Maryland, VII, 281

Style: the Great Style in painting, I, 253; Barry's *Inquiry into the Acquisition of the Arts* criticised, III, 99–100; style of Ladies' letters, V, 45, of Paine and Junius, VI, 304–5; on brevity and loquacity, VII, 79; advantages of the 'formless Letter', 103; fluency of, modern substitute for thought, 209, 359; the Light Style of Quack Medicines, 209–10; deplorable tendency to make written English different from spoken, 502, only Robertson free from the 'falsetto', 502–3; vice of poetic style, 503; style of William Smith's speech praised, VIII, 244. EB's style criticised by Philip Francis, VI, 86, 89, 91, by Cusack Smith, 304; his style difficult to convey in translation, 222; never had any hand at pretty turned Phrases, VII, 322; problems of Moral and Geometrical propriety in *Letter to a Noble Lord*, VIII, 398

Theory and practice, IV, 48–9; EB a dabbler in theories, I, 172, IX, 386; in governing colonies, III, 181–2; the contemplative virtue above the practical, 355; Theoretic plans the bane of France, VI, 219, pernicious theories for the first time reduced to practice there, 419; *see also* Abstract and concrete

Toleration: EB fears principles that leave no toleration for religion, II, 299,

Burke, Edmund (*cont.*)

426n1; expects spirit of intolerance to vanish by degrees, 310; ideas of, extend to Jews, Mahometans and Pagans, III, 111–12; all toleration on the same bottom, IV, 248; a steady friend to cause of, 261; attacked in Bristol for advocating, 263–4, 266hn, X, 40–1; 'early spring' of in England destroyed 'in its tender bud', IV, 372–3; the nature of Christian tolerance, VIII, 246. In Ireland: toleration of property for Catholics should be given precedence over religious, III, 454, 455, 463; supports toleration for Catholics and Dissenters, IV, 6–10, 17; EB's activities in support of, 241–2, 247–51; his plan too large for North, 251; danger of losing Ireland through intolerance, 261–2; Gardiner's Bill for, 405–18; becoming attitudes to, VIII, 246. In Scotland: resistance in Edinburgh to Toleration Act, IV, 45–6; intolerance of Scottish Dissenters, 85–7. *See also* Catholic Committee; Catholicism; Dissenters; Gordon Riots

Translations, IV, 48, VII, 427, 501–2, IX, 131–2; translation rights, 105

Trust: parliamentary representation as, III, 3, 436, 438, IV, 223; Established Church a public trust, III, 456; all representative stations public trusts, IV, 210; prosecution of Hastings a trust conferred on EB, V, 466–8; EB in trust to maintain rights and properties, VI, 93–4; Parliament as a trust cannot be limited by abstract principles, 102; King of France holds his power in Trust, 353

Women: their limiting effect on conversation, I, 24–5; female heroines, 41; the Passion vulgarly called love of a woman, 28; Ladies of a determined character better than a perpetual Coquette, II, 176; powerful wives and the absentee tax, 474, 477; the age distinguished for its extraordinary Women, V, 26; no good company but that of, 244; the Chivalrous Spirit and, VI, 90–1; the 'simple and genuine' women of London contrasted with the 'furies of Hell' in France, VII, 208–9; womanish invective, 287; Ladies with Nervous distemper, 351; usefulness of married women's portions, 594; Mrs Crewe impossible to keep seaworthy, VIII, 84tn; their charms called to the aid of Fitzwilliam, 188, 189; virtuous Wives and Mothers urged to save their families from the Clan of desperate and Wicked, 304

WORKS

Address to the King (1777), III, 309hn, 312, 314–15, 317tn

African Code, *see* 'Sketch of the Negro Code'

Annual Register: EB engaged to edit by Dodsley, I, 127hn, 174n2; change of publisher, IX, 96n1. 'Characters' in, I, 72n9. Reviews by EB: 1759, *Theory of Moral Sentiments* (Adam Smith), I, 129n2, *History of Scotland* (Robertson), III, 350n2, VII, 502n2, *Letter to d'Alembert* (Rousseau), VI, 81n2; 1760, 1761, Macpherson's Ossianic forgeries, I, 146n3; 1762, *Emile* (Rousseau), VI, 81n2; 1763, *Antiquities of Athens* (Stuart and Revett), I, 204n1; 1765, *Works* (Swift), 194n8; 1766, *Interesting Historical Events relative to ... Bengal ... and ... Indostan* (Holwell), V, 387n3; 1769, *History of Charles V* (Robertson), III, 350n2, VII, 502n2; 1772, *History and ... Discoveries relating to Vision, Light and Colour* (Priestley), V, 53hn; 1777, *History of America* (Robertson), III, 351n2. J. Z. Holwell on the Black Hole of Calcutta (1758), V, 387n2. Also mentioned, I, 174, 225hn, 329n7, III, 182n7, V, 373n2, VII, 98n2, VIII, 147n2, IX, 295, 470

Appeal from the New to the Old Whigs: undertaken as EB's defence against Foxite Whigs, VI, 275, 292hn, 331, VII, 51; printing arrangements, VI, 292, 298–9; a cancel, 307, 308; published (3 Aug. 1791), 308n4, 311dn; copy presented to King, 308–10, 316n3, 333, his 'flattering panegyric' on, 368n5; rejected by Prince of Wales, 310–11; copies for Fitzwilliam, 313, Mansfield, General Conway, and others, 314–15, RBJr, 317, Charlemont, 331, Weddell, VII, 50hn; French translation, VI, 329, EB not eager for Dupont to translate, 337–8, 341; 2nd edition in Press, 334–5, corrected, 360; sales lower than for *Reflections*, 335; 3rd edition in preparation, with revisions, 341, 360, published (2 Sept. 1791), 378; demand outruns supply, 378. Loughborough's worries over, 306n2; praised by Hawkesbury, 349n2, by Dundas, 360, by Fitzwilliam, 401hn, 402, IX, 438, by Mrs Bunbury, VII, 64n2; Party silent on, VI, 360, 369, 418;

Burke, Edmund (*cont*)

deplored by Portland, 369n2; King of Poland impressed by quotations from, in *Morning Herald*, 426hn, pleased with passage on Polish Constitution, VII, 76hn; passage quoted in support of Polish subscription, 164hn. EB on the subject matter, VI, 303–4, 416, 450, 'satisfied' with his defence, VII, 52. Also mentioned, IX, 445hn

'Case of the Suffering Clergy of France': corrected by Bishop of St-Pol-de-Léon, VII, 207hn; published in *Evening Mail* (17–19 Sept. 1792), 213hn, 219n2; also mentioned, 222, 420n1

Catholic Claims Discussed (Dublin, 1807), printed version of letter to William Smith (1795), VIII, 127–33

'Essay Towards an Abridgment of English History' (unfinished, 1763): EB said to be getting £300 for, I, 124n5; 'a sort of rent charge on my thoughts', 164; terms of agreement, 164n1; also mentioned, 202n3

'Funeral Oration on Dr Hill', a satire (1751), I, 140n2

'Heads for Consideration on the Present State of Affairs' (5 Nov. 1792), VII, 288, 517

'Hints for an Essay on the Drama' (unfinished, 1761), I, 143n1

'Letter to the Archbishop of Aix', published in *London Chronicle* and *General Evening Post*, 30 Aug.–1 Sept. 1791, VI, 293dn, 295tn, 477dn

Letter to Sir Hercules Langrishe (18 Feb. 1792): written to declare EB's sympathy with Catholic Committee, VII, 4; 'imperfect and clumsy, but the Stuff is right', 12; RBJr advised to be cautious in making it public, 48, sent to him before seen by Dundas, 49; Westmorland considers it inflammatory, 48n1; Hobart condemns publication, 49n4; EB thinks has been of service, 103. Published in Dublin (18 Feb. 1792), Byrne's blunders in, 94–5, 103; 2nd edition, 95n1, 95n4, 103n6. London edition (28 Feb. 1792), 95n3. Also mentioned, VII, 8dn, 40, VIII, 243n3, 272

Letter to a Member of the National Assembly: written (19 Jan. 1791) in answer to Menonville's letter, VI, 162hn, 169tn, 212; French translation, 228n5, 232–3, 241, 252hn, 253tn, Menonville's Preface to, 232;

English edition (21 May 1791), 253tn, 259n6; Grenville's favourable response, 252hn; the King very satisfied with, 252–3; Meyer questions arguments of, 256hn; Dupont on, 259–60. Rousseau denounced in, VI, 81n2, 214hn; Mounier and Lally-Tollendal reconsidered in, 166n4, 321hn; *comité des recherches* discussed, 169n5. Also mentioned, VI, 292

Letter to a Noble Lord: addressed to Duke of Bedford, VIII, 388; corrections to proof, 388–9; Windham objects to use of terms in, 392, 397; published (24 Feb. 1796), 388hn; immediate success, 388hn, 400; 'recommended' by the 'seasoning of personality', IX, 98; French Laurence's corrections for later printings, VIII, 392–4, 398; editions and translations up to 1796, 400n7; 'the little squib', 419; dispute with publisher over profits of sales, IX, 11n8, 97hn, 104n3. EB describes strains of his early days in Parliament, I, 239hn; on his love and admiration for Keppel, IV, 169n1; on unplumbing the dead, VIII, 339n10. Also mentioned, VIII, 342n3, 454, IX, 96n1

Letter to a Peer of Ireland, printed version of letter to Viscount Kenmare, 21 Feb. 1782, IV, 405hn, VIII, 143, 201

A Letter to Philip Francis (1788), reprinted from press version by supporters of Hastings, V, 371tn

Letter to the Sheriffs of Bristol, III, 334n2; written to justify conduct of the Party on Habeas Corpus Bill, 332hn, and on secession, 398hn; arrangements for printing in Bristol and London, 332–4, 338; shown first to Party leaders, 333; intended for the public as well as for Bristol, 334; last minute alterations, 334–5, 337–8; publication (8 May 1777), 337n4; General Oglethorpe's transports on reading, 343–4; copy sent to Dr Robertson, 352, and to Wm Richardson, 355; Lord Abingdon's *Thoughts* on, 369–70; Shelburne resents implied criticism in, 398hn; Paine described in, V, 415 n3; EB's fellow wanderers from the paths of rectitude listed in, VIII, 184n2

A Letter to Thomas Burgh (1780): written as defence against attacks on EB in Irish Parliament, IV, 181hn, 189; not intended for publication,

Burke, Edmund (*cont.*)

181hn, 201, 417; MS copy sent to Lady Rockingham, 191, and Rockingham 191, 192, 193; Brown's slips in copying, 194–5, 196; corrections in printed version, 194n8; Lady Rockingham 'not displeased', 194, 195–6, wishes to read again, 199; Thomas Burgh on, 201–2; approved by Hely Hutchinson, 201; Walter Hussey Burgh praised in, 202n3; John Scott offended by, 417n4, V, 50

'Letter to William Elliot, Esqr.' (1795), EB's answer to Duke of Norfolk's attack on him, VIII, 239

Letter to Viscount Rivarol (1791), VI, 265

Letters on a Regicide Peace:

Two Letters: prompted by Auckland's pamphlet, VIII, 333tn; hard at work on, 373–4, a great deal printed, 373; sheets sent to Windham, 379; corrections, 388–9; work on, suspended, 403; EB wishes he had read Gifford's book before writing, 408; concern at Bintinaye's proposal to translate from rough draft, 408–9; not yet certain of publishing, 409, 412, 415, 419; material for, from Anderson's *Origin of Commerce*, 413n9, 421; 'Two Letters' finished and in print, 413, 414–15; the pamphlet 'pre-occupied' by John Bowles's, 415; Chancellor wishes delay, 418, 421; Windham urges speedy publication, 447, IX, 64; ought not to wait much longer, VIII, 460; final printing arrangements, IX, 93, 94–6; amendments by French Laurence, 94–5; publication (20 Oct. 1796), 97; Owen's pirated version, 95n5, 97hn, 104n3, 105, 240; Peltier's unauthorised French translation, 104–5, 131–2, Abbé Bintinaye's authorised, 105n1, 131. Copies sent to Fitzwilliam, IX, 102, presented to Marquess and Marchioness of Buckingham, 128, to Duke of Württemberg, 318; approved of by Th. Townshend, VIII, 453tn, Mrs Crewe, IX, 106, Canning, 129–30; Portland said to approve of, 126; Pitt remains hostile to, 138, 217n4; has no effect on peace policy, 130; quoted in Commons by Sheridan, 180n1, 280n3, misquoted by Fox, 281; Mackintosh's articles on, 192hn. Contents referred to: hatred of Directory for English Government, VIII, 358n2; Mr Bird's interview with Delacroix, 376n7; England's 'diplo-macy of humiliation', IX, 89n4. Ed. 8, 105n5; ed. 11, 217n3; ed. 12, 105n5. Also mentioned, VIII, 399hn, 412n2, IX, 13dn, 48n1

Third Letter: begun, IX, 99; material for 186n4; directed against Malmesbury's peace mission, 211n2; advertised in Press, 217; still writing, 227, 302; incorporates passage from letter to French Laurence, 273–4; edited by Laurence and Walker King and published posthumously (13 Nov. 1797), 105n6

Fourth Letter: first attempt to answer Auckland's pamphlet, VIII, 333tn; addressed to Fitzwilliam, 367–8; published posthumously, 368n1

Letters of Valens (1777), contributions to, III, 233n3

Obituary of Sir Joshua Reynolds (Feb. 1792), VII, 75–6, 79, 322, VIII, 252, IX, 327n3

'Observations on the Conduct of the Minority' (1793): shown to Sir Gilbert Elliot, VII, 436; addressed to Portland and Fitzwilliam, 436hn, 497, as protest against their attitude to Jacobinism, 437–8; Portland's reply, 446–9; Owen's pirated edition, IX, 240n1, 243–4, 249n4; injunction against sale, 243, 244, 246n; authorised version (1802), 243n6; EB never intended for publication, 244–5, 248–9, but retracts nothing in it, 245; the paper well received, 242, 245n1, 247. An indictment of Fox, VII, 436hn, IX, 240n1, 245, 247, 249, 281n3

Observations on a Late State of the Nation (1769), II, 265n3, III, 307hn, VI, 10n2

Poems: 'Blackwater', poem on the scenes of EB's childhood, opening lines, I, 79–80; also mentioned, 75n1, 82, 85–6, 95, 96n1, 98. 'Panegyric on Damer', 28–9. 'Panegyric on Dr Taylor', 40n2. 'To Richard Shackleton on his Marriage' (1748), published in *A Collection of Poems by Several Hands*, 109n1. *Poems on Several Occasions*, EB's poems in, 64n3, 98n3

Preface to Brissot's *Address* (1794), VII, 426n7, 428n1

'Punch's Petition to Mr Sheridan' (?1747), I, 98n5

Reflections on the Revolution in France: addressed to Depont, V, 235hn, VI, 31hn, 158n2, 189n3; EB sends Depont

Burke, Edmund (*cont.*)

his first judgment on French Revolution, 39–50, writes *Reflections* in answer to Depont's reply, 61tn, 85hn; begins writing, 76n3, 81tn; shows MS draft and printed proofs to Francis, 85, and to other friends, 89n1; Francis criticises style, 86, 89, 142, 151, advises against publication, 150–1; Elliot reads early version, 149n2; completed (end of Aug. 1790), 137hn; published (Nov. 1790), 141–2. Copies sent to Calonne, 141, 221hn, Francis, 142, Windham 'as to an Asylum', 142–3, Sir Gilbert Elliot, 149–50, Bishop of Carlisle, 157hn, Richard Cumberland, 157–8, Dr Falconer, 160, Malone, 182, French Royal Family, 189, 199, 202, Bishop of Clermont, 211n2; Malmesbury asks for copy, 179, and Mme de Montrond, 213

EB on his purpose in writing, VI, 272–3, VII, 52; his object 'not France, but this country', VI, 141–2; intended as a warning against French Whiggism, VII, 52, but EB not 'the organ of any party', 52n3; approved by the 'old stamina of Whigs', VI, 161n2, 178, 450–1; recommended by Portland as containing true Whig creed, 161n2; pains taken to discredit it, in Party, 273; *Appeal* preferred to, 360; EB proscribed by Party on account of, VII, 52

approved by: Windham, VI, 143–4; Elliot, 'contains the fundamental Elements of all political knowledge', 156, his 'diplomacy' on, 356n3; Dr Falconer, 158–9; Lord John Cavendish, 160–1, 178; Portland, 178, 418n3, IX, 438; Fitzwilliam, VI, 178, 334; Duke of Devonshire, 178; Frederick Montagu, 178; Lady Anne Lindsay, 186–7; Abbé Maury, 190, 204; John Hatsell, X, 24; Oxford resident graduates wish to confer honorary degree on account of, VI, 193–5; success at French Court, 203–4, 205; Comtesse de Boufflers rapturous on, 205n3; John Trevor on, 216–17; George III compliments EB on, 219–20, 308–9; reports of reward for, 210n1; Calonne on, 221–3; a conversation with Prince Kaunitz on, 239–40; RBJr on, 254; Rivarol on, 265; Auckland on, 281tn; Mansfield on, 314n3; Charlemont's qualified ap-

proval, 332tn; Elector of Mainz praises, 345; admired by Catherine II, 442n4, IX, 439; EB congratulated by Pope on, VII, 420, 421n2; praised by Reynolds, IX, 327n3. Unfavourable opinions: Francis, 'the Wine too rich', VI, 151; Fox, 'entire disapprobation', 180tn, 254, 274, 335, X, 24; Mirabeau, VI, 225n4; Prince of Wales prejudiced against, 273, 310, VII, 58; Duke of Norfolk, VIII, 239n1; dispute over, at meeting of Revolution Society, VI, 159n5; Meyer's doubts on, 256hn; Rousseau and, 214hn

replies to: Paine, VI, 75tn, 246–7; 'a war of pamphlets with Dr Price', 86, 91–2; Mackintosh, 141n2, IX, 192hn; Christie, VI, 141n2, 273; 'Candour', 160tn; Menonville, 162–9; Mackenzie, 178n6; Mary Wollstonecraft, 214n1, VIII, 304n5; Rous, VI, 214n1, 273n1; Lofft, 214n1; Mrs Graham, 214n1; Sheridan intends answering, 178; a reply in verse, 317n3; EB doesn't read pamphlets critical of, 214–15, defends his religious views against critics, 215n1

contents: use of Priestley's term, 'fixed air', V, 54n3; Addison's *Cato* quoted, VI, 46n1; Necker on French finance, 74n2; artificial divisions in France, 74n6, 106n3; Marie Antoinette, 85n1, 204n5, passage dismissed by Francis as 'mere foppery', 86–7, defended, 89–91; slanders against the Queen, 90n1; error over Garde du Corps, 90n2, 372; attack on Society for Constitutional Information, 128n2; professional men, 159n3; *comité des recherches*, 169n5; ancient institutions, 222–3; King's return to Paris, 286, 287; homage to French clergy, 293n1; Lally-Tollendal, 321hn; Priestley ridiculed, VII, 153n1, 357hn; the swinish multitude, 340hn, VIII, 370, 407–8

editions and translations: eds 3 and 4, revised, with quotation from Calonne, VI, 141n2, 160, 179, 182; ed. 7, with additions due to Menonville, 163n1, 166n3; ed. 8, 227; ed. 10, 177n6. French translation by Dupont, 144hn, 162n1; ed. 2, includes EB's letter on Henri IV, 145hn, 189–90, errors not corrected, 189n5, 228; ed. 3, corrections asked for, 190, not made, 227, 227n5, Calonne's sharp comments on, 191n1; faults of translation, 221–2,

Burke, Edmund (*cont.*)

and his abode', IV, 240n6, to EB's hypothetical lectures in Dublin, VIII, 6n4

Thoughts and Details on Scarcity ... 1795 (pub. 1800), VIII, 337n1; sent to Pitt, 337–8, 344; possibly to be identified with 'Letter to Arthur Young', 459hn

'Thoughts on French Affairs' (1791), published posthumously (1797), VI, 440n4; occasioned by new French Constitution, VII, 517, its object the extinction of Jacobinism in France, 517–18; EB's 'last Effort', VI, 378n1, 408n1; MS shown to Comte de Conway, 314n4; returned by Grenville 'without a word', VII, 81, 'does not meet his ideas', 217–18, 291; sent to Pitt, 81; has no effect on Ministers, 313; Portland's views coincide with, 313. On French finances, VI, 412n; dissenters regarded as partisans of Revolution, 420n1; on the Frith Street Alliance, VII, 172n4

Thoughts on the Present Discontents (April 1770): first reference to writing of, II, 35hn; revising old papers for, 39, 49, 104; problems of composition, 52, 101, 102, 107, 108, 109, 113, 114, 118hn, 122; Rockingham urges completion, 89hn, 92, 95; EB's object in writing, 101; written at Richmond's 'pressing desire', IV, 235–6; 'System of Court' sent to Rockingham for comment, II, 108, 112hn, 114; EB's doubts on publishing, 108–9, stipulates for Party support on, 109, 118; Sir George Savile comments on draft, 118–21; advises against publishing, 119, 121; delays in getting views of Party leaders, 121hn, 122; Rockingham sends remarks on, to Dowdeswell, 123tn; publication, 123tn; well received, 136, 139–40, 149–50; 'the Political Creed of our Party', 136, 139–40; no systematic follow-up, 175; 'obloquy' suffered by EB on account of, IV, 236. WB and RBSr think parts 'too ludicrous', II, 109; Radicals hostile to, 139–40; Walpole on, 140n1; Catharine Macaulay's Answer to 140n1, 150; quoted by Fox against Windham, IX, 282; also mentioned, IV, 297n3, IX, 450

Three Memorials on French Affairs, published posthumously (Sept. 1797), VI, 440n4, VII, 517n4, VIII, 269n4,

IX, 132tn; French translation by Abbé de La Bintinaye, 132tn. *See also* 'Thoughts on French Affairs', 'Heads for Consideration' and 'Remarks on the Policy of the Allies'

'Tracts relative to the Laws against Popery in Ireland' [uncompleted]: begun in 1765, I, 202n3; consulted by Kenmare, IV, 204, X, 6–7; Irish Attorney General asks to see, IV, 205; French Laurence asks for, IX, 124

Two Letters on the Conduct of Our Domestick Parties (1797), VIII, 239n2

Two Letters on the Trade of Ireland (1778), III, 431–6, 440–4, IV, 224

A Vindication of Natural Society (1756): copied in MS by Joseph Emin, I, 121hn; published by Robert and James Dodsley, 127hn; referred to by Horace Walpole, 142n1; payment for, 190n4

other writings: 'Characters', of Reynolds (a Fragment), IX, 329, of RBJr and RBSr, VII, 580–600, of Samuel Dyer, II, 334n2. Epitaphs, for William Dowdeswell, III, 241–2, 243, IV, 27; for Garrick's Memorial, VII, 561, IX, 323–4, 360, 468; for Reynolds, VII, 322; for Rockingham, VI, 5–6. Inscriptions, for Reynolds's funeral cards, VII, 99–100, for bust of George Thicknesse, 38

unpublished writings: 'Sketch for Reynolds's collection of pictures', VII, 322–3, X, 46; verses, I, 5–7, 12–15, 18, 29

See also Junius

Burke, Mrs Edmund (Jane Mary Nugent, 1734–1812), wife of EB

correspondence with, listed above, p. 104

first acquaintance with EB, I, 115hn; his verses on her, 118; their marriage, 124; domestic life, 142, 143; on Ned's busy life, 236, IX, 389; goes with EB to Ireland, I, 264–5; her youthful appearance, 268; included in Strettel's 'inquiry', 274, II, 134–6; visits Plaistow, I, 287; keeps Rockingham informed on Bristol poll, III, 68–9, 71–2, 77; 'my ever dear Jane', 75; takes on some of EB's correspondence, 291–2, 424–5; survives the Gordon riots, IV, 241, 245–6; and EB's pension, 430, V, 10–11, VII, 575, 577, VIII, 13, 15, 16, 17, 18; concern for EB's low spirits, V, 111; visits Devon with EB, 113; acts as his copyist, 379hn, VII, 182hn, 472hn, VIII,

Burke, Richard Sr (*cont.*)

II, 9–10, VIII, 12n3; speculates in East India stock, II, 28hn, 29, 513n1; on the meeting to elect City Sheriffs, 31–5, 36n2; a present from the West Indies, 42; ordered back to Grenada, 109–10, 112, 122, 131, 134–5, 136, 137, 144, 149, 159, 181; and Governor of Dominica, 146hn; purchases lands in St Vincent, 227, 231, 328n1; returns from West Indies, 247, 250; writes part of reply to Markham's allegations against EB, WB and RBSr, 252hn, 271; defended by EB against charges of indiscretion, 277–80, 283–5; his retort, 278–9; his claim to Carib lands contested, 300, 307n3, 313–14, 409n2, 416n5, 472n3, seeks help from Fox, 370, 381–2, 450–1, 453, Lord North's bungling, 460–3; Memorials to Treasury on claim, 524–5, claim rejected, III, 162, 285; suspended from office in Grenada, 201–2, 211; granted further leave of absence, 203 tn, 285, IX, 412

writes EB's farewell letter to electors of Wendover, III, 55–6; deputises for EB at Bristol election, 64–5, 66, 72, 73–4; gives dinner to Committee, 74; presented with ring, 94; describes EB's speech on conciliation, 139–40; acts for EB on inquiry into arson at Bristol, 321–2; reports capture of New York, 300n3; goes bond with EB for WB, 372hn, 374hn, wins action on bond, IV, 77–8; on the temper of the people, III, 401

counsel in press-gang case, IV, 105hn; member of Bucks County Petition committee, 226hn; on EB's declining the poll at Bristol, 279, 280, 285; counsel for Burgoyne, 282n3; Rocking-ham wishes to see, 286, 301; on Bristol Tories, 329n1; goes on circuit, 335–6, 371, 430; becomes Secretary to Treasury, 430, 437; praised by Mansfield, 430n5, VII, 596; loses office, V, 10hn; on circuit again, 79–80, 273hn; returns to office, 82, 86, 100, 121hn; on life at the Pay Office, 101–2; appointed Recorder of Bristol, 113–14, 122, 283, 332, 443n3, VII, 598, VIII, 329, IX, 467; innuendoes on his 'public' income, V, 159–60; takes Deponts to Lord Mayor's Banquet, 235–8, VI, 31hn; mocks newspapers, V, 247n4; counsel for

prosecution against Hastings, 324, 398–9, VII, 109; goes abroad to escape creditors, V, 359–60; takes a gaol-delivery, 403–4; visits Stratford, 418, and Crewe Hall, 420–1; on circuit, VI, 131, 369, 455, VII, 92, 107; visits the Ladies of Llangollen, VI, 131–2; on the Prince of Wales's manners, 311tn; criticises Government inter-ference with Press, 461; his note on plan for relief of French clergy, VII, 222n3; on Archbishop's speech on Hastings, 369–70; his admiration for Fanny Burney, VIII, 462

kindness to relatives, II, 20, III, 391; takes care of Wat Nagle's funeral, IV, 93, IX, 427; friendship with Champion, III, 79, 87, 247, 253hn, IV, 149–50, their correspondence cited, III, 106hn, 119hn, 126tn, 131n1, 143–4hn, 220hn, 230hn, 233hn, 250n3, 298hn, IV, 329, 379n6, 419n2; consulted by EB on his letter to Champion, V, 173tn; warned of EB's anxiety over RBJr, 223; on Reynolds's death, VII, 74, 86–7, much affected by his funeral, 93

his health, IV, 370, 439, VI, 13; ought not to have attended Francis's festivities, V, 305, has been very ill, 339, 340; goes to Cheltenham, VI, 13; recovering, 33, 37; his illness described, 38; further reports, 137, 180, 334, 461, 465, VII, 12, 31, 98, 107; at Cheltenham for a scorbutic tumour, 195, 197; goes to Bath, V, 58, and Weymouth, VII, 204; two good nights, 516; his sudden death, 531, 563, 564, VIII, 12n3, 290n2; mentioned in RBJr's will, VII, 599, 600, and in EB's will, IX, 375; EB on his character, VII, 580, 595–8, a 'model for official Duty', 597; Fox thought him EB's natural superior, 596; mock epitaph on, II, 536n3

thinks parts of *Thoughts on the Present Discontents* too ludicrous, II, 109; arranges publication of *Speech on American Taxation*, III, 93–4, and of *Letter to the Sheriffs of Bristol*, 332–3; revises last sheets of *Appeal*, VI, 307; acts as amanuensis for EB, V, 373; letters in his handwriting, III, 69hn, IV, 117hn, 307hn, VII, 217hn, 246hn, 248hn, 254, 265hn, 279hn, 431hn, 527hn

Letters of Valens ascribed principally to, III, 233n3

Burke, Richard Sr (*cont.*)

also mentioned, I, 119, 134, 149, 245, 247, 251, 274, 277, 284n3, 351n1, II, 14n1, 16hn, 26, 84, 95hn, 107n2, 126, 179, 296, 301n3, 319–20hn, 412, 420, 454, 549, III, 22, 123, 231n1, 235n1, 287, 289, 364, 368, 376, IV, 58, 97, 240n6, 294, 298, 380, 381, V, 9, 34, 42n1, 87, 177, 201, 205tn, 206hn, 225, 246, 276hn, 285, 287, 293hn, 336, 349, 350, 380, 415n4, 438, VI, 56n6, 227, 259, 262, 290n2, 295, 299, 314n3, 316, 364, 409, 446, 472, VII, 49, 128, 206, 330, IX, 383, 387, 395, 396, 450, 456, 463, 465, 467, 472, X, 25

Richard's servant, VI, 394

Burke, Richard (RBJr, 1758–94), Edmund's son

correspondence with, listed above, p. 105–6

birth, I, 122n2, 136n1, VII, 118n1; Dr Markham godfather to, I, 225hn, II, 257, IX, 441; childhood, I, 135–6, 142n3, 154, 190, 228, 245, IX, 384; the 'young Julus', I, 191, 195; a seat at the pantomime, 234; birthday celebrations, 236, and baptismal, VII, 118; goes to school, I, 236, IX, 389; 'gone to domineer at his nurses', I, 287; his tutor, Thomas King, II, 27, 207, III, 28n1; studies Homer and writes Latin verses, II, 136; at Westminster School, 179, 227–8, V, 134n1, VII, 584, IX, 395; early taste for mathematics, VII, 580; awarded Studentship at Christ Church, Oxford, II, 393–5, 400–1, 409; to spend six months in France with his tutor, 401, 409, 411–13; stays at Auxerre with Parisot family, 419n2, 421–2, 424, 425n1, 426, 454, 458, 526, 534, V, 52n2, 104, VII, 588, 589, VIII, 25, 86; goes sightseeing, II, 414hn, 415, 417–18; a gift declined on behalf of, 418; fatherly advice to, 420; civilities shown to, 534

is bequeathed land in St John's Island, II, 517; offers it to *émigrés*, VII, 281–2, 297; large sums claimed for surveying barren land, IX, 44, 51–2, 110–11

in residence at Oxford, II, 537, 538tn, III, 74, 364, VII, 580; EB visits, III, 75, 78; at home on vacation, 285, 289, IX, 412; takes his B.A., II, 538tn, IV, 28hn, but not M.A., II, 538tn, IV, 369n3; his tutor's *Euclid* dedicated to, VII, 580; reads Greek with Nicolaïdes, 581–2; advice from Shackleton, IV, 58–9, 78–9; studies

for the Law, 28hn, 79, VII, 581; makes abstract of Irish revenues for Rockingham, IV, 158; reconstructs EB's speech on Economical Reform, 212; lives with his family at Beaconsfield, 234; on Shackleton's visit, 240n6; invited to appear with EB at Bristol, 245; goes with WB to Holland and France, 286n5, VII, 586–7; bears EB's withdrawal from Bristol with sense, IV, 290; goes on Circuit, 369, 371, 430, 437, V, 111hn, 112n3, 276, 332; advice on legal practice, 339–40; his Chambers, VI, 29

becomes Deputy Paymaster to EB, IV, 430, 437, loses office on EB's resignation, V, 10hn; appointed Joint Receiver General of Land Revenues for life, 8n2, 51–3, 82, 110n3, VI, 437n2, IX, 57; sends Fox his reflections on choice before Rockingham party, V, 3–5; proposed transfer of Clerkship of Pells to, 10–14; considers buying a library, 36; tours the North, 36, 221–2; visits Priestley in Birmingham, 54; regains office, 86hn; joins his parents in Devon, 113; innuendoes on his 'public income', 159–60; and Champion's debts, 170–1, 173tn; visits Holland and France again, 216, 222hn, 223, 225, 227, 231–5, 266, VI, 31, 366n7, 407; reported drowned, V, 225n3, 228, 261, 262, 284n5; stays with member of Artois household, 232; presented to Queen, 233–5, 261; goes to Ireland with EB, 284–90, 342, VI, 66n1, X, 36; acts as Committee Clerk for Hastings Impeachment, V, 378; takes holiday in West with EB, VI, 137, 138, sails up the Romantic Wye, 139n1; Oxford confers honorary degree on, 195tn; a member of Literary Club, 220

France and the Mission to Coblenz

receives letters from France on impending revolution, VI, 10n3, 16–20, 25–6; thinks badly of French plan for national bank, 50; describes Bastille Day celebrations in London, 295–7; Calonne suggests visit to Princes at Coblenz, 302tn, 342, 476; Dundas not encouraging, 306; starts on Mission, 314, 315hn, makes his will before he goes, VII, 599hn; warned to be prudent, VI, 315; rebuked for writing incautiously to O'Beirne, 315–16, 328–9, 339, 347, 353, 364–5, 366, 367, 384, 386n2; advice on how to proceed,

Burke, Richard Jr (*cont.*)

317–18, 333–4, 354–5, 358, 'the Cause is yours', 333; writes to Louis XVI for EB, 318–20, 326, 327, 372, warns him to rely only on help from abroad, 318–20, 326; in Brussels, 323, 326, 329, 333, 341, 347, 354, receives Address from Noblesse, 326, VII, 258–9; reports on plan to restore monarchy, VI, 323–30; is against immediate publication of Princes' Manifesto, 324, 359; on the French in exile, 325; on the state of the Austrian Netherlands, 327–8, 368; journeys to Coblenz, 326, 335, 342, received with civility, 343, 473–4; on the prospects of the French monarchy, 344–5; arranges for Bintinaye as London agent for Princes, 343, 373tn, 431–2, 434, 474–5; studies his Memorial, 423, wrote it himself, 431–2; Bintinaye thinks himself distrusted by, 434–5; plans for delivering Monsieur's letter to George III, 369–70; troubled by conduct of Hanover Regency, 369–70, 384, 393n2; disturbed that England opposes movement of Austrian troops from Netherlands, 378–84, 387, 400–1; appeals to Dundas for English intervention, 380–1, 387n2, 391, 400; fears Emperor's neutrality, 388, 405–8; his letter on Declaration of Pillnitz shown to Dundas, 404, IX, 437, quoted to Grenville, VI, 405–7; proposes to return to England, 388, 390n5, 398tn, 409n2; his insinuations on English in Paris, 395n4; Provence's gracious reception to, 400; Dundas refuses to discuss French affairs with, 404–5; witnesses meeting of Princes on Pont Volant, 406–7, VII, 474; EB wished him to stay at Coblenz, VI, 409, 414, proposes him for Berlin mission, 411; returns to England, 409n3, 417, 422, 424hn; his sacrifices for the Cause, 425; Calonne distrusts, 424–5, 433tn, sends Dillon to observe him, 425tn, receives unfavourable reports of, 446–8; EB's defence of, 474–7

Mission to Ireland

asked to draw up 'Appeal' by Irish Catholics, VI, 133, 134; appointed London Agent of Catholic Committee, 396–8, VII, 3hn; Dundas refuses to discuss plans with, VI, 429–30, 469–70, refers him to Irish Government, VII, 19–20, writes only as private person to him, 33, is not hostile to him as Agent, 34tn; sees Pitt, VI, 430, 436, 437, and Hobart, 463, 467hn; still in the dark, 471; sticks out for right of Franchise, 463; his proposed qualifications for Catholic electors, 464–5, memorial on, 467–8; goes to Ireland, 456, 471, VII, 3, 5, 7, 13; his supposed directions from England, 6, his role in Ireland, 35; deprecates Irish Government's attempt to divide Catholics, 6, 13–14, 18, 22–5, 29, 44, and their policy on Catholic relief, 26–7, 72–3, 87–8; accuses them of making a French revolution, 36; advice from EB on his mission, 10, 11–12, 16–17, 64–7, 82–4, 94, 203–5, 223–4, 284, 287, 289–90, 292–3; urged not to 'drink the draught to the dregs', 20–1, 31; draws up petition to parliament, 12n3, 17n1, 28, 32, bungling attempt to present, 45–6; takes little part in second petition, 69–71, 72, 73; negotiates with Hobart, 13–14, 18–20; Hobart's hostile tone, 18–19, indifference, 25–6, 28, 32; warned against him, 31, his treachery, 118; pursues aim of Catholic franchise, 19–20, 27–8, 39–40, 45, 71; Irish Ministers determined to resist, 39, 236, 239; hostility of Castle to Catholic cause and himself, 25, 30, 33, 36–7, 47, 66, 68–9, 72, 106n9, 130–1, 201–2, 295–6; English Ministers governed by Castle misrepresentations of, 80–1; not seen at Dublin balls, 107; the Irish government 'deaf as adders', 134

on the danger of junction between Catholics and Dissenters, VII, 25, 26, 242; repudiates use of violence, 35–6; Cork vote of thanks to, 72; drafts petition to King on Catholic relief, 82, 88, 119, 205, 274, 293n2; his letters to Dundas too long, 84; on confidential terms with Grattan, 100; Catholic Committee Dinner in honour of, 120tn; sends Declaration for King to Dundas, 126–8; goes to England, 126hn, 129; sees Dundas, 129, 130; considers answer to Declaration unacceptable, 130–2; Dundas refuses further discussion on Ireland, 138tn, 324hn, 325; gets his congé from Catholic Committee, 164–6, 201n6; returns to Ireland, 178hn, 185, 195, 586; regarded as spy of Dundas, 201n6; on the Protestant Ascendancy, 241–3, 255, his Declaration against,

Burke, Richard Jr (*cont.*)

255–6, deliverance of Ireland from, his unfulfilled goal IX, 85; believes English Ministers share his views on Ireland, VII, 245; engagements from Catholics and Protestants, 256, 268, 268; asks to be put on confidential footing with Ponsonbys, 257; 'commits a rape' upon the Committee, 268n5; gives the Ministry a good 'wipe' with his pamphlet, *Letter ... to a Gentleman of Cork*, 296; sends Memorials to Grenville, 297, and to Dundas, 324n2; thinks Catholics and Protestants ought to be reconciled, 297, 298–301

returns to England, VII, 302, 306, 321; warning on state of Ireland, 326–7; Grattan on his success, 362–3, 545, his 'triumph', 366; asked to draw up plans for education of Catholic clergy, 499–500, 507, 508tn, VIII, 5; thinks Ireland should be 'most favor'd nation' commercially, VII, 545–7; on her economic backwardness, 546; 'knew Ireland to the bottom', VIII, 23, 139; concerned for her up to his death, IX, 254

other references, VII, 86, 167, VIII, 147 203, IX, 134

Fitzwilliam and: 'goes out' with Topping in defence of Fitzwilliam, V, 131–3, VIII, 190; becomes his London agent, VI, 123n1, VII, 394hn; sends him his views on French Revolution and its English supporters, VI, 125–30; receives payments for EB from, 271n2, VII, 495n4; relations become strained over EB's quarrel with Fox, VI, 271n3; prospects with Portland and, 440–1; visits him at Wentworth, VII, 178, 181, 185–8, 235hn, reports on Irish politics to, 235–46; predicts Fitzwilliam for Lord Lieutenant of Ireland, 243, 257; Fitzwilliam's borough of Higham Ferrers not offered to, 394–5, VIII, 69n1; defends politics of EB and himself, VII, 396–410; thinks he is sacrificed to Fox, 398–9, 405–9, 418; asks only the 'old cloaths' of the late member, 405; could never adhere to any opinions but his father's, 417; remains Fitzwilliam's agent, 419tn; Fitzwilliam has complete confidence in him, 403n2; is offered Malton after EB's resignation, 553n1, 555–6, 559tn, 560; elected, 559, 568–9, VIII, 5, 373; alleged offer of post in Ireland,

4n2. Other references, VI, 37, 130, 178n2, VII, 574n4

Health: recovering from an illness, IV, 369, a kind of fever, V, 277; goes to Scarborough, 35–6; sickness spoils Irish visit, 288, 300; sea bathes at Brighton, 346–7, 349–50, 355, 418, 420, takes asses' milk, 350; takes the waters at Bristol, 403, 404, 406; taken ill on tour of West, VI, 138; goes to Margate, 292; convalescing, VII, 368; bathing again at Brighton, 460n1, 462hn, 477; his last illness, 561, diagnosed as consumption, 562; his deathbed, 563–6; quotes Milton, 564; funeral and pall bearers, 570, VIII, 140, IX, 374; his will, VII, 599–600; books from his library left to Maynooth College, 600n5, VIII, 265, 288n2

and his Father: EB's character the only inheritance he will have, II, 257–8, VI, 237–8; the family temper a fearful inheritance for, IV, 152; EB can only hope to exist in him, 152; his 'Son and friend', VI, 33; prudence not his forte, VII, 40, 48, but his temper and command better than EB's, 205; EB's Polish medal a testimony to him against calumny, 78; his Education given by the Old System, 161; set aside in everything for the sins of his father, 429; his acute eye for the political scene, 510; manages EB's affairs, 569hn, 591, delicate in revealing EB's debts, VIII, 18; 'All his severity was to himself', VII, 595; arrangements for, in terms of EB's pension, VIII, 15, 16, 18, 297

on the wisdom of his father's folly, VI, 92tn, 319; predicts his break with Opposition, 255, 316n1; desires to sit with his father as M.P., VII, 398–9; resents refusal of peerage, 550–2, 557; Windham communicates with EB through, 531–2; and Letter to Mayor of Bristol, III, 325hn; his intended translation of *A Representation*, V, 156n1, 246–7; and *Reflections*, VI, 90n2, 254, 372, 'our Book on French affairs', 334; and Dupont's translation, 144hn, 145, 149, 183, 227, 228, 262; advises on *Appeal*, 306n2, 307, 334–5, 343n6; advised to be cautious with *Letter to Langrishe*, VII, 48–9; and letter to Byrne, 224, 258, 273; intended to publish his father's works, 404; *Letter to a Noble Lord* written

Burke, Richard Jr (*cont.*)

to pay EB's debt to his memory, VIII, 395, 398

EB on the Treasure he has squandered, VII, 567–8, 592, VIII, 26; left an old withered stump, VII, 575tn; his son's death a calamity to EB and posterity, VIII, 3, 35, 128, IX, 255; a cartful of letters destroyed, VIII, 48; his desolation, 77, 279, increases with time, 81; 'died upon my Bosom', 159; EB has never dined out or visited since, 315–16, IX, 195, X, 30; every Saturday a sad Hebdomadary, VIII, 412, IX, 47; 'the best and dearest part of me', 12, 238; EB his unworthy and misplaced representative, 86; Tone on the grief of a father, 115n4; *émigré* boys at Penn his chief comfort, 226n2; feels for Laurence as for his son, 238; in EB's will, 375

Friends and relations: Keppel's partiality for, IV, 169; Adam Smith's kindness to, V, 302; fondness for his cousin Mary, 287; drinks lemonade with Cusack Smith, VI, 304n2; Reynolds attached to, VII, 41; charity to poor Irish relations, 106, visits them in the South, 197, makes up old women's quarrels, 282; advice to WB, 139–41, arranges for his debts, VIII, 359; interest in Mary Palmer, VII, 190; sends Mrs Haviland a present, 560; concern for Woodford, 571; his talent for friendship, 581, 583, 590; his 'Natural charities', 587, 595–6; friendship with Captain King, 588–90; filial piety, 590–1, affection for his mother, 591; 'did not like paltry people', VIII, 96; obtains commission for Henry King, 325, 326; respectful admirer of Fanny Burney, 462; his friends remembered by EB, 14, and in EB's will, IX, 377; Richard Bourke a favourite with, 369

Lord Bessborough on, IV, 369n3; Prince of Wales on, VI, 311tn; Dundas on, 380n5, VII, 429n5; Dillon on, VI, 436–8; Westmorland on, VII, 24n1, 46n6, 48n1; Langrishe on, 295; Portland on, 410tn. Tributes to, after his death, from Fitzwilliam, 567, Comte d'Artois, 573, Walker King, 581, Grattan, VIII, 3, Bishop of Auxerre, 78tn

Reynolds's portrait of, III, 8n4, VII, frontispiece; James Ward's engraving from Reynolds, VIII, 250, 289

opinions: states EB's ideas on French Revolution, VI, 125–30; on Establishments, 253–4; on Fox, 254–5; thinks Mackintosh 'Paine at bottom', 312; respect for the Aristocratic interest, VII, 240

A Letter from Richard Burke to a Gentleman of Cork, VII, 296, VIII, 139–40

also mentioned, I, 268, 295, II, 285n5, 296, III, 87n4, 325hn, 336, 368, 375, 376, 391, IV, 80, 101, 243, 380, 381, 382, 398hn, 458, V, 47, 55n1, 58, 126n5, 176n2, 177, 201, 217hn, 269, 279, 283, 301n3, 308, 336, 359, 369, 398, 415n4, 427, 453, 455, 464n3, VI, 13, 56n6, 115, 124, 186, 243, 244n1, 392, 403, 428n2, 443n1, 455, VII, 76n2, 293, 318, 486n1, 488n3, 501n2, VIII, 157hn, 314, 364, IX, 307, 450, 456, 463, 467

Burke, Richard, son of Walter Burke of Middleton

correspondence with, listed above, p. 106

Burke, Theobald (d. 1773): EB solicits Rockingham on behalf of, II, 30, 49; fails to get post as supercargo, 106; O'Hara on, 106n4; bequeathes land in St Johns to RBJr, 517hn; also mentioned, 95hn

Burke, Walter, great uncle of EB, II, 359n8

Burke, Walter (d. 1788), Captain of Sepoys, kinsman of EB, II, 359

Burke, Walter, mentioned in will of EB's father, II, 359n8

Burke, Will, cousin of EB, I, 125–6

Burke, William (WB, 1728–98), close friend and fellow law-student of EB, called by him 'cousin'

correspondence with, listed above, p. 106

friendship with EB, I, 103hn, II, 274–5, IV, 431, IX, 377, X, 13, 15; verse epistles to, I, 103–7, IX, 377; adventures at Monmouth with, I, 112–14; Dr Markham's advice to, on EB's début in parliament, 225–6; on EB in parliament 242–3, II, 126–9, 178n3, III, 336tn; plans trip to Italy with EB, I, 322; helps finance purchase of Gregories, 351n2, lives with EB there, 356, II, 26, 300, IV, 30, IX, 49; on EB's speech at Bucks County meeting, II, 80; on his London homes, 96n1, 301n3; visits Stowe with him, 104; thinks part of *Thoughts on Present Discontents* too ludicrous, 109; writes part of EB's reply to Dr Markham's strictures, 266, 269n5, 270n6, is defended by EB against Markham's charges,

C—, a young Divine, I, 106n

Cabarrus, Jeanne-Marie-Ignace-Thérèsa, *see* Tallien, Madame

Caddell, Thomas (1742–1802), London bookseller, V, 164, 165

Cadell, Thomas (1773–1836), printer, IX, 325

Cadogan, Charles Sloane (1728–1807), later (1776) 3rd Baron, M.P., Treasurer to Duke of York, I, 234, II, 56

Caesar, Caius Julius, VI, 47, 161

Caillaud, General John (*c.* 1724–1812), commander of East India Company troops in Bengal: complains against allegations concerning the capture of Ali Gauhar, VI, 243–4hn, EB's reply, 244–6; evidence to Committee on East India Company (1772), 245n8; also mentioned, V, 107n5, VI, 57n, VII, 148n3, VIII, 438n1

Cairnes, Major William (d. 1789), VII, 478n1

Cairnes, Mrs William, widow of the preceding, *see* Cuppage, Mrs William

Cairnes children, VI, 463

Calcraft, John (1726–72), M.P., army agent, I, 224n5; defeated at Rochester, 224; goes over to Chatham, II, 2n2, 115n4, 157n2, 160n2, 205n3; organises freeholders' petitions, 50n7, 115, 115n3; 'new friendship' with Lord Beauchamp, 92; also mentioned, I, 240n7

Calcraft, Thomas, M.P., petition against his return for Poole, II, 19n1

Caledonian Mercury, see Newspapers

Calgacus, Caledonian chief, IV, 45

Caligula, V, 151n2

Call, John (1732–1801), M.P., V, 197hn
correspondence with, listed above, p. 108

Calonne, Charles-Alexandre de (1734–1802)
correspondence with, listed above, p. 108
Controller-General of France, VI, 68n4; calls first Assembly of Notables, 68; introduces EB to Duc de Luxembourg, 106n1; *Reflections* sent to, 141; his sharp comments on French translation, 191n1, 221–2
becomes agent for French Princes in England, VI, 140hn, 301, 323, 431n3; discussions with EB at Margate, 206n2, 300, 356, 473–4, 476; sends Pitt his version of meeting, 425tn; RBJr's mission the outcome, 302; keeps up contact with RBJr, 346, 390n7, 423n1, 431n1, 433hn, 473hn; joins Artois in Turin, 216hn, 221;

advised by EB on Princes' Manifesto, 257–8, 291n1; distrust of England, 324, 370n1; Marie-Antoinette's dread of, 340n6, 348; goes to Vienna with Artois, 342, 344, 345, 347, 378hn; sends Dillon to spy on RBJr, 424–5; coolness to RBJr, 425tn; receives hostile reports on EB and RBJr, 436–8; the Bintinayes resent treatment by, 433hn, 434n2, 475–7; his letter to RBJr offends EB, 473–7; seeks conciliation with EB and RBJr, 477tn; improved relations with the Bintinayes, VII, 66; comes to England (1792), 225
ignores public opinion and the press, VI, 476; has newspapers in his pay, VII, 42
De l'état de la France: copy sent to EB, VI, 140; referred to in *Reflections*, ed. 4, 179; English translation dedicated to EB, 202–3; his eloquence in the cause of France, 212; his language too drastic for the disorder, 217n1; qualified approval given to, 218–19; to be reprinted, 228
also mentioned, VI, 172n3, 314n4, 409, 423n2, 431n2, 434n2, 438n2, 463

Calonne, Madame Charles-Alexandre de (Anne-Rose-Joséphine d'Harvelay, *née* de Nettine, *c.* 1740–1813), wife of the preceding
correspondence with, listed above, p. 108
her fortune and marriage to Calonne, VI, 140hn; RBJr visits, 342; also mentioned, 258

Calonne, Jacques-Ladislaus-Joseph de (1743–1822), Abbé de St Pierre de Melon, VI, 342

Calvert, Nicolson (*c.* 1725–93), M.P., his 'mad' speech on the peace proposals, I, 157

Camac, Lieutenant-Colonel Jacob (d. *c* 1784), II, 436
correspondence with, listed above, p. 108

Cambis, Vicomtesse de (Gabrielle-Françoise-Charlotte d'Alsace-Hénin-Liétard)
correspondence with, listed above, p. 108

Cambon, Joseph-Auguste, Chevalier de (b. 1722), VII, 431

Cambridge, Duke of, *see* Adolphus Frederick

Camden, 1st Baron, *see* Pratt, Charles

Camden, Baroness (Elizabeth Jeffreys), wife of the preceding, II, 1

Camden, 2nd Earl, *see* Pratt, John Jeffreys

Caritat, Marie-Jean-Antoine-Nicolas de, Marquis de Condorcet (1743–94): chosen as Dauphin's *governeur* by National Assembly, VI, 363, 477hn; his furious Jacobinism, 364; of the 'sect of Philosophic Robbers and Assassins', 478; Rougane's *Lettre* to, 478; his Report on Education, VII, 161; and the English Jacobins, 177; his end, VIII, 304; also mentioned, VI, 25n3, VIII, 242n6

Carleton, Elizabeth, *see* Shackleton, Mrs Richard

Carleton, General Guy (1724–1808), later (1786), 1st Baron Dorchester
correspondence with, listed above, p. 109
Commander-in-chief at Quebec, II, 304n1; settles boundary with New York, 304, III, 18; fails to get Niagara included, 19; has trouble raising troops, 191n1; to clear Canada of invaders, 240n1; surrenders at Ticonderoga, 410; considers Canada safe, IX, 417; returns from America, IV, 34n9; appointed Commander-in-chief in America, 404hn; his reported death, VIII, 367hn; also mentioned, IX, 416

Carleton, Hugh, 1st Viscount Carleton (1739–1826), Lord Chief Justice of Ireland, IX, 350, 355

Carlisle, Bishop of, *see* Douglas, John

Carlisle, 5th Earl of, *see* Howard, Frederick

Carlyle, Dr
correspondence with, listed above, p. 109

Carmarthen, Marquess of, *see* Osborne, Francis Godolphin

Carmichael, William (1702–65), Archbishop of Dublin, I, 230

Carnarvon, 1st Earl of, *see* Herbert, Henry

Carnatic, Nawab of, *see* Walajah Muhammad Ali

Carnot, Lazare-Nicolas-Marguerite (1753–1823), VIII, 149n4

Caroline Amelia Elizabeth of Brunswick-Wolfenbüttel, Princess of Wales (1768–1821): her marriage to the Prince of Wales, VIII, 216; strained relations, IX, 47n1; also mentioned, VIII, 84n2

Carr, John (1723–1807), architect: designs mausoleum at Wentworth Woodhouse, V, 46; Alderman of York, X, 18, 20; also mentioned, VI, 5n9

Carr, Richard Cooban, Solicitor to Dublin Customs Office, V, 52
correspondence with, listed above, p. 109

Carra, Jean-Louis (1742–93), radical revolutionary, VII, 177

Cartaine, Henry, VII, 104n4

Carte, Thomas (1686–1754): *History of England*, II, 282; *Life of James Duke of Ormonde*, III, 335n5

Carter, Mrs Elizabeth (1717–1806), friend of Mrs Montagu: accompanies Lord Bath on his travels, I, 173, IX, 387; also mentioned, I, 131hn

Carter, John
correspondence with, listed above, p. 109

Carter, Thomas, East India stockholder, V, 135n4

Carter, 'Little', his Indian adventure, X, 23

Carteret, 1st Baron, *see* Thynne, Henry Frederick

Carteret, John, 2nd Earl Granville (1690–1763), IX, 174; EB well known to, I, 124n5

Cartwright, Major John (1740–1824)
correspondence with, listed above, p. 109
attempts to convert EB on political reform, III, 328–9

Carysfort, 1st Baron of, *see* Proby, John

Carysfort, 1st Earl of, *see* Proby, John Joshua

'Case of the Suffering Clergy of France', *see* Burke, Edmund: Works

Casey, Charles, VII, 296n1

Cashel, Archbishop of, *see* Agar, Charles

Cashel, Dean of, *see* Palmer, Rev. Joseph

Castlereagh, Viscount, *see* Stewart, Robert

Castley, Thomas (1766–1860)
correspondence with, listed above, p. 109

Castries, Duc de, *see* La Croix, Armand-Charles-Augustin de

Castries, Marquis de, *see* La Croix, Charles-Eugène-Gabriel de

Castries's Corps, IX, 71n3

Cataline, I, 92

Cathcart, Charles, 9th Baron Cathcart (1721–76), British Envoy at St Petersburg, V, 122hn

Cathcart, David (d. 1829)
correspondence with, listed above, p. 109
asks EB's aid for Prof. Wilde, VIII, 98–9; also mentioned, 419n3

Catherine II, Empress of Russia (1729–96)
correspondence with, listed above, p. 109
her government preferable to tyranny of multitude, VI, 96; support against France uncertain, 324, 447n2; EB opposed to supporting Turks against, 377n9; her courtesy dangerous, 428tn; her foreign policy, 441hn, 443n1, n2; letter to on behalf of French *émigrés*, 442–5, not sent, 446–7hn, IX, 439; admires *Reflections*, VI, 442; her

Cavendish Bentinck, William Henry (*cont.*)
Bourbon monarchy, 221n2; Fitzwilliam wants coalition of Fox and, 352

America: power through reciprocal interests his principle, III, 226tn; and meeting of London merchants on America, 225–6; calls Party meeting on declaration of Independence, 291; discusses secession, 309hn, 311; approves plan to meet Franklin in Paris, 310; opposes joining in debate on Habeas Corpus Suspension Bill, 330n2; cannot understand anxiety for action, 399hn

India: urged to attend Parliament for East India Bill, II, 391–2, enters dissent against Bill, 392n3; his activity in East India business, 401; presents petition against Supervisors Bill, 408; stops publication of pamphlet on East India Company, v, 165, 166hn, 167; on Sheridan's Begums speech, 304; opposes indemnification of Hastings, VIII, 384hn; is given notice of EB's protest against Hastings's pension, 404

Ireland: appointed Lord Lieutenant (1782), IV, 454–5; resigns but wants Burgoyne to stay there, v, 55, 61; supports Catholic relief, has doubts about franchise, VII, 257n6; consulted in controversy over appointment of Provost of Trinity College, Dublin, 570hn, 571, 572, VIII, 10–11, 28, 37n2, 46, 47, 68n2; and Fitzwilliam's appointment to Lord Lieutenancy, *see above*, 'Party career'; relations with Grattan, 33–5; urged by Hussey to take action on behalf of Catholics, 153, 162–3; encourages Catholic education, 164, 179, 198, 200; approves of the Catholic Bill but fears for it, 185; always promised Beresford's dismissal, 185, 187; receives Catholic deputies, 193–4; accused by Grattan of deserting Ireland, 196–7; wants Hussey to stay and establish Colleges for Catholic clergy, 199–200, 215, IX, 345; sends Pelham to Ireland as Chief Secretary, VIII, 243, 352; Catholic Committee lose faith in, 352; confirms Hussey's appointment as Chaplain to Irish Catholic troops, IX, 82–3, never granted him a salary, 83, 182; all his actions in Ireland against his principles, 126, 159; salvation of Ireland his chief motive in taking office, 156, 158, and cp VIII,

197; still in his power to save her, IX, 157, 176; useless for Hussey to appeal to, on state of Ireland, 156, 159, 175–6, 180–1, 189, 190; petition of Catholic peers to, 331n1, 334n1

dispute with Lowther over lease of land in Cumberland, I, 341; Nullum Tempus Bill intended to help, 344n2, II, 195; triumphs over Lowther, 197–8, 200–1, 443–4, III, 289–90, 327–8; his Cumberland candidate wins petition against Lowther, II, 18

Regency crisis: the King's illness, v, 425; sends for Fox from abroad, 426n3; is reconciled to Prince of Wales, 427; and Regency arrangements, 431, 434hn, 435; EB's suggestions to, for Hanover, 445–6; advises Princes to accept Queen's invitation, 461n2

general: relations with Weymouth, I, 208, with Lord John Cavendish, 263, IX, 196; should give lead to Cumberland over petitioning, II, 102; and Westminster elections, (1770), 131–2, (1774), III, 32, 50, 58–9, supports EB as candidate, 51–3, 57–8, (1788), v, 408, 409, 414; asked to find seat for William Baker, III, 51; and Nottinghamshire election, 57, 63; supports 'natural Interests' in politics, 59, IV, 137; plans for reviving City as political centre, III, 194; Chatham falls upon his bosom, 427; attends Middlesex meeting, v, 188; replies to City thanks, 194–5; quarrels with King over Prince of Wales's finances, v, 99n1; sings praises of Sir James Harris, 355; apprehensions on Dissenters, VI, 84n3; subsidises Opposition newspapers, 130n2, VII, 321n4; 'not so ill at St James' nor 'so well at Carlton House' as Fox, 59–60; refuses to send Bishop to St Domingue, VIII, 91hn, 92–3, 103; alleged to have attended meeting on parliamentary reform, 109n1; 'marked for the Guillotine', 304; arranges seat for French Laurence, on terms, IX, 81–2; his inaction on Corsican affairs, 156n3

and the Burkes

willing to help find seat in Parliament for RBSr, II, 6, 9, 10, VIII, 12n3; helps Jane Burke's brother to employment in America, III, 331; appealed to, for seat for WB, 53, IV, 287; supports WB's petition against opponent's election, III, 153–4; urged to find

Cavendish Bentinck, William Henry (*cont.*)
post for WB in Bengal, 346hn, asked to safeguard his mission to Raja of Tanjore, IV, 305, 314, his safe arrival reported to, 379–80; WB on 'the One man whom Greatness doth not Spoil', 287hn; RBJr wants him to use influence with Ponsonbys, VII, 257; RBJr's claims on, 406; thinks RBJr unfit to bring into Parliament, 410tn; a pall bearer for RBJr, 570n1, VIII, 140 EB and Rockingham spend recess with, I, 287; visits EB, II, 3, 11, V, 177, 340; asked by EB to use influence with East India proprietors, II, 391; EB leases farm once his, 548; gets news of coup against Pigot from EB, III, 417–18; helpful on plan for economical reform, IV, 196–8; withdrawal from Bristol explained to, 266–75, 284hn; on EB's loss of seat, 286tn; EB asks place for bailiff's son as a gardener's boy, 382–3, recommends sister in Ireland to, V, 30, 32, and Boswell, 105, solicits post for little Zouch from, 110; Bulstrode and Beaconsfield will become inseparable, 216; perambulates EB round his Marybone Estate, 344; concern for EB's health, 407–8; EB dines with, 412, VI, 33; vexed at Oxford's mismanagement of honorary degree for EB, 195tn; news of Impeachment brought to Bulstrode, 197; EB attends levee with, 219hn, 238; his version of EB's difference with Fox, 248–9hn, 254n4, 272n; EB retains friendship with after break with Fox, 255, 331, 332hn, VII, 82, 122tn, 447, IX, 445hn; and EB's debts, VI, 271n2; RBJr thinks EB will break with, 316n1, 329n1, VII, 419tn; ought not to be incurably alienated, VI, 440; EB has never concealed anything from, 453; at ease with EB but avoids politics, VII, 3; fears the Burke leaning for the arduous and disputable, 4; EB will not be seen to vote differently from, 63; both attend dinner for Bintinayes, 107; EB attends his installation as Chancellor of Oxford, 207, 227–8; sends news of victory of Valenciennes, 380, and of the Glorious First of June, 549; and EB's pension, 451tn, and peerage, 550hn, 550n1, VIII, 287; EB and Fitzwilliam meet at his house, 76; EB solicits for Winstanley, 84–5, for Dr Morgan, 283; EB must choose

between Fitzwilliam and, 206; informs EB of duel between Fitzwilliam and Beresford, 275, 276, 282; appealed to, on behalf of a confidence trickster, 329–30; EB protests to, against settlement of refugee clergy in Penn, 317–18, 319–20, 323–4, orders countermanded, 322–3; EB has not seen for months, 383, 389, IX, 207, but has not broken with, VIII, 389n5; becomes a Trustee for *émigré* school at Penn, 397, 399, 442, IX, 13tn, 35, is asked to continue in EB's will, 379; a pall bearer for EB, 374

examines *Thoughts on Present Discontents*, II, 121hn; *Address to the King* shown to, III, 314, his Queries on, 317; thinks *Reflections* the true Whig creed, VI, 161n2, 178, IX, 438n4; danger to Fox–Portland group from *Appeal*, VI, 306, 369n2; says nothing to EB on, 415, 418, IX, 438; agrees with 'Thoughts on French Affairs', VII, 313; 'Observations on the Conduct of the Minority' addressed to, 436, told not to read it yet, 438, 446, 497; reads it, 446–7, 'perfectly at ease' about unauthorised printing of it, IX, 240n1, 243, 245; rumoured to have prevailed on EB not to publish *Regicide Peace*, VIII, 418n2

EB's unalterable affection for, III, 304, V, 33, 50, VII, 438, 447, 449, VIII, 323, IX, 160, names him as his friend in his will, 377; 'the best man and the best friend', V, 32, 'dearest and most honour'd name', 93; EB's implicit confidence in, 427; his virtuous, calm, steady character, VI, 11–12; unblemished honour, VIII, 36; as essentially bright as the sun but in eclipse, 206; thinks one way and acts in the contrary way, IX, 126; his irresolute conduct, 159; an '*excellent* person', but 'perplexed and inconsistent', 271

Personal

on the Quarto pamphlet, II, 114n1; ill with gout, 190n2; David Hartley his protégé, III, 24n1; Champion sends porcelain to, 142n4, appeals for assistance against Wedgwood, 451; robbed of his watch, 172n1; visits Keppel at Portsmouth, IV, 37hn; death of his brother-in-law, 375–6, 376–7; thrown from his horse, 400, V, 28–9, 31–2, 33, 36, and again, VII, 197, 204, 206; Kiernan owes his post

Cheveley, Jameneau
  correspondence with, listed above, p. 114
Chidley, Dick, accompanies EB to Dublin,
  I, 1
Chiswell, Richard Muilman Trench (1735–
  97), M.P., VIII, 241n7; commits
  suicide, IX, 235n4
Choiseul-Beaupré,   Charles-Antoine-
  Étienne, Marquis de (b. 1739): his
  children at *émigré* school, Penn, VIII,
  460n3, IX, 31
Choiseul-Beaupré, Eugène de, attends
  émigré school at Penn, IX, 31
Choiseul-Beaupré, Octave de, attends
  émigré school at Penn, IX, 31
Choiseul-Beaupré, Xavier de, attends
  émigré school at Penn, VIII, 460, IX,
  31
Choiseul-Stainville, Claude-Antoine- Gab-
  riel, Duc de (1760–1838): shipwrecked
  and taken prisoner, VIII, 376; also
  mentioned, VII, 486n1
Choiseul-Stainville, Étienne-François de,
  Duc de Choiseul (1719–85), Minister
  of Foreign Affairs: forms party against
  Madame Du Barry, II, 67–8; dismissed
  from office, 182n4; not returned to
  office on death of Louis XV, 539, III,
  24, 31; attack on in *Reflections*, VI,
  234hn; criticism modified in defer-
  ence to Mme de Choiseul, 234–7,
  285n1, 337; *Mémoires*, 235n1
Choiseul, Duchesse de (Louise-Honorine
  Crozat du Châtel, 1735–1801), wife
  of the preceding
  correspondence with, listed above, p. 114
  Burgoyne's appeal to, IV, 362hn; criticism of Choiseul modified in defer-
  ence to, VI, 234–7, 337; pays her husband's debts, 234; publishes *Mémoires
  de M. le duc . . .*, 235
Cholmley, Nathaniel (1721–91), M.P. for
  Boroughbridge: attends York County
  meeting, II, 63; offered seat at Malton,
  III, 48n2, IV, 183n3; opposes County
  petition, 183
Cholmley, Mrs Nathaniel (Anne Jessie
  Smelt), third wife of the preceding,
  IV, 183
Cholmondeley, George, 3rd Earl of
  Cholmondeley (1703–70), IX, 397n1
Cholmondeley, George James, 4th Earl of
  Cholmondeley (1749–1827)
  correspondence with, listed above, p. 114
  takes part in conversations with Grafton,
  IV, 143, 144; Shelburne's supporter,
  157; EB meets for first time, IX,
  397

Christian VII, King of Denmark, visit to
  England, II, 1, 15
Christie, Thomas (1761–96), editor of
  Analytical Review, V, 412
  correspondence with, listed above, p. 114
  Letters on the Revolution of France, an
  answer to *Reflections*, VI, 141n2, 273n3;
  also mentioned, VI, 451n2
Christ's Hospital, VIII, 293, X, 35
Chrysel, Christopher
  correspondence with, listed above, p. 114
Chudleigh, Elizabeth, *see* Kingston,
  Duchess of
Church, John Barker (*c.* 1746–1818), M.P.
  for Wendover, VI, 452; plan for escape
  of La Fayette, IX, 199
Church of England:
  EB's attachment to, II, 298–9, III, 111,
    IV, 84, baptized in, VI, 215, IX, 261;
    support for, does not exclude tolera-
    tion for Dissenters, III, 111, or for
    Catholics, IV, 248; EB prepared to
    vote for repeal of Sacramental test
    (1778), 7, 17; wants no alteration in,
    VI, 101–4; must be continued on firm
    foundation, VII, 118; when Establish-
    ment goes everything will go, VIII, 44;
    if Catholicism destroyed, the Church
    goes too, 131
  supported by Tories, II, 126; Dissenters'
    objections to, VI, 103–4, 420n4;
    Portland's attachment to, VII, 168,
    270, 571; Archbishop of Canterbury's
    fears for, VIII, 193
  clergy of: EB opposes relief from
    Thirty-Nine Articles for, II, 298hn,
    299, 309–10, 535, III, 111n2; import-
    ance of, to Whig interest in Bristol,
    IV, 350; raise funds for refugee clergy,
    VII, 390n2
  also mentioned, IV, 251tn, VI, 125n1, 233,
    VII, 300, 329, 405, IX, 442, 471
Church of Ireland: attitude to Catholics
  and Protestant Dissenters, VI, 462,
  VII, 119; proper attitude of Catholics
  to, 11, 12n3; ought to be continued
  on a firm foundation, 118, Government
  will allow no measure to shake it,
  131n2, superior offices of State and
  Army should be reserved for con-
  formers to, 350; declaration of Catholics
  on, 127–8; Catholics accused of de-
  signing its overthrow, 236; menaced
  by proposal to pay Catholic clergy out
  of State funds, 297–8; Catholic toleration regarded as danger to, 364, VIII,
  175, Archbishop of Canterbury sounds
  the alarm, 193; and Provostship of

Court (*cont.*)

IV, 449; abet iniquitous system in India, V, 155; Court People absent themselves from final vote on Impeachment, 314n1

EB and: attacks on, in *Thoughts on the Present Discontents*, II, 108–9, EB advised against publishing, 119, 122, political creed of Rockingham Whigs on Court system expressed in, 136, hostility to Courtiers, 150; Court writers charge EB with being Junius, 251; 'hue and cry' of the Court raised against him, 277; and *Address to the King*, III, 312–13; oppose EB's Welsh Bill, IV, 211; none but the staunchest Court Tories withstand Economical Reform, 219; EB will be looked on as victim of both Opposition and, 292; EB squibbed with 'a Court Tye', VI, 230n2

advantages to Bristol of Court candidate, III, 4; Bristol going to the Devil through manoeuvres of, 195; Court addresses in Bristol, 224; Bristol better served by EB than by Court members, IV, 50–1; and Bristol petition, 200; their candidate, Brickdale, 268

Grafton refuses 'Court employment', I, 205n5; Botetourt favoured by, II, 14n1; Bloomsbury gang at loggerheads with, 59n1; power of, in Sussex, 66–7; Lord Trevor supports, 77n2; interest in Buckinghamshire, 85; Sulivan goes over to, 106; Yorkshire opposed to, 155; Clive's abhorrence of, 181, driven to, 355, 'at the Bottom' of resolution on him, 433tn, if Court triumphs Clive will rule India, 472; Mansfield said to be supreme director of, 187–8; obliged to cling to Lord North, 207; Wilkes's triumph over, 221–2, assaulted by, 490; vexed by Cumberland match, 287; Germain's bias towards, 404; Earl of Ossory a supporter of, 472hn; Camden desperate with, III, 36; Lord Clare devoted to, 45; London Quakers hurt by contact with, 208; fails to get support in West country, 209; Archbishop of York their mouthpiece on Dissenters, 383; Fox not by nature a Court man, 385, no truth in talk of his making up to, IV, 29; Keppel censured by Court runners, 13, scandalous calumnies against him, 299, wins independence of Court at Surrey, 303; Burgoyne

persecuted by, 127–8, 154; and Richmond's scheme for parliamentary reform, 167; Wesley carries Methodists over to, 271; Whigs excluded from, 295, V, 167n1; Lascelles Court candidate for Yorkshire, IV, 301; North Party think themselves favoured by, V, 57; Pitt's predilection for, 130n3; Norwich carried by Court candidate, 282; Court majority in St Anne's parish, Westminster, reduced, 411; independence in Scotland being rooted out by, 424; 'Little Fry of Court Politicians' exult at Fitzwilliam's recall, VIII, 176, 228; Portland has no authority with, IX, 159

see also George III; King's friends

Court guides, II, 406

Court Jacobins, IX, 209

Court newspapers, the *Sun*, IX, 220–1

Court runners, IV, 13

Court writers, II, 251, 260

Court of St James: EB attends levees at, VI, 238–9, 333n1, 362–3, VII, 514, VIII, 30, 337

Courtenay, Anne, *see* Cork, Countess of

Courtenay, John (1738–1816), M.P.: a turtle dinner with EB, V, 269; member of Committee of Managers, 371; EB drops in at his party, 387; escapes with EB from Westminster election, 409; visits Beaconsfield, VI, 5n3, 15n2; mediates between Priestley and Fox, 15; member of Literary Club, 220; buffoonish reply to Laurence, IX, 270n2

The Rape of Pomona, V, 269n1

Courtenay, Michael (d. 1772), married to EB's cousin, I, 216n1, 328, 329, VII, 106n2, X, 3–4

Courtenay, Mrs Michael (Catherine Nagle), EB's cousin, wife of the preceding, I, 216; visits EB in London, 328–9, X, 3–4; EB sends money to, VII, 106; also mentioned, X, 42

Courtenay, William, 2nd Viscount Courtenay (1742–88)

correspondence with, listed above, p. 116

Chairman of Devon County Committee, IV, 258–60

Coutts, Thomas (1735–1822), banker, VII, 471

Cowles, William (d. 1778), partner of Joseph Harford, III, 79tn, IV, 224n3

Cowles, William, Bristol glass merchant, III, 367

Cowley, Abraham: 'Of Greatness', I, 32; EB will enter into a course of,

Cowley, Abraham (*cont*.)
147; Latin works of, sent by Dr Johnson, II, 145–6; 'On the Death of Mr Crawshaw', v, 211n5, X, 44

Cowper, Henry (1758–1840), Clerk Assistant to House of Lords: EB's aversion to, VIII, 113, 114; William Cowper's sonnet to, 113n1

Cowper, General Spencer (*c*. 1724–97)
correspondence with, listed above, p. 116

Cowper, William (1731–1800), poet, VIII, 113n1

Cowper, William (*c*. 1754–1823), Deputy-Resident at Lucknow, v, 417

Cox, Cornelius, Dublin merchant, I, 3n9, 52

Cox, Mr, Army agent, VII, 560n3

Coxe, Sir John, IV, 92hn

Coxe, Richard Hippisley (*c*. 1742–86), M.P. for Somerset, II, 127, III, 221n5, IV, 298
correspondence with, listed above, p. 116
James Nagle given introduction to, IV, 92

Crabbe, George (d. 1786), father of the poet, IV, 337

Crabbe, George (1754–1832)
correspondence with, listed above, p. 116
appeal to EB for help answered, IV, 337–9; EB sends *The Library* to Eden, 359, and to Dr Haliday, 361, assists him to ordination, 373hn; his good character, 374; becomes curate of Aldeburgh, 374n3, and later chaplain to Duke of Rutland, 453–4; a welcome visitor at the Burkes', v, 59, 261; sends EB MS of *The Village*, 59hn, and *The Newspaper*, 208; indignant at party writings against EB, 208n1; also mentioned, IX, 472

Crabbe, Mrs George (Sarah Elmy, 1751–1813), wife of the preceding, IV, 338n5, V, 208

Crabbe, George, son of the poet, v, 208n1

Craig, Captain James Henry (1748–1812), IX, 416

Cranborne, Viscount, *see* Cecil, James

Crane, Dr Edward (*c*. 1696–1777), Prebendary of Westminster, I, 151

Cranmer, John, I, 110n1

Craufurd, Charles Gregan (1761–1821), British representative with the Austrian Army, IX, 198, X, 39

Craufurd, James, 2nd Baronet
correspondence with, listed above, p. 117

Craufurd, John
correspondence with, listed above, p. 117

Craufurd, P. George
correspondence with, listed above, p. 117

Craufurd, Quintin (1743–1819): on EB's message to Marie-Antoinette, VI, 366tn; influences Dillon's opinion of EB and RBJr, 425tn, 436hn

Craufurd, Robert (1764–1812): his despatches on Mindelheim, IX, 107n3, on siege of Kehl, 188n2; his help asked for news of James Nagle, 198

Craven, Baroness (Lady Elizabeth Berkeley, 1750–1828)
correspondence with, listed above, p. 117

Craven, William, 6th Baron Craven (1738–91)
correspondence with, listed above, p. 117
anxious for EB's help with County petition, III, 234–5

Crawford, Mrs, I, 90hn

Creagh, Michael, III, 412n3

Creagh, Mr, I, 221

Crespigny, Philip [Champion, d. 1803, M.P.]
correspondence with, listed above, p. 117

Crewe, John (1742–1829), M.P. for Cheshire: his Bill to disfranchise revenue officers, IV, 219n3, 422, 447, v, 58n1, IX, 286; EB visits in Cheshire, V, 415, 424; a 'corrupted' partizan of Democracy (RBJr), VII, 187, supports Fox, VIII, 80hn; EB warns his wife against his democratic tendencies, 303–4, 399; remains friendly with EB after Whig schism, 401; supports repeal of game laws, IX, 106n6; says Portland approves of *Two Letters*, 126; heads Cheshire Volunteers, 207n2; also mentioned, IV, 398, VII, 182, 426, VIII, 83, 84, IX, 208

Crewe, Mrs John (Frances Anne Greville, d. 1818), wife of the preceding, Whig hostess and friend of EB, IV, 398
correspondence with, listed above, p. 117
included in EB's subscription plan for *Cecilia*, V, 26n1, VIII, 443, for *Camilla*, 462; entertains RBJr, v, 247, VII, 182n4, 197; dines with EB, v, 340; EB visits in Cheshire, 415, 424; a model of beauty and virtue, VI, 87; Jane Burke's bequest to, VII, 87n1; stays at Beaconsfield, 414, IX, 43, 44; scheme to raise money for French clergy, VII, 414, 424–6, Jane Burke's qualified participation in, 421–2, 424; asks EB for books, 426n5, 428n2
discussions with Whig politicians, VII,

Cumberland, Duchess of (*cont.*)
286–7; her language on public subjects, VI, 390

Cumberland, Richard (1732–1811), poet and dramatist
correspondence with, listed above, p. 117
praises *Reflections*, VI, 157–8

Cunliffe, Sir Ellis, 1st Baronet (1717–67), his house in Wimbledon bought by Rockingham, II, 218–19

Cunningham, Timothy (d. 1789), publishes *New and Complete Law Dictionary*, 1764–5, I, 201

Cunninghame, Robert (d. 1801), later (1796) 1st Baron Rossmore: A.D.C. to Halifax in Ireland, I, 192; Commander-in-Chief in Ireland, IX, 116n2; created Baron to remove him from command, 116, 182; his calm and moderate temper, 121; keeps Fitzwilliam informed on Ireland, 175

Cuppage, Rev. Burke, Rector of Coleraine, father of Capt. William Cuppage, IX, 450hn

Cuppage, Mrs Burke (*née* Kirkpatrick, d. 1792), wife of the preceding, IX, 450hn

Cuppage, Captain, later Major, William (1759–1832), cousin of WB, protégé of EB, VI, 13hn
correspondence with, listed above, p. 117–18
his budget of news, V, 374; Adjutant for his battalion at Woolwich, VI, 13; promoted Captain, 116n2; EB solicits post for, as Aide de camp to Howe, 116–17, VII, 142; his miraculous cure, VI, 116, VIII, 314; reported departure for Gibralter, VI, 137; at Margate with EB, 318; marriage, 463n4; stays at Beaconsfield, VI, 137, 318, VII 97; as his own son to EB, 142; in search of a French teacher, 506; bequeathed a ring by RBJr, 600; EB solicits Windham for employment in the Barrack line for, VIII, 314; acts with EB over WB's arrest for debt, 359, 360–1, 458–9; WB's allowances paid through, IX, 87, 92, 104
also mentioned, V, 277, VII, 3, 31, 74, 478, IX, 86n1, 450

Cuppage, Mrs William (Jane, d. 1832), wife of the preceding, widow of Major William Cairnes, VI, 463n4, VII, 478n1, 506

Curchod, Suzanne, *see* Necker, Madame Jacques

Curran, John Philpot (1750–1817), Irish M.P.: promises support for Catholic franchise, VII, 45; objects to wording of RBJr's petition, 46n6; moves for inquiry into Irish disturbances, IX, 122, 138; EB recommends as Counsel to Hussey, 358; also mentioned, VIII, 179n2

Curry, Dr John (*c.* 1702–80), Dublin friend of EB
correspondence with, listed above, p. 118
acts on behalf of Catholic Committee in proposed presentation to EB, IV, 117–18hn, 120tn; advised on attitude of Catholics to civil authorities, 118–19; approves EB's plan for Catholic education, 119n1
Historical Memoirs of the Irish Rebellion, EB's notes for London edition, I, 201–2; *A Candid Enquiry . . .*, 276n1

Cursetji Manuar, IV, 356n1
correspondence with, listed above, p. 118
see also Maratha Agents

Curson, Samuel
correspondence with, listed above, p. 118

Curt, Louis, Chevalier de (b. 1722), French *émigré* in England: appointed agent to Supreme Court of Justice in Martinique, VIII, 142, IX, 443

Curtin, Catherine (b. 1759), EB's cousin, I, 126n5

Curtin, Daniel (d. 1786), merchant in Cork, I, 126n5, III, 391n9

Curtin, Mrs Daniel (Margaret Nagle, d. 1798), EB's cousin, wife of the preceding, I, 126

Curtis, Rev. Charles (*c.* 1757–1829), Rector of St Martin's, Birmingham, VII, 333

Curwen, John Christian (*c.* 1756–1826), M.P.: attacks EB's pension, VIII, 339–41; supports repeal of game laws, IX, 106n6

Curwen, Samuel (1715–1802), American loyalist, III, 289n4

Curzon, Assheton (1730–1820), later (1794) 1st Baron Curzon, EB's country neighbour, VI, 120, VIII, 319
correspondence with, listed above, p. 118

Curzon, Nathaniel (1751–1837), M.P., III, 90n4

Cust, Sir John (1718–70), 3rd Baronet, Speaker of the House of Commons, I, 232, 233, 242n1

Customs, Collector of, *see* Burrows, Edward; Harson, Daniel

Customs, Commissioners of: satisfied with RBSr's conduct, I, 212; Collector of Hull sentenced by, 258

Cymmrodorion Society, IV, 239hn

Deane, Silas (*cont.*)
American army, III, 320n4; implicated in Bristol arson case, 327tn
Deane, Thomas, Bristol Alderman (*c.* 1717–98), IV, 243
Dease, Patrick, Dublin merchant, VIII, 164
Debating Society, later the Academy of Belles Lettres, forerunner of Trinity College, Dublin, Historical Society: starts slowly, I, 37–8, needs rousing from sleep, 44; 'our nonsense' too much for Shackleton, 50–1; all Friends in the Club, 53; becomes the Debating Society, 90hn; debates and proceedings, 91–4; EB's speech at (1747), 92n1; Shackleton the Anacreon of the Society, 101; and authorship of the *Reformer*, 102
Debrett, John (d. 1822), printer and publisher: publishes Elliot's speeches, v, 402–3, 413, 422, London edition of *Letter to Langrishe*, VII, 95, *Address from the General Committee of Roman Catholics*, 103; altercation between Secretary's Office and, VI, 461; delays in publication of Bintinayes' *Observations*, VII, 120, 129; also mentioned, v, 161n1, 162n2
de Burgh, John Smith, 11th Earl of Clanricarde (1720–82)
correspondence with, listed above, p. 114
his Galway estates, III, 255, IV, 438n1
Declonard, Masterson
correspondence with, listed above, p. 119
Decotte, Peter
correspondence with, listed above, p. 119
Decrétot, Jean-Baptiste (1743–1817), woollen manufacturer of Louviers and Deputy to Third Estate, VI, 10n3
correspondence with, listed above, p. 119
Defenders, Catholic agrarian organisation: conflicts with Peep of Day Boys, VII, 237n3, 285n4; sentences imposed on, 285n6; French sympathies, 361n1; Catholic business men charged as, VIII, 194n2; denounced by Catholic Archbishop, 351n5, IX, 344n3; the only restraint on Protestant Ascendancy, VIII, 378; members seized for the Navy, IX, 117n1; surprised in their Cabin fortresses, 163, scores and hundreds lose life or liberty, 228
Defoe, Daniel (*c.* 1661–1731), on the 'Long Room' at Customs House, v, 94n1
De Grey, Thomas, 2nd Baron Walsingham (1748–1818), v, 260n1

De Grey, William (1719–1800), later (1781) 1st Baron Walsingham, Attorney General, I, 345, X, 42
Delacroix de Contaut, Charles (1741–1805), Minister for Foreign Affairs in Revolutionary France: his lavish costume, VIII, 376; discussions with Malmesbury, IX, 101n5, 208, 219
De la Fontaine, Elias Benjamin, the Burkes' stockjobber, II, 35
De Lancey, Alice, *see* Izard, Mrs Ralph
De Lancey, Captain James (1732–1800), leading member of New York Assembly, II, 215hn
correspondence with, listed above, p. 119
invites EB to become New York Agent, II, 215; his marriage, 311; unable to find New England pacers for EB, 312, 399, 504–5hn, 506; EB writes to, as a friend, 329, 445; receives EB's power of attorney, 312, 329; asked for abstracts on controversial measures, 398, 445hn; jockeys from Rockingham's stable unobtainable for, 449, 458–9, 460, 505; efforts to conciliate Assembly and Governor, III, 137; sells his stud and retires to England, 195; also mentioned, II, 502, III, 364hn
De Lancey, Mrs James (Margaret Allen), wife of the preceding, II, 311n3, 330, 507, III, 138
De Lancey, Colonel, later General, Oliver (1749–1822), Barrack Master General: and housing for refugee clergy, VII, 492, VIII, 321n1, 322; William Cuppage recommended for deputy to, 314
De Lancey family, influence in New York politics, II, 215hn, III, 226hn
Delany, Joseph ('Josy', b. 1717), acquaintance of EB and Shackleton, I, 1, 16, 17
Delany, Mrs Josy, I, 16
Delaval, Sir John Hussey (1728–1808), later (1786) 1st Baron Delaval, M.P.: defeated for Northumberland, III, 23; granted British barony by Pitt, v, 250n3
Delawarr, 2nd Earl, *see* West, John
Deluc, Jean André (1727–1817), Reader to Queen Charlotte, VII, 138
correspondence with, listed above, p. 119
Deluc, Madame, wife of the preceding, VII, 138
Democracy, *see* Burke, Edmund, Opinions
Democritus, VIII, 420, IX, 237
Demosthenes, IV, 48hn; RBJr begins translation of [the *Philippics*, VII, 582

Dempster, George (1732–1818), M.P., Director of East India Company
correspondence with, listed above, p. 119
political connexion with Rockingham, II, 106, III, 25; keeps duty clear to East India Company and to party, II, 107; urges EB to accept Supervisorship, 321–3; sound principles as Director, 322, 401n2, resigns, 321n3; plan for reviving credit in Scotland, 339–40; approves of Dalrymple's pamphlet, v, 164; supports Warren Hastings, 164n1, opposes his impeachment, VII, 67n2, 68; EB's rival as candidate for Glasgow Rectorship, v, 187hn; retires from politics, VII 67hn; EB asks protection for young man sailing to India, 67; differs from EB on most public matters, 67, but remains friends with him, 68; and the Kinross election (1768), IX, 394
also mentioned, II, 307hn, 320hn

Dempster, Captain John Hamilton (d. 1800), takes EB's protégé on as midshipman aboard the Rose, VII, 67–8

Dempsy, Joannes
correspondence with, listed above, p. 119

Denbigh, 6th Earl of, see Feilding, Basil

Denham, Sir John, his poem 'Cooper's Hill' quoted, I, 95

Denham, Walter (d. 1780), Rockingham's Irish under-agent, IV, 163n2

Denis, Sir Peter, 1st Baronet (d. 1778), Vice Admiral of the Blue, II, 314

Dennis, Barneby, I, 88n3

Dennis, Mrs Barneby, wife of the preceding, I, 98

Dennis, William (c. 1730–74), friend and fellow student of EB
correspondence with, listed above, p. 119
on EB's unhappy life with his father, I, 66n2; pamphlet on the Kelly controversy, 88; activities in Debating Club, 90–4; writes on Aristotle's *Poetics*, 94hn, 95; on the pain in EB's hip, 94, IX, 46n3; in search of work, I, 99, 101; on sales of the *Reformer*, 102n1; friendship with EB, 108, 114, 167, 223; his poem, *Man's Redemption*, 124n5; reads *Sublime and Beautiful*, 123n4; on EB's visits to 'the great ones', 124n5; receives benefices from Macartney, 223n1, II, 300, 301; becomes a schoolmaster, I, 268; appointed chaplain to Chief Secretary, 334; WB sends story of EB's quarrel with Bagot to, II, 126–9; Jane Burke's poor opinion of, v, 158

also mentioned, I, 96n1, 97n3, 102n1 111, 123n2, 142, 241, 342, VIII, 155

Dennis, William, Jr (c. 1756–1815): EB gets him ordained, v, 158n2, recommends him for post, 158; remains Vicar of Kilculliheen, VIII, 155; Jane Burke's poor opinion of, v, 158n5; also mentioned, I, 96hn

Dennis, Mrs William, Jr (Ellen, c. 1755–1837), wife of the preceding, v, 158n4

De Peyster, Abraham, II, 302n2

Depont, Charles-Jean-François (1767–96), member of Paris Parlement
correspondence with, listed above, p. 119
Reflections addressed to, v, 235hn, VI, 31hn, 61, 85hn, 189n3, sent to, 189; his *Answer*, 189n3, 317n3
goes with RBSr to Lord Mayor's dinner and ball, v, 235–7, VI, 31, 33; visits Beaconsfield, 31, 39, 60; the flame of liberty first lighted in him by EB, 31, 40, 42, 59; elected to *comité patriotique* in Metz, 31hn; corresponds with EB on French affairs, 31–2, 40–50, 59hn; believes events in France inevitable, 60; his radical politics, 189; Minister Plenipotentiary to Elector of Cologne, 189n4; also mentioned, 78hn

Depont, Jean-Samuel (1725–1805), father of the preceding, Intendant at Metz, VI, 31hn; introduced to EB by Mme de Genlis, v, 226–7; goes with RBSr to Lord Mayor's dinner and ball, 235–7; a victim of pickpockets, 237, 238

Depont, Mme (Marie-Madeleine-Françoise Lescoureul de la Touche), wife of the preceding, friend of Mme de Genlis, v, 226

Derby, 11th Earl of, see Stanley, Edward

Derby, 12th Earl of, see Stanley, Edward Smith

Derby, Countess of (Lady Elizabeth Hamilton, 1753–97), wife of the preceding, v, 222

Derbyshire, see County meetings

Dering, Sir Edward, 6th Baronet (1732–98), M.P., IX, 410

Dermott, Anthony (d. 1784), treasurer of the Catholic Committee, IV, 117–18hn, 120–1
correspondence with, listed above, p. 120

Derry, Bishop of, see Hervey, Frederick Augustus

Desborow, Captain Lieutenant John
correspondence with, listed above, p. 120

Des Essars, Pierre (*c.* 1372–1413), VI, 111n1

Desfrançois, Abbé Louis-Antoine (*b. c.* 1728), French translator of *Sublime and Beautiful*, I, 187–8
correspondence with, listed above, p. 120

Desmond, 3rd Earl of, *see* Fitzgerald, Garrett

Desmoulins, John
correspondence with, listed above, p. 120

Despenser, 11th Baron Le, *see* Le Despenser

D'Estaing, Jean-Baptiste-Charles-Henri-Hector, Comte, *see* Estaing, Comte d'

Devaynes, John (*c.* 1727–1801), a Governor of Christ's Hospital, VIII, 293

Devaynes, William (*c.* 1730–1809), Chairman of East India Company, IV, 304n2; his attempted robbery of Tanjore revenues, 304, 306, 307, 308–11, 316; Hastings's letter to, VI, 63n1; EB appeals against his decision on Fowke's pension, 249–52; his interest sought as Governor of Christ's Hospital, VIII, 293

Devereux, James Edward (*c.* 1760–1845)
correspondence with, listed above, p. 120
member of Catholic Committee, VIII, 327hn; appeals to EB on behalf of James Semple Lisle, sentenced to transportation, 327–9; also mentioned, 273

Devereux, Rev. John (d. 1838), refugee from Douay: teaches English at *émigré* school, Penn, IX, 61n4, 128

Devereux, Robert
correspondence with, listed above, p. 120

Devereux, Sidney
correspondence with, listed above, p. 120

Devi Singh, Raja (d. 1805), revenue farmer in Rangpur, V, 372n3; his knavish character, 328n3, VII, 250; alleged bribery of Hastings, V, 372; his extortionate demands, 372hn, 384, 385, VII, 254; Hastings disclaims responsibility for his acts, V, 381hn, VII, 253n2; his defence, V, 385n1, 386tn, 'turns accuser into defender', 467; alleged agent of Hastings, VII, 249, 250

Devin, Jean-Jacques, Marquis de Fontenay (*c.* 1762–*c.* 1815), VIII, 376n2

Devisme, Louis (1720–76)
correspondence with, listed above, p. 120

Devonshire, *see* County meetings

Devonshire, Dukes of, *see* Cavendish, William

Devonshire, Duchess of (Georgiana Spencer, 1757–1806), wife of the 5th Duke, III, 41n1
correspondence with, listed above, p. 120
her interest in parliamentary proceedings, III, 421–3; supports Sheridan at Stafford, IV, 282n2; is sent *Speech on Economical Reform*, 212hn; included in subscription list for *Cecilia*, V, 26n1; takes M. Parisot de St Marie under her protection, 104; congratulated on Duke's maiden speech, IV, 213
Diary quoted: on Fox's Cabinet plan, V, 430n3; English Princes, 431n5; Regency crisis, 436hn, 438n1, 439n1; Fox–North coalition, 440n5; Mrs Fitzherbert, 444n1; Sheridan and Hastings's trial, 457n4
also mentioned, VI, 116hn

Deyzac
correspondence with, listed above, p. 120

Dickens, Rev. Dr Samuel (1719–91)
correspondence with, listed above, p. 120

Dickinson, John (1732–1808), heads battalion to reinforce General Lee, III, 265

Dickinson, William (1745–1806), M.P., goes over to Ministry, V, 374n6

Dickson, Rev. William (1745–1804), later (1783) Bishop of Down and Connor, friend of Fox: becomes First Chaplain to Lord Lieutenant of Ireland, V, 92

Diderot, Denis (1713–84), VI, 114, IX, 320n1

Diede, Wilhelm Christopher, Baron (1732–1807), Danish Minister in London, II, 15

Digby, Henry, 7th Baron Digby (1731–93)
correspondence with, listed above, p. 120
asks EB to renew his brother's deputy-paymastership in Minorca, IV, 445–6

Digby, Kenelm (*b. c.* 1754), Paymaster in East India Company's Southern Army, brings letters from WB in India, V, 344–5

Digby, Captain, later Admiral, Robert (1732–1815): witness at Keppel's trial, IV, 37; Commander-in-Chief in North America, 445–6

Dignan, David Brown (*c.* 1755–80), swindler
correspondence with, listed above, p. 120
EB helps to get him transferred from hulks, IV, 133–5, X, 5–6; his imaginary plot to kill the King, IV, 134n2, 135tn

Diler Himmat Khan, Nawab of Farrukhabad (d. 1796), Hastings accused of oppressive acts against, VIII, 160

Dillon, Arthur Richard (1721–1806), Archbishop of Narbonne: EB's acquaintance with, V, 266, VIII, 91n2; also mentioned, 236

Dillon, Governor Arthur Richard (1750–94), Governor of St Kitts, V, 266n7

Dillon, Charles-Edouard, Comte (1751–1839), friend of Marie-Antoinette, later Gentleman of the Bedchamber to Comte d'Artois, V, 266–7; sent as envoy of French Princes to London, VI, 424–5; instructed to observe RBJr, 425hn, 436tn, and to borrow money, 425n1; reports on EB and RBJr, 436–8; RBJr bound to support Bintinayes against, 438; attends Levee, 438n4; his regiment, VIII, 376n6

Dillon, Eleanor, see Osmond, Comtesse d'

Dillon, Henry, 11th Viscount Dillon (1705–87), his zeal as a Catholic, IX, 344; also mentioned, V, 266n7

Dillon, John (d. 1745), schoolfellow of EB at Ballitore, killed in a duel, I, 51
his wife and children, I, 51

Dillon, Sir John, Irish M.P., IV, 19n1

Dillon, Robert (1710–64), Irish banker settled at Bordeaux, VIII, 91n2; also mentioned, V, 266n6, VI, 199hn

Dillon, Roger-Henri de (1762–1831), Abbé d'Oigny, V, 266n6; an acquaintance of EB, 266–7

Dillon, Theobald, Comte de (1745–92), murdered by his troops, VII, 160n5

Dillon, William, Ballitore barber, his note, I, 9

Dillon Lee, Charles, 12th Viscount Dillon (1745–1813)
correspondence with, listed above, p. 120
speeches in Irish House of Lords, VII, 443n3, IX, 334n2; attacks Hussey's pastoral letter, 342; leading member of Secret Committee, 342, 345; his vindictive attack on Catholics, 344; 'the most contemptible wretch in Ireland', 345, 348

Diocletian, his cabbage garden, V, 150n2

Dionysius Cato, Disticha de Moribus, used at the émigré school, Penn, VIII, 461

Dionysius, the 'Younger', VIII, 216

Dissenters
in England: Rockingham Party supported by, I, 348n1, II, 492, III, 208, 383, deserted by in 1784, V, 471; EB supported by in Bristol, III, 3hn, 47; Bill for Relief of (1772), II, 310n2, petition for re-introduction, 423–4, III, 111–12; alleged disaffection to monarchy, IV, 8; support for Economical Reform, 202hn; Gordon riots and, 248; EB asked to support motion for repeal of Test and Corporation Acts (1789), V, 469, absents himself from debate, 470–2, again asked to support repeal (1790), VI, 82; Priestley's weight with, 15, 24; growing radical tendencies among leaders, 83–4, 91; relations with Fox, 84, 129, VII, 56–7, 151, 193; toleration claimed as 'natural right', VI, 100hn, 102; attempt to force test on candidates, 102–3; their French sympathies, 103, 419–22, VII, 119; lead celebrations at Crown and Anchor, VI, 125–6; and the Birmingham riots, 306–7; Yorkshire Dissenters adopt Priestley and his Cause, 420; their politics based on 'rights of man', 421; their radical ideas a danger to the Party, VII, 55–7; Jacobin sentiments, 177, Penn 'full of Jacobins and Dissenters', VIII, 321

in Ireland: Dissenters clause in Relief Bill, III, 459hn, 461, 464–5, IV, 6–8; militia open to, 8n1, 9, 17; unanimous for Catholic toleration, 401; danger of junction with Catholics, VII, 24–5, 26, 33, 64, 69, 72, kept aloof from them by Castle intrigues, 44, 88, 243; an incurable alienation not to be suffered, 118; continue supporting Catholics, 237, 242, 256, 268; affected by revolutionary principles, 294–5; greater advantages than in England, 350, VIII, 22, IX, 125; comparative numbers of Catholics, Episcopalians and, VIII, 55; 'professed democrates' in the North, 171; annual Government grant to increased, 203–4; 'Dissenting' secretary appointed by Catholic delegates, IX, 133n2

also mentioned, IV, 408, VI, 132hn, VII, 11, 164, 245, 480, IX, 255

Dixon, Jeremiah, Yorkshire follower of Rockingham, II, 116n1, III, 216n8

Dixon, Mary, III, 216n8

Dobinson, Robert, brings reports of Pigot's death in India, III, 417n4

Doctors' Commons: EB supports Ledwich's admission to, V, 15–16; French Laurence admitted to, VI, 65n5; also mentioned, IX, 270n2, 379

Dodge, Rev. Robert (*c.* 1758–97)
correspondence with, listed above, p. 120
recommended to Champion in Bristol, IV, 126; returns from Continent with letter for RBJr, V, 405; goes as tutor to Viscount Boyle on the Grand Tour, VI, 239hn, VII, 84–5; conversation with Prince Kaunitz on *Reflections*, VI, 239–40

Dodsley, James (1724–97), EB's publisher, IX, 96n1, X, 4
correspondence with, listed above, p. 120
publishes with Robert Dodsley, *Vindication of Natural Society*, I, 127hn, *Sublime and Beautiful*, 123n4, 127hn, 190n4; engages EB to edit *Annual Register*, 127hn, 174–5, 329n7, III, 182n7, V, 373n2, IX, 96n1; continues publishing business alone (1759), I, 174hn
works of EB published by, after 1759: *Speech on American Taxation*, III, 93hn; *Letter to Sheriffs of Bristol*, 334n2; *Two Letters . . . to Gentlemen in . . . Bristol*, 431hn; *Speech on the Nabob of Arcot's Debts*, V, 218–19; *Reflections*, VI, 150, 177n6; speeches at the Bristol election, ed. 2, 179n1; *Letter to a Member of the National Assembly*, 253tn; *Appeal*, ed. 3, 360, 378; *Works*, quarto ed., VIII, 201; 'Case' suggested for printing, VII, 222; presentation copies ordered from, VI, 196
his illness and death, IX, 96n1
also mentioned, II, 113n4, V, 208, VII, 95n3

Dodsley, Robert (1703–64), EB's publisher, IX, 96n1, X, 4
correspondence with, listed above, p. 120
published by James Dodsley and: *Sublime and Beautiful*, I, 123n4, 127hn, ed. 2, 128n4, terms of payment, 190n4; 'Abridgment of English History' (fragment), 164n1, 202n3; *Vindication of Natural Society*, 127hn, terms of payment, 190n4; engages EB to edit *Annual Register*, 127hn, IX, 470
EB recommends two friends to, I, 127, 128; introduces EB's writings to Shenstone, 128
also mentioned, I, 148n3, 288n4

Dodwell, Henry (d. 1784), man of letters
correspondence with, listed above, p. 120
spends Christmas with the Burkes, II, 177, 179; listed as Irish absentee landowner, 484

Dol-de-Bretagne, Bishop of, *see* Hercé, Urbain-René de

Dolphin, Hubert Thomas (*c.* 1771–1829), of Lincoln's Inn: his amazing progress, VII, 494, VIII, 295; stays at Beaconsfield, 295

Dolphin, Oliver (d. 1805), friend and neighbour of EB's sister in Ireland, father of the preceding
correspondence with, listed above, p. 120
acts as guardian to EB's niece, VI, 66–7, VII, 493–4, VIII, 295; also mentioned, IX, 467
his family, VI, 67

Dolphin, Mrs Oliver (Margaret Helena Collin), wife of the preceding, her parental care for EB's niece, VII, 493–4

Dolphin, Redmond (d. 1791), distant relative of EB, VI, 66

Dolphin, Mrs Redmond (Jane French), wife of the preceding, VI, 66n3

Dominica, *see* West Indies

Donaldson, Alexander (d. 1794), Scottish bookseller: opposes Bill for the Relief of Booksellers, X, 4n2

Doneraile, 1st Baron, *see* St Leger, St Leger

Doneraile, 4th Viscount, *see* St Leger, Hayes

Donoughmore, Baroness, *see* Hutchinson, Mrs John Hely

Donston, George [b. 1724]
correspondence with, listed above, p. 120

Doran, Felix, Liverpool merchant and friend of EB: arranges transport of bull to Ireland, II, 6, 12, 21

Dorchester, 1st Baron, *see* Carleton, General Guy

Dorchester, 1st Earl of, *see* Damer, Joseph

Dorset, *see* County meetings

Dorset, 3rd Duke of, *see* Sackville, John Frederick

Dorset, Duchess of (Arabella Diana Cope, 1769–1825), wife of the preceding, VI, 349n1, 396

Douce, William Henry, EB's attorney, partner of Henry Rivington
correspondence with, listed above, p. 121
engaged in suit against Owen, IX, 243n7, 245n6, 288n3; also mentioned, 102hn

Doughty, Catherine, *see* Lukin, Mrs George

Douglas, Archibald James Edward, 1st Baron Douglas, his Case, V, 373n5, also mentioned, II, 322n2, IX, 432hn

Dundas, Henry (*cont.*)

on Irish Catholics, 22–9, 33–7, 126–8, 130–8, 324–7, finds RBJr's letters too long to read, 84; supports Catholic relief, VI, 470n1, VII, 3hn, 9n2, 22, 34tn, 38n, later supports franchise for Catholics, 327–8tn, 342hn, 350n5; and 'Letter to Langrishe', 49–50; a cold interview with EB, 81; Keogh regards RBJr as spy of, 201n6; and petition of Fellows of Trinity College, Dublin, 453–4, VIII, 47; discusses Irish affairs with EB, 173, 177–80, 383, IX, 349, 443–4; other references, VI, 462n6, VII, 13n3, 47n4, 72n2, 84, 297n3, 508tn, VIII, 194

Home Secretary (1791–4): appoints Wentworth Governor of Nova Scotia, VII, 7–8; compromises on slave trade, 122, his proposals, 125tn; negotiates with Loughborough for broader bottom, 192–3, 206; and the Pattern Dagger, 328; offers Elliot a post, 429n1; is asked for place for RBJr, 429n5; supports jury trial for Reeves, VIII, 353–4, 355–6; other references, VII, 530, VIII, 389

Secretary for War (1794), VIII, 34, 71hn, IX, 207, 273n1; his part in the rupture in the Ministry, VIII, 65, 71–3; 'Duumvirate' with Pitt, IX, 65

and EB: succeeded by EB as Rector of Glasgow University, V, 137, 156n2; his generosity to WB, 215tn, 297, VI, 363; admires the *Appeal*, 333, 360, reads Fitzwilliam's letters on, 415, 428–9; EB dines with, 368, 376–7, 466, VII, 477n1; and EB's pension, 573, VIII, 309–10, 316, 337; his good will to EB, 290, 384, X, 28

also mentioned, V, 140n1, 161, 206tn, 336hn, 377n2, VI, 140hn, 313n1, 391, VII, 18n1, 19n1, 27n2, 47n4, 71n1, 72n2, 341n3, 365n3, 366n1, 503hn, 515n3, 524n4, VIII, 16, 122, 352, IX, 108n1, 369n1, X, 7, 46

Dundas, Lady 'Jane' (Lady Jean Hope, 1766–1829), wife of the preceding, IX, 108n1

Dundas, Robert, Lord Arniston (1713–87), V, 137n2

Dundas, Thomas (d. 1786), IV, 100n1

Dundas, Sir Thomas, 2nd Baronet (1741–1820), later (1794) 1st Baron, M.P., Fitzwilliam's brother-in-law
correspondence with, listed above, p. 123
his awkward disposition of Orkney boroughs, V, 229, 230n3; also mentioned, 221n2, VI, 417, VII, 107, VIII, 195, 196

Dundas, Lady Charlotte (Lady Charlotte Fitzwilliam, 1746–1833), wife of the preceding, V, 229n6

Dunk, George Montagu, 2nd Earl of Halifax (1716–71): Lord Lieutenant of Ireland, I, 138, 141, 142hn, 147n5, 151; his high reputation, 156; becomes First Lord of the Admiralty, 145n5, 168; supports plan to augment Irish army, 161; and EB's Irish pension, 166, 183, 184, 190, 192n1, 193; influences King on Regency Bill, 194n2; Garrick dines with, 355; his election interests in Northampton, 356n1; appointed Secretary of State for Northern Department, II, 185; his death, 219; his attempt to give protection to Catholics, VIII, 147; also mentioned, I, 132n3, 159, 160, II, 452

Dunkin, James, son of Rev. Dr William Dunkin, I, 350

Dunkin, William (d. 1807), barrister
correspondence with, listed above, p. 123
friendship with the Burkes, IV, 386, VI, 237; goes to Bengal, IV, 386n6, 431, V, 127, X, 13, returns, VI, 137; appointed Judge and knighted, 237

Dunkin, Mrs William (Elizabeth Blacker), wife of the preceding, VI, 137

Dunkin, Rev. Dr William: his bad piece, *Boeotia!*, I, 90; EB subscribes for *Selected Poetical Works*, 350

Dunmore, 4th Earl of, *see* Murray, John

Dunn, Mary, *see* Beattie, Mrs James

Dunning, John (1731–83), later (1782) 1st Baron Ashburton, M.P.
correspondence with, listed above, p. 123
Solicitor-General, II, 174n4, 189n2; advises on Jury Bill, 174; counsel for Massachusetts petition, 518, 521, 524, for Portland, III, 327, for Keppel, IV, 35n2

speeches in the Commons, II, 197, 199, 532, III, 167, 330n4, 423, IX, 399; seconds Bill for Catholic Relief, III, 449, 456, IX, 422n2; and EB's Welsh Bill, IV, 212; his motion on the power of the Crown, IV, 217tn; awarded Duchy of Lancaster, V, 82

Recorder of Bristol, III, 46, 209, IV, 105hn, 232, 252–3, 319n7; succeeded on his death by RBSr, V, 113

also mentioned, I, 345, II, 392hn, III, 171, VII, 557tn

East India Company (*cont.*)

Bill vetoes plan, 321hn, 390n1, 391–2, 402, 403, 405–6, 410, proprietors petition against Bill, 392, 405, 408; Parliament called early on account of Company affairs, 342–4, 349, 369, 381, 387hn, still no one knows Chatham's plan for, 346; debt to Government owing to loss of revenue from tea duty, 343n5, 379, 383–4, 385, 389, 399; problem whether to reduce dividend or borrow, 344, 346–7, 349–50, 358, 361, 364, 369, 381, 386–8, 399; Court eager to seize on patronage, 351, 358, 399, 407, 411, 503, gains ground in, 451; Colebrooke accused of jobbing with inside information, 354; fall of stock in 1772, 361, 365, 379, 384; election of Directors, 389n4; EB advocates borrowing and paying reduced dividend, 384–5, 387; Fetherstone's view as a stockholder, 389; Directors negotiate with North, 423; crisis over sale of surplus tea in America, 519hn, 527hn, 527n1

Select Committee, 1772, to investigate Indian abuses, II, 345, 354, 362n1, 365, 388, 402, 404, 408, 433hn; opposed by EB, V, 455n4; evidence, VI, 245–6; Burgoyne moves to revive, II, 388; Reports, 433hn, debate on, 434–6. Secret Committee, 1772–3, to examine Company books, 388, 389–90, 399, 402; proprietors petition against, 391; 1st Report, 390n1, 2nd Report, 383n1, 3rd Report, 423

Regulating Act of 1773: will bring Company into dependence on Crown, II, 429–30, III, 404n1; opposed by Company, II, 436–7, 460hn; an infraction of their Charters, 442; qualifying holding of stock for proprietor under, 451n4, V, 31hn, Richmond's plan for packing Court, II, 459; Instructions issued under, for Parliament Commission accepted by Directors but not by General Court, 494; rival instructions drawn up by committee under Richmond, 497n2, 523, debate on the two sets, 510–11; other provisions of Act: appointments, 471hn, 503n3, VIII, 430n2; election of Court of Directors, II, 515n2; powers of Supreme Council, V, 141n2; rules for correspondence, 310, 316; issue of warrants, 325n2; salaries, VII, 373n3, VIII, 441n2; Act renewed for a year in 1778, IV, 34n7; other references X, 11, 15

Regulating Act of 1781: Charter renewal due, IV, 310; incorporates EB's suggestions, 327–8tn; provision for payment of troops, V, 126n5; Bengal Council renewed, VIII, 429n1; compared with Act of 1773, X, 11

Select Committee, 1781–83, to examine administration of justice by Company in India, IV, 352hn; EB's dominant part in, 342, 344, 394, 402, 420tn, 422, V, 67hn, 106hn, 124, 204n3, 254–5, VIII, 429; leads to Bengal Judicature Act, IV, 352, 425hn, V, 141n3; evidence, IV, 356n1, 420–1, 431n2, V, 59–60, 95n2, 209n4, VII, 146–7; terms of reference extended (Dec. 1781), V, 59hn, VIII, 429n7; Chairman, Richard Smith, V, 304n4; resolutions against Sulivan, Impey and Hastings agreed to, IV, 447; Reports, V, 60tn, 66, 83–4, 115n3, 254, IX, 459; 1st Report, V, 254n3, 300n1; 2nd Report, 300n1; 7th Report, 83n1, 84tn, 209n4; 9th Report, 65n1, 95n2, written by EB, 107, 151n3, 254 n3, VI, 88n3, VIII, 418n1; 11th Report, written by EB, V, 254n3, 420n5, VI, 3n2, VIII, 418n1; other references, V, 317, VII, 248, 559, X, 11–12, 14

Secret Committee, 1781–82, to inquire into causes of Carnatic War, IV, 346n1, 394n1, VIII, 429n6; Committee report to House, IV, 447, V, 259hn; dominated by Dundas, IV, 447n6, V, 59hn, 67hn; inquiry extended to other wars, 245n6, 264tn; Reports, 115n3, 245, 1st Report, X, 11, 4th Report, V, 68n6, 5th Report, 245n6; other references, IV, 449, V, 244n2, VII, 248

Pitt's India Act, 1784, sets up Board of Control, V, 160–1, 196hn, 230, VIII, 261tn, 383, 427–8; petition of Company servants against, V, 308hn; protest meeting in Calcutta, 255n4; disputes between Board and Directors, 196–7, 199n1, 230n5, VIII, 260–1; India Act, 1786, Governor-General's powers under, V, 297n1, 309n5, VII, 252n3

Administration of Justice: attempt to form plan for Courts of Justice in Bengal in 1771, II, 337; Supreme Court established in 1773, IV, 352hn, Company petition against, V, 308hn; Bengal Judicature Bill, 1781, IV, 352hn, passes Commons, amended in Lords,

East India Company (*cont.*)

355, reduced to a triffle, v, 334, x, 12, and cp. IV, 424–5hn; provisions of Act: revenue administration, v, 141n3, appeals to Privy Council, 334n2, appeal in Patna Cause, 335, 376–7; Sir William Jones's Discourse and address to the Grand Jury at Calcutta, 127–8; Judicature Act, 1786, 163n3, 256n1, petition of Company against, 308hn

general: dissension over Madras Councillors' action in seizing Lord Pigot, III, 346–7, IV, 321, v, 206hn, IX, 414hn, 415; Company bring case against Rumbold, IV, 340, x, 10n2, and against Whitehill, IV, 431; and the Maratha Agents, 356–8, 361–2, IX, 430–1; elections of Directors, v, 30–1, 83–4; Company ignore recall of Hastings, 41n3; export licences granted by, 42n2; Macartney on the unsatisfactory System and Management in India, 41–3, 115, 124–7, must have wider powers if he returns to India, 260hn; acquisition of Nagore, 68; arrangements with rulers of Tanjore, 68n1, of Benares, 68n7, of Marathas, 148n5, of Oudh, 148n8, with the Mughal Emperor, 264n2, with Gangagobinda Sinha, 328n3; Commander-in-Chief dismissed, 114n7; influence of Company in Parliamentary elections, 135–6; approaching bankruptcy in 1784, 147; Eden criticises Directors' Report on state of finances, 147–8, a 'fictitious solvency', 150; plan for resolving debts, x, 16; revenues from Bengal, v, 148n2, from the Carnatic, 218n1; Hippisley's plan for reform, 218n1; war with Maratha Confederacy, 303n4; Correspondence, 310n2, n4, 324tn; reported capture of Seringapatam, VII, 139n1; 'Bengal Club' of Company servants, VIII, 382; prosecutions of servants for frauds in Bengal trade, 383hn; Company disfranchised three times for their bountiful dispositions to servants, 427–8; General Court, 1794, IX, 99hn

EB and: horror and contempt at Government plan in 1767, I, 303; has little influence with Company, II, 211, takes no part in their affairs except in Parliament, 513; has no interest with, IV, 93, v, 208–9, no weight at India House, IV, 334–5, no influence at all, VII, 511, VIII, 383; takes action against Sulivan's proposals on Tan-

jore, IV, 303–12, 315; objects to appointment of Macartney as Governor, 323–5; his plan for Indian territories, 324, 327–8; objects to Company taking Benfield back into service, 334, 347; East India business takes up every hour of his day, v, 102, he is called to a duty in a conflict with Tyranny, VI, 213; solicits on behalf of John Webb for Directorship, v, 30–1; the Company has laid a load upon his ashes, IX, 237

speculation in stock by WB and Verney, I, 269–70, 272, 351n2, II, 80, 410n1; WB sells his stock, 382–3hn; EB's advice on stock, 512–13, 'never had any concern' in himself, 513, buys stock to qualify in 1780, 513n1, IV, 316n3

see also Dundas, Henry; Fowke, Joseph; Fox, Charles; Hastings, Warren, Impeachment of; Impey, Sir Elijah; Maratha Agents; Pitt, William, the Younger; Rumbold, Sir Thomas; Sulivan, Laurence

East India Bills of Exchange, II, 350, v, 42n2, 147n1, n3

East India Bonds, v, 148

East India Company Army: II, 30n1, 359, 547, IV, 385n2, 386, 458; Recruiting Bill (1770–2), II, 389; discontent among troops, 332; a reported engagement, III, 417; included in Jenkinson's Budget, IV, 34; allowances to, from Indian rulers, 324, v, 68n1; purchase of commissions in, IV, 370; Commander-in-Chief, relation to civil Government of India, v, 42; pay arrangements, 42n4, arrears of pay, 148; relations of British and Company Services, 42n4, 214hn, 214n2; Hastings accused of hiring out, 245n4, of allowing officers to farm revenues, VIII, 160n7; seize palaces of Begams, v, 392n2; in Third Mysore War, VI, 454; power of Governor General to take command of, VII, 252n3; campaigns against Rohillas, VIII, 240n3; officers and men serving in, II, 30, 359, IV, 385n2, 386n1, 458, v, 104, 455n2, VI, 243hn, 245n5, VII, 147hn, 585, VIII, 434n2

East India Company shipping: shipping service, II, 19n4, 159, 179n2; East Indiamen, 211, 313n5, IV, 90, 267n5, 267n5; their ships exempted from Smuggling Bill, IV, 82n5; *Busbridge*, v, 124n4; *Chesterfield*, VI, 238n1; *Earl of Oxford*, v, 127n3; *Earl Talbot*, 345n1; *Hawkesbury*, VI, 238n1; *Leo-*

Edwards, Captain Thomas (d. 1815), gives evidence against Hastings, v, 392, 396

Eeles, Isaac, chairman of Buckinghamshire county meeting, IV, 226hn

Effingham, 3rd Earl of, see Howard, Thomas

Égalité, Philippe, see Orléans, Louis-Philippe-Joseph, Duc d'

Egan, John (c. 1750–1810), Irish M.P., VII, 46

Egerton, Ariana Margaret (c. 1752–1827), member of Queen's Household, v, 425

Egerton, Francis, 3rd Duke of Bridgwater, I, 336n5, II, 12n1

Egerton, Isabella Frances, see Master, Mrs Richard

Egerton, John, Bishop of Bangor (d. 1787), II, 12n1

Eglinton, 10th Earl of, see Montgomerie, Alexander

Egmont, Earls of, see Perceval, John

Egremont, 2nd Earl of, see Wyndham, Charles

Egremont, 3rd Earl of, see Wyndham, George O'Brien

Ekins, Rev. Jeffery, VI, 209n4

Elam, Samuel (d. 1777), Quaker merchant of Leeds, III, 194, 216

Eland, Mr, see Elam, Samuel

Eldon, 1st Earl of, see Scott, Sir John

Elgin, 7th Earl of, see Bruce, Thomas

Eliot, Edward Craggs (1727–1804), later (1784) 1st Baron Eliot, M.P., II, 6
correspondence with, listed above, p. 124
his six Cornish seats, II, 9, 10, 13; member of Literary Club, VI, 220; pall bearer for Reynolds, VII, 80n4

Elisabeth of Württemberg, wife of Francis II of Austria, IX, 318n4

Elizabeth I, Queen of England, I, 41, IV, 45n6; charter of, VIII, 6n2, 68n2; Act of Association in reign of, 104, 343

Elliot, Alexander (1754–78), v, 107n5

Elliot, Andrew (d. 1797), v, 231

Elliot, Anna Maria (1786–1855), her birth, v, 250

Elliot, Eleanor, see Eden, Mrs William

Elliot, George (1784–1863), his birth, v, 163, 166–7, 180

Elliot, Sir Gilbert (1722–77), later (1766) 3rd Baronet, M.P., a leading 'King's Friend', I, 160, 284, II, 145, 209, III, 118, IV, 106hn, IX, 410; supports Clive, II, 436, and Hastings, VIII, 429

Elliot, Lady (Agnes Dalrymple Murray Kynynmound), wife of the preceding, v, 168n3

Elliot, Sir Gilbert (1751–1814), 4th Baronet, M.P.
correspondence with, listed above, p. 125
a follower of EB and Fox, v, 106hn, 116, 178, 179; supports Fox's coalition, 134n2; loses seat at Roxburgh, 137, one of Fox's Martyrs, 224; no seat in Orkneys for, 137, 230n3; his 'scheme' to get in, 250; contests Berwick, 277, X, 17, wins, v, 279, 282, 298–9, 304tn; a 'Rockingham man', 299, 355, 426tn; reluctant to contest Berwick again, 353; candidate for Roxburgh, 423; returned for Helston, 423n5, VI, 156n2, 177n3; Opposition candidate for Speaker, 61n4, 176n3, 176–7; on the 'party', 180tn; and EB's break with Fox, 272n; refuses office, VII, 345n1, 429n1; claims a hand in Letter to Whig Club, 353hn, 355tn

sends report from France, IV, 233n1; introduces Mirabeau to EB, v, 190, VI, 63n6; his knowledge of France, v, 266, views on, 423; resists EB's views on France, VII, 121hn, 122tn; consulted by Pitt on war with France, 349tn, VIII, 50, wants discussions with Windham, VII, 438, 439; appointed Commissioner for Toulon, 429, 430–1, 471, 476n2, 477n5; his instructions, 476n3, 485n1; anxiety for his Mission, 484–6, 488–9; his despatch to Dundas, 524; Viceroy of Corsica, VIII, 105n1, IX, 135n3, 156n3, withdraws, 138

changes opinion on Hastings, v, 107n5; takes on charge against Impey, 299–300, 303n6, 367, 403n3, 424n3, VI, 61hn, 62, 150; his opening speech, v, 368hn, 368–9, 369n2; takes part in Hastings prosecution, 303, 331, VI, 56n2, 61hn; member of Committee of Managers, v, 371, VII, 278hn, 370hn

on the Prince of Wales's affairs, v, 329–30hn, 331; draws up defence for Prince, 451n1, 479n1; and the Regency crisis, IX, 457, 460

EB appeals to, on behalf of Adey, IV, 420tn, IX, 465, of Captain King, v, 178, 179; EB thinks him too modest, 279, 299, 'worth a battle', 304tn; his view of EB's ménage, 304n1; panegyric on EB, 368hn; on his 'grazing', VI, 62n5; sees Reflections in early stages, 89n1, 149n2, 155; receives a copy, 149–50; on his own and others' reactions, 150n, 155–6, 180tn;

Erskine, David Steuart, 11th Earl of Buchan (1742–1829)
correspondence with, listed above, p. 103
sends EB his 'Pastoral Roundelay', V, 265

Erskine, Henry (1746–1817): Lord Advocate, V, 106tn, 265; gives turtle feast for EB, 221n2; EB's 'landlord', 222; also mentioned, I, 156n2, VII, 482n3

Erskine, Sir James, 6th Baronet (1762–1837), M.P.: member of Committee of Managers for Hastings trial, V, 303, 308, 371; Adjutant General at Toulon, VII, 517n1, 524

Erskine, John (d. 1817), Commissary General at Toulon, VII, 517n1, 524

Erskine, Dr John (1721–1803), Minister of Old Greyfriars, Edinburgh
correspondence with, listed above, p. 126
defends Scottish clergy against charge of causing anti-Catholic riots, IV, 62–4, 83–8; his stand against popery, 102–5; pamphlets on Popery, 63n4, 85, 102hn, 103–4, on America, 63n5, 83

Erskine, Thomas (1750–1823), M.P.
correspondence with, listed above, p. 126
counsel for Keppel, IV, 35n2, for Lord George Gordon, 250n1, for John Stockdale, VI, 54n4, 199, VII, 111–12, VIII, 220n5, 381n5, for Paine, VII, 316, for Horne Tooke, VIII, 66n2, 81n4; relations with Prince of Wales, V, 426, VII, 59
dislikes Reflections, VI, 314n3; his radical opinions, VII, 157, 164, 187; 'outrageously French', 315, 482n3, 483n1; quotes EB on conciliation, VIII, 81n4, IX, 240–1
A View of the War with France, IX, 239, 242, 243, 302n1, 315; criticised by EB, 239–41, 265, by French Laurence, 249, 250
also mentioned, V, 265hn, VIII, 111n4

Erthal, Friedrich Karl Josef von (d. 1802), Archbishop Elector of Mainz, VI, 344

Esgrigny, Abbé Jouenne d' (d. 1815), royalist agent, VIII, 312

Essay Towards an English History, see Burke, Edmund, Works

Essex, see County meetings

Estaing, Jean-Baptiste-Charles-Henri, Comte d' (1729–94): in command of the Toulon fleet, III, 453; takes part in Franco–American action, IV, 15–16, 34; captures St Vincent and Grenada,

116n4; besieges Savannah, 155n1, 158

Este, Rev. Charles (1753–1829), editor of the World and the Oracle: his attacks on EB, VI, 473, 476n5

Esterhazy, Nicolas (1765–1833), VI, 443n1

Estrées, Gabrielle d', mistress of Henri IV, VI, 146n4, 147

Etherington, Thomas, Sr, VI, 282n2

Etherington, Thomas, Jr (b. 1758), protégé of EB, obtains ordination and curacy, VI, 282, 305, 308, VII, 213

Eton, William, secretary of Sir Charles Whitworth, IX, 247–8

Eton College: Fitzwilliam and Fox friends at, VII, 107n4; Fitzwilliam's son visits EB from, IX, 143, 147, 157; also mentioned, II, 215hn, V, 268n5, IX, 362

Etty, Rev. Andrew (d. 1784), VIII, 44 n2

Etty, Rev. James (c. 1771–1805), Rector of Whitchurch, Oxon, VIII, 44

Etty, Mrs James (née Middleton, d. 1804), wife of the preceding, VIII, 44n3

Euclid, VII, 580

Euripides: Iphigeneia in Taurica, V, 349; Hecuba, VI, 90; RBJr reads, VII, 581, 582; also mentioned, II, 484n4, VII, 549

Europe: EB hopes to send Representation to his Majesty to every country in V,, 155–6; Reynolds the first Master in, 184–5; collapse of France may damage, VI, 36, 459; balance of, 106, VII, 315, new France a danger to, VI, 218, VII, 191, 218, 383–4, 387–93, 522, VIII, 134, 254; effect of Marie Antoinette's death on general Cause of, VI, 309; meliorating itself upon its antient principles, 330, its present state of improvement, 385, VII, 159–60; Spirit and principles of in danger, 161; new malady of, 170; recoverable yet, 307; plans for recovery of Britain's former place in, 309–18; Liberties of, must be defended against French principles, 344; her independence in danger, 354; System of, 387, now at an end, IX, 307; only war can save, VII, 437, 498; must grow worse before it can be safe, 513; feeble in its efforts, 543; Pitt's power necessary for, VIII, 36, 45, 190, 291; Ireland and, 41–2, IX, 279; Government's indifference to, 337; her safety and liberty vital to Britain, 118; Emperor the only hope of, 182

Eustace, Rev. John Chetwode (c. 1762–

1815), Professor of Rhetoric at Maynooth, his verses, IX, 102

Evans, Caleb (1737–91), Baptist minister, IV, 271

Evans, George, 3rd Baron Carbery (d. 1783), I, 126

Evans
correspondence with, listed above, p. 126

Evatt, William, clerk to Committee on India, his salary, VII, 559n1

Events, see Burke, Edmund, Opinions

Everard, Charles, see Booth, Charles

Everton, John (d. 1795), Birmingham merchant, VII, 331

Ewart, Joseph (1759–92), diplomat, V, 307n4; Ambassador in Berlin, 307, VI, 323n4, 325, 360n6, 383, 411n1; his meddling nature, 356–7; also mentioned, X, 44

Ewart, Mrs Joseph (Elisabeth Sophia Frederica von Wartesleben, 1764–1817), wife of the preceding, VI, 356n4

Exeter, Bishop of, see Keppel, Frederick

Exshaw, Edward (d. 1748), bookseller, I, 72, 78

Exshaw, John (d. 1776), bookseller, printer and publisher, I, 72, 78

Eyre, James (1734–99), later (1772) Sir James: Recorder of City of London, II, 32; appointed Baron of Exchequer, IX, 400hn; Chief Justice, VIII, 113; presides at trial of Hardy and Tooke, 66hn

Eyre, James (1748–1813)
correspondence with, listed above, p. 126

Eyre, Vincent, VI, 313n1

Faizullah Khan (d. 1784): Hastings charged with harassing, V, 410hn, 463, VIII, 160, 240; dispute over his inheritance, 240n3

Falconer, Dr William (1744–1824), physician
correspondence with, listed above, p. 126
his paper on the French Revolution, VI, 159; 3rd edition of Reflections sent to, 160

Falconet, Étienne-Maurice (1716–91), sculptor, II, 417

Falkner, Mr, V, 175n3

Falkner, Mrs, wife of the preceding, see Ridge, Ann

Family, see Burke, Edmund, Opinions

Fane, John, 9th Earl of Westmorland (1728–74), III, 45

Fane, John, 10th Earl of Westmorland (1759–1841), Lord Lieutenant of Ireland: receives instructions from Dundas on Catholic relief, VI, 470, VII, 3hn; RBJr referred to for information, VI, 470, 471n1; achieves division among Catholics, VII, 6n1, 11n2, 18; hostility to RBJr and Catholic Committee, 24n1, 36n2, 37, 46n6, 48n1, 133–4, 135n3; unwilling to treat with him, 28–9, 32hn, 325; persuades Dundas to drop proposals on juries, arms, and franchise, 34tn; allows Protestants to defeat Catholic petition, 71; 'an accomplice' in the Protestant game, 238, 245; asks for troops, 292n3; no friend of Pitt's, 327, but yields unwillingly on juries and franchise, 328tn, 343n1, 352n3; Ireland 'a Farm terribly havockd by', VIII, 9; likely to turn Secretaryship of State into another job, 12; under the influence of the Junto, 34n3, 171; 'a Basha of Ægypt', 40

opposes claims of Fellows of Trinity College, Dublin, on Provostship, VII, 571n1; recommends his own Chaplain as Provost, VIII, 11n1, 28, 53–4; proposes giving bishopric to another chaplain, 59; and Fitzwilliam's appointment to Lord Lieutenancy, 38, 41, 43, 54, 58–9, 61, 154n5, 212; his speech against Fitzwilliam, 238

also mentioned, VII, 19n1, 27n2, 38n, 285n1, 365n3, VIII, 5n3, 60n, 80n1, 179n2, 217

Fant, William, letter on the White Boys, I, 147n5

Farming, see Burke, Edmund; Clogher; Watson Wentworth, Charles; Young, Arthur

Farnham, 1st Viscount, see Barry, Barry

Farquhar, George, The Recruiting Officer, I, 51; The Constant Couple, 92

Farr, John (d. 1797), Sheriff of Bristol, III, 332; Letter to the Sheriffs addressed to John Harris and, 333–4

Farr, Paul (d. 1794), Bristol merchant, friend and supporter of EB
correspondence with, listed above, p. 126
advises cooperation on triumphal entry, III, 123hn, 124, 126–7, 131; supplies American news, 161n5, 163n1; Master of Merchants Hall, 232n1, 260, 261, 301hn, 302; petitions to Parliament, 230, 248–9; urges EB to press for amendments to Colonial Trade Bill,

Farr, Paul (*cont*.)
238–9, 240n3; visit to London, 250; quarrels with Champion over Declaratory Act, 253–5, 259n8; refuses nomination to Common Council, 290, 366n8, 368; his dockyard, 302n1; goes bankrupt, 451
also mentioned, III, 133n2, 174, 176n4, 220–1, 233n1, 234, 261, 289n1, 300, 366, IV, 50n5, 53, 77, 105hn, 243, 263
Farr, Richard, his bankruptcy, III, 451hn
Farr, Thomas (d. 1791), Mayor of Bristol and friend of EB, III, 176, 208, 232, 288–9, 318, 321n4; his bankruptcy, 451hn
Farr, William, III, 233n1
Farrel, Mr, his unsuitability as a guardian, V, 191–2
Farrell, James, Irish Catholic executed on charge of treason, I, 249n4
Farrell and Jones, Virginia merchants, III, 248n2
correspondence with, listed above, p. 126
Farrukhabad, Nawab of, *see* Diler Himmat Khan
Fateh Sahi, a fugitive in Oudh, VII, 148
Fauconberg, 2nd Earl, *see* Belasyse, Henry
Faulkner, George (*c*. 1699–1775), publisher of *Dublin Journal*, I, 8, 79
correspondence with, listed above, p. 126
his wooden leg, IX, 130
Favras, Marquis de, *see* Mahy, Thomas de
Fawcett, General William (*c*. 1750–1826), denies Catholic soldiers forced into Protestant churches, IX, 304tn
Fawkener, William Augustus (1747–1811), Clerk of the Privy Council
correspondence with, listed above, p. 126
sent on special mission to Russia, VI, 442; conversations with Catherine II on *Reflections*, 442n4; also mentioned, IX, 306
Fawkes, Guy, VII, 88n6
Faÿ, Elizabeth (Hamilton), Comtesse de (b. *c*. 1730)
correspondence with, listed above, p. 126
Fay, Marie-Charles-César de, Comte de Latour-Maubourg (1757–1831): escorts the royal family from Varennes, VI, 287–8; taken prisoner by the Austrians, IX, 186
Fay, Mr, Irish Catholic, falsely charged with murder, VIII, 194
Faydel, Jean-Félix (1744–1827)
correspondence with, listed above, p. 126
Fear, John
correspondence with, listed above, p. 126

Fector, Peter (1732–1814), Dover merchant and packet-boat agent, II, 412, 413, VI, 315
Feilding, Basil, 6th Earl of Denbigh (1719–1800), leads opposition to Printers' Bill in Lords, II, 540
Fellows, Mr, the Mealman, IX, 290
Fénelon, Claude-Etienne Salignac de Fénelon, Chevalier de (b. 1774)
correspondence with, listed above, p. 126
Fenton, Richard (1708–88), Borough Bailiff of Malton, III, 56, 62
Ferdinand, of Brunswick, at Battle of Minden, I, 127n2
Ferdinand, King of Naples and King of Sicily (1751–1825), IX, 57
Ferdinand III, Grand Duke of Tuscany (1769–1824), IX, 57
Ferguson, Robert, Scottish adventurer, II, 284
Fergusson, Sir Adam, 3rd Baronet (1733–1813), M.P.: moves resolution for recall of Hastings, VIII, 429–30; also mentioned, II, 106n5, IX, 72, X, 43
Ferián-Núrez, Conde de, Spanish Ambassador in Paris, VI, 338n5
Fermanagh, Baroness, *see* Verney, Mary
Fermor, George, 2nd Earl of Pomfret, I, 290n2
Ferns, Dean of, *see* Marlay, Richard
Fernyhough, Rev. William (b. 1754)
correspondence with, listed above, p. 126
Ferris, Richard (1750–1828), secret agent, VII, 464–5
correspondence with, listed above, p. 126
Fersen, Hans Axel von (1755–1810), VI, 338n3
Fetherstonhaugh, Sir Matthew, 1st Baronet (*c*. 1715–74), M.P., friend of Richmond, II, 389; on EB's 'supplications' to Chatham, I, 286n2
Feuillants: formation of, VI, 339n1; Marie Antoinette and, 348hn; Emperor adds strength to, VII, 21; in concert with English Democrats, 187; Feuillant Language, 435; also mentioned, VI, 189n4, 322n1, VII, 180
Fielding, Henry (1707–54), II, 2
Fielding, Sir John (d. 1780), III, 382
Fife, 2nd Earl, *see* Duff, James
Finch, Daniel, 8th Earl of Winchilsea (1689–1769): loses office, I, 262; also mentioned, 348
Finch, Lady Elizabeth, *see* Mansfield, Baroness
Finch, George, 9th Earl of Winchilsea (1752–1826): Lennox's second in duel

Fitzgibbon, John (*cont.*)
despatches', 144tn; poisons the King's mind against Catholic concessions, 192n3; regarded as chief enemy by Catholic merchants, 194, 195; not fit to decide education of Catholic clergy, 202; insists on Fitzwilliam's staying till successor comes, 209hn; would teach the Irish submission, 225; nominated Lord Justice on Fitzwilliam's leaving, 229n5; stoned by mob, 232; repudiates Fitzwilliam's allegations, 238n5; a Trustee for Maynooth College, 263; defends measures to restore order in Ireland, IX, 294–5; his hostility to Catholics a hindrance to peace, 297; growing opinion that he must go, 350, 355, 363, 366

also mentioned, VII, 297n3, IX, 222n5, X, 42

Fitzherbert, Alleyne, 1st Baron St Helens (1753–1839), Ambassador at Madrid, VI, 324–5, 356n2, VII, 340

Fitzherbert, Mrs Maria Anne (1756–1837) correspondence with, listed above, p. 127
the Prince's connexion with, V, 329hn, 444, 478–9; her dislike of Fox, 427n3

Fitzherbert, Samuel, *see* Ruxton, Samuel

Fitzherbert, William (c. 1712–72), M.P., early friend and patron of EB
correspondence with, listed above, p. 127
introduces EB and WB to the Rockingham set, I, 207, 210; Dr Johnson on, 207n5; appointed to Board of Trade, 213; meets Garrick, 214; Wilkes and, 231n3, 256hn, 257, 259; on the Butes and the Bedfords, II, 5; Chairman of Society of Arts, 96 tn; suspects EB to be Junius, 249; also mentioned, I, 230, II, 11, 158

Fitzherbert, Mr, IX, 454

Fitzhugh, R. W., East India clerk, V, 251n2, 252

Fitzjames, Jacques-Charles, Duc de (b. 1743), colonel proprietor of Berwick Regiment, VI, 328

Fitzmaurice, John Hamilton, styled Viscount Kirkwall (1778–1820), VIII, 250

Fitzmaurice, Mary, *see* Shelburne, Dowager Countess of

Fitzmaurice, Thomas (1742–93), M.P., linen-merchant, half-brother of Marquess of Lansdowne: his Chancery suit against Lord Inchiquin, IV, 130, 340–1, 443; his domestic politics, VII, 191

Fitzmaurice, Lady Mary, wife of the preceding, *see* Orkney, Countess of

Fitzmaurice, William, *see* Petty, William

Fitzpatrick, John, 2nd Earl of Upper Ossory (1745–1818), M.P. for Bedfordshire
correspondence with, listed above, p. 185
his marriage, II, 5n5, 6; has a 'vein of Natural good-sense', 472; Fox brings into Opposition, IV, 135hn, 139n2, 174n3, VII, 197, IX, 410; his interest solicited for candidates in Ireland, IV, 135–6, 148, in Bucks, 138–9, 148; member of Literary Club, VI, 220; pall bearer for Reynolds, VII, 80; his Irish interests, 342–3; also mentioned, III, 452n3, IV, 442hn, VI, 452n1, VII, 107

Fitzpatrick, Richard (1748–1813), M.P. in British and Irish Parliaments, friend of Fox
correspondence with, listed above, p. 127
speaks on East India Company, II, 388, and on Canada, IX, 410; brings news from America, III, 452–3; serves in American war, IV, 442hn, V, 428
appointed Chief Secretary to Lord Lieutenant of Ireland, IV, 442hn; his success, 458, V, 50; EB recommends Marlay to, IV, 442, and Monck Mason, 450, V, 48, 49; member of Committee of Managers, 371; admires the French system, VI, 452; his motion on La Fayette's imprisonment, IX, 152n6, 185, his speech a 'chapter out of a Sentimental Novel', 188, 199, 200
also mentioned, IV, 135hn, 457, V, 25n1, VII, 408n1

Fitzroy, Augustus Henry, 3rd Duke of Grafton (1725–1811): dismissed from Lord Lieutenancy for opposing the peace, I, 162n7; refuses office from Cumberland, 205; Secretary of State for Northern Department in Rockingham Ministry, 210; speaks on repeal of Stamp Act, 244; wants to see Pitt at head of Administration, 248n3, 252n3; recommends EB to Pitt, 269n1; remains in office when Rockingham goes, 262n1, 263n3, 265n1, 277, 291n5, 303n2, 311n2; his horse beaten by Rockingham's, 309n3; goes over to Bute, 313; invites Rockingham to take office, 315–16, 320n4, II, 375–6; King wishes him to remain head of Administration, I, 317n3, 328, II, 3hn, 4, 51; holds on to the 'Bute bottom', I, 319, IX, 391; his domination contemptible and odious, II, 97

Fitzwilliam, William (*cont.*)

stands for, V, 17tn, recommends agent for, 338–9, gives notice of vacating, VI, 276, resigns, VII, 552–3, hopes to name successor for, 553n1; offered to and accepted by RBJr, 555–6, 558–9; his election, 560, 568; EB recommends French Laurence for, 574n4, IX, 67n2, 71n2; Baldwin succeeds to, on RBJr's death, VII, 574n4, VIII, 368; Lord Milton sits for, 367, 368; EB's happy days at, 373. Higham Ferrers, RBJr's hopes for, VII, 394–5; not offered to him, 396hn; borough blacklisted by Friends of the People, 405; Adair elected for, 408n1, VIII, 69n1. Peterborough, vacated by death of Benyon, IX, 67; offered to French Laurence on terms, 74–6, 77–8, 80–1; accepted, 81–2, 83, 88, 92–3, 101; terms carried out, 175n1, 219n2, 228–9, 250, 251, 252n3, 253, 284, 292–3, 296, 299, 335, 338; William Elliot returned for (1802), VIII, 157hn

EB and

on Bill for Economical Reform, IV, 336, V, 7; EB goes with, to Doncaster Races, 34, 35–6; concern for EB's agitation over RBJr, 223; sends EB a horse, and sheep for breeding, VI, 313–14, 401–2, 416, VII, 170, preserves his special breed after EB's death, III, 371n2

financial relations with EB, VI, 271n2, 449–50, 452–3, VII, 495n4, 551n2, VIII, 9n2, 13n3, 306–7; the 'generous delicacy', of his proceeding, VI, 271; political views no ingredient in his kindness, 449; EB cannot accept financial help from one whose cause he injures, 452–3; the debt of gratitude is never to be cancelled, VII, 495; acquits EB of all his bonds, VIII, 306–7; and EB's pension, VII, 562n1, VIII, 287–8, 298, 305

their friendship survives public break, VI, 255, 276, 331, 332hn, 453, 449, VII, 233; EB on the break, VI, 271–5, 450–2, VII, 496–7, IX, 243; his version, VII, 417–19; EB will never be seen to vote differently from, 63; is more cordial than ever, 82, IX, 445; his love and veneration for EB, VII, 403, 417, IX, 57, 267, 346, 'the brightest ornament' of the House of Commons, VII, 555; EB's political obligation to, 404, could never abandon him, VIII, 189–90; EB wished everything he

does to be 'splendidly Right', 10; his highmindedness and quick feelings, 40; consults EB before going to Ireland, 45–6, 48; stays at Beaconsfield, 107, IX, 355–6; EB's personal influence over, VIII, 173n2, IX, 353; their sentiment on foreign affairs identical, VII, 307; the nation that will not have him not worth struggling for, VIII, 403; on EB and Hastings's acquittal, 410–11; on EB's last visit to Lord John Cavendish, IX, 210tn; EB's dying message to, 373–4; a pall bearer at EB's funeral, 374; mentioned in his will, 377; EB's portrait of Keppel bequeathed to, IV, 169n1

patronage sought from by EB, VII, 573–4, VIII, 97–8, 274n3, 293n4, 298, 305

praises *Reflections*, VI, 161n2, 178, 334, 336; welcomes *Appeal*, 313, 401–2, 415–17, 418, 429, IX, 438; 'Thoughts on French Affairs' sent to but never read, VII, 313; sees 'Heads for Consideration', 288–9, 309, 310; 'Observations on the Conduct of the Minority' addressed to Portland and, 436hn, 497n1, unauthorised printing of, IX, 240n1, 243; *Regicide Peace* shown to in early stage, VIII, 368, 374, *Fourth Letter* addressed to, 368n1, EB's 'poor attempt to second' what he had done, IX, 102

Personal

seat at Milton, II, 497; makes allowance to O'Beirne, V, 30, 32, 33; visits Sheffield after riots (1791), VI, 313, (1795), VIII, 298, 305; entertains Paine at Wentworth, V, 415n4; his fête for the Prince of Wales, VI, 23; friendship with Sheridan, 128–9; entertains Bintinaye and Cazalès, VII, 96, 97, 107; subscribes to French refugee clergy, 224, 229; takes de La Robrie to masked ball, 531tn; his exalted but irritable mind, VIII, 174: 'the best man I ever knew' (Grattan), 196; his Irish estates, 199n, IX, 283n3, 284, advised to subscribe for unemployed Dublin tradesmen, IX, 331; notices an unwigged head, VIII, 377n1; 'inveterate enemy' of all innovation, IX, 75; believes in an Aristocratick system with alloy of Democracy, 144–5; his financial position, 146

A *Letter from a Venerated Nobleman ... to the Earl of Carlisle*, VIII, 209n2

also mentioned, I, 255n7, II, 486n1, III,

Forster, George (1754–94), son of Johan
Forster, sails with Captain Cook, II,
308n2
Forster, Johann Reinhold (1729–98)
correspondence with, listed above, p. 129
sails with Captain Cook, II, 308n2
Forster, John, Lady Fermanagh's legal
agent, VIII, 458
Forster, Rev. Dr John (c. 1707–88), Fellow
of Trinity College, Dublin: examines
EB, I, 66
Fortescue, Sir John (c. 1394–c. 1476), VIII,
455n2
Fortescue, William Henry, 1st Baron
Clermont (1722–1806), later (1771) 1st
Earl of Clermont, his Irish rents, II,
486
Fortescue Aland, John, *Reports*, II, 309n1
Forward, Elizabeth, *see* Nagle, Mrs Garrett
'Atty'
Foster, Lady Elizabeth (d. 1824), 'Journal'
quoted, V, 427n3, 432tn, 435tn, VI,
161n2, 178n1
Foster, John (1740–1828), later (1821) 1st
Baron Oriel, Irish M.P., Speaker of
Irish House of Commons: his 'declaration of War' against Catholic Committee, VII, 224, 282–3, 286–7, 290;
reprisals for a murder, 285; speaks
against Catholic Relief Bill, 364; an
active enemy of Catholics, VIII, 22–3,
195, 202; to be a Lord Justice on Fitzwilliam's recall, 229n5; his house
mobbed, 233n; more mischievous
than the Chancellor, IX, 355
Foster, Sir Michael (1689–1763), VII,
540n3
Fothergill, Dr John (1712–80), Quaker
friend of Rockingham, III, 113, 208
Foullon, Abbé Honoré-Charles-Ignace
correspondence with, listed above, p. 129
meets EB in London, VI, 263hn; his
horrid treatment in France, 263; also
mentioned, 227
Foullon, Joseph-François (1717–89), Controller-General of France: murdered
in Paris, VI, 10n1, 19n4, 107, 171n2,
263, IX, 186; handed over to the mob
by La Fayette, 154
Fountayne, John (1714–1802), Dean of
York, attends County meeting, II,
96–7
Fournès, Jules-Marie-Henri de Faret,
Marquis de (1752–1826)
correspondence with, listed above,
p. 129
Fowke, Francis (1754–1820), Resident at
Benares, V, 417, VI, 250n4, 251

Fowke, Joseph (1716–1806), East India
Company servant, V, 417
correspondence with, listed above, p. 129
EB takes up his case for pension, VI,
249–51; appears to win, 276–7; final
decision, 277tn
Fowke, Mrs Joseph, wife of the preceding,
VI, 251n5
Fowke, Louisa, daughter of Joseph Fowke,
VI, 251–2
Fowke, Randall (c. 1672–1745), father of
Joseph Fowke, fifty years in the
service of the East India Company,
VI, 251
Fowke, Sophia, daughter of Joseph
Fowke, VI, 251–2
Fowler, Rev. Henry Bond (1754–1829)
correspondence with, listed above,
p. 129
Fox, Caroline, Mrs Crewe's friend and
correspondent, IX, 207n2, 226n2,
234hn
Fox, Charles James (1749–1806), M.P. for
Westminster
correspondence with, listed above,
p. 129
In politics
supports Administration, II, 51; his
exertions in parliament, 301; motions
to amend Marriage Act, 305n2, IV,
355–6; appointed Lord of the
Treasury, II, 370, 382; supports EB
on America, 532, III, 165, 427hn,
joins Opposition over, 290hn, 291,
294; motion on failures in Quebec,
IX, 409–10; Ministry have no answer
to his speech on conciliation, III, 299;
breaks Rockingham's rule on absten-
tion and opposes Habeas Corpus Bill,
328n3; presents motion drafted by
EB on Royal Debts, 338–9; wants
settled Opposition plan, 380–1, 384,
385; attacks North on America, 419,
422–3; proposes Coalition government to curb power of Crown, IV,
38–41; rejects Grafton's proposal for
individuals joining Government, 154–
7; expects Rockingham to be called,
161; and Economical Reform Bill, 171
defeated at Bridgewater (1780), IV, 279;
elected for Westminster, 282–4, 291,
313, 'The Joy, the debauch', 293, 300,
scrutiny of votes, 301n1, 315; battle
for victory (1784), V, 134, 149,
229, holds Tain burghs in interim,
149n1, 230n3; (1788) by-election,
411–12, 414, VII, 406n3; defeats Horne
Tooke (1790), VI, 122n6, 124–5;

315

Fox, Charles (*cont.*)

lawyers, 410hn; wants adjournment after censure, 472hn; EB's defence to, of continuing trial, 472–4; actions for libel, VI, 54n4, 55n; differs from EB on Contracts Article, 57n5; still shares work with EB after break, VII, 82, 233n1; answers Law's challenge to EB, 252; other references, IV 431, V, 392, VI, 56n2, VII, 117, 532

EB and

his close and personal alliance with EB, III, 290–1, V, 427; intervenes to prevent duel between EB and Wedderburn, III, 406hn, 408; differences emerging, IV, 39; a night walk on the ramparts, 41tn; wastes his ability on long designs, 374; gains daily in esteem and popularity, 377, X, 13; EB consults on post for Boswell, IV, 445; his manly scheme of politics, V, 243; his great and difficult part, 429; gains credit for his moderation, 463; no real soreness over Hastings, 474; public break between, VI, 255, 273, 291, IX, 445–6; EB's feelings on, VI, 378, 416, VII, 82, 516, VIII, 335, IX, 113, regrets that politics can dissolve such friendships, VI, 472; defended by EB against invective of Dissenters, VII, 56; EB's resignation from Whig Club over, 353–5, IX, 243; EB has no personal animosity to, 79, but his politics are 'astray and absurd', 79; his 'tremendous consistency' on France a dreadful evil, 264; EB refuses deathbed reconciliation, 372–3, honours him as an example of virtue, 448

visits to EB, III, 173, 285, V, 240, to EB's Irish cousins, III, 390hn; EB breakfasts with, V, 107n7, prepares 'Infirmary' for at Beaconsfield, 433, 434hn

is shown 'Letter to the Sheriffs of Bristol', III, 333; suggests EB write Address for London Common Council, IV, 439; EB second only to, as Opposition speaker, V, 70n2; thinks *Reflections* the least perfect of his works, VI, 161n2, the worst he ever published, 178, 180tn, X, 24; no Whig dare praise *Appeal* for fear of, VI, 360; 'Observations on the Conduct of the Minority' an indictment of, VII, 436hn, IX, 240n1, 247, 249n2, 281n3; *Two Letters* directed against Pitt and, 98, 240n1, 247; misquotes EB in

parliament, 280–2, 285; reads all EB's pamphlets diligently, 282

other references, IV, 448, V, 52, 177, 239, VI, 110, 452, VII, 53, 361, 419, VIII, 437, IX, 313

and other Burkes: associated with RBSr as claimant to land in St Vincent, II, 370n2, 416, 450, 460hn, 461, 462, 463, 525, thought him superior in ability to EB, VII, 596; RBJr advised to consult on his Receivership of Land Revenues, V, 53; RBJr on his radical views, VI, 129, discusses him with Fitzwilliam in 'perfectly dispassionate' tone, VII, 186–7, thinks himself sacrificed to, 398–9, 400–1, 402, 405–9, 418

Personal

sport and gambling, II, 473, III, 290hn, IV, 374, 377n1, X, 13; travels abroad, III, 320, 323, V, 426, in Ireland, III, 380, 390hn; gives up Clerkship of Pells in exchange for pensions, 176–7, sharp exchange with Rose on reversion of office, IX, 286; stays at Chatsworth, III, 380hn; visits Keppel during his trial, IV, 37hn; appears at Court with EB, 91n1; his bust in Rockingham Mausoleum, V, 46n5; invited to be pall bearer for Dr Johnson, 205, 206tn; volume of Bellenden dedicated to, 293–4, 336hn; his establishment at St Anne's Hill, 304; his prudent attitude to France in 1787, 351; his bad health, 433n1, 435, 438, 442n2, 446; member of Literary Club, VI, 220; thinks himself as good an aristocrat as any, VII, 197; has been living with the Ladies of 'Monsr L'Egalité', 315

personal friends and supporters: Robert Adair, IX, 249n2, 285; Duke of Bedford, V, 78, VIII, 395n3; Coke of Norfolk, VII, 412n2; John Crewe, VIII, 80hn; John Debrett, VII, 120; George Dempster, V, 164n1; Duchess of Devonshire, III, 421hn, V, 439n1; Rev. Wm Dickson, V, 92n4; Sir Gilbert Elliot, 106hn; Thos Erskine, IX, 241, 249; Richard Fitzpatrick, III, 452n3, IV, 135hn, 442hn, VII, 342hn; Earl Fitzwilliam, VI, 129, VII, 107, 187, 398–9, 400–2, 405–9, 418, IX, 76, 364; Henry Fletcher, V, 209n3; Philip Francis, IX, 451; William Godwin, V, 64n1; Thos Grenville, 136n3, VIII, 59n2; Duke of Leinster, III, 386; Wm Mason, VI, 23n6; Dennis

Fox Party (*cont.*)
  Chronicle, VI, 451n3, its French news, 451n4
  also mentioned, VI, 418, 441, IX, 196
Fox–North Coalition (Apr. 1783–Dec. 1783)
  Fox and North parties combine to oppose Peace Preliminaries, V, 65hn; negotiations between North, Portland and the King, 69hn, 73, 74–5, 77–9, 84–5; EB's part in formation of coalition, 75n5; appointments, II, 18n2, V, 77hn, 82, 89–90hn, 96hn, 121hn, 145hn, 230n1, Great Seal put in commission, 66n3; RBSr returns as Joint Secretary to Treasury, 82n3, 86, with Sheridan, 121hn; EB becomes Paymaster General again, 86, IX, 459
  Pay Office Bill, V, 90, 93, 97, IX, 285; Bill for Sale of Forest and other Crown Lands, V, 95–6; Bill for Increase and Preservation of H.M.'s Wood and Timber, 96tn; and Ireland, 103; Dundas dismissed as Lord Advocate, 105hn; Peace Treaty with America signed, 111; Fox's India Bills, 116n4, defeated, 119hn, 146, 153n1; coalition dismissed, 119, 120hn, 121hn; EB's last act in office, 120; defeats and successes at general election, 135tn
  Abingdon opponent of, V, 103n2; EB's defence of in Commons, 153, 155–6, and in pamphlet, 156n1; defended by Lord Carlisle at York County meeting, 144hn; Dalrymple's pamphlet defends, 162; Godwin's defence of, 64n2; Dr Parr and Dr Homer express their sympathy for, 293hn. Relations with Hastings, 244n1, 254n4
  also mentioned, V, 53tn, 58n4, 62dn, 93dn, 98tn, 115n3, 134n2, 160hn, 242n1, 250n3, VI, 23n6, 335n3, VII, 405n1, 597n1, IX, 196n2, 433hn
Fox's India Bill, Speech on, see Burke, Edmund: Works
Foy, Mrs, *see* Lukin, Mary
Frampton, Rev. Matthew (b. *c.* 1719), friend of EB, I, 128
Français, Antoine, Comte (1756–1836): political 'godfather' to William Priestley, VII, 152; compares EB to Aristophanes, 153; his speech read at meeting of London Revolution Society, 358
France
  EB visits in 1773, II, 401, 409, 411–22, 424–5, III, 262, VI, 42; his poor

French, II, 425tn, V, 266, VI, 224, VII, 584, VIII, 237; the role of, in the balance of Europe, VI, 36, 106, 367, 459, VII, 161; national character, VI, 42, 213; greatness of, 419, VII, 54; family life more interesting than in England, VIII, 88
  L'Ancien Régime: 'a system of Court intrigue miscalled a government', VI, 479; Pranks of the Court at Versailles, V, 415; ill-judged acts of Monarchy, VI, 36; its prisons of despotism, 80; an 'abusive government', 97; attempt at unlimited monarchy, 172–3, 242, 266, a sort of despotism, 423; more favourable to liberty than new Government, 255, moderation of Monarchy in use of power, 400; crippled despite patronage, VIII, 49
  Constitution of: its 'antient Bases', VI, 219; true government of country by ancient estates, 258, 414; King cannot annihilate the Monarchy, holds his power in Trust, 353; fundamental constitution, 359–60, 'true antient Rights, Liberties, and privileges of the people', 360, fundamental Laws, 362; 'ancient order of methodized liberty', 400; Monarchy the 'Lawful prescriptive Government', VII, 434; EB hopes for a free constitution (1789–91), VI, 43–6, 97, 317, 360, 414, 423
  Constitution of 1791: prospect of a constitution democratic in form and spirit, VI, 25, 33; a conditional constitution absurd, 30, will ruin France if set up, 33; the 'collection of Democracies', 45; judicial system under, 107–8; 'a piece of French plate', 142; established not on the rights of men but their vices, 210–11; a degrading Tyranny, 217; Theoretic plans the bane of France, 219; fears of King accepting, 361–2; absurd and wicked, 363, VII, 183, 434–5; pernicious theories reduced to *practice*, VI, 419, hated by Portland as much as by EB, VII, 143–4. *See also* Louis XVI
  National Assembly: its limited powers, VI, 25, 36, dominated by Paris, 106n2; its arbitrary acts, 37, 44, 46; elections to, 53; will darken the air with its arrows, 91; EB's 'old prejudice' the Enemy of, 109; entertained with Mirabeau on EB, 225; should not be recognised, 258, 317; protests in, against suspension of King, 290; an

France, French Revolution (*cont.*)

EB's first reaction to storming of Bastille, VI, 10; a country undone, 36; thinks England not yet affected, 55; becomes alarmed, 78hn, 91–2; breaks with Paine over, 75–6tn, and with Fox, 255tn; makes public stand against, 81–2tn, 92–8, 105; stresses danger to England, 83–4, 357, 411, 419, VII, 55, 159, 170–1, 177, 192, 217–19, 317–18, 522; his sentiments spoken by RBJr, VI, 125–30; on the new philosophy, 136; the passive servility of France, 140–1; charges disorders on leaders, not Mob, 172; deplores destruction of Gentry and Property, 173, 179, fears contagion of Revolution, 211, 218; 'the French Pestilence', VII, 489; a new Evil, VI, 242, a revolt of innovation, 268, unprecedented in annals of Europe, 458, VII, 218; external force necessary to defeat it, VI, 211, 217–19, 257, 261; plan for Manifesto, 258, 317, 359–60; sends advice to Louis XVI, 319–20, fears his accepting Constitution, 341; writes to Queen of France, 348–52; French revolution compared to Polish, 426hn, 427tn, VII, 159–60; effects on EB's personal relations, VI, 330–1, VII, 121–2; his detestation of the Tyrranick and perfidious usurpation, VI, 399, 443, of the new doctrines, 418, the 'detestable faction', 458–9; thinks moment ripe for invasion, 412, 422; proposals for Bill of Rights when Monarchy restored, 413–14, 423; in despair over French affairs, 438; considers appealing to Catherine II, 441–5, IX, 439; on the imminent destruction of the Royal Family, VII, 171–2; advice to Grenville on relations with revolutionary leaders, 173–8; not the enmity, but the friendship, of France terrible, 176; whole Edifice of Europe shaken by the Earthquake, 191; the September Massacres, 203, 205–6, 281; the Catastrophe of the Tragedy completed, the execution of Louis XVI, 344, 473; madness of the French rabble more noble than the madness of the powers of Europe, 272; French arms and principles must be stopped, 292, 307, 310; measures to protect his corpse from French Revolutionaries, VIII, 339n10; Shakespeare and, 456

the French System of the Rights of man,

VII, 171; disposition of English Court the main support to, VI, 393; attempt to alter Frame of Society realized, 419; Europe indisposed to, 422; English disciples of, 452, detestable Doctrines of modern Whigs generated out of, 415; impossible to prevent growth of, 453; plan to assist Poland directed at finding Ally for, VII, 159; Hostility to, ought to be test for Fox, 194; a new System of Power, 277; attachment to, proof of malignant disposition, 304; in the West Indies, IX, 307

war with revolutionary France: offensive war necessary (Oct. 1792), VII, 261, VIII, 361–2; prospects of, VII, 278; EB consulted on, 348–9; at war with French Theory, 359, a War of Principle, 380–1, 383, the Cause worth the blood spilt, 385, the Cause of Humanity itself, 387, 452, to civilise France, 498, in defence of religion, VIII, 146; gains of the rich from, VII, 416; the whole scheme of, wrong, 422, 423, should be recognised as a Civil War, 432; EB as responsible as a Minister for, but not consulted on, 423; Toulon puts war on proper footing, 434; must be fought to an honourable end, 436; the only way of saving Europe from Jacobinism, 437–8, 518; action in the Vendée more important than in the Caribbean, 445–6, 449, 481; 'getting War on to a proper footing' still the problem after Maubeuge, 452; the retreat from Dunkirk, 457–9; whole plan based on false political principles, 460–1, 517, IX, 201; EB feels Pulse of City on the war, VII, 464; not the right moment for Declaration, 465–6; affair of Wissembourg 'one of the finest things in military History', 480; sickened by discrepancy of promise and achievement, 481; armed forces not being used for furtherance of Cause, 481, 485–6, 489; misfortunes of war all spring from spirit of chicane in politics, 490; flight from Toulon a calamitous and disgraceful affair, 514; EB's opinion asked by Ministers, 518, 525, 526–9; Fox's view of the war, 519–22; bears no resemblance to any former war, 521–2, all others games of Children in comparison, 522; perhaps the last struggle in favour of Religion, morality and property, 527–8; Portland right on, 529; the Glorious

France, French Revolution (*cont.*)

First of June, 548–9; surrender of Bois-le-Duc, VIII, 52; army should be raised in Papal States, 105; fears of French occupation of Cape of Good Hope, 122, IX, 211, 212; Holland lost to France, VIII, 134, IX, 212, 216; energy and enterprise needed more than experience, VIII, 149; the Country about to make its first natural and rational effort, 267–9, but the leader of the Great Business not to be trusted, 268–9, 273–4; the Civil War of Europe can be fought only on the plains of Picardy or Brittany, 345; Civil War threatened at home, 348; France impoverished and barbarised to gain territories, 363; dismal outlook of 1796, IX, 57; French Regiments saved from slaughter, 73, sent to Portugal, 135, 201, 206; war, the only way to reduce Republick to reason, 100; shameful flight from the Mediterranean, 109, 127, 164; domestic safety given priority over invasion, 117–18; use of Militia criticised, 118–19, 207, 278, and raising money by forced Loans, 119, 130; the absurd plan of passive defence, 124, 268, 272–4, 312–16, 317, 322, will ruin public credit, 278–9, puts our islands in a state of siege, 279; EB believes the War abandoned, 130; 'It is all over', 135; Pitt's 'kettle of fish' over Imperial Subsidy, 151, 173, 174, 178–9, 200; 'in a terrible way between our diseases and our Physicians', 182; things in a 'very trembling balance', 200; naval war mismanaged, 201; French expedition from Brest, 227, 249; intelligence service lacking, 272; Pitt's policy criticised, 300, 'resolved to make no war at all', 315; EB suspects plan to destroy French corps goes on, 301; wants casualty figures for this and other wars, 316; the Spithead mutiny, 317, 368, 370, the Revolution accomplished in, 333, 347; 'cowardice the principle of our War', 317, a 'false image of a War', 321

the Regicide Peace: negotiations should wait till Religion and Property restored, VII, 521; peace on French terms not to be thought of, VIII, 148–9; the Treacherous Cry of peace with France, 164; Pitt's 'plan of peace' in 1795, 230–1, his proposed negotiations, 357–8, 387–8; England's 'diplomacy of humiliation', IX, 89; Malmesbury's peace mission, 101–2, 106, 135, 203–6, 211, 216; Pitt's wish for a *plausible* peace, 151, his Jacobin peace efforts, 207–8, 212, 241; 'the cursed Peace' at the bottom of all the mad things done by Ministry and Opposition, 161; a peace disadvantageous to France to be hoped for, 188; 'we cannot make peace and we will not make war', 241, 300; Pitt's and Fox's plans compared, 265–6; EB expects a peace 'with a thousand wars in its womb', 306–7, the end of the 'system of Europe', 307

Revolutionary Army: their military success without military discipline, VI, 458; 'a kind of Democratick Military', VII, 55, the 'scum of a mercenary common soldiery', 160; their Generals' existence depends on constant new activity, 264; 'a Troop of strolling Players with a Buffoon at their head', 271; run away from the Prussian whisker, 276, 309; youth of their leaders, VIII, 149; Charette's successes against, 302–3; dependence of Regicide System on, IX, 100

Francis I, King of France, V, 9, VI, 224n4

Francis II, Holy Roman Emperor (1768–1835): elected King of the Romans, VII, 97; James Nagle joins his army, 376hn; prospects of political and military glory for, 383; his Declaration of Intent towards France, 391, 486n4; world hopes from, 393; does not recognise French princes, 333n1

Subsidy granted to by Pitt, VIII, 251n1; opposed in Commons, 148n8; a 'pretty kettle of fish' cooked up, IX, 151; Fox's vote of censure on, 173hn, 179; EB considers unconstitutional but not illegal, 173, 182; continuation of, recommended, 191n1; reduced, 200; Sheridan's motion against, 268n3, 296, 305

continues war after Prussia makes peace, VIII, 230; 'our only steadfast faithfull Ally', 388, IX, 263; his army saved by French gentlemen, 107; projected peace with Regicides, 127n2, 135, 161; and imprisonment of La Fayette, 154, 155, 160, 184, 185; the 'Tyrant Ally' pushes the war, 188; remains firm in spite of Republican temptations, 253; Pitt hostile to alliance with, 300; his submission to France feared 307, 314

George III (*cont.*)

Grenville's Administration, 206–7; Townshend proposed to, 207; tries Pitt again, 250, 252n1, 260, 263n6, 300, 311n2, n4; accepts resignation of Portland and other Ministers, 280; supports Grafton's attempt to get rid of Shelburne, II, 3hn, 4n1; Chatham's audience with, 43, 48; Rockingham party accused of ill-using, 260, 262; appoints Dartmouth Colonial Secretary, 331; Jenkinson's influence over, III, 90; fears a strong Ministry, IV, 40; views on Rockingham, 67tn; Grafton thinks him unwilling for great changes, 144; may send for Portland, 154, or for Rockingham, 156, 161; Rockingham's audience with, 194n8; negotiates through Thurlow, 422hn, 423hn, 427; appoints Rockingham First Lord, 428; Shelburne has his confidence after Rockingham's death, V, 3hn; allows Fox to stay for the present, 4n2; supports Shelburne against Fox's advice for First Lord, 5n3; a question whether his choice of Leader can validly be objected to, 6tn; appoints Shelburne First Lord on his sole authority, 24n4; asks Pitt to form government, 65hn; negotiates with North, 69hn, 73hn, with Portland, 74–9, IX, 433; insists on seeing whole Cabinet plan, V, 75hn, 76, 81–2; negotiations broken off, 79tn; turns to Pitt, 84hn; sends for North, 84; agrees to Portland's Cabinet including Fox and North, 84–5; uses Fox's India Bill to dismiss Fox and North, 119hn, Mirabeau on the dismissal, VI, 63, Cloots on, 110, 'our Tempest', 366; values Richmond's support, V, 150n1; urges Thurlow to settle differences with Pitt, VI, 34n7; not himself if not jealous of his First Minister, 35–6; Hawkesbury's declining influence with, 392n2; negotiations with Pitt for coalition with Fox fail, VII, 179, 194, 195; offers Loughborough the Great Seal, 344; alleged plot of Ministers against, VIII, 346; Pitt has his confidence more than anyone, IX, 207; Fox is 'to be forced upon', 265; Pitt a bad servant to, 315; 'Interest of his System' dearer to than the 'Interest of his Kingdom', IV, 156, 161

and Parliament: terms of Regency Bill, I, 194; repeal of Stamp Act a constitutional problem for, 244; on the Westminster election, II, 132n1; surprised at Burgoyne's vote on Spain, 199n1; averse to meddling with Printers, 209n10; against Absentee Tax, 499n3; on the Boston Port Bill, 533n1; offended by speech on royal debts, III, 338–9; thinks Opposition dictate to him, IV, 41tn; and Richmond's scheme of parliamentary reform, 165, 167; wants an early Dissolution, 253n2; intervenes in Windsor election, 283–4; offended by Speaker on Royal Household Bill, 319; reluctant to accept Economical Reform Bill, 434tn, 450, tries but fails to prevent its passing, V, 7n1, n2; Fox's India Bill a test of loyalty to, 119hn; thinks Windham's election a disaster, 153hn; mobbed on way to open Parliament, VIII, 338; EB on his relations to Parliament, 349–50, IX, 291–2; and the Royal Marriage Bill, 398hn

and City of London: Remonstrance to, II, 139, III, 312; approves Nash's election as Lord Mayor, II, 245hn; and City elections, 356n2

America: recommends compensation to faithful American subjects, II, 499n1; Boston Port Bill, 533n1; petition to, from First Continental Congress, III, 80n1; disapproves of taxing Americans, 80n1; will not send Hanoverians to America, 225; petitions from Bristol merchants to, 229; General Howe's audience with, IV, 3–4; supports continuation of war, 38hn; other references, III, 295–6, 392, IX, 418

France: French Princes' requests to, as Elector and as King, VI, 301hn; will maintain neutrality of Europe, 345, 381, 410, VII, 161, 176, 178tn, 218; earnest for the 'Cause of sovereigns' VI, 361; 'perfectly right' in the cause, 367; Monsieur's letter to, 370, his reply, 410; is sent RBJr's letter on French Princes and Emperor, 380n5; Bintinaye's letter, 393, 396hn, 398, 475; blamed for inaction against French rebels, 407; Princes try to borrow money from, 425n1; his declaration of Neutrality, 410n3; receives Bintinaye at Levee, VII, 106, is sent pamphlet by him, 152; considers recognising French Republic, 174; his recruiting idea, 339n5; firm in support of war,

George III (*cont.*)

power, 448–9; sees the Princes in presence of Queen, 450; resumes royal authority, 451; his total incapacity for business, 461; kept in ignorance of public affairs, 461; Dr Willis's diagnosis and treatment of, 462; convalesces at Weymouth, VI, 26–7

as Elector of Hanover: and plans to give Bremen and Verden to Sweden, II, 380; arrangements for his duties during illness, V, 431, 445; his role as Elector in European affairs, VI, 301hn, 325, 377; takes little interest in Electorate, 384; his real sentiments will be judged by the pulse of Hanover, 393

and EB: WB named to, for his part in debate, I, 302n2; 'Thoughts on the Approaching Executions' sent to, IV, 254; thinks EB 'flowry and no honesty in him', V, 430n2; EB's reckless remark about, VI, 7n2; compliments EB at Levee on *Reflections*, 219–20, 238–9; Menonville's letter shown to, 162hn, 252–3; *Reflections* modifies his view of Opposition, 272; conversations with EB on Boswell's *Life of Johnson*, 297–8, 300; *Appeal* presented to, 309–10, 311hn, 316n3, 341; reads it with satisfaction, 333; receives EB graciously at Levee, 362–3, conversation on Windsor Terrace, 368, VII, 50; reassured on attitude of Whigs by letters of Fitzwilliam and EB, VI, 428–9; prefers EB's letter not to be sent to Catherine II, 447–8, IX, 439; EB interrupts dramatic performance to toast his health, VII, 380hn; his warm feelings for EB and intention to reward him, 450, 451; EB serves his 'natural Sovereign', 473–4; French clergy threatened with eviction from his House, 490–1, 492; reported averse to peerage for EB, 550n1; and EB's pension, 574–5, 576, VIII, 13, 17, 18, 286, 291, 310, 340, 345; on EB's quality of gratitude, VII, 578tn; thanked for his goodness, VIII, 330–2; EB's general attachment to, 335; supports *émigré* school at Penn, IX, 53

personal: marriage to Princess Charlotte, I, 141n2; Wilkes's libel against, 171n, 231, 257; his Birthday Ball, II, 141; reviews the Fleet, 496n2; his cheerfulness, III, 184, 190; introduces summer wheat, 177n3; Sayre's plot

to seize his person, 234; an imaginary plot to kill, IV, 134n2; Smelt's adulation of, 179–80, 184, 185n1; Powney stands in the Kings Stalls, 285; at Weymouth, VI, 392; the Pope's high opinion of, VII, 421n2; recognises Edmund Nagle as a brother sportsman, VIII, 77; another attempt to seize, 338, 379; daily attempts on, 432; copy of Reynolds's *Journey to the Netherlands* for, IX, 325; thought by some 'as weak as he is bad', IV, 167

also mentioned, I, 261n1, II, 1n4, 206n2, 286n3, V, 443, VII, 373n1, 457, 482, VIII, 190, IX, 369n1, 436

see also Court; King's Friends

George Augustus Frederick, Prince of Wales (1762–1830), later George IV correspondence with, listed above, p. 186 his Governors and Preceptors, II, 306, III, 269, 272n2, IV, 176n2, 184, 185; quarrels with George III over debts and friendship with Fox, V, 307; visits Prince William at Plymouth, 374

disputes over his Regency rights, V, 426, 427–9, 431–2, 434, 445–6, 449; makes up quarrel with Fox and Portland, 427n3; Fox's advice to, 429tn; EB urges a spirit of command, 429, 437–8; accepts most of Pitt's restrictions, 435tn, 436hn, 446n2; Memorial to, from Opposition, 439, 441–2, 444; Address from Westminster electors in support of, 442n2; Irish Address to, 448hn, 448n3, 450–1, 458; plans to prevent change of Ministry by, 449; sees the King, 450; Charlemont's loyal message to, 459, 462; Queen's hostility to, 461; gains credit all round, 463

his relations with Sheridan, V, 442, VI, 128–9; and Mrs Fitzherbert, V, 329–30hn, 444; a Royal and official marriage essential (1789), 444–5; attends Royal Academy dinner, 465; memorial to King on his conduct considered, 478–9, VI, 2; his supporters in Ireland lose office, 4n6; Priestley dedicates *Experiments and Observations* to, 14–15, 24, 27–8; visit to Yorkshire, 23–4

Reflections intended for friends of, VI, 272; rejects EB's pamphlets, 273, 310–11, VII, 58; his 'known disposition' anti-Jacobin, VI, 358; supports Proclamation against seditious writings in his maiden speech, 358n2; his democratic friends and servants a

Gormanston, 12th Viscount, *see* Preston, Jenico

Gosford, 2nd Viscount, *see* Acheson, Arthur

Gosling, Francis, banker, VIII, 14

Gosling, William, banker, VIII, 14

Goujon, French publisher, VI, 183n2

Gowan, George, Dublin printer, I, 25n3

Gowan, Jonathan, Dublin printer, I, 25n3

Gower, Earl, *see* Leveson Gower, George Granville

Gower, 2nd Earl, *see* Leveson Gower, Granville

Gower, Lady (Elizabeth, *suo jure* Countess of Sutherland, 1765–1839), wife of the preceding: 'outrageously democratical', VI, 390, 395

Graeme, Catherine, *see* Hampden, Mrs Thomas

Graeme, Colonel David, later General (d. 1792), II, 77n2, IV, 137

correspondence with, listed above, p. 133

Grafton, 3rd Duke of, *see* Fitzroy, Augustus Henry

Grafton, Duchess of (Anne Liddell), divorced wife of the preceding, II, 5

Grafton, Duchess of (Elizabeth Wrottesley, 1745–1822), second wife of the 3rd Duke, II, 58n3, IV, 145

Grafton Administration (March 1767–Jan. 1770)

Chatham ceases to take further part in Administration (March 1767), I, 300n1; attempts to form new Administration with Rockinghams fail, 315–18, 319, 320, 322–3, II, 375–6, IX, 391; Grafton remains head of old Administration in absence of Chatham, I, 317n3, II, 3hn.; appointments, I, 318, 319, 330–1, 355; hold on to Bute bottom, 319; rumoured dissolution, 328; death of Charles Townshend, their 'real and efficient leader', 327; Conway draws in Edgcumbe, 334n3; attacked in amendment to Address for neglect of national concerns, 335–6; EB criticised for attacking Irish policy, 338; must triumph in approaching elections, 338, and in divided Opposition, 336; negotiations with Bedfords, 339; Portland the first victim of 'this unconstitutional administration', 341; too disunited to take action against Wilkes in Middlesex election (1768), 349, 353, Rockinghams will not provoke on issue, 352; centripetal force of disunion, 353

Grafton tries to force Shelburne's

resignation, II, 3–4; the 'strange incoherent composition' can't last long, 5; Rockingham and Savile club a sarcasm on their conduct, 11; City petitions on Middlesex election, 34; alarmed by addresses and petitions to King, 41, 44–5, 75hn, attempt to prevent them, 50–2, petitions stress distinction between virtues of King and vices of Administration, 53; reappearance of Chatham threatens change of Fabric, 43; assurances of support stronger than ever, 51; conflicts within Ministry, 59; their most indefensible act the decision in Middlesex election, 70; Yorkshire petition goes forward, 76; Bucks County meeting reported in Ministerial papers, 80tn; not expected to last long (Oct. 1769), 91; Court will probably try Chatham again, 92, 101; dinner at Thatched House demonstrates hostility to, 92; Temple urges union with Rockinghams to get rid of, 105; 'a dependent Administration' of 'the Court System', 105; Wilkes's attack on Grenville, a triumph for, 107; Chatham will challenge on Corsica, America and right of election, 112; succeeded by North Ministry, 126n2

America: recall of Amherst, Governor of Virginia, II, 14; repeal of Townshend duties, 45n2; accused of misconduct on, 47. Civil List expenditure, 41n3. Neglect of Corsica, 94, 112. East India Company, Dividend Bill, I, 340, 342, 343; influence with Company, II, 27–8. Ireland: augmentation of Irish Army, I, 330, 332, 337, 338, 340, II, 99, EB's speech on, I, 343; Bill defeated, 353n1; Supply Bills, 339; Septennial (Octennial) Act, 339, 342, II, 14; Irish Tea duties, I, 340. Oppose Nullum Tempus Bill, 344–5, II, 38

Camden goes over to, II, 4, veers towards Chatham, 51n4, 98n3; Chatham animated against, 98, 105, 112; Fox supports, 51n3; Thomas Harley supports, 34n4; Kent freeholders hostile to, 115n3; Lincolnshire opposed to, 48; Mansfield has no connection with, I, 347; Duke and Duchess of Northumberland move away from, II, 91, 101; Aldermen Plumbe and Kirkman support, 33n5, n6; hostility to Rockingham, 62; Sulivan goes over to, 106n1, n2; Temple's relations with, 58

Grafton Administration (*cont.*)
also mentioned, II, 22hn, 65, 84, 114n
Administration writers, II, 29n4
Graham, Mrs Catharine Macaulay, *Observations on...the Earl of Stanhope*, VI, 214n1. *See also* Macaulay, Mrs Catharine
Graham, James (1755–1836), styled Marquess of Graham, M.P., Chancellor of Glasgow University, v, 118, 156n2
Graham, Robert (1744–1836), counsel against the petition of Middlesex freeholders, II, 23
Graingorge d'Orgeville, François-Jean de, Baron de Mesnil-Durand (1729–99), writer, VIII, 409
Granby, Marquess of, *see* Manners, Charles; Manners, John
Grant, James
correspondence with, listed above, p. 133
Grant, Rev. Richard (*c.* 1745–1826), of Westminster School, VI, 34n4
Grant, Mrs Richard, wife of the preceding, VI, 34
Grantham, Barons, *see* Robinson, Thomas
Grantley, 1st Baron, *see* Norton, Sir Fletcher
Granville, 2nd Earl, *see* Carteret, John
Grattan, Henry (1746–1820), M.P. for Dublin in Irish Parliament
correspondence with, listed above, p. 133
and Irish constitution: moves for independent Irish parliament, IV, 231hn; regards settlement of 1782 as complete, 455n1; monument to, proposed by Irish Commons, 460; his support necessary to Administration, v, 92; loses influence to Flood, 103n1; leads Opposition in Regency dispute, 446hn, 453n1; presses need for constitutional reform, VII, 351n4; his resolutions on parliamentary reform, 352; a friend to the monarchy, 363; sketch of Irish politics, 544–5; on the danger of Ireland going with France, VIII, 150–1; accused of not consulting English Cabinet, 165–6; refuses to see Windham in London, 168–9, 174n2, 181–2, 197; only hope for Ireland an Opposition led by, 178; English Administration determined to seduce or destroy, 195, 232–3; violence prevented only by his opposition, 233, IX, 138; thinks the best manufacturer of an Irish Jacobin a british minister, VIII, 386n4; on relations between English and Irish parliaments, IX, 123; takes up parliamentary reform

again, 144, 373; his programme of administrative reform stolen by Pitt, 149–50; melancholy picture of Ireland, 188; approves plan to raise Irish question in English parliament, 189, 190; supports Absentee Tax, 283n2; denounces methods of British Government, 334; his project for new taxes on English goods, 365
and Catholic emancipation: consulted by Kenmare on Penal statutes, IV, 421; supports Catholic franchise, VII, 40n1, 45; revises RBJr's petition, 46, speaks in support of it, 70, 71, 83–4, 94; on good terms with RBJr, 100, 294, 362, 366; on the treachery of Irish Secretaries, 118; the Protestant Ascendancy, 289, 365, VIII, 207; supports all measures to maintain order, VII, 351n4; urges need for education of Catholic clergy, VIII, 28–9, 162; presents Dublin petition for total emancipation, 125; introduces Catholic Relief Bill, 150–1, 152, X, 30hn; wants Hussey to stay in Ireland, VIII, 162, 199, 215; his motions for Catholic relief stolen by Irish clique, 175, 232, X, 30; his Catholic Bill defeated in Irish Commons, VIII, 192n2; EB wishes all Catholics to be advised by, 249; abandons amendment to Indemnity Bill, IX, 122
and Fitzwilliam: his promise of support to Fitzwilliam 'worth all the Rest', VIII, 20; consulted over Lord Lieutenancy by Fitzwilliam, 31hn, by Pitt, 33, 34, 43, 57n2, 174n7, by Loughborough, 74–5, 76tn; advises Fitzwilliam to go to Ireland, 61, 78, supports him there, 154, urged by EB to persuade him to stay, 174; gives EB the facts, 185; on Fitzwilliam's achievements, 186–8; on Portland's betrayal of Ireland, 186–7; Fitzwilliam accused of acquiescing in his prejudices, 228n2; Fitzwilliam's estrangement from Portland on account of, IX, 75; not acting in concert with Fitzwilliam, 364–5
and EB: EB recommends Mr Shippen to, v, 453, Therry, VIII, 95–6, Kiernan, 96–7; visits to EB, VII, 289, VIII, 164; consulted by EB on Provostship of Trinity College, Dublin, 5–7, 19, 28, 46, 48; EB on his genius and patriotism, VII, 351–2, 360, 510, 4; his fire and humanity, 3; should have a 'never fading Garland' for his head,

Grattan, Henry (*cont.*)
  133; is 'far out of reach of Obloquy', 174; consoled by EB's approbation, 187–8; thinks there is wisdom in EB's ardour, 196; is sent print of RBJr's portrait, 289–90; EB's death-bed lament over, IX, 373
  also mentioned, VII, 568n1, VIII, 32n2, 37n1, 143, 155, 156, 176, 227hn, IX, 444
Grattan, Mrs Henry (Henrietta Fitzgerald, *c.* 1754–1838), wife of the preceding: visits to Beaconsfield, VII, 289, VIII, 164; RBJr visits in Ireland, VII, 547; her sympathy, VIII, 7; also mentioned, V, 453, VII, 353, 362, 366, VIII, 208, 233
Grattan, Mrs James (Mary Marlay, d. 1768), mother of Henry Grattan, V, 92, VIII, 20
Grave, Pierre-Marie, Chevalier de (1755–1823)
  correspondence with, listed above, p. 133
  his letter to the National Assembly, VII, 180, 181, 182, 183n1; accepts, and resigns from, Ministry of War in new French Constitution, 182–3
Graves, Admiral Samuel (1713–87), III, 250
Gravier, Charles, Comte de Vergennes (1719–87), French Foreign Minister, V, 52n3, VI, 172
Gray, James (d. 1796), joint-owner of *Morning Chronicle*, VI, 451n3
Gray, Dr John
  correspondence with, listed above, p. 134
Gray, Thomas (1716–71), poet, I, 164n1, IX, 325
Greaves, William (d. 1787)
  correspondence with, listed above, p. 134
Grecian coffee-house, I, 125
Green, Henry, Alderman, IV, 269n3
Greenwood, C. G.
  correspondence with, listed above, p. 134
Greenwood, John
  correspondence with, listed above, p. 134
Greenwood, Mr, election agent at Malton, VII, 560
Greeves, Mr, *see* Grieve, George
Gregory, Dorothea (*c.* 1756–1830), adopted daughter of Mrs Montagu, III, 266
Gregory, Robert (*c.* 1729–1810), M.P.
  correspondence with, listed above, p. 134
  contests Maidstone, I, 348; his horses, II, 316; Director of East India Company, 355n2, 381, 384, 386, 401n2, 423n6, IV, 308n4; Rockingham's high opinion of, II, 498;

elected to Committee of Proprietors, 497n2; loses Maidstone, III, 34, 49; visits Beaconsfield, 389; EB meets monthly at Thursday Club, IV, 334; resigns Directorship, V, 30hn
Grenada, *see* West Indies
Grenville, Sir Bevil (1596–1643), VII, 432
Grenville, George (1712–70), M.P.
  correspondence with, listed above, p. 134
  Secretary of State, I, 151n2, 206n1; becomes First Lord of the Treasury and Chancellor of Exchequer on Bute's resignation, 168n1; remains suspicious of Bute's influence, 169n3; the King's aversion to, 194n3, n4; fall of his Ministry, 204hn
  in opposition: his appointees dismissed by Rockingham, 214hn; opposes Ministry on America, 223–4, 229, 232, on Window Tax, 250, on the Embargo on export of corn, 278, 279n1; 'the Grand Financier', 225; plans coalition against Rockingham, 234, 235; not included in Pitt's Administration, 261; Rockinghams refuse to join, 263; his motion on relief of the poor, 278n5; views on East India question, 303n4, 305; relations with the Bedfords, 282, 284, 286–7, 302, II, 4; growing support for, from Rockingham followers, I, 309–10; proposed alliance, 317, 325n, 327; excommunicates Rockingham party over America, 336, 338; absents himself from House, 340, 343; supports Nullum Tempus Bill, 345; dines with Minority at Thatched House, II, 24, 92; 'a perfect coalition' with Rockinghams on the election issue, 26, 42
  the 'family system': reconciliation with Temple, I, 206, 261, 262; joins with Temple and Chatham, II, 46, 75; alliance with Rockingham uneasy, 87–8, 91, 93, 101, 105; gives limited support to County petitions, 48, 73; invites EB to Wotton, 72; supports, but does not attend, County meeting, 78–9; speech on Wilkes, 103, 104, 107; Wilkes's reply, 117; his Bill on controverted elections, 126, 138, III, 88; political effects of his death, II, 169hn, 175n1; his Stamp Act, III, 308n2
  RBSr recommended to, for Grenades post, I, 174tn; and EB's Irish pension, 189; his good relations with EB, II, 264–5, their common interest in Buckinghamshire roads, 125

Grenville, George (*cont.*)

supporters of: Wedderburn, II, 23n1, Clive, 106, 181, Suffolk, 185n2, T. Townshend, 407; his man of business, T. Whately, 55, 56, 63

also mentioned, I, 209, II, 23n4, 28, 60n2, 69n2, 71hn, 90n4, 112hn, 113n2, 449, 450, IV, 137, IX, 394, 450

see also Grenville Administration; Grenville Family; Grenville Party

Grenville, Mrs George (Elizabeth Wyndham, d. 1769), wife of the preceding, VII, 395

Grenville, George Nugent (1753–1813), later (1779) 3rd Earl Temple and (1784) 1st Marquess of Buckingham

correspondence with, listed above, p. 103

attends Buckinghamshire meeting, II, 78, 85; elected member for County, 450, III, 30, 33, 34n, 41; motion on French treaty with America, 419n1; becomes 3rd Earl Temple, IV, 129hn; puts up brother for County, 130; EB supports Verney against, 131–2; Portland defends his election policy, 136–8; his disposition dreaded in Bucks, 151–2; as Chairman of County Meeting opposes radical programme, 226hn, is given Mahon's proposals to read at meeting, 235

Lord Lieutenant of Ireland, V, 23hn, 29, 31, 32, 47, 60hn; resigns, 82; becomes sole Secretary of State on defeat of Fox's India Bill, 119hn; dismisses EB from office, 119; EB's political enemy becomes Marquess, 196n3; as Lord Lieutenant of Ireland again, refuses to transmit loyal address to Prince of Wales, 448, 450hn; his amnesty to signatories, 459hn, 464n4; opposition to, in Irish parliament, 460; Ponsonby will enter no engagement with, 464n3; resigns, 475

protests against proposed removal of French clergy from Winchester, VII, 491–2, 497–9, X, 29; a trustee for *émigré* school at Penn, VIII, 396, 397, 400, 442, 444, 448, 450, IX, 8, 12, 13tn, 14; visits school, 17, 42–3, 51; regarded as sole selector of boys by Bishop of St Pol, 18–19, 22–3, 25–6, 28–9, 34–5, 39–40; insists on EB's having final selection, 31–2, 36; sends clothes for boys, 32–3, 42; presents cannon and colours, 128–9; asked to continue support in EB's will, 379

also mentioned, VII, 71, 395n2, 396, VIII, 217n3, 374, IX, 403

see also Grenville Family

Grenville, Henry (1717–84), M.P. for Buckingham borough, II, 78, IV, 132, 132n3

Grenville, Mrs Henry (Eleanora Margaret Banks, 1723–93), wife of the preceding, IV, 132n3

Grenville, Hester, *see* Chatham, Countess of

Grenville, James (1742–1825), M.P. for Buckinghamshire, II, 436, IV, 132, 132n3, IX, 30, 39n2, 42

Grenville, Richard Temple Nugent Brydges Chandos, styled Earl Temple (1776–1839), VIII, 374, IX, 20

Grenville, Thomas (1755–1846), M.P. for Buckinghamshire, then for Aldeburgh

correspondence with, listed above, p. 134

at the Aylesbury Races, II, 450; rival candidate to Verney interest, IV, 129hn, 130–2, 140; Portland upholds his family right to seat, 137–8; elected unopposed, 148; EB defends his original stand against, 151–2; votes with Opposition, 153; supports County petition, 229; does not stand again, V, 136n3

sent by Fox on mission to France, V, 52; disapproves of Windham's negotiations with Government, VII, 288; his policy to await events, 313; abandons neutral position, 515n7; follows Portland and supports Administration, 529tn; sent on mission to Vienna, VIII, 59n2, 60, 62; his reported Peace Embassy to Paris, IX, 84; 'one of the most sensible men' EB knows, VIII, 183

also mentioned, VI, 248hn, 249tn, VII, 187n1, VIII, 68n3

see also Grenville Family

Grenville, William Wyndham (1759–1834), later (1790) 1st Baron, M.P.

correspondence with, listed above, p. 134

a leader of Court party, V, 85tn; defeats Verney for Buckinghamshire (1784), 143hn, VI, 120n7; re-elected unopposed (1789), IX, 436, elected with Verney (1790), VI, 120–1; succeeds EB as Paymaster of the Forces, V, 214n1; an ally of Hastings, 318; Speaker of Commons, IX, 435hn; Home Secretary, 436hn; sent on mission to France, V, 347–8; secures French neutrality towards Holland, 349–50; EB appeals to, on Borland's sentence, VI, 8–9, 12; recommends

Harford, Joseph (*cont.*)
326, thought him the best candidate, 329; commits the Club to backing Cruger, 333tn

EB recommends to Benjamin Franklin in Paris, v, 27; nominates RBSr as Recorder of Bristol, 114tn; is 'thoroughly master' of EB's views on Dissent, vi, 103, was once a Dissenter himself, 103n2; EB on his great merits, iv, 272, v, 27

also mentioned, iii, 61, 69hn, 79tn, 132n4, 260n3, 440hn, iv, 319

Harford, Mrs Joseph (Hannah Kill, 1741–1811), wife of the preceding, iv, 299

Harford, Richard
correspondence with, listed above, p. 135

Harford, Cowles and Co., Quaker iron merchants in Bristol
correspondence with, listed above, p. 135
disagreement with EB over Irish Trade Bill, iii, 440–6; EB's letter to, printed in *Two Letters to Gentlemen of Bristol*, 431hn, iv, 224n3

Hargrave, Christopher (*c.* 1710–87), Chancery solicitor
correspondence with, listed above, p. 135
his financial involvement with EB and WB, iii, 372–4, iv, 77–8, 106, vii, 551n2; also mentioned, iii, 251n5

Hargrave, Mrs Christopher (Ann Northey, d. 1782), wife of the preceding, iii, 373

Hargrave, Francis (*c.* 1741–1821), barrister, iii, 251

Hargrave, Major Richard, iii, 75n2

Harley, Lady Margaret Cavendish, *see* Portland, Dowager Duchess of

Harley, Thomas (1730–1804), M.P. for City of London, ii, 34n4; for Herefordshire, iii, 268n4, v, 97

Harness, Captain William (*c.* 1764–1804)
correspondence with, listed above, p. 135
expresses abhorrence of people of Dronfield at demonstration against EB, vii, 340–1

Harrach, Karl Borromäus, Graf von (1761–1829), dines with EB, vii, 429

Harris, Sir James (1746–1820), later (1787) 1st Baron Malmesbury
correspondence with, listed above, p. 152
British envoy in Holland, v, 277hn; his successful policy on Dutch internal politics, 355; becomes Baron Malmesbury, 355n2; asks for copy of *Reflections*, ed. 4, vi, 179; reports conversation between Portland and Fox, vii,

149n2, 150; 'wholly occupied' with Forest Bill, 151; discourses on coalition negotiations, 305; agrees with EB on foreign affairs, 307; at Portland's Whig dinner, 314; will support Government, 338; refuses office, 345n1

sent on peace mission to Paris, ix, 94hn, 96; his reception, 101n7; everything put blindfold into his hands by Ministers, 103, 106; his shameful terms, 109; 'sollicitor of disgrace', 126; fills EB with despair, 155; his mission must mean war against popery, 163; his peace terms refused by Directory, 202hn; kicked out of France, 203, 211; his humiliation, 204, 205; Mrs Crewe drinks his health, 208; *Two Letters* concerned with, 211n2; silent in debate on failure of peace negotiations, 216; King of Prussia's infamy in approving his terms, 298

his *Diary* quoted, vii, 149n2, 151tn, 193n2, 338hn, 345n1, ix, 96n2

also mentioned, v, 229n2, vii, 436, ix, 154, 219n4

Harris, Lady (Harriet Maria Amyand, 1761–1830), wife of the preceding: entertains EB with her sister at Minto, v, 229; also mentioned, 230, 355

Harris, John (*c.* 1726–1801), wine merchant, Sheriff of Bristol: and arrangements for publication of *A Letter to the Sheriffs of Bristol*, iii, 332, 333–4

Harris, W.
correspondence with, listed above, p. 135

Harrison, Edward
correspondence with, listed above, p. 135

Harrison, John (1738–1811), M.P.: his motion for the reduction of useless places, ix, 280, 285n3, the reverse of EB's reform, 281

Harrison, Joseph (1709–87): acts as EB's assistant in Rockingham's house, i, 240n4; has a rough time as Collector of Customs at Boston, ii, 12

Harson, Daniel (d. 1779), Bristol Collector of Customs: and Import of Irish Provisons Act, iii, 132n4, 141, 143, 144–5, ix, 406n2; despatches business for Champion, iii, 292–3, 330; EB gets his name included in Admiralty warrant, iv, 68, cp ix, 425–6

Hart, Major George Vaughan (1752–1832), Paymaster of the King's troops in Madras, vii, 427hn

Hastings, Warren, Impeachment of (*cont.*)
duration of speeches, v, 373, 379tn, VII,
93n7, n8, 94, 113, of Trial, 116,
Report on, 534, 538–40; EB's tenth
year of warfare, VI, 192

Publication of Proceedings: EB's plan
for complete printed record of trial,
VI, 63, VIII, 405, 413, 416–17, 418,
439, IX, 62–3, 237–8; Hastings publishes his side of Trial, VIII, 439n6

Hastings, William (d. 1808), Fitzwilliam's
agent at Malton, v, 339tn, VII,
568n2, VIII, 368n3

Haswell, Robert, publisher of *Morning
Post*, IV, 351hn

Hatsell, John (1733–1820), Clerk of the
House of Commons
correspondence with, listed above, p. 136
EB invited to meet, VI, 209: consulted
over EB's petition, VIII, 416–17; his
admiration for *Reflections*, X, 24; also
mentioned, III, 155n2, VI, 139

Hatsell, Mrs John (*née* Ekins, *c.* 1731–
1804), wife of the preceding: EB
invited to meet, VI, 209

Hatt, Elizabeth, *see* Noble, Mrs John

Hatt, Richard, X, 43

Hatton, Christopher (1540–91), VIII, 69

Hauteville, Jeanne-Caulet d', *see* Dupont,
Madame

Hautoÿ, Comtesse de
correspondence with, listed above, p. 136

Haviland, Mary, *see* Ruxton, Mrs Samuel

Haviland, Captain, later Major, Thomas
(d. 1795): in the West Indies, v,
278; dines at Beaconsfield, VII, 4;
promoted Major, 483; engaged to
EB's niece, 493; their marriage
settlement, 493n6; his frequent letters
to the Burkes, 560; EB recommends as
aide de camp to Fitzwilliam, VIII, 274;
dies at Martinique, 290, 292–3, 295,
297, 306; EB's love for, 294; birth
of his son, 312; also mentioned, v,
102n1, VI, 66n4, IX, 377, 453

Haviland, Mrs Thomas, *see* French, Mary
Cecilia

Haviland (later Haviland-Burke), Thomas
William Aston (1795–1852), son of
Mary French and Major Haviland,
last male representative of EB's
family, VIII, 312, 314

Haviland, General William (1718–84),
friend and neighbour of EB
correspondence with, listed above, p. 136
Commander-in-Chief at Plymouth, IV,
126n4; his death, v, 278; his house,
Tyler's Green, to be used for French

priests, VIII, 317, 320, 396, taken
over by EB for *émigré* boys school,
400, 444, 451, IX, 5n3; also mentioned, IV, 126, v, 238n4, VII, 4n6
493, IX, 453

Haviland, Mrs William (Salusbury Aston,
d. 1807), wife of the preceding,
mother-in-law of EB's niece
correspondence with, listed above, p. 136
death of her husband and her daughter,
v, 278; kindness to Dupont, VI, 262;
dines with the Burkes, VII, 4; the
soul of Beaconsfield, 85; and an old
friend's marriage, 190–1; sells her
house at Penn, 191n2; her property,
493; French Laurence writes to, on
RBJr's last illness and death, 562–3,
563–6; her son's death, VIII, 290, 294;
EB's love for, 294, and Jane Burke's
sympathy, 296; also mentioned, VI,
391, VIII, 353

Haviland family: visit to Beaconsfield, v,
374; also mentioned, 405, VIII, 401

Havré, Joseph-Anne-Auguste-Maximilien,
Duc d', et de Croy (1744–1839)
correspondence with, listed above, p. 136

Hawke, Sir Edward (1705–81), later (1776)
1st Baron: appointed First Lord of the
Admiralty, I, 283; resigns, II, 185;
Admiral of the Fleet, IV, 32; also
mentioned, I, 298

Hawke, Martin Bladen (1744–1805), M.P.,
intervenes as third candidate at
York, III, 62

Hawkesbury, 1st Baron, *see* Jenkinson,
Charles

Hawkesbury, Lord, *see* Jenkinson, Robert
Banks

Hawkesworth, John, his edition of Swift's
Works, I, 194

Hawkins, Rev. Dr James (*c.* 1724–1807),
Bishop of Raphoe
correspondence with, listed above, p. 136

Hawkins, Sir John (1719–89), on Samuel
Dyer, II, 334n2

Hawkswell, Richard, IV, 74n1
correspondence with, listed above,
p. 136–7

Hawley, General Henry, an early member
of the Debating Club in Dublin, I,
92

Hay, Edward (*c.* 1761–1826)
correspondence with, listed above, p. 137
brings Wexford Catholic petition to the
King, VIII, 264, 271; visits EB at
Beaconsfield, 264n5; takes books back
to Maynooth College, 264–5, 270,
288; his plan of enumeration, 264,

Heysham family, VI, 363

Hibernian Academy, Dublin, I, 91n3, IV, 458

Hibernian Antiquarian Society, V, 109, 110

Hickey, Ann (*c.* 1757–1826), EB's unofficial secretary, V, 238, 266, 267, VI, 14, 262, VII, 107, IX, 97, 110; 'good-natured and able', 207

Hickey, John (1751–95), sculptor
correspondence with, listed above, p. 137
commissioned for Dowdeswell's monument, III, 242, 454; recommended by EB to a patron, 453–4, and for the Grattan Monument, IV, 460; his bust of George Thicknesse, VII, 38hn; dies before finishing Garrick memorial, 561tn, VIII, 115, IX, 323–4

Hickey, Joseph (*c.* 1714–94), the Burkes' lawyer: left in the lurch as security for Lord Lisle, I, 230; and WB's speculations, II, 382hn; manages petition on American Acts, 432, 502; helps with campaign against Absentee Tax, 482hn, 484n1, 486, 487; goes bail for Walter Nagle, III, 391n4; undertakes EB's case against Haswell, IV, 351; his inconvenient dinner hour, V, 101; also mentioned, II, 416, 418, III, 75, IV, 159n2, VI, 14n1, 340n8, VII, 107n6, VIII, 401n8, IX, 440hn

Hickey, Joseph, Jr (1745–1827)
correspondence with, listed above, p. 137
brings news from Paris, VI, 340; recommended for office to Chancellor, IX, 440

Hickey, Sarah (*c.* 1757–1824), twin sister of Ann, V, 238

Hickey, William (1749–1809)
correspondence with, listed above, p. 137–8
anecdotes from *Memoirs*: a turtle feast in India, I, 236n1; the case of Robert Jones, II, 323hn; WB's speculations, 382–3hn; Ann and Sarah Hickey, V, 238n3; WB's duel, 345n2; Cuppage's wonderful cure, VI, 116n3; WB's horse, 454n5; Jane Burke's overdose, VII, 183hn

Hickman, Mary, *see* Charlemont, Countess of

Hickman, Miss, sister of Lady Charlemont, II, 333, 547; V, 343, 452, 462

Hickman, Thomas, father of Lady Charlemont, II, 24n2

Hiffernan, Paul (1719–77), his pamphlet *Tickler*, I, 102n2

Hill, Aaron (1685–1750), *Zara*, II, 1n4

Hill, Anne, *see* Gataker, Mrs Thomas

Hill, Arthur (1753–1801), styled Earl of Hillsborough, later (1793) 2nd Marquess of Downshire, Irish M.P.: election campaign against, VI, 123; cost of re-election, 125tn; chief enemy of Catholic Bill, VIII, 193–4; his intemperate counsels govern Ministry, 195, 201

Hill, Sir George Fitzgerald, 2nd Baronet (1763–1839), VIII, 186n15

Hill, Sir Hugh, 1st Baronet (1738–95)
correspondence with, listed above, p. 138

Hill, James (d. 1802), Sheriff of Bristol, III, 75
correspondence with, listed above, p. 138
Chairman of committee to oppose Bill on insolvent debtors, IV, 231–2

Hill, J., Jr ('Mr. Kill'), Spanish merchant: EB recommends to Benjamin Franklin, V, 27–8

Hill, Dr John (*c.* 1716–75), quack doctor, I, 140, VII, 209; EB's mock Funeral Oration on, I, 140n2

Hill, John Forster, reports on house for refugee clergy, VIII, 321n1

Hill, Joseph (*c.* 1720–1811), solicitor, Lord Inchiquin's legal adviser, VII, 153, 154–5, 190, IX, 439–40, 467
correspondence with, listed above, p. 138

Hill, [Sir] Richard [2nd Baronet, 1732–1808]
correspondence with, listed above, p. 138

Hill, Thomas (d. 1790), Fitzwilliam's London agent, VI, 123n1

Hill, Wills (1718–93), 1st Earl of Hillsborough, later (1789) 1st Marquess of Downshire
correspondence with, listed above, p. 138
Secretary of State for Colonies: his circular letters to American Governors, II, 14, III, 80; and the New York Assembly, II, 214hn, 216n2, 229, 230; EB attacks 'in a sober way', 268; election of colonial agents, 289; New York boundary dispute, 291, 292; resigns office, 327, 331, 348; receives English Earldom, 327
Secretary of State for Southern Department, IV, 161n5; EB's letters on India sent to, 303hn, 306hn, 307hn, 311; EB intercedes with, for Raja of Tanjore, 307–10, 316, and for the Maratha Agents, 356–8, IX, 430–1; unwilling for exchange of Burgoyne and Laurens, IV, 390tn; ready to consider treatment of Laurens, 391
his influence in Ireland, III, 386; advises against raising religious ques-

Hill, Wills (*cont.*)

tions, IV, 401n5; campaign to dethrone, VI, 123

also mentioned, II, 428hn

Hillsborough, 1st Earl of, *see* Hill, Wills

Hillsborough, 2nd Earl of, *see* Hill, Arthur

Hilton, William

correspondence with, listed above, p. 138

Hinchinbroke, Viscountess (Lady Elizabeth Montagu, d. 1768), I, 356

Hindus ('Gentoos'): Humund Rao sympathetically treated at Beaconsfield, IV, 368: their affairs cost EB sleepless nights, V, 124; indifference of the English to, 151; tried under their own law in civil suits, 367n3; also mentioned, IV, 411–12

'Hints for an Essay on the Drama', *see* Burke, Edmund: Works

Hipkis, Mr, Monmouth ironmonger, I, 111

Hippisley, John Coxe (*c.* 1748–1825), later (1796) 1st Baronet, M.P., friend of EB and WB

correspondence with, listed above, p. 138

Deputy to Resident at Tanjore, V, 400hn; brings letters from WB in India, 400; intervenes in EB's dispute with Caillaud, VI, 244n1; EB dines with, 332, 334; promotes contact between Papacy and Britain, VII, 420hn, 471, 483n1; his arrangements for mission questioned, 441, 482, 488, 513; defends his actions, 444–5; gets supplies for British Navy from Papal States, 440; induces Pope to take action on Ireland, 441, 443, 512; proposes a 'condoling visit' to Beaconsfield, VIII, 380; negotiates marriage of Princess Royal, IX, 318hn, 318n2

also mentioned, V, 218n1, 224hn, VI, 138hn

Hippisley, Mrs John Coxe (Margaret Steuart, 1755–99), wife of the preceding: her kindness to WB in India, V, 400; relations in Rome, VII, 420hn; proposed visit to Beaconsfield, VIII, 380; also mentioned, VII, 439hn, 444

Hippisley, Richard Coxe, *see* Coxe, Richard Hippisley

Hippocrates, I, 89, VIII, 420; Dr Sheridan the Irish, I, 362

Hirsinger, Yves (d. 1824), French chargé d'affaires, VII, 106

History, *see* Burke, Edmund, Opinions

Hoadly, Benjamin (1706–57), *The Suspicious Husband*, II, 1n4

Hobart, George (1731–1804), 3rd Earl of Buckinghamshire, VII, 507n1

Hobart, Henry (1738–99), M.P., elected for Norwich, V, 280n1, 282, IX, 43n1

Hobart, John, 2nd Earl of Buckinghamshire (1723–93): Lord Lieutenant of Ireland, I, 203n, III, 386n1, IV, 67hn; gives no support to Catholic Bill, 3n2; ought to follow advice of Speaker, 5, 9; the 'hero of non-resistance', 359

gives up hope of Norfolk petition, II, 50n8; his motion on Boston, 515, 523, III, 386

Hobart, Maria Frances Mary, *see* Guilford, Countess of

Hobart, Major Robert (1760–1816), later (1793) styled Lord Hobart, M.P. in English and Irish Parliaments

correspondence with, listed above, p. 138

Chief Secretary to Lord Lieutenant of Ireland, VI, 463n5; talks with RBJr on Catholic relief, 463; returns from London with full instructions, 470, VII, 6, 13n1, 16; was at Westminster School with RBJr, 6n6, 118; differences with RBJr on Irish Catholics, 13–14, 18–19, 25–6, 28–9, 30–2, 37, 87, 134, 202n, 295–6; warns Irish Commons of RBJr's presence, 47; on *Letter to Sir Hercules Langrishe*, 49n4; 'made by the Beresford Party', 71; visits to England, 120tn, 130, 365; insists on Protestant Ascendancy, 131, 238; has no need to be jealous of RBJr, 137; the genius of his politics purely Irish, 290; deputed to steer Catholic Bill through parliament, 350n5

becomes Lord Hobart and resigns office, VII, 507n1, 509hn; consulted on education of Irish Catholic clergy, 507; EB has never spoken to, 511; appointed Governor of Madras, then Governor-General of Bengal, 511n4, 545

also mentioned, VI, 467hn, 471n1, VII, 27n2

Hobart, Mrs Robert (Eleanor Agnes Eden, 1777–1851), wife of the preceding, IV, 360, IX, 209n2

Hobbes, Thomas, I, 111n2

Hobhouse, B., his canvassing methods at Bristol, IV, 267n4

Hoche, Louis-Lazare (1768–97), Republican general, VIII, 149n4, 299hn; his success at Quiberon, 299hn; orders execution of Bishop of Dol, IX, 164n3; Tone joins his staff, 115n3; in charge

Hoche, Louis-Lazare (*cont.*)
of French fleet in Brest, 164n2, expected to land in Ireland, 164, 221hn, 222, 224, 260, 335n2, 352

Hodgekinson, Francis (*c.* 1757–1840), Fellow of Trinity College, Dublin: goes to London with petition, VIII, 28n2, 47

Hodgson, William
correspondence with, listed above, p. 138

Hoensbroeck d'Oest, César-Constantin-François de, Prince-Bishop of Liége, VI, 217n3

Hogarth, William (1697–1764): Reynolds on, II, 17; *Analysis of Beauty*, IX, 471; also mentioned, 199

Hoghton, Sir Henry, 6th Baronet (1728–95), M.P., VII, 357
correspondence with, listed above, p. 138

Hoheb, Samuel, Jewish merchant at St Eustatius
correspondence with, listed above, p. 138
petition for redress of losses presented by EB, IV, 402–3; sends Memorial to Treasury, 452, receives nothing, 453tn

Hohenlohe-Kirchberg, Friedrich Wilhelm Fürst von (1732–96), promotes James Nagle, VII, 452, 459

Holbach, Paul Heinrich Dietrich, Baron d' (1723–89), I, 234

Holdernesse, Earl of, *see* D'Arcy, Robert

Holker, Lawrence, Deputy Governor of the Irish Society, II, 482n4

Holland: Dutch convoy seized (1780), IV, 180, 189; rupture with (1781), 333, X, 12; proposed mediation of Russia (1782), IV, 441, X, 12; ships taken at St Eustatius, IV, 343; EB sick of the war, X, 12; Patriot revolt in, suppressed by Prussian invasion (1787), V, 346, 347, 349n7, 352n, 354, 415n1, VI, 217; reported surrender of Amsterdam, V, 351; destruction of French Interest in, 354, 414, England's part in 355; Dutch crisis settled, 358n2

Triple Alliance between Prussia, Great Britain and (1788), VI, 118n5, VII, 30n3, 317n3, not 'quite prudent', VI, 118; ought to arm against France, VII, 317; France declares war against Great Britain and, 348hn, 353; driven out of Linselles, 415, defeated at Menin, 428n6; Treaty with, for subsidising Prussian troops, 542n2, IX, 200n4; their ships taken 'in Trust', VIII, 122; overrun by France, 135n2, 149, 369; Great Britain's power and commerce ruined by loss of, 134,

EB's Paper on loss, 135; Dutch Colony at Cape of Good Hope captured, 351, 388; French peace terms include non-interference in internal affairs of, 387n4; the strong to be allowed to 'scramble for the wreck' of, 388; no hopes of, as an Ally (1796), IX, 203, remains in the power of France, 212, 216; new christened the Batavian Republick, 265; French armament from, 272

Holland, 1st Baron, *see* Fox, Henry

Holland, 2nd Baron, *see* Fox, Stephen

Holland, Lady (Mary Fitzpatrick, d. 1778), wife of the preceding, IX, 403

Holliday, J.
correspondence with, listed above, p. 138

Holroyd, John Baker, 1st Baron Sheffield (1735–1821), M.P. for Bristol
correspondence with, listed above, p. 179
concern for French refugees, VII, 274; his news from Ireland, 285–6

Holt, Richard (d. 1783), Assistant Secretary to the East India Company, IV, 365

Holt, Robert, in the service of the East India Company: his evidence before Managers, V, 391hn; EB brings him off decently, 392–3; also mentioned, 396

Holwell, John Zephaniah (1711–98), *India Tracts*, V, 387; *Interesting Historical Events . . .*, 387n3

Homan, Richard, his ancient deer's head, V, 375–6

Homer: *Iliad*, EB examined in, I, 2, prescribed for Shackleton and RBSr, 69, young Kearney examined in, 97, young Richard forward in, II, 136, quoted, 510, V, 224, VI, 76, 90, VIII, 30, also mentioned, VII, 600; *Odyssey*, quoted, V, 72, VIII, 408, IX, 307; other references, I, 150, VI, 86, 224, X, 4

Homer, Dr Henry (1753–91), joint editor of Bellenden's *De Statu Libri Tres*, with dedications to Burke, Fox and North, V, 293–4, 336
correspondence with, listed above, p. 138

Hompesch's Hussars, VIII, 421n1

Hood, Alexander (1727–1814), later (1794) 1st Baron Bridport: his conduct at Keppel's court-martial, IV, 286; wins naval victory off l'Orient, VIII, 273; fails to intercept French fleet, IX, 222–3

Hood, Samuel, 1st Baron Hood (1724–1816), M.P.: returned for Westminster, V, 149n1; appointed Lord of Admiralty,

Howard, Charles (*cont.*)
lic (1778), IX, 422hn, gets EB to draft preamble for Catholic Relief Bill, 422–3; becomes an Anglican, IV, 242n1; member of Coalition Treasury Board, V, 82n4; moves for papers in debate on Fitzwilliam's recall, VIII, 238; attacks *Reflections* as subversive, 239, 413; witness for defence at O'Connor's trial, IX, 123n4

Howard, Frederick, 5th Earl of Carlisle (1748–1825)
correspondence with, listed above, p. 109
goes on Lord North's peace mission to America, III, 425n3, IV, 29n3, 34, 88n1; Eden's *Four Letters* to, 170hn; appointed Lord Lieutenant of Ireland, 358hn, 359; favours toleration, but unwilling to avow it, 401; his Popery Bill a credit to his government, 432; resigns on Rockingham's forming Administration, 432hn, 433tn; appointed Lord Steward of the Household, 446, 450n1; on EB's speech at Rockingham meeting, V, 9hn; Portland proposes for Privy Seal, 78; EB urges publication of his speech at York County Meeting, 144–5; a pall bearer for Reynolds, VII, 80; dines with EB and other Opposition members, 313
advises Fitzwilliam to modify his Irish policy, VIII, 172; Fitzwilliam's Letter to, 172n5, 180, 183hn, 275; his Letter in reply, 184n; Fitzwilliam's 2nd Letter to, 209, 211, 217, 224n3, 3rd Letter to, 227n1; sounds Fitzwilliam on new Irish government, IX, 350–1, 366, 367; EB on his 'impudence', 355
also mentioned, IV, 420tn, VI, 280n4

Howard, General George (1718–96), M.P., II, 199

Howard, [Sir] George [1718–96]
correspondence with, listed above, p. 139

Howard, Gorges Edmund (1715–86), Dublin solicitor
correspondence with, listed above, p. 139
on the sale of Gifford's estate, II, 140n4; EB sends dramatic pieces by, to Garrick, 333–4

Howard, Henry, 12th Earl of Suffolk (1739–79)
correspondence with, listed above, p. 182
becomes Lord Privy Seal, II, 185, 219; Secretary of State for Southern Department, 323hn; advises reprieve for Robert Jones after EB's inter-cession, 323–5; Secretary of State for Northern Department, III, 102n3; rejects conciliation with America, 102, 105, IX, 406; EB appeals to, against respite for wreck-plunderers, III, 212–13; receives Freedom of Bristol, 366, 367–8, 382, IV, 50; his death, 161n5
also mentioned, III, 157, IV, 134n2, 135tn

Howard, Henry Bowes, 11th Earl of Suffolk, II, 36n4

Howard, John, 15th Earl of Suffolk (1739–1820), VII, 539n3, IX, 294n2

Howard, John (*c.* 1726–90), prison reformer, VIII, 175n2

Howard, Martin, Jr (d. 1781)
correspondence with, listed above, p. 139
his losses in Rhode Island riots, IX, 458

Howard, Philip (1730–1810)
correspondence with, listed above, p. 139

Howard, Thomas (1721–83), later (1779) 13th Earl of Suffolk, II, 36

Howard, Mrs Thomas (Elizabeth Kingscote, d. 1769), wife of the preceding, II, 36

Howard, Thomas, 3rd Earl of Effingham (1747–91)
correspondence with, listed above, p. 124
resigns his commission, III, 166

Howard, William, 1st Viscount Stafford, impeached for complicity in Popish plot, VI, 175n3

Howe, John (d. 1769), VI, 116n5

Howe, Mrs John (Caroline Howe, *c.* 1721–1814), wife of the preceding, VI, 116n5

Howe, Admiral Richard, 4th Viscount Howe (1726–99), M.P.: Treasurer of the Navy, I, 219; his Nottingham interests, III, 121, 331hn; heads peace commission to America with General Howe, 272hn; makes rapid progress, 305, 309; Governor Johnstone intends impeaching, IV, 29; rumoured to be replacing Hardy as Commander of the Fleet, 107; to be included in Coalition Administration, 144, 154; the Glorious First of June, VII, 548, VIII, 100; his visit to mutinous seamen at Plymouth alarms EB, IX, 348; also mentioned, III, 428, IV, 334hn

Howe, General Sir William (1729–1814), M.P.: returned for Nottingham, III, 63n5; supports hosiery manufacturers' complaints, 121, presents their petition, 130
evacuates Boston, III, 263–5, 266; and Major Maxwell's court-martial, 272hn,

Howe, General Sir William (*cont.*)
273tn; reports Declaration of Independence, 291n1; victory on Long Island, 293, 294; advances up Hudson, 305, 309, takes Fort Washington, 315; advances towards Philadelphia, 316, political dangers of his victories, 377; John Nugent recommended to, 331, given 'a little office', 379, 428, VII, 142hn; whereabouts of his army unknown, III, 393; defeats Washington at the Brandywine, 394n4, 399, 401; public reaction to victories changes, 405; rumour of another battle with Washington, IX, 417–18; fortifies himself in Philadelphia, III, 410; junction with Burgoyne never made, 422; resigns American Command, IV, 3, 34; sees King, 4; Governor Johnstone intends impeaching, 29; Germain's charges against, 65n6
Lieutenant-General of the Ordnance, VI, 116n4; Captain Cuppage wishes to be aide-de-camp to, 116, VII, 142hn

Howison, Henry
correspondence with, listed above, p. 139

Hübner, Johann, his *New Geography*, I, 72

Hübner, Johann, Jr, his *Vollständige Geographie*, I, 72n5

Hudleston, John (*c.* 1749–1835)
correspondence with, listed above, p. 139
Secretary to Madras Select Committee, V, 126; should keep his sentiments concealed, IX, 307

Hudson, Robert, clerk in East India Company office, VI, 249n1
correspondence with, listed above, p. 139

Huet, Julien-Michel
correspondence with, listed above, p. 139

Huez, M., Mayor of Troyes, brutal murder of, VI, 19

Hughes, Rev. Dr David, of Jesus College, Oxford (*c.* 1754–1817)
correspondence with, listed above, p. 139
undertakes advertisement of French clergy subscription, VII, 270hn, 271; sends the Burkes honey and Aristotle, VIII, 67; stays at Beaconsfield, 123, has heard calumny against EB, IX, 441–2

Hughes, Admiral Sir Edward, 1st Baronet (1720–94): WB sails with, from India, IV, 32; Naval Commander in East Indies, V, 42n3; Macartney's differences with, 42–3; withdraws his ships to Bombay, 44n6; his fortune from the East Indies, 224

Hughes, Francis Annesley, of Ballitore School, I, 49

Hughes, Mary Walton, of New York, II, 230n1

Hughs, John (1703–71), prints 'Abridgment' fragment, I, 164n1

Huguenots: schoolboys at Ballitore, I, 17; also mentioned, VI, 154n1, VII, 214n2, VIII, 419

Huick, J.
correspondence with, listed above, p. 139

Huish, Mark, Nottingham hosier and town councillor
correspondence with, listed above, p. 139
his petitions on the effects of American war on trade, III, 121–2, 129–30; arranges recommendation for John Nugent to Sir William Howe, 331; writes on election politics to Bristol tradesmen, IV, 269

Hume, Sir Abraham, 2nd Baronet (1749–1838)
correspondence with, listed above, p. 139

Hume, David (1711–76), friend of EB, I, 129n1, VI, 81n1; sends Adam Smith's *Moral Sentiments* to EB, I, 129; his *History* puts a stop to 'Abridgment', 164n1; secretary to British Ambassador in Paris, 188n1; chooses French school for Gilbert Elliot, V, 190n4; succeeds WB as Conway's secretary, I, 297; also mentioned, 135n2, 201hn, 234n1

Hume family, of County Wicklow, II, 129n1

Humphreys, Sir Orlando (d. 1737), II, 76n3

Humund Rao, Bramin Maratha agent
correspondence with, listed above, p. 139
witness before Select Committee, IV, 356n1; entertained at Beaconsfield, 367–8; has trouble on way back to India, 372tn. *See also* Maratha Agents

Hungary, two gentlemen from: deliver P. Camper's letter to EB, III, 178–9

Hunt, Thomas (*c.* 1723–89), M.P., V, 374n6

Hunter, John (*c.* 1724–1802), director of East India Company, IV, 361

Hunter, John (1738–1821), Governor of New South Wales, VII, 463n3

Hunter, Dr William (1718–83), physician, his bequest to the University of Glasgow, V, 118

Huntingdon, 9th Earl of, *see* Hastings, Theophilus

Huntingdon, Countess of (Lady Selina Shirley, 1707–91), founder of the

Ireland (*cont.*)

his earliest instincts, 277; his 'inimitable work' for, VI, 253

EB's interest in proceedings of Irish Parliament grows less daily, II, 210; abused in, IV, 201, 224, not considered a friend to, 418, X, 8; pacification of, his great object, VII, 350; on the state of (1792), 233, (1796), IX, 112–15, 116–27

and England: Octennial Act (1768), I, 342–3; proposed tax on absentee landowners (1773), II, 459, opposed by EB, 464–70, 474–81, 482–4, 487–8, 489, IV, 348–9, IX, 401–2, his name on list of absentees, II, 464hn; Rockingham's activities against proposed tax, 471dn, 472, 480, 481–2hn, 484–7, 490–1, 495hn, 498–500, 506, IX, 402hn; supported by Flood, II, 466, 496, 509, opposed by Charles O'Hara, 501; rejected by Irish Parliament, 494, 495hn, 496, 501; Chatham's view of, 509; project revived (1779), IV, 158–9, (1797), IX, 283–4, 365

the two countries being brought to 'a perfect state of Uniformity' (1773), II, 495; could save England by action against American war, III, 218–19, 244–5, 271; union with, 'a great question of state', 434, 445, VIII, 20–1, IX, 336; beginning to be a Country (1778), IV, 15; legislative independence for, 204, 224, 454–5, 457, brought on by American war, VII, 204, EB never liked it, IX, 122–3; comparatively better off than England, IV, 455; her prosperity a principal part of the bond, V, 103; her importance to safety of succession, VI, 118; separation of, from England, VIII, 246–8, ought to be in close connexion, IX, 257; England not responsible for her evils, 114; her defence neglected, 223, 227

and Europe: importance of, in European politics, VIII, 41–2, IX, 121; Jacobin influence on, *see* Jacobins

people of Ireland: their character, I, 161, V, 50, their shrewdness, VII, 510; conversation of a good Irishman, 101; the Irish 'click', their ton or brogue, 509–10; a new set of 'Liberal Spirits', X, 7

army of, IX, 335, 346; Constitution, IX, 125n2, 336; history of, I, 68, 141, 201–2, II, 285, V, 108–10, 291–3, VI, 29, VII, 104–5, discovery of Sebright MSS, V, 108, 292; Jobb system in, VIII, 52, 53, 231, IX, 368; Post Office,

V, 475, VII, 21, VIII, 175, 177, 199, 208, 213, IX, 443–4; Protestant Ascendancy in, VII, 237n4, 241–3, 282–3, 287, 289, 290, 292, VIII, 138, 203, 254, X, 32, 34; Rebellion of 1641, II, 284–5

see also British Empire; Catholic Committee; Catholicism; Church of Ireland; Clogher; Commerce; Dissenters; Dublin

Ireland, Primate of all, *see* Newcombe, William; Robinson, Richard; Stone, George

Ireland, William Henry (1777–1835), Malone on his Shakespeare forgeries, VIII, 454, 455

Irish Academy, EB elected to, VI, 98

Irish Agent for Linen Board, I, 331

Irish Society, II, 482

Irland, John, Deputy Collector of Customs in Grenada: suspended from office with RBSr, III, 201–2

Irnham, 1st Baron, *see* Luttrell, Simon

Ironside, Colonel Gilbert (1737–1802), Indian Army officer, VI, 245

correspondence with, listed above, p. 140

visits Beaconsfield, VI, 245n4; subscribes to refugee clergy fund, VII, 205

Irving, John

correspondence with, listed above, p. 140

Irwin, Eyles (*c.* 1751–1817), despatch carrier for East India Company, IV, 304, 309, 379n2, n4, 380n

Irwin, General Sir John (*c.* 1728–88), M.P.: appointed Commander-in-Chief in Ireland, III, 152n4; loan to from Catholic merchants, IV, 373; contests Robert Adam's victory over him, IX, 394hn; EB's good opinion of, III, 152, IX, 394; also mentioned, I, 297n1

Isaac, Mr, estate agent of Portland properties, I, 341

Isaeus, William Jones's translation of, IV, 48hn

Isnard, Maximin (1751–1825), his speech on the King of France, VII, 169

Isted, Ambrose, I, 144hn

Italy: EB contemplates visit to (1767), I, 314, 349–50, II, 7, VI, 256n3; 'a sort of Native land to us all', 256; deprived of Power, but still has lessons to teach us, VII, 85; her elegance and taste, 85; French aggression towards, 264, 277, VIII, 105; EB considers taking refuge in, studies language (1795), 280n4; abandoned by England, IX, 135, 164, 167; EB's pleasure at hopes of relief

Kanna Ram, VI, 244n5

Karl Theodor (1724–99), Elector Palatine and Elector of Bavaria, VI, 323

Kaunitz-Rietberg, Wenzel Anton, Prince von (1711–94), principal Minister of the Emperor: praises *Reflections* at a dinner party, VI, 239–40, and to Lord Elgin, 240; calls for action in support of French King, 317n4, 323n4; is sent copy of EB's letter to Marie Antoinette, 350hn, 352tn; opposes intervention in France, 388, 409, IX, 438; his statement on Imperial policy, VII, 21n1; also mentioned, VI, 367n4, 368n1, n3, 389n6

Kavanagh, John, usher at Ballitore School, I, 98

Kearney, Alice, daughter of Mrs Elizabeth Kearney, II, 548

Kearney, Denis, ne'er do well farmer: EB takes over lease of his farm, II, 548; attempts of, to regain possession, 548–9

Kearney, Mrs Elizabeth, wife of the preceding II, 548

Kearney, Rev. John (1741–1813), Fellow of Trinity College, Dublin, VII, 105, VIII, 6n6
correspondence with, listed above, p. 142

Kearney, Mary, daughter of Mrs Elizabeth Kearney, II, 548

Kearney, Michael
correspondence with, listed above, p. 142

Kearney, Michael, barber-surgeon in Dublin, I, 4, 34, 39, 43; hears his boy read Greek, 97

Kearney, Mrs Michael, wife of the preceding: EB's encounters with, I, 97, 98

Kearney, Michael, Jr ('Michie', 1733–1814), early friend of EB, I, 4n1
correspondence with, listed above, p. 142
at Ballitore school, I, 34, 43; tested in Greek by EB, 97; elected Fellow of Trinity College, Dublin, 124

Kearsley, George (d. 1790), bookseller: publishes additions to Goldsmith's *Retaliation*, II, 536hn; also mentioned, V, 63

Keating, Geoffrey (*c.* 1570–*c.* 1644), *General History of Ireland*, V, 109, 291

Keating, Maurice (1690–1769), Irish M.P., I, 51n3

Keating, Maurice, Jr (d. 1777), kills a man in a duel, I, 51

Keck, Anthony Tracy (d. 1767), M.P. for pocket-borough of Woodstock, I, 149n2

Keeling, Eugene
correspondence with, listed above, p. 142

Keeling, Herbert
correspondence with, listed above, p. 142

Keene, Whitshed
correspondence with, listed above, p. 142

Keir, James (1735–1820), partner in alkali works, VI, 14n3

Keith, Sir Robert Murray (1730–95), British Ambassador at Vienna, VI, 383, 412n5, 414tn

Kelly, E., of Galway, gentleman: his grand theatrical squabble with Sheridan, I, 82–4; pamphlet on the controversy, 88n4, and a poem, *The Gentleman*, 90

Kelly, Henry, defeated with WB at Haslemere, III, 153hn

Kelly, John, II, 341hn
correspondence with, listed above, p. 142

Kelly, Rev. Lawrence (*c.* 1720–77), Rector of Irish College of the Lombard, Paris, IV, 410

Kelly, Thomas (d. 1809), Irish Judge, VI, 280, 281, VII, 5; EB's bondsman in Middle Temple, VI, 281n2

Kelly, Thomas, Jr (1769–1855), VI, 280n3; EB gives him introductions to ambassadors abroad, 280, 281

Kelly, William, his collection of books and MSS, VII, 104

Kelly, Mrs Mary, widow of the preceding, VII, 104n13

Kelyng, Sir John (d. 1671), *A Report of Divers Cases . . .*, VII, 540

Kemble, Sarah, *see* Siddons, Mrs William

Kemp, Rev. John (1745–1805), Scottish minister, IV, 104

Kempe, Mrs
correspondence with, listed above, p. 142

Kempenfelt, Admiral Richard (1718–82), IV, 397n1

Kenmare, 4th Viscount, *see* Browne, Thomas

Kenmare, 5th Viscount, *see* Browne, Valentine

Kennedy, Patrick (b. 1751)
correspondence with, listed above, p. 142

Kennedy, William, at Ballitore with EB, I, 110

Kennett, Brackley (d. 1782), declines opposing Admiral Keppel, III, 63

Kenney, Mrs, receives a gift from EB, V, 380

Kent, *see* County meetings

Kent, John
correspondence with, listed above, p. 142

Kent, Sir Thomas

correspondence with, listed above, p. 142

Kenyon, Lloyd (1732–1802), later (1788) 1st Baron Kenyon and Chief Justice

correspondence with, listed above, p. 142

consulted by EB on Welsh Bill, IV, 211–12; assists a clergyman's cause, 398–9; appointed Attorney General, 427, V, 8n2, 51hn, 90; becomes Lord Chief Justice, VI, 2n5; an incorrigible partisan of Hastings, 2, 3, 199, VII, 112, 541; his trial of Stockdale a Rehearsal for Hastings, 111

Kenyon, Mrs Lloyd (Mary Kenyon, 1741–1808), wife of the preceding: on EB and the Gordon rioters, IV, 246n2

Keogh, George Drew, stays at Beaconsfield as a schoolboy, VII, 180, 181, 196–7, 202n

Keogh, John, Sr (1740–1817), Dublin merchant, member of Catholic Committee

correspondence with, listed above, p. 142

deputed to invite RBJr to be Agent for Committee, VI, 397, 429hn, 436, returns with him to Ireland, 471, VII, 5, 7; Dublin Castle hostility to, 31, 37; letter to Hussey on Catholic claims, 82–3; loses faith in RBJr, 164hn, 201n6, 202n, 269n, 296n3; his sons invited to Beaconsfield, 180n2

goes with Catholic petition to King, VIII, 163, 168n1, 194, 213, IX, 112; delivers Hussey's letter to EB, VIII, 163n3, 168; becomes increasingly radical and anti-English, 245n3, 352; his report on Ireland after Fitzwilliam's recall, IX, 59–60; offers to visit EB and inform him on Ireland, 112, 115–16, 120, 123, 124; EB sends correspondence to Fitzwilliam, 120, 123–4, 138, and to Laurence, 126; his Jacobinical tendencies, 120, 123, 148n3, and his radical secretary, 115, 133; EB ready to see him, 133, 139, 144; wants him to see Laurence, 133, 148; his account of Ireland, 157

also mentioned, IV, 67hn, VII, 38n, 136n

Keogh, Mrs John (Mary Drew, d. c. 1813), wife of the preceding, VII, 197

Keogh, John, Jr, stays at Beaconsfield as a schoolboy, VII, 180, 181, 196–7, 202n

Keogh, Michael, stays at Beaconsfield as a schoolboy, VII, 180, 181, 196–7, 202n

Keppel, Admiral Augustus (1725–86), later (1782) 1st Viscount, M.P., follower of Rockingham

correspondence with, listed above, p. 142–3

as Lord of the Admiralty, I, 266; resigns office, 277n2, 282; dismissed as Groom of the Bedchamber, 283; discusses political outlook with EB and Richmond, 320–1; invited to meet Portland at Beaconsfield, II, 11; as Rockingham's close adviser, 65, 77, 89, 351, IV, 160, 161, 180; Chatham's overtures to, II, 88, 90, 91, 94, 100, 113; tours Sussex with EB, 220; his bad health, 348, 356, 388, recovers, 402

re-elected for Windsor, III, 63; urges action before Parliament meets, 195–6; receives sailing orders as Commander-in-Chief of Channel Fleet, 453; withdraws from Brest, IV, 3n3; has to wait in port for reinforcements, 3; military and political problems for, 11–12hn; indecisive action off Ushant, 12, congratulated by EB on, 13–14; refuses to exculpate Palliser for failing to obey orders, 30hn; court-martialled on Palliser's charges, 31; popular sympathy for, 34, 37–8; EB attends trial, 35–6, prepares defence speech, 35n2; his acquittal, 42–3; report of trial published, 42; resigns command, 91n7; Hood on his court-martial, 286n3

included in provisional plans for Rockingham Cabinet, IV, 144, 154; defeated by Powney for Windsor, 284, but still rides the High Horse, 285; nominated for Surrey, 283, 291, 'his second Trial', 299, wins, 302, congratulated by EB, 303, 313; appointed First Lord of the Admiralty, 451; remains in office after Rockingham's death, V, 24, 77, 78

Romney's portrait of, III, 238n1; Tassi's seal of his head, IV, 98; presents his portrait by Reynolds to EB, 169; his bust in Rockingham mausoleum, V, 46; 'the glory and the reproach' of his times, IV, 169; a saying of, VII, 308

also mentioned, II, 171, 199n7, IV, 51, 133, 369, 397, IX, 65n4, 66tn, 452hn

Keppel, Frederick (1729–77), Bishop of Exeter, I, 151

Keppel, George, 3rd Earl of Albemarle (1724–72), Governor of Jersey

correspondence with, listed above, p. 95

a close follower of Rockingham, I,

King's Friends (*cont.*)
Dyson, Martin, Stanley, Lord Rice, II, 209. *See also* Bute party; Court
Kingsland, Viscount, *see* Barnewall, Henry Benedict
Kingsley, William, Governor of Fort William (d. 1769), II, 99n4
Kingston, 2nd Duke of, *see* Pierrepont, Evelyn
Kingston, Duchess of (Elizabeth Chudleigh, *c.* 1720–88), bigamous wife of the preceding: her trial, III, 260–1
Kirby, Keeper of The Churn, Dublin, I, 36
Kirkman, Alderman John (d. 1780): stands for Lord Mayor of London, II, 33; Court candidate for Sheriff against Wilkes, 222; calls for City support against Regulating Act, 436–7
Kirkwall, Viscount, *see* Fitzmaurice, John Hamilton
Kléber, Jean-Baptiste (1753–1800), French commander, IX, 55n2
Klemens-Wenzel, Archbishop-Elector of Trier (1739–1812): offers refuge to Comte d'Artois, VI, 301hn, 342; RBJr visits, 345; his magnificent hospitality, 346; brings news of Peace of Sistova, 372; Emperor's statement of policy to, VII, 21n1
Knight, Richard Payne (1750–1824) correspondence with, listed above, p. 144
Knocklofty, County Tipperary, EB's early memories of, V, 289
Knowles, Admiral Sir Charles, 1st Baronet (*c.* 1704–77), II, 369
Knox, George (1765–1827), Irish M.P., proposal for Catholics in parliament, VIII, 21n2
Knox, William (1732–1810), Under-Secretary of State, II, 107n3, IV, 159n1 correspondence with, listed above, p. 145
Kolbel, Frances Lambertina, *see* Payne, Lady
Kriperam, John Paterson's secretary in India, V, 383, 384, 385
Kuprili, Muhammad, Grand Vizier (*c.* 1586–1661), V, 405
Kyalleram, Raja, *diwan* of Bihar, VII, 249
Kynynmound, Agnes Dalrymple Murray, *see* Elliot, Lady

Labilliere, Major Peter, II, 110–11
La Bintinaye, Agathon-Marie-René de, called Chevalier de La Bintinaye (b. 1758), *émigré* naval commander correspondence with, listed above, p. 145 first meeting with EB, VI, 185–6, 206;

his honourable wounds, 185hn, 241, 475; chosen as agent of French Princes in England, 242–3, 343; undertakes Mission, 371, 388, 405, 474–5, at RBJr's desire, VII, 163; his merits, VI, 400; brings Letter from Princes to George III, 393, arrangements to see Ministers, 393; fails to see Dorset, 394, 395; Dundas unwilling, but sees him, 475; received by Grenville, 398, 403, 412, 475, and by Pitt, 437; Grenville lays Letter before King, 398; receives the reply 'neutrality', 410, 412, 437, 476; his Memorial on restrictions of troop movements, 403tn; second Memorial, 414, 423–4; 3rd Memorial written by RBJr, 431–3; Grenville's dinner party for, 431, 434n1, 457
shilly-shallies about staying in England, VI, 431; complains of expenses and neglect, 433, 475, 477; EB's response, 433–5; his expenses paid, 438n2; RBJr's uncertain relations with, 437, 438; patience prescribed, 446; loses his French pension, 457, 475n5; dissatisfied with Calonne, 474; EB's defence of, to Calonne, 473–7; presented at Court, 457n2
answers attack in *Morning Chronicle*, VII, 42–3, 90–2, 95–6, 97–8, 120, 125–6, published as pamphlet, 128–9, copies for French King and Queen, 152–3; dines with Fitzwilliam, 97, 107; attends Court, 106–7; plans to leave England, 5, 66, 97, 98, 106, 128, leaves London, 138; Mr Ker given an introduction to, 152; his supposed death by drowning, 474
also mentioned, VI, 463, VII, 41, 160, 166, 167, VIII, 7–8, 86, 89, 106, IX, 438
La Bintinaye, Augustin-Marie-Xavier de (1749–1822), VI, 343n6
La Bintinaye, Abbé François-Marie de correspondence with, listed above, p. 145 his version of EB's Letter to Baron Cloots, VI, 135n3; translates *Appeal* for RBJr, 329; accompanies Chevalier Bintinaye to England, 371n1, 391, 392, 394, 403, prepares Memorial with him, 414; dissatisfied with reception in England, 433hn, 438; EB's candid reply to, 435; invited to Beaconsfield, 446, 463; defended by EB against Este, 473hn; could be useful on newspaper, 476; dines with Fitzwilliam, VII, 107; with Chevalier,

La Bintinaye, Abbé (*cont.*)
replies to attack in *Morning Chronicle*, 42–3, 90–2, 95–6; upset at EB's suggestions, 96; publication of reply as pamphlet, 120, 125, 128, 129; its success, 152–3, 166–7
welcomed back to England, VII, 302, VIII, 7–8; his scheme 'perfectly foolish', VII, 318; EB sends money and invitation to Beaconsfield, VIII, 24–5; asks help for Archbishop of Bordeaux, 86, 87, 90; more requests for money, 106; hopes to get passage for Abbé Esgrigny, 312; employment found for, 313
shows draft of *Two Letters* to Peltier, 409, IX, 104; starts translation without consulting EB, VIII, 408–9, 412; Peltier's vile version the result, IX, 104–5; EB's doubts on his translation, 131–2; translates *Three Memorials*, 132tn; his advice on diet, 371–2
also mentioned, VI, 341, 423n1, 424, 432, VII, 5, 41, 66, 97, 98, 106, 138n2, 474n4, VIII, 89
La Bintinaye, Gilles-François, Chevalier de (1727–1820), father of Agathon, VI, 186n1
La Bintinaye, Madame de (Marie-Anne-Angélique Champion de Cicé), wife of the preceding, VI, 186n1, VIII, 25n2
Laborde Méréville, François-Louis-Jean-Joseph de (1761–1801), his plan for a national bank, VI, 54n3
La Bourdonnaÿe, Comtesse de
correspondence with, listed above, p. 145
Lacratelle, Jean-Charles-Dominique de ('Lacratelle le Jeune', 1766–1855), calls for release of clergy, IX, 154
La Croix, Armand-Charles-Augustin de, Duc de Castries (1756–1842), his home pillaged, VI, 185
La Croix, Charles-Eugène-Gabriel de, Marquis de Castries (1727–1801), V, 262hn
Lactantius Firmianus (*c.* 260–*c.* 340), VI, 112
Ladbroke, Sir Robert (*c.* 1713–73), M.P. for City of London, II, 34n4; his death, 490n3, 492hn
Lady Huntingdon's Connexion, II, 298–9
La Fare, Anne-Louis-Henri de (1752–1829), Bishop of Nancy, VI, 211
La Fayette, Marquis de, *see* Du Motier, Marie-Joseph-Paul-Yves-Roch-Gilbert

La Fayette, Marquise de (Marie-Adrienne-Françoise de Noailles, 1759–1807), wife of the preceding: her imprisonment, IX, 199
Lafluy, his flute, I, 53
Lafon, Peter
correspondence with, listed above, p. 145
La Galissonnière, Augustin-Félix-Elisabeth Barrin de La Galissonnière, Comte de
correspondence with, listed above, p. 145
Lageard de Cherval, Abbé L. de
correspondence with, listed above, p. 145
La Grange, Bernardus, of New Jersey
correspondence with, listed above, p. 145
his boundary dispute, III, 226
La Haye, Denis de (*c.* 1629–1722), V, 405n2
Lake, General Gerard (1744–1808), IX, 295n3
La Lezardière, Louis-Jacques-Gilbert, Baron Robert de (1752–1801), his letter on proceedings in Poitou, VII, 432, 433
Lally-Tollendal, Trophime-Gérard, Comte de (1751–1830), constitutional monarchist, VI, 33n9
correspondence with, listed above, p. 145
a fugitive from Paris, VI, 33, a 'Senateur manqué', 115; his conduct praised by EB, 166, condemned by Menonville, 166–8, 321hn; recommends British Constitution for France, 168, VII, 167; his proposal on Rights of Men, VI, 167n4; his eloquence powerless to save France, 212; 'never . . . wrote any thing disobliging' to EB, VIII, 313
Lettre à Madame, VI, 210hn; *Quintius Capitolinus . . .*, effect on EB, 212, 321hn; copy sent to EB, 216hn; 'mild aperitives' not enough, 217; *Seconde Lettre à ses commettans*, quoted in *Reflections*, 321hn; *Lettre écrite au très-honorable Edmund Burke*, denounces revolutionaries, 321hn, VIII, 313n5; retracting of *Lettre* alienates EB irrevocably, VI, 321–2; *Post-Scriptum . . . à M. Burke*, 322tn, VIII, 315n5; *Seconde Lettre . . . à M. Burke*, 'not worthy of an answer', VII, 166–7, VIII, 313n5
La Luzerne, Anne-César, Marquis de (1741–91), French Ambassador to England, VI, 370
La Marche, Jean-François de (1729–1806), Bishop of St-Pol-de-Léon, leader of *émigré* clergy in England, VI, 294
correspondence with, listed above, p. 175
his pastoral letter denounced in Assem-

La Marche, Jean-François de (*cont.*)
  bly, VI, 457; raises funds for refugee clergy in England, VII, 198, 205, 212, 213; praises women of London for their help, 208–9; has two thousand clergy to house, 230; second relief fund entrusted to, 231, 276; arranges board, lodging and clothes allowances, 234, 425n5; 'Cet homme incomparable', 259; corrects 'Case of the Suffering Clergy of France', 207hn; special payments for bishops entrusted to, VIII, 87; and Catholic bishop for St Domingo, 90, 91hn
  takes part in organising *émigré* school at Penn, VIII, 400, 442, 445–6, 448–51; quarrels with Mrs Crewe over school, 453; his poor choice of staff, 460–1, IX, 9–10, 20, 30, 40, 48; unpleasantness between EB and, over admissions, 8–9, 9–11, 13hn, 14–16, 17, 18, 22–3, 23–8, 28–9; gives the cream to Marquess of Buckingham, the whey to EB, 33–4; Buckingham's version, 31–2; admission process explained, 34–5; dispute amicably resolved, 35–7; more trouble over running the school like a seminary for priests, 52–3; angers EB by terming himself a 'simple Clerk', 18, 19, 23, 24, 25, 27, 28, 34; is set against the laity, 21; recommends Buxton for EB, 72n5
  also mentioned, VII, 515, IX, 3hn
Lamballe, Prince de, *see* Bourbon, Louis de
Lamballe, Princesse de (Marie-Thérèse-Louise de Savoie Carignan, 1749–92), widow of the preceding, VII, 261, 376
Lambert, Abbé Bernard (1738–1813), consulted on place in France for RBJr, II, 414
Lambert, R. P.
  correspondence with, listed above, p. 146
  recommended by EB for Malton, V, 338–9
La Merlière, Nicolas de, his plan for a national bank, VI, 50hn
Lameth, Alexandre-Théodore-Victor, Comte de (1760–1829), constitutional monarchist, VI, 172, 338, 351
Lameth, Charles-Malo-François, Comte de (1757–1832), constitutional monarchist, VI, 172, 338, 351; wounded in a duel, 185n1
Lamoignon, Anne-Pierre-Chrétien, Vicomte de (1770–1827)

correspondence with, listed above, p. 146
EB meets in England, VI, 318
Lamoignon, Chrétien-François de (1735–89), of the 'famous Law name', VI, 318
Lamoignon, Marie-Charles-Guillaume de, (1767–95), EB meets in England, VI, 318
La Motte, Comtesse de (Jeanne de Saint-Rémy de Valois, 1756–91): and the Diamond Necklace affair, VI, 90n1; her escape to England, 348n1
La Motte-Picquet, Toussaint-Guillaume, Comte de (1720–91), IV, 90
Lanascal, Jacques-Yves-Joseph-Marie de Quemper, Marquis de (1759–1813)
  correspondence with, listed above, p. 146
Lanascal, Marquise de (Marie-Marguerite-Françoise-Julie de La Boessière)
  correspondence with, listed above, p. 146
Lancaster, EB refuses offer of a seat at, I, 326, 330, 332hn
Lancaster, Merchants at
  correspondence with, listed above, p. 146
Landon, James (1765–1850)
  correspondence with, listed above, p. 146
Landon, Dr Whittington (*c.* 1758–1838), Provost of Worcester College, Oxford, VIII, 283
Lane, John
  correspondence with, listed above, p. 146
Lane, Obadiah, VII, 182n3
Lane, Mrs Obadiah (Sarah Crewe, d. 1814), wife of the preceding, VII, 182, 188
Lang, Henrietta, *see* King, Mrs Edward
Langley, Benjamin, *see* Langlois, Benjamin
Langlois, Benjamin (*c.* 1727–1802), Secretary to Embassy at Vienna: RBSr's rival for seat, II, 6, 9, 10
Langlois, Christopher (1715–76), II, 10
Langlois, John (1716–89), II, 10
Langrishe, Sir Hercules, 1st Baronet (1731–1811), Irish M.P.
  correspondence with, listed above, p. 146
  early discussion with EB on Catholic affairs, VIII, 257, X, 35; EB's public *Letter* to, VII, 4, 5, 8hn, 12, RBJr advised to use cautiously, 40, 48, circulated among Ministers, 49; blunders in Dublin editions, 94–5, 103; London editions, 95n3, n4; thought inflammatory, 48, jesuitical, VIII, 243n3; also mentioned, 272
  supports seceders from Catholic Committee, VII, 6n1; supported by

Langrishe, Sir Hercules (*cont.*)
'respectable' Catholics, 27n2; his Bill for Catholic relief, 27, 47, 72, 73, 134n1, 135n1; 'mischievous and in-solent', 83; 'rational policy' beyond his mind, 189; his faction, 204; speech on the Catholic question, VIII, 253, X, 31; EB's letters on, VIII, 253–7, 270, 272, X, 31–5; his interest solicited for Kiernan, 36–8
also mentioned I, 195, V, 25n1, VII, 349dn, IX, 467, X, 46
Langton, Bennet (1737–1801), classical scholar
correspondence with, listed above, p. 146
his interest asked for William Ellis, III, 213–14; EB's memorable words to, V, 139; pall bearer for Dr Johnson, 205; also mentioned, X, 43
Langton, Stephen, Archbishop of Canter-bury, VI, 19n1
Lansdowne, 1st Marquess of, *see* Petty, William
La Queuille, Jean-Claude-Marie-Victor, Marquis de (1742–1810), *émigré* repre-sentative at Brussels, VI, 323n2, 446n2
correspondence with, listed above, p. 146
RBJr establishes contact with, VI, 323, 325–6, 328, 373; and La Bintinaye, 343, 433hn, 434, 438
Larkins, William (d. 1800), Accountant General to East India Company, his evidence in Hastings trial, V, 323, VI, 62, VII, 533
La Robrie, Joseph de (1770–95), his mission to England on behalf of Poitou Royalists, VII, 530–1, 532
Laroche, Sir James, 1st Baronet, M.P., Bristol merchant, III, 85n1, 240n3; introduces Henry Cruger into Com-mons, 85, 86; acts on behalf of Bristol, 320n1, 366, IV, 82n2; circu-lates American rumours, 252
La Rochefoucauld d'Enville, Louis-Alexandre, Duc de, VI, 25n3
La Rochefoucauld-Liancourt, François-Alexandre-Frédéric, Duc de (1747–1827), President of Committee of National Assembly: sends Olive Branch to the King, VI, 70; also mentioned, 191n3, 235
Lascaris, Constantine (*c.* 1434–1501), his Greek Grammar, VII, 581
Las Cases, Marie-Joseph-Emmanuel-Auguste-Dieudonné, Marquis de (1766–1842)
correspondence with, listed above, p. 146
Lascelles, Daniel (1714–84), M.P., II, 199

Lascelles, Edward (1740–1820), later (1796) 2nd Baron Harewood, M.P., II, 199
Lascelles, Edwin (1713–95), later (1790) 1st Baron Harewood, M.P. for Yorkshire, II, 37; supports Nullum Tempus Bill, 38; attends County Meeting, 63; declines standing at General Election (1780), IV, 285, 301; also mentioned, II, 162, 199
Lasmartres, [Gabriel b. 1745]
correspondence with, listed above, p. 146
La Touche, David (1729–1817), Irish M.P.: his motion to reject Catholic petition, VII, 70, 71nn1, 2; also men-tioned, 65n4, 69n1
La Touche, William George Digges (1747–1803), East India Company Resident at Basra, IV, 379
Latouche and Co., Dublin bankers, VIII, 162
La Tour d'Auvergne, Henri de, Vicomte de Turenne (1611–75), VI, 328n4
La Tour du Pin-Montauban, David-Sigismond, Marquis de (1751–1807), VII, 488–9, VIII, 31, IX, 14
Latour-Maubourg, Comte de, *see* Fay, Marie-Charles-César de
La Tour's Royal Étranger, foreign corps in West Indies, VIII, 421n1
La Trémoille, Duc de, *see* Tarente, Charles-Bretagne-Marie-Joseph, Prince de
La Trémoille, Duchesse de, *see* Tarente, Princesse de
Lauderdale, Earls of, *see* Maitland, James
Laugharne, Catherine Philipps, *see* Philipps Laugharne, Catherine
L'Aulne, Baron de, *see* Turgot, Anne-Robert-Jacques
Lauraguais, Comte de, *see* Brancas, Louis-Léon-Félicité de
Laurence, French (1757–1809), civil lawyer, protégé and literary executor of EB
correspondence with, listed above, p. 146–8
counsel for prosecution against Hastings, V, 324n3, 355, for the Managers, VII, 109n1; draws up Faizullah Khan charge, V, 410hn; sends EB papers on trial, VIII, 413–14; advises against petition on acquittal, 416–17; promises help with History of Impeachment, 417–18, 420; solemnly charged to see History through, IX, 62–3, 71, EB's dying request to finish it, 237–8, 242; on Mrs Warren Hastings's fortune, 235–6
his activity in Westminster election, V, 410–12, 414; completes his 'year of

Legge, William (*cont.*)
also mentioned, I, 307n2, II, 214hn, 262, III, 82n2, 109tn, 121n3, 161n6, 179hn, 182n2, 191n1, 216n6, 225, IV, 356hn
Leicester, Sir Peter, 4th Baronet (1732–70), M.P., Rockingham supporter, II, 102
Leinster, 1st Duke of, *see* Fitzgerald, James
Leinster, Duchess of (Lady Emilia Mary Lennox, 1731–1814), widow of the preceding: marries her children's tutor, III, 27; also mentioned, IV, 97n1, 98tn
Leinster, 2nd Duke of, *see* Fitzgerald, William Robert
Leland, John, son of Thomas Leland, EB solicits interest on behalf of, V, 97–8
Leland, Rev. Dr Thomas (1722–85), historian, friend of EB
correspondence with, listed above, p. 149
elected Fellow of Trinity College, Dublin, I, 65; EB assists in his *History of Ireland*, 202n2, V, 15n2, 108n1, 109, undertakes the *History* at EB's urging, II, 285, VII, 104; on EB's dispute with Rigby, II, 139n4; asks EB's help as candidate for Provostship of Trinity College, Dublin, 541–3, VIII, 48n2; asks EB's interest with Windham for his son, V, 97–8
also mentioned, I, 195, 225, 243, 245hn, 265, 267, 309n2, II, 24, 137n1
Le Mesurier, Paul (1755–1805), M.P., London merchant and prize agent, IV, 230
Lennon, Mr, V, 285
Lennox, Charles, 2nd Duke of Richmond, II, 6n1, 220n2
Lennox, Charles, 3rd Duke of Richmond (1735–1806)
correspondence with, listed above, p. 170
Aide-de-Camp to Prince Ferdinand, I, 128; Ambassador at Paris, 220n1; supports repeal of anti-Catholic laws, 244; loses office with fall of Rockingham, 262; his motion on Canada defeated, 313n4; his dislike of the Grenvilles, 317, 320, II, 115; disagrees with Rockingham's refusal to form Administration, I, 320–1, II, 371, 375–6; as Rockingham's leading supporter in Lords, 93, 117, 348, 423, IV, 143, 164, acts as Leader in his absence, II, 189hn, 190, 193, 195, 197, 199, 200
introduces resolutions on America in

Lords, II, 139; and Falkland Isles dispute, 142–3, 200; favours partial secession, 346, 351, 363, 366, 370–1, 375, 380, 383, 390, 407; will attend Parliament if EB advises, 386–7; rumoured action on Royal Marriage Bill, 402; thinks Germain wants Leadership of House, 404; opposes Absentee Tax, 487; reads Hillsborough's Letter in debate on taxation, III, 80n1; must be pressed to attend Parliament early, 89, 91, 99; speaks on Declaratory Act, 102–3; should present Merchants' petition, 106; suggests consulting Chatham, 108tn; urges Protests on America, 110, 299n1; speaks in support of New York Memorial, 166; believes loss of America will make millions free and happy, 170; consulted on Manifesto, 205, 216; his motion on conciliation defeated, 236; urges abandoning secession policy, 334hn; wants repeal of Declaratory Act, 398–9; moves State of Nation, 405; urges recognition of Independence, 419–20; speaks 'in great glory' against coercion, 427
activity in East India Company affairs, II, 371, 387, 389–92, 403, 408, 451; supports petition against Regulating Act, 436–7; wants supporters to buy qualifications in East India Stock, 459; appointed Chairman of new General Court Committee, 494, 510–11, 515; his campaign against Act ends in failure, 523
wants Party to stay in office after Rockingham's death, V, 9hn; remains in office as Master General of Ordnance, 24; Portland's Letter to, 24, VII, 448; resigns office on Coalition, V, 79n1, returns under Pitt, 79n1, 150; appears with Pitt at Lord Mayor's reception, 236; his rumoured post in a Pitt Cabinet, 351
his plan for parliamentary reform, IV, 165–8, 217hn, 296–7; includes annual elections, universal male suffrage at twenty-one, 166, 237n2, 296, and equal constituencies, 166, 237n2; proposes to annihilate the Freeholders, 296; proposes Associations to promote reform, 166, 167–8; introduces his Bill in Lords, 235hn; asks for EB's speeches against reform in preparing Bill, 235–6, EB unwilling for public controversy with, 235, 237;

Lennox, Charles (*cont.*)

called by Tooke as defence witness, as supporter of reform, VIII, 66n4

High Steward of Cheltenham and Lord Lieutenant of Sussex, III, 37n1; wants advice on County petitions, II, 44, 66hn; on why Sussex not ripe for petition, 66–7 and cp. 390–1; supports general remonstrance, 142; attacks proclamation on local defence, IV, 113; reform of parliament not supported in Sussex, V, 39

EB and: EB thinks will become a considerable man, I, 244; asks EB's interest for an exciseman, II, 142; EB stays with, at Goodwood, 220, 233, 316, 319hn, dines with, in London, 488; consulted by EB on Supervisorship in India, 319–21; refuses EB's request to support Verney interest in Bucks, III, 37, 38–40; asked by EB to persuade relations in Ireland to oppose Ministry, 217–20; EB's opinions of: 'Languid, scrupulous, and unsystematick', II, 373, not obstinate, 374, but 'tenacious', 544, dissipates his mind with minute pursuits, 374; on EB's wise and statesmanlike speech on conciliation, III, 171; tells EB some take his earnestness for private interest, 384; his love and esteem for EB, 37; commissions Romney to paint EB doing something, 237–8, V, 293hn, 336hn, and himself reading, III, 238

Personal: his experimental farming, II, 143, 233, 319, 338; supports his brother in court-martial, 221; patron of James Barry, 315; thinks his opinion of little weight with Friends in the Lump, 371; admires Milton, 378; has a fox-hunting House party, 387, 390–1; reads classics with Walker King, 525–6, III, 26hn, 198–200; his singular opinions on education, II, 544–5, III, 26hn, 199; ready to turn his nephew and heir wholly over to tutor, IV, 97–8; extremely mortified by his sister's marriage to her children's tutor, III, 27; grows sick of politics, 37, 40; thinks England in its natural old age, 170; prepares a refuge in France, 291tn, 296, gets his French peerage registered, 365; his entire despondency about public affairs, 388; Governor Johnstone stays with at Brighthelmstone, IV, 30; supports Keppel, 35n2, 37hn;

publishes his speech on Greenwich Hospital, 98; is satirised in the *Rolliad*, V, 150n1, and as Themistocles, 336hn; gives Cuppage promotion, VII, 142n2

also mentioned, II, 42, 79, 187n2, 188, 218n4, 262, 382, 483, 491n3, III, 36, 152n1, 309hn, 314, 328n3, IV, 29, 71n2, 134n2, 237n3

Lennox, Charles (1764–1819), later Colonel, nephew and heir of 3rd Duke of Richmond: his education under Walker King, II, 545, III, 26–7, 198–200, IV, 97–8; joins Sussex militia, 97n1; tutor and pupil like brothers, 98tn; quarrel with Duke of York, V, 476, leads to duel, 477; also mentioned, IV, 165n2, 168n1

Lennox, Lady Emilia Mary, *see* Leinster, Duchess of

Lennox, General Lord George (1737–1805), brother of the Duke of Richmond: court-martialled for not respecting superior officer, II, 220–1; M.P. for Sussex, IV, 168

Lennox, Lady Sarah, IV, 97n1, 98tn. *See also* Bunbury, Lady Sarah

Lenoir, Jean-Pierre-Charles (1732–1807), VI, 110

correspondence with, listed above, p. 149

Léon, Prince de, *see* Rohan-Chabot, Alexandre-Louis-Auguste, Duc de

Leonetti, Antonio, translator of *Reflections* into Italian, VII, 86

correspondence with, listed above, p. 149

Léon's Corps, IX, 72n

Leopold II, Holy Roman Emperor, (1747–92): completes suppression of Netherlands revolt, VI, 217n3, 266, 327, 382n3; leaves Hague Conference unconcluded, 327n5, 382n3, 412n5; his anti-clerical policy, 266–8, 'lust of philosophick spoliation, and equalization', 413; orders his sister, Regent of Netherlands, to be cold to *émigrés*, 344n3; his perfidious orders to Brussels *émigrés*, 446, 456n2, IX, 439

his relationship with Marie-Antoinette, VI, 309, 317; should warn her to stop her Cabal, 340; sends note to European powers on arrest of French royal family, 317n4; King needs no help from, 348; is sent copy of EB's letter to Queen, 350hn; raises troops for defence of French monarchy, 323; action contingent on general agreement, 323n9, 382; George III promises neutrality to, 345, 370, 373,

London Association (*cont.*)
City ought to be kept out of hands of, 224
London, Bishop of, *see* Lowth, Robert; Porteus, Beilby; Terrick, Richard
London Chronicle, Editor of
correspondence with, listed above, p. 150
see also Newspapers
London Corresponding Society, radical aims of, VIII, 66hn, 282n2
London Evening Post, see Newspapers
London Gazette, see Newspapers
Long, Charles (*c.* 1760–1838), M.P., Joint Secretary to the Treasury, VII, 584, IX, 52n, 222
correspondence with, listed above, p. 150
Long, Dudley (1748–1829), later (1789) Dudley Long North, Whig M.P.
correspondence with, listed above, p. 150
lends Crabbe £5, IV, 337n3, recommends him for ordination, 374; sheds tears over Sir Gilbert's speech, V, 369n1; a Manager for Hastings trial, 371, VIII, 428, IX, 214; EB's social relations with, V, 404, VI, 22, 26, IX, 213–14
Longfield, Richard (1734–1811), later (1795) 1st Baron Longueville, Irish M.P., a Governor of County Cork, VII, 66n2, VIII, 242
Longford, 2nd Baron, *see* Pakenham, Edward Michael
Longinus, EB buys copy of *On the Sublime*, I, 78, 86
Longman, Thomas Norton (1771–1842), bookseller, IX, 320hn
Longueville, 1st Baron, *see* Longfield, Richard
Lonsdale, 1st Earl of, *see* Lowther, James
Lorge, Duc de, *see* Durfort-Civrac, Jean-Laurent de
Lorne, Marquess of, *see* Campbell, George William; Campbell, John
Lorrain, Claude, *see* Claude Lorrain
Lort, Michael (1725–90), VI, 298n1
Loscombe, Benjamin (d. 1796), Sheriff of Bristol
correspondence with, listed above, p. 150
appeals to EB for distressed family, III, 231n2; supports EB for re-election, IV, 243
Lotbinière, Chevalier Michel Chartier de, claims lands in Canada, II, 303
Loughborough, 1st Baron, *see* Wedderburn, Alexander
Louis XIV, King of France (1638–1715): claims to Brabant, VI, 112n6; his *dragonnades*, 154n1; desire to dominate Europe, 260; treatment of

Huguenots, VII, 214n2; never took offence at aid to refugees from his rule, 216; territorial policy, VIII, 447; also mentioned, I, 2n3, VI, 171, VII, 261n2, IX, 70
Louis XV, King of France (1710–74): EB taken for spy of, I, 113; his mistress, II, 67; EB kisses his hand, 425n1; death of, 539; his ministers dismissed, III, 24n3; prodigality in war and peace, VI, 234hn; also mentioned, VI, 199hn, 228n6, VII, 273
Louis XVI, King of France (1754–93)
correspondence with, listed above, p. 151
his accession, III, 24n3; authorises assistance to America, 320n4; reads EB's *Speech on Economical Reform*, IV, 233; *Reflections* sent to, VI, 200, reported to have translated it, 326; his collection of coins, V, 118n1; asks for 'M. Burke' at levee, 234; understands English well, VI, 349
forced by finances to call Assembly of Notables and States General, V, 423, cp. VIII, 49; conditional constitution offered him 'an absurdity', VI, 30; his own programme of reform, 218n3, IX, 186; accepts limitation on veto, and single chamber, VI, 60; Paine thinks him on good terms with Assembly, 69; brought to Paris by mob, 70–1; Orléans' plot against, 73n5; a prisoner in the Palace, 79, 106, 'a captive King', 166n3, 217, 225; EB regards as deposed, 96; Favras's plot for his escape, 107n3; more victim than offender in ruin of France, 149; professes unity with Assembly, 200–1; deserted by *Gardes françaises*, 206–7; Calonne suggests accepting *Cahiers de doléances*, 218n3; prospects of European help to, 258, 260; the *journée des poignards*, 264; flight from the Tuileries, 278; his *Déclaration*, 341; arrested at Varennes, 279, 283, 289hn; bad effects on popular opinion, 284–5, 340n9; return to Paris, 286–8, 321hn; more a King in avowed prison than when at liberty, 290–1; Londoners rejoice at news of escape, 291, 316, so do the King and Prince of Wales, 358; warned against plans of *émigrés*, 293hn; pitiable conditions of imprisonment, 309; European powers promise to restore, 317, 324; Lally changes attitude to, 322; his friendship with La Queuille, 325; warned

Louis XVI (*cont.*)

that aid can come only from abroad, 318–20, 326; his relations with *émigrés*, 338n3, 344n6; distrusts Princes, 389

Assembly plan to set at liberty if Constitution accepted, VI, 340–1, 361–2, 363; tells Emperor he will sign, wants no help, 348; Marie Antoinette warned of consequences if he signs, 350–1; cannot annihilate Monarchy by signing, 353, would be a 'stuffed Skin of a Monarch', 362; signing implies an elective monarchy, 364, act of signing should be ignored, 369; his suspensive veto approved, 364n6; George III 'earnest' in favour of, 368; Comte de Provence's zeal for, 399; suspected of intriguing with foreign courts, 372, with perfidious nobility, 395; RBJr thinks he won't sign, 379; accepts Constitution, 388n4; will get 'some affluence and Liberty' at expense of Church and nobility, 413, 457, VII, 60; Declaration of Pillnitz sent to, VI, 413n2, 417n3, 431n2; EB distrusts Emperor's intentions towards, 413, VII, 169; in his Cause the Cause of all Sovereigns is tried, VI, 443; Pope refuses to discuss indemnity for lost lands with, 458n6; Monsieur to represent him during captivity, 475; Emperor hopes he will come to terms with constitutionalists, VII, 21n3

demands for his deposition, VII, 168hn; Swiss Guard massacred, 169hn; Royal Family prisoners in Legislative Assembly, 169hn, 171–2; suspended from Kingship, 171, 174; danger to, of new Declaration of European neutrality, 175, 218; George III's solicitude for, 178tn, 'final' plans for, 218; is a magic wand to keep all monarchs in thrall, 261–2; is deposed, 273n1; EB's false hopes for, 273; his execution, 344, 391, 482, 483; his royal domains seized, 389; copy of his will sent to EB, IX, 128; his portrait given to EB by Monsieur, 128; La Fayette's triple humiliation of, 153–4, 185n2

his character: without energy or initiative, VI, 36; mild and benevolent, 149, 154; well-intentioned but not bred for breaking prison, 241–2; only a cipher, 268; wavering and uncertain, 380n5; failed because he

never studied the 'Policy of Opinion', 459, despised in Paris, VII, 66; a King who loved his subjects, just and reasonable, 265; his dignity when on trial, 470; his fault an excessive unwillingness to punish wicked men, 472

also mentioned, I, 2n3, V, 232n6, VI, 140hn, 167, 301hn, 328, 343n4, 352tn, 373, 385hn, 425, 442, VII, 5n3, 486, 586–7, VIII, 123n5, 236hn, 268, 269n2, 301, 302, 313, 327hn, 408, IX, 5n4, 98n13

Louis XVII, King of France (1785–95): brutal treatment of, after execution of Louis XVI, VII, 391; Regent appointed for, 391n3; Emperor his chief hope for protection, 393; Toulon declares allegiance to, 423n7, Hood promises return of Toulon to, 423n6, 427n1, 481n1; still a prisoner, 475, 479; Marie-Antoinette's alleged indecencies with, 461n4, 490; Britain's bond of loyalty to, VIII, 303; his death, 303n3, IX, 69hn. *See also* Dauphin, The

Louis XVIII, *see* Provence, Comte de

Louis-Philippe (1773–1850), later King of the French, V, 227n5

Louise-Marie-Thérèse-Victoire, Princesse de Bourbon (1733–99), daughter of Louis XV, VI, 228n6

Lovat, 11th Baron, *see* Fraser, Simon

Lovebond, Henry, II, 154n2

Lovell, Michael, West Indian merchant, Chairman of the Livery at the Half-Moon, II, 33

Lovett, Verney (*c.* 1705–71), M.P. for Wendover, I, 154n1

Lowe, J.

correspondence with, listed above, p. 151

Lowenstein's Chasseurs, VIII, 421n1

Lowndes, Charles (*c.* 1700–84), M.P.: Secretary of the Treasury under Rockingham, I, 318; also mentioned, II, 157

Lowndes, Richard (*c.* 1707–75), M.P. for Buckinghamshire, III, 30n1; withdraws from 1774 election, 33–4, 41; also mentioned, 12

Lowndes, William (*c.* 1707–75), his appointment as Commissioner of Excise, I, 318

Lowth, Robert (1710–87), Prebendary of Durham, later (1777) Bishop of London

correspondence with, listed above, p. 151

his polemical *Letter* to Warburton, I, 222–3

Lowther, Sir James, 5th Baronet (1736–1802), later (1784) 1st Earl of Lonsdale, M.P. for Cumberland: Portland's electoral rival, I, 341n2; petitions for lease of part of Portland's Cumberland estate, 341n2, IX, 397–8; his claim not affected by Nullum Tempus Bill, I, 344n3; his election for Cumberland declared invalid, II, 18hn, 18n4; acts as second to Governor Johnstone, 172hn, 173n1; his claim to Portland's land debated in Commons, 197, 200hn, heard in Court of Exchequer, 443hn; compromise on electoral dispute, III, 36; loses all his suits against Portland, 289–90; refused a retrial, 327; his 'ninepins', VII, 398; also mentioned, III, 425n3, IV, 184n2

Lowther, Sir William (1727–56), I, 330n4

Loyd, Mr, his mortgage to EB, II, 206n5, 210

Lubersac de Libron, Abbé Charles-François (1730–1804)
correspondence with, listed above, p. 151
sends EB his pamphlets, *Hommages . . . de Léopold II . . . et de Gustave III*, and *Rapprochment et parallèle des souffrances de Jésus-Christ . . . avec celles de Louis XVI*, VIII, 236hn; EB has no useful comments on, 236–7

Lucan, *De Bello Civili*, II, 272; *Pharsalia*, V, 166, VI, 161, 378, VII, 17, 145, 361, VIII, 244, 345, 348, 412

Lucan, 1st Baron, *see* Bingham, Charles

Lucas, Dr Charles (1713–71), Dublin apothecary and pamphleteer, I, 139n1; strange influence of his hackneyed pretences, 139–40; his single medicine, 140; his pompous funeral, II, 287

Lucian, I, 69, II, 136

Lucretius, *De Rerum Natura*, II, 420, VII, 100

Luders, Alexander (d. 1819), Common Pleader of the City, V, 237

Ludgate, Robert
correspondence with, listed above, p. 151

Lukin, Rev. George (1739–1812), VII, 416n2

Lukin, Mrs George (Catherine Doughty, d. 1814), wife of the preceding, sends EB a turtle, VII, 416

Lukin, Kitty, (1775–1861): visits Beaconsfield, IX, 47; friendship with the Burkes, 65, 206

Lukin, Mary (later Mrs Foy, 1770–1800): visits Beaconsfield, IX, 47; friendship with the Burkes, 65, 206

Lukin, Robert (1733–1816), Agent to French Corps in British pay, VIII, 397

Lumley, Viscount, *see* Lumley Saunderson, George

Lumley Saunderson, George, styled Viscount Lumley (1752–1807), later (1782) 5th Earl of Scarbrough, II, 361
correspondence with, listed above, p. 151

Lumley Saunderson, Richard, 4th Earl of Scarbrough (*c.* 1725–82), Rockingham peer: resigns office on break with Chatham, I, 277n2, 280; abstains from voting, 307n; and Lincoln petition, II, 60, 102; ignores policy of non-attendance, 379; also mentioned, II, 380, III, 216

Lushington, Sir Stephen, 1st Baronet (1744–1807), M.P., Chairman of East India Company
correspondence with, listed above, p. 151
and pension for Fowke, VI, 249n1, 252tn; and compensation for Hastings, VIII, 241, 261tn, 384hn, 416

Lushington, William (1747–1823), M.P.
correspondence with, listed above, p. 151
his speech at East India House on war with France, IX, 99hn, EB replies to, 99–100

Lusigny, Lazare-Guillaume de Ganay, Comte de (b. 1725)
correspondence with, listed above, p. 151

Luther, John (*c.* 1739–86), M.P. for Essex, supports Freeholders' petition, II, 76

Luttrell, Anne, *see* Cumberland, Duchess of

Luttrell, Henry Lawes (*c.* 1737–1821), later (1787) 2nd Earl of Carhampton, M.P.
correspondence with, listed above, p. 109
declared elected for Middlesex in place of Wilkes, II, 22hn, 23; his election challenged at County meetings, 45, 97; the Court candidate, 199n2; presents petition from cabinet-makers, 306
takes up Caillaud's case with EB, VI, 243–4hn; his lenient and judicious measures as Lieutenant General on staff in Ireland, VIII, 271; appointed Commander-in-Chief in Ireland, IX, 116; his violent pacification of Connaught, 117; his odious and ignorant policy, 121–2, 134, 136, 139, 339, 348n3, 363; Portland criticised for appointing him, 126, 182; his rule a 'Luttrellade', 368

Markham, Dr William (*cont.*)
the public and private lives of WB, RBSr and EB, 252–86; warned EB to lower his ambitions, 254, 269–70, called him a useless declaimer of 'Bear Garden Talents', 263–4, 268, his house 'a Hole of Adders', 268, 273; charged all three with Jacobite leanings, 282

quarrel with EB made up, II, 294, 295; EB moves to his old house in Westminster, 301n3; arranges studentship for RBJr at Christ Church, Oxford, 393–4; receives him and Thomas King hospitably, 394–5, is pleased with RBJr's examination, 401, gives him year's leave of absence, 409; his interest asked for Thomas Leland as candidate for Provostship of Trinity College, Dublin, 541–3, VIII, 48

dismissed as Preceptor to Prince of Wales, III, 269; as Archbishop of York denounces Whigs and Dissenters from the pulpit, 383; supports Hastings in the Lords, V, 260n1, 341n1, VII, 146, VIII, 423; interrupts cross-examination to abuse EB, VII, 369–70, 405, VIII, 438, IX, 441–2

also mentioned, I, 202n2, V, 322n3

Markham, Mrs William (Sarah Goddard), wife of the preceding: and her children, II, 543

Markham, William, Jr (1760–1815), Resident at Benares, secretary of Hastings
correspondence with, listed above, p. 153
cross-examined on Hastings's private correspondence, V, 322; possible influence on his father, Dr Markham, 341n1, VII, 146–7; his fortune 'derived from the Spoil', VIII, 438; also mentioned, 312tn

Marlay, Mary, *see* Grattan, Mrs James

Marlay, Richard (1726–1802), Dean of Ferns, later (1787) Bishop of Clonfert and (1795) Bishop of Waterford, old friend of EB, IV, 442
correspondence with, listed above, p. 153
Fitzpatrick given introduction to, IV, 442, 458, and Shee, VI, 11n3; Windham recommended to, V, 91–3; connection with Grattan, 92, VIII, 20, 46n5, 154; member of Literary Club, VI, 220; fails to get Archbishopric, VIII, 20; becomes Bishop of Waterford, 148, 154–6; Joseph Palmer and William Dennis recommended to, 155; the 'best good man with the

worst-natured muse', 401; also mentioned, V, 93tn, 158n5

Marlay, Thomas (d. 1756), Lord Chief Justice in Ireland, I, 84, V, 91n1

Marlborough, 1st Duke of, *see* Churchill, John

Marlborough, 4th Duke of, *see* Spencer, George

Marlborough, Duchess of (Lady Caroline Russell), wife of the preceding, I, 149; her 'fine Still life' at Blenheim, IV, 97

Marner, Mrs Elizabeth (d. 1789), the Burkes' housekeeper, V, 101; death of, VI, 14

Marnières, Julien-Hyacinthe, Chevalier de Guer, comes to England with Cazalès, VII, 96

Marriott, Sir James (*c.* 1730–1803), Judge of the High Court of Admiralty, IX, 425
correspondence with, listed above, p. 153

Marsack (or Marsac), Major Charles (1736–1820), his evidence on conditions in Oudh, V, 397

Marseille, Antoine-Juste, Bishop of Auxerre's man of business, V, 232, VI, 208n4

Marsh, George (d. 1790), of the High Court of Admiralty, IV, 68, IX, 426

Marsh, John (d. 1817), Commissioner for American claims, VI, 11

Marshall, Captain Samuel, his evidence in favour of Keppel, IV, 37–8

Martial, *Epigrams*, V, 340, IX, 324, 444

Martin, James (1738–1810), M.P., V, 122n2

Martin, Joseph (1726–76), M.P., Sheriff of London: supports Wilkes in City, II, 222; attacked in office for Rockingham connexion, 240–3; also mentioned, 492

Martin, Abbé Noël-Paul (b. 1745), Superior of the French clergy establishment at Winchester, VII, 395–6

Martin, Samuel (1714–88), M.P., II, 209

Martin, William, Rockingham's steward at Wentworth, II, 297

Martin, Mr, of Dublin, I, 84

Martinique, *see* West Indies

Martinot, Jean-François, Captain of the *Marianne*, petitions for redress against Cornish plunderers, I, 219

Marvell, Andrew, 'On Mr Milton's Paradise Lost', VI, 23; EB receives Thompson's edition of *Letters*, IX, 411

Masères, Francis (1731–1824), Baron of the Exchequer, Quebec

Maxwell, Dr William (*cont.*)
from EB, 335tn; joins French army, 335tn; also mentioned, 215hn

Maxwell, Major William, his three court-martials, III, 272hn; EB solicits protection for, 272–3

May de Termont, Charles-Gilbert de, Bishop of Blois (d. 1776), II, 414

Mayne, Sir William, 1st Baronet (1722–94), Irish M.P., II, 295–6

Maynooth, St Patrick's College for Irish Catholic clergy: movement to establish, VII, 499–500, 506–8; RBJr's books given to, 600n5, VIII, 265, 270, 288; trustees of, 263; Hussey as President of, 308, IX, 20hn, 141, 147, 182, 304; EB's interest in, VIII, 322, 352, 380; also mentioned, IX, 102, 143, 161

Medical profession, *see* Burke, Edmund, Opinions

Mee, Mary, *see* Palmerston, Viscountess

Meeran, *see* Miran

Mellars, Mr, frequents the Orange Coffeehouse, VI, 279–80

Mellor, Lydia, *see* Shackleton, Mrs Abraham Jr

Melville, Lieutenant Colonel Robert (1723–1809), Governor of West Indian Conquered Islands, I, 177; his relations with RBSr, 212n1

Menaca, J. A. de, Master of *El Atrebido*, VII, 377

Mendip, 1st Baron, *see* Ellis, Welbore

Menonville, François-Louis-Thibault de (1740–1816), VI, 162hn
correspondence with, listed above, p. 154
mild protest against attack in *Reflections* on moderates remaining in National Assembly, VI, 162–9; *Letter to a Member of the National Assembly* EB's reply to, 169tn, 252hn, 259, 292; translates *Letter to a Member*, 232–3, adds Preface on Priestley, 232; translation published before English edition, 253tn; his criticism of Lally-Tollendal accepted in part by EB, 321hn
also mentioned, VI, 228n5

Mercer, Captain Thomas (*c.* 1733–1801), VI, 93n1
correspondence with, listed above, p. 154
shocked by EB's speech on Army Estimates, VI, 92–3hn; EB rejects his opinions, 93–7, but not his friendship, 98; also mentioned, X, 45

Merchant Venturers of Bristol, Society of, IV, 16n10; petition on America, III,

96, 97, 101, 103, 105–6, 107n1; oppose Smalls Lighthouse Bill, 128–9, 141n4, IX, 419–20; ask for action against plundering of wrecks, III, 140–1, 145, 212hn; favour Dudley Canal Bill, 145n1; instructions to EB on American trade, 240; Bristol Port Bill, 248–9, 259; damaged fruit, 259, 268n3; protection from impressment, 301–2, IX, 418–19; loyal addresses from (1777), III, 320n1, (1779), IV, 114hn; friendly hints to EB on their relations, III, 363; Memorial on arming vessels, 380, 382; object to Irish trade proposals (1778), 426, IX, 421, accept proposals (1779), IV, 172tn; EB defends his conduct in Parliament to, III, 431–6, 437, 439–40; rebuked for going over his head to Ministers, IV, 50–1, 52–3; presents of wine to EB, 73, 319, 380; objections to African trade proposals, 60–2, to Smuggling Bill, 81, 82–3, to Warehousing Bill, 82–3; petition to Privy Council on St Eustatius, 350n1; also mentioned, X, 43
Masters of, *see* Farr, Paul; Garnet, Henry; Miller, Michael; Powell, John; Span, Samuel; Smith, Robert

Mercy-Argenteau, Florimond-Claude, Comte de (1727–94)
correspondence with, listed above, p. 154
plenipotentiary of Emperor at Hague Conference, VI, 327, VII, 169n3; secret correspondence with Marie Antoinette, VI, 338n3, 340n6, 344n6, 367, 372, 377, carries EB's letter to her, 349hn; not in sympathy with *émigrés*, 352tn, 372n5, VII, 225n2
meets EB in England, VI, 366; their conversation at breakfast, 367, 377, 385–6, 408, VII, 386, IX, 438; thinks England unwilling to intervene in France, VI, 367; his supposed democratical leanings, 372–3, 389; denies his visit to England has public character, 385–6; his reported mission from King and Queen against Princes, 389; avoids politics with Ministers, 412; EB sees his influence everywhere, VII, 225, 269, 272; and restitution of *émigré* property, 391
appointed Emperor's representative in Netherlands, VII, 376hn, 389; James Nagle recommended to, 376, placed in regiment by, 386hn, 451, recommended to Hohenlohe by, 452
also mentioned, VII, 381hn, 484

Mithridates VI, of Pontus, II, 507

Moderation, see Burke, Edmund, Opinions

Moffatt, Dr Thomas (d. 1787), of New England, II, 12n3
correspondence with, listed above, p. 155
suffers from Stamp Act riots, IX, 458

Mohun, Matthew, first president of the 'Academy of Belles Lettres', Dublin, I, 91, 93

Moira, 2nd Earl of, see Rawdon-Hastings, Francis

Molesworth, Sir John (1729–75), of Cornwall, II, 50n3

Molesworth, Louisa, see Ponsonby, Mrs William Brabazon

Molesworth, Richard (1737–99), Pay Office Accountant, VII, 267
correspondence with, listed above, p. 155

Molesworth, Robert, 1st Viscount Molesworth (1656–1725), Irish and English M.P., IV, 19

Molesworth, Robert [1729–1813, later, 1793, 5th Viscount Molesworth]
correspondence with, listed above, p. 155

Molière (Jean Baptiste Poquelin), *Médecin malgré lui*, VI, 198

Molini, Peter (d. c. 1808), London bookseller and language master
correspondence with, listed above, p. 155
conducts Maratha Agents on their homeward journey, IV, 365, 371–2

Molyneux, Charles William, 8th Viscount Molyneux (1748–95), M.P., II, 74n1

Molyneux, Sir Thomas (c. 1724–76), Usher of the Black Rod, I, 287

Monarchy, see Burke, Edmund, Opinions

Monboddo, Lord, see Burnett, James

Monbrun, Alexandre de
correspondence with, listed above, p. 155

Monck, George, 1st Duke of Albemarle (1608–70), VI, 164

Monckton, Colonel Henry (1740–78), killed at Sandy Hook, IV, 16

Monckton, John, 1st Viscount Galway (1695–1751), V, 247n3

Monckton, Mary, see Cork, Countess of

Monckton, General Robert (1726–82): appointed a Commissioner for India, II, 320hn, 322, 345, 348, 358; will do nothing to leaven a heavy piece of dough, 355; receives for his services lands in St Vincent claimed by RBSr, 460hn, plan for repurchase from, 461, 462, 463, 472; finally sells land, 463n4

Monmouth, EB's life at, in 1751, I, 111–13

Monmouth, Duke of, see Scott, James

Monroe, James, American minister in Paris, VIII, 358n2

Monsey, Dr Messenger (1693–1788), physician, friend of Mrs Montagu, I, 121hn, 132
correspondence with, listed above, p. 155

'Monsieur', see Artois, Charles-Philippe de Bourbon, Comte d'; Provence, Louis-Stanislas-Xavier de Bourbon, Comte de

Monson, John, 2nd Baron Monson (1727–74), resigns office with Rockingham on break with Chatham, I, 277n2, 280; also mentioned, 307n2

Montagu, 1st Duke of, see Brudenell Montagu, George

Montagu, Lady Barbara, I, 132n3

Montagu, Edward (d. 1775), husband of Mrs Elizabeth Montagu, I, 132, 170, 173, II, 456, 457, IX, 387

Montagu, Mrs (Elizabeth Robinson, 1720–1800), friend and admirer of EB
correspondence with, listed above, p. 155
EB seeks help of, for Madrid consulship, I, 131–2; has no influence with Ministers, 133; goes to Tunbridge, 137; EB tries to be an agreeable correspondent to, 170, IX, 385; 'news' is his passport to, I, 171, IX, 385; his satirical sketch of, I, 172–3, IX, 386; on EB's divine speaking, I, 242n1
invitation to her Evening, II, 19; a Pattern of Virtue, 224; visits Beaconsfield, 225; on RBJr at school, 394n1; offers to stand security for EB, III, 249–50; takes up WB's interest, 265–6; EB's long friendship with, VI, 196; entertains EB and Abbé Foulon, 263; best person to raise subscription list for Fanny Burney, VIII, 443; a Saturday engagement with, IX, 456
her other friends and protégés: Joseph Emin, I, 121hn, V, 456, VI, 12hn; Lord Bath, I, 163, IX, 384, takes a trip to the Continent with him, I, 173n2; Lord Lyttelton, II, 454–8, on EB's masterly portrait of him, 456; Duchess of Portland, III, 304n1
also mentioned, I, 187hn

Montagu, Frederick (1733–1800), M.P., leading Rockingham supporter
correspondence with, listed above, p. 155
speaks for Nullum Tempus Bill, I, 345; reports on changes in Administration, II, 174; one of the 'conciliabulum', in Rockingham's neighbourhood, 343, 356, III, 210, 291tn; speaks for Nottingham hosiers' petition, 122;

Murray, William (*cont.*)
  314n3; said to dislike *Reflections*, 314n3
  also mentioned, I, 306n4, II, 267, IV, 161n5, 162
Mustapha Khan, Raja: motion for inquiry into execution of, rejected, VI, 99–100
Musters, John (1753–1827), withdraws as Tory candidate for Nottinghamshire, III, 83–4tn
Myers, Dorothy, *see* King, Mrs Edward
Mysore, rulers of, *see* Haidar Ali; Tipu Sultan

Nabakrishna, Maharaja (d. 1797), 'Nobkissen': allegations in Presents Article on Hastings's loan from, VIII, 434–5, 441; 'Nobkissen versus Hastings', 434n5, 435n1
Nabakrishna, Maharaja, son of, VIII, 435n1
Nabob of Arcot's Debts, Speech on, see Burke, Edmund, Works
Nagle family, EB's maternal relations: genealogical table, III, 466; EB's boyhood spent with, I, 54, 79n3, 125hn; Catholic connections among, 147n5, III, 414; 'considering yourselves as one family', the burthen of his song, 371–2; disputes on claims to Clogher estate among, 411–17
Nagle, Ann, III, 412n3
Nagle, Anne, *see* Hennessy, Mrs John
Nagle, Athanasius, of Ballylegan, EB's uncle, I, 135n3
  correspondence with, listed above, p. 157
  his son abducts an heiress, I, 216; asks EB to act as guardian for young Therry, II, 180, 231, 244, IX, 396; asks EB to provide for his son Walter, II, 211; also mentioned, I, 228, 314n1, 315n2, 330n1, II, 123n3
Nagle, Athanasius ('Atty'), cousin of EB, I, 315
Nagle, Catherine, daughter of Garrett Nagle of Clogher, I, 315n3
Nagle, Catherine, suitor in case of Robert Nagle (1763), III, 412n3
Nagle, Catherine, *see* Carey, Mrs Joseph
Nagle, Catherine, *see* Courtenay, Mrs Michael
Nagle, David (1718–1800), of Ballygriffin and Bath, I, 119
Nagle, Edmund (d. 1763), EB's cousin, I, 216n6; loved by EB, 228, II, 19; also mentioned, III, 284n4
Nagle, Edmund, Sr, of Clogher: held main lease of Clogher estate, III, 414n1; estate sold to, X, 42

Nagle, Mrs Edmund, Sr, of Clogher (Catherine Fitzgerald), widow of the preceding, allegedly brought to beggary by Robert Nagle, III, 414
Nagle, Edmund, Jr, son of Garrett of Clogher: EB disposes interest in Clogher estate to, III, 417tn
Nagle, Edmund (1757–1830), later (1794) Sir Edmund, EB's cousin and favourite: EB helps plan his career at sea, I, 216–17, 228, 289, 347; joins East India Company Shipping Service, II, 19n4; promoted midshipman, 159; transfers to Navy, 179n2; Captain Stott's good opinion of, 179, IX, 395–6; in Madeira, II, 235; goes into Mediterranean, 314; cruises off St Helena, III, 284–5, IX, 412; praised by his captain, III, 371; promoted Lieutenant, 391; in the West Indies, IV, 28; brings the *Syren* from Newcastle, 94, IX, 428; returns from America, as Captain, V, 152; the 'flip-prescriber', 303; Admiral Pigot speaks kindly of, 348; visits Stratford with the Burkes, 418; robbed by highwaymen, VI, 31n; and William Baker's election campaign, 120, 121, 122; goes with RBJr to Coblenz, 347, 387n1, 388, 391, 400, 404, 405, 409; stays at Beaconsfield, VII, 31, 41, 97, 107, 167; asked to escort Artois to England, 368–9; brings letters through storm, VI, 454; RBJr's bequest to, VII, 600
  distinguishes himself in action, VIII, 66–7; returns to Beaconsfield in poor health, 70; is knighted, 76; received by King as his Brother Sportsman, 77; EB thanks First Lord of Admiralty on behalf of, 101; EB recommends to protection of Lord Spencer, 102; his ship's company laid up with scurvy, 312
  also mentioned, VI, 262, 465, VIII, 325, 326, IX, 270n1
Nagle, Edward, of Clogher, defendant in lawsuit (1754), III, 412n3; main leaseholder of Clogher estate, with his brother Edmund, 414n1
Nagle, Edward (1758–1826), son of Garrett and Betty Nagle, at school in Dublin, I, 289
Nagle, Edward James (d. 1802), called 'Edmund', son of Wat Nagle, clerk in the War Office, EB's kinsman and 'friendly secretary'
  correspondence with, listed above, p. 157
  at a Catholic school in Staffordshire,

Newspapers and Periodicals (*cont.*)

83, VIII, 249; 'the present age and reign of', VII, 105; dexterity in reporting cannibal acts in France, 210; wicked industry of Jacobin papers, 216, 229, 260, 'Newspapers of Hell', 225; 'almost perishing by the Press', 359; abused by supporters of Hastings, 372, VIII, 220, 438n2; no person once convicted safe from, 328; mischiefs done by, in Spithead mutiny, IX, 333

EB and: mistake or misrepresent EB's speeches, II, 178, 452, 532, IV, 394, V, 58, 254, 296, EB teased over misrepresentation, 247n4; scurrilous attacks on him for pleading unpopular causes, II, 325tn; Scottish papers filled with abuse of him, 358; misrepresented for his zeal in the Whig cause, III, 289; attacks ignored by EB as 'triffling amusement', V, 117; reported to be dangerously ill, 225n3, and RBJr lost at sea, 228; not frightened or flattered out of his principles by their Libels and panegyrics, 411; calumnies on his loyalty, VI, 7; he neither knows nor cares what they make him say on France, 97; his *voluntary* declaration of principles at Bristol finds its way in all papers, 178; and his proposed honorary degree at Oxford, 194hn; passage on Marie-Antoinette quoted in, 204n5; reported to be receiving reward for *Reflections*, 210n1, 333n1, and for *Appeal*, 333n1; correspondence with Archbishop of Aix published in, 295tn; reported to have solicited Provostship for himself, VIII, 6, 46; 'I never take up a Newspaper', 112, 338, 406, IX, 47, breaks his rule, VIII, 339; extracts from *Letter to a Noble Lord* printed in, 388hn; libels on him in every paper, 426; kept from him over Swift's piracy, IX, 239, 240n1, 244; Windham's references to EB ignored by, 307

EB and particular newspapers: *Ami du Roi*, EB's letter to Woodford printed in, VI, 223dn, 228n3; *Caledonian Mercury*, its version of Edinburgh Catholics' petition, IV, 53–4; *Courier de l'Europe*, read in France on economical reform, 233n1; *Gazetteer*, EB condemns Horne's letter in, II, 241, admires article on election of City Chamberlain, III, 280–1, opposes prosecution of editors for libel, VI, 54n5;

deplores their hostility to Aristocrates, 336; *London Chronicle*, their version of Rockingham's address criticised, I, 267; EB's letter to, on Jury Bill, II, 186–8; EB undertakes inquiry into their offensive attack on the Ladies of Llangollen, VI, 131hn, 132; *London Evening Post*, Shackleton's account of EB published in, II, 129–31, 133–5, 135–6; their account of debate on Jury Bill challenged, 201–3; essays by Valens published in, III, 233; *London Gazette*, its 'contemptuous appellation' for General Arnold, III, 246; false account of fighting in America, 305; Howe's victories put in proper perspective by, 410, shows true posture of affairs in America, IV, 313; its reports incomplete, 366; EB's appointment as Paymaster General announced in, V, 86; Ministers not likely to authorise publication of French Princes' Memorial by, VI, 432; 'our happiness or Misery dependent on', VII, 427; EB asks to be heard on Declaration before it appears in, 466; justice done to Edmund Nagle in, VIII, 67; EB sits up till past one for *Gazette Extraordinary*, VII, 483; *Monthly Review*, 'unjust censure' of EB's work answered by Falconer, VI, 160tn; editor of, VII, 503n3; articles by James Mackintosh on *Regicide Peace* (Nov., Dec. 1796), IX, 192hn; *Morning Chronicle*, Foxite paper subsidised by Opposition, VI, 130n2, 336n1, 451; EB acts' barbarously' in detaining, V, 161; backs Fox against EB, VI, 271hn, 450; EB suggests reply from Bintinaye to the 'infamous paper', VII, 42–3, 90hn; taken in by EB, 159; articles on Poland, 159, 160; its version of events in France, 172, 179, 203, omits EB's speeches on French atrocities, 323; accuses him of deserting liberty, 407; Fitzwilliam reported in, VIII, 238, 239; Wilmot urged to renounce and defy, X, 26; *Morning Herald*, and Holt's evidence in Hastings Trial, V, 391–2; EB protests against prosecution of, for libel, VI, 54n5; *Appeal* quoted in, 426hn; *Morning Post*, EB brings action for libel against, IV, 350–1, IX, 246n1; taken in by EB, VI, 34n6, 55n2, 231, 296n1; *North Briton*, EB sketches out a *golden number* on Mrs Montagu, I, 171–2, IX, 386; Number Forty-Five, V, 279; *Oracle*, squib on

Nisibis, Archbishop of, *see* Brancadoro, Césare

Nivernais, Duc de, *see* Mancini-Mazarini, Louis-Jules-Barbon

Noailles, Emmanuel-Marie-Louis, Marquis de (1743–1822), French Ambassador, III, 421; La Fayette presented at Court by, IX, 153n4

Noailles, Louis-Marie, Vicomte de (1756–1804), President of National Assembly: his house a rendezvous for English democrats, VI, 395; Grenville declines offer of services, VII, 339n7; also mentioned, VI, 356n3

Noailles, Marie-Adrienne-Françoise de, *see* La Fayette, Marquise de

Noailles, family of, VI, 235n2

Noales, Mr, schoolmaster, I, 49n2

'Nobkissen', *see* Nabakrishna, Maharaja

Noble, John (1743–1828), Bristol merchant and member of Common Council, a leading supporter of EB, III, 74

   correspondence with, listed above, p. 158

   hostility to Henry Cruger, III, 116n3; urges EB not to join in triumphal entry, 117, 123hn, avoids appearing himself, 125; presses EB to visit Bristol, 288hn, 290; and ministerial address, 317–18, 320n1; doubts on EB's Irish policy, 437–8; plans for 1780 elections, IV, 243–5; his ideas same as EB's, 325–7, 330; finally supports Cruger, 333tn

   elected Sheriff, III, 293; on the Freedom voted to Sandwich and Suffolk, 367; opposes subscriptions to raise volunteers, IV, 122; and proposed Bristol petition, 200; EB agrees with plan to limit Union Club, 312–13, 315; advised to get support of clergy for Whigs, 350; wants EB to move for alterations in Corporation Act, VI, 100hn, EB demurs, 101–4

   his interest in Labrador fisheries, III, 117hn, 173hn, 353, 366; gets protection for ships against pressganging, 424, IV, 66, 68, 263–4, IX, 425–6; loses ships to American privateers, IV, 23n3, 75n2, 381, IX, 464; little hope of compensation for, IV, 26, 49–51, 52, 76; EB tries to get protection on the high seas for his ships, 22–3, 52; proposal that Navy use his ships for defence in Labrador, 66, 68, IX, 425; Admiralty takes his ship, IV, 75; his prize-ships, 230, 253; problem of salt for fisheries, 342, 347–8, 350; EB will take up his plan

for securing Newfoundland fisheries, 381; has heavy losses, VIII, 235hn; Portland promises help, 235hn, 389

   sends EB a cheese, III, 117; is 'charged with a foreigner' by EB, 353; suffers from gout, IV, 264, 298, 312; chooses best wines for EB, 319; his support asked for Gloucestershire candidates, V, 121–2; dines with EB at Duke of Portland's, VI, 33; is asked to get smooth-eared corn and two-rowed barley for EB, 101; EB wants a dairymaid who understands cheese and butter, VIII, 390

   also mentioned, III, 176, 260, 261, 292, 298, 321, 324, 440n1, IV, 90, 240, V, 114, X, 43

Noble, Mrs John (Elizabeth Hatt, d. 1792), III, 118, 174, 366, IV, 77, 253, 264, 312, 342, 348, 381, V, 122, VI, 104, IX, 426; stays at Beaconsfield, VI, 33; EB's Gossip at a baptism, X, 5; also mentioned, 43

Noble, John Hatt, son of the preceding, wine merchant at Oporto

   correspondence with, listed above, p. 158

   recommended to British Minister at Naples, IV, 266, 380, X, 8–9; asked to procure Spanish wheat for Beaconsfield farm, VI, 101; also mentioned, X, 44

Noble, Richard (1778–1849), brother of the preceding: gets clerkship in Home Office, VIII, 235hn, 389

Noble and Pinson, John Noble's trading partnership to Labrador, III, 424

Nodin, J.

   correspondence with, listed above, p. 158

Nollekens, Joseph (1737–1823): statue of Rockingham at Wentworth, V, 46n5, 343n4, VI, 5–6; bust of Rockingham for Charlemont's Dublin house, 5–6

Norfolk, *see* County meetings

Norfolk, Dukes of, *see* Howard, Charles

North, Brownlow (1741–1820), Bishop of Winchester, VII, 443n3

North, Lady Catherine Anne, *see* Douglas, Lady Catherine

North, Dudley Long, *see* Long, Dudley

North, Frederick (1732–92), styled Lord North, later (1790) 2nd Earl of Guilford, M.P. for Banbury

   correspondence with, listed above, p. 158

   Home: refuses promotion from Pay Office to Chancellor of Exchequer, I, 298n3, accepts on Townshend's death, 328, IX, 392; succeeds Conway as Minister in Commons, I, 339n4;

North Administration (*cont.*)

422–3; reject proposals to accept American sovereignty, 427; still refuse to consider peace without submission, 427, IV, 89–90; motion on conduct of the war – a bad day for Ministers, 65; in high spirits over America, 89; Spanish charges against, 91; hostility towards their plans for volunteer defence, 108–9, 113, 122–5; Rockingham condemns Militia Bill, 110–11; their blunders and neglect of Navy, 115; people seem readier to lose colonies than the Ministry, 116–17; 'very dull in their expectation about America', 116; have brought the country to the verge of ruin, 124–5, 163; the only men at ease, because their emoluments are safe, 126, 156; refuse to recognise Congress, 127hn; demand Burgoyne's return to America after defeat, 127–8, 362hn, refuse to exchange him with Laurens, 378, 383–5, 388–92, 395–6; fears of Jamaica invasion, 165; stunned by military weakness in America, 313; attempt to raise troops in Germany and Ireland, 314; Germain forced to retire from Ministry, 404hn, 406n3; Conway's motion on ending the war brings Administration to an end, 419, 422hn

India: intervention in the East India Company likely, II, 343–6, 349–51, 369, 387–8, 389–90; Government measures against, 398–9, 402; negotiations with Company, 423; Ministry call of the House will bring Company into entire dependence on Crown, 429–30; compensation for General Monckton, 461–2; submission of Company expected, 493–4, 523; Directors in connexion with, 497; and election of Directors, 515n2; make difficulties for WB going to India, III, 347; and the seizure of Lord Pigot in India, 417; EB presses for intervention in Sulivan's Tanjore project, IV, 304, 306–10; appear to support abuses in East India Company, 320–1; EB proposes discussions of Indian affairs with, 325tn; treatment by, of Maratha Agents, 356hn, 357, 362, IX, 431; danger of Shelburne's rallying 'routed corps' of, in a jobbing Indian policy, IV, 449; Macartney on the fallen Administration, V, 41. For Select and Secret Committees, Regu-

lating Act of 1773, *see* East India Company

Ireland: their Irish Trade Bill not a Ministerial Jobb, III, 441; have thoughts of rejecting Irish Toleration Bill, IV, 6–7, IX, 423; blunders and imbecility of their Irish policy, IV, 71, 89n3; support resolutions from Committee on Trade with Ireland, 1778, IX, 421; Ireland takes independent action on trade IV, 162, 223–4; their Irish policy censured by EB, 181–2; supported by Irish Parliament 189; EB knows nothing of Ministry plans for Irish Toleration Bill, 406–7; legislative Independence of Ireland grows from American troubles created by, VII, 204n6, cp III, 441; Irish Mutiny Act, VII, 365n4

Relations with Rockingham Party: non-attendance proposed on measures that mortgage House to Court, II, 362–3, 367, 387, 407; the Party should put no confidence in, 411; divided over support of Ministry on Indian policy, 411, 425–6; should have an alternative system ready, III, 88, 107–8, ought to have 'good intelligence of the Enemies' motions', 89–90; Ministers have no answer to Fox, 299; the Party should ensure a Gallery when they speak against, 314; negotiations to bring individual members of Party into Government, 420tn, 421hn; Opposition not accepted by people generally as an alternative government, IV, 25, 141; Fox wants coalition with, 40–1; alternatives open to Opposition in dealing with, 142; EB draws up articles of impeachment against, 142n1; Grafton goes through 'the whole Conduct' of, with leaders of Opposition, 143–4, suggests individuals should accept office if offered, and on conditions, 144, 154, 157, 161; Fitzwilliam favours coalition of all opposition groups against Court and, 146; Opposition not popular, but Ministry odious to the people, 153; Fox wants total change of Ministry, 156; succeeded in 1782 by Rockingham–Shelburne coalition, 423tn, V, 41

EB and: defends Opposition against, to Dr Markham, II, 259; has no influence with, 542, IV, 135, V, 63; has problems in carrying on constituents' affairs with, IV, 50; was always in opposition

North Administration (*cont.*)
 to, but began Indian business during, v, 255; Ministers convinced EB is Junius, II, 250

 Bristol supporters: vote loyal address, III, 220hn, fail to carry it, 319n2; defeat Whigs in Gloucester and Hereford, 268n4; use Volunteers as test of party, IV, 113, will exclude Whigs from, 122n5; plan for joint candidate at Bristol, 238n3, canvassing policy, 267n4; distribute Wesley's pamphlet on American taxation, 271n5

 Brickdale and Daubeny support, IV, 342n5; Clive's relations with, II, 181, 355n3, 434hn, 452, 472, V, 456n1; John Durbin supports, III, 420hn; Eden a critic of, IV, 170hn; Flood won over to, III, 176n6, 177; Lord George Germain's connexion with, II, 404–5, III, 246; Granby's relations with, II, 153n2; Grenville's disciples in, 449–50; City of Hull supports, IV, 129tn; Governor Johnstone's relations with, II, 437n4, IV, 29; James Macpherson writes for, V, 165n2, other writers in pay of, II, 251, 288; Lord Ongley supports, IV, 139n2; Andrew Pope a supporter, III, 321n4; Sir John Trevelyan an opponent of, IV, 298n2; hostility to Wilkes, II, 132, 351, 356n1. Court connexions, II, 150, 181, 429–30, IV, 50–1; measures 'mortgaged to', II, 363; all depend on the King, IV, 156, 161. Election candidates: for City of London, II, 492hn, for Lord Mayor, 356; for Middlesex, IV, 159n3, Gloucester, 281hn, Westminster, 282hn, Windsor, 303hn

Northampton, 8th Earl of, *see* Compton, Spencer

North Briton, see Newspapers

Northcote, James (1746–1831), portrait painter
 correspondence with, listed above, p. 159
 paints 'Death of Wat Tyler' for Alderman Boydell, V, 465n1; his interest solicited for John Sanders, X, 23–4

Northcote, Rev. Thomas ('Regulus', d. 1787), political journalist, III, 276–7

Northey, Ann, *see* Hargrave, Mrs Christopher

Northington, Earls of, *see* Henley, Robert

Northumberland, 2nd Earl and 1st Duke of, *see* Percy, Hugh Smithson

Northumberland, Duchess of (Lady Elizabeth Seymour), first wife of the preceding, Lady of the Bedchamber to the Queen, II, 5n3; resigns position, 91n1; visits Rockinghams, 152

Northumberland, 2nd Duke of, *see* Percy, Hugh

Northumberland, Duchess of (Frances Julia Burrell, 1752–1820), second wife of the preceding, V, 419

Norton, Sir Fletcher (1716–89), M.P., Speaker of the House of Commons, later (1782) 1st Baron Grantley
 correspondence with, listed above, p. 159
 Chatham attempts to fix, I, 319n6; Townshend will probably try for, 319, IX, 391; speaks for, but does not vote on, Nullum Tempus Bill, I, 345; opposes Middlesex petition, II, 24; intervenes between EB and Rigby, 124hn; examines public records, 224n2; and the *Endeavour*'s expedition to the South Seas, 308; admittance to Commons asked for Beattie, 457n2; finds entry to Commons blocked by crowd, III, 236tn; his Speech before the King on Bill for Royal Debts offends King but pleases House, 338–9, IV, 319; his illness causes House to adjourn, 232; North tries to get rid of, 319; nominated by Opposition, 319n6; on Royal Marriage Act terms, IX, 400; also mentioned, II, 198, 436, III, 155hn, VII, 588

Norwich, Bishop of, *see* Horne, George; Young, Philip

Nott, John, Button Burnisher, pseudonym of John Morfitt (c. 1757–1809), barrister and loyalist pamphleteer
 correspondence with, listed above, p. 159
 receives orders for Liberty Buttons following Daggers order, VII, 328–9

Nottinghamshire, *see* County meetings

Nugent, C.
 correspondence with, listed above, p. 159

Nugent, Dr Christopher, F.R.S. (1698–1775), Irish physician, EB's father-in-law, I, 115hn
 correspondence with, listed above, p. 159
 EB marries his daughter, I, 115hn; EB's early poem addressed to, 115–18; the Doctor who restored EB's life and taught him how to live, 117; settles in London, 139–40; EB's family live with, 141–2; payment by Dodsley to EB made through, 175; his high opinion of Flood, 195; an original member of the Literary Club, 220n2, III, 237hn; 'goes his rounds', I, 245; has the gout, 247, II, 223, 507,

O'Bryen, Dennis (*cont.*)
EB cannot help, but would like to meet, IV, 425–6; friendly relations with EB, V, 269; claims to have seen draft of *Reflections*, VI, 89n1; becomes close friend of Fox, VII, 157, IX, 265
Utrum Horum? The Government or the Country, IX, 265
'Observations on the Conduct of the Minority' (1793), *see* Burke, Edmund, Works
Observations on a Late State of the Nation see Burke, Edmund, Works
O'Connor, Arthur (1763–1852), Irish M.P.: an enthusiast for Rousseau, but tractable, VIII, 242; speaks out in parliament, 242n6; his speech not warmed with the fire of heaven, 245; his radical election address, IX, 122; lived in close association with Fox in England, 123; Fitzwilliam's fears of, 145
O'Connor, Mrs Arthur (Eliza de Caritat, daughter of Condorcet), wife of the preceding, VIII, 242n6
O'Conor, Charles (1710–91), Irish anti-quary
correspondence with, listed above, p. 159
affection for EB, I, 203; thinks ancient Chronicles of Ireland should be edited, translated and printed, V, 109; work on Sebright MSS, 292; also mentioned, 293tn
Dissertations, III, 275hn
O'Conor, Charles (1764–1828)
correspondence with, listed above, p. 159
O'Conor, Patrick (d. *c.* 1812), later (1795) Sir Patrick, Cork merchant, VII, 258
correspondence with, listed above, p. 159
a pall bearer for RBJr, VII, 570, VIII, 140; knighted by Fitzwilliam, IX, 111; sends news of French ships in Bantry Bay, 221n3; also mentioned, 340tn
O'Conor, Mrs Patrick, later Lady (Eliza-beth Therry, EB's cousin), wife of the preceding, VII, 258, IX, 111
O'Donel, Hugh
correspondence with, listed above, p. 159
O'Donovan, Ellen, *see* Nagle, Mrs Patrick
Ogier, Mrs, *see* Augier, Mrs
Ogilvie, Thomas
correspondence with, listed above, p. 159
Ogilvie, William (1740–1832), tutor to children of widowed Duchess of Leinster: marries the Duchess, III, 27n2; also mentioned, V, 221n1, 282n2

Ogle, Hester Jane, *see* Sheridan, Mrs Richard Brinsley
Ogle, Ralph, 3rd Baron Ogle (1468–1513), VIII, 342n6
Oglethorpe, General James (1696–1785), founder of Georgia
correspondence with, listed above, p. 159
popularises Indian corn in England, II, 183n4; in transports with *Letter to the Sheriffs of Bristol*, III, 343–4; EB happy to have known, 344
O'Gorman, Chevalier Thomas (d. 1809)
correspondence with, listed above, p. 160
O'Halloran, Sylvester (1728–1807)
correspondence with, listed above, p. 160
O'Hara, Charles, Sr (*c.* 1715–76), Irish M.P.
correspondence with, listed above, p. 160–3
friendship with EB, I, 206, 233tn, II, 147, 235, 425, 451, III, 243, 255; EB feels the loss of his company, I, 210, longs for an hour with, 247, for the Cordial of his presence, II, 495; EB speaks without reserve to his private ear, I, 241, his letters the only agreeable thing from Ireland, 254, their correspondence 'a refuge from Solitude', 251. Sees EB in Ireland, 144; advises him to 'manage' persons so that he avoids personal attacks on himself, 338; meet over 'a little Stirabout' at St James Street, 139; visits EB's father, 139, is friendly and prudent with him over EB, 139; warns EB against his temper, 233tn; fails to meet during EB's visit to Ireland, 264, 271; urged to visit the new home, Gregories, II, 13–15, all the odd set there his friends, 26; stays at Beaconsfield, 57hn, the 'communion of Friendship', 137; friendship with Mrs Burke's father, Dr Nugent, 286, receives medical advice from him, 508, III, 185
on the dangers of retirement, I, 144–5, 147; his Curragh solitude, 145, II, 206; rural amusements, I, 141, 145, 151, riotous life as gambler, sportsman and horseman, 208n4; Ranger of the Curragh, 145n4; on the people and ancient ruins of Enish Murray, his island, 146, 147, EB wants drawings of the ruins, 148; divides a mountain farm into four villages, 146; his London card-playing, 152; loves a *bon mot*, 244; sends his race-horse Hirpinus to Rockingham's stable in Newmarket, 339, 349, II, 16; his

O'Hara, Charlotte, *see* Trench, Mrs Eyre

O'Hara, James, 2nd Baron Tyrawley (1690–1773)
correspondence with, listed above, p. 185

O'Hara, Mary, *see* Ponsonby, Mrs James Carrique

O'Hara, William Henry King (*c.* 1750–80), Naval officer, younger son of Charles O'Hara, Sr
correspondence with, listed above, p. 163
education in England, I, 139, 145; returns to Ireland, 210; visits Beaconsfield, 139, II, 86, 'charms everyone', 98, 'couldn't help loving him', III, 151; meets Thomas King on Marine tour, II, 238; sent to Mediterranean, III, 151; also mentioned, II, 501, III, 72

O'Keefe, James, Bishop of Kildare (d. 1797), establishes seminary at Carlow, VIII, 265

O'Keefe, T.
correspondence with, listed above, p. 163

O'Kelly, John James, Comte O'Kelly (1749–1800): resigns as French Minister at Mainz, VII, 29; talks with EB, 30; takes letter to RBJr, 29

Old Hall Green Academy, founded for exiles from Douay, IX, 45hn, 46tn, 60n2, 61n4

Old Whigs, *see* Burke, Edmund, Works: *Appeal*; Newcastle Party

Oldys, Francis, *see* Chalmers, George

O'Leary, Arthur
correspondence with, listed above, p. 163

Oliff, John, Sr (*c.* 1689–1760), of Henbury, farmer, IV, 117n4

Oliff, John, Jr, farmer, IV, 117n4

Oliff, Mrs John (Betty Crocker, Mrs Burke's dairy maid), wife of the preceding, IV, 117

Oliver, Andrew (1706–74), Lieutenant Governor of Massachusetts, petition for removal of, II, 518, 519hn, 521–2

Oliver, Richard (1735–84), West India merchant, M.P. for London: defeated by Wilkes for Sheriff, II, 221n5; as Sheriff later, accused of sharp practice by Wilkes, 359n2; votes with Opposition on East India Company Bill, 392; EB wants to keep City out of such hands as, III, 224; his livery and himself corrupt, 281; also mentioned, II, 33n11

O'Malony, John (1617–1702), bequest to Irish College of the Lombard, IV, 410n4

Ompteda, Dietrich Heinrich Ludwig, Freiherr von (1746–1803), Hanoverian delegate to Imperial Diet: his supposed opposition to intervention in France, VI, 325, 329, 377; RBJr finds explanation for, 384, EB remains puzzled, 386, 393

O'Neale, Michael
correspondence with, listed above, p. 163

O'Neil, Rev. Arthur (b. *c.* 1711), Chaplain at Bencoolen, I, 109–10; his unbecoming behaviour, 110n1

O'Neil, Rev. Felix (*c.* 1713–*c.* 1787), usher at Ballitore School, I, 11n1, 23n3; over-solicitous for his brother's health in Sumatra, 109–10

O'Neill, Charles
correspondence with, listed above, p. 163
assists EB in general affairs, III, 416

O'Neill, John (1740–98), Irish M.P.: goes to England as Commissioner to carry Address to Prince of Wales, V, 450n3

O'Neill, Owen Roe (*c.* 1590–1649), VII, 104

O'Neill, Sir Phelim (*c.* 1604–53), and the Irish Rebellion of 1641, VII, 104n6, 105

O'Neill, Turlogh, and the Irish Rebellion, VII, 104n6

Ongley, Robert, 1st Baron Ongley (*c.* 1724–85), M.P. for Bedfordshire, IV, 139

Onslow, Arthur (1691–1768), M.P., Speaker of the House of Commons, III, 76n1

Onslow, George (1731–1814), M.P., Lord of the Treasury: gets damages for insults from Horne Tooke, II, 148; more sensible than newspapers on EB's speeches, 178; brings printers before House for breach of privilege, 208; EB's altercation with, 265n2; and Absentee Tax, 484; also mentioned, I, 231n3

Onslow, Colonel George (1731–92), M.P.: opposes Middlesex petition, II, 24; with his cousin brings printers before House for breach of privilege, 208n1

Onslow, Thomas (1754–1827), M.P.: throws up contest for Surrey, IV, 302, 303hn; goes over to Ministry, V, 374n6

Opie, John (1761–1807), portrait of EB, 1792, VI, frontispiece

Opposition, *see* Burke, Edmund, Opinions

Oracle, see Newspapers

Ord, Daniel, V, 299n1

Orde, Thomas (1746–1807), M.P. for Aylesbury, protégé of Dundas

Overton, John (*cont.*)
reads EB's dagger speech, VII, 328hn; sends information on daggers, 331n1, 334n3

Ovid: *Amores*, I, 176, IV, 273, VI, 1; *Ars Amatoria*, VII, 4; *Fasti*, III, 355; *Heroides*, I, 15n1; *Metamorphoses*, I, 15, 32, 78, II, 136, IX, 366; his exile, I, 259

Owen, John, bookseller and printer: examined on authorship of *Thoughts on the English Government*, VIII, 355, IX, 104n3; refuses to publish defence of *Thoughts*, VIII, 456hn; joint publisher of *Letter to a Noble Lord*, IX, 11n8, 12n; goes bankrupt, 51, 244tn; brings out pirated edition of *Regicide Peace*, 95n5, 97hn, 98; Bill filed against him, 104, 105; his counterclaim, 104n3; injunction against sale, 105n3; 'little great rogue of a publisher', 106; publishes EB's 'Conduct of the Minority', 240n1; injunction sought to prevent sale, 240; news broken to EB, 242–3; delays in proceedings against, 245–6, 288, 306

Oxford, 1st Earl of, *see* Harley, Robert

Oxford, Resident Graduates of, their Address to Burke, VI, 194–5

Oxford, University of: decrements at, I, 65n3; Hungarian Protestants at, III, 179; Boy-Professor of, V, 112hn; Regius Professor of Greek, 113n1; Portland elected Chancellor, VII, 167–8, 195, 571n4, VIII, 11, 47, 85, 93n1, his installation, VII, 207, 227–8; combines with City and County for relief of French clergy, 269–71; Captain King attends lectures at, 588; French Laurence becomes Professor of Civil Law, VIII, 354n3; corrupting Indian influence at, IX, 441–2; University prizes, X, 35

EB and: M.A.s' Address of thanks to, VI, 144tn; honorary degree for, refused by Caput, 193hn, 195tn, later offered and refused, 195tn; resident graduates' Address to, 194–5, X, 163; RBJr receives honorary degree, VI, 195tn

Bodleian Library, VII, 65n3; Christ Church, RBJr awarded studentship at, II, 394–5, IV, 28hn, 58, 369n3, III, 74, VII, 580–1, 584; Corpus Christi, Walker King at, III, 27, 198hn, 199; St John's College, Bristol Common Council appoint to scholarship at, IV, 244; Worcester College, Dr Morgan recommended by EB for Provostship, VIII, 283

other references, III, 368hn, V, 38n1, 462, VIII, 67hn

Oxford, Vice-Chancellors of, *see* Cooke, John; Wills, John

Ozier, Mrs, *see* Augier, Mrs

Page, Richard, Repton's Red Book for estate of, VII, 330

Paine, Thomas (1737–1809), V, 412hn correspondence with, listed above, p. 163 stays with EB at Beaconsfield, V, 412, 415; his iron bridge project, 415, VI, 67–8, 313; on EB's tardy recognition of revolution in France, 10n2; optimistic view of the new Constitution, 68–75; agrees to meet EB if topic of France avoided, 76tn

Rights of Man his reply to *Reflections*, VI, 246, 253n1; celebrated by Unitarians at Crown and Anchor, 247; EB's alarm at, 249; its principles gain ground in Portland party, 273, 336; William Smith's *Examination* of, 302hn, 303, VII, 3n1; EB on its style and content, VI, 303–4; Mackintosh 'Paine at bottom' (RBJr), 312; nothing can make Fitzwilliam a disciple of, 402; *Rights of Man*, Part II, VII, 119; John Quincy Adams's *Answer* to, 504; Duke of Norfolk condemns both *Reflections* and *Rights of Man*, VIII, 239n1; EB's heart said to be broken by Paine's book, IX, 115n4

charged with sedition, VII, 229n2; given French citizenship, 229; Fox helps with brief for his defence, 315–16; effigies of, burned by Loyalists, 340; William Smith's allegory on 'Ainep' and 'Rekub', 355; 'elevated from a Staymaker to a fine Gentleman' in Paris, VIII, 362; publishes *Age of Reason*, 362n2; outlawed from England, IX, 261n2; held up as a warning to Dissenters, 261; hostility to Christian religion, 320n1

also mentioned, VI, 78hn, 109hn

Painting, *see* Burke, Edmund, Opinions

Pakenham, Edward Michael, 2nd Baron Longford (1743–92), Captain of the *America*, III, 461

Palliser, Admiral Sir Hugh, 1st baronet (1723–96), M.P., a Lord of the Admiralty correspondence with, listed above, p. 164 fails to rejoin line at Ushant, IV, 12hn; dispute with Keppel over his inaction,

Parliament (*cont.*)

present troubles, III, 235–6, second plan for Conciliation, 237, 246; on New York Remonstrance, 164–5; brings in Wrecks Bill, 220–1, 222, 258, 261; draws up amendment to North's Conciliatory Bill, 299; secedes during debate on Habeas Corpus Suspension Bill, 330, IV, 393n2; on Civil List Debts, III, 334hn; supports petition of Africa Company Committee, 340–2, 345hn, 346tn; speech on Irish Trade Bill, 448n2, IV, 455n3; answers Burgoyne on American defeats, IX, 410; draws up preamble for Catholic Relief Bill (1778), 423; on the arrest of Lord Pigot, 432–3

opposes tax on postchaises, IV, 47n4; speech on petition of Edinburgh and Glasgow Catholics, 54n1; revises Camden's motion on Irish trade, 70n1; on Spain, 90n4, 91n1; strain of Parliament on his health and spirits, 92; lashes Lord Temple on Buckingham Church Bill, 131n3; speech on Address to the King, 171n1

Bills for Economical Reform (1779–82): first sketch of plan, IV, 171; notice given of Bills, 174–5, V, 14n1, 172n1; first speech on, IV, 175; further preparation, 190, 196–9; presents plan to Commons, 203tn, 212–13; clauses defeated, IV, 214hn, 215n1, 217tn, 219; Committee proceedings, 214–15; 'the whole systematic part of the Bill rejected', 214, 219–20; 'disposed of and melted away', 240, 302; asked to reintroduce Bill, 258–60, 265; brought in for second time, 336; passed in attenuated form (Civil List Act), 433–4, 447, V, 7, 100, 330; support for plan at York County Meeting, IV, 176hn, in Bristol, 200, 244; City thanks Savile but not EB for Bill, 205; thanked by County Committees, 206–9, 210–11, 225, and by Common Council of London, 209–10; adopted by Westminster Committee, 282hn; acceptance of Bill a condition for Rockingham's taking office, 434tn; Walpole on, V, 14n1; speech on the King's Message on, 35n1; French Laurence on, IX, 281; Fox's criticism answered, 285–8; anonymous praise for, 315n3; other references, I, 138n2, IV, 233hn, V, 106hn, VI, 23n6, 95n2, IX, 280n3, X, 7

speech on Ireland (1780), misinterpreted, IV, 181hn; introduces Welsh Bill, 211–12, 239–40; speaks against pillory sentences, 230hn; confers with Committee on Insolvent Debtors Bill, 231–2; opposes Sawbridge's motion on parliamentary reform, 235, 237, 238; speech on petition of Protestant Association, 246; resolutions on toleration after Gordon riots, 248–51, defends Ministerial Address condemning riots, 251tn, opposes North's resolution, 251tn; willing to serve again but never wishes to set foot in Parliament again, 316–17; moves for inquiry on seizure of property in St Eustatius, 343, 387, 402hn, 402n7, presents Hoheb's petition, 402–3; opposes Fox's Marriage Bill, 355n4; speech on Laurens in the Tower, 385tn, 394, presents his petition, 393, brings in Bill to facilitate exchange of prisoners, 394hn, 438; speech on Irish trade, 455n3

Act for Reforming the Pay Office (1782), V, 22, new Bill (1783), 73–4, 76, 85, 90, 93, VI, 95n2, IX, 287; speech on proposed Bill to prevent appeals from Irish to English Courts, V, 58n2; appointed member of Select Committe on India (1782), 59–60, *see also* East India Company; defends his conduct in reappointing Powell and Bembridge, 91tn; Bill for Sale and Disposal of Forests, 95–6; speech on Fox's India Bill, 123n1, 129hn; motion in defence of Coalition, 153, 155–6; speeches on Pitt's India Bill, 165–6, 308–9, 311n1, moves for inquiry into Reports of Select Committee, 165–6; speech on Nawab of Arcot's debts, 207n1, 211–12, VIII, 428; his policy on motions for papers, V, 253, moves for papers on Almas Ali Khan, 253–4; on the price of a seat, 300; makes 'quite a riot' about Elliot, 304tn; too busy to attend to the Wool business, 401; opens debate on Regency arrangements, 440n4, opposes Regency Bill, 446n2, VI, 7n2, n5, called to order, 7n3; prepared to vote for repeal of Test and Corporation Acts (1789), V, 470–1, attitude hardens against repeal (1790), VI, 82–3, 101–4, speech on, 100hn

speech on Army Estimates, VI, 81–2tn, 97, 106n2, 124, 331n1, attacked on, by Sheridan, 127n1; speeches 'cut up'

Petty, William (*cont.*)

Grafton tries to get rid of, II, 3hn; Camden gives him up, 4; dispute over Turin ambassador, 4n1; James Townshend supports, 26n2, 175n2, 222n1, 359, IV, 159n2; Isaac Barré a follower, II, 26n2, 211; sends secret mission to Corsica, 35n2; Dunning close friend of, 174n4, III, 209n3; Corporation of London possessed by his faction, II, 175; suffers defeats in London, 222, III, 281; more popular in City than Rockingham, II, 241, becomes Master of City, 359; rôle in possible new Ministry, 297; disapproves of Absentee Tax, 465, attitude altered by Chatham, 472n1, 498n3, said to have used Goldsmith to write for the tax, 482, 491n3, his double game, 483, 491, 509, disapproves of Rockingham's resolution on the tax, 498n3; supports Chatham's prospective son-in-law for Westminster, III, 50; agrees with Rockingham on America, 102, 108tn, 205, 398hn, 419–20; appears to support EB's Conciliation Bill, 236; proposes subscription for American prisoners, 411hn; disgusts everyone with his prevarication in debate on America, 427

Grafton thinks ought to accept office if asked, IV, 144; and parliamentary reform, 167, 217tn; proposes committee on public expenditure, 185n2, 194, IX, 281n2, terms of motion, IV, 174n1; promised no clash with EB's motion, 174; thanked by City, 194, 205; policy on County meetings, 189, 193, 194n1, alleged to encourage associations only where he has no property, V, 39; agrees with Rockingham to preserve unity of Opposition, IV, 217tn; breach over Dunning's motion, 218tn; approached in vain by North, 422hn; forms coalition as Secretary of State with Rockingham, 423tn; impedes passage of EB's Economy Bill, 434tn, 450, V, 7n2, IX, 287; makes Lord Advocate's protégé his secretary, IV, 448; gets Marlborough's support, 450n1; Catholic Committee submit Memorial to, 459n1

asked by King to lead Administration after Rockingham's death, V, 3hn; possible relations of Rockingham's followers with, 4; EB's advice to Fox on his war with, 5; Richmond wants

Party to serve under, 9hn; Cavendish refuses to support, 10n1, 17hn; and Barré's 'pay office' pension, 17–18; offers Lord Lieutenancy to Temple, 23hn; Richmond ceases to attend Cabinet, 24n1; disagrees with Fox on American Independence, 27n1; 'bringing round the old System', 35; comparative strengths of Fox, North and, in Commons, 57; resigns on Preliminary Articles of Peace, 65hn, 354, IX, 286n5; establishes friendly relations with Gower, V, 81n2; accuses Ministers of laying counterfeit plots on radical clubs, VIII, 346n7; thinks 'Belgium' ought to be insisted on, IX, 294; included in 'sole option' if Pitt's Administration falls, 337

India: Sulivan friends with, I, 301, breaks with, II, 106; thinks East India Company ought to be allowed to borrow more, 347; has more weight than EB with Company, IV, 425; correspondence with Indian Princes in his hands, 431; supports Hastings, 447n6, V, 314n2, 342; makes bargain with Dundas on India, IV, 448–9; supporters of, in East India Company, V, 31tn; promises William Jones Bengal judgeship, 37, faithful and just to his promises, 38, 66, 67tn; his alleged Indian designs, 342; speech in favour of Hastings, VIII, 219

And EB: speaks highly of EB, I, 264; EB refuses to intervene over East India Stock crash, II, 140–1; his cunning, 210, tricks, 483; polite to EB, but EB has no interest with, 211–12, III, 284, IX, 411–12; Garrett Nagle wishes to be Irish agent to, II, 211, III, 283–4; Abbé Morellet criticises EB to, II, 425tn; resents *Letter to the Sheriffs*, III, 398hn; EB calls on, IV, 66; offers himself 'to sale by sample', 157; EB visits, 193; EB despairs at power delivered into hands of, V, 20; 'neither Whigg nor Tory' – Boswell ought to get on well with, 34; 'demolished', at a cost to the Kingdom, 72; old Rockingham Whigs adhere to the spirit, he to the letter of the Constitution, 295; EB's dislike of, VI, 64n3, hatred of, for his radical tendencies, 91–2

Personal: returns from France, III, 296; named in imaginary plot as conspirator against King, IV, 134n2; Crabbe fails to

Pitt, William, the Elder (*cont.*)

Election, 112, 160; does not go all the way with his brothers, 115; preferred to Rockingham or Grenville at Court, 157; 'Systematick Hostility' towards Rockinghams, 175, 210; not whole-heartedly opposed to Administration, 406; intoxicated by the Closet, but disposed to move towards Rockinghams, III, 89; his bad health, 186, 194, 205; perfectly recovered (Sept. 1775), 210; his theatrical appearances in Parliament wrapped in flannel, 400; his last speech and seizure in House of Lords, 427

External Affairs: stands out against Ministry on Ireland, I, 141; speech against the peace, 160; battle between Pride and Patriotism, 194; declares against right to impose interior taxes on colonies, 231–2, 240; 'the great Commoner' opposes West Indian freeports, 251; views on repeal of Stamp Act, 280n1, II, 88n1, III, 254n2; plan for India (1766), I, 281, 291–2, 297–9, 300–1; the only leader able to conduct a war, II, 173; no fixed plan for India (1772), 346–7; supports Irish Absentee Tax, 466, 472n1, 498n3, 509; the *sacra anchora* of the Ministry, III, 31; considers Declaratory Act of 1766 responsible for all American troubles, 91–2; moves for removal of troops from Boston, 101, 104, IX, 405; raises question of supreme sovereignty and right of taxing, III, 102–3; discussions with Franklin on conciliation, 108–9, 111n1; his 'fatal' tax on tea, 120n3, 185–6; never did America any service yet they cling to him, 195; his conciliatory motion on America (1777), 342–3; on the war situation, 398hn

Home Affairs: seconds motion for repeal of Cyder Act, I, 244; speech on the dispensing power, 286; on rights of freeholders, II, 92, 94, 105; supposed author of City of London Remonstrance, 140; opposes triennial parliaments, 142, 150; changes his view, 142n3; difference with Rockinghams on juries and libel, 160, 170, 189, 190; will assent to nothing but a Declaratory Bill on juries, 193, 199; merchants' petitions to be kept out of his hands, III, 106; supports motion on the State of the Nation, 405

EB and: EB applies to, for Madrid consulship, I, 131, 133; praises EB's

speech on colonial taxation, 238, 241, 243; disapproves of EB's trade maxims, 269n1; attack on, omitted from *Thoughts on the Present Discontents*, II, 109; plan for EB to visit Hayes, 164

relations with Beckford, I, 281, II, 34n4; with Calcraft, 2n2; with Camden, 4n2, 51n4, 199–200, VIII, 191; with Dunning, III, 209n3; with Keppel, II, 88, 113; with William Hamilton, I, 240

Personal: created Earl of Chatham, I, 263, takes formal possession of his 'new Freehold', 279; his daughter's marriage to Lord Mahon, III, 32, 50, 91

his style of politics: a 'hero of the Mob', I, 349; hovers in Air over all Parties, II, 103; 'that great being who *never dines*,' 197; makes use of all parties without engagement to any, IV, 79–80; always adhered to the letter of the Constitution, EB to the Spirit, V, 295; considers all mankind as fit only for his slaves, VIII, 225

Godwin's biography of, V, 63

also mentioned, I, 148n2, 316, 317n3, II, 120, 153n2, 176, 187n2, 204hn, 205n3, 267, 297, 323hn, 465n3, 515n4, III, 328n3, 384n2, IV, 70, VI, 416n1

see also Chatham Administration, Chatham Group

Pitt, William, the Younger (1759–1806), M.P.

correspondence with, listed above, p. 166

Home Affairs

maiden speech on EB's Bill for Economical Reform, IV, 336tn; takes Fox's seat on Government Bench (July 1782), V, 9; motion for committee on representation defeated, 40n2; will not make RBJr's Receivership permanent, 51hn; his subservience to North, 56; attempt to reconcile Fox and, 58n4; declines to form Ministry, 65hn, 84hn; withdraws Custom House Reform Bill, 93hn, 94

1st Ministry (Dec. 1783), V, 119; takes office as First Lord of the Treasury, 121tn; success in general election, 135hn, 295n5; Carlisle deplores way he became Prime Minister, 144hn; his African Bill cut to pieces in Lords, 405; plans addresses in support of Ministry, 433n4; possible coalition with Fox, 440; York traders support, VI, 15n7; dissensions with Thurlow

Pitt, William, the Younger (*cont.*)

william always intended acting in concert with, 74, their reputations inseparable, 75; his misconceptions on Ireland, 156, 173; dispute over appointments, 157-8; mutual dislike of Fitzwilliam and, 181, IX, 75-6, 364; appoints Camden Lord Lieutenant, VIII, 191; his Irish policy attacked by Fitzwilliam, 225, by EB, IX, 134; his Irish Bill, VIII, 243; supports parliamentary reform for Ireland, IX, 149; dominates his Home Secretary on Irish matters, 176; has no fixed plan for Ireland, 367; other references, VII, 135n3, IX, 137, 350n2, 353. Relations with Gratton, VIII, 33n3, 43, 185, 196-7

Foreign policy

will support Prussia if France intervenes in Holland, V, 347n1, 349n7, 352; commercial treaty with France, VI, 22n1; speech on the future of France, 82tn; and EB's speech on the French Constitution, 249tn; mission to Paris, 356n3

prepares for war with Spain over Nootka Sound, VI, 118n2; Convention with Spain, 189n1; his policy towards Spain criticised, VII, 277-8; EB's talks with, 319

failure of Russian Armament, VI, 355n5, VII, 30n3, 158; relations with Imperial Envoy, VI, 368, 377, 389; talks no foreign politics, 387-8, 389n6; mistakes disposition of Emperor, 411

relations with Calonne and the French Princes, VI, 300hn, 301hn, 356, and with RBJr as their Agent, 436-8; alleged to be in sympathy with French democrats, 355-6; won't be moved from neutrality, 410, 422; dead to effects of French Revolution on England, 411; believes war imminent, VII, 338hn, takes EB's advice on outbreak of war, 348-9, 423n1; prefers forming frontiers to an invasion, 411; Windham supports war policy 439tn, EB urges cooperation, 448n1; discussions with EB, 501n2, 525; accepts Prussian offer of troops, 542n2; French Corps Bill, 537; his power necessary for existence of Europe, VIII, 36, 45, 190; answers Wilberforce's plea for peace, 112

overtures for peace (Dec. 1795), VIII, 357n1; 'no longer a question of treating, but a question of terms',

387; stresses importance of Cape of Good Hope, 388n1; his French policy shabby, mean, selfish, IX, 79; disgraced by evacuation of Mediterranean, 109; still seeking peace, 121; concentrates on home defence instead of action abroad, 130, 268, 278, 300; his Jacobinical peace, 145-6, mingles the bully with submission to France, 160; difficulties over Imperial subsidy, 150hn, 151, 155, Fox's censure of, 173-4, debate on, 178, 184, 186n1; EB supports subsidy, 179, King recommends paying, 191; failure of peace negotiations, 211, 212; always intended to restore Bourbons, 221n2, *cp* 313; 'cannot make peace and he will not make war', 241, 300; disbelief in French intentions in Ireland, 251; his peace policy compared with Fox's, 252-3, 264, 266, a half-hearted policy, 269, 315; other references, VI, 423n2, VII, 122

The King's Illness

sends circular letter to M.P.s, V, 425; will resign if Prince of Wales a Regent, 426; Prince's hostility to, 427hn; resolutions on restricting Regency powers, 432tn, 434hn, 436tn; restrictions accepted by Prince under protest, 435tn; condemned by Pelham, 437n2, supported by City, 443n1, adopted in Commons, 436hn, opposed in Ireland, 446hn; takes the lead instead of the Prince, 438; proposes to invest control of the King in Queen, 440n2; changes mind over resigning, 441; supported by Buckingham, 475n3; Regency Bill attacked by EB, VI, 7n3; supported by Queen, 35; other references, V, 450n1

and EB

EB on the 'sour and severe insolence' of a boy of twenty, V, 279; EB inclined to join (June 1791), VI, 316n1, dines with, 363, 376, 381n3, 410, VII, 477n1, not one word of politics at dinner, 414; never converses with EB on Pay Office topics, VI, 374; EB accused of delivering himself into hands of, VII, 418, RBJr's retort, 419tn; EB laboured for junction with, VIII, 49, 50, 174

consulted on Canadian plan for *émigrés* VII, 310, on refugee clergy, X, 28-9; supports *émigré* school at Penn, VIII, 396hn, 400, 442, 444, 445, IX, 16hn; arbitrates on local possession of school building, 5, 16; asked to

Pitt Administration (*cont.*)

first moves towards peace, VIII, 336, 357, 358n4, 387, canting a Jacobin Peace, 414; Fitzwilliam's protest against, 361–2; Treasonable Practices Bill, 343, Seditious Meetings Bill, 343, 346n6; policy on food scarcity, 344; accused of manufacturing plots to scare people into compliance, 346–7; prosecution of Reeves, 357tn; hatred of Directorate against, 358n2; Windham's view of, 377; the Duumvirate who direct all, IX, 65; a Ministry without principle, 89; the Nation deadened by, 90; affairs of Europe put blindfold into Malmesbury's hands at peace conference, 103, 106, 126, 163, 202hn; withdraw from Mediterranean and evacuate Corsica, 103n2, 109, 163; go the same Jacobin way as their Allies the Opposition, 106, 283, want to conciliate with the Regicides, 151; forced loan proposed, 119n1, 130, 145n3, 149; and La Fayette, 153, 184, 200n2; censured for subsidy to Emperor, 155n2, 173, 296; the 'cursed peace' of a mad Ministry, 161; squabbles among, 176–7; failure of peace negotiations, 203, 204–5, 211; destruction of French system the original base of Coalition, 218, 220, 221n1, n2; Laurence's motion in support of war, 250n2; Fitzwilliam fears change of Ministry might mean change in Constitution, 252n3; and a Third party, 275; London and Southwark petition King to dismiss his Ministers, 293; have prostrated the public mind, 296; Bank Indemnity Bill, 299n3; speculation on duration of Ministry, 300; spirit of Royalty dim among, 313; must replace defence with action, 316; suspension of cash payments, 340n2; debts on their Civil List, 337–8; Ministers imbecile, 333, treacherous and pusillanimous, 357; alternative governments considered, 337, 349, 352–3, 354–5, 356; indifference to general liberty of Europe, 337; Spithead mutiny mishandled by, 338–9, 347–8, Bill to prevent further mutinies, 368

émigrés: relief for, VII, 214–15; too concerned 'whether Charity be politick', 216; take active measures for, 223, 225; provide a house but no beds, 274; miss opportunity to rouse public against French principles, 281; not interested in classifying scheme, 339; grants to *émigrés*, VIII, 87n2, 88, 396; problem of housing, VII, 491–2, 497–8, VIII, 317, X, 28–9; adopt plan for *émigré* school at Penn, VIII, 397, 461, IX, 4, 5n3, 10, 14, 18, 19, 20, 24, 25, 28, 29, 34n4, 41, 45, 108; provide funds for school, VIII, 400, 445, 450, 451, 461, IX, 11n6, 16n4, 33, 37–9, 42, 44, 51n6, n8, 53, 68, 346

India: not expected to dispute East India affairs, V, 150–1, abet company's iniquitous system, 155; set up Board of Control, 160–1; and the Nawab of Arcot's debts, 196–8; relations with Hastings, 202, 207tn, 254n4, 259, 264tn, Hastings faction a danger to, 314, 391; oppose Francis as Manager, 360–3; support Hastings's petition against EB's language, 469; not represented on Committee of Managers, VI, 174n1; support resumption of trial, 197–8; have no influence over system of Indian delinquency, VII, 372–3; will be discredited by an acquittal, 374; dishonour themselves by appointing Shore Governor General, 247–8, 254; agree to annuity for Hastings, VIII, 240

Ireland: RBJr appointed by Catholic Committee to negotiate with, VI, 396–7; attempts at negotiation, VII, 3hn, 5n8, 19–20, 22–3, 32, 239, 362; Ministers pressed by Irish Government not to insist on proposed concessions, 33hn; RBJr accused of stirring up trouble between Irish and English Governments, 37; Irish Government will not receive lessons from, 43–4, stop Catholics having direct approach to, 133–5, 165, 238–9; refuse to deal with Catholics except through Irish Government, 137–8tn; Crown and, the only protection for Irish subjects, 242; authority of, rejected by Lord Lieutenant, 245; effects on, if civil war comes to Ireland, 245; Ministers governed by Castle, 283, abandon Ireland to Junto of Robbers, 290, VIII, 40–1, 49, 55, 207, do not intend sending more troops there, VII, 292; send instructions on Catholic Relief Bill, 342hn, 343n1, 349–50; urged to provide for education of Catholic clergy, 507, 508tn; appointment of Fitzwilliam as Lord Lieutenant, VIII, 8hn, *see also* above,

Pius VI, Pope (*cont.*)
   not to be squeamish about accepting *munitions de guerre* from, 440; letter to the Irish on obedience to Government, 441, 443; his emissary arrives in England, 471n5; Jacobinised Catholics pay little regard to, 513
   puts his ports in French hands, IX, 57; terms of Directory to, 127; praised by Laurence for playing Priam, 133n4; English cut their own throats by warring against, in Ireland, 133, 162, 164; Bonaparte's deadly blows against, 162–3, 259–60; Wilde thinks him Antichrist, 205
   also mentioned, VI, 293hn, 391, 465
Pizarro, Francisco, I, 147
Plato, *Timaeus*, III, 351n1; *Republic*, VI, 358
Plautus, his humour, I, 89–90
Pliny, Arria's first Stab compared with WB's, II, 274
Plumb, Thomas
   correspondence with, listed above, p. 166
Plumbe, Alderman Samuel (d. 1784), candidate for City Sheriff against Wilkes, II, 222; horridly hissed, 33
Plumer, Thomas (1753–1824), Hastings's counsel: opens defence to Benares charge, VII, 93, 94n4; lays down 'a sort of publick Law' for India, 113
Plumer, William (1736–1822), M.P.
   correspondence with, listed above, p. 166
   returned for Herts, VI, 121n2, n6; also mentioned, III, 33
Plunkett, Arthur James, 8th Earl of Fingall (1759–1836): the only Catholic peer in Ireland qualified to take a seat if eligibility granted, VIII, 22; presents Memorial to Lord Lieutenant, IX, 331
Plutarch: perhaps EB's favourite author, I, 358, 362; *Lives*, Dryden's translation, VII, 549; *Moralia*, VIII, 342
Podesta, Gio[vanni] Bat[tis]ta
   correspondence with, listed above, p. 166
Poems on Several Occasions, see Burke, Edmund: Works
Poetry, *see* Burke, Edmund: Opinions
Poignaud, Dr Louis (*c.* 1746–1809), physician-accoucheur in Middlesex Hospital, attends EB's niece, VIII, 296
Poissonier-Desperrières, L.
   correspondence with, listed above, p. 166
Poland: partition of (1772), II, 310, 359, 429, VII, 159, 'Poland but a breakfast', II, 514; her new Constitution

praised in *Appeal*, VI, 426–7, VII, 76–8, 158, 164; her revolution contrasted with the French, VI, 426hn, 427tn, VII, 159–60; EB awarded medal by King of Poland, VI, 426–7, VII, 66–7, 76, 78–9, sends King his Writings in Three Quartos, 163; the Polish subscription, 157–8, 162, 163–4; EB declines subscription, 216, opposed to war in supposed aid of, 157–63
Poland, King of, *see* Stanislaus Augustus (Poniatowski)
Polastron, Yolande-Martine-Gabrielle, *see* Polignac, Duchesse de
Polignac, Diane, Comtesse de (b. *c.* 1747): entertains RBJr at Fontainebleau, V, 234; visits England, 340
Polignac, Duc de, brother of Diane de Polignac, V, 234n3
Polignac, Duchesse de (Yolande-Martine-Gabrielle Polastron, 1749–93), wife of the preceding: RBJr's letter of introduction to, V, 104; an intimate friend of Marie-Antoinette, 233; RBJr at her *reveillon*, 247; visits England, 340; also mentioned, VIII, 376
Polignac family, visit to England, V, 340
Politi, Demetrio, recommends Nicolaïdes to RBJr, VII, 584
Politics, *see* Burke, Edmund, Opinions
Pollen, George Augustus (*c.* 1775–1807), M.P., IX, 307n2
Pollock, John
   correspondence with, listed above, p. 166
Pomeroy, John (d. 1790), O'Hara's neighbour, I, 273
Pomfret, 2nd Earl of, *see* Fermor, George
Poniatowski, Prince Michael George (1736–94), brother of the King of Poland, Primate of Poland, VI, 427
Ponsonby, Lady Charlotte, *see* Fitzwilliam, Countess
Ponsonby, Frederick, styled Viscount Duncannon (1758–1844), later (1793) 3rd Earl of Bessborough: returned for two constituencies, VI, 123n1; signs Fitzwilliam's protest, VIII, 235hn
Ponsonby, George (1755–1817), Irish Opposition M.P., son of John Ponsonby: opposes franchise for Catholics, VII, 71; presents his brother's Bill for more equal representation, 353n, IX, 351; promises support from his Friends for Catholic Bill, VIII, 151; and Gosford's inflammatory paper, 374, 386; also mentioned, VIII, 61, 374
see also Ponsonby Group

439

Rawdon-Hastings, Francis (*cont.*)
Force, VII, 465tn, 504, 506, 515;
returns to Cowes, 518; accused of
using *émigré* officers, 531n2, and
Hessian troops, 542n6; supports Fitzwilliam in Lords, VIII, 238, IX, 444;
Artois stays with, VIII, 269n2; moves
for intervention of King in Ireland,
IX, 292n2, 335n2; 'irregular' in his
ideas, 292

Rawlinson, Abraham (1709–80), merchant
correspondence with, listed above, p. 170
sounds EB on candidature for Lancaster,
I, 326; and Shackleton's sketch of EB,
II, 131

Raynal, Abbé Guillaume-Thomas-Fran-
çois (1713–96)
correspondence with, listed above, p. 170
entertained by EB, III, 363; recommended to Champion in Bristol, 353,
363–4; letter attributed to, read at
National Assembly, VI, 262; disowns
letter, 262n5
Histoire des deux Indes, III, 353, VI,
262n5

Rayneval, Joseph-Matthias Gérard de
(1746–1812), visits England as agent
of French Foreign Minister, V, 51hn,
52, 53

Read, John, and ownership of Clogher
estate, III, 412n3, 414n1

Read, Theodosius, condemned to pillory
for attempted sodomy, EB intervenes on behalf of, IV, 230–1

Reddy, Dr Richard (b. *c.* 1718), friend of
EB, I, 225

Reed, Isaac, and *Abridgment of English
History*, I, 164n1

Rees, Dr Abraham (1743–1825), dissenting
minister: celebrates Fall of Bastille,
VI, 125n3; disclaims sentiments of
Revolution Society, VII, 357

Reeve, Elizabeth, *see* Kill, Mrs

Reeve, William (d. 1778), Bristol merchant:
confirms Rockingham's impression of
general desire for peace, II, 191;
supports Ministry, III, 233n1

Reeves, Mrs Eliza
correspondence with, listed above, p. 170

Reeves, John (*c.* 1752–1829), legal historian, VIII, 346n3
correspondence with, listed above, p. 170
EB supports his campaign against
levellers and republicans, VIII, 346;
charged with violating privilege of
Parliament in a pamphlet, 347; ought
to petition, 348; an Exordium for,
349–51; Dundas supports his cause,

353; defended by Laurence, 354;
accepts responsibility for publication,
356; Commons ask Crown to prose-
cute, 369hn; charges against, ridiculed, 370–3; found not guilty,
373tn; Moser's pamphlet in defence
of, 456hn, 456n3, 457
Thoughts on the English Government,
346n3; written to serve both Crown
and Parliament, 350; irreverend,
but not libellous, 354; Select Committee names Reeves as author of,
353n5, 355hn; Sheridan's motion for
burning defeated, 357tn; also mentioned, 398

Reeves, Mr, VI, 184. *See also* Grieve,
George

Reflections on the Revolution in France,
see Burke, Edmund, Works

Reformer, The, see Burke, Edmund, Works

Regicide Peace, Letters on, see Burke,
Edmund, Works

Regulus, pseudonym of political journalist,
III, 276

Reid, Colonel John (*c.* 1720–1807), and
the New Hampshire Patent, III, 136

Reilly, Michael
correspondence with, listed above, p. 170

Religion, *see* Burke, Edmund, Opinions

'Remarks on the Policy of the Allies', *see*
Burke, Edmund: Works

Report on the Lords Journals, see Burke
Edmund: Works

Reports from the Select Committee, see
Burke, Edmund: Works

Representation to his Majesty, see Burke,
Edmund: Works

Repton, Humphry (1752–1818), landscape gardener
correspondence with, listed above, p. 170
his correct views on buildings and
plantations, VII, 330; the 'Red Book',
330hn, 330n2; debt to *Sublime and
Beautiful*, 330n5

Retz, [Jean-Georges], Vicomte de [d. 1804]
correspondence with, listed above, p. 170

Réverseau, Intendant of La Rochelle in
1789
correspondence with, listed above, p. 170

Revett, Nicholas (1720–1804), joint author
of *Antiquities of Athens*, reviewed by
EB in *Annual Register*, I, 204n1

Revolution Society: Price's sermon to,
VI, 55n2, 81tn, 83n1, 100hn, VII,
357hn; correspondence with National
Assembly, VI, 59, 81tn, 83n1; *Reflections* EB's response to, 81tn, 141,
142n1, VII, 357hn; members of,

Reynolds, Sir Joshua (*cont.*)
153, 156, 335–7, IX, 308, 310–11
his 'amiable qualities' and 'ingenuity', III, 275; ornament of his country and delight of society, VII, 64; dislike of 'Adam-wits', IX, 310n3; his debt to Dr Johnson, 326, and to Mr Mudge, 326–7, 329; 'a great generaliser', with a 'strong turn for humour' 329

EB's 'character' or obituary of, VII, 75–6, 322, VIII, 251–2, IX, 327n3, translated into French, VII, 79; RBJr on his loss, 86; bequest to RBJr, 87, to EB, 87n2, 141–2, IX, 328n3; mentioned in RBJr's will, VII, 600; RBJr's Baskerville *Horace* a present from, 600n5, VIII, 288n2

Works: Paris diary, II, 415n5. 5th *Discourse*, abominably printed, 416–17; EB re-reads *Discourses*, IX, 326. Malone's edition of *Works*: EB's proposed memoir, VIII, 252; Malone's 'Memoir', IX, 308, 326; EB's advice asked on Motto for, 309; copy for EB, 325, other presentation copies, 325; ed. 2, part of EB's letter printed in, 327n2. *Journey to the Netherlands*, IX, 309, 325, 326

also mentioned, II, 535, IV, 239hn, V, 101, 227n8, 333, 474tn, VII, 81, 502n2, VIII, 155, IX, 218n1, 439hn, 464, X, 23hn

Reynolds, Mary, *see* Palmer, Mrs John
Reynolds Moreton, Thomas, 2nd Baron Ducie (1733–85), III, 297
Reynolds, Getly & Co.
correspondence with, listed above, p. 170
Rhames, Joseph, Dublin printer and bookseller, I, 62
Ribouville, Jean, his translation of Francis's speeches, V, 161n1
Riccoboni, Marie-Jeanne (1714–92), novelist: on RBSr, I, 233–4
Rice, Dom.
correspondence with, listed above, p. 170
Rice, George (*c.* 1724–79), M.P., Treasurer of the King's Chambers
correspondence with, listed above, p. 170
a King's Friend, II, 209; his handsome behaviour, 265; supports American Acts, 532; chairman of committee on Bristol election, III, 119
Rice, Mr, presented at Court, II, 415
Rich, Field-Marshall Sir Robert, 4th Baronet (1685–1768), Governor of Chelsea Hospital: death of, I, 342

Richard I, King of England, Blondel's song to, VI, 30n2
Richards, Rev. George (1767–1837), Fellow of Oriel College, Oxford: EB solicits interest on behalf of, VIII, 293, 298, 305–6, X, 35
Richardson, Francis, and alleged plot to seize the King's person, III, 234
Richardson, William (1743–1814), Professor of Humanity at Glasgow University
correspondence with, listed above, p. 170
sends poems and studies of Shakespeare to EB, III, 353–4; adopts suggestion of writing on Shakespeare's faults, 354, V, 122hn; *Letter to the Sheriffs* sent to, III, 355: sends *Anecdotes of the Russian Empire* and further *Essays* on Shakespeare, V, 122–3; EB traces relation between his Muscovite and his Lear, 123; *Speech on Fox's India Bill* sent to, 123
Richelieu, Cardinal, I, 104
Richelieu, Duc de, *see* Vignerot du Plessis, Louis-François-Armand
Richie, Robert, British Consul in Venice, IV, 368n2, 372tn
Richmond, 2nd Duke of, *see* Lennox, Charles
Richmond, 3rd Duke of, *see* Lennox, Charles
Richmond, Duchess of (Lady Mary Bruce, d. 1796), wife of the preceding
correspondence with, listed above, p. 171
her marriage, I, 321n4; wants EB's advice on education of heir, III, 26hn; EB dines with, 99; arrangements with tutor, 200; also mentioned, II, 545
Rickards, John
correspondence with, listed above, p. 171
Ridge, Ann (b. *c.* 1768), later Mrs Falkner: and her sister Catherine's pension, V, 174–6, 182–7, 190–5; beauty begs in the streets of Dublin, 181, 185–6, 193, 194; her own 'fortune', 183, 184, 185, 186, 194; EB's indignation and compassion, 187; arrangements to get her clothed and lodged, 190–1, 192, 193; her animosity against Catherine, 193, 195; ultimately gets a third of the pension, 195tn
Ridge, Catherine (*c.* 1758–*c.* 1839), later Mrs Jonathan Bagnall: EB obtains Irish pension for, III, 279, V, 152hn, 174hn, as an aid to a reputable marriage, 185; visits London with her father, 174n1, 184, EB's personal knowledge of, 174–5, 182, 184–5;

Rockingham, Marchioness of (*cont.*)
  impatient for news of, 200; better, 207, but still in distressing state, 209; gradually mending, 218, 296, 349, very well, 402, 424, 459; deceives her husband on her health, IV, 176, 178; other references, II, 510, 515, 523, 540, III, 26, 76, 296, 316, IV, 98
  political activities: EB reports Opposition motion on India Committee to, I, 304–5, asks her to ensure attendance of member for Malton, 310; takes messages to Marquess, 348; summons EB to see Chatham's letter, III, 108–9; explains EB's conciliation proposals to Governor Wentworth, 146–7; is sent authentic news of Boston, 262–4; shows EB Admirals' letter, IV, 32; gets account of EB's travels through London and Warley Camp, 129, 140–4, 155; Rockingham habitually talks politics in presence of, 145; remains in London as link between Rockingham and his friends, 176–7, 178, 179–80, 188, 190, 192; EB told to see, 183; 'mortified' as a Yorkshire woman by petition, 180, is sent copies to distribute, 187; 'obeys orders without commenting upon them', 188; receives 'boxes' from Wentworth, 190, 195; put in charge of Shelburne's lists of Peers, 194–5, 205; undertakes to explain Portland's situation in Ireland to Townshend, V, 31, 47; EB reports Edgcumbe's refusal of office to, IX, 392, and debate on Fox's Quebec motion, 409–10; sends EB news of Watson's election, 408–9; gathers support for Pigot, 414, 415; her part in Rockingham's services to the country, V, 46
  personal: dislike of Grenville, I, 305n5; invited to Danish Masquerade, II, 15–16; purchase of coach-horses from Chatham, 52–3; presses Dowdeswell to go abroad, III, 48–9; her carriage almost overturns, IV, 28; stays at Portsmouth during Keppel's trial, 37–8; protests at burning effigy of Palliser, 43tn; presents seal of Keppel to Walker King, 97–8, and to her steward, 98n2; and the Gordon riots, 241n1; her charity greater than her faith, 205–6; consolatory letter to Keppel on his defeat at Windsor, 284n5; advises Portland to consult her physician, V, 33; goes to Brighton,

40, 45; purchases house near Beaconsfield, 216; on Nollekens's method of working, 343n4; Walker King stays with, 373, VI, 5n2; much affected by Charlemont's plans for Memorial to Rockingham, 117; thinks coalition with Pitt hazardous, VIII, 40n1
  and the Burkes: a present from RBSr, II, 42; thought of asking EB's advice on Wimbledon house, 219; EB's affection and esteem for, 386, III, 146, VI, 124; her admiration and esteem for EB, III, 146; EB breakfasts with, at Wentworth, 68; congratulates EB on Bristol election, 77, wants to see his 'aloetic Pill' to Malton constituents, 116; *Speech on American Taxation* presented to, 99; her opinion asked on sketch for Dowdeswell's epitaph, 243; arranges for Mrs Governor Wentworth to watch trial of Duchess of Kingston with EB's party, 260hn; signs WB's congratulatory letter to Portland, 327hn; invites EB to Rockingham's birthday party, IX, 457; admits EB into her privileged Council, IV, 74–5, will not deputise her correspondence with him for anyone, 179; *Letter to Thomas Burgh* sent to, 191, 194, 195–6, 199; consolatory letter to EB on withdrawal from Bristol, 284–6; invites him to Wentworth, 285–6, 301; RBSr visits, V, 101, dines with, 349; EB engaged with, 239; EB reports to, on Rockingham papers, 45–7; her own papers not to be destroyed, 45, the 'easiness and spirit of the style', 45; continues visiting Burke family during mourning period, 47tn; provides Mrs Burke with dinner and dessert, VI, 5; draft epitaph on Rockingham submitted to, 5; asks EB to support Governor Wentworth for Nova Scotia, VII, 7–8
  copies of letters in her hand, II, 61hn, 342hn, 347, 348, 382, 459, 471, III, 203hn, IV, 193hn; letters to and from Rockingham cited, I, 303n6, 304n3, 305n4, 306n3, 307n3, II, 53n1, 484n6, 489n2, III, 383n1, IV, 98n2, 129tn, 194n1
  also mentioned, II, 12, III, 23n4, 231n3, 282, 297n1, IV, 37hn, 322n3, V, 38n4, 79, 112n2, VII, 495n3, IX, 471
Rockingham Administrations
  1765–6: formation of, I, 193, 204–5, 206–8, 209–10; Bute and, 169n3,

Rockingham Party (*cont.*)
burne), 398hn; accused of langour and inactivity, 400

negotiations for coalition fail, IV, 38hn, 41tn; attempt to create breach in, 157, 161; Shelburne's ambiguous relations with, 449–50, V, 5n2, 24n1, 72; resignations after Rockingham's death, 6tn, 9hn, 24; Fitzwilliam accepted as his political heir, 6–7; Portland regarded as Leader of Group, 5, 25; RBJr on principles of the party, VI, 127

activities and views of Party: Absentee Tax, II, 468, 487, III, 193; America as a party issue, III, 88–9, 102, 104–5, 108tn, 192, 204–6, 210, 211, 214–16, 295–6, 309, 315–16, 318–19, 343, 381, 383, 398hn, IV, 65, IX, 418; Clergy subscription, II, 299; Election Act, 1770, III, 88; Falkland Islands, II, 189hn, 200n2; General Warrants, 39, 42, 195; Habeas Corpus Bill, III, 330n2, 332hn; India, I, 281, 304–5, 307, 342, II, 351, 362, 364–6, 382hn, 385, 390, 392hn, 401, 403, 407, 425, 433tn, 434hn, IV, 33n1, 339–40, V, 41n3, 255n3; Juries, II, 170–1, 175, 186–8, 189, 190, 196hn, 193–5, 199, 201–3, 210; Land Tax, I, 296–7; Non-attendance, II, 362–3, 366, 367, 368–9, 370, 371, 375, 407, III, 291n4, 308hn, 311–12, 313, 314, 330n2, 332hn, 334, IV, 142n2, 164; Parliamentary reform, IV, 166, 167–8, 294hn, VIII, 109n1; Penal Laws, IV, 204; Petitions of Freeholders, II, 35hn, 37, 43–4, 155; Power of the Crown, 194, IV, 39–40, 177n1; Wilkes, I, 352, II, 23–4, 87hn, 92, 155, 157, 169hn, 192, 218, 222n4, 492hn

and EB: Markham's allegations against, answered by EB, 258–63, 268; EB glories in his connexion with, 263; difference of view on Thirty-Nine Articles, 299; EB's lecture to Richmond on, 372–8; EB accepts Bristol candidature as member of, III, 3, 66, 395, his continuing in Parliament important for, 48; accused of not introducing Cruger among, 85–6; impatient at inaction of, 218, draws up Address to King from, 309hn, 312, 314–15, 317tn; EB's love for, 385, IV, 80; and his withdrawal from Bristol, 273, 275; and his Economy Bill, V, 7n2, IX, 287; his sway over, V, 75n5

Thoughts on the Present Discontents, party justification of refusing junction, II, 101; the 'political creed of our party', 136, 139–40; ought to have been followed up by, 175; party obloquy suffered by EB on account of, IV, 236

members, supporters, critics, connexions: Brook Watson, IX, 109; Cartwright, III, 328–9; Lord John Cavendish, IV, 70n1, IX, 177n7; Cornwall, II, 24n11; Dempster, II, 106n5, VII, 67hn; Dowdeswell, II, 24n7, 404, III, 21hn; Fetherstonehaugh, II, 389n2; Flood, IV, 181; Germain, II, 404–5, 406, III, 152n3; Gregory, II, 316n4; Harrison, II, 12n3; Governor Johnstone, V, 297n3; Duke of Manchester, II, 131hn; Lord Mansfield, I, 347, II, 153n3, 187; Meredith, 21hn, 210; Fred. Montagu, 174n1, IV, 70n1; Lord Pigot, III, 346hn, IX, 414hn; Richmond, II, 66hn, 189hn, 197; Savile, III, 23, 28; Trecothick, II, 157n3, 245; Chas Turner, V, 39n3; Verney, III, 39; Horace Walpole, III, 383n1; Wedderburn, II, 23n1. Relations with City of London, II, 157, 192, 203–5, 218, 222, 241, 242–3, 245, 492hn, III, 194

Rockingham Volunteers, of County Wicklow, IV, 186n2

Rocquefeuille, Jacquette de, *see* Du Gage, Marquise

Roden, 1st Earl of, *see* Jocelyn, Robert

Rodney, Admiral George Brydges (1719–92), later (1782) 1st Baron Rodney
correspondence with, listed above, p. 174
raises siege of Gibraltar and is knighted, IV, 108; Administration candidate for Westminster, 282hn, tops poll, 283, 284tn; takes St Eustatius, 343, EB protests against confiscation of property, 343tn, 350n1, 387n1, 402–3, 452; victory at Battle of Saints ends hope of redress, 453tn; his recall censured, 456; Biron's generous behaviour to, VII, 587; also mentioned, V, 348n8

Roe, Richard, Izaak Walton's fishing friend, V, 107

Rogers, Bayley
correspondence with, listed above, p. 174

Rogers, George, Keppel's secretary, IV, 31

Rogers, James, & Co., Bristol merchants, III, 418

Rogres de Champignelles, Charles-Casimir de (1709–81), VI, 136

Rouse, Charles (*cont.*)
and Bengal Judiciary Bill, IV, 355, X, 12; agrees with EB on treatment of Maratha Agents, IV, 357, 358, IX, 430, 431; Secretary of Board of Control, V, 319n2

Rousseau, Jean-Jacques (1712–1778): EB thinks him deranged, VI, 81; visits England, 81n1; quoted by artisans in Paris, 114; his view on government considered similar to EB's, 214hn; comments on in *Letter* to Menonville please George III, 253; admired by O'Connor, Jr, VIII, 242; also mentioned, VII, 346n3
Contrat Social, leaves little impression on EB, VI, 81; *Letter to d'Alembert* and *Émile* reviewed by EB in *Annual Register*, 81n2; *La Nouvelle Héloïse*, 270

Rowan, Archibald Hamilton (1751–1834), United Irishman, VIII, 257, X, 34

Rowe, M.
correspondence with, listed above, p. 175

Rowe, Nicholas (1674–1718), *The Fair Penitent*, I, 83, V, 168n5

Rowley, Clotworthy (d. 1781), Irish M.P., III, 450

Rowley, Hercules (*c.* 1714–94), Irish M.P., III, 450

Roxburghe, 3rd Duke of, *see* Ker, John

Royal Academy: Barry exhibits at, I, 324n2; Reynolds becomes President, II, 9n1, considers resigning, V, 167hn; John Hickey exhibits at, III, 453n8; EB recommends a painter for, V, 284; Royal Academy Dinner (1789), a tradesman toasted, 465; John Sanders a Gold Medallist of, VI, 78; used for guests at Reynolds's funeral, VII, 79n4, members pay part of funeral costs, 93, EB's speech in Council Chamber, 93n2; Academy Travelling Scholarship, VIII, 126n6, X, 23–4; copy of Reynolds's *Discourses* deposited at, IX, 325
members of: Geo. Barret, II, 9n2, James Barry, 315hn, Richard Cosway, VI, 78
also mentioned, VII, 336n2, X, 19

Royal Asiatic Society of Bengal, V, 128n1

Royal Irish Academy
correspondence with, listed above, p. 175
EB elected honorary member of, VI, 98–9, 117, 119; his zeal for, 99; also mentioned, V, 375n1

Royal Society: Priestley's paper on experiments with gases presented to, V, 54n4; and Paine's iron bridge, VI, 68n2

Royal Society of Arts, *see* Society for the Encouragement of Arts, Manufactures and Commerce

Royds, John
correspondence with, listed above, p. 175

Royou, Thomas-Marie (1743–92), his *Reflexions* sent to EB, VI, 318n3

Royston, Viscount, *see* Yorke, Philip

Rozier, Jean-François Pilâtre de, *see* Pilâtre de Rozier

Ruffhead, Owen (1723–69), II, 50n2

Rumbold, Sir Thomas, 1st Baronet (1736–91), M.P., Governor of Madras, IV, 343
correspondence with, listed above, p. 175
dismissed from Governorship for financial misconduct, IV, 309n5, 323hn, V, 44, X, 10n2; denies plan to partition Tanjore, IV, 339n1; EB's former service to, 340, and regard for, 344; East India Company Chancery suit against, 340; praised for discountenancing Maratha War, 344; censured for continuing ill policies of Madras government, 346–7; Resolutions against in Commons, 448; trial under Pains and Penalties adjourned and not revived, VI, 56, 58, X, 11; also mentioned, V, 68

Rush, Samuel (d. 1783), Rockingham's landlord, II, 218

Russel, C.
correspondence with, listed above, p. 175

Russell, Lady Caroline, *see* Marlborough, Duchess of

Russell, Francis, styled Marquess of Tavistock (1739–67), dies after riding accident, I, 301, 302, 306

Russell, Francis, 5th Duke of Bedford (1765–1802): his house at Streatham, II, 543n1, 544; property in Buckinghamshire, IV, 139; follower of Fox, V, 78, VIII, 395n3, IX, 337; moves for peace, VIII, 336; protests against EB's pension, 342, 400; his protest ridiculed in *Letter to a Noble Lord*, 394, 395; EB never read his attack, 406; appears crop-headed in Lords, 377; motion on foreign subsidies, IX, 204

Russell, Francis (d. 1795), Solicitor to Board of Control, VIII, 311

Russell, John, 4th Duke of Bedford (1710–71): goes to Paris to conclude peace treaty, I, 145, 148, 159; his daughter marries Marlborough, 147hn, 149; insists on Gower as Lord Chamber-

Sanders, John (1768–1826), architect: EB solicits membership of Royal Academy for, VI, 78, X, 23–4; Sir John Soane's first pupil, VI, 78n2

Sandford, General Robert (d. c. 1795), takes pamphlets to Brussels for EB, VI, 317

Sandouville, Monsieur de
correspondence with, listed above, p. 176
asks assistance for his brother, Abbé de St Albin, VII, 258

Sands, Edward, school fellow of EB at Ballitore, I, 20, 21

Sandwich, 4th Earl of, see Montagu, John

Sandys, Edwin, 2nd Baron Sandys (1726–97), II, 131hn

Sandys, Madam, and short cuts, III, 377

Sangster, Robert, EB appeals to Attorney General against his sentence to the pillory, IV, 230

Sankey, Hon. Edward (d. 1786), Lord Mayor of Dublin
correspondence with, listed above, p. 176
conveys offer of Freedom of Dublin City to EB, I, 295

Santerre, Antoine-Joseph (1752–1809), radical revolutionary, VII, 177

Sappho, I, 98

Sardinia, King of, see Victor Amadeus III of Savoy

Sargent, John (c. 1715–91), merchant, III, 113

Sarlabus, Jean-Antoine de Mun, Marquis de (1753–1843)
correspondence with, listed above, p. 176

Sarpi, Paul, III, 97

Sarsfield, Jacques-Hyacinthe de Sarsfield, Comte de (d. 1789)
correspondence with, listed above, p. 176

'Satire in 1753, A', see Burke, Edmund: Works

Saturninus, Lucius Appuleius, VI, 47

Saunders, Sir Charles (c. 1713–75), M.P., follower of Rockingham
correspondence with, listed above, p. 176
rumoured resignation as First Lord of Admiralty, I, 266; resigns on Rockingham's break with Chatham, 277n2, 282; becomes Admiral, II, 65; supports petition to Crown, 77n4; Chatham's interest in, 88, 90, 91, 94, 100; assists Wolfall in gaol, 168hn; tours Sussex with EB and Keppel, 220; disapproves of non-attendance, 368; visits Germain with EB, 388; speaks in support of Clive, 436; agrees with Baker on City politics, 492; loan to EB, 550, VIII, 443; and the General Election of

1774, III, 52, 62, 63; thinks Party should do something before Parliament meets, 195–6
also mentioned, II, 89, 356, 369

Savignac
correspondence with, listed above, p. 176

Savile, Barbara, see Scarbrough, Countess of

Savile, Sir George, 8th Baronet (1726–84), M.P. for Yorkshire
correspondence with, listed above, p. 176
questions punishment of Hull collector, I, 258; motion on Nullum Tempus, 344, 345, II, 38n2, IV, 239; one of Rockingham's inner conciliabulum, II, 11, 170, 195, 196, 346, 348, 356, 379, 380, 470, 477–8, III, 204–5, 210, 215, 216, 291tn, 392hn, IV, 65, 88; supports Portland against Lowther, II, 18; speaks against Luttrell, 25; Grand Jury of Yorkshire confidence in, 37, 38; concern in General Warrants question, 39; and County meetings, 62–3, draws tears by speech at, 97; Vice-President of Society for Encouragement of Arts, 89; his idea of Nottinghamshire, 102n4; letter from County meeting to, 162; promises vigilance, 163; doubts on Jury Bill, 199, seconds Bill, 203; secedes from Parliament with EB, 205; on the untainted honour of City Sheriffs, 242–3; falls from his horse, 288; his unsavoury simile for Conway, 355
and party action on East India Company, II, 361–2; refuses membership of Select Committee on India, 362n1, 366, 408; views on secession, 367, 368; stays away from Parliament, 408; and Absentee Tax, 477–8, 484n6, 500; opposes Massachusetts Bills, 532; presents petitions from Yorkshire booksellers, 540hn; would like to retire from Parliament, III, 23–4, 28; his protégé, David Hartley, 24n1, IV, 430n6, and Hartley's motion on cost of American war, III, 256–7; speaks on hosiery trade, 121hn; and revival of City as political centre, 194; EB's Wrecks Bill, 222, 258; too inclined to sit still, 257, 296; thinks Opposition can do nothing, 317; attends Parliament to oppose Habeas Corpus Bill, 328n3, 330n2; a real friend to his country (Baker), 388hn; Bill for repeal of penal laws, 449, 450, 456, 461, IX, 422n2

Sheridan, Richard Brinsley (*cont.*)
activity in Regency crisis, 435tn, 436
441–2, 457n2, IX, 457hn; and the
Irish Deputies, V, 450–1; publicly
rejoices in French Revolution, VI,
126, 128, VII, 57–8; RBJr's opinion
of, VI, 127–9, VII, 409; EB's opinion,
VI, 127n1; Elliot's poor opinion of,
180; moves postponement of Quebec
Bill, 249tn; an ardent admirer of the
'French System', 452; resents Dissenters' treatment of Fox, VII, 57;
Fox and, lead 'the new French Whigs',
63, 232; ought to be satiated with
French massacres, 172; his Bill to
reform Scottish boroughs, 316; his
radical line in Parliament, 400; Fox
will never break with, 400; opposes
French Corps Bill, 537
opposed to junction with Pitt, VIII, 40;
Mrs Crewe's conversations with,
84tn; moves for repeal of Habeas
Corpus Suspension Act, 108n2, 112;
attack on Windham, 108n3, 113, 135;
'low policies' of 'Sheridanism', 109;
regards Prince of Wales as a Gentleman, not a Prince, 266; abuses his
connection by marriage with Portland,
342; condemns Reeves's pamphlet as
malicious libel, 346n3, secures revival
of Committee on authorship, 355–6,
presents 2nd Report of Committee,
356n1, motion for burning pamphlet
defeated, 357tn
witness for defence of O'Connor, IX,
123n4; and Budget Day, 152; attacks
Pitt for allowing EB the Pensioner to
slander Courts of Justice, 180;
opposes sending specie to Emperor,
268n3; motion against loan to Emperor, 296, 305; among 'sole options'
if Pitt's Ministry falls, 337; Ministers
'coquetting' with, 369
habit of procrastination, IV, 361; his
'forty-eight pounder Philippics', IX,
180; his mind 'takes an Eagle flight
by itself', V, 454
also mentioned, I, 82n3, V, 64n2, 464n2,
VI, 106n2, 110, VII, 532, IX,
186n1
Sheridan, Mrs Richard Brinsley (Elizabeth
Ann Linley, 1754–92), first wife of
the preceding
correspondence with, listed above,
p. 179
her health keeps Sheridan from Committee, V, 377–8; urged by EB to
persuade Sheridan to act on Presents

Article, 454, prevented by her husband
from answering EB's letter, 457, 458
Sheridan, Mrs Richard Brinsley (Hester
Jane Ogle, *c.* 1771–1817), second wife
of Sheridan: her Portland connection,
VIII, 342n6
Sheridan, Thomas (1719–88), manager of
the Theatre Royal, Dublin: his
grand theatrical squabble with Mr
Kelly, I, 82–4, 90n2; crowned by
'Dulness', 88n2; urged to put on *The
Lawsuit* by Brenan, 98n5; EB's
'Punch's Petition' to, 98n5; rumoured
to be losing his house, 102; 'a pitiful
fellow', 102; also mentioned, VI, 128
Sheridan, Dr, 'the Irish Hippocrates', I,
358; also mentioned, 362
Sheriffs of Bristol, Letter to, see Burke,
Edmund, Works
Sherlock, Thomas
correspondence with, listed above, p. 179
Shiffner, Henry (1721–95), M.P., I, 193
Shipley, Jonathan (1714–88), Bishop of
St Asaph, friend of EB, V, 127, 140
Shippen, Thomas Lee, of Pennsylvania
(1765–98)
correspondence with, listed above, p. 179
on the grand tour of Europe, V, 452n1;
given letters of introduction by EB,
452, 453, 455
Shippen, Dr William, Jr (1736–1808),
Philadelphia physician, father of the
preceding, V, 452n1
Shirley, Lady Selina, *see* Huntingdon,
Countess of
Shoolbred, John, Africa merchant, III,
345hn
correspondence with, listed above, p. 179
Shore, John (1751–1834), later (1792) 1st
Baronet: an expert on Bengal revenue
problems, V, 328, VII, 249n6, 275n2;
asked by Hastings to collect 'testi-
monials', V, 416n4; reported next
Governor General of Bengal, VII,
233; his 'dreadful delinquencies', 233;
EB protests against appointment,
246–55, 266, 273–4, 278–9, VIII, 383;
EB's mistaken view of, VII, 246hn;
'among the worst of Mr Hastings's
Instruments', 248, 249, 251; member
of Hastings's Committee of Revenue,
233n3, 249, 250, 251n3; Gunga
Govind Sing's instrument, 250; said
to have written defence on Revenue
Article, 253n1; Managers have no
personal animosity against, 253;
alleged maladministration of Revenue
Board, 266; appointment upheld of

Shore, John (*cont.*)
'one of the ablest, and most upright Servants of the Company', 267tn; Dundas on his ability and integrity, 275–6; created baronet, 279; EB remains unconvinced, 279–80; his successor, 511n4

Short, William (1759–1849), American Chargé d'Affaires in Paris, VI, 75

Shuckburgh, Sir George Augustus William, 6th Baronet (1751–1804), M.P., VII, 331

Shuja-ud-daula, Nawab Wazir of Oudh (ruled 1754–75): conquest of Rohillas by, IV, 345n1, VIII, 240n3; Hastings accused of hiring out Company troops to, V, 245n4

Shuldham, Admiral Molyneux (*c.* 1717–98), M.P., Rear-Admiral of the White, III, 183

Shute, William Wildman Barrington, *see* Barrington Shute, William Wildman

Siddons, Mrs William (Sarah Kemble, 1755–1831), EB attends her benefit, IX, 433

Silburn, Thomas (d. 1788), VIII, 461n1, IX, 9n3

Silburn, Mrs Thomas (Dorothy Robinson, d. 1823), widow of the preceding: helps with French *émigré* boys at Penn, VIII, 461, IX, 9, 10, 12, 68, 105, 346

Sillery, Marquis de, *see* Brulart, Charles-Alexis-Pierre

Sillery, Marquise de, *see* Genlis, Comtesse de

Sinclair, Sir John, 1st Baronet (1754–1835), M.P.
correspondence with, listed above, p. 179
and Hastings's trial, VI, 56n7, 57n1; President of Board of Agriculture, sends pamphlets to EB, VIII, 459hn, IX, 361; leads 'armed neutrality' against Pitt, 271n1, 275

Sindhia, Mahadaji (Madhava Rao), Maratha ruler, V, 148, 312n1

Singleton, John, Rockingham's trainer at Newmarket, I, 339; unable to find a jockey for export to America, II, 449, 450, 458, 459, 505

Siraj-ud-daula, Nawab of Bengal, II, 434hn

Sisson, Richard (d. 1767), Irish painter: one of EB's triumvirate in Dublin, I, 52, 55, 70, 71; friendship with Shackleton, 55, 62, 67, 71; portraits of Irish Speaker and the Ikerrin family, 71; EB commissions portrait of Shackleton from, 166n2, 271; his death, 309;

EB provides for his son, 309n2; his miniatures of EB, III, 8; also mentioned, I, 241

Sisson, Mrs Richard (*née* Smith), widow of the preceding, I, 309n2

Sixtus V, Pope (1585–90), IV, 45

Skene, Philip Warton, II, 446, 493, 502

Skinner, Thomas (1737–1806), City Alderman, comes to rescue of RBSr at Lord Mayor's Banquet, V, 237

Skynner, John (*c.* 1724–1805), barrister, M.P., I, 226
correspondence with, listed above, p. 179
acts as peacemaker between EB and Dr Markham, II, 294; Counsel before Board of Trade in boundary dispute between Canada and New York, 441

Slater, John, EB's schoolfellow at Ballitore: his 'madness' turns to melancholy, I, 16–17; his aunt, 17

Slaughter, Thomas, Duke of Portland's steward in Bucks, I, 341n1, III, 41, IV, 132

Slavery, *see* Burke, Edmund, Opinions

Sleigh, Dr Joseph Fenn (1733–70), of Cork, friend of EB, I, 124
correspondence with, listed above, p. 179
introduces James Barry to EB, I, 203–4; his continued interest in Barry's career, 294, II, 87

Sloane, Hans (1739–1827), M.P., VI, 139

Sloper, Lieutenant General Robert
correspondence with, listed above, p. 179

Sloper, W[illiam, *c.* 1708–89]
correspondence with, listed above, p. 179

Smelt, Anne Jessie, *see* Cholmley, Mrs Nathaniel

Smelt, Leonard (*c.* 1719–1800): dismissed from post as sub-Governor to Prince of Wales, III, 269; influence on the Prince deplored, IV, 184, 185; his curious speech on the Patriot King, 176, 177, a Bouquet from Bute's garden, 179–80; his speech hissed, 184; now '*walking* Cabinet counsellor' to the King, 185; his speech printed in *York Courant*, 188, good effects expected from it, 189; Mrs Burke's *Dish of Smelts*, 190; also mentioned, 183

Smith, Adam (1723–90)
correspondence with, listed above, p. 179
finds *Sublime and Beautiful* full of promise, I, 129hn; concern with Scottish bank crisis, II, 339hn; asked to use interest with Buccleuch for Champion's China Patent, III, 152–3; tutor to 3rd Duke of Buccleuch, 153n2, IV, 448n6; North's budget influenced

Steele, Thomas (1753–1823), M.P., Secretary to the Treasury
correspondence with, listed above, p. 181
protests against costs of Impeachment, v, 388; refers clerical bill to EB, 402; and Pitt's Regency restrictions plan, 434; also mentioned, vii, 427hn

Steell, M. G.
correspondence with, listed above, p. 181

Stennett, Rev. Dr Samuel. (1729–95)
correspondence with, listed above, p. 181

Stephens, Philip (1723–1809), M.P., Secretary to the Admiralty
correspondence with, listed above, p. 181
EB's dealings with, on behalf of Bristol merchant vessels, iii, 301hn, 361, 374, 424, iv, 22–3, 51–2, 59n3, 68, 75, 81n6, ix, 425; his assiduity and kindness, iii, 376; responsible for Edmund Nagle's promotion, 391; takes up case of Capt. Fraser, war prisoner, iv, 117; speaks kindly of Nagle, v, 348; offers passage for Chevalier de Sade, vii, 489; arranges release of impressed Bristol pilots, ix, 419

Stepney, Sir John (1743–1811), British Minister at Dresden, v, 307n4

Sterling, Rev. James, i, 362n7

Sterne, Laurence (1713–68), iii, 265n5

Steuart, Margaret, see Hippisley, Mrs John Coxe

Steuart, Miss, vii, 444

Stevens, Joseph, First Clerk of the Excise Office, iv, 26n8
correspondence with, listed above, p. 182

Stevenson
correspondence with, listed above, p. 182

Stewart, Alexander, 6th Earl of Galloway, ii, 30n4

Stewart, Archibald, London wine merchant, ii, 35n2

Stewart, Lady Catherine, see Murray, Lady Catherine

Stewart, Charles, styled Lord Linton (1744–1827), later (1779) 7th Earl of Traquair
correspondence with, listed above, p. 185
EB meets in London, iv, 45n3, his high opinion of, 56; presents loyal address from Catholics, ix, 423n2

Stewart, Charles Edward [1751–1819]
correspondence with, listed above, p. 182

Stewart, James (c. 1760–1827), Irish M.P., a Commissioner to bring Address from Irish Parliament to Prince of Wales, v, 450n3

Stewart, John, London wine merchant, partner of Archibald Stewart, ii, 35n2

Stewart, John (d. 1778), ii, 35n2
correspondence with, listed above, p. 182
applies to Rockingham for secretaryship to Supervisors, ii, 35, 39, then for post as Secretary to Society for Encouragement of Arts, 89, 94–6; attempt to pack election for, foiled, 95hn; recommended unsuccessfully by EB, 95–6; 'too much abilities for their paltry Business', 103, cp. 358; becomes Bengal Secretary under Hastings, 357hn; sends EB wines and canes, 357–8; WB and Emin committed to his protection, 359–60

Stewart, Robert (1739–1821), Irish M.P.:
opposes Catholic Relief, iii, 450; objects to copying British Parliament, 460n2

Stewart, Robert (1769–1822), later (1789) 1st Baron Londonderry and (1795) styled Viscount Castlereagh: defeats Hillsborough for County Down, vi, 124–5; his motion respecting Catholic clergy, vii, 65

Stockdale, John (c. 1749–1814), publisher: acquitted on charge of publishing libel on Commons, vi, 54; significance of acquittal for Hastings trial, 54n4, vii, 111, viii, 220n5, ix, 246n2; his prosecutors, counsel and judge, vi, 199n4; author of the alleged libel, viii, 381n7

Stockdale, Percival (1736–1811)
correspondence with, listed above, p. 182

Stokes, Rev. Dr John (c. 1721–81), Fellow of Trinity College, Dublin, i, 65

Stone, Andrew (1703–73), M.P., appointed Queen's Treasurer, i, 141

Stone, George (c. 1708–64), Archbishop of Armagh, Primate of all Ireland: would be a loss to Ireland, i, 152; EB's Irish pension on his list, 167, 183, Hamilton denies it, 189, 190; his death, 208n3

Stone, John Hurford (1763–1818), member of Society of Friends of the Revolution, settled in Paris, viii, 304n4, 423n5

Stone, William Hurford, tried and acquitted on high treason charge, viii, 423, 440

Stonehewer, Richard (c. 1728–1809), Under-Secretary of State for Northern Department, friend of EB
correspondence with, listed above, p. 182
his help asked for sufferers from Stamp Act riots, ix, 458; Reynolds's bequest to, 325

Thrale, Mrs. Henry (*cont.*)
between Johnson and Burke, IV, 47n3; also mentioned, V, 25hn, 113n4

Three Memorials on French Affairs, see Burke, Edmund: Works

Throckmorton, Sir John Courtenay, 5th Baronet (1753–1819), chairs meeting of Friends of the People, VII, 482–3

Thugut, Johann Amadeus Franz de Paula, Baron (1736–1818), Austrian Minister of Foreign Affairs, IX, 314

Thurlow, Edward, 1st Baron Thurlow (1731–1806), M.P.

correspondence with, listed above, p. 184

Attorney General: appealed to in case of Robert Jones, II, 325tn; RBSr's claims in St Vincent submitted to, 416n8, 525, III, 162; supports Massachusetts Bills, II, 532; declines answering Fox's speech, III, 299; moves adjournment after Rigby quarrels with Speaker, 339; becomes Lord Chancellor, 455n1

consults EB on Irish Toleration Bill, IV, 6; against combining measures for Catholics and Dissenters, 9; included in Weymouth's proposed Administration, 38hn; Rockingham thinks King has no confidence in, 161, will be less active in debate, 162; asked by EB to limit executions after Gordon riots, 254, 255; Crabbe fails to find a patron in, 337hn; and plural livings, 398–9; King negotiates with Rockingham through, 422hn, 423hn; speaks handsomely of Keppel, 451; refuses to fix Great Seal on RBJr's Warrant of Office for life, V, 51–3

India: alleged personal animosity to Clive, II, 433tn, supports charge against him, 435, 436; consults EB on Bengal Judiciary Bill, IV, 355, later 'reduces' Bill, V, 334, X, 12; reluctant to give judgeship to William Jones, IV, 425, V, 66, 67; Hastings's 'professed friend', 66n4, 202, 204, 260n1, his closest ally, VI, 3n1, VIII, 439n6, prophesies peerage for him, V, 203n3; negotiates with EB on Nabob of Arcot's debts, 196–9, 201–5; presides at Hastings trial, VI, 3, IX, 435; adjourns trial for EB, V, 464; delays resumption, VI, 62, 199n5; advises 'a calm mode of Enquiry', 197, 198; questions validity of Presents Article, 198n5; thinks Bribes a 'very nasty business', 199n1, n2; in

unequivocal conjunction with Hastings's agents, VII, 372; increasing hostility over trial between EB and, VIII, 113, 177–8, 219, 422–3, 437; opens every debate in Lords, 178n1; spends every evening with Major Scott, 178n1, is his Squire, 218, directed by him in observing on evidence, 219; disgraces Commons by rejecting Articles, 221

gets life pension on resignation of Ministry, V, 72; King insists on his remaining Chancellor, 74–5; attends Lord Mayor's Banquet, 236; 'taken off' in Preface to Bellenden, 336hn; and Pitt's Africa Bill, 405; and the King's illness, 429tn, 434hn, 438, 448n4, 450n1; in conflict with Pitt, VI, 34, 35, 198, his weight with the King dust in the balance against Pitt's with the Queen, 35; reported to favour peerage and pension for EB, 210; Pitt forces his resignation, VII, 143hn, 193; King unwilling to dismiss him, 179n2; goes into Opposition, 314

his firm and systematic mind, III, 455, IV, 9; 'a plain and decided tone' works best with, V, 52; 'wild beast', 'Caliban' (William Jones), 66; 'a glorious fellow' (Scott), 203n3; 'false and formal', VI, 62, 64; his profanity, 251n3

also mentioned, II, 24, III, 423, V, 73hn, 393tn, IX, 465, X, 7

Thursday Club, political club of the Opposition meeting at the Thatched House, IV, 334; *see also* Thatched House

Thynne, Henry Frederick, 1st Baron Carteret of Hawnes (1735–1826), dismissed from office, VI, 35

Thynne, Thomas, 3rd Viscount Weymouth (1734–96), later (1789) 1st Marquess of Bath

correspondence with, listed above, p. 188

seconds Egmont's Address in the Lords, I, 158; as absentee Lord Lieutenant of Ireland, 195hn, 198n, 208, 245n2; EB's view of, 197–8; Horace Walpole's view of, 197–8n; his Bedford connexion, 197, 272n5, II, 296, 297, 327, 375n3, leader of Bedford party in Lords, IV, 65n4

becomes Secretary of State for Southern Dept (1767), I, 339n4; his terms for sending naval force to India, II, 54; resigns office over Falkland Islands,

Tomlinson, Ralph, attorney, IV, 443

Tomlinson, Robert
correspondence with, listed above, p. 184

Tone, Theobald Wolfe (1763–98), assistant secretary of Irish Catholic Committee: his diary quoted on RBJr in Ireland, VII, 164hn, 197n1, 201n6, 242n5, 256n1, 268n5, 296n3; alleged connexions with United Irishmen, VIII, 256n2, IX, 115n2; goes with Catholic Delegation to England though not a Catholic, 115, 133; meeting with EB, 115; on the effect of his son's death on EB, 114n4; joins Gen. Hoche, 115n3

Tonge, Thomas R.
correspondence with, listed above, p. 184

Tonson, William (1724–87)
correspondence with, listed above, p. 184

Tooke, John Horne, see Horne, John

Topham, Captain Edward (1751–1820), founder of *The World*, V, 410n2

Topping, James (1756–1821), lawyer on Northern Circuit with RBJr
correspondence with, listed above, p. 184
challenged by RBJr for insulting Fitzwilliam, V, 130–3

Torcy, Marquis de, see Colbert, Jean-Baptiste

Tories: Rockingham ought to be prepared to take in (1765), I, 208; united on Land Tax, 297; attachment to new Court, II, 66; support Bill on Controverted Elections, 126–7; always flourish in the decay of a country's glory, III, 268–9; resurrected by American war, 382–3; agree with Whigs on rights of property, 456; angry with Ministry, IV, 25–6; have overfed the Government, 46; consider fate of Ministry their own, 115; Portland's election policy towards, 137–8; Fitzwilliam favours coalition with, 146; Tory language and Whig measure, the Genius of the Constitution, V, 35; EB ready to be called a Tory if his principles are, IX, 446
in Bristol, III, 43–4; supported by tradesmen and manufacturers, 45; country gentlemen vote for 'high party', 67; their manoeuvres driving Bristol to the devil, 195; thoroughbred, Sunshine and Temperate brands of, 207; half Corporation Tory, 219; 'warm' part resolved on War address, 223, eager to congratulate the King, 318–19, 319–20; Fast-breakers not safe from Tory mob, 303; *Letter to*

Sheriffs of Bristol not to be toned down for, 333; proposed Volunteer plans entirely in interest of, IV, 123n, 126, EB's letter on, may be shown to Moderates, 126; EB to stand jointly with Tory candidate, 238n3, 266hn; their two candidates put him in difficult situation, 267–72, 273; sober Tories dread election of Cruger, 276, are not EB's friends, but are fair enemies, 281; their victory not glorious, 294–5; many ready to turn Bristol into Treasury Borough, 325; their policy in by-election of 1781, 325hn, 328n1, 329, 332, 333tn; EB had not a single vote from, VI, 178
use of term Tory in America, VI, 68; Boswell's Tory soul, V, 35, 138; Buckinghamshire Tories stay away from county meeting, II, 78, their strong interest, 85, Temple's desire to conciliate, 450, Rockingham candidate depends on support from, III, 33, will gain from Whig disunion, IV, 131; Mr Drake supports, III, 34; Essex Tories support Bute, II, 76; Fox fears growth of Tory principles, VII, 315; triumphant at Gloucester and Hereford, III, 268–9; Nottingham Tories represent neither manufacturers nor Corporation, 123tn; Portland stands better with, than any man in England, IV, 147; Shelburne neither Whig nor, V, 34; Capt. Spencer Stanhope born a Tory, IV, 184; Earl of Strafford a Tory, VI, 23n5; stay away from York County meeting, II, 97
also mentioned, I, 82, 157, II, 282, III, 294, IV, 279

Torrington, Lucy (née Boyle), Viscountess (1744–92)
correspondence with, listed above, p. 184

Totnes, 1st Earl of, see Carew, George

Touchet, John
correspondence with, listed above, p. 184

Towers, Dr Joseph (1737–99), Dissenting minister, VI, 125n3

Townsend, Captain, of the *Glasgow*, III, 161n5

Townsend, James (1737–87), M.P., Alderman, Sheriff, and Lord Mayor of London, II, 26n2
correspondence with, listed above, p. 184
dines with minority at Thatched House, II, 24n1; dines with EB, 26; Alderman for Bishopsgate, 32; elected Sheriff,

Trevenen, Captain James (1760–90), 'marked for some extraordinary destiny', VII, 590; dies from wounds at Viborg Bay, 590n3

Trevor, 4th Baron, see Hampden, Robert

Trevor, John (1749–1824), British Minister at Turin

correspondence with, listed above, p. 185

sends EB Lally-Tollendal's pamphlet, VI, 212n5, 217, 321hn; praises *Reflections*, 216; his Dutch allegory, 217n1; difference with, on correct policy towards France, 218

Trevor, Mrs John (Harriet Burton, c. 1751–1829), wife of the preceding: devours *Reflections* with enthusiasm, VI, 216

Trier, Archbishop-Elector of, see Klemens-Wenzel

Trimble, James, usher at Ballitore School, I, 62, 96, 98

Trimbuck Sambagee

correspondence with, listed above, p. 185

Trimleston, 13th Baron, see Barnewall, Thomas

Trimleston, 14th Baron, see Barnewall, Nicholas

Trinity College, Dublin

EB and: student days at, I, 1–103; examined on entry, 2; his reading, 4, 74, 288n4, X, 42; lectures, I, 8–9, 23, 40, 44; the day's round in verse, 12–15; walks in College Park, 23; degree examinations, 11, 32; Evening Prayer, 36; subjects for Modern History, 38; 'Mother Price's convent', 47; a student cautioned with a Vix, 49; EB gets proemium in his Division, 51–2, wins Scholarship, 64, 65–6; remains in College, 72, 74; 'furor mathematicus' cured by study, 89; receives honorary degree (1790), VI, 192–3, in a gold box, 384–5; rumoured to be next Provost, VII, 570, reported to have solicited office for himself, VIII, 6–7

general: proposal to admit Catholics to, IV, 401, 411, 435; Sir John Sebright's Irish MSS presented to, V, 15n2, 292n5, their publication advised, 110; College lads suspected of destroying Parliament House, VII, 88n6; Catholics not to be admitted to Fellowships, 350n1; relations between Fellows and Lord Lieutenant, 571n1; the University of the Establishment, VIII, 193; ought not to have control of Catholic education in Ireland, 202, 263

Divinity School, I, 23n4; Library, VII, 104; Museum, V, 375; Provostship, controversy over appointment of unstatutable layman, III, 103–4, 105tn, VII, 453–4, 572, VIII, 10, 19, 46–8, 54, IX, 404–5

also mentioned, I, 267, II, 24n3, 479n1, III, 152n3, 275hn, 304hn, IV, 458, V, 375hn, 375n1, VI, 280n3, VII, 65, 103, 499hn, VIII, 201, 452hn, IX, 92n1

Trinity College, Dublin, Provosts of, see Andrews, Francis; Baldwin, Richard; Hutchinson, John Hely; Murray, Richard

Trinity College, Dublin, Historical Society, I, 37n3, 93n2. *See also* Debating Society

Trinity House: proposal for employment of criminals by, III, 251; supports Smalls Lighthouse Bill, 430n3, IX, 420; EB dines at, 459–60

Trinity House, Hull, I, 258n1

Troward, Richard (d. 1815), prosecution solicitor in Hastings trial, V, 390, 420–1, VI, 173, VII, 108–9, 539, 553n3, VIII, 111, 167, 219, 222n1, 413, 448, IX, 63, 237, 308, 435

correspondence with, listed above, p. 185

directions for preparation of briefs, VIII, 117–18, 160, 221; his fees held up, 177; recommended for Solicitor to Board of Control, 311; controls two seats in Parliament, 311; prepares Abstract of trial proceedings, 416; and EB's personal finances, 443, IX, 308n1; and epitaph for Garrick's monument, 323–4, 360–1

Troward, William (1755–1826), VIII, 448

Troy, John Thomas (1739–1823), Catholic Archbishop of Dublin

correspondence with, listed above, p. 185

signs Kenmare's minority Address, VII, 6; persuades other bishops to support Kenmare, 44n3; informs Hobart of Catholic intention to petition King, 295–6; on need for Catholic colleges, 507; thanks EB for books presented to Maynooth College, VIII, 288; anxiety over freedom of worship for Irish Catholic soldiers, 288, 289; denounces Defenders in pastoral letter, 351n5, IX, 344n3, 345; deplores Hussey's pastoral, 341–2hn; alleged to have taken oath of United Irishmen, 344, 345; a 'timid, passive and inert man', 345; also mentioned, 358n5

Troyes, Mayor of, see Huez, M.

Unitarians (Socinians): case for toleration for, IV, 102; Priestley as Unitarian minister, VI, 14n5; EB toasted by, 247, 249tn; a threat to the Constitution, 247tn; responsible for French faction among Dissenters, VII, 119; petition for repeal of Trinity Act, 119n3; eligible for Parliament, VIII, 21

United Irishmen: suspected of destroying Parliament House, VII, 88n6; their only fault urging separation from England, 283; Arthur O'Connor becomes member, VIII, 242n6; think their grievances originate from England, 246, IX, 142, 165, 190, 365; unite all the discontented to produce disorder, VIII, 248n1; Catholic leaders said to be in contact with, 256n2, Dr Troy alleged to have taken their oath, IX, 344; the country being Jacobinised through them, 142; proclamation against, 363n1

Report on Popery laws, IX, 124

Unknown
  correspondence with, listed above, p. 191–4
  Letters to, from EB: II, 21–2, 304–5, III, 11–12, 70–1, 417, 453–4, 454–6, IV, 214–15, 231, 242, 242–3, 320–1, 333, V, 45, 64, 115–16, 209–10, 358, 416, 464–5, VI, 78–82, 138–9, 196–7, 202–3, 214–16, 479–80, VII, 167–8, 210–11, 349–51, 358, 523, VIII, 107–8, 363, 364–5, 365–6, 381–2, 390, IX, 12, 13–14, 84–5, 253–63, 369–70, 372, 397, 400–1, 429, 432, 459–62, 463, 464, 465, 466, 467, 468, 469, 471, 472, X, 40–1
  Letters to, from RBSr, IX, 472, from RBJr, 466

Unknown Journal, letter to, II, 201–3

Unwin, Samuel, Sr, and the hosiers' petition, III, 123tn, 130

Unwin, Samuel, Jr., and the hosiers' petition, III, 123tn, 130

Upper Ossory, 2nd Earl of, see Fitzpatrick, John

Upper Ossory, Countess of (Anne Liddell, 1738–1804), wife of the preceding, former wife of Duke of Grafton, IV, 136; also mentioned, III, 319n3, IV, 149, VII, 190n7

Vachell, William (1735–1807), signs Round Robin, III, 274n1

Valence, Comte de, see Timbrune-Thiembronne, Jean-Baptiste-Cyrus-Marie-Adélaïde de

Valence, Comtesse de (Edmée-Nicole Pulchérie Brulart de Genlis, 1767–1847), wife of the preceding, V, 231–2

Vallancey, Colonel Charles (1721–1812), antiquary
  correspondence with, listed above, p. 185–6
  links Irish civilization with Phoenician, V, 108hn, 291; his use of Sebright MSS, 108n1; leading spirit of 'Society of Seven', 109n6; should translate and publish Irish Historical documents, 109, 291–2
  Collectanea de Rebus Hibernicis, volume of, sent to EB, V, 108, 292n4; *Vindication of the Ancient History of Ireland*, sent to EB, 290, EB's qualified approval used to attack the author, 292–3tn, VI, 29

Van Baal, Jan Hendrickse, his boundary dispute in New York, III, 226n2

Vanbrugh, Sir John: *Aesop*, I, 82; *The Provoked Wife*, II, 1n4; his epitaph, X, 13

Van Cortlandt, Philip, of New York, II, 230

Van der Noot, Henri-Charles-Nicolas (1735–1827), lawyer: calls Brussels to arms, VI, 38n

Vane, Frederick (1732–1801), M.P., II, 436
  correspondence with, listed above, p. 186

Vansittart, Henry (d. 1769), M.P.: goes out to India as Supervisor, II, 35n2; lost at sea in the *Aurora*, 227

Vassy, Claude-Marie-Alexandre de (b. 1755), French Army Officer: EB supports his application to join British forces, VII, 503–4; captured and executed, 503n4

Vattel, Emmerich von (1714–67): on the law of nations, IV, 403n; *Le Droit des gens* quoted by EB, VI, 261n2, 317, VII, 479n1

Vaubrun, Abbé de (c. 1666–1746), donor to Irish College of the Lombard, IV, 410n4

Vaudreuil, Comte de, see Rigaud, Joseph-Hyacinthe-François de Paule

Vaughan, Benjamin (1751–1835), M.P., his political essays on Poland, VII, 159

Vaughan, General John (c. 1748–95), M.P.
  correspondence with, listed above, p. 186
  becomes Governor of Fort William, IV, 154n4; assists in capture of St Eustatius, 343hn; his seizure of private property questioned by EB, 387n1, 452, 453n1; Hoheb's petition against, 402–3, read at Treasury, 452n3; his action against law of

Watson Wentworth, Charles (*cont.*)
motion on American Teaships, 515–16; dilemma on Printers' Bill, 540–1; rights of parliament over colonies, III, 25; American troubles blamed on his Declaratory Act, 91–2, stands by Act, 102; declares against use of troops in Boston, 102; urged to take action by EB, 105–8, 189–96; presents Merchants' Petitions, 106, 109, advises against petition to King, 113–14; suggests motion on tobacco revenues, 114–15; assists New York Memorial in Lords, 166; 'America is yours', 193; tentative plan of action, 205–6, non-attendance revived for debates on America, 206, 311, 314; signs Protest against Bill prohibiting trade with colonies, 239n2; friendly union with Colonies his policy, 295–6; EB urges action after Saratoga, IX, 418; and Grenville's Election Act, III, 88; acts as arbitrator on Champion's China Patent Bill, 157–9; answers Dublin Address, 206, 211; moves amendment to Lords' Address, 299; absent from debates on Habeas Corpus Suspension Bill, 328n3; supports repeal of penal laws, 449n2; presents petition on Irish grievances to King, IV, 67, 194n8, presents motion on, in Lords, 69–72, 194n8; attacks terms of Militia Bill, 110–14; always justified Irish Associations, 186, thanked for patronage of Volunteers, 186n2; will be blamed for Irish troubles (Shelburne), 189, stunned by events in Ireland, 191; opposed to annual parliaments and additional County members, 216hn, perturbed by County support for, 216, his difficult position, 217tn, in general agreement with EB on, 297; views on Fox's Marriage Bill, 355–6; never approved of Proclamations during Gordon riots, IX, 295; enters Protest against Royal Marriage Act, 399n1

as Leader of Party: his 'true honour and reputation' in and out of office, I, 266; his temper the first of his political virtues, 309; on a Leader's duty, 317; meets his 'inner council', 321n5, II, 132, 159, 379, III, 291; 'we should be cautious', II, 117; 'should come to town' (1769), 121–2, (1772), 364, 366, 370, 378–9; speaks regularly in Lords, 139, joins in debates with difficulty, 541; confined by his

'principles of delicacy', 155, 175–6, 197; never takes up a grievance unless he means to reform it, 160; hopes best of 'Bill of Rights gentry' will join them, 163; his Secret Service Books, 167–8hn; his policy to stress Ministerial negligence, 188, 191–2; prefers Men to Measures, 297; thinks 'a winter's soiling' good for politicians as well as for horses, 402; the only person who can bring the Party into order, 408, 411, III, 311; argues from reason and experience against the hot and violent, II, 497–8; should not take things too anxiously, 523; views on foreign affairs, III, 24–5; finds politics an unfruitful and unthankful concern, 50, must wait for events to take their course, 176, 203, 282, 380hn, 401, EB disagrees, 190–2; must have firm plan before Parliament meets (1775), 210–11, (1777), 309, 311, 314, (1779), IV, 145, 153, 157–8; plans a Protestation, III, 214–16; returns unwillingly, 297; despair for country, 297, IV, 162; wishes his principal friends would do more and indulge him in a little rest, III, 296; ought to risk Address to King, 312–14; the Public must not be hurried, 392–3, 398–9hn; 'we must be governed by events', 401n3; salvation of country depends on him (Fox), IV, 29n2; proposes Resolution against prorogation, 88–9; on the political situation in 1779, 160–3, 168–9; plan of campaign, 164; on the human heart and public opinion, 196

friends and connexions: Lord Abingdon, III, 370tn, 378; William Baker, II, 240–1, III, 388hn, V, 153hn; Lord Camden, III, 36; Lord John Cavendish, II, 24n5; Richard Champion, III, 43hn, IV, 369–70; Lord Charlemont, 270hn, V, 343, VI, 117–18; Sir George Colebrooke, II, 332, 365, 547; Stephen Croft, IV, 176hn; Lord Dartmouth, II, 327n1; James De Lancey, III, 137hn; George Dempster, 25, V, 164n1; William Dowdeswell, II, 70, 113n4, III, 24, 35, 48–9; William Fitzherbert, I, 207n5; Lord George Germain, II, 406, IV, 404–5; Joseph Harrison, II, 12; Admiral Keppel, III, 453n3, IV, 11–12, 14, attends his trial, 30–1, 35–6, 37hn, celebrates his acquittal, 42hn, 43tn; John Lee, II, 23n2, III, 12hn, IV, 184, 427, V, 77hn,

Watson Wentworth, Charles (*cont.*)
VII, 405n1; London merchants, I, 267; City of London, II, 157–8, 240–1, IV, 194; Mr Mackinnon, II, 110; Lord Mansfield, I, 347, II, 153n3, 469; James Murray, II, 30n4; Duke of Newcastle, I, 324n3, 325, II, 376; George Pigot, IX, 414; Duke of Richmond, I, 320, II, 371, 374, 386, 497–8; Sir George Savile, II, 288, 408, III, 23–4, 28, 90, 194, 204; Charles Townshend, I, 310; Barlow Trecothick, II, 34n4; Charles Turner, V, 39; Alexander Wedderburn, I, 336n2; Governor Wentworth, supports him against Peter Livius, II, 444–5, 463–4, 469, claims him as distant kinsman, III, 146n1, VII, 7–8; John Wilkes, I, 231, 256hn, 257, 260tn, II, 192. Hostility to House of Grenville, I, 317n2, 336, II, 48

relations with the King, I, 317n3; Lord of the Bedchamber, 290n2; on the corrupt and increasing power of the Crown, II, 194, 344–5, IV, 163, 174hn, 192, 217tn; the King on his 'huddled speech' in Audience, 67tn

In Yorkshire

dismissed from Lord Lieutenancy for opposing peace preliminaries, I, 162n7, acts again as Lord Lieutenant, IV, 110; as Custos Rotulorum deals with clippers and coiners in Halifax, II, 116; always absorbed in York affairs during summer, III, 22hn; attends Sheffield Cutlers Feast, 25–6; as Admiral of the Coast allays alarm at Paul Jones's frigates, IV, 128–9, 139–40, 160; finds Yorkshire Committee of Association grows moderate, 382; his memory cherished, V, 46

his boroughs: perplexed to find suitable candidates, I, 348n2; finds one with thumping landed property, II, 13; by-election at Scarborough, 152–3; EB elected for Malton (1774), III, 48, 56–7, 61–4, IV, 277; Malton offered to Cholmley, 183n3, occupied by cousin and brother-in-law (1780), 322hn, one seat vacated for EB, 322, 428–9; objects to strangers in Yorkshire seats, 277, 331–2; pleased with elections, 285–6, but a strain on him, 301; Higham Ferrers (Northants), 286tn, IX, 414n1; expensive campaign at Hedon, 408–9

County Meetings: (1769), freeholders' rights the issue, II, 37–9, 40–1; wants middle way, 37, 46; prefers Assizes to calling meeting, 37; suggestions for an Address, 37–9, 40, 44, 51; ought to take lead in County petition, 44, 51; no petition voted at Assizes, 46–7; his suspicion of petitions, 48; and the High Sheriff's Letter, 47, 49; urged by EB to accept petition, 50–1, gives way, 60–1, 75; Meeting arranged, 61–5, advised as peer not to attend, 65n5, 77; the Meeting, 71–2, 77, 154–5, X, 43, a lead to other counties, II, 73–4; York scruples unknown in the South, 79; petition delayed, 115; Meeting (1770), and right of election, 151hn; against Remonstrance, 152–3, 164; plans for Meeting, 156, 160–1; Chairman's Letter to County M.P.s, 162–3; (1775), disposition on America to be reviewed at York Races, III, 183–4; (1779), petition for Economical Reform voted, IV, 176, 180, 183–5, 192–3; his success, 177; on Mr Smelt's speech, 179, 184; petition not signed by peers, 185, 192; same petition and resolutions adopted by Middlesex, 188; (1780), and Economical Reform, 214hn; perturbed by support for parliamentry reform, 216

EB and

appoints EB his unpaid secretary, I, 211, 230, 260tn, disputed origins of connexion, II, 274, IX, 177n7, 442; wants assurance EB is not dangerous Roman Catholic, I, 216n4, 333n7; and EB's Irish pension, 226n3, V, 32; EB lives with, I, 240n4, feels neglected by, 264, is deeply committed to, 285n4, spends recess with, 287; takes EB on tour of Welbeck and Wentworth, 289hn; reads Shackleton's letter in praise of EB, 351; discusses Meredith's pamphlet with him, II, 25, 39; sees his letter on election of City Sheriffs, 36; EB stays with, 85; Walpole thinks EB his 'governor', 140n1; consulted on EB's appointment as New York Agent, 215hn; Markham's allegations against him refuted by EB, 260–2; was never told of EB's 'Mad Ambition' for Office, 269–70; his apparent indifference to Supervisorship hurts EB, 319, 320–1; EB sends him his present of Constantia wine, 358; discusses EB's election arrangements with Portland, III, 57–8; EB breakfasts with, 66hn, 68; follows EB's campaign at

Webster, Mrs William (*cont.*)
    Burke, VI, 292; her tender care of RBJr, VII, 564; resists inroads on her larder, IX, 41n4

Weddell, William (1736–92), Rockingham's brother-in-law, M.P. for Hull, later for Malton

correspondence with, listed above, p. 187

serves on Yorkshire Grand Jury, II, 47; might need Malton, III, 48n2; visits Wentworth, 297; succeeds EB at Malton (1775), 297n1; joined by EB (1780), IV, 322, V, 17tn; joins Yorkshire Association, 38hn; warned against dangers of County meeting, 39–40; forced to decline poll (1784), 295n5, VII, 51n1; EB's public 'Letter' to, VI, 440, VII, 50–63, sent in reply to thanks for *Appeal*, 50hn, intended for circulation, VI, 440n6, VII, 63; one of Fox's martyrs in 1784, 50n1; also mentioned, V, 47, VI, 81n1, 84n5, IX, 393n1

Weddell, Mrs William (Elizabeth Ramsden, d. 1831), wife of the preceding, half-sister of Lady Rockingham, III, 297, V, 38, 40, VI, 261n3, IX, 393

Wedderburn, Alexander (1733–1805), later (1780) 1st Baron Loughborough, M.P., I, 173–4hn

correspondence with, listed above, p. 150–1

on Northern Circuit, I, 318; connexions with Grenville and Rockingham, 336, 342; supports Opposition on Middlesex election, II, 23, 24; consulted on Dowdeswell's pamphlet, 25, 69n4, 113n4; encourages petition movement in Yorkshire, 63, 65, 115n2, 151; Whiggissimus in speech at County meeting (1769), 97; attends meeting again (1770), 152; turning towards Administration, 181; accepts office as Solicitor General under North, 175n1, 433hn, VIII, 65n1; acts for Lowther against Portland, II, 443hn, 444; acts for Governors against Massachusetts petitions, 518, 521–2, 524, his furious philippic against Franklin, 518, 519hn, 522, 524, V, 54hn; opposes Dunning on Royal Marriage Act, IX, 399

and North's 'conciliatory' propositions to American colonies, III, 118; replies to Fox on America (Feb. 1776), IX, 410, declines replying (Nov. 1776), III, 299; motion on Burgoyne's defeat, 423; succeeds Thurlow as Attorney General, 455n1; becomes Chief Justice

and Baron Loughborough, IV, 247, V, 21; gains confidence in speaking, 340; his long speech in Douglas case, 373; meeting with Prince of Wales, 447; refuses Pitt's offer of Great Seal, VII, 143hn, negotiates with Pitt and Portland, 143–4, 149–50, 150–1, 186n4, VIII, 49–50; negotiates with Dundas for comprehension of parties, VII, 192–3, 195; includes Fox in Cabinet plan, 194; joins in conversations with EB and Windham, 288hn, 291–2, 418, 501n2; again declines Great Seal, 303–4, 305; shares EB's views on foreign affairs, 307, wants action against France, 310–11, 312; despairs of Portland's giving up Fox, and accepts Chancellorship, 318–19, 320, 338, 344–5, VIII, 43hn, 50

approved by Grattan, VII, 352, 510; Mgr Erskine received by, 513n2; thinks Fitzwilliam ought not to dismiss Irish Chancellor, VIII, 32hn; influenced by Jobbery of Irish connexions, EB fears, 52, 65; takes up Dublin Provostship, 46, 48, 68; fetches up EB as mediator with Fitzwilliam, 70–1, 73–5, meeting with Fitzwilliam, 76tn; expects much from new French constitution, 336, but was misled, 418; thinks Fayettism ought to be driven out of the House, IX, 179–80; his grave illness, 322, 323tn

India: wants to know EB's line on Clive, II, 433, conducts defence of Clive ably, 435, 436; and Bengal Judiciary Bill, IV, 355; asked to stop Sulivan's despatch on Tanjore, 305; disagrees with EB on Macartney's appointment, 323–5; agrees with EB's plans for settling India, 323–5, V, 255; and Hastings trial, VI, 62, 64n4, VII, 372, 541, VIII, 112, 114–15, 240–1; signs Protest at Lords' Resolution, VII, 539; voted Hastings guilty on thirteen counts, VIII, 423n2, 435; concurred in temporary disfranchisement of East India Company, 427; his Letter justifying 'compensatory' pension for Hastings, 413, IX, 62n2, 'monstrous and provoking', VIII, 419, EB's draft replies to, 422–35

personal relations with the Burkes: supports RBSr's claim to post in Grenades, I, 174; and RBSr's claims to land in St Vincent, III, 162n1; quarrels with EB over Germain,

Wedderburn, Alexander (*cont.*)
406–8; invites EB's views on Toleration Bill and Dissenters clause, IV, 5–6, 248–50; moved by EB's appeal against pillory sentences, 230–1, and by his appeal to limit executions after Surrey riots, 255–7; arranges meeting between North and EB, 327–8tn; concern at EB's loss of office, V, 15; consulted on EB's letter to Chancellor, 198tn; RBJr meets in Brighton, 349–50; and *Appeal*, VI, 306, 311tn; supports EB's plan for refugee clergy, VII, 211–12, and for classifying *émigrés*, 339–40; keeps EB in touch with Pitt on war situation, 516–19, 524–5; and EB's pension, 562n1, VIII, 14, 16, 392, 397, defends pension against Bedford's attack, 406–7; EB's Threnodia to, 43–50, 52; appoints nominee of EB to living, 43; appealed to, for Prof. John Wilde, 98–9; EB seldom sees, 383–4; shows EB's letter to French Laurence, 416; and *Regicide Peace*, 418; grants injunction against Owen, IX, 105n3, 243n5; appealed to, on behalf of Archbishop of Paris and Bishop of Amiens, 322–3, of Joseph Hickey, 440–1, of Walker King and Tremamondo, the royal fencing master, 455

his long friendship with EB, I, 173–4, VIII, 45, 406n1, 427; early visits to Beechwood together, V, 19; visits Beaconsfield, VIII, 45; EB thinks him 'a good humoured, friendly man', 52; pall bearer for EB, IX, 374n3; *émigré* school at Penn committed to his care, 379

also mentioned, II, 51n, V, 205tn, 251n4, 347, VII, 180hn, 529hn, 574, VIII, 363n2, IX, 93, 471, X, 7, 42, 46

Wedgwood, Josiah (1730–95): rivalry with Champion over china patent, III, 43hn; political influence, 142; stirs up potters to petition against patent, 153; opposes Patent Bill on 'public' grounds, 156hn, 163; tries to see specification, 158–9, foiled by change of date, 159tn; his pamphlets against Champion's patent, 163; makes copy of Portland vase, X, 22

Wells, Mrs Mary (fl. 1781–1812), Drury Lane actress: EB praised in her papers, V, 410

Welsh School, London, IV, 239

Wendover, borough of Lord Verney, I, 154; EB returned for (1765), I, 222–3,

225, 228, (1768), 347, 351; his colleague, II, 148, 151, 154, V, 69hn; by-election (1770), II, 157, 158; seats put up for sale (1774), III, 33–4, 61; EB's farewell letter to his constituents, 55–6

Wentworth, Lady Anne, *see* Fitzwilliam, Countess

Wentworth, Charles-Mary (b. 1775), godson of the Rockinghams, III, 146n1

Wentworth, Lady Charlotte Watson (1732–1810), sister of Rockingham, VII, 30
correspondence with, listed above, p. 187

Wentworth, Frances, *see* Wentworth, Mrs John

Wentworth, Hugh (d. 1787), Rockingham's estate agent in Ireland, I, 338hn, IV, 163n2

Wentworth, John (1737–1820), Governor of New Hampshire, distant relation of Rockingham
correspondence with, listed above, p. 187
Peter Livius's petition against, II, 444hn; appeals to Privy Council against decision, 444hn, supported by Rockingham, 444–5, 463; Lord Mansfield's opinion on case, 469; EB's testimonial for, VII, 7–8; appointed Governor of Nova Scotia, 8tn; also mentioned, III, 146, 147, 260hn

Wentworth, Mrs John (Frances Wentworth, widow of Theodore Atkinson, d. 1813): Lady Rockingham's letter to, submitted to EB for approval, III, 146–7; visits England, 146n1, 262hn; joins EB's party at trial of Duchess of Kingston, 260hn

Wentworth, Paul (d. 1793), Agent for New Hampshire, III, 81n1, 308n1

Wentworth, Thomas, 1st Earl of Strafford (1593–1641), EB explores his unpublished papers, I, 202n2, VIII, 184, 190–1

Wentworth, William, 2nd Earl of Strafford (1722–91), entertains Prince of Wales at Wentworth Castle, VI, 23

Wesley, Rev. Charles (1707–88), Henry Cruger seen with, IV, 252

Wesley, Rev. John (1703–91): carries over Methodists to the Court on America, IV, 271; also mentioned, 252n7

Wesleyans, *see* Methodists in Bristol; Lady Huntingdon's Connexion; Wesley, John

West, Benjamin (1738–1820): exhibits at Society of Artists (1766), I, 254; Rock-

Whately, Thomas (*cont.*)
79n1, 90n4, 112hn, 113n2; on Amherst's pension, 14n2; invited to Gregories, 55–6, IX, 394–5, his visit, II, 60, 71–4; supplies information on Bucks County meeting, 56–7, 59–60, 71–3, 79n1; passes on news from America, 77; letters from American Governors stolen after his death, 519hn

Whetham, Rev. John, Dean of Lismore (1733–96), chaplain to Westmorland, VIII, 59n4, X, 46

Whig Club
correspondence with, listed above, p. 188
foundation, VI, 9n2; hypothetical meeting with Revolution Society, 128; confused with Club of Constitutional Whigs, 465n4; Fox's speech on reform at, VII, 320; vote of confidence in Fox, 353hn, 436hn, IX, 243; EB, RBJr and others resign, VII, 354–5, IX, 245; fails to get Addresses for peace, 281

Whig Club (Ireland): foundation, VI, 9; takes up parliamentary reform, IX, 144; also mentioned, VII, 297

Whigs: resolved to try for an Administration by themselves (1765), I, 206; the Liberty and power of doing good – the whole of Whiggism (Savile), II, 121; 'modern Whiggs', not interested in Liberty, III, 290; early attendance on America urged, 294n3; consider secession on America, 308–9hn, 334hn, 343n2; could be mediators for peace, 310; might consider impeachment of Ministers, 313; state of, in 1777, 383; attacked in Archbishop's sermon for supporting American cause, 383n1; should not 'over hurry' public opinion (Rockingham), 398hn; EB's Whig principles, 438, 456, IX, 446; agree with Tories on rights of property, III, 456; Toleration Bill first started by, IV, 6; never proposed repeal of sacramental test, 7; would never have survived disgraces suffered by North Ministry, 115; their cause would be promoted by coalition against Court and Ministry (Fitzwilliam), 146; 'twenty-eight years of Systematick endeavours to destroy', V, 429n4; *Reflections* approved by Old Stamina of Whigs, VI, 161n2, 178, contains the true Whig creed (Portland), 161n2, partially aimed against frenchified Whiggism,

VII, 52; 'Mr Burke's New Whig quasi Wig', VI, 230n2
split between old and new Whigs over Fox–Burke dispute, VI, 271hn, 275, 292hn, 336, 418n3, VIII, 401n5; Fox declares for French Whiggism, VI, 273; detestable doctrines of modern Whigs, 415–16; EB's sentiments those of the 'rational Whiggs', 309, his doctrine that of the 'classic' Whigs, 331; he will never act with new-modelled Whigs, 452, VII, 63, considers himself censured by their granting Freedom of York to Fox, 51n4; Old Whigs ought to support Government, 143, VIII, 49n3; a possible Whig Administration with Pitt, VII, 186; Old Whigs support Pitt openly, 529tn

in Bristol, III, 10hn, 43, 44; two branches of, 43hn, 45; Sunshine Tories profess attachment to, 207; their influence in Corporation, 288hn, 289, 290, 366, 368; the Whig Cause toasted on Fast day, 303; must consider counter-petition to Tory loyal address, 318; Common Council controlled by, IV, 114hn; excluded from Volunteers, 122n5; real picture of principal Whigs in, 245; impossible to carry two Whig members (1780), 266hn, 267; divided irretrievably, 268; Whig merchants strongly for EB, 268; Tories and, in Bristol, 270; Bristol party must be brought into concert with 'the rational and sober Whiggs', 275; Union Club extended to 'honest part' of Whigs, 276n1, 328–9; support for EB, 280; Cruger party deserted by, 293; taught a lesson by EB's defeat, 295; one Whig member assured, 300; advised on by-election (1781), 326, 328–9, 330, 331n1, 332; Cruger adopted by, and defeated, 333tn; support of clergy essential to, 350; EB's Whig principles declared in 1774, VI, 178–9

Adey not an old Court Whig, IV, 291; Bowes's Whiggism, VII, 102; disunion of, in Bucks, IV, 131–2, 137; RBSr educated 'in the utmost Severity of Whig Principles', II, 284; WB classed both as Swiss and, I, 283n4; Camden an Old Whig, VI, 333n3; Canning, Whig supporter of Pitt, IX, 267hn; Chatham's Whig principles, II, 112; Mrs Crewe, noted Whig hostess, IV, 398n1, VI, 87n4, VIII, 84tn,

Willis, Dr Robert Darling (1760–1821), son of Dr Francis Willis, assists in treatment of George III, v, 462

Willis, Rev. Thomas (1754–1827), son of Dr Francis Willis, assists in treatment of George III, v, 462

Willoughby, Thomas (1728–81), M.P., III, 83hn

Wills, John (1741–1806), Vice-Chancellor of Oxford, VI, 195tn

correspondence with, listed above, p. 188

Wilmot, John, 2nd Earl of Rochester, *Satires* quoted, VIII, 401

Wilmot, Sir John Eardley (1709–92), Chief Justice, expected to succeed Camden as Chancellor, II, 98, 103

Wilmot, John Eardley (*c.* 1749–1815), M.P., Chairman of Committee for French Refugee Clergy, VII, 207–8hn, IX, 11n1, X, 28

correspondence with, listed above, p. 189

his zeal and charity, VII, 213, VIII, 140, X, 26; arranges first meeting of committee, VII, 219n2; EB's advice to, on space and clothing for clergy, 226–7, and pocket-money, 231–2; advice accepted, 234–5; 'will do everything that he ought', 498; shares EB's view on peace with France, VIII, 148–9

see also French Refugee Clergy

Wilmot, Sir Robert (d. 1772), I, 167n5

Wilmot Committee, *see* French refugee clergy

Wilson, Alexander (1714–86), Professor of Practical Astronomy at Glasgow University, v, 156

Wilson, Charles Henry: publishes 'Letter to Michael Smith' in *Beauties of Burke*, I, 357–9

Wilson, Patrick (1743–1811), son of Professor Wilson: appointment as Assistant Astronomer, v, 156–7

Wilson, Rev. Thomas (1703–84), Rector of St Margaret's, Westminster

correspondence with, listed above, p. 189

approaches EB on standing for Bristol, III, 3–4, 10hn, 11, 46, 149

Wiltshire, *see* County meetings

Wimpffen, Louis-Félix, Baron de (1744–1814), Girondist, VIII, 268, 273

Winchester, Bishop of, *see* North, Brownlow

Winchilsea, 8th Earl of, *see* Finch, Daniel

Winchilsea, 9th Earl of, *see* Finch, George

Windham, William (1750–1810), M.P., friend and disciple of EB

correspondence with, listed above, p. 189–90

does not agree that Whig conduct must be governed by events, III, 401n3; defeated for Norwich (1780), VII, 412n1, elected (1784), v, 153hn, 280, 282, 463, VI, 21, 26n3, re-elected (1796), IX, 43; seconds EB's motion in defence of Coalition, v, 153hn, 156n1, VIII, 135n1; suspicions of North, v, 229n5; and Regency crisis, 433, strongly opposed to limitations, 436hn, EB unburdens his mind on, 439, 445; and Norwich Address on King's recovery, 463; in favour of Loughborough's taking Great Seal if asked, VII, 150; eager for political activity, 288hn; joins EB and Loughborough in negotiations with Ministers for action in Europe, 288–9, 291, 310–14, 418n1, n2; more optimistic than EB, 291, 292, 466; pledges support to Pitt if action taken, VIII, 50; agrees with EB and Fitzwilliam on foreign affairs, VII, 307; prepared to go farther than Proclamation against Seditious Writings, 314; finds Fox unaltered by events in France, 315, 316, 318; refuses office, 345n1, 412n6, 440; consulted by Pitt and Dundas on outbreak of war, 349tn, 423; takes Chair at meeting of anti-Fox Whigs, 353hn, resigns from Club, 355, attacked by Sheridan for break with Fox, VIII, 108n3

approves 'frontier' plan in war, VII, 411–12; tours army in Flanders, 411n1; on anti-war feeling in Norfolk, 411–12; exchange of views with EB on state of war, 413–16, 461; advises Elliot on Toulon Governorship, 429, 439tn; on the Declaration, 479, 480–1, 487; discusses war with Pitt and EB, 501n2; his wish for open support of Pitt accepted by Portland Whigs, 525–6; takes up cause of compensation for de La Robrie, 530n4; and the First of June, 548–9; becomes Secretary at War, 570hn

goes to Breda, VIII, 14, 16, 30; establishes Comte d'Hector's Corps, 31; has done more good in Office than he could have in Opposition, 82; speech on repeal of Habeas Corpus Act, 108–9, 112; and parliamentary reform, 109; on acquittals by juries, 109, 112; his Norwich constituents petition for peace, 134; warned never